P9-DFW-055

HANDBOOK OF FATHER INVOLVEMENT

Multidisciplinary Perspectives

HANDBOOK OF FATHER INVOLVEMENT

Multidisciplinary Perspectives

Edited by

Catherine S. Tamis-LeMonda
New York University

Natasha Cabrera
*National Institute of Child Health
and Human Development*

2002

LAWRENCE ERLBAUM ASSOCIATES, PUBLISHERS
Mahwah, New Jersey   London

Editor:	Bill Webber
Editorial Assistant:	Erica Kica
Cover Design:	Kathryn Houghtaling Lacey
Textbook Production Manager:	Paul Smolenski
Full Service & Composition:	Black Dot Group / An AGT Company
Text and Cover Printer:	Sheridan Books, Inc.

This book was typeset in 10/12 pt. Times Roman, Bold, and Italic.
The heads were typeset in Americana, Americana Bold, and Americana Bold Italic.

Lawrence Erlbaum Associates, Inc., Publishers
10 Industrial Avenue
Mahwah, New Jersey 07430

Library of Congress Cataloging-in-Publication Data

Handbook of father involvement: multidisciplinary perspectives / [edited by] Catherine S.
Tamis-LeMonda and Natasha Cabrera.
      p. cm.
   Includes bibliographical references and index.
   ISBN 0-8058-3702-7 (alk. paper)
      1. Fathers. 2. Fatherhood. 3. Father and child. I. Tamis-LeMonda, Catherine S.
(Catherine Susan), 1958-   II. Cabrera, Natasha J.
   HQ756 .H359 2002
   306.874'2—dc21   2002019170

Books published by Lawrence Erlbaum Associates are printed on acid-free paper, and
their bindings are chosen for strength and durability.

Printed in the United States of America
10 9 8 7 6 5 4 3 2 1

For Anthony Francis Tamis, my father, and Richard James LeMonda, my husband—two generations of loving and devoted fathers.

Catherine S. Tamis-LeMonda

For Jeffrey Ian Ross, the best father in the world.

Natasha Cabrera

And for all the fathers who struggle on a daily basis to be the best parent they can be.

Natasha Cabrera and Catherine S. Tamis-LeMonda

Contents

Multidisciplinary Perspectives on Father Involvement: An Introduction

Social, economic, and political events of the past 30 years have placed fathers in the national spotlight, leading to changes in the ways that federal, state, and local agencies and researchers conceptualize and collect data on fathers. These changes, in turn, have had an impact on how men and women perceive fatherhood and on how policies are designed to promote father involvement in the lives of children. Today, fathers are more likely to share in the care of their children; participate in child care or school-related activities; and ask for joint custody of their children. Public policies, which in the past have been "mother focused," are becoming more "father friendly." Child support legislation is now beginning to integrate visitation rights, courts are more willing to grant joint custody, and welfare reform legislation permits states to use some of their funds to design programs that promote positive father involvement.

These events have led to an unprecedented surge of research on fathers in various scientific disciplines, including demography, developmental psychology, sociology, evolutionary psychology, economics, and public policy. Although *unique* methodological approaches, guiding assumptions, theoretical frameworks, levels of analysis, and research foci characterize these diverse scientific traditions, the aims of description, explanation, prediction, and modification of human behavior are shared by all. Specific to the topic of fatherhood, describing and understanding the nature, antecedents, and consequences of father involvement across biological status, family structure, culture, and stages in children's development lie at the heart of fathering studies, as well as at the core of this text.

However, as is often characteristic of the social sciences, the study of father involvement continues to be an insular enterprise, with exciting progress generally occurring within rather than across fields. Consequently, neither threads of similarity nor points of tension have been identified or pursued. The overarching goal of this handbook is to address this limitation by highlighting the challenges that face researchers of father involvement across disciplines. We seek to build on the commonalities across disciplines by offering a multidisciplinary view on the status of current research as well as a prospective vision of the promises of future interdisciplinary collaboration. This integrative approach is fundamental to a comprehensive understanding of human development generally, and to fathering more specifically. It is also timely because it dovetails with the heightened appreciation of multidisciplinary research as a means to achieve both breadth and depth in scientific inquiry.

SHARED THEMES ON FATHERHOOD

In the context of their unique vantage points, all contributors shared the charge of considering how their research inquiries shed light on the meaning of father involvement for developmental outcomes in children. Consequently, four salient themes/questions, regarding the nature, determinants, and outcomes of father involvement inspire thought and recur throughout the book: (a) What is father involvement, what dimensions comprise the construct, and how are those dimensions changing over time? (b) What factors contribute to and/or play a role in explaining father involvement, within and across time? (c) Which outcomes in children are affected by which dimensions of father involvement at which stages in development? and (d) How and why might father involvement vary across culture and ethnicity?

With respect to the first theme, the complexities and challenges of defining father involvement lie at the core of its understanding. What is positive father involvement? What taxonomies are useful to its conceptualization? How do those taxonomies change with children's developmental stages? Though, by necessity much of the research presented throughout this handbook emphasizes a specific dimension of father involvement, researchers agree that multiple dimensions of fathering act in concert as part of a complex, multifaceted system. Moreover, it is critical to consider how and why different dimensions of father involvement do or do not change and are or are not stable over the course of fathers' and children's development. It does not suffice to describe or identify a particular pattern or direction of change across two or more ages. Rather, descriptive portrayals must be balanced by emphases on theory and explanation. Researchers of human development ask *why* a particular pattern exists and what mechanisms or processes underlie the observed change. The nature of changes in father involvement over time, the laws or factors that govern those changes, and the rules by which changes occur are all of primary interest.

The second theme emphasizes the factors that contribute to and/or provide the background context for understanding father involvement. What factors support and predict positive father involvement? What factors obstruct involvement? The study of fathering is a study of nested levels of influence. Fathers, children, and families are not isolated entities, but rather exist within developmental, situational, contextual, cultural, and historical contexts. Families, schools, communities, and the overarching beliefs, ideologies, and practices of cultures and subcultures operate simultaneously in affecting fathering, as do the corelations that exist among these systems. Additionally, children themselves are active participants in their own experiences, and children's temperament, age, gender, and other characteristics no doubt affect fathering. Because of the numerous contextual dependencies that exist in the father–child relationship, determining the extent to which findings from a specific population of fathers and children, studied within a specific context, can or cannot be generalized is a challenge. Consequently, researchers are appropriately cautious in their interpretation of findings and prudent in applying them to fathers, families, and children in other ecological contexts.

The third theme—fathers' effects on children—is at the heart of all studies on fathers. Research on and interventions with fathers are primarily motivated by individual and societal concern about and commitment to children's well-being. Policymakers, researchers, practitioners, educators, and parents share interest in when, under what circumstances, and how father involvement affects positive outcomes in children. A thorough understanding of the mechanisms that underlie fathers' effect on children is critical. Fathers exert both direct and indirect effects, and both pathways of influence are key to a comprehensive understanding of fatherhood. Fathers' involvement and actions directly affect children's thoughts and actions as well as affect other persons in children's lives, such as mothers, who in turn are key to children's well-being. Moreover, certain aspects of fathering, such as the provision of material resources, undoubtedly affect the environmental and economic circumstances of children's development and may be fundamental to children's experiences beyond the quality of the father–child relationship.

The final theme—cultural and ethnic variation in fatherhood—is key to the conceptualization and definition of who is a good father and what fathering means for children and families in various settings. Acculturation, ethnic identity, and generational status play critical roles in shaping fathering patterns. Given the increased diversity of the U.S. population, in parallel with a global trend toward cultural diversity in most countries, it is imperative that researchers, policymakers, and educators increasingly understand the cultural construction of fatherhood. Fathering is a social construct, yet little progress has been made toward defining the cultural boundaries of fathers' and mothers' roles and of disentangling cultural norms from more universally accepted forms of childrearing. Is there a set of universal patterns in how fathers and mothers should rear their children? How do men across different cultures function in families? In some cultures men other than a child's biological father play an important fathering role. Additionally, family formation and the role of men in families from other societies may be influenced by factors different from those prevalent in the United States. In some countries, fathers' economic contribution is linked to marital stability, and men who cannot provide for their families often abandon them. In such cultures, fathers may be defined as disciplinarians, and nurturance may be culturally unacceptable. An understanding of cultural variation in fathers' roles and influence is central to advancing theories of human development.

MULTIDISCIPLINARY PERSPECTIVES ON FATHERHOOD

The structure of this handbook is somewhat unique with respect to more traditional handbooks, so as to heighten the value of its multidisciplinary orientation. Rather than inviting contributors ourselves, we collaborated with invited section editors who provided expertise in the scientific disciplines comprising the handbook. In consultation with us, each section editor was responsible for framing their section and for inviting noteworthy researchers to contribute to their area. This approach resulted in a collection of chapters that span demographic, developmental, sociological, evolutionary, economic, and policy perspectives. Each discipline brings to the study of fathers its tools, methods, theoretical orientations, and epistemological assumptions.

The book is divided into six sections, entitled: (I) The Demography of Fathers, (II) Father Involvement and Child Development, (III) Father Involvement: Sociological and Anthropological Perspectives, (IV) Father Involvement: Evolutionary Perspectives, (V) Father Involvement: Economic Perspectives, and (VI) Father Involvement: Social Policy and Intervention. As a segue to these sections, the opening chapter poses methodological challenges to fatherhood research, including that of sampling, recruitment, theoretical approaches, measurement, design, and analysis from an interdisciplinary perspective. The closing chapter summarizes and integrates salient themes from the six sections.

Sandra Hofferth of the University of Michigan is the editor of the first section, "The Demography of Fathers." Traditionally, demographic researchers have focused on the processes that determine population size, growth, composition, and distribution and the determinants and consequences of those processes for society. Research on fathers within family demography, therefore, has focused mainly on the distribution and characteristics of fathers and fathering in the population. In the past, demographic research on fathers has had a number of methodological and conceptual limitations. National surveys often excluded men by design, leading to a paucity of data from men about their family lives. In instances in which men were included in surveys, minority and low-income men were often missed, leading to biased representation. This section first provides an overview of the social, economic, and demographic characteristics and circumstances of fathers living with children ages 0 to 17 in the home and of fathers who are not living with any of their children, based on new national data. Demographic research can do a good job of describing not only what fathers look like, but also what fathers do in the lives of their children Three central components of father involvement include paternal engagement, accessibility, and responsibility. The second chapter in this section focuses on overall measures of the frequency of engagement and involvement of fathers with children. It describes the time fathers spend in developmental activities with children, particularly playing with, caring for, and reading to them, and the quality of the relationship. In contrast to earlier studies, men report on their own behaviors and relationships with their children. An important feature of this chapter is that it distinguishes between the behavior of fathers who are related in diverse ways to the child, including stepfathers and partners to mothers. Based as they are on nationally representative surveys, the two chapters in this section provide a detailed up-to-date representative picture of the population of U.S. fathers and their involvement in their children's lives.

Michael Lamb of the National Institute of Child Health and Human Development (NICHD) is the editor of the second section, "Child Development." A key emphasis of developmental psychologists has been on change and stability in social, emotional, motor, personality, linguistic, and cognitive functioning from infancy through adulthood. Development across these domains is viewed as a transactional process in which environmental and biological factors affect one another and codetermine trajectories of individuals' lives. At the core of much developmental research lies a focus on the relationship and interactions between parents and their children. Although the bulk of investigators have focused on mother–child dyads, a substantial body of research has examined the role of fathers in the lives of their children and families. These studies have embraced a range of topics, including the effects of father presence/absence on children's development; associations between various forms of father involvement and children's cognitive abilities, social-emotional development, school achievement, and sex role development; studies of children's early attachments to their fathers; and the indirect effects of father involvement through its association with factors such as mothering and family socioeconomic status. In general, research indicates that fathers fulfill multiple roles and exert both direct and indirect effects on children. Developmental research, however, is characterized by several limitations, including the study of small, nonrepresentative samples; the use of mothers as proxies for fathers; a predominant focus on fathers from middle-class, intact households; the utilization of unidimensional conceptualizations of fatherhood; few prospective, longitudinal studies; and limited exploration of ethnic and cultural variations in fathering. Ongoing research is addressing some of these limitations by incorporating developmental measures into larger-scale studies; assessing fathers directly; probing the experiences of fathers from low-income, ethnically divese populations; applying richer, multidimensional definitions of fathering; and examining the course and consequences of fathering for fathers, children, and families over development. The four chapters in this section represent these strengths.

The third section, "Sociological and Anthropological Perspectives," is edited by Linda Burton of Pennsylvania State University. In this section, the focus is on sociocultural processes and the role of culture in shaping father involvement and its effect on children and families. The dynamic interactions among culture, social expectations, and the family processes that allow role negotiation are critical to understanding how fathers and children construct the meaning of parenting. Sociologists often utilize survey methods, which rely on large, nationally representative data sets to study population-based trends, patterns of fathering behavior, and the impact of fathering on children. At the other end of the spectrum are sociologists who employ ethnographic methods in an attempt to capture people's beliefs, values, and attitudes and the development of behaviors, social roles, and perceptions in specific physical, social, and cultural niches. Through in-depth interviews with fathers (and mothers), students of culture shed light on the meaning and perceptions of fatherhood; the roles fathers perform in their children's lives; the factors that determine the nature, level, and quality of fathering; the patterns that characterize the paternal role over time; and how various contexts and cultures influence "who fathers," "when fathering occurs," and "how fathers father." The main limitation of this body of research rests in its generalization to larger, representative populations, although ethnographic data are valuable in generating hypotheses and interpreting findings from large-scale studies. Recently, investigators have combined quantitative and ethnographic data in an effort to understand how families function in different social, cultural, and political contexts.

The fourth section, "Evolutionary Perspectives," is edited by Frank Marlowe of Harvard University. Evolutionary psychologists assert that social behaviors and emotions represent heritable adaptations that were selectively advantageous during our ancestral human environments. Family groupings have a biological basis and are formed under specific ecological and demographic conditions. Although a high degree of cooperation is expected among family members because of their genetic ties, conflict is expected and intensified in stepfamilies. From studies of altruism and selfless behavior to studies of why people invest not only in their own offspring but also in distant kin, evolutionary psychologists attempt to model and provide a biological explanation for family behavior. Why do some people form families while others cut their ties to their children as fast as possible? Why do individuals behave differently in different kinds of family structures, and are such behaviors predictable? Evolutionary theorists attempt to predict family behavior and relative stability of extended families, biological families, stepfamilies, single-parent families, and families with resources as compared to those without. Some evidence exists to support the theoretical predictions that stepparents invest less in offspring from previous marriages and that children in stepfamilies are more likely to be physically abused. Because this body of work has been slowly accumulating, there is little research that has applied an evolutionary theory of family to the study of fathers. However, ongoing research uses this approach to understand the roles and type of investment that biological, "biological social" fathers (uncles, grandparents, etc.), and stepfathers make on behalf of their children. Another line of work looks at age at first reproduction and reproductive strategies as a function of father presence/absence to explore evolutionary attachment theory. Others explore the effects of fathers' time spent with children, on children's human capital, and on the long-term intergenerational effects of men's marital status on their children and grandchildren's survivorship and reproduction. A limitation raised by critics is that an evolutionary perspective is essentially based on models of animal behavior (mainly birds) or alternatively on small samples. Although an evolutionary perspective is not widely integrated into psychological thinking about fathering, it provides a unique and compelling perspective regarding the causes of family function and hypotheses about situations under which conflicts arise.

Irv Garfinkel of Columbia University edits the fifth section, "Economic Perspectives." Economists working in the family area have postulated that fertility and family formation can be analyzed within the choice-theoretical framework of neoclassical economics. This approach has provided the basis for innovative models that aim to explain patterns of nonmarital paternity and involvement among disadvantaged men. Like many social–demographic studies of marriage behavior, economists rely on structural–functionalist models of role specialization within families and the factors that have reduced the value of role specialization and incentives for marriage (such as women's economic interdependence and men's earning capacities). Traditionally, economic models have evolved from static lifetime formulations to life cycle dynamic models. More recently, new approaches to modeling household decision making recognize the importance of individual decision makers who comprise the household. Economists also model the effects of welfare, child support enforcement, and labor markets on father noninvolvement and attempt to incorporate economic theory in understanding social trends and the outcomes of divorce, separation, and nonmarital births. The three chapters in this section apply economic principles and models to the areas of parental bargaining, child support and visitation, and even to fathers' emotional investment in their children and families.

The final section, "Social Policy and Intervention," is coedited by Jeanne Brookes-Gunn of Columbia University and Sara McLanahan of Princeton University. This section provides a synergistic view of how psychological research informs program design and implementation as well as public policies. Psychological research on the ways that fathers, especially low-income and nonresidential men, can promote child well-being is a central component of public policies aimed at improving the lives of families and children. Social policies and programs both drive and are driven by ongoing research, leading to dynamic, synergistic relationships. The four chapters in this section address the intersection between research and policy in several areas, including the effects of welfare reform and child support policies on child well-being; the consequences of child custody policies on fathering and child development; the role of government in promoting father well-being; the consequences of current policies on the developmental trajectories of fragile families; and the effects (and noneffects) of different types of fatherhood programs on fathers, families, and children.

In closing, each section of this handbook presents current perspectives and challenges to research on father involvement within a specialized scientific discipline. This handbook will appeal broadly to professionals and advanced students who seek to better understand the nature, processes, and outcomes of father involvement, child development, parenting, and family processes within nested ecological settings. Through the merging of diverse, sometimes conflicting, sometimes complementary theoretical frameworks and methodological approaches, we seek to stimulate new insights on fathers, children, and families and to provide the impetus for innovative, dialogic, interdisciplinary research efforts well into the future. We hope that readers of this handbook, whom we anticipate will represent a variety of scientific disciplines, share our excitement and enthusiasm toward this collection of interdisciplinary chapters.

Catherine S. Tamis-LeMonda, Ph.D.
New York University

Natasha Cabrera, Ph.D.
National Institute of Child Health
and Human Development

September 2001

ACKNOWLEDGMENTS

We wish to acknowledge our colleagues in the Early Head Start (EHS) Father Studies Work Group, who are our partners in the commitment to advance an understanding of the roles of fathers in young children's lives. The seeds of thought to edit a book on father involvement in part emanated from the shared discourse among members of our group. The EHS Father Studies Work Group members represent the funding agencies (Administration on Children, Youth, and Families; National Institute of Child Health and Human Development; Office of the Assistant Secretary for Planning and Evaluation in DHHS; and the Ford Foundation); the local research universities participating in the Early Head Start Research Consortium; the national Early Head Start evaluation contractor (Mathematica Policy Research and Columbia University); and program directors from the Early Head Start programs participating in the national evaluation. We also thank Jacqueline Shannon for her thoughtful contributions. Finally, thanks go out to the many fathers who have participated in our research; their stories have illuminated the complexity of what it means to be an involved father and directly speak to the value that multidisciplinary collaboration brings to the study of fathering.

1

Methodological, Measurement, and Design Issues in Studying Fathers: An Interdisciplinary Perspective

Lori A. Roggman
Utah State University

Hiram E. Fitzgerald
Michigan State University

Robert H. Bradley
University of Arkansas at Little Rock

Helen Raikes
U.S. Department of Health & Human Services and The Gallup Organization

BEGINNING OUR RESEARCH: WHY STUDY FATHERS?

Fathers may make important contributions to child development, and in turn, the experience of fathering may make important contributions to adult development. These are sufficient reasons to study fathers and fathering. Although the number of studies of fathers has increased substantially in the past three decades, most research methods for studying parents have been developed for studying mothers, especially in early childhood, and not all of those methods work as well for studying fathers. To understand more about fathers and fathering, we need methodological approaches that are appropriate to study fathers directly and as part of a family system.

1

This chapter provides a framework for discussion of the pertinent methodological issues and themes that arise in the course of designing and conducting research on fathers. It is reasonable to suppose that many of the methods used for studying mothers and mothering can be adapted to study fathers and fathering, but it is equally reasonable to expect new issues, problems, and concerns to arise that are unique to the study of fathers. A key difficulty that researchers face when trying to study fathers is that much of the literature on parenting is framed by a conception of caregiving built around maternal parenting, or what is called the "maternal template" (Marsiglio, Amato, & Day, 2000). Using a methodological "mother template" may be useful initially to explore similarities and differences between parents that may contribute to our understanding of family systems or child outcomes. Nevertheless, in some ways, using the mother template may create as many problems as it solves with respect to systematic research on fathers.

Several limitations are likely to confront those doing research on fathers. These limitations include the lack of a common definition of fathers and fathering, a lack of focused theoretical models regarding fathers, little recognition in the research literature of the cultural embeddedness and variability of fathering, barriers to the participation of fathers in research as well as in parenting, and limited psychometric quality of the tools typically used for studying fathers. We are aware of many of these limitations because we have shared the common experience of designing and conducting studies of fathers of infants and toddlers participating in the national evaluation of Early Head Start. Throughout this chapter, we will draw on these experiences to discuss methodological approaches to studying fathers and fathering.

In approaching our research on fathers, we face several fundamental questions. Who should we study? What should we study about them? How should we study them? After briefly addressing the problem of defining fathers, we will discus theoretical, cultural, evolutionary, and policy perspectives and then focus on selecting methods for studying fathers. Our discussion of methods will include quantitative and qualitative approaches; cross-sectional and longitudinal designs; procedures for sampling, recruitment, and retention; instrument development; and data analysis.

Defining "Fathers": Who Should We Study?

This seems to be a simple question, but it is not. Is the father the child's biological father, a man who becomes invested in the child as a stepfather or adoptive father, a relative who oversees the development of the child, or any and all of the above? Who do we study to assess the impact of fathers on children? As researchers, we can move beyond a traditional view of "father" as biological, living with the child, and married to the mother and instead use a definition more open to the many ways fathering functions in various contexts to influence children. Demographic changes in families are making traditional definitions less useful. (See Section II of this volume for more on this issue.) By defining fathering in terms of particular functions, such as caregiving, playing, teaching, providing support, or acting as role models or authority figures, we can make informed choices about whom to study in cultures that are quite different from our own. Cultural diversity in functions ascribed to fathers requires that an adequate definition take into account multiple aspects of their functions in the family system (Loukas, Twitchell, Piejak, Fitzgerald, & Zucker, 1998).

Fathering also may be defined in terms of a role (cf. Lamb, 1987) that is played out in relation to particular children; as part of a family system; in a particular community circumstance, cultural milieu, and historical era; and during a particular point in the life course. When studying fathering, the questions of who needs to be studied and how they need to be studied depend on the aspects of the role with which a researcher is most concerned. If fatherhood is a role, where does it fit in the course of an individual man's life, and what does it mean in the life of a particular child? Variations in family structure suggest that the study of fathers must reflect the rich diversity that characterizes a man's biological relationship and availability to a child. A loose typology that captures most father roles can be based on a combination of residence and biology: biological resident fathers, biological nonresident fathers, and nonbiological fathers (sometimes termed "social" fathers). Regardless of how fathers, fathering, and fatherhood are defined, the meaning of such definitions are embedded in the dynamics of family, society, and cultural–historical contexts.

The definition of *father* varies across cultures because cultural groups enact parenting functions differently, for fathers even more than for mothers (Lynn, 1974). Father behavior is shaped by social networks within a local culture, which may be part of a minority culture within a larger dominant culture. Thus, there are sometimes substantial variations in fathering within cultures just as there are variations between cultures. Who the fathers are, where they live, and whom they live with may limit the kinds of research that can be done or the kinds of procedures that would be appropriate. Approaching the study of fathers and fathering from the cultural perspective of one group may miss the meanings and functions embedded within the cultural perspectives of another group, unless investigators make efforts to learn more about the culture being studied, perhaps by hiring research staff from that culture. This is especially important because many scientists studying children and families in minority cultures of the United States may have limited experience with those cultures (Johnson, 2000). Diversifying the sources of information about family functioning is essential if we are to capture the richness of cultural diversity in America's families.

Culture may take on different meaning and require different methods of studying fathers in various disciplines. The constructs of *father* and *culture* may be used differently in the traditional methodologies of various disciplines. Furthermore, the research questions, types of data, procedures of data collection, and roles of data collectors may vary depending on the discipline. Anthropologists may focus on ethnographic qualitative descriptions of fathers' disciplinary function within a society, whereas psychologists may focus on the direct effects of fathers' discipline strategies on the child's acting-out behavior in the context of a structured laboratory situation. Rich descriptions of traditions of fathering within a particular cultural group may be interesting to some researchers but not to others who may be more interested in microanalytic patterns of father–child interactions. Some researchers may be concerned about the "big picture," whereas others focus on the "critical details." Different perspectives on what to study about fathers and how to study them can lead to different conclusions about how to identify and recruit fathers to participate in research. For example, a researcher interested in the impact of fathers on children with particular problems (e.g., those with behavior problems) could focus on children in that group and attempt to recruit their fathers into the research project. Alternatively, a researcher interested in fathers with particular problems could attempt to recruit them into a study on the presumption that their children would be at risk for related problems (e.g., Zucker et al., 2000). Depending on their perspectives and their goals, some researchers may be searching for universal features of fathering across cultures by using standardized procedures, whereas others may be studying features within specific cultural contexts using a concomitant variety of methods. Because of the interaction between culture and discipline in relation to father research, different disciplinary approaches may use different definitions, ask different questions, and obtain different kinds of outcomes.

Answers to questions about fathers may have been constrained by the traditional approaches of particular disciplines. Creative integration of seemingly disparate approaches, for example, qualitative and quantitative methods, may be usefully employed to provide a better understanding of cultural factors in relation to fathers and fathering. A broader awareness of definitions, cultural context, and disciplinary traditions for studying fathers and fathering may help researchers consider the implications of various methodological choices.

ASKING QUESTIONS: WHAT SHOULD WE STUDY ABOUT FATHERS?

Theoretical Perspectives in Father Research

The crucial questions of science should be driven by theory, by policy, or by a perspective derived from careful observation, not by methods. The questions researchers ask about fathers arise in the context of a given theoretical perspective or a perspective based on extensive encounters within a culture. An international economist may question why a national increase in the economic power of women predicts father absence (Mackey, 1996), whereas a developmental psychologist may ask why father presence in a family predicts children's academic achievement (Coley, 1998). (See Section VI of this volume for more on economic perspectives and Section III for more on child development outcomes.) The questions and the level of analysis will differ depending on the scientist's culture, discipline, and theoretical point of view. The questions and the level of analysis then dictate specific methodological approaches. Different disciplines using different methodologies can, in effect, ask the same question. At a broad level of inquiry, there might be few disparities, and different methodological approaches may produce the same general answer. However, at a more specific level, the choice of a particular methodological approach might constrain the answers. Questions come from theory, observation, or policy, but answers might be limited by methods.

Methods and analytic strategies vary depending on whether investigators are variable oriented or person oriented in their perspectives (von Eye & Schuster, 2000). A variable-oriented researcher may focus on the degree to which parental physical punishment is related to the number of child aggressive acts on the playground. A person-oriented researcher may focus on the extent to which children reared by antisocial alcoholics are at high risk for biobehavioral disregulation when compared to children of nonantisocial alcoholics (Fitzgerald, Davies, & Zucker, in press). In the variable-oriented example, the investigator most likely would select a cross-sectional strategy using observations of specific behavioral acts to link to something such as frequency of parental spanking. In the person-oriented example, the investigator may use a longitudinal strategy to assess the impact of a particular parental typology (antisociality) on children's later risk for poor outcomes.

Choosing the methods needed to study fathers depends on having a coherent conceptual framework as a guide. Otherwise, study results are apt to be incomplete, perhaps even misleading. For example, there is a general belief that paternal involvement in the lives of children is good for children's well-being. But what does that mean? Such generic, inchoate beliefs do not tell us what kind of involvement or how much involvement matters, nor does it tell us if paternal involvement matters more under some conditions or at certain points in a child's life or in relation to specific child outcomes. Posing questions about fathers in the absence of a guiding theory or a framework based on extended field observations runs the risk of obtaining answers that are difficult to interpret. An organizing conceptual framework, whether derived from theory or field observations, is important because it gives structure and, ultimately, meaning to scientific inquiry.

A theory provides a set of propositions to unite the parts of the questions such that the approach used to gather information about one part takes into consideration all parts. From the standpoint of this chapter, a theory can provide guidance regarding the methods needed to study fathers. It can offer a framework for choosing the constructs to be measured, for selecting the sample and the study design, for developing the data-gathering instruments and the schedule of measurement, and for employing the best-suited analytic strategies. Indeed, curiosity may provide the impetus to study a particular question about fathers, but theory gives the question the kind of shape that has scientific value (i.e., precision and perspective). Unfortunately, for doing research on fathers and selecting methods to study them, one of the limitations is a lack of a theory to address the fathering role in a precise and comprehensive way that tells us what is the best way to study fathers, in context, in relation to families and children, along a life course.

There is no Grand Unifying Theory of fatherhood to effectively guide research on fathers. For that matter, there is no Grand Unifying Theory of motherhood either, or even parenthood more generally. There are, nonetheless, several classes of theories that can give shape to the rapidly evolving field of father studies. There is a class of theories that may help explain paternal attitudes and beliefs, including identity theory, gender role theory, socialization theory, social learning theory, life-span developmental theory, and cultural theory. Another class of theories may help explain the impact of fathers on children, most particularly theories pertaining to the development of competence, adaptive functioning, and attachment. Attachment theory, in particular, may offer a perspective regarding fathers as caregivers with whom infants are likely to form attachments varying in security. A class of theories that may help explain paternal behavior includes reinforcement theory, exchange theory, conflict theory, the functionalist theory of emotions, environmental theory (i.e., affordances), and cultural theory, which address behavior in terms of individual experiences. Paternal behavior may also be explained by ethological and evolutionary theories, which address the adaptive advantages of behaviors, and by various systems theory approaches, family systems theory, general systems theory, and developmental systems theory, which address behavior in terms of the interplay of forces between and across the systems in which fathering takes place.

Developmental systems theory (Ford & Lerner, 1992; Sameroff, 1983; von Bertalanffy, 1968), because of its potential to integrate multiple levels of analysis and thereby reflect the emphasis domains of multiple disciplines, may offer a bridge for an interdisciplinary methodological approach to studying fathers. Even when the question primarily concerns the construction of fathers' belief systems, the reference to systems theory concepts (centralization, equifinality, self-regulation and stability, and permeability) may help inform such critical decisions as what sample to select and what control or moderator variables to use. The value of systems theory (or chaos theory, as it is sometimes called) is not well understood in fatherhood studies, perhaps owing to its relative newness in science (Gleick, 1987). But rapid changes in fathering and fatherhood since World War II make certain dynamic systems principles potentially quite attractive. Such principles help account for sudden sharp reorganizations in family functioning. They also may help explain why small initial changes in the state of things, such as the behavior of one family member, can lead to substantial later changes for several family members. The notion of strong deep attractors may help explain why certain family processes and configurations seem to operate within rather narrow limits despite efforts to perturb them. It may even help explain why relatively small amounts of paternal involvement (in terms of direct care) can still have important effects on children.

But currently, the lack of a Grand Unifying Theory makes the choice of methods and solutions for methodological problems more challenging. The methodological choices and solutions for studying fathers are not prescribed by theory, including systems theory. Nonetheless, the field of father studies is likely to benefit by utilizing the principles of one or more theories, particularly developmental systems theory, to help organize and direct each study. Such an approach is preferable to the largely atheoretical approach used in the previous history of studies on fathers.

Much of the early research on fathers used the conceptual frameworks, research questions, and methodological strategies that researchers found useful for studying mothers. To wit, Greenberg and Morris (1974) labeled fathers' reactions to their newborn infants as "engrossment" and offered it as the father equivalent to bonding (Klaus & Kennel, 1976). Certainly, some of the ideas, questions, and methodological approaches developed for studying mothers are likely to also work well when studying fathers because they have been carefully refined over decades of research on mothers. For example, methods used for research on infant attachment were derived directly from a strong theoretical basis that focused initially almost exclusively on the infant–mother relationship (Bowlby, 1969). These methods have been usefully adapted to study the infant–father relationship as well, but may not always be the best choice for studying infant–father relationships. The infant–father relationship may offer unique adaptive advantages other than the emotional security of attachment, such as playfulness and problem solving, that researchers are just beginning to develop methods for studying (Grossmann, Grossmann, & Zimmermann, 1999). When there is a demand for mothers to play a strong economic role in the family, there may be more demand for fathers to do "parenting" like mothers, and the mother template may be useful (Mackey, 1996). However, fathers may adapt to this demand in ways that may make the template inappropriate.

Cultural and Evolutionary Perspectives in Father Research

Contemporary research on fathers is not guided by an overarching theory, nor is the impetus for contemporary concern for fathers and fathering grounded in any historical theoretical tradition that gave rise to the past 50 years of research on infant-mother attachment. Indeed, a case can be made that contemporary concern for fathers reflects changes in western culture related to increases of the educational status of women and their increasing presence in the workforce. Amato (1998) notes that in the mid-20th century, the role of the father in the United

States was relatively clear; they were providers, disciplinarians, and role models for the work ethic and achievement. The sociological description of father advanced by Parsons and Bales (1955) soon was displaced by cultural changes in women's education, employment, and unwillingness to bear large numbers of children. Thus, "as women became more like fathers, so men were expected to become more like mothers" (Amato, 1998, p. 241). So, as Patricia Draper (1998) asks, why should fathers father?

A cultural-economic answer may emphasize the importance of children as a labor force for working on the farm, whereas a biological determinist view may emphasize the importance of carrying on the bloodline and the continuation of the gene pool. Although subsistence living and high infant mortality continue to be related to high birthrates in underdeveloped countries, industrialization, the decline of the family farm, and improvements in health care clearly played a role in the decline in family size that occurred in nearly every developed country during the 20th century. Thus, when men in the United States are asked what motivates them to want to have children, they are more likely to stress the love and emotional satisfaction children bring into their lives than the fact that the bloodline may persist (Mackey, 1996).

Evolutionary theory has contributed one of the few theoretical efforts to explain why fathers should be invested in their offspring. (See Section I of this volume for more on evolutionary perspectives.) Trivers (1972) proposed that parental care is regulated by parental investment and parental certainty. Parental investment was defined in terms of activities that would increase the offspring's chances of survival or reproductive success: *substitutive activities* (typical of females), such as transporting, feeding, and retrieving infants, and *complementary activities* (typical of males), such as territorial defense, play, and role modeling (Snowdon & Suomi, 1982). Trivers's (1972) theory implies a parental certainty hypothesis, which means that the extent to which fathers are invested in their offspring will be affected by the extent to which they are certain of their paternity. Studies of nonhuman primates provide only partial support for the parental certainty hypothesis with respect to paternal behavior, whereas support is stronger among humans (Snowdon & Suomi, 1982) because of the high degree of substitutive behaviors in predominately monogamous family (breeding) systems. Research on fathers' parental investment has often stressed substitutive activities. "Our society tends to define parental investment in terms of the amount of time spent with offspring and the quality of that time spent. It defines parental care in terms of maternal care" (Snowdon & Suomi, 1982, p. 66). However, time spent by fathers with their children is often in complementary activities. Fathers of toddlers enrolled in Early Head Start report that they perform some substitutive behaviors, but that the most time spent with their toddlers is in the complementary activity of play, particularly rough and tumble play (Fitzgerald et al., 2000; Fitzgerald & Montanez, 2000).

In anthropology and comparative psychology, there are models of male parenting that diverge substantially from maternal behavior and reflect both diversity and commonalities across cultures and even across species (particularly among nonhuman primates). (See Section V of this volume for more on anthropological and cross-cultural perspectives.) There appear to be more universals for mothers than for fathers, although culture influences both substitutive and complementary behaviors. The greater diversity in fathering implies a more dynamic response, or a greater adaptive capacity to respond to environmental and cultural change. Fathering may involve behavior to sustain systems that support mothering. From an evolutionary perspective, the family system evolved because it contributed some adaptive advantage for pair mates to sustain a relationship in order to enhance chances for offspring to survive. Indeed, the normative family involves at least one man and one woman responsible for child care, even if neither is the biological parent (Lynn, 1974). As predicted from the parental certainty hypothesis, the stronger the biological relatedness of parent to offspring, the more invested parents should be in their care. For fathers in particular, this should translate into greater involvement in substitutive activities. It is clear that when circumstances restrict men's access to their children (through divorce or separation), parental investment is markedly compromised (Lerman & Sorensen, 1996; Mackey, 1996). Viewing these roles and behaviors across cultures can be helpful in exploring their meaning.

Cross-cultural studies of mothering have often focused on commonalities, but that may not be the best strategy for cross-cultural studies of fathering. Looking at fatherhood as more adaptive and dynamic suggests that it may be the variations in fathers/fathering across cultures and species that are more important to view than the commonalities. Although the parental certainty hypothesis has difficulties, it may provide an anchor around which to organize studies of the cultural impact on fathers' connectedness to the family system and to their substitutive and complementary parental activities. For example, it would lead to rather clear predictions about the involvement of residential biological fathers, nonresidential biological fathers, and nonbiological "social" fathers with respect to their investment in the care of children.

Social Policy Perspectives in Father Research

What researchers learn about father involvement as caregivers or providers will have implications for social policy and social programs. Research and theory can influence policy and programs, but the reverse is also true; policy and programmatic needs to know can both determine what we will study and stimulate advances in methodology. Although it is not the purpose of this section to explicate the role of policy and program in a new science of father research (see Section VII of this volume for more on these topics), its purpose is to make apparent the role that policy and programmatic needs to know are playing in defining methodological challenges and opportunities that contribute to the methodological frontier of father research. A further purpose for including policy in the discussion of methods for studying fathers is to demonstrate the dynamic interplay among policy, theory, and methods in general. Methodological challenges arise from recent policy initiatives.

Recent policies stemming from the Personal Responsibility and Work Opportunities Reconciliation Act (PRWORA) illustrate how fatherhood policies may affect research methodology in studies requested by the federal government. PRWORA stressed the importance of *biological* father involvement in children's lives for purposes of financial and, in some cases, emotional support. Prior programs targeting efforts to involve fathers of children, such as Head Start, may have emphasized *male* involvement with children and with program activities. Thus, research conducted in the earlier context may have investigated whichever father or male was involved with a child, and sometimes at a single point in time. However, more recently, the central role of the *biological* father in policies emphasizes different research questions with new methodological challenges for investigators. For example, consider the program/policy question, "Can birth-to-three programs such as Early Head Start increase the chances that biological fathers in fragile families will stay involved with their children?" Research designed to address this question must incorporate identification of the biological father at or near birth and *follow* that father over time. The study is further complicated if other romantic figures enter the mother's life or other father figures enter the child's life. Thus, earlier research methodology to answer questions about father involvement with children has shifted from a point-in-time assessment of the male in a child's life to a more complex study that may involve locating multiple fathers and disentangling their complex influences over time.

A shift in the reference point—from fatherhood as a role to the father of a specific child—can change the methodology of study. Policy and programmatic needs for defining the sample may drive the methodological framework in ways that would not be anticipated if only theory were the guiding factor. For example, many policy and program-related studies, such as the Early Head Start study and others, select samples based on children. In these studies, fatherhood is defined in relation to a specific child or children and only secondarily in terms of a man's own life course development. The methodological picture is further complicated when studying young children for whom the father must be named by the *mother.* Although many important questions must necessarily begin by sampling the children and their mothers, the unique challenges introduced by talking to the mother before talking to the father must be acknowledged and addressed. Methodological challenges are introduced by using mothers as informants while attempting to avoid introducing a bias into the sample if some mothers screen fathers out of the study. Using mothers as informants necessitates studying corroboration of mother and father on paternity; that is, do men *and* women agree on who is the biological father or the father figure? Methodological techniques must be refined to determine how to gain information from the mother about the father while minimizing chances that the mother will make the final decision about the father's participation in the research. Further techniques are needed to move away from deficit assumptions and look to fathers for strengths, for example, focusing on the impact of the father's presence rather than his absence and on what he does when he is with his child rather than what happens when he is gone (Fitzgerald et al., 2000; Fitzgerald & Montanez, 2000).

Challenge is also encountered when there is a methodological deficit around an urgent policy question, and opportunity exists for methodological innovation when the deficit is identified. Here we introduce the broad example that father researchers encountered in seeking measures that were not based on a mother template. Recognized deficits such as reliance on a mother template may be difficult to correct without intentional methodological efforts, resources, and coordination among investigators such as the DADS (Cabrera et al., 2001) group that has sought to systematically develop and promulgate promising methodology and instrumentation. This group identified key mother template measures that would allow direct comparisons of fathers with mothers but also identified new measures unique to father investigation to avoid missing important information about what is distinctive about fathers. Imperfect though the efforts driven by policy are, when efforts are intentional and coordinated and resources are expended across agencies, they provide important opportunities for methodological advances.

One such opportunity is for interdisciplinary collaborations. Current policy initiatives to develop new forms of programs bring a mixture of disciplines to the table and thereby drive interdisciplinary studies requiring new mixes of paradigms and methods. Whereas a policy question may determine the methodology used, more commonly, the policies may also stir up assumptions about the important questions to ask and the important paradigms to frame the study. By doing so, policy-guided research may lead to the development of hybrid and new methodologies. For example, the Office of Child Support Enforcement and the Early Head Start program collaboration to increase father involvement in children's lives around birth called for measures to assess community collaboration efforts as well as measures to assess effects on children and fathers. Thus, methods used by sociologists and developmental psychologists were both relevant. In turn, methodological or theoretical variations in approaches to studying fathers have a potential impact on policy regarding appropriate intervention. Psychological data may imply an intervention at an individual level, sociological data at a community level, and economic data at a national level. Altogether, during this current dynamic period of father research it is important to acknowledge that some methodological challenges and opportunities, as well as advances, are being driven by policy and programmatic considerations.

SELECTING METHODS: HOW SHOULD WE STUDY FATHERS?

General Methodological Approaches

How do our methodological choices influence the answers to our questions? If we continue to use perspectives developed for studying mothers yet take an approach that mothers and fathers have different roles or that fathering has different functions, then we need to develop methods that are sensitive to those differences in the context of family relationships. For example, if we ask mothers and fathers the same questions about the amount of time spent playing with the child, we may miss the qualitative differences between mothers and fathers in the ways that they play with their children. If we ask about types of play and fathers report more rough and tumble play, we may miss what that does for a child or for the father–child relationship unless we observe the interactions more directly. When we observe directly, we may see very different behavior (e.g., play vs. caregiving) serving very similar functions (e.g., helping regulate emotions). Focusing on either just the behavior or just the function may blind us to the other unless we take a broader approach. Using only the traditional methods of our particular discipline may also limit our vision. One way to ensure a broader approach is to conduct research in interdisciplinary teams. An advantage of working together from different disciplinary traditions, is the opportunity to explore new methods or integrate various methods and approaches in ways that help us better understand our data. For example, quantitative researchers may explore qualitative methods, researchers who have done large-scale studies may explore the advantages of small-scale studies, and those who have done cross-sectional studies may explore the possibilities of longitudinal studies.

Qualitative and Quantitative Methods. Research on fathers can benefit from creatively combining qualitative and quantitative approaches to inform our multiple perspectives on fathers, fathering, and fatherhood. There are challenges and opportunities inherent in each approach. Qualitative methods help us to understand the deeper meaning of our constructs to the subjects of our studies, but qualitative data can be a challenge to collect, time and labor intensive to analyze, and inappropriate to generalize. Quantitative methods offer the opportunity for objectivity, statistical testing accounting for chance effects, generalizability, and testing of formal hypotheses and models, but quantitative data can emphasize group trends that mask individual variation and be difficult to interpret. By combining the two approaches, both sets of advantages can be maintained while offsetting their disadvantages.

In particular, integrating quantitative and qualitative data may be valuable in helping us understand how fathering may be defined differently by fathers in different cultures or contexts (cf., Fitzgerald et al., 1999). Interviews of common-law couples in low-income Jamaican families revealed that both mothers and fathers believe that mothers should be primary caregivers and managers of the household and that fathers should focus on economic provision for the family (Roopnarine et al., 1995), whereas the Aka hunter-gatherers of the Central African Republic would likely find such nonegalitarian attitudes about involvement in child care to be quite strange indeed (Hewlett, 1992). Within the United States, African-American mothers report higher levels of father caregiving involvement with their children than white mothers report in a national data set (John, 1996), but not in a more local population area (Hunter, Pearson, Ialongo, & Kellam, 1998). Finally, a study of Mexican-American women's recollections of their fathers indicated that they remembered their fathers, uncles, and grandfathers as much more involved with play activities than the women caregivers in their lives (Lopez & Hamilton, 1997).

In much of the research on young children, fathers are ignored and only mothers are questioned about the "caregiving environment." As researchers involved with the national evaluation of Early Head Start, we have learned that fathers are typically very willing to talk to researchers about their parenting experiences with their infants and toddlers. This is especially true in qualitative interviews when they are encouraged to talk about what fathering means to them. Nevertheless, we have also learned that it is sometimes not appropriate to use the mother template and ask fathers the same kinds of questions we have asked mothers or to conduct observations of fathers and children the same way we structure observations with mothers and children. For example, in an interview with a series of parenting questions about the frequency of activities such as feeding and bathing, one frustrated father asked, "Why don't you ask me about how hard I work to support them?" In setting up observations with mothers, we asked the mother and child to sit together in a restricted area and play with toys while we videotaped their interactions. This kind of interaction is probably more typical for mothers than fathers, so when we asked fathers to do the same thing, the interactions sometimes appeared awkward and unnatural. When we asked fathers to do whatever they "enjoy doing" with their child, the interactions were often more active and innovative (e.g., chasing games, making noises with body parts, moving the child's body like an airplane).

The question of whether to collect qualitative or quantitative data carries implications for the size of the sample studied. Disciplinary traditions suggest that the sample size deemed appropriate by a demographic sociologist will be much different from that deemed appropriate by an ethological psychologist. Interdisciplinary research may challenge our accepted notions of the proper scale for our studies. Large random samples using standardized quantitative measures offer high generalizability and statistical testing of hypotheses, whereas small in-depth studies of a few participants may offer rich qualitative descriptions or detailed observational data that generate new ideas for interpreting the quantitative data. An obvious advantage to interdisciplinary research teams is the potential for linking quantitative and qualitative methods in the same study by selecting, from a large-scale study, a small subgroup for more in-depth interviews or observations. (See Section IV for perspectives of fathers from quantitative and qualitative data; also see chap. 20 for further discussion of the integration of quantitative and qualitative work.)

Cross-Sectional and Longitudinal Studies. Cross-sectional designs enable researchers to answer questions about the current father and fathering in a child's life and how these are related to current child developmental outcomes for children of different ages or for fathers of different ages. Longitudinal designs enable researchers to ask about the long-term experience of having a father or of being a father, about the importance of father involvement over time to both fathers and children. Longitudinal studies allow father researchers to begin building a coherent picture of father involvement in relation to both child and adult development. Indeed, a longitudinal study of fathers and children is really two longitudinal studies, a study of father effects over time on child development and a study of changes in fathers over time. But longitudinal methods present some thorny methodological issues, because fathers can change their residential status, more than one father can become involved in a child's life, and one father can be involved in many children's lives.

Despite the difficulty and cost of longitudinal research, there are particular advantages to this approach in studying fathers. If we only look at fathers cross sectionally, we may learn what proximal issues they have to deal with at different ages, but we will not learn much about how transforming these experiences may be over time in terms of how fathers relate to their children. Longitudinal analysis of fathers can then be particularly revealing. For example, if fathers do play a unique role in socializing young children, perhaps through their differential play interactions, then we are likely to learn something unique about this role if we look at it over time, versus looking only at the proximal case. Even in longitudinal studies, proximal factors may be the best predictors of outcomes, but any particular proximal or concurrent variable derives from a history of development. Long-term outcomes may not manifest until later in childhood or adolescence. Many policy questions require longitudinal study, so there is likely to be more funding in this area in the future. Among many other important questions, policy questions influence this methodological issue during different stages of child development. For example, policy concerns about fragile families during infancy point to the importance of studying the factors involved in the initial formation of the father–child relationship over the first year.

Both cross-sectional and longitudinal studies of fathers share the challenge of defining key constructs at different ages of the children. Some characteristics of fathers may be more important at some ages than others. Perspectives, values, and attitudes may change for fathers as children get older. Indeed, fathering may become more distinct from mothering by adolescence. The role of fathers may be important for the transition to adulthood, which is culturally defined and for some individuals very long. The research literature has been dominated by studies of fathers of infants and young children, and more research is needed on fathering of adolescents and young adults and the experience of fathering at different times in a man's life.

Studies of fathers at one time or over time may also encounter problems depending on the ages of the fathers themselves. It may mean something different to study fathers who are at different ages when they become fathers. Age differences among fathers may be confounded by several factors including maturity, education, income, and health. A father still in his own adolescence may interact quite differently with his infant than a father in his forties. By the time the infant becomes an adolescent, the younger father would be in his thirties, whereas the older father could be approaching 60 and interacting with his teenage son in a much different way.

Age of father may thus interact with age of child. Fathers' roles may change across developmental eras, and mothers and fathers may regulate each others' roles differently depending on both their child's and their own age. In addition, longitudinal studies may show how changes in family composition over time—a new infant in the family, a grown child leaving home, divorce, remarriage, or other household changes—affect fathering and father–child relationships differently at different ages. These complex age interactions have not been studied enough to understand what happens in family systems in relation to developmental change. Cross-generational studies may offer a glimpse at fathering across generations, and a longitudinal cross-generational study could reveal interactions of historical change with the age of father and the age of child. By using different methodologies and asking different questions during different developmental eras, we may learn more about interactive age effects and their meaning at different points in historical time.

Procedures

Sampling. The goal of every sampling plan, regardless of the topic of research, is to draw a sample that adequately represents the population of interest. Thus, the first question a researcher interested in studying fathers must answer is: What group of fathers am I interested in? In some studies, fathers have been defined as those men with a direct biological relationship to the child; that is, men who have literally "fathered" the children of interest. In other cases, fathers are defined as those men with an intimate caregiving relationship to a child, regardless of whether there is a biologic linkage ("social" father). The role of fatherhood is socially constructed. Even so, identifying a particular man as a father does not necessarily mean that he enacts every aspect of the role as it is socially constructed.

Studies of biological fathers may misidentify some of those fathers. Since the advent of DNA testing, there has been a reliable method of determining biological paternity. However, most studies of biological fathers have not utilized DNA testing, relying instead on reports by the supposed biological father or by the child's mother. As a result, some of the studies have not been truly representative of the population of interest. This does not mean that future studies of biological fathers must rely on DNA analysis to establish actual paternity, but it is critical that researchers acknowledge the potential limitations attached to other means of identification.

Studies of social fathers have been even more fraught with risk. Social fathers are typically thought of as men who spend time with a child and who have established a caregiving or guidance relationship with the child. But, it is often difficult to define how much involvement and what type of involvement a man must have with a child in order to be considered a social father. What is a social father and who determines when a man fulfills the role? The man himself? The child's mother? The child? To designate a man a "social father," is it sufficient to say that the man has a relationship with the child's mother and lives with the child? Seldom have researchers actually derived their operational definitions of social fathering from a strong conceptual framework. There is no set answer on what group of men belongs to the population called social fathers.

The answer to the sampling question, "Who belongs to the population, fathers?" depends partly on the overall research question and partly on the conceptual framework that guides the study. In the Early Head Start longitudinal study, we were interested in the impact of paternal involvement on child well-being. We operated on the assumption that fathers influence the development of children (beyond their genetic influence) primarily through their "involvement" with a child in one or more of the ways defined by Lamb (1997). We also operated on the assumption that a man did not have to live with a child in order to perform these functions. Because of the larger context of the study, we had to first inquire of mothers whether any man was playing such a role in the life of our target child. That process may have inadvertently eliminated some men from being identified as social fathers due to their relationship with the child's mother or the mother's own disposition regarding his participation in the study. Thus, our study almost certainly includes some bias, and the findings may not fully reflect the influence of social fathers on their children.

For some studies, the definition used in the Early Head Start study may not be useful. For example, if a researcher's purpose is to determine how much time fathers spend helping children with homework and whether that type of paternal involvement matters in terms of children's achievement, it probably makes little sense to include nonresidential fathers in the sample. If the researcher is asking whether the quality of paternal involvement is related to children's social development, then it probably makes little sense to include men in the sample who do not have at least some minimal level of regular contact with the child because the impact of variations in quality of care almost certainly depends on providing some minimal quantity of care. In the NICHD Study of Early Child Care (1997), one of the research questions pertained to the impact of paternal care in families that routinely used some type of nonmaternal care. The sample included fathers who routinely provided at least 10 hours of care per week to the target child when mothers were not present.

Depending on how a researcher defines fathers, the study may end up including more fathers than children, because for some children more than one man plays a fathering role. One child may have a nonresident biological father, a resident stepfather, and another male relative (e.g., grandfather) who functions as a "father figure" for the child. In a longitudinal study, such a problem can become particularly acute because "who the father is" can change across time. If the research question is, "What is the impact of father involvement on children's well-being?" should researchers follow the original father (i.e., the one first identified as father during the longitudinal study), use whatever man plays the role of father at any given time, or include all men who play the role of father at any time? The anomaly of having more than one father could pose no problem if the goal is to document how much contact a child has with a father during a specified period of time. But it could present almost intractable difficulties if the goal is to determine the association between a particular type of involvement and some aspect of child well-being. Almost no theory of parenting would stipulate that the association would be the same irrespective of the number of relationships or the exact nature of each relationship between any particular "father" and child. (See Section III of this volume for more on this issue.)

The current interest in studying fathers, important as it is for understanding children's well-being, family life, and adult male development, suffers from the highly politicized climate that gives rise to some of that interest (Marsiglio et al., 2000). There is a tendency often not fully realized even by the researchers themselves to define the population of interest in keeping with the researcher's own political views about what constitutes fatherhood. For certain research questions, that tendency may actually serve the interests and validity of the study. However, the history of science indicates that such tendencies often lead to false information about the subject being studied. For most studies, researchers who study fathering would generally be well served by selecting members of their father samples conservatively, including only those men who clearly meet the criteria for being a father implied by the research question and the conceptual framework that guides the research. A more conservative approach to population definition and sample selection is particularly important in an area of inquiry that is not only highly politicized but also relatively new. As the area of inquiry matures, there is less danger that a more liberal approach to sampling will lead to inaccurate conclusions. Indeed, a more liberal approach during later stages may help expand and test the limits of some theory or set of findings.

Even in studies where researchers have clearly and definitively defined a population of fathers they wished to study, rarely has the sample been representative of the population stipulated. Most studies have utilized samples of convenience, such as fathers participating in a particular program, class, or organization or fathers whose wives volunteer to participate in a study. Almost all such convenience samples are obtained in a single locale and dominated by a single ethnic or social class group, sometimes even a single religious affiliation. What those samples represent is often difficult to determine—and too often it is not even discussed. The problem with convenience samples is not so much who was included (more often middle-class European-American men living with the child) as who was left out. Due to the costs and complexities of recruiting them, incarcerated and homeless fathers, fathers in the military or with jobs that keep them away from home, fathers loosely attached to households or relationships within the family, fathers from small minority groups, and the like have often been omitted from study samples. National studies of fathers have been plagued with what may be called an "undercount problem," such as has historically been the case with population censuses. Sampling strategies (and, perhaps more accurately, recruitment strategies as will be discussed later) need to be implemented that include these "missing" or "invisible" groups of fathers. Otherwise results will reflect only a restricted subgroup of fathers: those who are easy to identify and locate, in more stable situations, of higher status, and more trusting of researchers. For this reason, the Federal Interagency Forum on Child and Family Statistics (1998) strongly recommended the inclusion of nonresident fathers in future studies of fatherhood. Such approaches to sampling, of course, entail substantially greater costs.

The other difficulty with most samples of fathers is the small number of fathers included. In simple descriptive studies, a small sample size may not be a huge problem if the sample is otherwise representative of the population. But even in descriptive studies, estimating population diversity may be difficult if the researcher has only a small number of cases. For studies about statistical relations, a small sample can often severely limit statistical power. The literature on "paternal effects" seldom includes evidence of what is technically called a "large effect." Detecting small (but meaningful) effects generally requires a relatively large sample. As a result the canon of father studies probably includes a disproportionate number of Type II errors. Relatedly, many studies with "null findings" have probably never seen the light of day (what is referred to as the "file drawer problem"). Small sample size also severely restricts the researcher's ability to test the complex models of parenting and family functioning implied in developmental systems theories.

Recruitment and Retention.   Studying fathers has historically proven more difficult than studying mothers partly because men have been harder to recruit as participants. There are often logistical or legal problems involved when recruiting and retaining fathers who do not reside in their children's homes or are incarcerated. Although there are numerous tomes on sampling methodology, there is no handbook on recruitment or blueprint for how to get it done. As a consequence, many father studies have samples limited in their ability to produce representative, meaningful findings (Marsiglio et al., 2000).

Researchers may increase the likelihood of successfully recruiting a representative sample of fathers if they ask themselves the following questions and consider what the answers imply in terms of recruitment strategies: (a) What is the purpose of the study? (b) Will men see the study as legitimate? and (c) Will men see their involvement in the study as worth their time and effort? If the purpose of the study is to determine paternal effects on child development, the researcher may benefit by first recruiting a sample of children with the hope that once the child is recruited, the father can also be recruited. By comparison, if the purpose of the study is to delineate the father's role in the family, a researcher may find it useful to recruit a sample of mothers (our experience suggests that mothers are often easier to recruit), with the hope again that once the mother agrees to participate, the father will also agree. These steps are rarely sufficient to attain a large enough representative enough sample of fathers.

Even if a researcher is successful in recruiting a group of children or mothers, that is no guarantee that fathers will subsequently agree to participate. Some men, because of their investment in the fathering role or because they feel they (or fathers in general) have been excluded, may be eager to participate. In general, however, men are less inclined to accede with requests just by virtue of being asked or if the justification for participation is primarily social. Several strategies have been used to persuade such reluctant men to participate: (a) using their wives as conscriptors in the process, (b) using others whom they might respect (other fathers in their community, ministers in their churches) as conscriptors, and (c) financial inducements. Some researchers have found success by providing services to the men themselves, such as support groups or educational programs, but that strategy carries the danger that the service actually constitutes a kind of intervention that affects the very processes that are the target of study.

Men are more likely to agree to participate if they perceive the research as having a legitimate purpose. Demonstrating the legitimacy of the research is critical to successful recruitment. The study may seem more legitimate if the request comes from someone whom the father trusts and respects, if data collection is to occur on the father's own turf or someplace with a clear connection to the role of fathering (laboratory assessments may seem strange), and if the manner and type of data collection have "face validity" (certain types of structured encounters and questionnaires may be off-putting). The methods that have historically been used to study mothers may sometimes interfere with studying fathers by alienating the men.

Even if a man sees the request to participate as legitimate and even if that man is generally inclined to participate, he will still evaluate his decision to participate in terms of the perceived cost of participation (i.e., how much time and effort will it take in relation to the anticipated benefits or value derived). For this reason, father researchers have tried to keep the burden of participation light. Rarely does the amount of data collection done require more than an hour or so or require the father to make special arrangements to participate (i.e., efforts are made for the father's convenience). Monetary or other tangible inducements to participate are often required. For men who may have concerns about privacy, researchers might also consider using a computer assisted self-interview (CASI), which allows the respondent to receive questions via a headset and then enter the information directly on a computer. If men are told that they will be able to give potentially sensitive information in this way, they may be more inclined to participate.

Concerns about response burden in the Early Head Start study meant limiting the number of measures used with fathers and being very flexible in terms of the times and places where data were gathered. For fathers working long or variable hours, it was particularly important to maintain flexibility in scheduling appointments and sometimes in segmenting them into a series of shorter sessions in order to complete the data collection. Likewise, we allowed fathers substantial opportunity to tell their own story in their own way, rather than constricting them to completing a long series of paper-and-pencil instruments. We also arranged for fathers to provide data to us when not in the presence of mother, fearing that the partner's presence may unduly constrain the father's responses. Although we attempted to ask penetrating questions about paternal beliefs and practices, we attempted to ask them in ways that would not be perceived as embarrassing or accusatory. These efforts to meet men on their own terms seems to have resulted in an experience that most men found acceptable and even pleasant. The vast majority of these fathers participated in a second round of data collection and were willing to continue their participation in the study.

For recruiting and tracking fathers, the most common gateway is through mothers, a strategy with both potential advantages and potential disadvantages. As stated earlier, mothers can often persuade fathers to participate, thus increasing the likelihood of a large enough, good enough sample. However, in some groups, recruiting fathers by contacting mothers may backfire and make fathers less willing to participate if they perceive themselves as solely responsible for such decisions. Mothers can also be excellent sources of information regarding the whereabouts of nonresidential fathers for those trying to conduct longitudinal research on fathers. But, although they are the gateway, mothers can often function as gatekeepers as well. Mothers may buffer some men from participation, exclude some men from participation, or finger some men as fathers who do not identify themselves as a father. An alternative is to directly recruit fathers to bring their families into the study and obtain adequate contact information directly from the fathers themselves. In a longitudinal study of children at risk for alcoholism, fathers were recruited directly because of their characteristics in order to look prospectively at risk and protective factors related to children and their development (Fitzgerald et al., in press).

Retention of fathers in a longitudinal study may depend on their interactions with data collection staff. Some fathers are more comfortable if data collectors are from their own community, ethnic background, or gender. There are often trade-offs to consider among building rapport, utilizing local knowledge, hiring trained research staff, and minimizing observer bias. Disciplines differ in terms of the importance attached to minimizing potential bias or the value of having data collector and research participant tightly "matched," and unfortunately there is inadequate data on how much the characteristics of data collectors affect subject retention or the quality of data obtained. Clearly, given the diversity of backgrounds among fathers, careful attention to the background and training of data collectors and their importance in engaging men in the data-collection process is central for retaining fathers in a longitudinal study.

Measurement Instruments

Measures Unique to Fathers.   Studies on fathering have often adapted, many times with scant modification, measures used in research on mothers. Simple modifications include substituting a more male-oriented activity for a more female-oriented activity to create a measure of paternal involvement, changing the observation context from a mother–child friendly setting to one that is more father–child friendly when measuring father–child relationship quality, and adjusting the wording of an attitudinal indicator somewhat so that it seems to be more reflective of how fathers feel or believe rather than how mothers feel or believe about the process of parenting. Adapting instruments developed for studying mothers has the advantage of using measures with a longer history of validation and reliability testing. However, these simple adaptations have been met with growing skepticism, partly as a function of findings that didn't quite mesh with expectations, partly as a function of qualitative studies of fathers, and partly as a function of advances in conceptualizations about male parenting. Measures that work well with mothers may contain some questions that would not be appropriate for fathers or do not reflect the ways fathers think, feel, or act. Validity inheres in every property of a data-collection instrument. Thus, when considering whether to use a measure that has a good track record with mothers, researchers must not only evaluate the measure in terms of content appropriateness, but also the response options available and the opportunities afforded fathers to express themselves in characteristic ways. Moreover, it is critical to conduct psychometric studies of the measures to ensure validity.

Consider, just for illustration, how to measure parenting efficacy in men. Summing items from a newly converted measure of parenting efficacy (one on which items have been adjusted to be more father-oriented) may not result in a score that captures paternal efficacy beliefs as validly as the original scale captured maternal efficacy beliefs. Deeper feelings about parenting efficacy may not be as fully reflected in responses to how well fathers can get their kids to do a series of particular everyday things as might be the case with mothers, whose tasks of parenting more often involve trying to accomplish just such small, everyday goals. If fathers' roles are more distal and family context bound, then a more holistic approach to assessing efficacy will be required.

In the Early Head Start study of fathers, we grappled with the issue of how to measure paternal sensitivity. The traditional way of measuring maternal sensitivity is to place mother and child in a structured situation where there is a goal to accomplish. The mother and child are then observed in a series of small exchanges pertinent to that goal. Such an approach may not be fully ecologically valid, but it may work well as a window on mother–child relationship quality in that mothers and children frequently engage in small exchanges around goal-oriented activities, and most mothers share a number of common goals pertaining to everyday living. Fathers tend to spend much less time engaged in small exchanges connected to everyday goals, and there is far less commonality across households in what fathers do vis-à-vis their children. An alternative approach is to put fathers and children in a free-play situation and then design a new set of observation codes to index paternal sensitivity—an imperfect solution probably, but one that moves in the direction of measuring fathers without relying completely on the mother template. The methodological father template is not yet as finely hewn as the mother template. Thus, researchers will often struggle when constructing measures for fathers. Even so, the excellent efforts to define paternal involvement by Lamb (1997; in press) and others may offer useful guidance.

Measures for Various Kinds of Fathers.   Not only are different instruments and protocols needed for fathers than for mothers, but different instruments may be needed for different kinds of fathers: residential biological father, nonresident biological father, stepfather, and so forth (see chap. 3). There may well be something constant about what men bring to the role of parent, but different roles often mean different kinds of behaviors and attitudes with respect to children and families. Thus, there is a challenge to measure the same (or at least similar) constructs in men who play different fathering roles. For example, fathering may mean something quite different for stepfathers, given that their behavior toward a child may be dependent on the age of the child or the length of time in the relationship. Moreover, the same man may be more than one kind of father, a biological father to one set of children and a stepfather to another, thus questions and measures need to be designed accordingly. For example, is "sensitive fathering" reflected in the same behaviors of resident and nonresident biological fathers? Or does sensitivity in non-resident fathers include more attention to indirect/supportive behaviors and more consideration of the off-again, on-again nature of contact between father and child than is the case with resident fathers? For stepfathers, is sensitivity more defined by timing of entry into the family, duration of the union, and even age and gender of the child? Might the same behavior that is considered sensitive in a resident biological father be considered intrusive or even inappropriate for a stepfather?

Cultural differences may necessitate different types of instruments as well as different data collection approaches. Most of the research on fathers was designed by and tested on middle-class Europeans and Americans living in the 20th century, in effect, the group of men moving toward what has been defined as the "new fatherhood" (Lamb, 1997). As such, the meaning and measurement of fathering has been constricted by the cultural script that fits mostly middle-class white people living in individualistic capitalist societies. That script does not even fit all Americans, much less residents of other countries. The importation of a parenting script constructed for one culture to be used in another culture has been descried for studies of mothers, where there might be greater convergence of roles and responsibilities across cultures (Masten, 1999). But importing the white, middle-class script of fathering to most groups of men is likely fraught with greater dangers in that fathering tends to be even more diverse across times and places.

Partly as a hedge against overreliance on currently available measures of fathering, in the Early Head Start study of fathers, we included a series of open-ended questions aimed at allowing men to define their own perceptions about being a father. Many poor men, when asked about what support they needed in their role as parents, responded with surprise and denial: "I don't need any support. No one supports me." Qualitative open-ended questions such as this one allowed greater individual and cultural variations in responses to emerge.

Measures Using Multiple Informants. Many studies may need to learn about fatherhood across multiple informants. Fundamentally, fathering is about relationships—the relationship between father and child, but also between father and other family members, and even between father and community. Although it is often easy and inexpensive to obtain maternal reports about fathers, it is also often valuable to include information from multiple informants when studying complex constructs pertaining to fatherhood. Certainly, information about fathering from the fathers themselves is critical, but the mothers' perspectives are also important. Mothers and fathers tend to have different views and only modest agreement about the same phenomena including their parenting activities. Fathers do not always provide accurate or complete information about their own behavior but that information can be usefully supplemented by others who observe them. Moreover, for certain research questions, the views of mothers or children may have value in their own right. Thus, for some research questions, obtaining information from multiple informants can be quite useful, even critical.

In the Early Head Start study we often asked mothers and fathers the same questions (or complementary questions) about key aspects of fathering. In so doing, we hoped to explicate the meaning of fatherhood in low-income men by looking at both individual and corroborative responses. The field is clearly moving toward the use of multiple informants on studies of fathers. There is a particular need to develop ways of obtaining meaningful information about fathers from their children, especially in early childhood, an age for which there are fewer reliable measures. Of particular relevance to the study of fathers are problems entailed in obtaining information from children on subjects where there is high emotional salience and cultural ideation that tends to shape how children respond.

Adapting and Developing New Measures. To date, there has been too little attention given to the technology of measurement in father studies. Developing new instruments for studying fathers means that research time will need to be allocated for testing the stability, reliability, and validity of the measures derived. There is a wealth of information on how to measure attitudes, beliefs, and behaviors that has gone largely untapped when constructing (or selecting) measures for fathers—the measurement of father–child interaction is a partial exception to this general rule. Each measurement process carries with it assumptions about the experiences, competencies, and dispositions required for valid assessment. Fathers play such a diversity of roles and engage in such a variety of responsibilities vis-à-vis their children that many fathers have very little experience with the issues and activities included on parenting measures, even those that are well regarded. As a general rule, researchers are advised to include a significant number of indicators in a measure to ensure the reliability of the measure. However, if men tend to have little experience with some indicators, then it may be advisable to limit the items to only those for which fathers can provide valid responses. Sometimes reliability can be gained by changing the item format (e.g., using more response alternatives or more carefully anchoring them) so that reliability can be maintained with fewer items. In contrast, for some parenting measures, a small number of prototypical behaviors reflect maternal parenting, but for fathers, a much more extensive array of indicators may be needed to capture the same parenting phenomenon.

Different concerns about reliability arise with different kinds of measures. Lists of discrete activities that fathers engage in with their children tend to be included in measures of father involvement because of their presumed relation to child well-being. For the most part, these lists are "cause" indicators (see Bollen & Lennox, 1991, for a discussion of this issue) with no assumptions about the underlying covariance structure or unidimensionality of items on the list (i.e., each stands alone), so there is little reason to use factor analysis or coefficients of internal consistency. It is perfectly proper to sum items from an activity measure containing cause indicators even when coefficient alpha is low, so long as the summary score is correlated in expected ways with those child outcomes the activities purportedly affect (for a good example of how this works, look at risk indices and measures of stressful life events). By contrast, measures designed to reflect some underlying paternal characteristic (e.g., investment, sensitivity) are "effect" indicators with an assumption of both an underlying covariance structure and undimensionality, so factor analysis and alpha or another internal consistency measure may be useful. All in all, coefficient alpha tends to be overused, subject to misinterpretation (Cortina, 1993), and too dependent on the number of items examined.

Instruments developed for research on fathers need to include aspects of fathering that are important to men, important to their families, and important to their children. Our understanding of fathers will be enriched by developing not only good standardized survey instruments but also reliable behavioral measures, valid attitude scales, and the kinds of questions and prompts that elicit thoughtful subjective qualitative responses from fathers. Inviting fathers to define the questions and determine the conditions under which they are studied will help refine measurement practice in studying fathers. As researchers develop better measures of fathering, theories about fatherhood are likely to advance. Likewise, policy efforts are likely to benefit more fathers and their families. For the short run, researchers need to concentrate on construct validation of father measures. Otherwise, even movements away from the mother template and efforts to expand the cultural scripts used to guide measurement may yield little about fathering and how it affects children's lives.

Data Analysis

Father research will benefit from further development of statistical methods that permit analyses of dyadic interactions, test models of behavior over time, examine intergenerational effects and contextual support, and account for selection effects. Analytic techniques developed for longitudinal developmental methods (von Eye & Schuster, 2000) may help analyze father data collected as part of developmental studies that included not just dyadic, but also more complex interactions over multiple time points. The fact is that there is nothing unique to fathers in any statistical technique.

What is valuable for the study of fathers is the extraordinary increase in analytic techniques that have been developed in the past 30 years or more. For example, von Eye and Schuster (2000) note that at the beginning of the 20th century, cluster analyses, log-linear modeling, classic or probabilistic test theory, configural frequency analysis, structural equation modeling, time-series analyses, Markov models, or nonparametric statistics were not available. Today we not only have these analytic techniques, but we also have hierarchical linear modeling, survival analysis, logistic regression, prediction analysis, dynamical systems modeling, and so forth. Moreover, we can use models that combine categorical and continuous indicators of latent variables (Muthen, 1984), models that can analyze synergistic influences on designated outcomes (von Eye, Schuster, & Rogers, 1998), or multilevel models involving data collection at different points in time (Schuster & von Eye, 1998). New techniques appear almost geometrically as quantitative-minded social and behavioral scientists actively engage challenges to the measurement of change (von Eye, 1998).

Among these analytic techniques, several hold great promise for study of the father's impact on child development. For example, using survival analysis to determine the impact of father's presence at childbirth, his death, parental divorce, years of absence, unemployment, and so forth will enable investigators to isolate event occurrence and impact over the life course. Survival analysis may prove especially helpful in estimating the effects of proximal and distal influences on child behavior, particularly with respect to issues related to risk and resilience. Is father presence in the home during the early years of life a protective factor with respect to risk for biobehavioral disregulation? If so, what specific factors provide protection? Complex techniques such as structural equation modeling allow the testing of explanatory models separately for mothers and fathers to examine both direct and indirect causal paths. Simple comparisons of means, such as tests of outcomes in children with fathers present versus those with father absent, offer less understanding.

Data from multiple informants, that is, responses from mothers about fathers, fathers about mothers, mothers about children, and fathers about children, have sometimes been examined as multiple measures of the same thing. However, reliability estimates suggest only a small portion of variance in common to such perceptions, although the correlations between mother and father perceptions of their children's behavior increase as the amount of time fathers spend with their children increases (Fitzgerald, Zucker, Maguin, & Reider, 1994). We must be cautious before rejecting low-order correlations to parental perceptions of their children's behavior as meaningless. In effect, we must apply the same logic to these correlations as is applied to current concerns about p values versus effect size in relation to sample size and statistical power (Cohen, 1977). It is possible that explaining 1, 5, or 8% of the variance will be all that we can accomplish for a given variable or set of variables.

Analytic strategies, of course, depend on conceptual models. Data from fathers may show moderator effects that require either looking beyond direct effects to whatever fathers do to moderate or change the impact of causal variables or the reverse, looking at how the impact of fathers may be moderated by other factors. The influences of marital conflict, custody decisions, and unemployment come to mind. Appropriate models also include tests of mediator effects that look beyond merely father presence/absence to what it is that fathers actually do to influence children or what specific experiences of fatherhood affect fathers. Fathers' involvement with substitutive caregiving behaviors, for example, is likely to mediate the impact of father presence on children. The quality of the father–child relationships, in turn, is likely to mediate any effects of caregiving involvement on child outcomes. Selection and attrition effects may offer more than just missing data—having a father leave is interesting on its own and analytic strategies should be used to explain as well as control for it. Researchers interested in fathers in relation to child development need to include child data in statistical models as well. To capture complex relations between any one aspect of fathering and any other variable, analysis techniques are needed that allow researchers to include variables that embrace all of these things, to test moderator and mediator effects appropriately, while also aggressively pursuing analysis of change over time in individual and family development.

Finally, we cannot emphasize enough the importance of qualitative analyses of the stories that fathers tell about their lives and about their beliefs and perceptions related to their paternal role. We have not practiced well the ethologist's dictum to "know thy organism" when it comes to studies of human development in general and fathers in particular. If we confine our investigations of fathers to studies of father–infant structured interactions in a university laboratory, we may miss his impact on child development in everyday life. In order to compile a natural history of fatherhood, we need to speak to fathers, to have them share their perceptions of their roles and articulate their perceptions of barriers that prevent or interfere with their ability to fulfill these roles. Qualitative analyses of ethnographic databases that include men from a range of socioeconomic levels and cultures may provide the inspiration necessary to generate father templates and thereby enable researchers to construct a more complete understanding of human development, not just the father's impact on child development.

GOING FORWARD: WHAT SHOULD WE DO?

Researchers using new directions and interdisciplinary approaches can build bridges across disciplines, integrating strategies of different methodological approaches from various disciplines. (See chap. 22 for more on interdisciplinary approaches to studying father involvement.) Theoretical approaches such as Ford and Lerner's Developmental Systems Theory (1992) may facilitate integration of constructs from sociology, anthropology, psychology, pediatrics, education, and policy perspectives. How will systems theory facilitate the study of fathers? It provides a framework for conceptually organizing what we know about fathers in multiple roles, relationships, and contexts. For example, it may suggest critical hypotheses based on the type of parenting a child receives from a father in different cultures in relation to the child's later self-regulatory system. Lamb (1997) suggests that one way to look at fathering is not only directly at what they do but also indirectly at how they affect what others do, that is, how they influence what mothers and communities do for children. These indirect effects occur at multiple levels in the hierarchical relations implicit in systems theory. Although some hypotheses may be generated from a systems theory approach, this approach is most useful for conceptualizing complex models. What is needed is a focused yet multilevel theory of fathers, fathering, and fatherhood

One multilevel direction for future research is the examination of social change in relation to men's confusion about their roles as fathers, as men, and as individuals. As men are trying to understand their roles and where they fit, changing circumstances may require changes in their patterns of fathering. We need studies designed to test explicit hypotheses about social change in both fathers' and mothers' roles, not just to describe attributions about those roles. For example, fathers who define their roles as providers versus those who define themselves otherwise may have different impacts on their children's development and their families' stability. Studying fathers in the 21st century may be like trying to hit a moving target. Men, in their roles as fathers, may have more flexibility than mothers in adapting to prevailing circumstances, so we may see more diversity in how fathers adapt, how they father, and how they are involved with their children. Indeed, fathers' adaptation to circumstances may result in a proliferation of many different patterns of fathering.

As father researchers, we have been challenged to include fathers in studies that previously focused only on mothers and children—intervention studies, child development studies that interview the "primary caregiver," and impact studies of myriad social programs. Many programmatic areas with concomitant disciplines undergirding them are simultaneously looking to include father research. Methods developed to date for studying fathers are not completely adequate to answer the rush of questions these new works will call for, and we will need to develop new methods by working across disciplines and beyond traditions toward building a new field of father studies.

REFERENCES

Amato, P. R. (1998). More than money? Men's contributions to their children's lives. In A. Booth and A. C. Crouter (Eds.), *Men in families: When do they get involved? What difference does it make?* (pp. 241–278). Mahwah, NJ: Lawrence Earlbaum Associates.

Bollen, K. A., & Lennox, R. (1991). Conventional wisdom on measurement: A structural equation perspective. *Psychological Bulletin, 110*, 305–314.

Bowlby, J. (1969). *Attachment*. New York: Basic Books.

Cabrera, N., Moore, K., West, J., Tinkew, J., Halle, T., Brooks-Gunn, J., Reichman, N., Teitler, J., Ellingsen, K., Nord, C., Boller, K., and the Early Head Start Fathers Working Group (2001, February). *The DADS initiative: Measuring father involvement in large scale surveys*. Paper prepared for the Workshop on Measuring Father Involvement, Bethesda, MD.

Cohen, J. (1977). *Statistical power analysis for the behavioral sciences* (rev. ed.). New York: Academic Press.

Coley, R. L. (1998). Children's socialization experiences and functioning in single-mother households: The importance of fathers and other men. *Child Development, 69*, 219–230.

Cortina, J. M. (1993). What is coefficient alpha? An examination of theory and applications. *Journal of Applied Psychology, 78*, 98–104.

Draper, P. (1998). Why should fathers father? In A. Booth & A. Crouter (Eds.), *Men in families. Why do they get involved? What difference does it make?* (pp. 111–121). Mahwah, NJ: Lawrence Erlbaum Associates.

Federal Interagency Forum on Child and Family Statistics. (1998). *Nurturing fatherhood: Improving data and research on male fertility, family formation, and fatherhood*. Washington, DC: Author.

Fitzgerald, H. E., Berlin, L., Cabrara, N., Coker, D., Pan, B. A., Raikes, H., Roggman, L. A., Spellman, M., Tamis-LeMonda, C., & Tarullo, L. (2000, July). *Paternal involvement in infant and toddler development: Insights from Early Head Start*. Presented at the biennial meeting of the International Society on Infant Studies as part of symposium, "Twenty-four months of fatherhood: Low-income men and their toddlers" (L. Roggman & K. Boller, Chairs). Brighton, UK.

Fitzgerald, H. E., Davies, W. H., & Zucker, R. A. (in press). Growing up in an alcoholic family: Structuring pathways for risk aggregation. In R. MacMahon & R. DeV Peters (Eds.), *Children of disordered parents*. Boston: Kluwer.

Fitzgerald, H. E., & Montanez, M. (2000, October). *Infant mental health and Early Head Start: Building capacity for father engagement*. Paper presented at the Head Start Infant Mental Health Forum Panel on "Addressing mental health needs of infants, parents, and families in Early Head Start and Migrant Head Start: Lessons from the scientific community" (R. Cohen, Chair). Washington, DC.

Fitzgerald, H. E., Zucker, R. A., Maguin, E. T., & Reider, E. E. (1994). Time spent with child and parental agreement about ratings of child behavior. *Perceptual and Motor Skills, 79*, 336–338.

Fitzgerald, H. E., Johnson, R. B., Van Egeren, L. A., Castellino, D. R., Johnson, C. B., & Judge-Lawton, M. (1999). *Infancy and culture.* New York: Falmer Press.

Ford, D. H., & Lerner, R. M. (1992). *Developmental systems theory.* Newbury Park, CA: Sage.

Gleick, J. (1987). *Chaos: Making a new science.* New York: Penguin Books.

Greenberg, M., & Morris, N. (1974). Engrossment: The newborn's impact upon the father. *American Journal of Orthopsychiatry, 44*, 520–531.

Grossmann, K. E., Grossmann, K., & Zimmermann, P. (1999). A wider view of attachment and exploration: Stability and change during the years of immaturity. In J. Cassidy & P. R. Shaver (Eds.), *Handbook of attachment: Theory, research, and clinical applications* (pp. 760–786). New York: Guilford.

Hewlett, B. S. (1992). Husband-wife reciprocity and the father-infant relationship among Aka Pygmies. In B. Hewlett (Ed.), *Father–child relations: Cultural and biosocial contexts* (Vol. 8, pp. 153–176). New York: Aldine de Gruyter.

Hunter, A. G., Pearson, J. L., Ialongo, N. S., & Kellam, S. G. (1998). Parenting alone to multiple caregivers: Child care and parenting arrangements in black and white families. *Family Relations, 47*, 343–353.

John, D. (1996). Women's reports of men's childcare participation: An examination of African-American and white families. *Journal of Men's Studies, 5*, 13–30.

Johnson, D. J. (2000). Disentangling poverty and race. *Applied Developmental Science, 4*, 55–67.

Klaus, M. H., & Kennel, J. H. (1976). *Maternal infant bonding.* St. Louis, MO: Mosby.

Lamb, M. E. (Ed.). (1987). *The father's role: Cross-cultural perspectives.* Hillsdale, NJ: Lawrence Erlbaum Associates.

Lamb, M. E. (1997). *The role of the father in child development* (3rd ed.). New York: Wiley.

Lamb, M. E. (in press). Research on father involvement: An historical overview. *Marriage and Family Review.*

Lerman, R., & Sorensen, E. (1996, October). *Father involvement with their nonmarital children: Patterns, determinants, and effects on their earnings.* Paper presented at the NICHD Family and Child Well-Being Network Conference on Father Involvement. Bethesda, MD.

Lopez, L. C., & Hamilton, M. (1997). Comparison of the role of Mexican-American and Euro-American family members in the socialization of children. *Psychological Reports, 80*, 283–288.

Loukas, A., Twitchel, G. R., Piejak, L., Fitzgerald, H. E., & Zucker, R. A. (1998). The family as a unity of interacting personalities. In L. L'Abate (Ed.), *Family psychopathology: The relational roots of dysfunctional behavior* (pp. 35–59). New York: Guilford.

Lynn, D. B. (1974). *The father: His role in child development.* Monterey, CA: Brooks/Cole.

Mackey, W. C. (1996). *The American father: Biocultural and developmental aspects.* New York: Plenum.

Marsiglio, W., Amato, P., & Day, R. D. (2000). Scholarship on fatherhood in the 1990s and beyond. *Journal of Marriage and Family, 62*, 1173–1191.

Masten, A. S. (Ed.). (1999). *Cultural processes in child development: The Minnesota symposium on child psychology, Vol. 29.* Mahwah, NJ: Lawrence Erlbaum Associates.

Muthen, B. O. (1984). A general structural equation model with dichotomous ordered categorical and continuous latent variable indicators. *Psychometrika, 49*, 115–132.

NICHD Early Child Care Research Network. (1997). Familial factors associated with the characteristics of non-maternal care for infants. *Journal of Marriage and Family, 59*, 389–408.

Parsons, T., & Bales, R. (1955). *Family, socialization, and interaction process.* New York: Free Press.

Roopnarine, J. L., Brown, J., Snell-White, P., Riegraf, N. B., Crossley, D. Z., & Webb, W. (1995). Father involvement in child care and household work in common-law dual-earner Jamaican families. *Journal of Applied Developmental Psychology, 16*, 35–52.

Sameroff, A. J. (1983). Developmental systems: Contexts and evolution. In P. H. Mussen (Ed.). *Handbook of child psychology, Vol. 1. History, theory, and methods* (pp. 237–294). New York: Wiley.

Schuster, C., & von Eye, A. (1998). Determining the meaning of parameters in multilevel models for longitudinal data. *International Journal of Behavioral Development, 22,* 475–491.

Snowdon, C. T., & Suomi, S. J. (1982). Paternal behavior in primates. In H. E. Fitzgerald, J. A. Mullins, & P. Gage (Eds.), *Child nurturance: Vol. 3. Studies of development in nonhuman primates* (pp. 63–108). New York: Plenum.

Trivers, R. L. (1972). Parental investment and sexual selection. In B. Campbell (Ed.), *Sexual selection and the descent of man, 1871–1971* (pp. 136–179). Chicago: Aldine.

von Bertalanffy, L. (1968). *General systems theory.* New York: Braziller.

von Eye, A. (1998). Statistical analysis of longitudinal data: The benefit of progress. *International Journal of Behavioral Development, 22,* 447–451.

von Eye, A., & Schuster, C. (2000). The road to freedom: Quantitative developmental methodology in the 3rd millennium. *International Journal of Behavioral Development, 24,* 335–343.

von Eye, A., Schuster, C., & Rogers, W. M. (1998). Modelling synergy using manifest categorical variables. *International Journal of Behavioral Development, 22,* 537–557.

Zucker, R. A., Fitzgerald, H. E., Refior, S. K., Puttler, L. I., Pallas, D. M., & Ellis, D. A. (2000). The clinical and social ecology of childhood for children of alcoholics: Description of a study and implications for a differentiated social policy. In H. E. Fitzgerald, B. M. Lester, & B. Zimmerman (Eds.), *Children of addiction: Research, health and public policy issues* (pp. 109–142). New York: Routledge Falmer.

I

The Demography of Fathers

Sandra L. Hofferth
University of Maryland

What does demography offer to students of fathers that is unique from other disciplines? Demography offers the big picture—national representation. One of the discipline's core beliefs is that knowledge requires accurate and adequate representation of the phenomenon or populations of interest. To obtain that information, it is important that rigorous sampling designs be used and that any known biases be exposed. The reason that studying fathers has been so difficult is precisely that it is difficult, if not impossible, to select a national sample of all men who have ever been fathers or who are current fathers of children under age 18. This is because, in contrast to mothers, not all fathers live with their children. In addition, fathers may not even be aware that they have fathered a child. Thus, Hernandez and Brandon (chap. 2) take special pains to identify populations they may miss in their national surveys and to estimate the potential population of nonresidential fathers.

An alternative way to identify fathers is to start with their children. Because children had both a mother and a father at conception, identifying the parents of living children is an alternative approach. This is the approach taken by chapter 3, which is used to form a national picture of the involvement not only of children living with fathers, but also children of nonresidential biological fathers. This chapter provides national estimates of the level of involvement of such fathers in their children's lives in the late 1990s, the most recent estimates currently available.

Besides national representation, demography offers a picture of fathers based on common categories that are important to children's lives and children's well-

31

being and on which there is widespread agreement regarding measurement. These categories include parental education, age, income, employment, race/ethnicity, family size, and marital status. These same categories are used in both chapters. Education, employment, and income are clearly important because they provide the resources available to children, in terms of both human and financial capital. Whereas parental age and family size affect the personal energy parents can devote to each child, the age of the child indicates the amount and type of attention that is required. Race and ethnicity define potential cultural differences, though they also reflect differences in income and education when used by themselves without simultaneous controls for the latter. Marital status is a key factor, as children have been shown to be much better off with two parents compared with a single mother (McLanahan & Sandefur, 1994). Chapter 2 focuses on differences among fathers according to these demographic categories and to the categories jointly with race and ethnicity. As they so clearly point out, the increase in the representation of Hispanic and other ethnic minorities in the United States as a result of continued immigration is rapidly changing the nature of fatherhood. Studying minority populations will be crucial to understanding fatherhood.

Although Hernandez and Brandon focus on who these fathers are in the demographic sense of describing their basic characteristics and the significance of changes in these characteristics for children's lives, chapter 3 goes to the next step to provide a national picture of what fathers do with their children. This chapter focuses on a distinction not often used in demography, but that originates from evolutionary psychology, along with one of the major demographic distinctions that has been shown to be linked to children's development. This is, first, the biological relationship of the child to the father and, second, the marital relationship between the mother and this father. Although father involvement has been shown to be linked to positive child development, this chapter focuses on the relationship of child and parent rather than on the outcomes of this relationship. It examines the time parent and child spend engaged in certain activities and the quality of the relationship. Drawing from evolutionary psychology, it examines differences in investments of fathers in children who are biologically related and whose relationship to the mother is marital or cohabitational. Finally, it focuses on examining the involvement of nonresidential fathers in their children's lives, again showing differences by the marital status of the child's residential mother.

These chapters present an important new national picture of what fathers look like and what they do that is drawn from recent national data sets.

REFERENCE

McLanahan, S., & Sandefur, G. (1994). *Growing up with a single parent: What hurts, what helps.* Cambridge, MA: Harvard University Press.

2

Who Are the Fathers of Today?

Donald J. Hernandez
New York State University at Albany

Peter D. Brandon
University of Massachusetts

All children have two parents, a mother and a father. Yet, only during the past two decades have social scientists and policymakers begun to direct substantial attention toward understanding men's experience with children and the role that fathers play in child development through the resources, care, and nurturing they give to their children (see Cabrera, Tamis-LeMonda, Bradley, Hofferth, & Lamb, 2000; Eggebeen, in press). The early focus first on the changing circumstances and activities of mothers, and more recently on the lives of children, can be understood as a response to the dramatic increases during the past half-century in mothers' labor force participation, divorce, out-of-wedlock childbearing, and mother-only family living arrangements (see Hernandez, 1986; 1993). But increasing evidence indicates that fathers' circumstances and behaviors are consequential for the well-being and development of children and for their transition to adulthood (for overviews, see Cabrera et al., 2000; Hernandez, 1993).

Fathers' educational attainments, occupations, and income have long been known to influence educational and occupational attainments of their children when the children reach adulthood. Family composition, both the presence or absence of the father and mother in the home and the number of siblings in the home, has similar consequences. More immediately, the well-being, cognitive development, and social competence of young children is influenced by fathers'

emotional investment in, attachment to, and provision of resources for their children. Whether or not fathers live with their biological children, fathers' age, family poverty status, and financial support from nonresident fathers also influence
children's well-being along such dimensions as academic achievement, psychosocial problems, delinquency, and crime. Changing gender roles, differences across
cultural groups, and the rapidly increasing racial, ethnic, and cultural diversity of
fathers in the United States all suggest the need for increasing attention to the circumstances and behaviors of fathers and their consequences for children.

To provide the national-level context for detailed analyses in subsequent chapters of this volume, this chapter presents new results that portray the demographic, family, and socioeconomic circumstances of the fathers of the 1990s who are
coresident with their children, and it highlights key issues concerning men whose
children are not living with them. More specifically, we begin by focusing on men
who have at least one biological, step, or adopted child in the home, because the
U.S. Census Bureau's Current Population Survey (CPS) can be used to study
these fathers in detail. Next, we distinguish between fathers with biological, step,
and adoptive children, using data from the U.S. Census Bureau's Survey of
Income and Program Participation (SIPP). Finally, we focus briefly on issues
regarding fathers who do not live with their biological children, as well as men
who may be fathers, but for whom available data are quite limited.

DEMOGRAPHIC PORTRAIT OF FATHERS
WITH CORESIDENT CHILDREN

Men Residing With Their Children

To what extent did men in the United States have at least one of their children living in their home during the 1990s? Although a majority of males age 15 and
older did not currently live with a child, nearly 4 in 10 (35 to 37%) had a coresident child in the home at the beginning, middle, and end of the 1990s (Table 2.1).
Distinguishing men by the ages of their children, nearly 3 in 10 (27 to 29%) lived
with one or more of their dependent children under age 18, whereas about 1 in 10
(11 to 12%) lived with one or more of their children age 18 or older. Among
fathers with at least one coresident child, about two thirds (67 to 68%) only had
children under age 18 in the home, about one tenth (11%) lived with both younger
and older children, and more than one fifth (21 to 22%) lived only with children
who were age 18 or older (Table 2.2).

Thus, many fathers maintaining households with coresident children provide
financial support and a home for children who are beyond the typical age for
completing high school, but who have not yet set up an independent household.
Because children under age 18 are both financially dependent and legally dependent on their parents (or other adults), subsequent sections of this chapter usually
focus on the two thirds of fathers with coresident children who have children
under age 18.

TABLE 2.1

Presence of Children in Home for Men 15 Years and Older: 1990, 1996, 1999

Number and Ages of Children in Home (numbers in percent)	1990	1996	1999
Total	100.0	100.0	100.0
None	63.3	64.9	65.4
One or more any age	36.7	35.1	34.6
One or more ages 0–17 only	24.7	24.0	23.4
One or more ages 0–17, and one or more age 18+	3.9	3.7	3.7
One or more age 18+ only	8.2	7.5	7.5
One or more ages 0–17	28.6	27.7	27.1

RACIAL, ETHNIC, AND IMMIGRANT DIVERSITY

Fathers with coresident children under age 18 (hereafter referred to as fathers with coresident dependent children) became increasingly diverse during the 1990s with regard not only to their race and ethnicity, but also to their own, or their wives', country of birth. Between 1990 and 1999, the proportion of fathers with coresident dependent children who were non-Hispanic Whites declined from 78% to 73%, with a corresponding increase from 22% to 27% in fathers who were non-White or Hispanic (Table 2.3). Reflecting the overall level of immigration and the fact than many immigrants to the United States are young adults, by 1999 one of every five fathers (20%) with coresident dependent children was foreign born or was living with a foreign-born wife. Fathers who are foreign born or who live with a foreign-born wife are, hereafter, referred to as living in immigrant families, whereas those who are native born and who are not living with a foreign-born wife are referred to as living in native-born families.

Among non-Hispanic White fathers with coresident dependent children in 1999, about 8% lived in immigrant families, and this amount climbed to 13% for non-Hispanic Blacks, 66% for Hispanics, and 76% for other non-Hispanics. Combining race and ethnicity with immigrant status, by 1999 only 67% fathers with coresident dependent children were non-Hispanic Whites in native-born

TABLE 2.2

Presence of Children in Home for Fathers 15 Years and Older with at Least One Child in Home: 1990, 1996, 1999

Ages of Children in Home (numbers in percent)	1990	1996	1999
Total, any age	100.0	100.0	100.0
One or more ages 0–17 only	67.4	68.3	67.8
One or more ages 0–17, and one or more age 18+	10.5	10.5	10.6
One or more age 18+ only	22.1	21.2	21.6

TABLE 2.3
Race, Hispanic Origin, and Immigrant Family Status of Fathers with Children
0–17 Years in Home: 1990, 1996, 1999

Race, Hispanic Origin, and	Percent Distribution			Number (in thousands)		
Family Status	1990	1996	1999	1990	1996	1999
Total						
White, non-Hispanic	78.4	75.7	73.2	20620	20642	20248
Native-born family	—	69.7	67.1	—	19025	18575
Immigrant family	—	5.9	6.1	—	1617	1673
Black, non-Hispanic	8.4	8.2	8.5	2215	2234	2345
Native-born family	—	7.0	7.4	—	1914	2050
Immigrant family	—	1.2	1.1	—	320	295
Hispanic	9.3	11.4	13.3	2441	3114	3676
Native-born family	—	3.7	4.5	—	1000	1253
Immigrant family	—	7.8	8.8	—	2114	2423
Other, non-Hispanic	3.9	4.7	5.1	1017	1291	1396
Native-born family	—	1.0	1.2	—	275	339
Immigrant family	—	3.7	3.8	—	1016	1057

Notes:
Native-born family: Father is native born and if wife is present, she is native born.
Immigrant family: Father is foreign born or if wife is present, she is foreign born.
Immigrant status not available in 1990.

families; 33% of fathers with coresident dependent children were non-White or Hispanic, or they lived in immigrant families. As the 21st century begins, then, fathers in the United States are extremely diverse in their race, ethnicity, and immigrant circumstances.

Looking to the future, projections of additional increases in the racial and ethnic diversity of fathers are not available. But the U.S. Census Bureau has projected the future racial and ethnic composition of children, which reflects, in turn, the future racial and ethnic composition of fathers and mothers. U.S. Census Bureau projections indicate that between 2035 and 2040 the proportion of children who are Hispanic or non-White will rise to and then surpass 50%, as the historic minorities become the numerical majority population among children (U.S. Census Bureau, 2001b). This transformation in the race and ethnic origin of children is occurring mainly because most future growth in the U.S. population is projected to occur as a result of immigration and births to immigrants and their descendants and because most immigrants are Hispanic or nonwhite. For example, as of 1990, about one half of children in immigrant families were Hispanic and about one fourth were Asian. The implications of this increasing racial, ethnic, and cultural diversity of fathers, mothers, and children are potentially quite profound (Hernandez, 1999; Hernandez & Charney, 1998).

Father's Age

The vast majority of fathers with coresident dependent children throughout the 1990s (75 to 77%) were 30 to 49 years old (Table 2.4). But with the aging of fathers born during the baby boom, a substantial shift toward older ages occurred during the decade. As fathers born during the peak baby boom year of 1959 became 40 years old in 1999, the proportion of fathers with coresident dependent children who were 40 years old and older increased from 39% in 1990 to 47% in 1999. Because no more than 1% of fathers with coresident dependent children were under age 20 in 1990, 1996, or 1999, the corresponding decline in the proportion of fathers under age 40 occurred within the range of 20 to 39 years, and approximately equal declines occurred for fathers in their 20s and 30s.

Non-Hispanic White fathers with coresident dependent children were, as of 1999, somewhat more concentrated in the age range of 40 to 49 years than were corresponding non-Hispanic Black fathers. Hispanic fathers with coresident dependent children were, however, much more likely than the other two groups to be in their 20s and substantially less likely to be in their 40s.

FAMILY PORTRAIT OF FATHERS WITH CORESIDENT DEPENDENT CHILDREN

Number of Dependent Children in the Home

The number of dependent children in the homes of fathers changed little during the 1990s either overall or for non-Hispanic Whites and Blacks (Table 2.5). Compared to non-Hispanic Whites, however, non-Hispanic Blacks were slightly more likely to have only one child or at least four children in the home. In 1999, for example, the differences were 45 versus 41%, with only one child in the home, and 8 versus 4% with at least four children in the home. Hispanic fathers with coresident dependent children in the home were still more likely than the non-Hispanic Whites and Blacks to have larger families. In 1999, 28% of Hispanic fathers with coresident dependent children in the home had three or more children in the home, compared to 22% for non-Hispanic Blacks and 19% for non-Hispanic Whites. Among Hispanics, fathers in immigrant families were substantially more likely than those in native-born families to have three or more dependent children in the home, at 31% and 22%, respectively, in 1999.

Father's Marital Status

Throughout the 1990s, more than 9 of every 10 fathers with coresident dependent children were married, with spouse present, although the proportion declined slightly from 95% overall in 1990 to 93% in 1996 and 1999 (Table 2.6).

TABLE 2.4

Age of Fathers With Children 0–17 Years in Home, by Race, Hispanic Origin, and
Immigrant Family Status: 1990, 1996, 1999 (*numbers in percent*)

1990		White, Non-Hispanic			Black, Non-Hispanic	Hispanic		
Father's Age	*Total*	*Total*	*Native-Born Family*	*Immigrant Family*	*Total*	*Total*	*Native-Born Family*	*Immigrant Family*
Total	**100.0**	**100.0**	—	—	**100.0**	**100.0**	—	—
15–29	**16.8**	**15.6**	—	—	**21.0**	**25.8**	—	—
30–39	**44.3**	**45.3**	—	—	**42.0**	**40.6**	—	—
40–49	**30.3**	**31.2**	—	—	**26.0**	**24.0**	—	—
50+	**8.6**	**7.9**	—	—	**11.0**	**9.6**	—	—

1996		White, Non-Hispanic			Black, Non-Hispanic	Hispanic		
Father's Age	*Total*	*Total*	*Native-Born Family*	*Immigrant Family*	*Total*	*Total*	*Native-Born Family*	*Immigrant Family*
Total	**100.0**	**100.0**	100.0	100.0	**100.0**	**100.0**	100.0	100.0
15–29	**13.3**	**12.1**	12.3	9.4	**14.4**	**22.5**	23.0	22.3
30–39	**41.9**	**41.9**	42.1	39.5	**40.9**	**44.5**	45.9	43.8
40–49	**35.8**	**37.5**	37.4	38.5	**34.0**	**24.2**	23.7	24.5
50+	**9.0**	**8.6**	8.2	12.7	**10.7**	**8.8**	7.5	9.4

1999		White, Non-Hispanic			Black, Non-Hispanic	Hispanic		
Father's Age	*Total*	*Total*	*Native-Born Family*	*Immigrant Family*	*Total*	*Total*	*Native-Born Family*	*Immigrant Family*
Total	**100.0**	**100.0**	100.0	100.0	**100.0**	**100.0**	100.0	100.0
15–29	**13.0**	**11.6**	12.0	7.9	**13.6**	**21.9**	24.8	20.5
30–39	**39.7**	**39.2**	39.4	37.0	**41.1**	**42.1**	37.7	44.4
40–49	**36.3**	**38.3**	38.2	39.3	**32.6**	**26.9**	28.9	25.9
50+	**11.0**	**10.9**	10.5	15.8	**12.6**	**9.0**	8.7	9.2

Notes:

Native-born family: Father is native born and if wife is present, she is native born.

Immigrant family: Father is foreign born or if wife is present, she is foreign born.

Immigrant status not available in 1990.

TABLE 2.5

Number of Children Age 0–17 Years in the Homes of Fathers with Children
0–17 Years in Home, by Race, Hispanic Origin, and Immigrant Family Status:
1990, 1996, 1999 (*numbers in percent*)

| *1990* | | | | Black, Non-Hispanic | | | |
| | | White, Non-Hispanic | | | Hispanic | | |
Number of Children	*Total*	*Total*	Native-Born Family	Immigrant Family	*Total*	*Total*	Native-Born Family	Immigrant Family
Total	**100.0**	**100.0**	—	—	**100.0**	**100.0**	—	—
1	**40.4**	**40.7**	—	—	**43.2**	**36.4**	—	—
2	**39.1**	**40.3**	—	—	**33.7**	**33.9**	—	—
3	**14.8**	**14.5**	—	—	**15.0**	**18.3**	—	—
4+	**5.7**	**4.5**	—	—	**8.1**	**11.4**	—	—

| *1996* | | | | Black, Non-Hispanic | | | |
| | | White, Non-Hispanic | | | Hispanic | | |
Number of Children	*Total*	*Total*	Native-Born Family	Immigrant Family	*Total*	*Total*	Native-Born Family	Immigrant Family
Total	**100.0**	**100.0**	100.0	100.0	**100.0**	**100.0**	100.0	100.0
1	**39.5**	**39.6**	39.7	38.4	**43.9**	**35.1**	38.5	33.4
2	**40.2**	**41.4**	41.4	41.7	**34.7**	**36.1**	37.9	35.2
3	**14.6**	**14.1**	14.1	15.1	**15.2**	**18.6**	15.1	20.2
4+	**5.7**	**4.9**	4.8	4.8	**6.2**	**10.2**	8.5	11.2

| *1999* | | | | Black, Non-Hispanic | | | |
| | | White, Non-Hispanic | | | Hispanic | | |
Number of Children	*Total*	*Total*	Native-Born Family	Immigrant Family	*Total*	*Total*	Native-Born Family	Immigrant Family
Total	**100.0**	**100.0**	100.0	100.0	**100.0**	**100.0**	100.0	100.0
1	**40.1**	**40.7**	39.9	42.4	**45.1**	**35.3**	40.4	32.7
2	**38.8**	**40.0**	39.9	40.6	**33.0**	**36.9**	37.8	36.4
3	**15.5**	**15.2**	15.4	12.7	**14.3**	**19.2**	15.7	21.0
4+	**5.6**	**4.1**	4.8	4.3	**7.6**	**8.6**	6.1	9.8

Notes:
Native-born family: Father is native born and if wife is present, she is native born.
Immigrant family: Father is foreign born or if wife is present, she is foreign born.
Immigrant status not available in 1990.

TABLE 2.6

Marital Status of Fathers with Children 0–17 Years in Home by Race, Hispanic
Origin, and Immigrant Family Status: 1990, 1996, 1999 (*numbers in percent*)

1990		White, Non-Hispanic			Black, Non- Hispanic	Hispanic		
Marital Status	*Total*	*Total*	*Native- Born Family*	*Immigrant Family*	*Total*	*Total*	*Native- Born Family*	*Immigrant Family*
Total	**100.0**	**100.0**	—	—	**100.0**	**100.0**	—	—
Married, spouse present	**94.8**	**95.4**	—	—	**90.2**	**94.3**	—	—
Not married, spouse present	**5.2**	**4.6**	—	—	**9.8**	**5.7**	—	—
Never married	**1.3**	**1.0**	—	—	**3.3**	**2.6**	—	—
Divorced	**2.7**	**2.7**	—	—	**4.1**	**1.6**	—	—

1996		White, Non-Hispanic			Black, Non- Hispanic	Hispanic		
Marital Status	*Total*	*Total*	*Native- Born Family*	*Immigrant Family*	*Total*	*Total*	*Native- Born Family*	*Immigrant Family*
Total	**100.0**	**100.0**	**100.0**	**100.0**	**100.0**	**100.0**	**100.0**	**100.0**
Married, spouse present	**93.1**	**94.0**	93.6	97.5	**85.8**	**92.6**	88.3	94.7
Not married, spouse present	**6.9**	**6.1**	6.4	2.5	**14.2**	**7.4**	11.7	5.4
Never married	**2.1**	**1.3**	1.4	0.3	**6.6**	**3.6**	5.3	2.7
Divorced	**3.3**	**3.5**	3.7	1.3	**2.8**	**2.1**	4.2	1.1

1999		White, Non-Hispanic			Black, Non- Hispanic	Hispanic		
Marital Status	*Total*	*Total*	*Native- Born Family*	*Immigrant Family*	*Total*	*Total*	*Native- Born Family*	*Immigrant Family*
Total	**100.0**	**100.0**	**100.0**	**100.0**	**100.0**	**100.0**	**100.0**	**100.0**
Married, spouse present	**92.5**	**93.2**	92.8	97.5	**86.1**	**92.3**	88.1	94.5
Not married, spouse present	**7.5**	**6.8**	7.2	2.5	**13.9**	**7.7**	11.9	5.5
Never married	**2.5**	**1.8**	1.9	0.4	**5.8**	**4.3**	5.9	3.5
Divorced	**3.4**	**3.6**	3.9	1.1	**4.9**	**1.6**	3.4	0.6

Notes:

Native-born family: Father is native born and if wife is present, she is native born.

Immigrant family: Father is foreign born or if wife is present, she is foreign born.

Immigrant status not available in 1990.

Differences by race, ethnicity, and immigrant status are, however, noteworthy. Among non-Hispanic White fathers with coresident dependent children in native-born families in 1999, 93% were married, spouse present, compared to 98% for those in immigrant families. The corresponding proportion was substantially smaller for non-Hispanic Blacks, at 86%. Thus, non-Hispanic Black fathers with coresident children in the home were substantially more likely than corresponding non-Hispanic Whites to not have a wife present in the home (14 vs. 7%).

Hispanic fathers with coresident dependent children differed greatly by immigrant status. Among Hispanics in native-born families, 12% did not have a wife in the home, about the same as among non-Hispanic Blacks, but this drops to 6% among Hispanics in immigrant families, a level similar to non-Hispanic Whites in native-born families. Thus, within these race-ethnic groups, fathers in foreign-born families are more likely to be married, spouse present, and among those in native-born families, both Hispanic and non-Hispanic Black fathers are about twice as likely as white fathers to not have a wife in the home.

Among non-Hispanic White fathers with coresident dependent children but without wives in the home, divorce is the most common marital status, whereas among corresponding non-Hispanic Black fathers and Hispanic fathers, the most common marital status is never married. It is important to note, however, that many fathers with dependent children have none of their children in their home, because the children reside with their mothers, as discussed later in the chapter. Nonetheless, especially among fathers with coresident dependent children who are non-Hispanic Black or Hispanic living in native-born families, substantial proportions have no wife present in the home, 14 and 12%, respectively, in 1999.

Finally, it should be noted that the CPS data reported here do not explicitly identify, as such, fathers who are cohabiting with their children's biological mother. If the father maintains the household, he is classified as living with his child(ren) and by his legal marital status (other than married, spouse present). If the mother maintains the household, he is not identified as living with his biological child(ren). See Bumpass and Lu (1999) for a discussion of cohabitation and children.

SOCIOECONOMIC PORTRAIT OF FATHERS WITH CORESIDENT DEPENDENT CHILDREN

Father's Educational Attainments

Fathers with coresident dependent children are extremely diverse in their educational attainments (Table 2.7). At the extremes in 1999, about 5% had completed no more than 8 years of schooling, and nearly 9% had attended but not graduated from high school. Thus, a total of 13% were not high school graduates, whereas 11% had earned a degree beyond the bachelor's. The remaining fathers were

TABLE 2.7
Educational Attainment of Fathers With Children 0–17 Years in Home,
by Race, Hispanic Origin, and Immigrant Family Status: 1990, 1996, 1999
(*numbers in percent*)

1990		White, Non-Hispanic			Black, Non-Hispanic	Hispanic		
Educational Attainment	*Total*	*Total*	Native-Born Family	Immigrant Family	*Total*	*Total*	Native-Born Family	Immigrant Family
None–8th grade	**6.5**	**3.3**	—	—	**6.4**	**31.9**	—	—
9th–11th grade	**9.1**	**7.9**	—	—	**13.9**	**15.8**	—	—
High school graduate	**37.6**	**38.7**	—	—	**43.1**	**29.3**	—	—
Some college, no bachelor's degree	**20.0**	**20.7**	—	—	**21.1**	**14.1**	—	—
Bachelor's degree or more	**26.9**	**29.4**	—	—	**15.4**	**8.9**	—	—
Bachelor's degree	**14.5**	**15.7**	—	—	**9.3**	**4.7**	—	—
Postbachelor's degree	**12.4**	**13.7**	—	—	**6.1**	**4.2**	—	—

1996		White, Non-Hispanic			Black, Non-Hispanic	Hispanic		
Educational Attainment	*Total*	*Total*	Native-Born Family	Immigrant Family	Hispanic *Total*	*Total*	Native-Born Family	Immigrant Family
None–8th grade	**5.4**	**1.7**	1.5	3.5	**3.7**	**29.4**	6.9	40.1
9th–11th grade	**8.6**	**6.7**	6.8	4.7	**12.7**	**18.4**	17.6	18.8
High school graduate	**31.8**	**32.3**	33.2	22.2	**39.2**	**27.3**	40.8	21.0
Some college, no bachelor's degree	**26.2**	**27.0**	28.1	26.5	**28.2**	**16.7**	23.9	13.3
Bachelor's degree or more	**28.1**	**31.4**	30.4	43.1	**16.3**	**8.1**	10.9	6.9
Bachelor's degree	**17.4**	**19.5**	19.0	24.9	**11.5**	**5.3**	6.0	4.9
Postbachelor's degree	**10.7**	**12.0**	11.4	18.2	**4.8**	**2.9**	4.9	2.0

(Continued)

TABLE 2.7   (Continued)

1999 Educational Attainment	Total	White, Non-Hispanic			Black, Non-Hispanic Hispanic Total	Hispanic		
		Total	Native-Born Family	Immigrant Family		Total	Native-Born Family	Immigrant Family
None–8th grade	**4.9**	**1.4**	1.2	4.3	**2.5**	**25.1**	7.0	34.5
9th–11th grade	**8.5**	**6.2**	6.4	4.6	**11.4**	**19.1**	16.6	20.4
High school graduate	**31.1**	**31.3**	32.1	22.5	**39.5**	**28.6**	37.9	23.8
Some college, no bachelor's degree	**25.7**	**26.8**	27.2	22.7	**29.8**	**17.7**	27.4	12.7
Bachelor's degree or more	**29.8**	**34.2**	33.2	45.8	**16.7**	**9.4**	11.2	8.5
Bachelor's degree	**18.7**	**21.6**	21.3	24.0	**11.7**	**6.5**	7.7	5.9
Postbachelor's degree	**11.1**	**12.7**	11.9	21.9	**5.0**	**2.9**	3.5	2.6

Notes:
Native-born family: Father is native born and if wife is present, she is native born.
Immigrant family: Father is foreign born or if wife is present, she is foreign born.
Immigrant status not available in 1990.

approximately equally divided among those with high school degrees (31%), some college (26%), and a bachelor's degree (30%). Between 1990 and 1999, the educational distribution of fathers with coresident dependent children shifted upward by several percentage points.

Differences across racial, ethnic, and immigrant groups were quite large. Among fathers with coresident dependent children in 1999, only 1 to 4% of non-Hispanic Whites and Blacks had completed no more than 8 years of education. However, this rose to 25% for Hispanics, mainly because 35% of those in foreign-born families had completed no more than 8 years of education. The figure for Hispanics in native-born families was 7%, which was nearly twice the level experienced by non-Hispanic Blacks. Large differences also exist for attending but not graduating from high school. Among non-Hispanic Whites, a total of 8 to 9% had not graduated from high school, compared to 14% for non-Hispanic Blacks, 24% for Hispanics in native-born families, and 55% for Hispanics in immigrant families.

At the upper educational levels, differences by race, ethnicity, and immigrant status also are very large. The proportion of fathers with coresident dependent children in 1999 who had completed at least a bachelor's degrees was 33% for non-Hispanic Whites in native-born families and 46% for non-Hispanic Whites in foreign-born families, but only 17% for non-Hispanic Blacks, 11% for Hispanics in native-born families, and 9% for Hispanics in immigrant families. Thus, the educational experiences that fathers with coresident dependent children bring to their children and to the labor market vary enormously by race, ethnicity, and immigrant status.

Fathers' and Mothers' Labor Force Participation

Labor force participation is nearly universal among fathers with coresident dependent children, at 90% or more regardless of race, ethnicity, and immigrant status (Table 2.8). Many do not, however, work full-time year-round, and substantial differences distinguish non-Hispanic Whites from other groups. Because the employment data reported here, as well as the income, poverty, and program participation data reported later, pertain to the years immediately preceding the year during which respondents were interviewed, employment and income results are presented for 1989, 1995, and 1998, which correspond to the CPS data collection years of 1990, 1996, and 1999.

Ninety-five percent of fathers with coresident dependent children in 1999 worked during the preceding year, but only 83% worked full-time year-round. The proportions of fathers with coresident dependent children who were working full-time year-round were 85% for non-Hispanic Whites in native-born families and 82% for those in immigrant families, but this fell to 79% for Hispanics in native-born families, 76% for Hispanics in immigrant families, and 75% for non-Hispanic Blacks.

These results suggest that fathers with coresident dependent children have strong work ethics, regardless of race, ethnicity, or immigrant status, but that many fathers are unable to find full-time year-round work, especially if they are Black or Hispanic. Fifteen percent of non-Hispanic White fathers in native-born families with coresident dependent children worked less than full-time for the full year or not at all in 1998, and this rose to 18% for non-Hispanic Whites in immigrant families, 22% for Hispanics in native-born families, 24% for Hispanics in immigrant families, and 26% for blacks. Although full-time year-round employment increased noticeably between 1989 and 1998 by 3 to 4 percentage points for non-Hispanic Whites and blacks and by 7 percentage points for Hispanics, many fathers with coresident dependent children, especially minority fathers, were not fully employed during 1998.

For many, an employed coresident wife sharply increases the overall amount of labor force participation in the family. In 1998, 88% of fathers with coresident dependent children lived in families with at least one parent working full-time year-round, and 32% lived in families with both parents working full-time year-round (Table 2.9). Families with both parents working full-time year-round

TABLE 2.8

Employment for Fathers With Children 0–17 Years in Home, by Race, Hispanic
Origin, and Immigrant Family Status: 1989, 1995, 1998 (*numbers in percent*)

| *1989* | | | | | Black, Non-Hispanic | | | |
| | | *White, Non-Hispanic* | | | | *Hispanic* | | |
Employment	*Total*	*Total*	*Native-Born Family*	*Immigrant Family*	*Total*	*Total*	*Native-Born Family*	*Immigrant Family*
Full-time year-round	**79.5**	**81.6**	—	—	**70.6**	**70.5**	—	—
Part-time or part-year	**16.5**	**15.2**	—	—	**20.7**	**24.1**	—	—
None	**4.1**	**3.2**	—	—	**8.7**	**5.5**	—	—

| *1995* | | | | | Black, Non-Hispanic | | | |
| | | *White, Non-Hispanic* | | | | *Hispanic* | | |
Employment	*Total*	*Total*	*Native-Born Family*	*Immigrant Family*	*Total*	*Total*	*Native-Born Family*	*Immigrant Family*
Full-time year-round	**80.4**	**83.3**	83.7	78.9	**71.1**	**71.2**	74.0	69.9
Part-time or part-year	**14.5**	**12.9**	12.6	15.8	**18.6**	**21.9**	18.4	23.6
None	**5.0**	**3.8**	3.7	5.3	**10.4**	**6.9**	7.7	6.5

| *1998* | | | | | Black, Non-Hispanic | | | |
| | | *White, Non-Hispanic* | | | | *Hispanic* | | |
Employment	*Total*	*Total*	*Native-Born Family*	*Immigrant Family*	*Total*	*Total*	*Native-Born Family*	*Immigrant Family*
Full-time year-round	**82.6**	**84.8**	85.1	81.9	**74.5**	**77.1**	78.6	76.3
Part-time or part-year	**12.8**	**11.5**	11.3	13.7	**15.9**	**17.6**	15.5	18.7
None	**4.6**	**3.7**	3.7	4.5	**9.6**	**5.3**	6.0	5.0

Notes:

Native-born family: Father is native born and if wife is present, she is native born.
Immigrant family: Father is foreign born or if wife is present, she is foreign born.
Immigrant status not available in 1989.

were most common among non-Hispanic Black fathers with coresident dependent children at 40%, followed by Whites (regardless of immigrant status) and
Hispanics in native-born families at 30 to 33%, whereas only 22% of Hispanics
in foreign-born families lived in families with both parents working full-time
year-round.

TABLE 2.9
Employment of Fathers and Their Wives with Children 0–17 Years in Home,
by Race, Hispanic Origin, and Immigrant Family Status: 1989, 1995,1998
(*numbers in percent*)

1989		White, Non-Hispanic			Black, Non-Hispanic	Hispanic		
Employment	*Total*	*Total*	*Native-Born Family*	*Immigrant Family*	*Total*	*Total*	*Native-Born Family*	*Immigrant Family*
Both parents full-time year-round	**26.3**	**26.0**	—	—	**34.2**	**20.5**	—	—
One parent full-time year-round	**58.6**	**60.7**	—	—	**45.3**	**56.4**	—	—
None full-time year-round, at least one part-time or part-year	**12.9**	**11.7**	—	—	**15.9**	**20.1**	—	—
Neither employed	**2.2**	**1.6**	—	—	**4.6**	**3.1**	—	—
1995		White, Non-Hispanic			Black, Non-Hispanic	Hispanic		
Employment	*Total*	*Total*	*Native-Born Family*	*Immigrant Family*	*Total*	*Total*	*Native-Born Family*	*Immigrant Family*
Both parents full-time year-round	**29.3**	**29.4**	29.7	26.0	**37.0**	**22.8**	28.9	20.0
One parent full-time year-round	**57.1**	**59.3**	59.4	59.1	**45.0**	**53.8**	51.3	55.0
None full-time year-round, at least one part-time or part-year	**11.2**	**9.5**	9.3	11.8	**14.0**	**19.4**	14.6	21.7
Neither employed	**2.5**	**1.8**	1.6	3.1	**4.0**	**4.0**	5.2	3.4

(Continued)

TABLE 2.9 (Continued)

1998		White, Non-Hispanic			Black, Non-Hispanic	Hispanic		
Employment	Total	Total	Native-Born Family	Immigrant Family	Total	Total	Native-Born Family	Immigrant Family
Both parents full-time year-round	31.7	31.5	31.7	30.2	39.7	25.9	32.8	22.3
One parent full-time year-round	56.1	58.0	58.1	57.1	44.6	56.2	51.1	58.9
None full-time year-round, at least one part-time or part-year	10.1	9.0	8.8	11.2	11.0	14.9	12.5	16.2
Neither employed	2.1	1.5	1.5	1.6	4.8	3.0	3.7	2.7

Notes:
Native-born family: Father is native born and if wife is present, she is native born.
Immigrant family: Father is foreign born or if wife is present, she is foreign born.
Immigrant status not available in 1989.

Because the proportions with only one full-time year-round worker tended to be smaller among minorities than among non-Hispanic Whites, however, minorities were most likely to have only part-time workers or no workers present in the home, at 19% for Hispanics in foreign-born families and 16% for non-Hispanic Blacks and Hispanics in native-born families, compared to 13% for non-Hispanic Whites in immigrant families and 10% for those in native-born families.

Official Poverty

Official poverty rates among fathers with coresident dependent children were unchanged during the 1990s at 8% in 1989, 1995, and 1998 (Table 2.10). Similarly, the proportion in deep poverty with an income-to-poverty-threshold ratio under 0.75 was unchanged at 5%, whereas the proportion near-poor or poor with an income-to-poverty-threshold ratio under 1.50 increased from 16 to 17% between 1989 and 1995, and then declined to 15% in 1998.

Reflecting differences in education and employment discussed in the preceding sections, as well as race and ethnic differences in earnings among men with similar educational attainments (Mare, 1995), poverty rates differ substantially by race, ethnicity, and immigrant status. The poverty rate for non-Hispanic Whites in 1998 was only 5 to 6%, depending on immigrant status, but twice as great at 11% for blacks, about three times as great at 15% for Hispanics in native-born families, and four times as great at 23% for Hispanics in immigrant families. Similar-

TABLE 2.10
Ratio of Income to Poverty Threshold for Fathers With Children 0–17 Years in Home, by Race,
Hispanic Origin, and Immigrant Family Status: 1989, 1995, 1998 (*numbers in percent*)

1989		White, Non-Hispanic			Black, Non-Hispanic	Hispanic		
Ratio of Income to Poverty Threshold	*Total*	*Total*	*Native-Born Family*	*Immigrant Family*	*Total*	*Total*	*Native-Born Family*	*Immigrant Family*
Under 0.75	**4.5**	**3.2**	—	—	**8.2**	**11.2**	—	—
Under 1.00	**7.8**	**5.5**	—	—	**14.5**	**20.0**	—	—
Under 1.50	**15.8**	**11.8**	—	—	**26.6**	**37.8**	—	—

1995		White, Non-Hispanic			Black, Non-Hispanic	Hispanic		
Ratio of Income to Poverty Threshold	*Total*	*Total*	*Native-Born Family*	*Immigrant Family*	*Total*	*Total*	*Native-Born Family*	*Immigrant Family*
Under 0.75	**5.2**	**3.2**	3.1	4.6	**7.6**	**14.6**	8.6	17.4
Under 1.00	**8.4**	**5.5**	5.3	8.2	**11.0**	**23.4**	13.8	27.9
Under 1.50	**16.9**	**11.7**	11.4	15.2	**23.9**	**42.8**	27.0	50.3

1998		White, Non-Hispanic			Black, Non-Hispanic	Hispanic		
Ratio of Income to Poverty Threshold	*Total*	*Total*	*Native-Born Family*	*Immigrant Family*	*Total*	*Total*	*Native-Born Family*	*Immigrant Family*
Under 0.75	**4.6**	**3.1**	3.0	4.2	**5.9**	**10.8**	9.2	11.6
Under 1.00	**7.7**	**4.9**	4.7	6.3	**11.0**	**20.1**	14.5	23.0
Under 1.50	**15.1**	**9.8**	9.7	11.4	**22.9**	**37.6**	24.3	44.5

Notes:
Native-born family: Father is native born and if wife is present, she is native born.
Immigrant family: Father is foreign born or if wife is present, she is foreign born.
Immigrant status not available in 1989.

ly, only 3 to 4% of non-Hispanic Whites lived in deep poverty, compared to 6% of
Blacks, whereas 9 and 12% were poor among Hispanics who were, respectively,
in native-born and immigrant families. Many fathers with coresident dependent
children live in near-poor or poor families. One in ten non-Hispanic Whites (10 to
11%) were poor or near-poor. This increased to nearly one in four (23 to 24%) for
non-Hispanic Blacks and Hispanics in native-born families and to nearly one half
(45%) for Hispanics in immigrant families.

Income From the Market Economy and Public Benefits

The total amount of economic resources available to fathers and their families for necessary goods and services is determined not only by the amount of income they receive in return for work they perform in the market economy, but also by the amount of tax (e.g., income, sales) they pay to governments and by the benefits they receive from government sources in the form of cash (e.g., earned income tax credit), near-cash benefits (e.g., food stamps), or in-kind benefits (e.g., housing subsidies). To assess the importance of government taxes and income sources, U.S. Census Bureau estimates using the CPS are used here to calculate key statistics for fathers with coresident dependent children (Table 2.11).

Questions about the effect of resources from government sources have become especially prominent since federal welfare reform, which was enacted through the Personal Responsibility and Work Opportunity Reconciliation Act of 1996, and two subsequent pieces of legislation (the Balanced Budget Act of 1997 and the Agriculture Research, Extension, and Education Reform Act of 1998). These laws mandated, or allowed states to set, new restrictions on eligibility for public benefits under the Temporary Assistance to Needy Families program (TANF), which was formerly the Aid to Families with Dependent Children program (AFDC), Food Stamps, and Supplemental Security Income (SSI). Simultaneously, however, the federal government expanded and increased the monetary value of the Earned Income Tax Credit (EITC) to provide additional economic incentives, beyond income earned on the job, to motivate low-income persons to increase their labor force participation. The focus here is primarily on these four programs, as well as on public housing subsidies, which represent a fifth major public benefit program for low-income persons and families. Because eligibility for these programs is means-tested, that is, because eligibility depends of the level of economic resources available to a family from market sources, these programs are referred to hereafter simply as means-tested programs or as welfare programs.

Another aim of income transfer programs, generally, is to provide economic resources to persons with limited economic means. It is important, therefore, to assess how changes in these programs affect poverty rates. In this context, it is important to note that during the past two decades, scholars and policymakers have expressed increasing concern about problems with the official poverty measure. Among the weaknesses identified by a recent National Research Council panel is the fact that the income measure used in calculating the official poverty rate does not reflect the effects of major government policies that alter the disposable income available to families, including the effect of near-cash or in-kind public benefits, such as food stamps, and the effect of the tax code, including the EITC (Citro & Michael, 1995). The U.S. Census Bureau has been aware of these problems and since 1980 has calculated estimates of the value of EITC, food stamps, and public housing subsidies, which are available on the CPS public-use microdata sets. These estimates are used here. Because the determination of

TABLE 2.11

Market Income Poverty and Nonmarket Income Poverty for Fathers With Children 0–17 Years in Home by Race, Hispanic Origin, and Immigrant Family Status: 1989, 1995, 1998 (*numbers in percent*)

1989

Poverty Rate	Total	White, Non-Hispanic			Black, Non-Hispanic Total	Hispanic		
		Total	Native-Born *Family*	Immigrant *Family*		*Total*	Native-Born *Family*	Immigrant *Family*
Based on market and non-means-tested income	9.2	6.7	—	—	15.7	23.2	—	—
Based on market, non-means-tested, and means-tested income	7.1	5.1	—	—	11.7	18.8	—	—
Effect of means-tested income	**−2.1**	**−1.6**	**—**	**—**	**−4.0**	**−4.4**	**—**	**—**

1995

Poverty Rate	Total	White, Non-Hispanic			Black, Non-Hispanic Total	Hispanic		
		Total	Native-Born *Family*	Immigrant *Family*		*Total*	Native-Born *Family*	Immigrant *Family*
Based on market and non-means-tested income	9.6	6.4	6.1	9.5	13.0	25.7	14.5	31.0
Based on market, non-means-tested, and means-tested income	6.0	3.8	3.6	6.0	7.6	18.3	9.5	22.4
Effect of means-tested income	**−3.6**	**−2.6**	**−2.5**	**−3.5**	**−5.4**	**−7.4**	**−5.0**	**−8.6**

1998

Poverty Rate	Total	White, Non-Hispanic			Black, Non-Hispanic Total	Hispanic		
		Total	Native-Born *Family*	Immigrant *Family*		*Total*	Native-Born *Family*	Immigrant *Family*
Based on market and non-means-tested income	8.6	5.6	5.4	6.9	12.1	21.9	14.8	25.6
Based on market, non-means-tested, and means-tested income	5.6	3.5	3.4	4.5	7.4	14.7	10.8	16.6
Effect of means-tested income	**3.0**	**−2.1**	**−2.0**	**−2.4**	**−4.7**	**−7.2**	**−4.0**	**−9.0**

Notes:

Native-born family: Father is native born and if wife is present, she is native born.

Immigrant family: Father is foreign born or if wife is present, she is foreign born.

Immigrant status not available in 1989.

poverty is based on family income, these income sources for all family members are used in deriving the estimates that follow.

Finally, it should be noted that non-means-tested sources of income from the government, such as Social Security, also provide important resources, especially to the elderly. Because market and non-means-tested income sources are often viewed as rightly earned by recipients, whereas means-tested benefits are often viewed as more akin to government charity, for ease of presentation here, the combined income from market sources and non-means-tested benefits are sometimes referred to hereafter simply as market income.

Market Work, Means-Tested Public Benefits, and Poverty

Without means-tested income, the poverty rate for fathers with coresident dependent children would have declined slightly from 9.2% in 1989 to 8.6% in 1998 (Table 2.11). But taking into account the effect of mean-tested programs, the decline was from 7.1% to 5.6%. Thus, the effect of means-tested programs in reducing poverty among fathers with coresident dependent children increased from 2.1 percentage points in 1989 to 3.0 percentage points in 1998. This overall effect actually occurred before welfare reform, because by 1995 the means-tested programs were acting to reduce the poverty rate for fathers with coresident dependent children by 3.6 percentage points. The pattern of change was generally similar for non-Hispanic Whites, non-Hispanic Blacks, and Hispanics, with most of the change occurring for non-Hispanic Whites by 1995, and all of the change for non-Hispanic Blacks and for Hispanics occurring by 1995. Distinguishing fathers with coresident dependent children according to their immigrant status, non-Hispanic Whites, non-Hispanic Blacks, and Hispanics in native-born families experienced little or no change in market-based poverty between 1995 and 1998, whereas non-Hispanic Whites and Hispanics in immigrant families experienced notable declines, respectively, of 2.6 and 5.4%. Changes in means-tested programs had essentially the same effect or less effect in 1998 than in 1995 in reducing market-based poverty among these four groups.

The magnitude of the effect of means-tested programs is greater for non-Hispanic Blacks than for non-Hispanic Whites in each year, reflecting the much higher market-based poverty rate among non-Hispanic Blacks and the still larger rate among Hispanics, whose market-based poverty rates are approximately twice as great as non-Hispanic Blacks. Similarly, the magnitude of the effect within specific race-ethnic groups tends to be greater for fathers in immigrant families than fathers in native-born families. The greater effect of means-tested programs for groups with higher market-based poverty rates is consistent program eligibility criteria, which are designed to provide assistance to persons with low market-based incomes.

What changes occurred in benefit receipt from specific programs? Among fathers with coresident dependent children, the AFDC/TANF participation rate increased slightly between 1989 and 1995, and then declined by one half as of 1998 (Table

2.12). The pattern was similar for food stamps, although the post–welfare reform decline was less striking. For non-Hispanic Blacks and for Hispanics the magnitude of the drops in participation rates for AFDC/TANF and food stamps are especially striking. Because these two groups had especially high proportions receiving benefits in 1989 and 1995, declines of about one half between 1995 and 1998 imply comparatively large drops in the proportion receiving benefits—4 to 6 percentage points, compared to declines of 1 to 2 percentage points for non-Hispanic Whites.

The situation regarding EITC is quite different, but a cautionary note is in order. U.S. Census Bureau estimates of participation in AFDC/TANF, food stamps, SSI, and housing subsidies are based on questions asked of respondents regarding whether or not they received benefits, but EITC participation is based on the assumption that all eligible persons are receiving benefits. Insofar as this assumption is not fully accurate, results for EITC also will not be fully accurate. Perhaps especially suspect is the extraordinary estimate that 57 to 59% of fathers with coresident dependent children in Hispanic immigrant families received benefits under the EITC. Hence, it may be best for particular groups, most notably immigrants, to view the program effects as those that would occur if all eligible persons received the tax credit. It should also be noted that the overall effect of various programs in reducing poverty will be exaggerated insofar as the effect of the EITC is overestimed.

With this caveat in mind, Census Bureau estimates suggest that the proportion who were eligible for EITC increased substantially between 1989 and 1995 by 4% overall and by 3, 3, and 10%, respectively, for non-Hispanic Whites, non-Hispanic Blacks, and Hispanics. Little change or slight declines then occurred between 1995 and 1998 for these groups, regardless of their immigrant status. Hence, the EITC may have had an increased effect in reducing poverty among fathers with coresident dependent children of about 1% between 1989 and 1998, overall, and by 1 to 3% for non-Hispanic Whites, non-Hispanic Blacks, and Hispanics. Except for non-Hispanic Blacks, the increase occurred between 1989 and 1995.

PORTRAIT OF FATHERS BY TYPE OF RELATIONSHIP WITH CORESIDENT CHILDREN

The type of family relationship linking a father to his child depends on the pathway by which the relationship is established. Biological fatherhood results from the birth of a child whom the man has fathered through a sexual union with his wife or nonmarital partner. Stepfatherhood occurs through the marriage of a man to a woman who brings to the marriage her biological child conceived with a different man. The legal adoption of a child leads to adoptive fatherhood, and the bringing a foster child into the home leads to foster fatherhood.

The demographic, family, and socioeconomic circumstances of fathers distinguished by the type of relationship linking them to their coresident dependent children are portrayed here with data from the 1991 and 1992 panels of the U.S. Cen-

TABLE 2.12

Receipt of Means-Tested Public Benefits and Effect on Poverty for Fathers
With Children 0–17 Years in Home by Race, Hispanic Origin, and Immigrant Family
Status: 1989, 1995, 1998 (*numbers in percent*)

1989		*White, Non-Hispanic*			*Black, Non-Hispanic*		*Hispanic*	
Receiving Benefits	*Total*	*Total*	*Native-Born Family*	*Immigrant Family*	*Total*	*Total*	*Native-Born Family*	*Immigrant Family*
AFDC/TANF	3.1	2.2	—	—	7.9	4.5	—	—
Food stamps	5.4	4.1	—	—	11.8	9.5	—	—
SSI	1.2	0.9	—	—	3.3	1.7	—	—
Housing subsidies	1.7	1.0	—	—	5.6	3.6	—	—
EITC	17.4	13.7	—	—	27.3	40.0	—	—
1995		*White, Non-Hispanic*			*Black, Non-Hispanic*		*Hispanic*	
Receiving Benefits	*Total*	*Total*	*Native-Born Family*	*Immigrant Family*	*Total*	*Total*	*Native-Born Family*	*Immigrant Family*
AFDC/TANF	3.6	2.3	2.2	3.4	7.3	7.8	7.3	8.0
Food stamps	6.6	4.6	4.5	5.2	11.6	15.1	12.6	16.3
SSI	1.8	1.3	1.4	0.9	3.1	2.6	2.5	2.6
Housing subsidies	2.0	1.1	1.0	1.6	6.0	5.0	4.8	5.1
EITC	21.7	16.4	16.3	17.2	30.6	49.9	30.3	59.2
1999		*White, Non-Hispanic*			*Black, Non-Hispanic*		*Hispanic*	
Receiving Benefits	*Total*	*Total*	*Native-Born Family*	*Immigrant Family*	*Total*	*Total*	*Native-Born Family*	*Immigrant Family*
AFDC/TANF	1.7	1.1	1.1	1.4	2.5	3.4	2.5	3.9
Food stamps	4.0	2.7	2.7	2.5	6.9	9.1	9.0	9.2
SSI	1.7	1.2	1.2	1.3	3.1	2.0	2.2	1.9
Housing subsidies	1.9	1.2	1.1	1.6	3.9	4.7	4.8	4.6
EITC	20.9	14.8	14.6	17.2	29.1	48.0	30.3	57.1

(Continued)

sus Bureau's Survey of Income and Program Participation (SIPP). The data were collected between 1991 and 1994, and the results represent the weighted average of fathers with coresident dependent children in each successive 4-month data collection period for these surveys (see Appendix 2A for additional methodological discussion). Differences between the nature of this SIPP sample and the CPS sam-

TABLE 2.12   (Continued)

1989 Effects of Poverty	White, Non-Hispanic			Black, Non-Hispanic	Hispanic		
	Total	**Total**	Native-Born Family	Immigrant Family	**Total**	**Total**	Native-Born Family	Immigrant Family

Effects of Poverty	**Total**	**Total**	Native-Born Family	Immigrant Family	**Total**	**Total**	Native-Born Family	Immigrant Family
AFDC/TANF	−0.6	−0.4	—	—	−0.9	−0.8	—	—
Food stamps	−0.5	−0.4	—	—	−1.3	−0.6	—	—
SSI	−0.1	−0.1	—	—	−0.4	−0.3	—	—
Housing subsidies	−0.1	−0.1	—	—	−0.4	−0.2	—	—
EITC	−0.8	−0.6	—	—	−1.4	−2.1	—	—

1995	White, Non-Hispanic			Black, Non-Hispanic	Hispanic		

Effects of Poverty	**Total**	**Total**	Native-Born Family	Immigrant Family	**Total**	**Total**	Native-Born Family	Immigrant Family
AFDC/TANF	−0.6	−0.2	−0.2	−0.1	−1.1	−1.1	−0.6	−1.2
Food stamps	−0.6	−0.5	−0.5	−0.4	−0.9	−1.6	−2.0	−1.4
SSI	−0.2	−0.1	−0.1	0.0	−0.5	−0.3	−0.1	−0.4
Housing subsidies	−0.1	−0.1	−0.1	0.0	−0.3	−0.6	−0.3	−0.8
EITC	−2.1	−1.7	−1.7	−2.1	−1.4	−4.8	−2.9	−5.8

1999	White, Non-Hispanic			Black, Non-Hispanic	Hispanic		

Effects of Poverty	**Total**	**Total**	Native-Born Family	Immigrant Family	**Total**	**Total**	Native-Born Family	Immigrant Family
AFDC/TANF	−0.3	−0.2	−0.2	−0.4	−0.8	−0.5	−0.2	−0.7
Food stamps	−0.6	−0.4	−0.4	−0.7	−1.3	−1.2	−1.1	−1.3
SSI	−0.1	−0.1	−0.1	0.0	−0.3	−0.1	−0.2	−0.1
Housing subsidies	−0.2	−0.1	−0.1	−0.1	−0.5	−0.7	−0.7	−0.7
EITC	−2.1	−1.5	−1.5	−1.5	−2.9	−5.5	−2.6	−7.0

Notes:
Native-born family: Father is native born and if wife is present, she is native born.
Immigrant family: Father is foreign born or if wife is present, she is foreign born.
Immigrant status not available in 1989.

ples for various years imply that results presented here from the two surveys are not directly comparable. However, although the SIPP results do not reflect the circumstances of fathers in any specific year, they do accurately reflect the nature and magnitude of differences in circumstances during the early 1990s among fathers linked to their children through various types of family relationships.

At the outset, six major combinations of father–child relationship types are distinguished for fathers with at least one coresident dependent child. During the early 1990s, the vast majority of fathers with coresident dependent children (87%) lived with biological children only (including biological fathers who were cohabiting with their children's biological mothers). Next most common were equal proportions (5%) that lived with both biological and stepchildren and with stepchildren only. Between 1 and 2% lived with adopted children only or with both biological and adopted children, whereas 0.4% lived with foster children (including in most cases a child with another relationship). Thus, among fathers with coresident dependent children in the early 1990s, about 93% lived with biological children. Although only 7% of fathers with coresident dependent children were not living with any of their biological children, twice that proportion (14%) had dependent children in the home who were not their biological offspring; that is, about one in seven fathers were caring for step, adopted, or foster children. The pattern of relationships is the same for non-Hispanic Whites and Hispanics, but non-Hispanic Black fathers were less likely, at 80%, to have only biological children in the home, and more likely, at 8 to 9% each, to have only stepchildren or both biological and stepchildren in the home. Thus, one in five non-Hispanic Black fathers were caring for nonbiological children in their homes in the early 1990s.

How do fathers with various arrays of parent-child relationships differ in their demographic, family, and economic circumstances? Because of limits associated with the small samples for three arrays of parent–child relationships, the focus here is on fathers with biological children only, both biological and stepchildren, and stepchildren only (Table 2.13).

Fathers with coresident dependent children who have both biological and stepchildren in the home tend to differ from fathers with only biological or only stepchildren in the home. Compared to fathers with only one type of child in the home, fathers with both biological and stepchildren are younger on average (37 vs. 42 years old) and more likely to be non-Hispanic Black (11% vs. 6 to 9%). The average number of children they have in the home is greater (2.8% vs. 1.5 to 1.8%), at least partly because in order to have both a biological and a stepchild in the home, they must have at least two children.

Fathers with both biological and stepchildren also are more likely to have completed high school only and not to have attended college (62% vs. 53 to 57%). Despite the slightly greater proportion of fathers with both biological and stepchildren who are employed (90% vs. 86 to 87%), they are, consistent with their lower educational attainments, less likely to be employed in high-prestige professional or sales/administrative positions (32% vs. 42 to 47%) and more likely to live below the official poverty threshold (14% vs. 6 to 9%), below 125% of the official poverty threshold (20% vs. 9 to 14%), and below 150% of the official poverty threshold (30% vs. 13 to 18%).

Fathers with coresident dependent children who have only biological children also are distinguished from the other two father types in several ways. They are less likely to be married, spouse present (92% vs. 100%), a difference explained by the fact that the other two father types can obtain stepchildren only through marriage,

TABLE 2.13
Characteristics and Circumstances of Fathers with Biological or Stepchildren
0–17 in the Home: Early 1990s (*numbers in percent unless otherwise noted*)

Characteristics and Circumstances	Biological Children Only	Stepchildren Only	Both Biological and Stepchildren
Mean age (*number*)	41.9	42.4	37.2
Marital status			
Married, spouse present	92.2	99.7	99.7
Never married	1.7	0.1	0.0
Divorced	3.7	0.1	0.1
Widowed	1.4	0.0	0.0
Separated	0.9	0.0	0.1
Education			
None–11th grade	17.9	18.1	19.3
High school graduate	34.8	38.8	42.9
Some college, no bachelor's degree	20.2	25.2	23.4
Bachelor's degree or more	27.2	17.8	14.3
In school	2.8	3.2	4.9
Race and Hispanic origin			
White, Non-Hispanic	78.9	82.3	75.1
Black, Non-Hispanic	5.6	8.7	10.5
Asian, Non-Hispanic	4.0	0.8	1.1
Employment and income			
Employed	86.0	87.0	90.0
Hours worked (*mean hours*)	43.3	43.5	43.4
Earnings (*monthly mean dollars*)	$2,685	$2,386	$2,207
Occupation			
Professional	25.5	24.1	17.2
Sales/administration	21.3	18.1	14.3
Service	14.4	11.0	14.1
Agriculture	5.8	8.3	8.7
Craft	1.7	1.3	2.2
Laborer	16.1	17.4	20.8
Other	15.2	19.9	22.7
Households			
Number of own children (*mean number*)	1.8	1.5	2.8
Ratio of income to poverty threshold			
Under 1.00	9.5	6.1	13.7
Under 1.25	13.6	8.9	20.3
Under 1.50	18.3	13.2	29.9

Note: Weighted estimates.
Source: The Survey of Income and Program Participation (Household Relationship Module, Wave 2, 1992 and 1993 panels).

although some of these fathers are in a nonmarital cohabiting union with the children's biological mother. Fathers with only biological children are more likely to have completed college (27% vs. 14 to 18%), more likely to be Asian (4% vs. 1%), and to have higher average earnings (13 to 22% greater), but they also have a slightly higher poverty rate than fathers with only stepchildren. The preceding patterns generally hold true for non-Hispanic whites, but the sample sizes are too small to provide the basis for meaningful comparisons for non-Hispanic black and Hispanic fathers who have only stepchildren or who have both biological and stepchildren.

FATHERS NOT LIVING WITH THEIR CHILDREN

Many dependent children do not have a father in the home. The CPS, for example, estimates that about one fourth (23%) of children in 1998 lived in mother-only families where the mother was not widowed, with corresponding proportions of 16, 55, and 27%, respectively, for non-Hispanic White, non-Hispanic Black, and Hispanic children (U.S. Census Bureau, 1998). These estimates only approximate the proportion of children who actually do not reside with their living biological father, however, because step and adoptive fathers are included as fathers in these CPS estimates, and because some biological fathers are not included in the count of fathers if he is not himself maintaining a household but is instead cohabiting with, but not married to, the mother of his child(ren).

Little is known about fathers not living with their dependent biological children, because major national surveys seldom ask men whether they have fathered children or whether they have children not currently residing in their homes. (However, for new information about fathers not living with their children see the following results that were derived by Sorensen & Wheaton, 2000, as well as chaps. 3 and 16.) Especially prominent in discussions of fathers not living with their children are Black fathers, because the proportion of Black children not living with fathers is quite high, compared to non-Hispanic Whites and Hispanics. Three key sets of facts regarding the circumstances of Black fathers that are seldom mentioned in social research or public policy discussions merit special attention here.

First, many young Black men who may be fathers are not counted or interviewed in the Decennial Census of the Population or in major national surveys. For example, in the 1990 census, the proportion uncounted among Black males was 6% for ages 20 to 24, and 11 to 14% for various 5-year age groups between the ages of 25 and 59 (Hogan & Robinson, 1993). Although CPS weighted estimates are adjusted for the undercount of Black men and other groups, the adjustment effectively assumes that uncounted men are similar in their demographic, family, and socioeconomic circumstances to men who are counted during the regular enumeration process. Because the uncounted population tends to be of lower socioeconomic status than the counted population, however, undercount-adjusted estimates tend to overestimate educational and economic resources and to underestimate poverty, especially among those who are most likely to be uncounted, including Black men. (For the effect of the undercount on child poverty, see Hernandez & Denton, 2001.)

A second issue relevant to studying the circumstances of fathers not living with their children is the large number of men, especially Black men, who are in prison or jail and the enormous increase in this number during the past two decades. The number of non-Hispanic Black men in jail in 1985 was 309,800, but this count more than doubled as of 1997 to a total of 753,600. Because non-Hispanic Black men in jail in 1997 accounted for 3.6% of all non-Hispanic Black men and an additional 3.2% were in prison, a total of 6.8% of all non-Hispanic Black men were in jail or prison by 1997 (Pastore & Maguire, 2000). As of 1999, 3.4% of all non-Hispanic Black men were in prison alone, with proportions of 7.3% for ages 20 to 24, 9.4% for ages 25 to 29, 8.4% for ages 30 to 34, and 7.3% for ages 35 to 39 (Pastore & Maguire, 2000). Because the prison population accounted for slightly less than one half of all non-Hispanic Black men who are in either prison or jail, it seems plausible that perhaps 14 to 18% of non-Hispanic Black men between the ages of 20 to 39 were either in prison or in jail by 1999. Many of these men became fathers before they were incarcerated (Sorensen & Wheaton, 2000). Insofar as this is the case, many non-Hispanic Black fathers are not available to provide a home or financial resources to their children, although they may continue to interact with dependent children who visit them in prison or jail. The proportion of non-Hispanic White men ages 20 to 39 in prison in 1999 was much smaller, at 0.8 to 1.1%, but substantially larger among Hispanic men in this age range, at 2.3 to 3.1%. Thus, perhaps as few as 2% of non-Hispanic White men in these prime childrearing ages are in prison or jail, compared to 4 to 6% of Hispanic men and 14 to 18% of non-Hispanic Black men.

Finally, a substantial number of young men ages 20 to 39 are in the military. As of March 1, 2000, 2 to 4% of non-Hispanic White men, 3 to 5% of non-Hispanic Black men, and 1 to 3% of Hispanic men in their 20s and 30s were serving in the military (U.S. Census Bureau, 2001a, c). Some of these men also are fathers, but their demographic, family, and socioeconomic circumstances are not measured in most national surveys, because these surveys use households as the sampling unit, and few of these men live in households.

All told, then, it appears that between 20 and 40% of non-Hispanic Black men in the prime childrearing ages of 20 to 39 are not counted or interviewed in the household population because they are uncounted or in prison, jail, or the military. Given the overall differentials in undercount rates (U.S. Census Bureau, 2001a), it appears that perhaps 15 to 25% of Hispanic men and 5 to 10% of non-Hispanic White men in the prime childrearing ages are not counted or interviewed in the household population. Insofar as these men are fathers and insofar as the characteristics of these men differ from men who are included in household surveys, national data collection systems tend to provide biased estimates of the characteristics of all fathers in the United States. Of course, not all of these men are fathers, and in addition, some fathers in national surveys are not identified as such.

In an effort to develop improved estimates pertaining to the circumstances of fathers not living with their children, Sorensen and Wheaton (2000) used 1993 SIPP data pertaining to men who reported having fathered at least one child and additional data on their age, marital history, and financial support for children outside their household to (a) identify fathers not living with their children, (b) estimate the number of such fathers missing from the SIPP, and (c) develop new weights to apply to these fathers. This methodology allows 78% of fathers not living with their children to be identified in the SIPP, with a figure of 86% for Whites and 59% for Blacks. Overall, this methodology compares favorably to other surveys which identify between about one-half of fathers not living with their children (the Panel Study of Income Dynamics and the National Survey of Families and Households) and about 70% of these fathers (National Survey of American Families) (Sorensen, personal communication, April 13, 2001). Thus, 22% of fathers not living with their children could not be identified in the SIPP or were not interviewed in the SIPP because they were in prison, jail, other institutions, military barracks, or overseas military service, with a figure of 14% for whites and 41% for blacks.

Sorensen and Wheaton (2000) go on to develop "data records" and weighting procedures for the remaining fathers not living with their children in order to develop overall estimates of the characteristics of these fathers. Based on plausible assumptions about their income levels in 1993, Sorensen and Wheaton suggest that fathers not living with their children are, on average, financially better off than the custodial mothers, with about two thirds of the latter and two fifths of the former having family incomes below 20% of the official poverty threshold. The 20% poverty rate for these fathers is only about half as great as the rate of 37% for the mothers, but substantially greater than the poverty rates of 6 to 14% for fathers living with biological and/or stepchildren derived here (Table 2.13) from the SIPP for the early 1990s.

CONCLUSION

Burgeoning research on fathers, especially during the past two decades, has demonstrated that fathers have important influences on their children. The demographic and family circumstances, the socioeconomic resources, and the nature and quality of father–child interaction that fathers bring to their children's lives have consequences for the well-being, cognitive development, social competence, academic achievement, and adult educational and occupational attainments of their children. The enormous and increasing diversity in the demographic, family, and socioeconomic circumstances of fathers are reflected in the results presented in this chapter.

As gender roles of fathers and mothers continue to be transformed, the United States is simultaneously experiencing a dramatic rise in the race, ethnic, and cultural diversity of fathers, mothers, and children. With one in five fathers with dependent children living in immigrant families and most immigrants hailing from Hispanic or Asian countries of origin, the cultural content and meaning of fathering is, and will no doubt continue, changing in complex and unanticipated ways. Importantly, racial, ethnic, and cultural diversity intersect with sometimes large differences in family structure and with socioeconomic disparities.

Hispanic fathers, and especially Black fathers, are less likely than White fathers to be living with their children, but if they are, Black fathers are much more likely to be caring not only for their own biological children but also for stepchildren in a blended family situation. In addition, if they are living with children, both Black and Hispanic fathers are more likely to be living with a larger number of children, especially Hispanic fathers in foreign-born families, and White and Hispanic fathers in foreign-born families are more likely to be living in a married-couple family than are fathers in native-born families.

The socioeconomic resources available to Black and Hispanic fathers in rearing their children are, however, often comparatively limited. Despite labor force participation rates of 90% or more, the limited educational attainments of many Black fathers with dependent children, and especially of many Hispanic fathers with dependent children, restrict their opportunities for finding full-time year-round employment. The result is poverty rates among Black and Hispanic fathers with dependent children in native-born families that are two or three times greater than the rates for non-Hispanic White fathers. Hispanic fathers with dependent children in immigrant families are even more likely to find themselves in pressing circumstances as they seek to provide economic resources to their children. Means-tested public benefits serve to reduce the magnitude of this economic deficit, but posttax, posttransfer poverty rates for Black and Hispanic fathers with dependent children continue to be two to four times greater than the poverty rate for White fathers living with dependent children.

In addition, little is known about fathers not living with their children, in part because most household surveys do not collect information from fathers who are uncounted, incarcerated, or in the military. In the 1993 SIPP, for example, 14% of White fathers and an extraordinary 41% of Black fathers were, for these reasons, not interviewed. Although detailed information is not available about these fathers, available evidence suggest that they experience much higher poverty than fathers living with their children and, hence, a more restricted ability to provide economic resources to their children.

In sum, fathers are extremely and increasingly diverse in their demographic, family, and socioeconomic circumstances and resources. The nature and quantity of these resources have been shown to carry important consequences for children. Increasing cultural diversity seems likely to bring potentially important changes in the meaning and content of fathering as practiced in the United States during the next few decades. The neglect of men as fathers in studies and policies focused on families and children has, thankfully, begun to be redressed during the past two decades. This chapter ends as it began, by emphasizing that all children have two parents. The well-being and future prospects of children depend on continuing research and policy attention to both mothers and fathers, to the resources they provide to families, to their relationships with each other, and to the nature and quality of their relationships with their children.

REFERENCES

Bumpass, L., & Lu, H-H. (1999). Trends in cohabitation and implications for children's family contexts in the U.S. Working Paper NSFH 83. Madison: Center for Demography and Ecology, University of Wisconsin.

Cabrera, N. J., Tamis-LeMonda, C. S., Bradley, R. H., Hofferth, S., & Lamb, M. E. (2000). Fatherhood in the 21st century. *Child Development, 71*(1), 127–136.

Citro, C. F., & Michael, R. T. (Eds.). (1995). *Measuring poverty: A new approach.* Washington, DC: National Academy Press.

Eggebeen, D. J. (in press). The changing course of fatherhood: Men's experience with children in demographic perspective. *Journal of Family Issues.*

Hernandez, D. J. (1986). Childhood in sociodemographic perspective. In R. H. Turner & J. F. Short, Jr. (Eds.), *Annual Review of Sociology: Vol. 12* (pp. 169–180). Palo Alto, CA: Annual Reviews.

Hernandez, D. J.(1993). *America's children: Resources from family, government, and the economy.* New York: Russell Sage Foundation.

Hernandez, D. J. (Ed.). (1999). *Children of immigrants: Health, adjustment, and public assistance.* Washington, DC: National Academy Press.

Hernandez, D. J., & Charney, E. (Eds.). (1998). *From generation to generation: The health and well-being of children in immigrant families.* Washington, DC: National Academy Press.

Hernandez, D. J., & Denton, N. A. (2001). Child poverty rates in the 1990 Census: Implications of the undercount for states, cities, and metropolitan areas. Unpublished manuscript prepared for the U.S. Census Monitoring Board, Presidential Members.

Hogan, H., & Robinson, G. (1993). What will the Census Bureau's coverage evaluation programs tell us about differential undercount. *Proceedings, 1993 Research Conference on Undercounted Ethnic Populations.* Washington, DC: U.S. Census Bureau.

Mare, R. D. (1995). Changes in educational attainment and school enrollment. In R. Farley (Ed.), *State of the union, America in the 1990s, Volume One: Economic Trends* (pp. 155–213). New York: Russell Sage Foundation.

Pastore, A. L., & Maguire, K. (Eds.). (2000). *Sourcebook of criminal justice statistics* [online]. Retrieved February 20, 2001, from Bureau of Justice Statistics Web Site: http://www.albany.edu/sourcebook/

Sorensen, E., & Wheaton, L. (2000). Income and demographic characteristics of nonresident fathers in 1993. Retrieved April 11, 2001, from http://aspe.hhs.gov/hsp/nonresfathers00/

U.S. Census Bureau. (1998). Current population survey (CPS) reports, Unpublished tables—Marital status and living arrangements: March 1998 Update; Table 6, Living arrangements of children under 18 years, by marital status and selected characteristics of parents: March 1998 (pp. 36–55). Retrieved from http://www.census.gov/population/www/socdemo/ms-la.html

U.S. Census Bureau. (2001a). 1990 Census undercounts and undercount rates—U.S. http://www.census.gov/dmd/www/90census.html

U.S. Census Bureau. (2001b). National population projections (NP-D1-A): Annual projections of the resident population by age, sex, race, and Hispanic origin: Lowest, middle, highest, and zero international migration series, 1999 to 2100. Retrieved from http://www.census.gov/population/www/projections/natdet.html

U.S. Census Bureau. (2001c). Monthly population estimates, 1990 to 2000. Collected from "Monthly Postcensal Resident Population plus Armed Forces Overseas" and "Month Postcensal Civilian Population." Retrieved from http://eise.census.gov/popest/archive/national/nat_90s_detail.php

APPENDIX

Data from the 1991 and 1992 panels of the Survey of Income and Program Participation (SIPP) are used in this chapter. The SIPP is a nationally representative, longitudinal survey of a random sample of the U.S. population (U.S. Census Bureau, 1991). Data collection in these two SIPP panels spanned 1991 through 1994, with each wave of the survey conducted quarterly. Because respondents were reinterviewed at 4-month intervals, the surveys provided 36 months of data for each household. Interviewees were asked about their economic experiences (income, employment, and so forth) over the past 4 months, including benefits received from welfare programs. In addition to detailed information on income sources and employment, data on household composition and related demographic information were collected.

The SIPP is well suited for the purposes of the present chapter because it included specially organized topical modules that asked about the relationships among individuals in the same household and about the fertility histories of men and women. In the "Household Relationships" topical module, exact relationships are pinpointed for households of three or more members. The module establishes a matrix indicating how each household member is related to every other household member. Interviewers guide the household reference person[1] through the various possible types of relationships, which are specified precisely. In the "Fertility History" topical module, males 18 or older are asked the number of children they have fathered.

The detailed demographic information on males matched to data collected on them from the "Household Relationships" and "Fertility History" topical modules meant that we could identify different types of fathers and examine the characteristics of the various fatherhood types. In fact, the household relationships matrix generated such a rich array of fatherhood types that we had to exclude males with multiple fatherhood types (e.g., males who simultaneously were fathers of biological, adoptive, and stepchildren) because their small numbers and multiplicity of roles prohibited meaningful comparisons.

To describe variation in fatherhood types, we identified males age 18 or older and classified them into six (mutually exclusive) fatherhood categories. As stated, fatherhood type is based on the precise relationship between an adult male and a child age 17 or younger residing in the same household. The six fatherhood types are: (a) biological father only, (b) stepfather only, (c) adoptive father only, (d) foster father[2], (e) biological-stepfather only, and (f) biological-adoptive father only. To prevent the exclusion of cohabiting fathers and stepfathers from our sample, we avoided distinguishing fathers based on their marital status. By doing so, we could identify cohabiting biological fathers and stepfathers in addition to married biological fathers and stepfathers. Our final sample of the six different types of fathers numbered 13,287.

---

[1] In the survey, a person who owned or rented the dwelling was termed the "household reference person." They provided information on all household members.

[2] This category includes two types of fatherhood combined into one. We altered our sample rules in this particular case because most foster fathers are required to have other children present. Restricting the foster father subsample to those without other children present would have reduced the subsample to about nine foster fathers.

3

The Demography of Fathers: What Fathers Do

Sandra L. Hofferth
University of Maryland

Jeffrey L. Stueve
University of New Mexico

Joseph Pleck
University of Illinois

Suzanne Bianchi
Liana Sayer
University of Maryland

In order to gain perspective on fathering in the 21st century, it is important to understand the extent of fathers' involvement in their children's lives today, their involvement in the recent past, and how father involvement is linked to social and demographic characteristics of fathers and families. This chapter focuses not only on overall measures of involvement with children, but also on more detailed indicators of the time parents spend in specific activities with children, particularly caring for, playing with, and reading to them. Paternal play and reading have particular significance in promoting cognitive development. The chapter also includes measures of the warmth of the relationship between a father and his children, his monitoring of their behavior and the degree of parenting responsibility he takes, and other contributions he makes to their welfare.

Demographers often assess how trends in the population might affect family behavior at a future point in time. Increases in divorce have produced a higher proportion of children living with a stepfather, and increases in cohabitation over the past several decades have led to increases in residence with a biological mother and her partner (Smock, 2000). An important feature of this chapter is that it distinguishes between the behavior of fathers who are related in diverse ways to the child, including stepfathers and unmarried partners to the mother. The discussion is not restricted to married fathers residing with the biological children of both parents, the group on which the bulk of prior research was based. We examine not only the involvement of fathers but also discuss reasons for differences among different types of fathers in involvement with their residential and nonresidential children. Much of this chapter is focused on the child. In the first part we examine children living with a father in the home. We examine the activities and relationship between father and child in all father-present families, including biological, stepfather, and cohabiting families. In the second portion of the chapter, we look at children with a nonresidential father—the frequency of contact and the types of activities fathers do with their children—by the type of family in which the child lives. Our major source is the 1997 Child Development Supplement to the Panel Study of Income Dynamics because it contains measures of the amount and quality of children's involvement with residential fathers and provides data on nonresidential fathers' involvement as well. Three other surveys of adults, the 1995 National Survey of Adolescent Males (NSAM) (Third Wave), the 1998 Trends in Time Use Study, and the 1999 National Omnibus Study, provide additional information about resident fathers' time with children. The NSAM represents a cohort of contemporary young fathers. These data permit classification of fathers jointly according to their biological relationship to the child and their marital status in relation to the child's mother. The strengths of the 1998 Trends in Time Use Study include data collection using time diaries, the inclusion of child-related secondary activity time, and reports of time expenditures obtained directly from a sample of mothers and fathers. The National Omnibus Study provides information on perceived responsibility of fathers and mothers for children.

BACKGROUND

In the United States at the beginning of the 21st century, the majority of children live with fathers. According to standard Census Bureau tabulations from the 1999 March Current Population Survey, 68% of children under age 18 in 1998 lived with two parents, and 4% lived with their father only, for a total of 72% living with a father. Twenty-three percent lived with a single mother, and 4% lived with neither parent (Federal Interagency Forum on Child and Family Statistics, 2000, Table POP5.A). This is the standard way of classifying children's living arrangements. Although distinguishing between two-parent and one-parent families is important, it is only a first step. Two-parent families are not homogeneous. Some fathers have married the children's mothers and others are simply cohabiting with them. Some men have a biological and others a nonbiological or "social father" standing. Some children have nonresidential biological fathers with whom they share time and attention, and some children's residential nonbiological fathers have nonresidential biological children competing for their time and attention. As such alternative relationships have become more numerous, they affect an increasing number of children and are likely to have a substantial impact on the types of activities and investments their parents make, yet little is known about them.

Using data from the 1996 Survey of Income and Program Participation (SIPP) (Federal Interagency Forum on Child and Family Statistics, 2000, Table POP5.B), it is possible to take the distinction between biological and stepparenthood into account and to determine how many children's single mothers and fathers live with an unmarried partner. Table 3.1 focuses on family types of children under age 18. In 1996, 64% of children lived with two biological parents including about 2% with biological parents who were cohabiting but had not married. Another 7% lived with one biological and one stepparent. Twenty-three percent lived with a single mother, and 2% lived with a single father. Some of these single parents are actually living with a partner—about 2% of children live with a single mother and her unmarried partner, and 0.4% live with a single father and his part-ner. A small proportion, 4%, do not live with either parent. In addition, there are two major differences by race/ethnicity: (a) A higher proportion of White than Hispanic children and Hispanic children than Black children live with two bio-logical parents. (b) Both Hispanic and Black children are more likely to live with only one parent. Hispanic children are one and a half times more likely (26%) and Black children are over three times more likely (53%) than White children (16%) to live with a single mother. The vast majority of children living with a single par-ent or a single mother and stepfather have a biological father living elsewhere.

If one assumes that most children living with one biological parent and one stepparent are living with a stepfather and one includes children living with a mother and her unmarried partner, the 1996 SIPP data suggest that about three fourths of children live with a father, an estimate fairly close to that from the 1999 Current Population Survey. The SIPP data go further than the standard Census Bureau classification of children's living arrangements in distinguishing between

TABLE 3.1
Relationship of Children to Their Parents, all U.S. Children Under Age 18

	All Races	White	Black	Hispanic
two bio parents	**64.2%**	**71.5%**	**31.7%**	**62.9%**
Married parents	62.4%	70.1%	29.9%	58.7%
Unmarried parents	1.8%	1.4%	1.8%	4.2%
one bio, one stepparent	**6.7%**	**7.5%**	**5.2%**	**5.2%**
single bio mom	**22.7%**	**15.5%**	**52.5%**	**25.7%**
Mother only	20.6%	13.4%	50.2%	23.3%
Mother and partner	2.1%	2.1%	2.3%	2.4%
single bio dad	**2.5%**	**2.8%**	**2.0%**	**1.7%**
Father only	2.1%	2.4%	1.7%	1.3%
Father and partner	0.4%	0.4%	0.3%	0.4%
no bio parent	**3.9%**	**2.7%**	**8.5%**	**4.4%**
Total	**100.0%**	**100.0%**	**100.0%**	**100.0%**

Source: 1996 SIPP data, reported in America's children: Key national indicators of well-being, Federal Interagency Forum on Child and Family Statistics, 2000

Note: The small group of children with adoptive parents are included with those with biological parents.

biological and stepparenthood and identifying unmarried partners. In this chapter, a more complete understanding of the demography of fatherhood requires taking into account whether the male parent (biological or step) is married to the child's mother and how this alters the parent–child relationship. Although these data go farther than standard Census Bureau data in showing the variety of fathers, they do not address the proportion of children who have nonresidential fathers nor the proportion of children living in families sharing their father's time and resources with nonresidential children.

The first part of this chapter focuses on the involvement of children with their residential fathers, biological and nonbiological, whether married to the mother or not. The second part of this chapter focuses on the involvement of children with their nonresidential fathers.

INVOLVEMENT OF CHILDREN WITH RESIDENTIAL FATHERS

In this section we discuss types of father involvement, what factors motivate fathers to be involved with their children, the measurement of father involvement and fathering from the four different surveys, and our findings.

Types of Father Involvement

A major part of children's learning occurs through interacting with and observing parents, leading to two important aspects of father involvement: (a) the time parents spend engaged with or accessible to children overall or in specific activities and the responsibility they take for them,[1] and (b) the quality or nature of the relationship (Lamb, Pleck, Charnov, & Levine, 1985; Pleck, 1997). Previous research on two-parent families has shown levels of engagement by fathers with young children of about 2 to 2.8 hours per day, not distinguishing type of day (Pleck, 1997). Fathers (and mothers) spend more time with young children than with adolescents. Estimates of paternal engagement with adolescents have ranged from 0.5 to 1 hour for weekdays and 1.4 to 2 hours for Sundays (Pleck, 1997). Recent research (Yeung, Sandberg, Davis-Kean, & Hofferth, 2001) found that fathers in

---

[1]Three central components of father involvement, according to recent writings (Lamb, Pleck, Charnov, & Levine, 1985; Lamb, Pleck, Charnov, & Levine, 1987; Pleck, Lamb, & Levine, 1986), are paternal engagement, accessibility, and responsibility. Paternal engagement includes direct interaction with children, and accessibility includes time the father is available to children, but not directly interacting with them. The degree of responsibility a father assumes for his children encompasses the management of the child's welfare—making sure that the child is fed, clothed, housed, monitored, managed, examined by physicians, and cared for when needed. Although Lamb and Pleck recognized fathers' economic contributions to their children as part of fathering, they did not include breadwinning within the narrower construct of father involvement (Pleck, 1997), and this chapter follows their usage. (For an alternative view, see Christiansen & Palkovitz, 2001.)

intact families spent about 1 hour and 13 minutes on a weekday and about 3.3 hours on a weekend day with children under age 13. Because both parents' times may vary, relative levels of involvement may provide a better sense of father involvement. Based on data from the 1980s and 1990s, fathers' time engaged in activities with their children is about two fifths of mothers' time. Fathers are accessible to their children about two thirds as often as mothers (Pleck, 1997). These figures are higher than in the 1970s and early 1980s. And a recent study from the mid-1990s shows that fathers' time engaged with children on a weekday is about two thirds of mothers' time, and on a weekend day it is almost 90% of mothers' time, additional evidence for increased father involvement (Yeung et al., 2001). In these more recent data, the ratio of fathers' to mothers' time accessible to their children is about the same as that of engaged time. As children become older and the absolute amount of parental time declines, fathers' time rises as a proportion of mothers' time with children (Yeung et al., 2001).

Of course the increasing ratio of fathers' to mothers' time since the 1970s could be due to either a decline in mothers' or an increase in fathers' available time. However, one comparison between 1965 and 1998 suggests that mothers' time with children has remained fairly constant (Bianchi, 2000), and hence, the rise in the ratio of fathers' to mothers' time with children is not due to a decline in mothers' time, at least in two-parent families. Other research also suggests that fathers' time with children has risen in two-parent families where the average amount of time children spent with fathers rose by about 3 hours per week between 1981 and 1997, and time with mothers rose as well (Pleck, 1997; Sandberg & Hofferth, 2001). The time children spent with fathers did not rise significantly over all families because of the offsetting increased number of single-parent families and because nonresidential fathers are less involved with their children (Sandberg & Hofferth, 2001).

Although the overall amount of time may be important to child development, developmental psychologists are concerned about the nature of those activities. As has been found in several studies, play and companionship account for the largest fraction of time children spend with their fathers. According to recent research, about 39% of children's engaged time with fathers is spent in play and companionship on a weekday or weekend day (Yeung et al., 2001). Household work and social activities comprise a relatively small fraction of children's time engaged with their fathers, about 15% on a weekday and 30% on a weekend day. The time children spend in learning and educational activities with their fathers is quite small, averaging only 3 to 5% of engaged time.

A fourth important category is personal care received by the child from the father, about 25% of the father's engaged time on a weekend day and 35% on a weekday. Child care by fathers when mothers are working is an important aspect of caregiving. In the United States a substantial minority of dual-earner parents keep their use of nonparental care to a minimum by adjusting their work schedules so that a parent can care for their children when needed. About one-third of working parents in two-parent families with a preschool child work different schedules and can share care (Presser, 1989). The proportion of fathers who care for children during the hours when mothers work rises to three quarters as the number of nonoverlapping hours increases (Brayfield, 1995). Other evidence that fathers' time in child care is responsive to available time is that, during the 1991 recession in which more men were presumably out of work or working fewer hours, the proportion of men who provided child care as a primary or secondary provider while their wives were working rose by one third. It declined again following the end of the recessionary period (Casper & O'Connell, 1998).

Much of what parents do for children demands time indirectly, through management of their lives and activities—the extent of responsibility fathers take for their children (McBride & Mills, 1993; Pleck, 1997; Radin, 1994). Fathers can participate in a wide variety of managerial and supervisory activities, including selecting doctors and child-care programs, managing appointments, arranging transportation, coordinating with schools, and monitoring children's activities (Cabrera, Tamis-LeMonda, Bradley, Hofferth, & Lamb, 2000). Whereas fathers take less responsibility than mothers, and few fathers take sole responsibility for any parenting tasks (Sandberg, 2000), fathers are likely to share direct care, to transport children to activities, and to participate in choosing activities and selecting a child-care program, preschool, or school. They are less likely to be involved in purchasing clothing and in selecting and making appointments for doctor visits (Sandberg, 2000).

An additional aspect of fathering considered in this chapter is the quality of the father–child relationship. Most developmental psychologists argue that the quality of parenting and of the parent–child relationship are crucial to developing competent children (Cabrera et al., 2000; Pleck, 1997). Although a variety of measures of quality could have been tapped, the combination of responsiveness with control has been shown by research to be linked to optimal child development (Maccoby & Martin, 1983; Steinberg, 2000) and is our focus. In this chapter, measures of parental warmth tap the responsiveness dimension by providing information on the emotional content of the interaction between parent and child. Control is measured by indicators of parental monitoring, which includes setting rules and enforcing them.

What Factors Motivate Fathers to Be Involved With Their Children?

Family Structure. Although there are a number of factors that might explain fathers' involvement, this chapter focuses on family structure. Family structural variables are expected to be associated with paternal involvement because they may influence fathers' motivation to participate. Particularly important are the relationship of the male to the child (biological/other) and to the mother (married/cohabiting). From the point of view of evolutionary psychology, genetic benefits arise from fathering and investing in one's own natural offspring (Kaplan, Lancaster, & Anderson, 1998). Such "parenting investment" increases the reproductive fitness of the next generation. Stepfathers gain little genetic benefit by investing in the care of stepchildren, and such investment detracts from time they might otherwise spend ensuring the fitness of their own biological progeny. However, many examples of caring behavior by stepparents exist (Hofferth & Anderson, 2001), suggesting that paternal investment is not restricted only to biological offspring. One of the mechanisms behind such investment is "relationship investment." By investing in their spouse's children from a prior union, remarried men increase the prospect of further childbearing as well as continuation of supportive exchanges with their partner. Thus, investment in one's partner's children may have payoffs. However, there is also less normative support for involvement by stepfathers than biological fathers (Cherlin, 1978; Daly & Wilson, 1998), consistent with findings that stepfathers are behaviorally less involved (Pleck, 1997). It is likely that cohabiting (especially nonbiological cohabiting) fathers also receive less normative support for being involved. In addition, both stepfathers and cohabiting fathers may receive less support for involvement from the child's mother. Because of the importance of the biological and marital relationship and in order to compare across different data sets, we present our results (when sample sizes permit) by biological relationship to child and, among nonbiological fathers, by marital relationship to the mother.

Social and Demographic Factors. Biological, stepfather, and mother's cohabiting partners are likely to differ on a variety of social and demographic factors that could also be linked to father involvement. For example, fathers' motivation for involvement with older children may be greater because interaction with them is more gratifying. On the other hand, as children age into adolescence, they may become less interested and less motivated to spend time with their father. Older fathers may be more motivated to spend time with their children. Cultural variation also exists. Recent research found African-American and Hispanic fathers taking more responsibility for managerial tasks than White fathers (Hofferth, in press), even after adjusting for differences in socioeconomic and demographic characteristics. African-American fathers are less warm and more controlling than White fathers, and Hispanic fathers are equally warm but less controlling than White fathers. Better-educated fathers may have more positive fathering attitudes and more equitable gender-role attitudes, which may relate to greater engagement with children. Their expectations may also be higher. On the other hand, fathers with longer work hours will be constrained from spending more time with their children. Fathers' income could be positively or negatively related to engagement with children, depending on whether the level of income is a function more of education or work hours.

Measures of Paternal Involvement and Fathering

Each study used slightly different samples and definitions of variables. These are described in this section.

The Panel Study of Income Dynamics—Child Development Supplement (PSID—CDS)[2]

Whether the child was genetically related or not and the marital status of the parents was obtained as follows: The primary caregiver answered a series of questions as to whether the child lived with his/her biological or adoptive mother, biological or adoptive father, a stepfather, a stepmother, or a father figure. If the child lived with a biological father, the child is a biological child of the father. If the child lived with a male identified as a stepfather, the child is a stepchild. If the child lives with a male caregiver who is a partner or boyfriend of the mother, then the child lives with the mother's partner (nonbiological cohabiting father figure). Adoptive children were classified with biological children on the grounds that adopted children are more similar to biological children than to stepchildren, because they are chosen by the two parents. It should be noted that biological fathers could be married or unmarried to the child's mother. For nonbiological children (except adopted children), whether the male is married to the child's mother was the basis for distinguishing stepfathers from mothers' partners.

Time Children Spend Engaged With or With Access to Their Father. The primary caregiver completed one diary for one weekday and one weekend day for each child age 0–12 in the family.[3] Although it is true that children's activities vary over the course of the week, their sampled days tend to be representative— 62% of respondents reported that the day selected was either very typical or typical (on a 5-point scale). Only 7% reported that the day was not typical at all. Time diaries are relatively easy to obtain from children, although complicated and expensive to code. The time diary asked about the child's flow of activities over a 24-hour period beginning at midnight of the randomly assigned designated day. These questions ask the child's primary activity that was going on at that time, when it began and ended, and whether any other activity was taking place. Two additional questions—"Who was doing the activity with the child?" and "Who else was there but not directly involved in the activity?—when linked to activity codes such as "playing" or "being read to," provide details on the extent of one-on-one interactions of others with the child. For this analysis, times in which the

---

[2]Detailed descriptions of the four data sets can be found in Appendix 3A.

[3]Sixty percent were completed by the mother, 12% by mother and child together, 6% by the child alone, and 15% by someone else in the family.

father (father, stepfather, foster, or adoptive father) was engaged in activities with a child were coded as father engaged. Times in which the father was present (e.g., at home) but not actively involved with the child were coded as father accessible. Times engaged and accessible were summed over all activities for weekdays and weekends for each child. Weekly time was computed by multiplying weekday time by 5 and weekend-day time by 2. To obtain daily estimates, the weekly estimate was divided by 7. These totals include children with whom the father spent no time. Besides total time, this paper also examines the time children spend with their fathers in three specific activities—personal care, playing, and reading with the father. These are subcategories of the aggregate time children spend with fathers.[4]

Types of Activities With Parents. Besides gathering data in a time diary, the CDS asked fathers directly about 13 different activities parents and children, age 3 and older, may do together. These include washing or folding clothes; doing dishes; cleaning house; preparing food; looking at books or reading stories; talking about the family; working on homework; building or repairing something; playing on the computer or video games; playing a board game; card game, or puzzle; and playing sports or outdoor activities. The total score reflects the number of activities fathers reported doing with their children in the past month and has a reliability coefficient of 0.78.[5]

Responsibility. The eight responsibility items used here focus on the care of children, including bathing, playing with, and disciplining children; buying them clothes; selecting a child-care program or pediatrician; and choosing and driving them to activities. Response categories are: (a) I do this, (b) another household member does this, (c) I share this task, and (d) someone else does this task. If the respondent did the task, the response was coded 2, if the respondent shared it, it was coded 1; otherwise the task was coded 0. Scores were summed over all items. Overall scale reliability was 0.73.

Parental Warmth. Parental warmth is a six-item scale developed by Child Trends for use in measuring the warmth of the relationship between child and parent. The questions, asked about all children, ask how often the parent hugged the child, told the child they love him/her, spent time with child, joked or played with child, talked with child, and told child they appreciated what he/she did. The response categories range from (1) not in the past month to (5) every day. A scale was created by summing the number of behaviors that the parent said they did with the child in the past month. The reliability coefficient was 0.77.

---

[4]Personal care will be underestimated for school-age children because we did not ask who was helping them with such care.

[5]All reliabilities are measured using Cronbach's alpha.

Paternal Monitoring and Control. Parental monitoring is measured by a set of nine items asking fathers of children age 3 and older whether they have rules setting limits on their children's activities, their schedules, their food, their whereabouts, and their homework, and whether they discuss these rules with their children. In contrast to the other scales, this scale measures control across all children. The response categories (reverse coded) range from (1) never to (5) very often, with 45 the highest possible score. The reliability coefficient was 0.73.

Background Variables. We examined how characteristics of the child and family were associated with biological and marital status of the father. Included are the age of the child and the age of the father, the education, earnings, work hours, and family income of the father, and race/ethnicity measured as White, Black, or Hispanic.

The 1995 National Survey of Adolescent Males (NSAM), Third Wave

In contrast to the CDS, in which the child is the point of reference, the *father* is the reference person in the NSAM. Thus, a somewhat different categorization of subgroups of fathers is needed than was used previously (e.g., a child usually lives with only a biological father or a stepfather, but a father can live with both biological children and stepchildren). Three categories of relationship to the children in the household were distinguished: (a) biological fathers, (b) stepfathers, and (c) "mixed" fathers (living with both biological and stepchildren). Biological fathers (weighted $n = 212$) were those living with only biological child(ren). These fathers may or may not be living with the child(ren)'s biological mother. Fathers in this group who are living with female partners may or may not be married to them. Following Cherlin (1996, p. 387), stepfathers ($n = 48$) were operationally defined to include adult men who are not biological parents to the child(ren) living with them, but who nonetheless function as "social" fathers to these children, whether or not they are married to the child(ren)'s mother. It should be noted that stepfathers who live with a female partner may or may not be married to her, and if living with a partner, she may or may not be the child(ren)'s biological mother. Mixed fathers ($n = 22$) live with both biological and stepchildren. In addition, three adoptive fathers also had biological children residing with them and are included in the mixed group. This categorization differs from the CDS, where adoptive and biological children are grouped together.

An important difference between the NSAM father groups and the CDS father groups is that the NSAM groups are based only on the father's biological relationship to his child(ren). In contrast, among nonbiological fathers in the CDS analysis, those married to the children's mothers (stepfathers) could be distinguished from those living with her nonmaritally (mothers' partners, or nonbiological cohabiting fathers). A more minor difference is that adoptive children in the CDS were grouped with children of biological fathers, whereas in the NSAM analysis they were included in the mixed father group, as those fathers also had biological children.

Time Fathers Spend Engaged With Their Children. In contrast to the time-diary methodology used in the CDS, the NSAM assessed fathers' engagement time by asking fathers to *estimate* how much time they spent with their children per day in the three engagement activities: play, reading, and care.[6] The items, adapted from the National Survey of Families and Households (NSFH), Wave 1, were: "Thinking about your child(ren) under 10 who are living with you, about how much time in a typical day do you spend playing with (him/her/them)?"; ". . . spend reading to (him/her/them)?"; and ". . . spend taking care of their physical needs, including feeding, bathing, dressing, and putting (him/her/them) to bed?" It should be noted that a measure of total engagement time (comparable to that provided by the CDS data) is not available in the NSAM. The CDS time-diary methodology yielded time engaged in a broader set of activities than care, play, and reading. The NSAM provides fathers' estimates of their time only in these three specific activities, so that their total engagement time cannot be estimated.

Background Variables. The relationship of fathers' and partners' age, fathers' and partners' education, fathers' ethnicity, fathers' work hours, number of children, and age of youngest child to family structure as sociodemographic background variables was examined. Education was collapsed to four levels: high school graduate or less, some college or vocational school, college degree, and more than college degree (1–4).

The 1998 Family Interaction, Social Capital, and Trends in Time Use Study

Specific Engagement Activities. In this study, parents provided one-day diaries of all their activities and, in addition, indicated "with whom" they did each activity. The 1998–99 data collection was the first time since the mid-1980s that a national sample of U.S. adults was asked to report on not only what they were doing the previous day but also "with whom" they did each activity. For each activity that a respondent reported as their main or primary activity, the interviewer probed as to whether the respondent was doing anything else during

---

[6]The data obtained using standard questions asked in a number of surveys are generally considered inferior to those collected using time diaries because of increased social desirability (Hofferth, 1999b; Juster & Stafford, 1985). Absolute levels of time are likely to be less meaningful than the relative comparisons across family types.

that time. Responses to the "anything else" probe are referred to in the time-diary literature as "secondary activities." A set of nine codes (20–29) capture child care directly (20 Baby care; 21 Child care; 22 Helping or teaching; 23 Talking/reading; 24 Indoor playing; 25 Outdoor playing; 26 Medical care—child; 27 Other; 28 (not used); 29 Travel/child care).

Sum of Engagement and Accessibility. The diary data collection in 1998–99 permits an overall measure of all time parents spent with children. For each activity a respondent did during the day, he or she reported with whom that activity was done. This we call "daily hours with children," and this measure is comparable to the sum of engagement and availability from the CDS. However, much of the existing time-diary literature on parents' time with children focuses solely on the time spent in the primary activity of child care. Hence, the second measure of time with children that we construct is just the hours in the diary day that a respondent reported that he or she was engaged in activities coded as direct care of children (the nine codes listed previously). We refer to this as primary child-care time. Bryant and Zick (1996) used data collected in the late 1970s in 11 states in two-child, two-parent households to show that secondary child-care time comprises about one third of all parental child-care time. Robinson and Godbey (1997) report an even more dramatic increase if secondary child-care time is added, up to 50 percent in total child-care time when secondary time is added. Hence, the third measure of parental investment in children that we construct is the combination of primary and secondary time spent in activities coded as direct child care. The fourth measure we examine is the total number of minutes on the diary day that a respondent reported playing with or teaching children (code 22) as primary or primary + secondary activity.

Responsibility. In a fourth survey of adults, the 1999 National Omnibus Survey, respondents answered a series of questions about who is mainly responsible for six parenting domains. The mothers were asked: "In parenting your children, who is mainly responsible for disciplining the children? Mainly you, mainly the children's father, or both about equally?"; fathers were offered analogous response categories: "mainly you, mainly the children's mother, or both about equally?" The five other dimensions of parenting were asked in the same manner, with the same response categories: "Who is mainly responsible for providing financial support for the children?" "Who is mainly responsible for playing with or having fun with the children?" "Who is mainly responsible for taking care of the children's daily needs, like meals, clothing, and transportation?" "Who is mainly responsible for providing emotional support for the children?" "Who is mainly responsible for monitoring the children's activities and friends?"

Results

Sociodemographic Comparisons—PSID—CDS

In Table 3.2, we show the characteristics of the fathers of children under 13 living with their children, obtained from the CDS. We see that, overall, children's fathers are very similar in age, except that stepfathers were about one year younger on average than biological fathers. Educational levels are slightly lower for stepfathers and cohabiting fathers than for biological fathers. Consistent with their lower educational levels, fathers' earnings and total family income are lower for children in nonbiological father families than for children in biological father families. There are substantial race/ethnic differences in family structure—60% of biological fathers are white compared with 40% of stepfathers and 53% of cohabiting fathers. A correspondingly higher proportion of stepfathers and mother's partners are Black. A similar proportion of biological fathers and stepfathers are Hispanic. Few mother's partners are Hispanic.

Children living with biological fathers are the youngest group of children, with children of nonbiological cohabiting dads about a year older and children of stepfathers about two years older than children living with a biological father. This is because cohabitation often occurs following divorce, and remarriage occurs even later.

Sociodemographic Comparisons—NSAM. Demographic similarities and differences between NSAM fathers and CDS fathers should first be noted. NSAM fathers are substantially younger on the average (23.6 years) than CDS fathers (36.5 years), due to the NSAM's restriction to fathers age 21–27 in 1995 (15–19 in 1988) (Table 3.3). Following from this difference, NSAM fathers' children are considerably younger; whereas CDS fathers are reporting on their involvement with a child age 6 on the average, NSAM fathers are reporting on a child whose average age is about 2.5. However, employment hours appear comparable between the two samples. Fathers' education was coded differently in the two samples, but here too the results seem comparable.

In comparing the three father groups within the NSAM, it should be noted that the NSAM sample sizes are considerably smaller than those of the CDS, resulting in less statistical power to detect differences among groups. Nonetheless, stepfathers and/or mixed fathers differed significantly from biological fathers on partner's age, respondent's ethnic background, partner's education, number of children, and age of youngest child. Biological fathers had younger partners than both stepfathers and mixed fathers. Biological fathers' partners also had completed more education than stepfathers' partners. Biological fathers had fewer children than the other two groups of fathers. Finally, biological fathers had a youngest child who was significantly younger than the two other groups. Additional analysis within the mixed father subgroup, not shown in Table 3.3, indicated that their

TABLE 3.2
Father Involvement and Characteristics, by Relationship of Father to Child, CDS

	All children	Biodad	Stepdad	Mother's partner
Paternal involvement:				
Daily hours engaged	2.1	2.2	0.8*	1.4*
Daily hours available	1.8	1.8	0.8*	1.7
Daily hours Dad cares	0.10	0.11	0.02*	0.04*
Daily hours Dad plays	0.51	0.53	0.19*	0.56
Daily hours Dad reads	0.06	0.06	0.04*	0.01*
n	2067	1866	129	72
# of activities at least once a week	9.1	9.2	7.9*	7.6*
n	998	921	59	18
Paternal warmth	5.0	5.1	4.3*	4.0*
n	1306	1220	61	25
Paternal monitoring & control	32.2	32.2	32.5	28.1*
n	1079	1003	57	19
Motivation:				
Involvement of father's father	3.1	3.1	2.9	3.0
Positive attitudes to fathering	26.1	26.1	25.4*	25.6
Skills				
No parenting class	75.0%	75.0%	78.0%*	71.0%
Dad learned to parent from dad	56.0%	56.0%	50.0%	29.0%*
n	1290	1207	60	25
Partner support				
Partner–partner conflict	2.9	2.8	3.4*	3.5*
Conflict over child	4.9	4.8	5.8*	5.6*
n	1206	1122	58	26
Institutional barriers				
Work Hours	43.6	43.8	43.5	39.6*
n	2531	2265	162	104
Sociodemographic factors				
Dad's education (years)	13.1	13.1	12.7*	12.6*
Dad's earnings	$34,920	$35,720	$28,320*	$27,710*
Family income	$54,000	$56,180	$39,800*	$28,670*
Dad's age (years)	36.5	36.6	35.5*	36.8
White	58.0%	60.0%	40.0%*	53.0%
Black	28.0%	26.0%	47.0%*	42.0%*
Hispanic	9.0%	9.0%	8.0%	1.0%*
Other	4.0%	4.0%	5.0%	4.0%
Age of child (years)	6.0	5.9	7.8*	6.9*
Father pays child support	4%	4%	3%	5%
n	2531	2265	162	104

*statistically significant at p < .05 compared with children living with their biological father

TABLE 3.3

Paternal Engagement and Other Measures by Family Type, NSAM 1995

	All Dads	Biodads	Stepdads	Mixed
Engagement				
Daily hours dad cares	4.5	4.8	3.0*	4.3
Daily hours dad plays	2.9	2.9	2.5	3.4
Daily hours dad reads	0.51	0.46	0.57	0.82*
Motivation				
Alienation	1.5	1.5	1.4	1.4
Cost of children	2.9	2.9	2.8	2.8
Male gender role attitudes	2.8	2.9	2.8	2.6*
Skills				
Paternal competence	3.4	3.4	3.3	3.3
Partner support				
Say about raising child	2.8	2.8	2.3*	3.0
Agreement w/partner about children	3.6	3.6	3.6	3.7
Institutional barriers				
Work hrs/week	42.4	43.5	37.6	42.3
Worked fewer hrs because of child	26.2%	28.0%	15.2%	31.4%
Sociodemographic factors				
Father's age (years)	24.3	24.3	24.4	24.4
Partner's age (years)	23.6	23.2	24.5*	25.4*
Black	16.4%	14.6%	22.9%	19.0%
White	66.2%	69.3%	50.0%	71.4%
Hispanic	13.5%	14.6%	12.5%	4.8%
Other	3.9%	1.4%	14.6%	4.8%
Father's education (years)	1.4	1.4	1.3	1.5
Mother's education (years)	1.5	1.6	1.2*	1.3
Number of children	1.4	1.3	1.5*	2.4*
Age of youngest child (months)	30.6	25.9	52.2*	28.0
Married	70.2%	79.7%	31.3%	63.6%
Number of cases	282	212	48	22

*statistically significant at $p < .05$ compared with children living with their biological father

youngest child was usually a biological child of the father. Mixed fathers had more children than did other father groups, in large part because to have both a biological and stepchild (and therefore be included in the mixed category) required having a minimum of two children.

In the chapter's treatment of residential fathers to this point, we have emphasized the distinction between biological and nonbiological fathers, and among the latter, between those married versus not married to the child's mother. However, for biological resident fathers, the NSAM sample provides some additional insight into patterns of marital status. Of the sample's biological fathers, 37 (17.5%) were cohabiting with rather than married to the mother, and 6 (2.8%) were not living with a wife or partner. Of fathers living with both biological and nonbiological children (mixed fathers) (22), 8 (36.4%) were cohabiting. In addition, of the 67 cohabitating fathers, 45 (67.1%) were living with biological children (including 8 living with both biological and nonbiological children). Thus, among young cohabiting fathers, the majority are biological fathers. Although the sample size does not permit comparing married versus cohabitating biological fathers in terms of sociodemographic factors or paternal involvement, the relatively high prevalence (at least among the younger fathers represented in the NSAM) of cohabiting biological fathers suggests that this group should receive more research attention than it has to date.

Children's Time With Fathers: PSID—CDS

Two general patterns are evident, each with limited exceptions: First, residential biological fathers tend to be more involved than other fathers; second, mothers' partners (or cohabiting father figures tend to be more involved than stepfathers. The two broadest measures, engagement time and availability time, illustrate both patterns. Across all ages, children under age 13 spent 2.2 hours per day talking, playing, and otherwise engaged with their biological father and 1.8 hours in close proximity (Table 3.2). Children spend the next most amount of time with their mother's partner or other father figure—almost 1.4 hours per day engaged and 1.7 hours in proximity, on average. In contrast, children spend the least time with stepfathers—only about eight-tenths of an hour (48 min) per day engaged and the same amount of time in proximity. Fathers' time in caregiving again illustrates both gradients, although estimates for stepfathers and mothers' partners are not very different.

However, play time and reading time depart from one or both patterns. Children with biological fathers do not spend any more time playing with their fathers than children living with a partner of the mother, although children living with stepfathers spend significantly less time playing with their father than the other two groups. In contrast, reading time with stepfathers exceeds that with nonbiological cohabiting father figures, although children of biological fathers spend the most time reading with their fathers. The average amount of time children read with their fathers is low for all three groups, however.

Finally, the number of regular weekly activities children, age 3 and over, do with their fathers illustrates the first gradient, but not the second. Biological fathers average 9 out of 13 weekly activities with their children, compared with 7.8 for stepfathers and 7.6 for nonbiological cohabiting father figures. The general pattern that biological fathers are the most involved on most indicators is not surprising, as prior research generally finds biological fathers to be more involved than stepfathers (Pleck, 1997). In interpreting the relatively lower involvement of stepfathers, it should be noted that in many cases children's nonresidential father is also involved in the child's life, perhaps making up for the shortfall in fathering by stepfathers (Hofferth & Anderson, 2001). The stepfather may also have a biological child he is not living with and with whom he spends time, detracting from potential time with his stepchild.

What is perhaps more surprising in these results is that, on the majority of indicators, nonbiological cohabitating father figures show greater involvement than stepfathers. Fathers in neither group have a biological relationship to the child. Within nonbiological fathers, one might have expected that having the more normatively legitimated relationship to the mother signified by marriage would be associated with fathers' being more involved. Several interpretations are possible. First, cohabiting fathers are far less likely than stepfathers to have such competing obligations to their own biological children living elsewhere (Hofferth & Anderson, 2001). Second, although the marriage of a nonbiological father to the child's mother introduces some degree of normative approval into the father–child relationship, it may introduce tensions as well (i.e., that the child now has to accept the male as married to his or her mother) (Hetherington & Jodl, 1994). In addition, nonbiological unmarried fathers living with the child and mother may more actively try to be more involved, in order to gain acceptance from the child and approval from his partner. If marriage has occurred, however, the issue of the child's acceptance of the father has either become moot or taken on an entirely new dimension that is not facilitated by the father being more involved. Third, there may be more than one such father figure, such as a partner as well as a grandfather, in the household.

Quality of Relationship With the Father

The story is somewhat different for the relationship quality. Consistent with our prediction that children's biological parents are most committed to and will be most involved with their children, parental warmth is lower for both stepfathers and cohabiting fathers than for biological fathers. Although stepfathers report similar levels of monitoring and control as biological fathers, cohabiting father figures report the lowest levels. This provides further support for our hypothesized lack of an institutionalized relationship that could make monitoring by unmarried partners legitimate. Thus, although we see that stepfathers and cohabiting fathers are similar in warmth, we see stepfathers exhibiting more monitoring and control, with cohabiting partners much less involved in this dimension of childrearing. These data show no significant differences by relatedness in the degree of responsibility that children's fathers take for them, suggesting that responsibility is a different dimension from either engagement or quality of the relationship.

Fathers' Time With Children—NSAM

Fathers estimated they spent 4.5 hours per day in physical care, 2.9 hours per day playing with their child or children, and 0.51 hours reading to them. Biological fathers reported significantly less time reading to children than mixed fathers, but not significantly less time than stepfathers. However, biological fathers reported more time in physical care than stepfathers. Because the age of the youngest child is lowest for biological fathers, this may account for biological fathers spending more time in physical care and less time reading. The CDS also finds children of biological fathers obtaining more care than nonbiological children, though in the CDS they are also more likely to be read to. Differences in child age—biological children are younger—may explain greater care time in the CDS, but not the greater time being read to. Overall reading time is small in both studies, and ability to detect small differences is weak.

Time Fathers Spent With Children—Trends in Time Use Study

Looking at the overall time fathers spent on a daily basis with children in 1998 (Panel A, Table 3.4), we see that married fathers spent about 3 hours and 46 minutes with children in 1998, including both engaged and available time. This is very similar to the sum of engaged and available time (3.9 hours) that an individual child is reported to spend with his/her father on an average day, according to the PSID—CDS (Table 3.2, all children). This estimate is also similar to the estimate of the daily time the father cared for children overall in the NSAM, about 4.5 hours per day (Table 3.3). In comparison, married mothers spent almost 6 hours per day with children in 1998.

The daily time the father spends in primary child care (defined earlier) amounts to about 1 hour per day, and if the time when the father is caring for the child and doing something else at the same time is included (primary + secondary), it increases to 1 hour and 20 minutes per day. This estimate is larger than the CDS estimate, but in the latter, direct care time is known to be underestimated for older children and time is reported on a per child basis rather than across all children. In comparison, married mothers spend twice as much time in primary and secondary child-care activities as do fathers: married mothers spent 1 hour and 46 minutes per day in primary child care and close to 3 hours per day in primary and secondary child care in 1998. The time parents spend in play or teaching activities is more equivalent across mothers and fathers. According to the 1998 Family Interaction, Social Capital, and Trends in Time Use Study, married fathers' play and teaching time amounts to about 24 minutes per day, either as primary time or as secondary time, whereas married mothers' primary or secondary play and teaching time amounts to around 30 minutes per day. These results are similar to results reported for the time children spend playing with fathers in the CDS. In the CDS, children were reported as spending about one-half hour playing with the father per day, on average. Daily times spent playing with children are much larger in the NSAM data set, again, coming from direct paternal estimates rather than diaries. The NSAM estimated that fathers spend almost 3 hours playing with children on an average day. The Trends in Time Use data set coding did not allow determining the time the father read with the child separately from talking with the child.

TABLE 3.4

Father Involvement and Parental Responsibility, 1998 Family Interaction, Social
Capital, and Trends in Time Use Study and National Omnibus 1999 Study

Panel A: Time with Children (hours:minutes)	Married Fathers	Married Mothers
Paternal involvement:		
Daily hours with children	3:46	5:52
Daily hours in child care (primary)	0:59	1:46
Daily hours in child care (primary + secondary)	1:20	2:57
Daily hours plays or teaches (primary)	0:23	0:27
Daily hours plays or teaches (primary + secondary)	0:24	0:34
N[a]	141	194

Panel B: Parental Responsibility	Father's Report	Mother's Report
Who is mainly responsible for:		
Basic caregiving?		
Mainly father	10.0%	2.0%
Both	35.0%	34.0%
Mainly mother	55.0%	64.0%
Playing with children?		
Mainly father	17.0%	5.0%
Both	73.0%	73.0%
Mainly mother	10.0%	22.0%
Emotional support?		
Mainly father	6.0%	1.0%
Both	74.0%	65.0%
Mainly mother	20.0%	34.0%
Monitoring?		
Mainly father	5.0%	0.0%
Both	76.0%	68.0%
Mainly mother	19.0%	32.0%
Discipline?		
Mainly father	19.0%	6.0%
Both	77.0%	59.0%
Mainly mother	4.0%	35.0%
N[b]	126	108

[a]Data in Panel A are from the 1998–99 Family Interaction, Social Capital, and Trends in Time Use Study.

[b]Data in Panel B are from the 1999 National Omnibus Study.

Responsibility for Children. Although the CDS showed no differences in fathers' overall responsibility by relationship to child and marital status, in the National Omnibus study there are differences across domains in the extent of responsibility fathers take and in the perceptions of mothers and fathers. Panel B of Table 3.4 presents data on mothers' and fathers' perceptions of who is mainly responsible for six parenting domains: mainly the mother (father), mainly the children's father (mother), or both about equally. Time need not be directly related to the degree of responsibility fathers take for children; however, on few tasks do fathers take primarily responsibility. On basic caregiving there was substantial agreement between mothers and fathers, with 34 to 35% saying it was shared and 64% of mothers and 55% of fathers reporting that it was mainly the mother. There was also substantial agreement on playing, where 73% said that it was the responsibility of both fathers and mothers. However, disagreement was common. For the most part fathers (mothers) reported themselves to be more responsible than the mothers (fathers) reported them to be. The largest difference in reporting occurred for discipline, where 77% of fathers and only 59% of mothers said both were responsible. Thirty-five percent of mothers reported that they were mainly responsible, whereas only 4% of fathers reported that to be the case. Nineteen percent of fathers said they were primarily responsible for discipline, whereas only 6% of mothers said that was the case. For the rest of the tasks, the couple agreed that mothers did it or it was shared. In contrast, the only parenting task for which fathers reported themselves as primarily responsible was financial support (not shown). Fifty-four percent of mothers and 61% of fathers reported that the father was mainly responsible, with most of the respondents saying that it was a shared responsibility.

INVOLVEMENT OF CHILDREN WITH NONRESIDENT FATHERS

Data from the PSID Child Development Supplement were used to examine the degree of engagement of nonresidential fathers with their children, by the family structure of the child's residential household, as reported by the primary caregiver (Table 3.5). These data are representative of all U.S. children in 1997 (see Appendix 3A for a description of the Child Development Supplement) and provide the most up-to-date national picture of the involvement of nonresidential fathers. The questions were answered by the child's primary caregiver (usually the mother) about the child's involvement with the nonresident father. Thus, although these data accurately represent U.S. children, the responses are based on the primary caregiver's perception, not the father's actual responses. With this limitation in mind, we report that about 28% of primary caregivers of U.S. children under age 13 report that the child's biological father does not live with them, and 96% of these children have a father alive and living elsewhere.

Most nonresidential fathers were in touch with their children. Mothers reported that during the past 12 months, one third of the children had no contact with the father, including telephone calls or letters. Almost half (48%) were in touch at least once a month, and 72% of the mothers reported that their child had seen the father in the past 12 months. Of this 72%, more than two thirds (68%) had contact with their father at least once a month. Children were more likely to have frequent contact with their father if their mother had not remarried.

TABLE 3.5
Involvement of Nonresidential Fathers, by the Family Structure
of the Child's Household

	All Children	Stepdad	Cohab Mom	Single Mom	Number of Cases
Father not in household	27.7%	89.0%	92.0%	99.0%	3,558
Father alive	96.0%				1,223
No contact with father in past year	33.2%	32.0%	18.2%	34.2%	1,160
Contact once a month or more	47.8%	44.8%	55.3%	48.4%	1,160
Saw dad in last 12 months	72.1%	67.0%	76.3%	72.8%	1,162
If so, contact once a month or more	68.4%	63.7%	71.7%	69.0%	870
PCG talks with father about child at least monthly	64.1%	56.1%	53.3%	67.3%	881
Father's influence on decisionmaking is none	52.3%	60.8%	63.9%	48.8%	881
Never has conflict with father over:					
where child lives	79.8%	86.3%	82.7%	78.0%	882
how child is raised	63.4%	67.1%	61.6%	62.0%	881
discipline	66.2%	72.5%	71.1%	62.5%	879
how you spend money on child	73.8%	84.9%	84.2%	69.1%	879
how he spends money on child	63.5%	77.5%	68.5%	59.1%	878
the time father spends with child	52.0%	52.4%	41.8%	50.7%	879
his visits with the child	55.2%	51.0%	50.4%	55.1%	880
the father's financial contribution	49.6%	42.0%	46.6%	48.2%	880
father's use of alcohol/drugs	73.8%	64.1%	66.2%	76.1%	880
the father's friends	74.9%	69.0%	77.8%	75.0%	880
Spends time with father once a month or more:					
in leisure activities	42.6%	32.7%	53.0%	44.1%	869
in religious activities	11.7%	16.6%	12.9%	10.9%	871
working or playing together	46.1%	42.7%	52.7%	45.7%	865
in school activities	16.2%	13.9%	13.5%	17.4%	865
Father has done these in the past year:					
Bought presents	78.9%	85.0%	79.9%	77.1%	881
Paid for camp or lessons	16.3%	22.2%	13.6%	16.2%	879
Took child on vacation	25.4%	26.9%	23.4%	27.3%	879
Paid medical expenses	22.4%	38.9%	32.0%	19.9%	879
Paid medical insurance	28.0%	33.3%	38.6%	27.8%	881

Of children who saw their father at least once in the past year, mothers were asked about their communication with and the influence of the father. Two thirds reported talking with their child about their father at least once a month. Again, this is influenced by the presence of a new father figure in the household. Children living with a single mother are much more likely to have had their mother discuss their father with them than children living in a family in which the mother has remarried or has a new partner.

In influencing their decisions about such things as education, religion, and health care, nonresidential fathers do not have much influence, however. Only 19% reported that the dad had a great deal of influence, 29% reported some influence, and half (52%) reported they had no influence at all. Again, nonresidential fathers have more influence over children living with a single mother than children living with a stepfather or whose mother is cohabiting.

The primary caregiver reported on the frequency of conflicts with the nonresidential father over childrearing issues. The fewest conflicts were reported on where the child lived, how the mother spent money on the child, father's drug use (because few used drugs), and father's friends. The most conflicts were reported over the time the father spent with the child (48%), father visits (45%), and the father's contribution to the child's support (50%). Discipline, childrearing, and lifestyle were the next biggest sources of conflict. Conflict was somewhat more frequent among families headed by a single mother than other families, particularly over financial issues.

The primary caregiver was asked about the frequency with which children did things with their father. About 43% of fathers spent time in leisure activities in the past month. Only about 11% spent time in religious activities. About 46% spent time playing together at least once a month. Sixteen percent spent some time with their child in school activities. Again, children of single mothers tended to spend more time with their fathers than children living with stepfathers. Children with cohabiting mothers spend slightly more time in leisure and play activities with their fathers than children living with a single mother or with a remarried mother.

Finally, the primary caregiver was asked about nonmonetary contributions of the nonresidential father to the child, including clothing or presents, paying for camp or lessons, taking child on a vacation, paying for dental or medical expenses, paying for medical insurance, and other things. Mothers reported that 79% of children received presents from their fathers. This was the most common type of expenditure. Only 16% paid for camp or lessons, 25% took the child on a vacation, 22% paid medical expenses, and 28% paid for medical insurance. Differences by family type were small, but there was one large difference—children's fathers were twice as likely to pay medical expenses if the child lived with a stepfather than if the child lived with a single mother. Single mothers may be more likely to have their own health plan through an employer or welfare office.

SUMMARY AND CONCLUSIONS

This chapter described the involvement of residential fathers with biological and nonbiological children living with them and nonresidential fathers with their biological children who do not live with them. It examined differences in involvement according to the biological relationship of children and their fathers and the marital status of the mother. Demographic factors such as the age of the child, education, and paternal work hours are also likely to affect involvement indirectly, through motivation.

This chapter compared estimates of the time children and fathers spent together obtained from four different data sets with different strengths and weaknesses. The strength of the Child Development Supplement and the Trends in Time Use Study is their collection of data in a diary format. Estimates collected through direct questions are generally larger in magnitude than those collected through diaries. For example, fathers appear to overestimate the time they spend playing with and reading to children in the NSAM compared with the time use studies. The advantage of the NSAM is its focus on young men in their prime childbearing and childrearing period. The NSAM data also call attention to the relatively high prevalence of residential biological fathers who have not married the child's mother among younger parents (i.e., biological as opposed to nonbiological cohabiting father figures). Further research is needed on this group.

Estimates of the total time fathers and children spend together per day is comparable across the three studies, if time spent caring for children in the NSAM is assumed to be a reasonable measure of this time. According to these measures, fathers spend between 3 and 4.5 hours per day in direct contact with or available to children. When comparing children of biological fathers, stepfathers, and mother's partners (nonbiological father figures), we found, as expected, that children spend the most time with their biological father. In both studies that were able to separate stepfather from biological-father families, children spend much less time with stepfathers than biological fathers. Surprisingly, rather than spending even less time with the partner of the mother, children spend more time with cohabiting father figures than with stepfathers, though still not as much time as with biological fathers. This may be because stepfathers more often than cohabiting, nonbiological fathers have nonresidential children for whom they are also responsible. In addition, although it may be that being married to the child's mother introduces some degree of normative approval into the relationship between a child and a nonbiological father, it may introduce tensions as well. Finally, some children may have several cohabiting father figures who spend time with them.

Though we provide great detail about the time fathers and children spend together, the literature is clear that the quality of the father–child relationship may be as important or more important to child development than the amount of time. For this reason we also provide information on the warmth of the relationship, the extent to which fathers monitor children's behavior, and the extent of responsibility fathers share. Here again, as with time, we find biological fathers to be warmer and to monitor their children more than other fathers. Both stepfathers and partners are rated lower on warmth than biological fathers. In addition, cohabiting father figures rate lower on monitoring and control. This suggests that although partners may spend time with the child, their role is a more permissive one. Stepfathers, in contrast, may fall more on the authoritarian side, with less warmth in their relationship to stepchildren than biological fathers but equal control.

On responsibility, fathers do not differ significantly by relationship to child and marital status. Fathers are primarily responsible only for financial support of the family, outside of our concept of paternal involvement in this chapter. Mothers are primarily responsible for basic caregiving. Playing with children, emotional support, monitoring, and discipline tend to be shared by mothers and fathers.

In summary, the relationship of child to the father and the marital status of the mother have an influence on the time residential fathers spend with their children and on the quality of their relationship. Biological fathers are the most involved in terms of time and quality of the relationship. The cohabiting father figure is more similar to biological father in terms of time, whereas stepfathers are lower. Both stepfathers and cohabiting fathers are low on warmth. Cohabiting fathers are lowest on control. The marital status of the mother also influences the involvement of nonresidential fathers with their biological children. For nonresidential fathers, fathers' involvement is lower when children's mothers have remarried or are cohabiting. Involvement is greater, but conflict also higher when the mother is single. Ultimately, it will be important to examine how time and quality of relationship are linked to the well-being of the children. This is especially important with the growth of nonmarital cohabitation and the increasing incidence of child-rearing within cohabiting relationships. As family structures change, our data collection efforts need to reflect these new realities.

REFERENCES

Bianchi, S. M. (2000). Maternal employment and time with children: Dramatic change or surprising continuity? *Demography, 37*(4), 401–414.

Brayfield, A. (1995). Juggling jobs and kids: The impact of work schedules on fathers' caring for children. *Journal of Marriage and the Family, 57,* 321–332.

Bryant, W., & Zick, C. (1996). Are we investing less in the next generation? Historical trends in time spent caring for children. *Journal of Family and Economic Issues, 17*(3/4), 365–392.

Cabrera, N., Tamis-LeMonda, C., Bradley, R., Hofferth, S., & Lamb, M. (2000). Fatherhood in the twenty-first century. *Child Development, 71*(1), 127–136.

Casper, L., & O'Connell, M. (1998). Work, income, the economy, and married fathers as child-care providers. *Demography, 35,* 243–250.

Cherlin, A. (1978). Remarriage as an incomplete institution. *American Journal of Sociology, 84*(3), 634–650.

Cherlin, A. (1996). *Public and private families: An introduction.* New York: McGraw-Hill.

Christiansen, S., & Palkovitz, R. (2001). Why the "good provider" role still matters: Providing as a form of paternal involvement. *Journal of Family Issues, 22,* 84–106.

Daly, M., & Wilson, M. (1998). *The truth about Cinderella: A Darwinian view of parental love.* New Haven, CT: Yale University Press.

Federal Interagency Forum on Child and Family Statistics. (2000). *Trends in the well-being of America's children and youth, 1999.* Washington, DC: U.S. Department of Health and Human Services.

Fitzgerald, J., Gottschalk, P., & Moffitt, R. (1998). An analysis of sample attrition in panel data: Michigan Panel Study of Income Dynamics. *Journal of Human Resources, 33*(2), 251–299.

Hetherington, E. M., & Jodl, K. (1994). Stepfamilies as settings for child development. In A. Booth & J. Dunn (Eds.), *Stepfamilies: Who benefits? Who does not?* (pp. 55–79). Hillsdale, NJ: Lawrence Erlbaum Associates.

Hofferth, S. L. (in press). Race/ethnic differences in father involvement in two-parent families: Culture, context, or economy. *Journal of Family Issues.*

Hofferth, S. (1999b, May). *Family reading to young children: Social desirability and cultural biases in reporting.* Paper presented at Workshop on Measurement of and Research on Time Use, Committee on National Statistics, Washington, DC: National Research Council.

Hofferth, S. L., & Anderson, K. (2001, February). *Biological and stepfather investment in children.* Conference on Measuring Father Involvement, Bethesda, MD.

Hofferth, S., Davis-Kean, P., Davis, J., & Finkelstein, J. (1999). *1997 user guide: The Child Development Supplement to the Panel Study of Income Dynamics.* Ann Arbor, MI: Institute for Social Research, University of Michigan.

Juster, F., & Stafford, F. P. (1985). *Time, goods, and well-being.* Ann Arbor: Institute for Social Research, University of Michigan.

Kaplan, H. S., Lancaster, J. B., & Anderson, K. G. (1998). Human parental investment and fertility: The life histories of men in Albuquerque. In A. Booth & A. C. Crouter (Eds.), *Men in families: When do they get involved? What difference does it make?* (pp. 55–109). Mahwah, NJ: Lawrence Erlbaum Associates.

Lamb, M. E., Pleck, J. H., Charnov, E. L., & Levine, J. A. (1985). Paternal behavior in humans. *American Zoologist, 25,* 883–894.

Lamb, M., Pleck, J., Charnov, E. L., & Levine, J. (1987). A biosocial perspective on paternal behavior and involvement. In J. Lancaster, J. Altman, A. Rossi & L. Sherrod (Eds.), *Parenting across the lifespan: Biosocial perspectives* (pp. 11–42). New York: Academic Press.

Maccoby, E., & Martin, J. (1983). Socialization in the context of the family: Parent–child interaction. In E. M. Hetherington (Ed.), *Handbook of child psychology, Vol. IV* (pp. 1–101). New York: Wiley.

McBride, B., & Mills, G. (1993). A comparison of mother and father involvement with their preschool age children. *Early Childhood Research Quarterly, 8,* 457–477.

Milkie, M. A., Bianchi, S. M., Mattingly, M. J., & Robinson, J. P. (2000, May). The stalled revolution at home: Ideal versus actual father involvement and parental well-being Revised version of paper presented at the annual meeting of the American Association of Public Opinion Research, Portland, OR.

Pleck, J., Lamb, M., & Levine, J. (1986). Epilogue: Facilitating future change in men's family roles. In R. Lewis & M. Sussman (Eds.), *Men's changing roles in the family* (pp. 11–16). New York: Haworth Press.

Pleck, J. H. (1997). Paternal involvement: Levels, sources, and consequences. In M. E. Lamb (Ed.), *The role of the father in child development* (pp. 66–103). New York: Wiley.

Presser, H. (1989). Can we make time for children? The economy, work schedules, and child care. *Demography, 26*(4), 523–543.

Radin, N. (1994). Primary-caregiving fathers in intact families. In A. Gottfried & A. Gottfied (Eds.),

Redefining families: Implications for children's development (pp. 55–97). New York: Plenum.

Robinson, J. P., & Godbey, G. (1997). *Time for life: The surprising ways Americans use their time.* University Park: Pennsylvania State University.

Sandberg, J. F. (2000, March). *Modeling multi-dimensionality of involvement in two parent families: A latent class analysis of paternal responsibility.* Paper presented at the Annual Meeting of the Population Association of America, Los Angeles.

Sandberg, J. F., & Hofferth, S. L. (2001, August). Changes in parental time with children. *Demography, 38*(3), 423–436.

Smock, P. (2000). Cohabitation in the United States: An appraisal of research themes, findings, and implications. In *Annual Review of Sociology* (pp. 1–20). American Sociological Association.

Sonenstein, F., Pleck, J., & Ku, L. (1989). Sexual activity, condom use, and AIDS awareness among adolescent males. *Family Planning Perspectives, 21,* 152–158.

Steinberg, L. (2000, April). Presidential Address. Society for Research on Adolescence Annual Meeting. Chicago.

Yeung, W. J., Sandberg, J., Davis-Kean, P. E., & Hofferth, S. L. (2001). Children's time with fathers in intact families. *Journal of Marriage and the Family, 63*(1), 136–154.

APPENDIX: DESCRIPTION OF DATA SETS USED IN THE CHAPTER

The 1997 Child Development Supplement to the Panel Study of Income Dynamics

The primary data for this chapter come from the Panel Study of Income Dynamics (PSID), a nationally representative sample of U.S. men, women, children, and the families in which they reside, which has been followed for more than 30 years. During the spring and fall of 1997, information on up to two randomly selected 0- to 12-year-old children of PSID respondents was collected from the primary caregivers, from other caregivers, and from the children themselves (Hofferth, Davis-Kean, Davis, & Finkelstein, 1999). The Child Development Supplement (CDS) completed interviews with 2,394 child households and about 3,600 children. The response rate was 90% for those families regularly interviewed in the core PSID and 84% for those contacted the first time in 1997 for an immigrant refresher to the sample, with a combined response rate for both groups of 88%. When weights are used, as is done throughout this paper, the results have been found to be representative of U.S. individuals and their families (Fitzgerald, Gottschalk, & Moffitt, 1998). Case counts represent actual sample sizes. Weights are also applied to adjust for differential nonresponse across instruments.

The sample for analysis of residential paternal involvement with children consists of 2,500 children, of whom 2,067 have time diaries, as the majority but not all families completed time diaries. The response rate for this part of the instrument is the same as for the full study, 88%, because these questions were asked of primary caregivers (generally the mother) about each child. The sample size including those with complete information on the control variables ranges from 937 to 1,077, children, depending on the number of complete responses to the parenting measures and on the ages of the children measured. The sample size for the analysis of nonresidential involvement consists of 1,167 children with a living nonresidential father. The study attempted to interview these non-residential fathers by telephone to obtain direct reports on their involvement with their nonresidential children. However, interviewers were successful in reaching only about 25% of fathers by telephone; responses from that sample would have been biased because the fathers who were not reached were unlikely to be in contact.

National Survey of Adolescent Males

The Third Wave of the National Survey of Adolescent Males (NSAM), conducted in 1995, provides additional information on young fathers' engagement time with children for three subgroups of resident fathers: fathers living with only biological children, fathers living with only stepchildren (whether married to the children's mother or not), and fathers living with both biological children and stepchildren. The First Wave of the NSAM, collected in 1988, included 1,880 never-married males ages 15 to 19, representing the noninstitutionalized never-married male population in this age group in the contiguous United States. The sample was stratified to overrepresent black and Hispanic respondents. The use of sampling weights makes the results representative of the national population. The response rate for those eligible to be interviewed was 73.9%. Additional information on the sample, design, and procedures is provided in Sonenstein, Pleck, and Ku (1989). At the third interview in 1995, the sample ranged in age from 21 to 27. In 1995, 74.8% of those first interviewed in 1988 were successfully reinterviewed. Attrition analyses indicated that respondents lost to follow-up were more likely to have been sexually active in 1988 (73.0%) than those retained in the sample (65.3%), but they did not differ in ethnicity.

This analysis uses the subsample of 309 males ages 21 to 27 in the 1995 NSAM, who live with at least one child under 10 years of age (a) who is either their biological, step, or adopted child, or (b) to whom they consider themselves to "be like a father." Males in this subsample may or may not have a female partner living with them; if they do, the male may or may not be married to her, and she may or may not be the child's mother. The results reported here use the weighted sample, which adjusts for the oversampling of Black ($n = 106$) and Hispanic young men ($n = 76$) in the original frame, compared to White males ($n = 112$) and to males of other ethnicities, predominantly Asian ($n = 15$). With adjustment for sample weights, the analysis sample has a weighted $n = 282$.

1998 Trends in Time Use Study

In 1998–99, with funding from the National Science Foundation as part of the "Family Interaction, Social Capital, and Trends in Time Use Study", time-diary data were collected from a nationally representative sample of adults (Bianchi & Robinson, 1998). Interviewing was done by the Survey Research Center at the University of Maryland. Using random digit dialing and computer-assisted telephone interviewing (CATI) procedures, a total of 1,151 interviews were conducted with a national probability sample of adults, age 18 and over. The overall response rate was 56%. The weaknesses of the data include the small sample size, which restricts the focus to married residential fathers and the fact that fathers cannot be distinguished by their biological relationship to the child.

National Omnibus Study

The data on parental responsibility are drawn from a national Omnibus probability study of 1,001 adults conducted by computer-assisted telephone interviews (CATI) in the spring of 1999 at the University of Maryland's Survey Research Center (Milkie, Bianchi, Mattingly, & Robinson, 2000). Respondents were selected using random digit dialing of residential telephone numbers; within each sample household, the target respondent was selected at random from among all adults residing in the household. Of eligible households, 18% of focal respondents were not able to be contacted after a minimum of 20 attempts, 21% refused, and 4% were unable to be completed for other reasons such as respondent illness or language difficulties, resulting in an overall response rate of 57%. The distributions of these respondents' answers on key well-being variables are within a few percentage points of the distributions of respondents' answers to duplicate questions from the 1996 General Social Survey, which has a 76% response rate. Of the 1,001 respondents completing telephone interviews, only the 234 married parents with children under 18 currently living in their household are included in our sample.

II

Father Involvement
and Child Development

Michael E. Lamb
National Institute of Child Health
and Human Development

As the heterogeneous contents of this handbook demonstrate, there are many ways of examining fathers and fatherhood. In this section, we focus narrowly on the ways in which fathers influence child development. This in itself covers an array of topics, few of which can be given attention in this wide-ranging anthology. We thus devote chapters to four especially significant topics: (a) the initial development of relationships between fathers and their children in infancy; (b) the effects of father–child relationships on the child's integration into social relationships outside the family; (3) the diverse faces, facets, and consequences of father involvement; and (4) the role of nonresidential fathers in their children's lives.

Because developmentalists are frequently interested in understanding the earliest emergence of important phenomena or formative experiences, they frequently scrutinize the first months or years of life with special care. It is not surprising, therefore, that we pay special attention here to the formation of relationships between fathers and infants. The topic is particularly pertinent because psychologists doubted for many years that infants formed significant relationships with anyone other than their mothers. They further opined, following Freud's assertion, that the mother–infant relationship had a singularly important impact on all later development, but as Lamb shows in chapter 4, there is now unequivocal evidence that most infants form attachments to both of their parents at roughly the same age. Mothers continue to assume a disproportionate share of the responsibility for child care, however, and this seems to ensure both that infants develop preferences for their mothers and that mother–child relationships have greater formative significance than father–child relationships.

When the concept of paternal involvement first gained prominence in the 1970s, it was typically operationalized in terms of such participation in child care, but as Palkovitz points out in chapter 5, scholars now recognize that paternal involvement needs to be viewed in much broader context because parenting involves so much more than child care. There is great variability with respect to the ways in which involvement is conceptualized by different parents, and as a result, measures that focus only on the level of involvement in physical child care may fail to capture important difference among fathers and families.

In addition, as Parke and his colleagues point out in chapter 6, paternal influences on child development reflect not only features of the father–child relationship itself, but also maternal and family characteristics that shape the parents' relationship and mutual responsibilities. The evidence reviewed in this chapter documents the ways in which fathers shape children's social skills and thus affect the successfulness of their efforts to develop relationships with peers and others outside their families.

Because fathers play diverse roles in the family, of course, the effects of their absence are broad and varied depending on the nature of the roles they might have played. As a result, there is great variability among the roles played by nonresidential fathers and in the impact—for good and for ill—that they have on their children's development. As pointed out in chapter 7, we have come a long way from the time when father absence was viewed as a demographic or structural variable with easily understood implications.

Indeed, all of the chapters in this section underscore that it is impossible to identify *the* role of the father in child development because fathers play different roles in different families, and their possible influence varies as a result. These contributions demonstrate that fathers have a considerable impact on child development, but that we still have much to learn about the complex developmental processes involved.

4

Infant–Father Attachments and Their Impact on Child Development

Michael E. Lamb
*National Institute of Child Health
and Human Development*

Since 1970, there has been considerable research on the development of father–infant relationships. The majority of studies have involved affluent Euro-American families in the United States, and generalization to other groups will remain uncertain until they have been studied more extensively. This limitation notwithstanding, our impressive knowledge of father–child relationships is readily apparent in this chapter.

Developmental theorists tell us that the formation of relationships depends on both the quality and amount of interaction. As a result, the first two sections of this chapter deal with, first, paternal responsiveness or sensitivity and, second, the extent of father–infant interaction. As I conclude, the evidence shows clearly that the average father is sufficiently sensitive to foster the development of attachment relationships and that the amount of time fathers tend to spend with their infants allows relationships to develop in the first months of life. The focus then shifts to the developmental course of infant–father attachments; here, the evidence shows that mother– and father–infant attachments develop in parallel and on similar schedules, although as explained in Section IV, they have distinctive characteristics. Parent–child relationships are believed to have substantial formative importance, and the final two substantive sections deal with direct and indirect patterns of paternal influence on child development.

PATERNAL SENSITIVITY

Bowlby (1969) proposed that human infants are biologically predisposed to emit signals (e.g., cries, smiles) to which adults are biologically predisposed to respond. When adults respond promptly and appropriately to infant signals, infants come to perceive them as predictable or reliable, and secure infant–parent attachments result, whereas insecure attachments may develop when adults do not respond sensitively (Ainsworth, Blehar, Waters, & Wall 1978; Lamb, 1981; Lamb, Thompson, Gardner, & Charnov, 1985). When adults respond rarely, no attachments at all may develop, and it is thus crucially important to determine whether fathers are appropriately responsive to their infants.

Even though new mothers experience more life changes and obtain more satisfaction from their new role than fathers do (Dulude, Wright, & Belanger, 2000), most fathers report being elated when their infants are born (Bader, 1995; Greenberg, 1985; Greenberg & Morris, 1974; Lewis, 1986), frequently visit hospitalized newborns (Marton & Minde, 1980; Levy-Shiff, Sharir, & Mogilner, 1989), and continue to feel emotionally connected to their infants, such that fathers and mothers are equivalently anxious about leaving their babies and toddlers in someone else's care (Deater-Deckard, Scarr, McCartney, & Eisenberg, 1994; Hock & Lutz, 1998, although see Wille, 1998 for contrasting results). New fathers behave just as mothers do when introduced to their newborn infants (Rödholm & Larsson, 1982) and are effective sources of heat for neonates (Christensson, 1996). The nurturant attentiveness of new fathers may reflect the fact that mothers and fathers experience similar changes in hormonal levels (increasing levels of prolaction and cortisol and decreased levels of testosterone and estradiol) around the birth of their infants (Storey, Walsh, Quinton, & Wynne-Edwards, 2000).

When blindfolded and denied access to olfactory cues, Israeli and American fathers were able to recognize their infants by touching their hands after only 60 minutes of exposure (Bader & Phillips, 1999; Kaitz, Lapidot, Bronner, & Eidelman, 1992; Kaitz, Shiri, Danziger, Hershko, & Eidelman, 1994). Fathers could not recognize their infants by touching their faces, however, whereas mothers could do so (Kaitz et al., 1994; Kaitz, Meirov, Landman, & Eidelman, 1993), perhaps because the mothers had spent more time with their infants prior to testing (12.6 hours vs. 6.8 hours on average). Interestingly, both mothers and fathers were better at identifying their own newborns by touching their hands than by touching their faces.

Kaitz, Chriki, Bear-Scharf, Nir, and Eidelman (2000) reported that Israeli mothers soothed their newborns more effectively than new fathers did, regardless of parity, whereas American fathers and mothers both responded appropriately to infant cues when observed feeding their infants (Parke & Sawin, 1977). Fathers and mothers both adjust their speech patterns when interacting with infants— speaking more slowly, using shorter phrases, imitating, and repeating themselves more often when talking to infants rather than adults (Blount & Padgug, 1976; Dalton-Hummel, 1982; Gleason, 1975; Golinkoff & Ames, 1979; Kokkinaki &

Kugiumutzakis, 2000; Lewis et al., 1996; Rondal, 1980). Infant-directed singing has more exaggerated features than simulated singing or normal singing (Trehub et al., 1997; Trehub, Hill, & Kamenetsky, 1997), and Warren-Leubecker and Bohannon (1984) reported that fathers increased their pitch and frequency range even more than mothers did when speaking to 2-year-olds. Although they can discriminate among male voices, however, 4-month-olds do not show preferences for their fathers' voices (Ward & Cooper, 1999).

Some researchers have found no differences between levels of maternal and paternal sensitivity. In the face-to-face and still-face paradigms, for example, mothers and fathers were equally sensitive with their 4-month-olds, and the infants showed equivalent patterns of affect and self-regulation (Braungart-Rieker, Garwood, Powers, & Notaro, 1998), although boys were more negative with their fathers when their mothers were employed (Braungart-Rieker, Courtney, & Garwood, 1999). Both parents are sufficiently sensitive to developmental changes in their children's abilities and preferences that they adjust their play and stimulation patterns accordingly (Crawley & Sherrod, 1984), although Israeli fathers of 6-month-olds expect cognitive maturity and social autonomy to be acquired more slowly than mothers do (Mansbach & Greenbaum, 1999). In addition, fathers appear highly attuned to their toddlers' interests when playing with them, although their tendencies to tease can be disruptive (Labrell, 1994). Notaro and Volling (1999) reported no differences in the sensitivity and responsiveness of mothers and fathers who were observed interacting with their 1-year-olds for 3 minutes while the parents were preoccupied completing questionnaires.

Others have reported contrasting results, however. When observed playing with their 8-month-olds, fathers were less sensitive to cues regarding the infants' interests and activities than mothers were (Power & Parke, 1983), prohibited their infants' activities and talked more (Brachfeld-Child, 1986), and were somewhat less likely to retrieve their crying infants than mothers were (Donate-Bartfield & Passman, 1985). Likewise, Heermann, Jones, and Wikoff (1994) reported that fathers were rated lower than mothers on several multifactorial scales and at every age. In another study, fathers of both full- and pre-term infants appeared less sensitive than mothers when the infants were 3 and 12 months old (Harrison & Magill-Evans, 1996).

Individual Differences in Responsiveness

Belsky, Gilstrap, and Rovine (1984) reported that, although fathers were less actively engaged in interaction with their 1-, 3-, and 9-month-old infants than mothers were, the differences narrowed over time. Individual differences in paternal engagement were quite stable over time, especially between 3 and 9 months, and it is obviously important to determine why fathers differ in their sensitivity and engagement. Fathers' recollections of their own childhood relationships play an important role in shaping fathers' sensitivity: Researchers have shown that fathers who had loving and secure relationships with their parents were more sensitive, attentive, and involved than fathers who recalled poor relationships (Cowan, Cohn, Cowan, & Pearson, 1996). Perceived psychological well-being on the part of fathers is associated with paternal sensitivity (Broom, 1994), but it is not clear whether and how symptoms of depression affect paternal sensitivity: McElwain and Volling (1999) found that depressed fathers were less intrusive when observed playing with their 12-month-olds, whereas Field, Hossain, and Malphurs (1999) reported that depressed fathers did not interact with their infants more negatively than nondepressed fathers did. Infants with depressed mothers have more positive interactions with their nondepressed fathers, however, as though they were seeking relationships to make up for less-satisfying interaction with their mothers (Hossain, Field, Gonzalez, Malphurs, & Del Valle, 1994). In addition, paternal depression appeared to mediate the adverse effects of paternal alcohol abuse on paternal attitudes and behavior (Das Eiden, Chavez, & Leonard, 1999; Das Eiden & Leonard, 2000). Paternal responsiveness also appears to vary depending on the degree to which fathers assume responsibility for infant care: Caretaking experience appears to facilitate parental responsiveness (Donate-Bartfield & Passman, 1985; Zelazo, Kotelchuck, Barber, & David, 1977), and fathers who are more involved in the treatment of their medically compromised infants appear to interact with them more positively than those who were more distressed by their infants' ill health (Darke & Goldberg, 1994). This may explain why low-income fathers who lived with their infants appeared more sensitive than those who did not (Brophy-Herb, Gibbons, Omar, & Schiffman, 1999). There is also an intriguing association between paternal reactivity to infant signals and the magnitude of the hormonal changes experienced by new fathers (Storey et al., 2000).

Because fathers interact with their infants less and assume less responsibility for child care than mothers do, we might expect paternal sensitivity to decline over time relative to that of mothers, but the available evidence does not reveal a clear developmental pattern of this sort. Variations and developmental changes notwithstanding, most fathers are sufficiently responsive to their infants that attachments should form provided that a sufficient amount of father–infant interaction takes place.

THE EXTENT OF FATHER–INFANT INTERACTION

Many efforts have, in fact, been made to determine how much time fathers spend with their infants, but there is considerable variability among the reported estimates, no doubt attributable to cultural variability and the opportunistic sampling procedures employed in many studies. In one of the earliest studies, for example, American mothers reported that the fathers of 8- to 9 1/2-month-old infants were home between 5 and 47 hours per week at times when the infants were awake

(Pedersen & Robson, 1969). The average was 26 hours, and the fathers reportedly spent between 45 minutes and 26 hours each week actually interacting with their babies. From interviews with the parents of 6- to 21-month-olds in Boston, meanwhile, Kotelchuck (1976) determined that mothers spent an average of 9 waking hours per day with their children, whereas fathers spent 3.2 hours. The parents interviewed by Golinkoff and Ames (1979) reported figures of 8.33 and 3.16 hours, respectively, whereas the fathers interviewed by Lewis and Weinraub (1974) reported an average of only 15 to 20 minutes of interaction per workday.

Studies conducted outside the United States likewise yield widely varying estimates. Interviews with Israeli parents of 9-month-old infants thus suggested that the average father spent 2.75 hours available to his infant each day, with 45 to 50 minutes spent in actual interaction (Ninio & Rinott, 1988). These Israeli fathers averaged one caretaking task per day, but seldom (once every 10 days) took sole responsibility for their infants. English fathers interviewed by Lewis (1984) reported engaging in one activity with their children each day—strikingly more than their own fathers, although less than the Israeli fathers or the Irish fathers studied by Nugent (1987). German and Italian fathers, by contrast, appear much less involved than the Israeli, English, or Irish fathers (New & Benigni, 1987; Nickel & Köcher, 1987). Swedish fathers in dual-earner families are probably most highly involved (Hwang, 1987); they reportedly spent an average of 10.5 hours per nonworkday and 7.5 hours per workday with their children—almost as much as the mothers did (Haas, 1992, 1993).

The variability among these estimates can be attributed to socioeconomic, cultural, and demographic differences among the populations studied, with maternal employment status as one possible source of variation. Like Gottfried, Gottfried, and Bathurst (1988), Crouter, Perry-Jenkins, Huston, and McHale (1987) reported that fathers in dual-earner families were more involved in child care than were fathers in single-earner families, although the mothers' employment status did not affect paternal involvement in leisure activities, and fathers' sex role attitudes did not predict the types of paternal involvement (McHale & Huston, 1984).

The extent of paternal involvement may also differ depending on the amount of encouragement and support fathers receive: Lind (1974), for example, found that Swedish fathers who were taught how to care for their newborns and were encouraged to do so were more involved with their infants three months later, whereas Parke and Beitel (1986) reported that the greater burdens imposed on families by the birth of preterm babies facilitated paternal involvement. Other paternal characteristics surely affect involvement, too: Levy-Shiff and Israelashvili (1988) found that Israeli fathers who were rated prenatally as warm and interested played more with their 9-month-olds, whereas prenatal perceptiveness, sensitivity, and a tolerance for external intrusions were correlated with greater involvement in caretaking. McHale and Huston (1984) reported that fathers who perceived themselves as more skillful were more involved later, but knowledgability affected involvement differently among Mormon and non-Mormon fathers, leaving uncertainty about the association between involvement and knowledge of child development (Roggman, Benson, & Boyce, 1999). Short-term interventions for new fathers do not appear to influence paternal behavior or involvement (Belsky, 1985; Pannabecker, Emde, & Austin, 1982; Parke & Beitel, 1986) although Myers (1982) reported that fathers became more knowledgeable and more involved when they were shown how to conduct standardized assessments of their newborns, and Israeli fathers who were more involved with their 9-month-olds attributed the greatest levels of competence to them (Ninio & Rinott, 1988). Apparently, perceptions of infant competence and paternal involvement reinforce one another. Grossmann and Volkmer (1984) reported that the predelivery desire of German fathers to be present during delivery had a greater impact on their reported involvement than did actual presence during childbirth. This outcome was not surprising in light of Palkovitz' (1985) conclusion that birth attendance, in and of itself, does not appear to have consistent, clear, or robust efforts on paternal involvement or behavior. On the other hand, birth attendance followed by extensive postpartum father–infant interaction in the hospital may stimulate greater paternal involvement and engagement (Keller, Hildebrandt, & Richards, 1985).

Infant gender also affects the extent to which fathers interact with their infants. Many researchers have shown that fathers interact preferentially with their sons from shortly after birth (Cox, Owen, Lewis, & Henderson, 1989; Gewirtz & Gewirtz, 1968; Kotelchuck, 1976; Lamb, 1977a, 1977b; Lewis, 1986; Parke & Sawin, 1980; Rendina & Dickerscheid, 1976; Weinraub & Frankel, 1977; West & Konner, 1976; Woollett, White, & Lyon, 1982).

Whatever factors influence fathers' tendencies to be more or less involved in interactions with their infants, there appears to be substantial stability, at least during the period from birth through the first 30 months (Hwang & Lamb, 1997; Lamb et al., 1988; Nugent, 1987; Pruett & Litzenburger, 1992). Not surprisingly, work demands played an important role in determining how involved the Swedish fathers in Lamb et al.'s (1988) study were, just as they did in a later study conducted in the United States (Hyde, Essex, & Horton, 1993). In addition, of course, it is important to remember that paternal involvement is a multifaceted construct, and that time-based measures ignore these other aspects of involvement (Pleck & Stueve, in press; Palkovitz, chap. 5).

THE DEVELOPMENT OF FATHER–INFANT ATTACHMENTS

Even before most of these studies on the amounts of time that fathers spent with their children were conducted, Schaffer and Emerson (1964) asked whether and when infants formed attachments to their fathers. Mothers reported that their infants began to protest separations from both parents at 7 to 9 months and that by age 18 months, 71% protested separation from both parents. Babies formed attachments to those with whom they interacted regularly regardless of their involvement in caretaking. Pedersen and Robson (1969) also relied on maternal reports, although their focus was on responses to reunion rather than on separation protest. Seventy-five percent of the mothers reported that their infants responded positively and enthusiastically when their fathers returned from work, with the intensity of greeting by boys correlated with the frequency of paternal caretaking, paternal patience with infant fussing, and the intensity of father–infant play. Among daughters, however, intensity of greeting was correlated only with reported paternal "apprehension" about the girls' well-being.

Separation protest was the preferred measure when observational studies of father–infant attachment began in the 1970s. Kotelchuck (1976) reported that 12, 15-, 18-, and 21-month-old infants predictably protested when left alone by either parent, explored little while the parents were absent, and greeted them positively when they returned. Few infants protested separation from either parent when the other parent remained with them. A majority of the infants were more concerned about separation from their mothers, but 25% preferred their fathers, and 20% showed no preference for either parent. Later research confirmed, not suprisingly, that infants and toddlers also protested being left by either parent in nursery school settings (Field et al., 1984). Somewhat unexpectedly, however, babies who experienced a great deal of interaction with their fathers started to protest separation later than those whose fathers were uninvolved (Lester, Kotelchuck, Spelke, Sellers, & Klein, 1974), and the phase during which protest occurred was briefer when involvement was greater (Kotelchuck, 1976; Spelke, Zelazo, Kagan, & Kotelchuck, 1973). These counterintuitive correlations suggest that the intensity of separation protest may not index the intensity of attachment. On the other hand, low paternal involvement in caretaking was associated with reduced interaction and proximity seeking in the laboratory (Spelke et al., 1973), and when paternal involvement increased at home, there was a concomitant increase in the amount of father–infant interaction in the laboratory (Zelazo et al., 1977). Measures of separation protest were unaffected.

Feldman and Ingham (1975), Lamb (1976b), and Willemsen, Flaherty, Heaton, and Ritchey (1974) all reported no preferences were expressed by children for either parent in different laboratory procedures focused on responses to separation and reunion. Distress did not discriminate between mothers and fathers in a study by Cohen and Campos (1974) either, but on measures such as the frequency of approach, speed of approach, time in proximity, and use of parents as "secure bases" from which to interact with strangers, 10-, 13-, and 16-month-old infants showed preferences for their mothers over their fathers, as well as clear preferences for fathers over strangers. Likewise, Ban and Lewis (1974) reported that 1-year-olds touched, stayed near, and vocalized to mothers more than to fathers in 15-minute free play sessions, whereas no comparable preferences were evident among 2-year-olds.

By the mid-1970s, therefore, there was substantial evidence that children developed attachments to their fathers in infancy. It was unclear how early in their lives infants formed these attachments, however, because there were no data available concerning the period between 6 and 9 months of age during which infants form attachments to their mothers (Bowlby, 1969). There was also controversy concerning the existence of preferences for mothers over fathers, and there were no data available concerning father–infant interaction in naturalistic settings. Lengthy home observations subsequently revealed that 7-, 8-, 12-, and 13-month-old infants in traditional Euro-American families showed no preference for either parent over the other on attachment behavior measures, although all showed preferences for the parents over relatively unfamiliar adult visitors (Lamb, 1977c). Similar patterns were evident in a later study of 8- and 16-month-old infants on Israeli kibbutzim (Sagi, Lamb, Shoham, Dvir, & Lewkowicz, 1985). Patterns of separation protest and greeting at home also showed no preferences for either parent in the North America study, but the situation changed during the second year of life when many of the infants began to show preferences for their fathers. According to attachment theory (Bowlby, 1969), preferences among attachment figures may not be evident when infants do not need comfort or protection from attachment figures, but infants focus their attachment behavior more narrowly on primary attachment figures when distressed. When infants are distressed, the display of attachment behaviors increases, and infants organize their behavior similarly around whichever parent is present (Lamb, 1976a, 1976c). When both parents are present, however, distressed 12- and 18-month-olds turn to their mothers preferentially (Lamb, 1976a, 1976c), whereas 8- and 21-month-olds show no comparable preferences (Lamb, 1976b). Especially between ages 10 to 20 months, therefore, mothers appear to be more reliable sources of comfort and security, even though fathers are more desirable partners for playful interaction, especially with boys (Clarke-Stewart, 1978; Lamb, 1977a, 1977c).

In a longitudinal study of less-involved and highly involved Swedish fathers and their partners, Lamb, Frodi, Hwang, and Frodi (1983) found that 8- and 16-month-olds showed clear preferences for their mothers on measures of both attachment and affiliative behavior, regardless of the fathers' relative involvement in child care. One reason for this unexpected result may have been that these Swedish fathers were not especially active as playmates. Lamb et al. speculated that playfulness may serve to enhance the salience of fathers, and that in the absence of such cues infants develop clear-cut preferences for their primary caretakers. Frascarolo-Moutinot (1994) reported that Swiss fathers and mothers were both used as secure bases and sources of security only when the fathers were unusually involved in a variety of everyday activities with their infants. By contrast, Swiss infants with traditional fathers clearly obtained more comfort and security, even at home, from their mothers than from their fathers. Increased paternal involvement thus does seem to strengthen infant–father attachment, but when mothers assume primary responsibility for child care, they are preferred attachment figures. Most infants, however, clearly form attachments to their fathers.

CHARACTERISTICS OF MOTHER– AND FATHER–INFANT INTERACTION

Even in the first trimester, fathers and mothers appear to engage in different types of interactions with their infants. When videotaped in face-to-face interaction with their 2- to 25-week-old infants, for example, fathers tended to provide staccato bursts of both physical and social stimulation, whereas mothers tended to be more rhythmic and containing (Yogman, 1981). Mothers addressed their babies with soft, repetitive, imitative sounds, whereas fathers touched their infants with rhythmic pats. During visits to hospitalized premature infants, mothers were responsive to social cues, fathers to gross motor cues (Marton & Minde, 1980), and although Israeli mothers visited and interacted with hospitalized preterm infants more than fathers did (Levy-Shiff et al., 1989), fathers were consistently more likely to stimulate and play with their infants, and less likely to engage in caretaking.

When observed with infants and toddlers, American fathers tend to engage in more physically stimulating and unpredictable play than mothers do (Clarke-Stewart, 1978; Crawley & Sherrod, 1984; Dickson, Walker, & Fogel, 1997; Lamb, 1977c; Power & Parke, 1979; Teti, Bond, & Gibbs, 1988), although rough physical play becomes less prominent as children grow older (Crawley & Sherrod, 1984). Because these types of play elicit more positive responses from infants, young children prefer to play with their fathers when they have the choice (Clarke-Stewart, 1978; Lamb, 1977c). Mothers are more likely to hold their 7- to 13-month-old infants in the course of caretaking, whereas fathers are more likely to do so while playing or in response to the infants' requests to be held (Belsky, 1979; Lamb, 1976b, 1977c). It is thus not surprising that infants respond more positively to being held by their fathers than by their mothers (Lamb, 1976a, 1977c). On the other hand, Frascarolo-Moutinot (1994) and Labrell (1994) reported that French and Swiss fathers were also more intrusive than mothers were, and all researchers agree that most of the differences between mothers and fathers are not large. Both parents encourage visual exploration, object manipulation, and attention to relations and effects (Power, 1985; Teti et al., 1988).

Fathers and mothers do not simply play differently; play is an especially salient component of father–infant relationships. According to Kotelchuck's (1976) informants, mothers spent an average of 85 minutes per day feeding their 6- to 21-month-olds, 55 minutes per day cleaning them, and 140 minutes playing with them. The comparable figures for fathers were 15, 9, and 72 minutes, respectively. According to parental diaries (Yarrow et al., 1984), the average father spent

6 and 7.3 hours per week playing with his 6- and 12-month-old, respectively (43% and 44% of the time spent alone with the infant) compared with 17.5 and 16.4 hours by the average mother (16% and 19%, respectively, of the time she spent alone with the infant). Clarke-Stewart (1978) and Rendina and Dickerscheid (1976) also suggested that fathers were consistently notable for their involvement in play and their lack of involvement in caretaking.

It is not only affluent Euro-American fathers who specialize in play: Middle-income African-American (Hossain, Field, Pickens, Malphurs, & Del Valle, 1997; Hossain & Roopnarine, 1994) and Hispanic (Hossain et al., 1997) fathers were also more likely to play with their infants than to feed or clean them despite claiming (like many Euro-American fathers) that parents should share child-care responsibilities (Hyde & Texidor, 1988). English fathers are also more likely than mothers to play with rather than care for both normal and handicapped infants and toddlers (McConachie, 1989), and similar differences are evident in India, regardless of whether or not mothers are employed (Roopnarine, Talukder, Jain, Joshi, & Srivastav, 1992), as well as in France, Switzerland, and Italy (Best, House, Barnard, & Spicker, 1994; Frascarolo-Moutinot, 1994; Labrell, 1996). By contrast, Taiwanese fathers reported that they rarely played with their children (Sun & Roopnarine, 1996), and fathers on Israeli kibbutzim did not play with their 8- and 16-month-olds more than mothers did, although the mothers were much more actively involved in caretaking and other forms of interaction than the fathers were (Sagi, Lamb, Shoham, Dvir, & Lewkowicz, 1985). Likewise, German (Best et al., 1994), Swedish (Frodi, Lamb, Hwang, & Frodi, 1983; Lamb, Frodi, Hwang, & Frodi, 1982; Lamb et al., 1983), and Aka (pygmy) (Hewlett, 1987) fathers are not notably more playful than mothers. Interestingly, Zaouche-Gaudron and Beaumatin (1998) argued that French fathers who differentiated between maternal and paternal roles tended to have a more positive impact on their children's development than those whose roles were less distinctive.

Patterns of parental behavior may differ when both parents work full-time during the day (Pedersen, Cain, Zaslow, & Anderson, 1982). Working mothers stimulated their infants more than nonworking mothers did, and they were far more active than their husbands were. As expected, fathers with nonworking wives played with their infants more than mothers did, but this pattern was reversed in the families with working mothers. Likewise, Field, Vega-Lahr, Goldstein, and Scafidi (1987) reported that employed mothers were much more interactive in face-to-face interactions with their infants than employed fathers were.

What happens when fathers are highly involved in infant care? Field (1978) reported that primary caretaking fathers behaved more like mothers than secondary caretaking fathers did, although fathers engaged in more playful and noncontaining interactions than mothers did regardless of their involvement in child care. Pruett (1985; Pruett & Litzenburger, 1992) only studied fathers who were highly involved in infant care but repeatedly remarked on the distinctive playfulness of these fathers. Frascarolo-Moutinot (1994) reported no differences in playfulness between "new fathers" and "traditional" fathers, although the wives of the new fathers were less intrusive and controlling than the wives of traditional fathers. Lamb and his colleagues (Lamb, Frodi, Frodi, & Hwang, 1982; Lamb, Frodi, Hwang, Frodi, & Steinberg, 1982a, 1982b) reported that mothers were more likely than fathers to vocalize, display affection to, touch, tend to, and hold their infants whether or not their partners took a month or more of paternity leave.

Overall, these findings suggest that the distinctive maternal and paternal styles are quite robust and are still evident when fathers are highly involved in infant care. Fathers are not universally more playful then mothers, however.

PATERNAL INFLUENCES ON INFANT DEVELOPMENT

In response to consistent evidence concerning the impact of mother–infant interaction on cognitive development, many researchers have explored paternal influences on cognitive and motivational development. Yarrow et al. (1984) reported that paternal stimulation played an especially important role in the development of boys' (but not girls') mastery motivation in the first year of life, whereas Wachs, Uzgiris, and Hunt (1971) reported that increased paternal involvement was associated with better performance on the Uzgiris-Hunt scales. Magill-Evans and Harrison (1999) reported that the sensitivity of both mothers and fathers to their 3- and 12-month-olds predicted individual differences in the linguistic and cognitive capacities of the children when they were 18 months old whereas Yogman, Kindlon, and Earls (1995) reported that infants with more involved fathers had higher IQs than those whose fathers were less involved, even after controlling for socioeconomic differences. Finnish fathers who read more often to their 14- and 24-month-old infants had children who were later more interested in books (Lyytinen, Laakso, & Poikkeus, 1998). In addition, Labrell (1990) reported that paternal scaffolding (i.e., providing indirect rather than direct help) promoted independent problem solving by 18-month-olds. Symbolic activity by 30- and 42-month-olds was predicted by maternal but not paternal distancing strategies in a later study (Labrell, Deleau, & Juhel, 2000), however.

In her observational study of 15- to 30-month-olds, Clarke-Stewart (1978) found that intellectual competence was correlated with measures of maternal stimulation (both material and verbal), intellectual acceleration, and expressiveness, as well as with measures of the fathers' engagement in play, their positive ratings of the children, the amount they interacted, and the fathers' aspirations for the infants' independence. However, examination of the correlational patterns over time indicated that the mothers affected the children's development and that this, in turn, influenced the fathers' behavior. In other words, paternal behavior appeared to be a consequence of, not a determinant of, individual differences in child behavior. Similarly, Hunter, McCarthy, MacTurk, and Vietze (1987) reported that, although the qualities of both mother– and father–infant interaction in play sessions were individually stable over time, the paternal variables were not associated with differences in the infants' cognitive competence, whereas the indices of maternal behavior were predictively valuable. These findings illustrate a notion we pursue in the next section—that children develop within family systems, in which all parties affect and are affected by one another. Influences do not always run directly from parents to children.

Although mothers and fathers both adjust their speech characteristics when speaking to infants, some differences between maternal and paternal communicative patterns remain. Gleason (1975) and Rondal (1980) have suggested that, because fathers use more imperatives, attention-getting utterances, and stated sentences than mothers do, they contribute in unique, though still poorly understood, ways to linguistic development. Infants clearly view both parents as potential sources of information. In ambiguous settings, they look to either parent for clarification, and they are equally responsive to information from mothers and fathers (Dickstein & Parke, 1988; Hirshberg & Svejda,1990).

The Security of Infant–Father Attachment

Attachment theorists believe that maternal sensitivity determines the security of infant–mother attachment and thus of subsequent psychological adjustment (Ainsworth et al., 1978; Lamb, 1987; Lamb et al., 1985), and it seems reasonable to assume that individual differences in paternal sensitivity influence the security of infant–father attachment. As expected, Cox, Owen, Henderson, and Margand (1992) reported that fathers who were more affectionate, spent more time with their 3-month-olds, and had more positive attitudes were more likely to have securely attached infants 9 months later. Caldera, Huston, and O'Brien (1995) likewise reported that infants were more likely to appear insecure in the Strange Situation at 18 months when their fathers appeared more detached in a semistructured laboratory situation 12 months earlier. Notaro and Volling (1999), however, reported no significant associations between assessments of mother– and father–infant attachment in the Strange Situation and near contemporaneous measures of parental responsiveness in a brief (3-minute) session. These findings were consistent with an earlier report that measures of father–infant interaction at home when infants were 6 and 9 months of age were unrelated to the security of infant–father attachment in the Strange Situation (Volling & Belsky, 1992) and with Rosen and Rothbaum's (1993) observation that measures of both maternal and paternal behavior were weakly associated with the Strange Situation assessment of attachment security. By contrast, Goosens and Van IJzendoorn (1990) had reported that the sensitivity of fathers in a free play session was correlated with near contemporaneous assessments of infant–father attachment in a sample of Dutch fathers, and a meta-analysis of eight studies concerned with the association between paternal sensitivity and the quality of infant–father attachment in the

Strange Situation revealed a small but statistically significant association (Van IJzendoorn & De Wolff, 1997) that was significantly weaker than the association between maternal sensitivity and the security of infant–mother attachment. Father–infant attachments are more likely to be insecure when fathers report high levels of stress (Jarvis & Creasey, 1991).

Steele, Steele, and Fonagy (1996) reported that mothers' perceptions of their attachment to their own mothers predicted the security of their infants' attachments to them, whereas fathers' perceptions of their childhood attachments predicted the security of their infants attachments to them. Consistent with this, Van IJzendoorn (1995) reported an association between the security of infant–father attachment and the fathers' representation of their own childhood attachments.

The effects of infant–father attachment on subsequent behavior have also been studied. In a study of infants on Israeli kibbutzim, Sagi, Lamb, and Gardner (1986) reported that the security of both mother– and father–infant attachment were associated with indices of the infants' sociability with strangers: Securely attached infants were more sociable than insecure-resistant infants. Earlier, Lamb, Hwang, Frodi, and Frodi (1982) reported that Swedish infants who were securely attached to their fathers were more sociable with strangers, although there was no association between the security of infant–mother attachment and sociability in their sample. Main and Weston (1981) found that the security of both mother–infant and father–infant attachments affected infants' responses to an unfamiliar person (dressed as a clown). Unfortunately, it was not possible to determine which relationship had the greater impact because the clown session took place at the same time as the assessment of the mother–infant attachment— 6 months before assessment of the father–infant attachments. Belsky, Garduque, and Hrncir (1984), however, reported that the security of both attachment relationships, but especially the infant–mother attachment, affected executive capacity, an index of cognitive performance. Main, Kaplan, and Cassidy (1985) reported that earlier and concurrent assessments of mother–child attachment had greater impact on children's attachment-related responses than earlier and concurrent assessments of child–father attachment, and similar results were reported by Suess, Grossmann, and Sroufe (1992), who studied associations between parent–infant attachment security and the quality of the children's later interaction with peers. Interestingly, although the parents' sensitivity toward their 12-month-olds did not predict later behavior problems in one study (Benzies, Harrison, & Magill-Evans, 1999), Verschueren and Marcoen (1999) reported that the security of child–mother attachments had a greater effect on the positive self-perceptions of 5- and 6-year-olds than did child–father attachments, whereas child–father attachments had a greater effect on behavior problems. In either case, secure attachments to one parent partially but not completely offset the effects of insecure attachment to the other, and we might expect the same to be true in infancy.

Fagot and Kavanagh (1993) underscored the importance of considering the quality of attachment to both parents. Both parents found interaction with insecurely attached infants less pleasant, and both tended to become less involved in interactions with insecurely attached boys, a factor that may explain the greater likelihood of behavior problems among boys. Interestingly, fathers had unusually high levels of interaction with insecure-avoidant girls, who received the fewest instructions from their mothers. In a study of 20-month-olds, Easterbrooks and Goldberg (1984) found that the children's adaptation was promoted by both the amount of paternal involvement and, more importantly, the quality or sensitivity of their fathers' behavior, but neither the security of infant–mother nor infant–father attachment influenced the adjustment at age 5 of infants raised on traditional kibbutzim (those with central dormitories for children), although the security of the infant–caretaker relationship was influential (Oppenheim, Sagi, & Lamb, 1988).

Contrasting Patterns of Paternal and Maternal Influence

Recent research also suggests that fathers and mothers may have distinct influences on the development of peer relationships. MacDonald and Parke (1984), for example, found that physically playful, affectionate, and socially engaging father–son interaction was correlated with the boys' later popularity, whereas mothers' verbal stimulation was associated with popularity. In addition, rejected-aggressive boys reported receiving less affection from their fathers (but not from their mothers) than did rejected-nonaggressive and neglected boys. And although the security of infant–father attachment did not predict the quality of later sibling interaction, there was a nonsignificant tendency for sibling interaction to be more positive if fathers had positive relationships with the older children when they were 3 years old. Parke et al. (1989) argued that father–child interactions teach children to read their partners' emotional expressions and that these skills are later displayed in interactions with peers. Similarly, Youngblade and Belsky (1992) found no significant associations between the security of infant–father attachment and the quality of father–child interaction when the children were 3 years old, although those children who had more positive interactions with their fathers at age 3 interacted more positively with peers 2 years later. Interestingly, the security of infant–father attachment at age 1 was inversely associated with indices of peer play at age 5, leading Youngblade and Belsky to speculate that unsatisfying parent–child relationships lead children to look outside their families for more rewarding relationships. These associations were not replicated when infant–father attachment was assessed using the Attachment Q-sort rather than the Strange Situation: secure infant–father attachments were then associated with more positive interactions with peers (Youngblade, Park, & Belsky, 1993) leaving some confusion about the pattern of predictive associations.

DIRECT AND INDIRECT EFFECTS

Fathers not only influence children directly; they also affect maternal behavior, just as mothers influence paternal behavior and involvement (Cummings & O'Reilly, 1997; Lamb, 1997). Indeed, the quality of the marital relationship affects the behavior of both parents. Fathers are consistently more involved in interaction with their infants when they were highly engaged in interaction with their partners (Belsky et al., 1984) and when both they and their partners have supportive attitudes regarding paternal involvement (Beitel & Parke, 1998), whereas Grych and Clark (1999) reported that marital quality predicted the amount of appropriate paternal stimulation of 4- and 12-month-olds. Similarly, Durrett, Otaki, and Richards (1984) found that the Japanese mothers of securely attached infants reported greater levels of spousal support than did the mothers of insecurely attached infants. By contrast, infants whose fathers abused alcohol tended to have insecure attachments to their mothers (Das Eiden & Leonard, 1996). Goldberg and Easterbrooks (1984) reported that good marital quality was associated with both more sensitive maternal and paternal behavior as well as higher levels of functioning on the part of the toddlers studied.

After controlling for individual differences in the fathers' psychological adjustment, Cox et al. (1989) reported that fathers in close, confiding marriages had more positive attitudes toward their 3-month-old infants and toward their roles as parents than did fathers is less-successful marriages, whereas mothers in close, confiding marriages were warmer and more sensitive. Similar results were reported by Levy-Shiff and Israelashvili (1988), although Crouter and her colleagues (1987) reported that, at least in dual-earner families, increased paternal involvement in child care was often at the expense of marital happiness. Other researchers have likewise reported that maternal employment may alter the relationships between fathers and infants. For example, Braungant-Riecker et al. (1999) reported that fathers in dual-earner families were less sensitive toward their 4-month-old sons and that the boys were more likely to become insecurely attached to their fathers than to their mothers. Grych and Clark (1999) reported that fathers with unemployed or part-time employed mothers were more sensitive when they were involved, whereas fathers whose wives were employed full-time behaved more negatively when they were more highly involved.

Gable, Crnic, and Belsky (1994) reported powerful associations among marital quality, the quality of parent–child relationships, and child outcomes in a study of 2-year-olds. Infants characterized by negative emotionality early in the first year tended to become more positive when they had active, sensitive, and happily married mothers, whereas some infants became more negative when their fathers were dissatisfied with their marriages, insensitive, and uninvolved in their children's lives (Belsky, Fish, & Isabella, 1991). Meanwhile, Heinicke and Guthrie (1992) reported that couples who were well adapted to one another provided better care than parents whose spousal adaptation was poor or declining, and similar findings were reported by other researchers (Durrett, Richards, Otaki, Pennebaker, & Nyguist, 1986; Engfer, 1988; Jouriles, Pfiffner, & O'Leary, 1988; Meyer, 1988). Belsky, Gilstrap, and Rovine (1984) and Lamb and Elster (1985) both reported that fathers' interactions with their infants were influenced by the ongoing quality of interaction with their partners much more profoundly than mothers' behavior was. This may be because paternal behavior and engagement are somewhat discretionary, whereas maternal behavior is driven by clearer conventions and role definitions. In any event, marital conflict appears to have a more harmful impact on socioemotional development than does parent–child separation or father absence (Hetherington & Stanley-Hagen, 1999).

CONCLUSION

Clearly, fathers can no longer be deemed "forgotten contributors to child development" (Lamb, 1975), because the relationships between fathers and infants have been studied quite intensively, especially in the United States. Of course, many important questions remain unanswered, but at least some issues have been resolved. First, there is substantial evidence that both mothers and fathers are capable of behaving sensitively and responsively in interaction with their infants. With the exception of lactation, there is no evidence that women are biologically predisposed to be better parents than men are: Social conventions, not biological imperatives, underlie the traditional division of parental responsibilities. Second, the amounts of time that fathers spend with their infants vary quite widely depending on individual characteristics, family characteristics, and cultural prescriptions. Third, most infants form attachments to both mothers and fathers at about the same point during the first year of life, although there appears to exist a hierarchy among attachment figures such that most infants prefer their mothers over their fathers. These preferences probably developed because the mothers were primary caretakers; they might well disappear or be reversed if fathers shared caretaking responsibilities or became primary caretakers, which few have done. Fourth, the traditional parental roles affect styles of interaction as well as infant preferences. Several observational studies have now shown that fathers are often, but not always, associated with playful—often vigorously stimulating—social interaction, whereas mothers are associated with caretaking. These social styles obviously reflect traditionally sex-stereotyped roles and may play some role in the early development of gender role and gender identity.

In the immediate future, the most conceptually important advances will involve attempts to determine how patterns of interaction within the family system affect the course of infant development. It is clear that the way either parent interacts with the infant is determined jointly by his or her personality, relationship with the spouse, and the infant's unique characteristics, but we do not know just how these diverse influences complement and supplement one another.

REFERENCES

Ainsworth, M. D. S., Blehar, M. C., Waters, E., & Wall, S. (1978). *Patterns of attachment.* Hillsdale, NJ: Lawrence Erlbaum Associates.

Bader, A. P. (1995). Engrossment revisited: Fathers are still falling in love with their newborn babies. In J. L. Shapiro, M. J. Diamond, & M. Greenberg (Eds.), *Becoming a father* (pp. 224–233). New York: Springer.

Bader, A. P., & Phillips, R. D. (1999). Fathers' proficiency at recognizing their newborns by tactile cues. *Infant Behavior and Development, 22,* 405–409.

Ban, P., & Lewis, M. (1974). Mothers and fathers, girls and boys: Attachment behavior in the one-year-old. *Merrill-Palmer Quarterly, 20,* 195–204.

Beitel, A. H., & Parke, R. D. (1998). Parental involvement in infancy: The role of maternal and paternal attitudes. *Journal of Family Psychology, 12,* 268–288.

Belsky, J. (1979). Mother–father–infant interaction: A naturalistic observational study. *Developmental Psychology, 15,* 601–607.

Belsky, J. (1985). Experimenting with the family in the newborn period. *Child Development, 56,* 407–414.

Belsky, J., Fish, M., & Isabella, R. (1991). Continuity and discontinuity in infant negative and positive emotionality: Family antecedents and attachment consequences. *Developmental Psychology, 27,* 421–431.

Belsky, J., Garduque, L., & Hrncir, E. (1984). Assessing performance, competence, and executive capacity in infant play: Relation to home environment and security of attachment. *Developmental Psychology, 20,* 406–417.

Belsky, J., Gilstrap, B., & Rovine, M. (1984). The Pennsylvania Infant and Family Development Project, I: Stability and change in mother–infant and father–infant interaction in a family setting at one, three, and nine months. *Child Development, 55,* 692–705.

Benzies, K. M., Harrison, M. J., & Magill-Evans, J. (1998). Impact of marital quality and parent–infant interaction on preschool behavior problems. *Public Health Nursing, 15,* 35–43.

Best, D. L., House, A. S., Barnard, A. L., & Spicker, B. S. (1994). Parent–child interactions in France, Germany, and Italy—The effects of gender and culture. *Journal of Cross-Cultural Psychology, 25,* 181–193.

Blount, G. B., & Padgug, E. J. (1976). Mother and father speech: Distribution of parental speech features in English and Spanish. *Papers and Reports on Child Language Development, 12,* 47–59.

Bowlby, J. (1969). *Attachment and loss: Vol. 1. Attachment.* New York: Basic Books.

Brachfeld-Child, S. (1986). Parents as teachers: Comparisons of mothers' and fathers' instructional interactions with infants. *Infant Behavior and Development, 9,* 127–131.

Braungart-Rieker, J., Courtney, S., & Garwood, M. M. (1999). Mother– and father–infant attachment: Families in context. *Journal of Family Psychology, 13,* 535–553.

Braungart-Rieker, J., Garwood, M. M., Powers, B. P., & Notaro, P. C. (1998). Infant affect and affect regulation during the still-face paradigim with mothers and fathers: The role of infant characteristics and parental sensitivity. *Developmental Psychology, 34,* 1428–1437.

Broom, B. L. (1994). Impact of marital quality and psychological well-being on parental sensitivity. *Nursing Research, 43,* 138–143.

Brophy-Herb, H. E., Gibbons, G., Omar, M. A. & Schiffman, R. P. (1999). Low-income fathers and their infants: Interactions during teaching episodes. *Infant Mental Health Journal, 20,* 305–321.

Caldera, Y., Huston, A., & O'Brien, M. (1995, April). *Antecedents of father–infant attachment: A longitudinal study.* Paper presented to the Society for Research in Child Development, Indianapolis, IN.

Christensson, K. (1996). Fathers can effectively achieve heat conservation in healthy newborn infants. *Acta Paediatrica, 85,* 1354–1360.

Clarke-Stewart, K. A. (1978). And daddy makes three: The father's impact on mother and young child. *Child Development, 49,* 466–478.

Cohen, L. J., & Campos, J. J. (1974). Father, mother, and stranger as elicitors of attachment behaviors in infancy. *Developmental Psychology, 10,* 146–154.

Cowan, P. A., Cohn, D. A., Cowan, C. P., & Pearson, J. L. (1996). Parents' attachment histories and children's externalizing and internalizing behaviors: Exploring family systems models of linkage. *Journal of Consulting and Clinical Psychology, 64,* 53–63.

Cox, M. J., Owen, M. T., Henderson, V. K., & Margand, N. A. (1992). Prediction of infant–father and infant–mother attachment. *Developmental Psychology, 28,* 474–483.

Cox, M. J., Owen, M. T., Lewis, J. M., & Henderson, U. K. (1989). Marriage adult adjustment, and early parenting. *Child Development, 60,* 1015–1024.

Crawley, S. B., & Sherrod, R. B. (1984). Parent–infant play during the first year of life. *Infant Behavior and Development, 7,* 65–75.

Crouter, A. C., Perry-Jenkins, M., Huston, T. L., & McHale, S. M. (1987). Processes underlying father-involvement in dual-earner and single-earner families. *Developmental Psychology, 23,* 431–440.

Cummings, E. M., & O'Reilly, A. W. (1977). Fathers in family context: Effects of marital quality on child adjustment. In M. E. Lamb (Ed.), *The role of father in child development* (3rd ed., pp. 49–65, 318–325). New York: Wiley.

Dalton-Hummel, D. (1982). Syntatic and conversational characteristics of fathers' speech. *Journal of Psycholinguistic Research, 11,* 465–483.

Darke, P. R., & Goldberg, S. (1994). Father–infant interaction and parent stress with healthy and medically compromised infants. *Infant Behavior and Development, 17,* 3–14.

Das Eiden, R., Chavez, F., & Leonard, K. E. (1999). Parent–infant interactions among families with alcoholic fathers. *Development and Psychopathology, 11,* 745–762.

Das Eiden, R., & Leonard, K. E. (1996). Paternal alcohol use and the mother–infant relationship. *Development and Psychopathology, 8,* 307–323.

Das Eiden, R., & Leonard, K. E. (2000). Paternal alcoholism, parental psychopathology, and aggravation with infants. *Journal of Substance Abuse, 11,* 17–29.

Deater-Deckard, K., Scarr, S., McCartney, K., & Eisenberg, M. (1994). Paternal separation anxiety: Relationships with parenting stress, child-rearing attitudes, and maternal anxieties. *Psychological Science, 5,* 341–346.

Dickson, K. L. Walker, H., & Fogel, A. (1997). The relationship between smile type and play type during parent–infant play. *Developmental Psychology, 33,* 925–933.

Dickstein, S., & Parke, R. D. (1988). Social referencing in infancy: A glance at fathers and marriage. *Child Development, 59,* 506–511.

Donate-Bartfield, D., & Passman, R. H. (1985). Attentiveness of mothers and fathers to their baby cries. *Infant Behavior and Development, 8,* 385–393.

Dulude, D., Wright, J., & Belanger, C. (2000). The effects of pregnancy complications on the parental adaptation process. *Journal of Reproductive and Infant Psychology, 18,* 5–20.

Durrett, M. E., Otaki, M., & Richards, P. (1984). Attachment and the mothers' perception of support from the father. *International Journal of Behavioral Development, 7,* 167–176.

Durrett, M., Richards, P., Otaki, M., Pennebaker, J., & Nyquist, L. (1986). Mother's involvement with infant and her perception of spousal support, Japan and America. *Journal of Marriage and the Family, 68,* 187–194.

Easterbrooks, M. A., & Goldberg, W. A. (1984). Toddler development in the family: Impact of father involvement and parenting characteristics. *Child Development, 53,* 740–752.

Engfer, A. (1988). The interrelatedness of marriage and the mother–child relationship. In R. A. Hinde & J. Stevenson-Hinde (Eds.), *Relationships within families: Mutual influences* (pp. 104–118). New York: Oxford University Press.

Fagot, B. L., & Kavanagh, K. (1993). Parenting during the second year: Effects of children's age, sex, and attachment classification. *Child Development, 64,* 258–271.

Feldman, S. S., & Ingham, M. E. (1975). Attachment behavior: A validation study in two age groups. *Child Development, 46,* 319–330.

Field, T. (1978). Interaction behaviors of primary versus secondary caretaker fathers. *Developmental Psychology, 14,* 183–184.

Field, T., Gewirtz, J. L., Cohen, D., Garcia, R., Greenberg, R., & Collins, K. (1984). Leave-takings and reunions of infants, toddlers, preschoolers, and their parents. *Child Development, 55,* 628–635.

Field, T. M., Hossain, Z., & Malphurs, J. (1999). "Depressed" fathers' interactions with their infants. *Infant Mental Health Journal, 20,* 322–332.

Field, T., Vega-Lahr, N., Goldstein, S., & Scafidi, F. (1987). Interaction behavior of infants and their dual-career parents. *Infant Behavior and Development, 10,* 371–377.

Frascarolo-Moutinot, F. (1994). *Engagement paternal quotidien et relations parents-enfant* [Daily paternal involvement and parent-child relationships]. Unpublished doctoral dissertation, Universite de Geneve, Switzerland.

Frodi, A. M., Lamb, M. E., Hwang, C. P., & Frodi, M. (1983). Father–mother–infant interaction in traditional and nontraditional Swedish families: A longitudinal study. *Alternative Lifestyles, 5,* 142–163.

Gable, S., Crnic, K., & Belsky, J. (1994). Coparenting within the family system: Influences on children's development. *Family Relations, 43,* 380–386.

Gewirtz, H. B., & Gewirtz, J. L. (1968). Visiting and caretaking patterns for kibbutz infants: Age and sex trends. *American Journal of Orthopsychiatry, 38,* 427–443.

Gleason, J. B. (1975). Fathers and other strangers: Men's speech to young children. In D. P. Dato (Ed.), *Language and linguistics* (pp. 289–297). Washington, DC: Georgetown University Press.

Goldberg, W. A., & Easterbrooks, M. A. (1984). The role of marital quality in toddler development. *Developmental Psychology, 20,* 504–514.

Golinkoff, R. M., & Ames, G. J. (1979). A comparison of fathers' and mothers' speech with their young children. *Child Development, 50,* 28–32.

Goosens, F. A., & van IJzendoorn, M. H. (1990). Quality of infants' attachments to professional caregivers: Relations to infant–parent attachment and day care characteristics. *Child Development, 61,* 832–837.

Gottfried, A. E., Gottfried, A. W., & Bathurst, K. (1988). Maternal employment, family environment, and children's development: Infancy through the school years. In A. E. Gottfried & A. W. Gottfried (Eds.), *Maternal employment and children's development: Longitudinal research* (pp. 11–58). New York: Plenum.

Greenberg, M. (1985). *The birth of a father.* New York: Continum.

Greenberg, M., & Morris, N. (1974). Engrossment: The newborn's impact upon the father. *American Journal of Orthopsychiatry, 44,* 520–531.

Grossmann, K. E., & Volkmer, H. J. (1984). Fathers' presence during birth of their infants and paternal involvement. *International Journal of Behavioral Development, 7,* 157–165.

Grych, J. H., & Clarke, R. (1999). Maternal employment and development of the father–infant relationship in the first year. *Developmental Psychology, 35,* 893–903.

Haas, L. (1992). *Equal parenthood and social policy: A study of parental leave in Sweden.* Albany: State University of New York Press.

Haas, L. (1993). Nurturing fathers and working mothers: Changing gender roles in Sweden. In J. C. Hood (Ed.), *Men, work, and family* (pp. 238–261). Newbury Park, CA: Sage.

Harrison, M. J., & Magill-Evans, J. (1996). Mother and father interactions over the first year with term and preterm infants. *Research in Nursing and Health, 19,* 451–459.

Heermann, J. A., Jones, L. C., & Wikoff, R. L. (1994). Measurement of parent behavior during interactions with their infants. *Infant Behavior and Development, 17,* 311–321.

Heinicke, C. M., & Guthrie, D. (1992). Stability and change in husband–wife adaptation and the development of the positive parent–child relationship. *Infant Behavior and Development, 15,* 109–127.

Hetherington, E. M., & Stanley-Hagen, M. M. (1999). The effects of divorce and custody arrangements on children's behavior, development, and adjustment. In M. E. Lamb (Ed.), *Parenting and child development in "nontraditional" families* (pp. 137–160). Mahwah, NJ: Lawrence Erlbaum Associates.

Hewlett, B. S. (1987). Intimate fathers: Patterns of paternal holding among Aka pygmies. In M. E. Lamb (Ed.), *The father's role: Cross-cultural perspectives* (pp. 295–330). Hillsdale, NJ: Lawrence Erlbaum Associates.

Hirshberg, L. M., & Svejda, M. (1990). When infants look to their parents: I. Infants' social referencing of mothers compared to fathers. *Child Development, 61,* 1175–1186.

Hock, E., & Lutz, W. (1998). Psychological meaning of separation anxiety in mothers and fathers. *Journal of Family Psychology, 12,* 41–55.

Hossain, Z., Field, T. M., Gonzalez, J., Malphurs, J., & Del Valle, C. (1994). Infants of depressed mothers interact better with their nondepressed fathers. *Infant Mental Health Journal, 15,* 348–357.

Hossain, Z., Field, T., Pickens, J., Malphurs, J., & Del Valle C. (1997). Fathers' caregiving in low-income African-American and Hispanic American families. *Early Development and Parenting, 6,* 73–82.

Hossain, Z., & Roopnarine, J. L. (1994). African-American fathers' involvement with infants: Relationship to their functional style, support, education, and income. *Infant Behavior and Development, 17,* 175–184.

Hunter, F. T., McCarthy, M. E., MacTurk, R. H., & Vietze, P. M. (1987). Infants' social-constructive interactions with mothers and fathers. *Developmental Psychology, 23,* 249–254.

Hwang, C. P. (1987). The changing role of Swedish fathers. In M. E. Lamb (Ed.), *The father's role: Cross-cultural perspectives* (pp. 115–138). Hillsdale, NJ: Lawrence Erlbaum Associates.

Hwang C. P., & Lamb, M. E. (1997). Father involvement in Sweden: A longitudinal study of its stability and correlates. *International Journal of Behavioral Development, 21,* 621–632.

Hyde, J. S., Essex, M. J., & Horton, F. (1993). Fathers and parental leave: Attitudes and expectations. *Journal of Family Issues, 14,* 616–641.

Hyde, B. L., & Texidor, M. S. (1988). A description of the fathering experience among Black fathers. *Journal of Black Nurses Association, 2,* 67–78.

Jarvis, P. A., & Creasey, G. L. (1991). Parental stress, coping, and attachment in families with an 18-month-old infant. *Infant Behavior and Development, 14,* 383–395.

Jouriles, E. N., Pfiffner, L. J., & O'Leary, S. G. (1988). Marital conflict, parenting, and toddler conduct problems. *Journal of Abnormal Psychology, 16,* 197–206.

Kaitz, M., Chriki, M., Bear-Scharf L., Nir, T. & Eidelman, A. I. (2000). Effectiveness of primiparae and multiparae at soothing their newborn infants. *Journal of Genetic Psychology, 161,* 203–215.

Kaitz, M., Lapidot, P., Bronner, R., & Eidelman, A. L. (1992). Parturient women can recognize their infants by touch. *Developmental Psychology, 28,* 35–39.

Kaitz, M., Meirov, H., Landman, I., & Eidelman, A. L. (1993). Infant recognition by tactile cues. *Infant Behavior and Development, 16,* 333–341.

Kaitz, M., Shiri, S. Danziger, S., Hershko, Z., & Eidelman, A. L. (1994). Fathers can also recognize their newborns by touch. *Infant Behavior and Development, 17,* 205–207.

Keller, W. D., Hildebrandt, K. A., & Richards, M. E. (1985). Effects of extended father–infant contact during the newborn period. *Infant Behavior and Development, 8,* 337–350.

Kokkinaki, T., & Kugiumutzakis, G. (2000). Basic aspects of vocal imitation in infant–parent interaction during the first 6 months. *Journal of Reproductive and Infant Psychology, 18,* 173–187.

Kotelchuck, M. (1976). The infant's relationship to the father: Experimental evidence. In M. E. Lamb (Ed.), *The role of the father in child development* (pp. 329–344). New York: Wiley.

Labrell, F. (1990). *Educational strategies and their representations in parents of toddlers.* Paper presented at the Fourth European Conference on Developmental Psychology, Sterling, UK.

Labrell, F. (1994). A typical interaction behavior between fathers and toddlers: Teasing. *Early Development and Parenting, 3,* 125–130.

Labrell, F. (1996). Paternal play with toddlers: Recreation and creation. *European Journal of Psychology of Education, 11,* 43–54.

Labrell, F., Deleau, M., & Juhel, J. (2000). Fathers' and mothers' distancing strategies towards toddlers. *International Journal of Behavioral Development, 24,* 356–361.

Lamb, M. E. (1975). Fathers: Forgotten contributors to child development. *Human Development, 18,* 245–266.

Lamb, M. E. (1976a). Effects of stress and cohort on mother– and father–infant interaction. *Developmental Psychology, 12,* 435–443.

Lamb, M. E. (1976b). Interactions between two-year-olds and their mothers and fathers. *Psychological Reports, 38,* 447–450.

Lamb, M. E. (1976c). Twelve-month-olds and their parents: Interaction in a laboratory playroom. *Developmental Psychology, 12,* 237–244.

Lamb, M. E. (1977a). The development of mother–infant and father–infant attachments in the second year of life. *Developmental Psychology, 13,* 637–648.

Lamb, M. E. (1977b). The development of parental preferences in the first two years of life. *Sex Roles, 3,* 495–497.

Lamb, M. E. (1977c). Father–infant and mother–infant interaction in the first year of life. *Child Development, 48,* 167–181.

Lamb, M. E. (1981). The development of social expectations in the first year of life. In M. E. Lamb & L. R. Sherrod (Eds.), *Infant social cognition: Empirical and theoretical considerations* (pp. 155–175). Hillsdale, NJ: Lawrence Erlbaum Associates.

Lamb, M. E. (1987). Predictive implications of individual differences in attachment. *Journal of Consulting and Clinical Psychology, 55,* 817–824.

Lamb, M. E. (1997). Fathers and child development: An introductory overview and guide. In M. E. Lamb (Ed.), *The role of the father in child development* (3rd ed., pp. 1–18, 309–313). New York: Wiley.

Lamb, M. E., & Elster, A. B. (1985). Adolescent mother–infant–father relationships. *Developmental Psychology, 21,* 768–773.

Lamb, M. E., Frodi, A. M., Frodi, M., & Hwang, C. P. (1982). Characteristics of maternal and paternal behavior in traditional and nontraditional Swedish families. *International Journal of Behavioral Development, 5,* 131–141.

Lamb, M. E., Frodi, A. M., Hwang, C. P., & Frodi, M. (1982). Varying degrees of paternal involvement in infant care: Attitudinal and behavioral correlates. In M. E. Lamb (Ed.), *Nontraditional families: Parenting and child development* (pp. 117–137). Hillsdale, NJ: Lawrence Erlbaum Associates.

Lamb, M. E., Frodi, M., Hwang, C. P., & Frodi, A. M. (1983). Effects of paternal involvement on infant preferences for mothers and fathers. *Child Development, 54,* 450–458.

Lamb, M. E., Frodi, A. M., Hwang, C. P., Frodi, M., & Steinberg, J. (1982a). Effects of gender and caretaking role on parent–infant interaction. In R. N. Emde & R. J. Harmon (Eds.), *Development of attachment and affiliative systems* (pp. 109–118). New York: Plenum.

Lamb, M. E., Frodi, A. M., Hwang, C. P., Frodi, M., & Steinberg, J. (1982b). Mother– and father–infant interaction involving play and holding in traditional and nontraditional Swedish families. *Developmental Psychology, 18,* 215–221.

Lamb, M. E., Hwang, C. P., Broberg, A., Bookstein, F. L., Hult, G., & Frodi, M. (1988). The determinants of paternal involvement in primiparous Swedish families. *International Journal of Behavioral Development, 11,* 433–449.

Lamb, M. E., Hwang, C. P., Frodi, A. M., & Frodi, M. (1982). Security of mother– and father–infant attachment and its relation to sociability with strangers in traditional and nontraditional Swedish families. *Infant Behavior and Development, 5,* 355–367.

Lamb, M. E., Thompson, R. A., Gardner, W., & Charnov, E. L. (1985). *Infant–mother attachment: The origins and developmental significance of individual differences in Strange Situation behavior.* Hillsdale, NJ: Lawrence Erlbaum Associates.

Lester, B. M., Kotelchuck, M., Spelke, E., Sellers, M. J., & Klein, R. E. (1974). Separation protest in Guatemalan infants: Cross-cultural and cognitive findings. *Developmental Psychology, 10,* 79–85.

Levy-Shiff, R., & Israelashvili, R. (1988). Antecedents of fathering: Some further exploration. *Developmental Psychology, 24,* 434–440.

Levy-Shiff, R., Sharir, H., & Mogilner, M. B. (1989). Mother– and father–preterm infant relationship in the hospital preterm nursery. *Child Development, 60,* 93–102.

Lewis, C. (1984, September). *Men's involvement in fatherhood: Historical and gender issues.* Paper presented at the meeting of the British Psychological Society (Developmental Section), Lancaster, UK.

Lewis, C. (1986). *Becoming a father.* Milton Keynes, UK: Open University Press.

Lewis, C., Kier, C., Hyder, C., Prenderville, N., Pullen, J., & Stephens, A. (1996). Observer influences on fathers and mothers: An experimental manipulation of the structure and function of parent-infant conversation. *Early Development and Parenting, 5,* 57–68.

Lewis, M., & Weinraub, M. (1974). Sex of parent × sex of child: Socioemotional development. In R. Richart, R. Friedman, & R. Vande Wiele (Eds.), *Sex differences in behavior* (pp. 165–189). New York: Wiley.

Lind, R. (1974, October). *Observations after delivery of communications between mother-infant–father.* Paper presented at the meeting of the International Congress of Pediatrics, Buenos Aires.

Lyytinen, P., Laakso, M. L., & Poikkeus, A. M. (1998). Parental contribution to child's early language and interest in books. *European Journal of Psychology of Education, 13,* 297–308.

MacDonald, K., & Parke, R. D. (1984). Bridging the gap: Parent–child play interaction and peer interactive competence. *Child Development, 55,* 1265–1277.

Magill-Evans, J., & Harrison, M. J. (1999). Parent–child interactions and development of toddlers born preterm. *Western Journal of Nursing Research, 21,* 292–307.

Main, M., Kaplan, N., & Cassidy, J. (1985). Security in infancy, childhood and adulthood: A move to the level of representation. *Monographs of the Society for Research in Child Development, 50,* 66–104.

Main, M., & Weston, D. M. (1981). The quality of the toddler's relationship to mother and to father: Related to conflict behavior and the readiness to establish new relationships. *Child Development, 52,* 932–940.

Mansbach, I. K., & Greenbaum, C. N. (1999). Developmental maturity expectations of Israeli fathers and mothers: Effects of education, ethnic origin, and religiosity. *International Journal of Behavioral Development, 23,* 771–797.

Marton, P. L., & Minde, K. (1980, April). *Paternal and maternal behavior with premature infants.* Paper presented at the meeting of the American Orthopsychiatric Association, Toronto.

McConachie, H. (1989). Mothers' and fathers' interaction with their young mentally handicapped children. *International Journal of Behavioral Development, 12,* 239–255.

McElwain, N. L., & Volling, B. L. (1999). Depressed mood and marital conflict: Relations to maternal and paternal intrusiveness with one-year-old infants. *Journal of Applied Developmental Psychology, 20,* 63–83.

McHale, S. M., & Huston, T. L. (1984). Men and women as parents: Sex role orientations, employment, and parental roles with infants. *Child Development, 55,* 1349–1361.

Meyer, H. J. (1988). Marital and mother–child relationships: Developmental history, parent personality, and child difficultness. In R. A. Hinde & J. Stevenson-Hinde (Eds.), *Relationship within families: Mutual influences* (pp. 119–139). Oxford, UK: Clarendon Press.

Myers, B. J. (1982). Early intervention using Brazelton training with middle-class mothers and fathers of newborns. *Child Development, 53,* 462–471.

New, R. S., & Benigni, L. (1987). Italian fathers and infants: Cultural constraints on paternal behavior. In M. E. Lamb (Ed.), *The father's role: Cross-cultural perspectives* (pp. 139–167). Hillsdale, NJ: Lawrence Erlbaum Associates.

Nickel, H., & Köcher, E. M. T. (1987). West Germany and the German-speaking countries. In M. E. Lamb (Ed.), *The father's role: Cross-cultural perspective* (pp. 89–114). Hillsdale, NJ: Lawrence Erlbaum Associates.

Ninio, A., & Rinott, N. (1988). Fathers' involvement in the care of their infants and their attributions of cognitive competence to infants. *Child Development, 59,* 652–663.

Notaro, P. C., & Volling, B. L. (1999). Parental responsiveness and infant–parent attachment: A replication study with fathers and mothers. *Infant Behavior and Development, 22,* 345–352.

Nugent, J. K. (1987). The father's role in early Irish socialization: Historical and empirical perspectives. In M. E. Lamb (Ed.), *The father's role: Cross-cultural perspectives* (pp. 169–193). Hillsdale, NJ: Lawrence Erlbaum Associates.

Oppenheim, D., Sagi, A., & Lamb, M. E. (1988). Infant–adult attachments on the kibbutizm and their relation to socioemotional development 4 years later. *Developmental Psychology, 24,* 427–433.

Palkovitz, R. (1985). Fathers' birth attendance, early contact, and extended contact with their newborns: A critical review. *Child Development, 56,* 392–406.

Pannabecker, B., Emde, R. N., & Austin, B. (1982). The effect of early extended contact on father–newborn interaction. *Journal of Genetic Psychology, 141,* 7–17.

Parke, R. D., & Beitel, A. (1986). Hospital-based intervention for fathers. In M. E. Lamb (Ed.), *The father's role: Applied perspectives* (pp. 293–323). New York: Wiley.

Parke, R. D., MacDonald, K. B., Burks, V. M., Carson, J., Bhavnagri, N., Barth, J. M. & Beitel, A. (1989). Family and peer systems: In search of the linkages. In K. Kreppner & R. M. Lerner (Eds.), *Family systems and life-span development* (pp. 65–92). Hillsdale, NJ: Lawrence Erlbaum Associates.

Parke, R. D., & Sawin, D. B. (1977, March). *The family in early infancy: Social interactional and attitudinal analyses.* Paper presented at the meeting of the Society for Research in Child Development, New Orleans.

Parke, R. D., & Sawin, D. B. (1980). The family in early infancy: Social interactional and attitudinal analyses. In F. A. Pedersen (Ed.), *The father–infant relationship: Observational studies in a family setting* (pp. 44–70). New York: Praeger.

Pedersen, F. A., Cain, R., Zaslow, M., & Anderson, B. (1982). Variation in infant experience associated with alternative family roles. In L. Laosa & I. Sigel (Eds.), *Families as learning environments for children* (pp. 203–221). New York: Plenum.

Pedersen, F. A., & Robson, K. (1969). Father participation in infancy. *American Journal of Orthopsychiatry, 39,* 466–472.

Pleck, J. H., & Stueve, J. L. (in press). Time and paternal involvement: Reconsideration and new data. In K. Daly (Ed.), *Minding the time in family experience: Emerging perspectives and issues.* Greenwich, CT: JAI Press.

Power, T. G. (1985). Mother– and father–infant play: A developmental analysis. *Child Development, 56,* 1514–1524.

Power, T. G., & Parke, R. D. (1979, March). *Toward a taxonomy of father–infant and mother–infant play patterns.* Paper presented to the Society for Research in Child Development, San Francisco.

Power, T. G., & Parke, R. D. (1983). Patterns of mother and father play with their 8-month-old infant: A multiple analyses approach. *Infant Behavior and Development, 6,* 453–459.

Pruett, K. (1985). Oedipal configurations in young father-raised children. *Psychoanalytic study of the child, 40,* 435–460.

Pruett, K., & Litzenberger, B. (1992). Latency development in children of primary nurturing fathers: Eight-year follow up. *Psychoanalytic Study of the Child, 4,* 85–101.

Rendina, I., & Dickerscheid, J. D. (1976). Father involvement with first-born infants. *Family Coordinator, 25,* 373–379.

Rödholm, M., & Larsson, K. (1982). The behavior of human male adults at their first contact with a newborn. *Infant Behavior and Development, 5,* 121–130.

Roggman, L. A., Benson, B., & Boyce, L. (1999). Fathers with infants: Knowledge and involvement in relation to psychosocial functioning and religion. *Infant Mental Health Journal, 20,* 257–277.

Rondal, J. A. (1980). Fathers' and mothers' speech in early language development. *Journal of Child Language, 7,* 353–369.

Roopnarine, J. L., Talukder, E., Jain, D., Joshi, P., & Srivastav, P., (1992). Personal well-being, kinship tie, and mother–infant and father–infant interactions in single-wage and dual-wage families in New Delhi, India. *Journal of Marriage and the Family, 54,* 293–301.

Rosen, K. S., & Rothbaum F. (1993). Quality of parental caregiving and security of attachment. *Developmental Psychology, 29,* 358–367.

Sagi, A., Lamb, M. E., & Gardner, W. (1986). Relations between Strange Situation behavior and stranger sociability among infants on Israeli kibbutzim. *Infant Behavior and Development, 9,* 271–282.

Sagi, A., Lamb, M. E., Shoham, R., Dvir, R., & Lewkowicz, K. S. (1985). Parent–infant interaction in families on Israeli kibbutzim. *International Journal of Behavioral Development, 8,* 273–284.

Schaffer, H. R., & Emerson, P. E. (1964). The development of social attachments in infancy. *Monographs of the Society for Research in Child Development, 29*(94).

Spelke, E., Zelazo, P., Kagan, J., & Kotelchuck, M. (1973). Father interaction and separation protest. *Developmental Psychology, 9,* 83–90.

Steele, H., Steele, M., & Fonagy, P. (1996). Associations among attachment classification of mother, fathers, and their infants. *Child Development, 67,* 541–555.

Storey, A. E., Walsh, C. J., Quinton, R. L., & Wynne-Edwards, R. E. (2000). Hormonal correlates of paternal responsiveness in new and expectant fathers. *Evolution and Human Behavior, 21,* 79–95.

Suess, G. J., Grossmann, K. E., & Sroufe, L. A. (1992). Effects of infant attachment to mother and father on quality of adaptation in preschool: From dyadic to individual organization of self. *International Journal of Behavioral Development, 15,* 43–65.

Sun, L. C., & Roopnarine, J. L. (1996). Mother–infant, father–infant interaction and involvement in childcare and household labor among Taiwanese families. *Infant Behavior and Development, 19,* 121–129.

Teti, D. M., Bond, L. A., & Gibbs, E. D. (1988). Mothers, fathers, and siblings: A comparison of play styles and their influence upon infant cognitive level. *International Journal of Behavioral Development, 11,* 415–432.

Trehub, S. E., Hill, D. S., & Kamenetsky, S. B. (1997). Parents' sung performance for infants. *Canadian Journal of Experimental Psychology, 51,* 385–396.

Trehub, S. E., Unyk, A. M., Kamenetsky, S. B., Hill, D. S., Trainor, L. J., Henderson, J. L., & Saraza, M. (1997). Mothers' and fathers' singing to infants. *Developmental Psychology, 33,* 500–507.

Van IJzendoorn, M. H. (1995). Adult attachment representation, parental responsiveness, and infant attachment: A meta-analysis of the predictive validity of the Adult Attachment Interview. *Psychological Bulletin, 117,* 387–403.

Van IJzendoorm, M. H., & De Wolff, M. S. (1977). In search of the absent father—meta-analyses of infant–father attachment: A rejoinder to our discussants. *Child Development, 68,* 604–609.

Verschueren, K., & Marcoen, A. (1999). Representation of self and socioemotional competence in kindergartners: Differential and combined effects of attachment to mother and to father. *Child Development, 70,* 183–201.

Volling, B., & Belsky, J. (1992). Infant, father, and marital antecedents of infant–father attachment security in dual-earner and single-earner families. *International Journal of Behavioral Development, 15,* 83–100.

Wachs, T., Uzgiris, I., & Hunt, J. (1971). Cognitive development in infants of different age levels and from different environmental backgrounds. *Merrill-Palmer Quarterly, 17,* 283–317.

Ward, C. D., & Cooper, R. P. (1999). A lack of evidence in 4-month-old human infants for paternal voice preference. *Developmental Psychobiology, 35,* 49–59.

Warren-Leubecker, A., & Bohannon, J. N., III (1984). Intonation patterns in child-directed speech: Mother–father differences. *Child Development, 55,* 1379–1385.

Weinraub, M., & Frankel, J. (1977). Sex differences in parent–infant interaction during free play, departure, and separation. *Child Development, 48,* 1240–1249.

West, M. M., & Konner, M. J. (1976). The role of the father: An anthropological perspective. In M. E. Lamb (Ed.), *The role of the father in child development* (pp. 185–216). New York: Wiley.

Wille, D. (1998). Longitudinal analyses of mothers' and fathers' responses on the maternal separation anxiety scale. *Merrill-Palmer Quarterly, 44,* 216–233.

Willemsen, E., Flaherty, D., Heaton, C., & Ritchey, G. (1974). Attachment behavior of one-year-olds as a function of mother vs. father, sex of child, session, and toys. *Genetic Psychology Monographs, 90,* 305–324.

Woollett, A., White, D., & Lyon, L. (1982). Observations of fathers at birth. In N. Beail & J. McGuire (Eds.), *Fathers: Psychological perspectives* (pp. 72–94). London: Junction Book.

Yarrow, L. J., MacTurk, R. H., Vietze, P. M., McCarthy, M. E., Klein, R. P., & McQuiston, S. (1984). Developmental course of parental stimulation and its relationship to mastery motivation during infancy. *Developmental Psychology, 20,* 492–503.

Yogman, M. (1981). Games fathers and mothers play with their infants. *Infant Mental Health Journal, 2,* 241–248.

Yogman, M. W., Kindlon, D., & Earls, F. (1995). Father involvement and cognitive-behavioral outcomes of preterm infants. *Journal of the American Academy of Child and Adolescent Psychiatry, 34,* 58–66.

Youngblade, L. M., & Belsky, J. (1992). Parent–child antecedents of 5-year-olds' close friendships: A longitudinal analysis. *Developmental Psychology, 28,* 700–713.

Youngblade, Y. M., Park, K. A., & Belsky, J. (1993). Measurement of young children's close friendship: A comparison of two independent assessment systems and their association with attachment security. *International Journal of Behavioral Development, 16,* 563–587.

Zaouche-Gaudron, C., Ricaud, H., & Beaumatin, A. (1998). Father–child play interaction and subjectivity. *European Journal of Psychology of Education, 13,* 447–460.

Zelazo, P. R., Kotelchuck, M., Barber, L., & David, J. (1977, March). *Fathers and sons: An experimental facilitation of attachment behaviors.* Paper presented at the meeting of the Society for Research in Child Development, New Orleans.

5

Involved Fathering and Child Development: Advancing Our Understanding of Good Fathering

Rob Palkovitz
University of Delaware

The purpose of this chapter is to review theoretical and empirical literature pertinent to two questions that have generated growing attention and debate over the past 40 years. The interrelated questions are: (1) What do we mean when we say "more father involvement" and "less father involvement"? and (2) What are the effects of varying degrees of father involvement on child development?

On the surface, these questions sound relatively straightforward, and after 40 years of increasingly focused interest, theory, instrumentation, and systematic research, straightforward answers would be expected. We have amassed literally hundreds of research studies that address these questions to greater and lesser degrees, and through selected lenses, the answers are relatively clear cut. However, as the theories, data and public discourse have unfolded across time, what appear to be simple questions have proven to have elusive answers complicated by an intricately interdependent array of definitional, methodological, ethical, and sociopolitical issues. Because these questions are not as straightforward as they initially appear through a different set of lenses, we do not have much to offer in the way of definitive answers. The first question will receive primary attention in this chapter, and the second will be briefly discussed in relation to the first.

In an introductory chapter to a recent collection of papers on fatherhood, Peters and Day (2000, p. 1) noted that despite strong and persistent interest and concern about fathers, we are far from understanding the complex ways in which fathers make contributions to their families and children. In order to consider the two central questions of this chapter with the integrity that they deserve, it is first necessary to explicitly address some of the issues inherent in the questions. In a brief analysis, this chapter will demonstrate that it is first necessary to consider the diversity of contexts and qualities of father involvement. To understand father involvement, we must consider who fathers are. Further, we must take into account many aspects of the demographics, the father's personal characteristics, developmental status, and preparation for fatherhood as well as the child's (or children's) characteristics. In considering what is meant by more or less involvement, I will argue that, in actuality, it is not the amount of involvement that is crucial for our understanding. Rather, the more critical factor is the overall quality of father involvement over time. I will further demonstrate that though the zeitgeist suggests that "more father involvement is better" for child development outcomes, in individual cases or under specific circumstances, the "more is better" perspective represents serious misconceptions. I will demonstrate that the generalized discussion of "more involved fathering" is really a proxy for "good fathering." We currently have the data to describe good fathering and to demonstrate that good fathering is correlated with positive child development outcomes. Thus, I will argue that what is needed is not more involvement; what is most beneficial is "good fathering."

WHO ARE FATHERS?

Marsiglio, Day, and Lamb (2000) recognized that definitions of fatherhood and conceptualizations of paternal involvement are inextricably interwoven. If we are to advance our conceptualization of fatherhood and paternal involvement while improving our understanding of its implications for children and families, we must update our perception of the diverse forms of fatherhood and the complex ways in which conceptualizations affect paternal involvement (Marsiglio et al., 2000). When we ask questions regarding father involvement as though fathers are a homogenous group, we mask the great diversity of fathers, the contexts of their involvement, their developmental characteristics, the challenges they face, and their responses to these variables at any given time as well as patterns across time. Peterson and Steinmetz (2000) eloquently stated that "diversity has become the norm that defines our domestic relations" (p. 316). Other writers have urged that policies and interventions for fathers must respect the enormous socioeconomic, cultural, and demographic diversity among fathers (see Hewlett, 2000). Peterson and Steinmetz (2000) summarize the diversity of fatherhood, fatherhood meanings, and fathering contexts by noting that

> fatherhood is no simple phenomenon, but a complex tapestry of many things . . . the reality [is] that fatherhood is not a static phenomenon, but more like at a moving target, only some of which has constant meaning. (p. 315)

The "seemingly simple and somewhat rhetorical question" of "Who are fathers?" is "fraught with conceptual ambiguity" because considering the question from biological, social, psychological, and legal perspectives brings different issues into play (Marsiglio et al., 2000, p. 273). Independent of disciplinary boundaries, fathers are only fathers because of relationships. A man becomes a biological father as a result of a relationship to the child's birth mother. Biological fathering is the result of a biological act with differing degrees of planning, intentionality, emotion, and commitment across different relationships. However, becoming a social father, making the transition to fatherhood (Cowan, 1991), is a different process, entailing different functions and dynamics (Daniels & Weingarten, 1988). A father is only a social father in relation to a child. Doherty, Kouneski, and Erickson (1998) assert that sociological and historical analyses clearly establish that, beyond insemination, fathering is "fundamentally a social construction" (p. 278), with each cohort shaping its own conception of fatherhood. Garbarino (2000) observed that we are currently reinventing social fatherhood.

Social fathering is a decision that can be made independent of biological status. To embrace social fathering, a man must engage in a significant reorganization of both identity and role enactment (Cowan, 1991). LaRossa (1988) noted the discrepancy between the ideals that cohorts set forth (the culture of fatherhood) and the ways that fathering roles are actually enacted (the conduct of fatherhood). Similarly, Lamb (2000) noted the discrepancies between images of nurturant and active fathers presented by journalists and filmmakers and the diversity of role conceptualizations and enactments of fathers in everyday activities.

Demographic analyses indicate that the prevalence of social fatherhood is increasing as a growing array of men are being perceived to have fatherlike roles in children's lives, in part because increasing numbers of biological fathers are disengaging from their children or were never actively involved (Marsiglio, Day, & Lamb, 2000). Involved fathering across time is a commitment that reflects an ongoing set of decisions that have behavioral, cognitive, and affective components (Palkovitz, 1997) as well as developmental consequences for both fathers and their children across time and contexts (Palkovitz, 1996).

The distinctions between biological and social fathers, residential and nonresidential, and legal fathers and men with no legal fathering rights are elucidated elsewhere in this volume (see chap. 3); the important point for our focus in this chapter is that fathering, at its core, entails relationships. Because scientific inquiry involves collection and analysis of data, it has been necessary to operationalize involvement in ways that yield observable categories and frequencies of behavior. This is artificially reductionistic because involvement is a component of relationships between a father and a child. Relationships are dynamic, developmentally fluid, contextually embedded, multifaceted, and complex. They have a developmental history and changing meaning over time (Palkovitz, 1996) as well as across cohorts (Hareven, 2000). Though the father's primary relationship is in regard to one or more children, fathering is significantly affected by other relationships, most notably to the children's mother, other family members, and other persons (e.g., friends, neighbors, coworkers). The supports and roadblocks that are introduced through these relationships influence both the culture and the conduct of father involvement for individual men.

DIVERSITY OF FATHERING CONTEXTS

The variability in contexts of father involvement is quite extensive. Men engaging in fathering roles vary by marital status, marital quality, type of fathering relationship to child, legality of paternal status, residential status, educational level, employment status, income, relationship with own father, supports and hindrances toward involvement, personality, health, range and types of involvement engaged in, predominant parenting style, beliefs about the fathers' role, cultural background, individual skill levels, and motivation. Although this list is not exhaustive, it does represent variables that are frequently reported in various studies of father involvement and begins to show the reasons that answers to our questions regarding father involvement and child development are complex and require careful consideration. Table 5.1 depicts some of the characteristics which affect fathers' involvement across time. Thus, when answering the question, "What does it mean when we say that a father is more or less involved?" the answer to the question partially depends on the current status of an individual father at the time that we are assessing his involvement in an interdependent and dynamic array of relationships to the child and others in the family and community context.

WHAT IS FATHER INVOLVEMENT?

Ross Parke (2000) posits that a "key element is to recognize how difficult it is to define the complexities of father involvement" (p. 43). Palm (1993) reduces much of the complexity by stating that men who are involved in the day-to-day responsibilities of parenting and value the importance of these activities are considered involved fathers. The literature on father involvement spanning the past 40 years is filled with different definitions of this central term and different strategies for measurement of involvement. Part of the variability in conceptualization and metrication is attributable to multidisciplinary interest in father involvement. Marsiglio et al. (2000) observed that "anthropologists, economists, family scientists, legal scholars, developmental psychologists, and sociologists specializing in family and gender studies tend to approach father involvement in unique ways, emphasizing certain features while downplaying others" (p. 276). Yet even within disciplinary boundaries, different studies employ different conceptualizations and different metrics on nonrepresentative samples in varying

TABLE 5.1

A Partial Listing of Sources of Variability in
Father Involvement Contexts

Child Characteristics	**Father's Personal Factors**
Age	Functionality
Gender	Preparation for Fatherhood
Developmental Status	Experience in Caregiving
Health	Knowledge of Child Development
Personality	Relational Style
	Authoritative
Father's Demographic Factors	Authoritarian
Age	Indulgent/Permissive
Education	Indifferent
Income	Motivation
Adequacy	Personality
Percentage of Family Provision	Skills/Abilities
Contributed	View of Father Role
Other Support Obligations	Cultural Background
Alimony	Fathering Identity
Child Support	
Marital Status	**Competing or Complementary Role**
Single	**Demands**
Cohabiting	Family
Engaged	Husband
Married	Son
Separated	Brother
Divorced	Uncle
Recohabiting	Work
Remarried	Hours Working
Relationship to Child(ren)	Job Security
Biological Father	Job-Related Stress
Social Father	Community
Legality	Involvement in Organizations
Residential Status	
Coresidential	**Relational Factors**
Nonresident, but nearby	Partner/Significant Other
Nonresident and distant	Marital Status
Timing of Transition to Fatherhood	Relational Quality
Early	Degree of Gatekeeping
On-Time	Relationship with Own Father
Late	Primacy of Modeling vs. Reworking
Employment Status	Degree of Warmth vs. Emotional
Voluntarily Unemployed	Distance
Involuntarily Unemployed	Level of Conflict
Part-Time Employed	Siblings/Extended Family
Full-Time Employed	Social Supports
Multiple Jobs	
Cultural Identity	**Father Involvement**
Religiosity	Frequencies
	Range of Behaviors
	Quality of Interactions
	Meaning of Involvement

contexts. Some studies distinguish between absolute levels of father involvement versus involvement relative to other caregivers (Parke, 2000), whereas others focus on the quality versus the quantity of paternal involvement (Palm, 1985; Parke, 2000).

In the past decade, the conceptualization and measurement of father involvement has received increasing attention. To give full consideration to this issue is beyond the scope of this chapter. Several recent reviews and conceptual papers have encapsulated the primary issues (Dollahite, Hawkins, & Brotherson, 1997; Hawkins & Dollahite, 1997; Hawkins & Palkovitz, 1999; Lamb, 2000; Palkovitz, 1997; Parke, 2000; Pleck, 1997). A fair summary would be that although our understanding and our operationalization of fatherhood and father involvement have changed over time, fatherhood has always been a multifaceted concept (Lamb, 2000). The net result is that father involvement has been viewed and indexed in different ways at different times and in different studies, making comparisons across studies difficult at best.

Much of the research on father involvement has been focused on elucidating relationships between patterns of paternal behavior and child development outcomes. Pioneering research in the field of developmental psychology linked patterns of paternal behavior and infant development. For that reason, conceptualizations and measures of father involvement focused on fathers' overtly observable behaviors—behaviors that have meaning to a sensorimotor stage child and behaviors that can reasonably be measured and quantified by observers or captured through time diaries (Hawkins & Palkovitz, 1999).

Recently, however, Palkovitz and his colleagues (Christiansen & Palkovitz, 2001; Hawkins & Palkovitz, 1999; Palkovitz, 1994, 1997) have pointed out the limitations of conceptualizations and measures that narrowly focus on paternal behaviors while ignoring the cognitive and affective domains of father involvement. Moreover, the *meaning* of various forms of father involvement has been highlighted as a needed focus for researchers and theorists to develop more fully (Christiansen & Palkovitz, 2001). The greatest point of consensus at this time is that further conceptualization is needed regarding the nature, origins, sources, and meanings of paternal involvement (Lamb, 2000; Parke, 2000; Pleck, 1997). Developing appropriate metrics is yet another challenge.

There are no widely accepted conceptual frameworks of paternal involvement that have been translated into extensively used, psychometrically reliable and valid measures. Though conceptualization has rapidly advanced in recent years, our understanding of important components of father involvement have far outstripped standardized metrics for tapping these dimensions. Significant measure development efforts have been launched by interdisciplinary teams of scholars working from emerging conceptual models (see Hawkins et al., 1999), but initial data from nationally representative samples of fathers indicate that the measures require significant refinement to capture the variability that we know exists in father involvement across diverse contexts.

Clearly, family scientists continue to struggle with what it means to be an involved father. One of the factors that has prolonged this struggle is the common failure to distinguish between structural or demographic variables that are proxies for residential status or economic provision and the social construction of fathering, which is more centered on the nature and quality of father–child interactions. Men having the same value on demographic variables (e.g., residential, full-time employed) can be at opposite ends of a continuum regarding the social construction of fathering (e.g., highly functional, authoritative vs. dysfunctional, authoritarian). Grouping fathers by similarity in structural or demographic variables masks variability in involvement levels and paternal styles. Though large-scale, nationally representative data sets are valuable resources in many regards, they have lacked qualitatively meaningful measures of father involvement. As advances are made in our understanding of meanings and contexts of father involvement, it will be crucial for family scientists to incorporate measures of paternal style and quality into large, representative samples of fathers varying across contexts. We currently know more about quantities of father involvement than we do regarding qualities of father involvement.

One of the most frequently cited and utilized frameworks for studying father involvement was proposed by Lamb, Pleck, Charnov, and Levine (1985, 1987). It conceives father involvement as including three components: (a) *paternal engagement* (direct personal interaction with the child in the form of caretaking, play, teaching, or leisure); (b) *accessibility or availability* to the child (i.e., temporal and proximal positioning that would allow the child to enter into engagement if desired or necessary); and (c) *responsibility* for the care of the child (making plans and arrangements for care as distinct from the performance of the care). Prior to the formulation of this tripartite construction, one line of research regarding the paternal behaviors and characteristics studied in father-present families tended to focus on "qualitative ones such as masculinity, power, control, warmth, responsiveness, independence training, playfulness, and the like" (Pleck, 1997, p. 67). A distinctly separate line of research considered father's engagement in specific caregiving tasks (e.g., the number of diapers changed, time spent in verbal interaction, amount of physical contact between fathers and children) (see Palkovitz, 1980; Rebelsky & Hanks, 1971). By comparison, employing the categories of engagement, accessibility, and responsibility allows a content-free construction of involvement, concerning only the quantity of fathers' behavior, time, or responsibility with their children (Pleck, 1997).

The fact remains that most empirical studies focus primary attention on a limited range of father–child interactions that are a subset of the category of engagement (Hawkins & Palkovitz, 1999; Palkovitz, 1997). Although we have a growing body of literature that looks at distinctions between various components of father involvement, the database is limited and does not comprehensively address the cognitive and affective domains of involvement or the meanings of involvement. Furthermore, studies have not systematically assessed the degree to which each of these components make unique contributions to children's developmental outcomes (Parke, 2000; Tamis-LeMonda & Cabrera, 1999).

Because involvement takes place in the context of relationships, the meaning of involvement can be quite different to the different parties involved. A father may provide what he perceives to be a high degree of involvement, whereas in his spouse's or partner's view, he contributes only a small amount of involvement. Further, what may be of primary importance from the child's perspective may not be the degree of involvement but the *quality* of father–child interaction. (Was the interaction happy? Was it fun? Did the interaction make the child feel good or competent? Conversely, did the encounter bring emotional pain, isolation, or embarrassment?) The texture of father–child interactions and their meanings are influenced by fluctuating emotional currents across time, as well as moods, expectations, and perceived needs. Thus, the developmental contributions of father involvement are cumulative, irregular, and change and compound across time with the development of the father, the child, and others in the relational context. Though we have the conceptual sophistication to recognize this, existing measures of father involvement have not captured each of these characteristics, masking some of the meanings and effects of involved fathering. Perhaps considerations such as these contributed to Joseph Pleck's (1997, p. 66) question, "How good is the evidence that fathers' *amount* of involvement, without taking into account its content and quality, is consequential for children, mothers, or fathers themselves?"

WHAT IS MEANT BY MORE OR LESS FATHER INVOLVEMENT?

Because of the lack of a universally accepted conceptualization of father involvement, answers to this question vary from study to study. However, because of the nature of the bulk of the available data, when social scientists discuss "more involvement," we commonly mean more time (Blair & Hardesty, 1994; McBride, 1990), higher frequencies of behavior (Marsiglio, 1991), or greater levels of engagement, accessibility, and/or responsibility (Lamb et al., 1985).

However, because father involvement also carries an array of significant qualitative components—the quality, sensitivity, developmental appropriateness, emotional climate, degree of connection, mutual delight, and meaning—more involvement is not always better (Palkovitz, 1994, 1997; Parke, 2000). It is theoretically possible for fathers and children to hit developmental ceiling effects or saturation points where more father involvement does not yield enhanced child development but is simply redundant (see Palkovitz, 1996, for an expanded discussion of these concepts). In such instances, more involvement represents a drain on resources of fathers' time and energy that may be more fruitfully invested elsewhere. The contexts and temporal fluctuations of paternal involvement need further consideration in future investigations.

These concerns notwithstanding, the term *more involvement* has been used to mean a wide variety of things, including more time invested in child-centered activities (Kotelchuck, 1976; McBride & Mills, 1993), more father–child contact (Palkovitz, 1980), more financial support (U.S. Census Bureau, 1987), more activities engaged in (Palkovitz, 1980), more caregiving (Haas, 1993), and more father–child play (Clarke-Stewart, 1978; MacDonald & Parke, 1986). More involvement can also mean more thinking, planning, feeling, caring, monitoring, evaluating, and praying; more energy invested; and more worrying (Palkovitz, 1997, 2000). It can also mean more priority, greater commitment, more responsibility, more of a place in the overall scheme of roles and facets of the self, more father identity (Ihinger-Tallman, Pasley, & Buehler, 1993). More involvement often means more relationship. More involvement has meant more affection, more touch, more smiles, more warmth (Palkovitz, 1980). More involvement has been conceptualized as more commitment, more sacrifice, more other-centeredness, and more investment in the next generation (Dollahite et al., 1997; Snarey, 1993). More involvement is often associated with more sensitivity to subtle signals (Nash & Feldman, 1981); more willingness to work at "getting it right"; and more motivation to build relationships, encourage children, and facilitate development (Palkovitz, 1980). More involvement can mean more mutuality, interdependence, intimacy, and resources, both psychologically (Biller & Kimpton, 1997) and economically (Tamis-LeMonda & Cabrera, 1999). Because more involvement usually entails more time in relationships across various contexts, more involvement can mean more diversity in relational styles experienced, greater potential for redundancy in meeting developmental needs, more occasions for discrimination learning (Palkovitz, 1987), and more occasions for children to model instead of engaging in reworking (Snarey, 1993) because there is a greater sample of paternal behavior from which to choose. More involvement can mean more life satisfaction for both fathers (Palkovitz, 2000) and children (Biller, 1974). More involvement can help to establish a secure base for exploration (Cohen & Campos, 1974) with different realms of movement and activity (Lamb & Sherrod, 1981) and new and different styles and worlds to explore. More involvement can mean more training, more teaching, more coaching, more instruction, more discipline, and more exposure to different contexts and perspectives for both fathers and children (Field, 1978).

From children's viewpoints, more involvement means more resources, more contrast, different styles, new perspectives, opportunities, caring, security, and encouragement. More involvement is more likely to build trust, to encourage initiative, to support industry, to enhance identity, to support the attainability of intimacy, and to create the potential for generativity (Snarey, 1993). In some studies, more father involvement has been associated with enhanced social skills (MacDonald & Parke, 1984; Pedersen, Rubenstein, & Yarrow, 1979), cognitive ability (Snarey, 1983), self-confidence (Amato, 1987), and exploration (Lamb & Sherrod, 1981) in children. Caution needs to be exercised in compiling such a list of findings because the studies reported implicitly and explicitly address only a sub-set of paternal involvement as described. Nonetheless, in each of these studies, more involvement tends to be characterized as developmentally facilitative for children. A key question would be, "What are the mechanisms by which these patterns of father involvement affect children's development?"

All of these characterizations assume that fathers are coming to the relation-ship with positive, developmentally faciliative interactions. In short, studies pub-lishing the listed meanings of more involvement assume that positive qualities are operating in the father (Pleck, 1997) and that they are present in sufficient quanti-ty to be passed on to his child. Even the best of fathers has flaws and weaknesses, aspects that need development, healing, working through, enhancement, or extraction. Clearly, more father involvement would provide a context for greater harm, greater detriment, and higher risk when men are functioning poorly, when they manifest multiple deficits, or when they model negative behaviors and inflict physical or psychological injury. Under these conditions, more involvement is not better. There is also a point where some levels and styles of involvement may become "overinvolvement," enmeshment, "smothering," "sheltering" or overly protective. When involvement reaches these levels, it may hinder children's development by suppressing appropriate independence, responsibility, and oppor-tunities to practice competencies for themselves.

In contrast, less involvement has been used to denote less engagement, acces-sibility, and responsibility; lack of resources—time, confidence, ability, skill, motivation; less role fulfillment; and less interdependence, identity, intimacy, and generativity (Snarey, 1993). Less involvement often reflects and results in more emotional and relational woundedness, both in fathers and children. Less involve-ment means less enjoyment and less development for both parties. Less involve-ment implies missed opportunities, unreached potential, and unfulfilled needs. Less involvement can mean deficits in resources for both fathers and children.

In contrast to the predominant usages in the professional literature, what is meant by the term *more involvement* has only tenuous ties to frequencies or dura-tions of involvement—its meaning has more to do with the quality, texture, depth, character, centrality, consistency, pervasiveness, and relational qualities of father-ing, call them what you will. Snarey's (1993) four-decade study of how fathers care for the next generation brought Erikson's (1963) construct of generativity and the associated virtue—care—to the attention of fathering scholars. In short, fathers who are more involved are characterized as more caring. Doherty and his colleagues (1998) and Dollahite et al. (1997) have emphasized an array of ethical components of involved fathering. The qualitative work of Cohen and Dolgin (1997) highlighted various psychological (e.g., degree of identification and prior-itization of fathering roles) and affective components (e.g., depth of perceived closeness between fathers and children) of father involvement. Pasley and her col-leagues (Ihinger-Tallman et al., 1993; Minton & Pasley, 1996) have linked identi-ty theory and father involvement to explore men's internal conceptions of appropriate paternal behavior. These studies have drawn attention to the salience of father identity and men's commitment to that identity in juxtaposition with men's engagement in directly observable interaction or time invested in their children. These perspectives, when coupled with qualitative investigations of the perceived effects of fatherhood on men's development (Palkovitz, 2000), demonstrate that men think of father involvement as multidimensional, relationally based, encompassing an array of indirect and less-observable components, multiply determined, and contextually and temporally influenced. Clearly, it is reductionistic to focus primarily on directly observable frequency tallies or time spent in direct engagement while ignoring the meaning, salience, and appropriateness of fathers' involvement with their children (Hawkins & Palkovitz, 1999; Palkovitz, 1997). However, most empirical studies report data that portray father involvement in time or frequency counts (Palkovitz, 1997). Such portrayals can lead to the "more involvement is better" perspective that is prevalent in ongoing prescriptions for fathers' engagement with their children.

In regard to father involvement, the reason that the "more is better" myth is so pervasive in our culture is because: (a) the studies that report positive relationships between father involvement and child development outcomes are grounded in the assumption that involvement is positive in quality (Pleck, 1997) and (b) so many of our children are not getting a perceived minimum daily requirement of involvement from a positively engaged father. It is true that many children would benefit from more father involvement, but only if it was appropriate, positive, building, developmentally facilitative, loving, warm, and sensitive. When we assess the relationships between varying levels and styles of paternal involvement and child development, we draw on data that reflect developmental outcome models.

WHAT ARE DEVELOPMENTAL OUTCOMES?

A long-established tradition of developmental psychologists is to assess the maturation and adaptability of people as indicators of well-being, success, or appropriate development. Because it has long been the assumption that parental influence on child development is of paramount importance, one way to assess the quality of fathering a child receives is to assess the child's developmental outcomes.

Developmental outcomes are reports of maturational or adaptive status at a particular time of data collection and are often empirically linked to another factor such as father involvement. Though most linkages reflect correlational data due to design complexities and ethical considerations, we frequently make causal inferences regarding the relationship between children's current developmental status and patterns of past or concurrent paternal involvement. In making such assessments, both the child's developmental status and the degree and/or quality of paternal involvement must be conceptualized and measured before statistical relationships between the two can be assessed.

Because significant variability exists in constructions and measures of involvement and because development is multiply determined and plastic (Magnusson & Cairns, 1996), it is somewhat hazardous to get too specific regarding relationships between patterns of paternal involvement and child development outcomes. In focusing on child outcomes, we often ignore the fact that patterns of father involvement are only one factor in a large and diverse array of possible contributors to developmental outcomes. Clearly, children's development is influenced by mothers, teachers, siblings, peers, other caregivers, other relatives, and countless other socialization agents. Beyond persons as socialization agents, other contextual factors contribute significantly to children's developmental status. The existing database does not allow us to conclusively partial out the effects of father involvement on child outcome variables.

In the same way that we evaluate the performance of other roles by product outcome evaluations (e.g., a good mechanic reliably repairs and maintains my automobile, a good teacher has students who demonstrate mastery of the subjects they have been taught), a good father has children who "turn out" well. That is, good fathers produce children who manifest positive developmental characteristics and reach achievement levels that indicate success. Looking at children's achievement in school, popularity, adjustment to friendships, and histories with penal and mental health systems is a common metric for gauging success in regard to developmental outcomes.

WHAT DO THE DATA TELL US?

What are the relationships between more and less father involvement and children's developmental outcomes? It is no longer possible to comprehensively review the literature on the effects of father involvement on child development in a chapter-length manuscript. Despite the already enormous and rapidly growing volume of published work examining the relationship between father involvement and child development, we still have a long way to go before we can confidently elucidate what is really happening. The truth is that precisely articulated relationships that hold across fathering types, child characteristics, and father–child relationship contexts are only available at "global," demographic or qualitative levels—and those answers look remarkably like common sense, conventional wisdom, and family centered ideologies.

There is a strong consensus among developmentalists who have reviewed father-involvement literature that the more extensive a father's emotional investment, attachment, provision of resources, and involvement with his children, the more beneficial it is for children in terms of cognitive competence, school performance, empathy, self-esteem, self-control, well-being, life skills and social competence (see Lamb, 1997; Marsiglio et al., 2000, MacDonald & Parke, 1984; McKeown, Ferguson, & Rooney, 1998; Pleck, 1997; Pruett, 1983; Radin, 1982, 1994). "Conversely, children are less likely to become involved in delinquent behavior if their fathers are sensitive and attentive to them; even the children of fathers who have a criminal record are less likely to become delinquent if the father spends a lot of time with them" (McKeown et al., 1998, pp. 86–87).

Parke and Brott (1999) state that "researchers over the past two decades have been nearly unanimous in their findings: "Fathers matter. And they matter a lot" (p. 5). Although no one completely understands the processes involved (Palkovitz, 1996; Parke & Brott, 1999; Tamis-LeMonda & Cabrera, 1999), involved fathering clearly benefits children, mothers, and fathers themselves (Palkovitz, 1996; Parke & Brott, 1999). Thus, encouraging fathers to be positively involved—and supporting them in their efforts to do so—is an investment that could yield important psychosocial dividends for all stakeholders.

Again, it is important to reiterate that the quality of father involvement influences the direction of child development outcomes. Pleck (1997) observes that the "more is better" nature of these findings result from defining father involvement that really reflects what he calls positive father involvement. McKeown et al. (1998) focus on the quality of fathering received as well by pointing out that:

> "authoritative" fathering, which involves providing consistent values and boundaries and relating to the child with warmth and confidence, is beneficial to the child but "authoritarian" fathering, which involves excessive discipline, control and aloofness from the child, is not. (p. 87)

In a similar vein, Parke and Brott (1999) emphasize that the quality of a father's involvement is crucial.

> Simply being there is not enough; being available and involved is what really counts. . . . kids whose fathers are cold and authoritarian, derogatory, and intrusive have the hardest time with grades and social relationships. They are, says John Gottman, even worse off than kids who live in homes with no father at all. Kids with nonsupportive dads and dads who humiliate them were the ones most likely to be headed for trouble, he says. They were the ones who displayed aggressive behavior toward their friends, they were the ones who had trouble in school, and they were the ones with problems often linked to delinquency and youth violence. (pp. 9–10)

Lamb (1997) refocuses our attention on the broader family system by asserting that "the benefits obtained by children with highly involved fathers are largely attributable to the fact that high levels of paternal involvement created family contexts in which parents felt good about their marriages and the child care arrangements they had been able to work out" (p. 12). This summary reflects the interdependent nature of fathering relationships with other relational contexts. Fathers who have histories of high levels of ongoing involvement with their children have maintained social supports and circumstances that are facilitative of high paternal involvement or they have made necessary adjustments and have overcome obstacles in their contexts. It is likely that men who are highly motivated to remain actively engaged in their children's lives and who have resilient personalities have greater capacities to accommodate changes and challenges to their involvement than less-motivated or resilient men.

WHY IS FATHER INVOLVEMENT SUCH A CHARGED TOPIC?

In recent years, growing attention has focused on father involvement as a central issue in impassioned discussions of gender equity (see Coltrane, 1996) and "family decline" (see Popenoe, 1993). In both contexts, increased father involvement has been forwarded as a fundamental part of the solution to social injustices. In regard to gender equity, men's contributions to child care and household labor as fathers are compared to women's investments as mothers. In the family decline discussions, father absence is associated with a range of negative child outcomes and challenging living conditions for families. In these contexts, arguments have been advanced to imply that, in general, men are not sufficiently engaged in father involvement. Though such assessments may be warranted in some cases, discussions of more and less father involvement can also reflect the value-charged issues of gender bias, racism, classism, or cultural elitism. Discussion of how men exceed or fall short of idealized levels of father involvement brings an evaluative component that can be threatening to families because the status quo is challenged, and the implication is that *someone* is not performing their role adequately. In short, the discussion of father involvement is inescapably value laden.

Some social scientists would charge that reviewing the data in a manner that emphasizes quality and relational contexts is prescriptive and insensitive to individual differences in fathering styles or contexts. Such views stand in stark contradiction to our tendencies as developmentalists to embrace postformal reasoning during adulthood as an achievement that furthers cognitive adaptability (King & Kitchener, 1994). Kail and Cavanaugh (2000) state that

> Postformal thought is characterized by a recognition that the truth (the correct answer) may vary from situation to situation, that solutions must be realistic in order to be reasonable, that ambiguity and contradiction are the rule rather than the exception, and that emotion and subjective factors usually play a role in thinking. (p. 342)

In postformal thinking, developmentalists esteem the superiority of the integration of multiple perspectives and the integration of cognitions, emotions, and behaviors. Positive value is placed on reasoning that goes beyond available data and integrates cognitive and emotional components. In short, postformal reasoning is viewed to be a hallmark of a well-functioning adult mind (Kail & Cavanaugh, 2000). Yet, at times, when we apply this manner of thinking to social science questions, we may be accused of forwarding personal agendas. Because of the variety of conceptualizations of father involvement, the plethora of measures, and the diversity of fathering contexts studied, in the end, the only conclusions that are meaningful result from meta-analysis. Perhaps it is time that we look beyond the traditional discourse and engage in some postformal reasoning with regard to this field.

In different sectors of parenting literature, we have terms that are associated with positive outcomes in children's development: authoritative, highly warm, moderately controlling, positive role modeling, responsible fathering, provision, connectedness, sensitivity, involvement, engagement, generativity, marital stability, and coparental cooperation. If we looked at these terms through a slightly different lens, it would appear that prescriptions for ethical relationships bear good fruit, whereas violating them brings harm. After reviewing all of this literature, in my view, the "best" level of father involvement is one that mirrors a high degree of direct interaction, instruction, and relating, coupled with intangibles such as love, mutual respect, and mutual delight (having fun), all in a manner that is consistent with ethical principles of the "golden rule" adjusted for developmental differences between fathers and children and tailored to the individual needs of each child. Men who consistently do this across time and contexts are "good fathers" who tend to have children who are developing positively.

ADVANCING AN UNDERSTANDING OF "GOOD FATHERING"

The term *involved father* is a historically derived proxy for the broader term *good father*. This is clear from the prevalence of the discourse regarding more involvement as a panacea and the assumption implicit in the literature that the involvement that fathers provide is positive (Pleck, 1997). Social scientists have avoided defining "good fathering" because such a label may be argued to be prescriptive, moralistic, and value laden. Though social scientists have been reticent to use the term, laypersons frequently employ it in statements such as, "Paul is a good dad." If pressed, they are also able to elaborate on the specific qualities that resulted in the assessment.

In fact, there has already been a call for researchers to elaborate on this construction in the professional literature. Marsiglio et al. (2000), stated:

> Researchers should also strive to develop a more systematic portrait of how men, women, and children from different family structure, class, and race/ethnic backgrounds view aspects of fatherhood. How is "good" fathering defined and how are these definitions conditioned by individual, interpersonal, and more macro or cultural level factors? (p. 288)

Taking into account variability in contextual and developmental resources and norms, we are now in a position to begin to synthesize the various definitions and meanings of father involvement, good dads and bad dads (Furstenberg, 1988), responsible fathering (Doherty et al., 1998), and generative fathering (Hawkins & Dollahite, 1997) and to couple them with practice that we know to be developmentally faciliative, such as authoritative styles and parenting characteristics associated with secure attachments, and to outline components that are central to defining "good fathering." Although there is undoubtedly considerable variability in what may merit such a label overall, there is a core cluster of features that are positively valued. It is essential to recognize that no father will exhibit all of these characteristics, and that considerable variability would exist in what components individual men value and aspire to achieve. The bottom line is that when men do "enough" of the things in this list and when they achieve above expectation for the resources they have or for the norms of their community, they are viewed in "heroic" manner and called "good dads"—who are venerated as models for others in similar circumstances to emulate.

Though different people hold different definitions of "good fathering," and some would assert that even naming such a construct is inappropriate, most people operate on implicit assumptions about good fathering. They would prefer to have a good dad for a father, a partner, and a father of their children. They would readily recognize one when they saw him, and they would, on reflection, be able to specify the attributes that make the individual a "good dad." Though there has been great resistance to making these values explicit, an honest assessment of the contemporary literature reveals a less-explicit and value laden content as well. Specifically, the language of involved fatherhood is couched in terms that already reflect these underlying values to varying degrees.

We are quick to talk about respecting differences and about the political correctness of various constructions of involvement, but responsible people would not espouse that "whatever a man wants to do is acceptable." Extreme examples would be that physical abuse is not tolerable, nor is teaching children drug dependence tolerable. It is easy to espouse the position that we must respect diversity and individual choice, but we really mean that we respect those values within limits that are determined by other cultural norms and a sense of ethics and values. Such norms and values shape the way we view "positive involvement," "developmentally appropriate practice," "generative fathering," and other constructs that bear on this discussion.

Fathering scholars have begun to make their assumptions more explicit. Pleck (1997) elaborated on Lamb et al. (1985) construct of the "involved father" to advance the concept of positive involvement. Doherty and his colleagues (1998) have discussed responsible fathering. Dollahite et al. (1997) have advanced the notion of generative fathering. Doherty et al. (1998) used the term *responsible fathering,* originally used by the Department of Health and Human Services in commissioning their work, to describe some elements of what I would more inclusively label "good fathering." Doherty et al. (1998) assert that their use of this term reflects a contemporary shift away from "value-free" language and suggest an "ought," a "set of desired norms," a "moral meaning," and an explicit statement of long-standing and often implicit values that men should be more committed, nurturant, and involved in children's lives. Some social scientists justify the use of these terms by virtue of their association with positively valued outcomes such as social competence, fairness, and fewer behavior problems—outcomes that would be endorsed quite unanimously. These are value judgments as well.

Other writers have begun to espouse values regarding father involvement as well. Marsiglio et al. (2000) conceptualized father involvement by "emphasizing men's positive, wide-ranging, and active participation in their children's lives" (p. 276). Pleck (1997) noted that

> The development most affecting the study of both sources and consequences [of paternal involvement] is the tacit shift in measurement noted throughout this chapter from paternal involvement per se to positive paternal involvement. . . . Since most measures used currently incorporate a substantial component of positive content, they actually assess positive paternal involvement. These measures tap the dimension of paternal behavior that actually should be of primary interest. Positive paternal involvement means high engagement, accessibility and responsibility with positive engagement behaviors and stylistic characteristics. In essence, positive involvement means not just "going through the motions" of fatherhood. (p. 102)

In one of the most clear and explicit statements of values regarding father involvement, Dollahite et al. (1997) set forth a "conceptual ethic" of generative fathering. In doing so, they clearly stated that generative fathering is meant to be viewed as a framework that is intended to suggest what is possible and desirable. Generative fathering is presented as a moral call for men to meet the needs of their children.

"Good fathering" reflects the synthesis of the affective, cognitive, and behavioral attributes of involved fathering just reviewed, positive father involvement, responsible fathering, and generative fathering. These characteristics and relational qualities characterize the practice of good fathering in behavior, affect, and cognitions across time and contexts (Palkovitz, 1997). In short, good fathering is characterized by a high degree of engagement with, accessibility to, and responsibility for children, each of which reflects fathers' sensitivity, mutual delight, developmentally facilitative practice, and other-centered ethics. Good fathering entails men investing in ongoing, adaptive relationships with their children in an appropriate level (quantity) of child-centered (quality) care. Good fathering is reflective of child-centered developmentally appropriate and developmentally facilitative practice.

Recent qualitative data have documented that men who have made the commitment to good fathering and who persevere across time, contexts, and life's inevitable hurdles tend to consider the costs inconsequential in comparison to the overall gains for children, families, self, and communities (Palkovitz, 2000). For some, the decision is deliberate, carefully weighed, and well-articulated and becomes an enduring and central role and prescription for ongoing involvement. Good fathering becomes a central organizing tendency, a prime objective, a principal value. For others, the commitment to good fathering that seemed clear and promising at one time in their lives loses its luster in the face of deteriorating relationships with former spouses or partners, hurdles, pain, failures, substance abuse, or other ongoing issues. Instead of embracing a vision of good fathering and operationalizing it through making it a life rule or central value, some men have merely glimpsed it as a good idea or an ancillary to marriage, cohabitation, employment, or residential status. Perhaps some families can be helped by programs that assist men in making plans and decisions about how to maintain positive involvement across time and contexts in the face of great challenges. In a manner that parallels the literature on "good marriages," what appears to be most needed for good fathering is a value for relationships that endure and transcend shifting contexts.

CONCLUSIONS

This review of research literature could lead to the mistaken belief that by listing all of the external characteristics associated with good fathering, we can "build a better dad." Placing men into the external conditions or contexts that recreate positive contexts for fathering will ultimately not be a panacea. Contexts of development certainly facilitate or hinder the expression of father involvement, but good fathering reflects a commitment to building enduring and positive relationships. Social fathering requires an ongoing set of decisions. Putting a man in a residential, married context may enhance the likelihood of expression of certain paternal behaviors, but the context is neither necessary nor sufficient. Countless men, despite being neither married nor coresidential, nonetheless exhibit exemplary paternal involvement (whether they are biological fathers or not, or legal fathers or not). Marital and residential status are not sufficient to elicit good fathering because untold numbers of wives and children in homes with resident married fathers suffer from lack of father involvement, neglect, or harmful patterns of father involvement. Although active, good fathering is undoubtedly easier to maintain in some sets of circumstances (e.g., happy marriages, residential status, employment with a living wage, education, health) than others (e.g., divorce, illness, unemployment, nonresidential status, low educational attainment), good fathering can be maintained without these supports if there is sufficient motivation and perseverance. We have all observed men in challenging circumstances who overcome roadblocks and persist in good fathering. We have seen the developmental benefits in the lives of their children, regardless of age, gender, or developmental status.

These facts would lead us to conclude that, although contexts of fathering can support good fathering, there are factors beyond context that play a determinative role. Perhaps it would serve us well to study men who view good fathering along the lines of a "calling," a "destiny," an axis mundi, or a "regula" that produces consistently positive paternal involvement across contexts, time, and developing and changing relationships.

In specifying the characteristics of father involvement that potentially yield positive developmental outcomes for children, it is important that we not mask individual variability in what is needed in specific relationships. Though we can delineate the general qualities associated with good fathering, it is imperative that we do not apply the constructs in a universal "recipe," ignoring the unique relational characteristics and cultural and contextual distinctives. Further, it is essential to recognize that there are costs associated with good fathering. Good relationships can be costly—to the self, to individualism, to independence, to spontaneity, to responsibility, to order, to predictability, to control, to disposable cash, to leisure time, and to educational and career attainment, among other dimensions. Involved fathers are able to articulate the costs and benefits of engagement in their children's lives, but involved fathers perceive that the costs of not engaging in good fathering are even more costly (Palkovitz, 2000).

There are legitimate reasons to want to know what different patterns of paternal involvement contribute to the development of children so that we can provide training and supports for the corequisite skills, so that we can enhance contexts for father–child relationships, and so that we can create policies that will yield the greatest probability for positive outcomes. But in the end, there are a lot of qualitative intangibles that are not reducible to numbers and that are not predictable in the realm of social science. Some would argue that these have little bearing in the scope of scientific writing. But the quality of life, the changing texture of relationships, and the fruit that they bear, are the fabric that make up families and our society.

Many components of good fathering are largely a matter of the heart. Explicit statements concerning the value of good fathering for children, for families, for men, and for communities may bring shifts in the culture of fatherhood that will forerun parallel shifts in the conduct of good fathering.

REFERENCES

Amato, P. R. (1987). Children in Australian families: The growth of competence. Upper Saddle River, NJ: Prentice Hall.
Biller, H. B. (1974). Paternal deprivation: Family, school, sexuality, and society. Lexington, MA: Lexington.
Biller, H. B., & Kimpton, J. L. (1997). The father and the school-aged child. In M. E. Lamb (Ed.), *The role of the father in child development* (3rd ed., pp. 143–161). New York: Wiley.
Blair, S. L., & Hardesty, C. (1994). Paternal involvement and the well-being of fathers and mothers of young children. *Journal of Men's Studies, 3,* 49–68.

Christiansen, S., & Palkovitz, R. (2001). Providing as a form of paternal involvement: Why the "good provider" role still matters. *Journal of Family Issues, 22,* 84–106.

Clarke-Stewart, K. A. (1978). And daddy makes three: The father's impact on mother and young child. *Child Development, 49,* 466–478.

Cohen, L. J., & Campos, J. J. (1974). Father, mother and stranger as elicitors of attachment behaviors in infancy. *Developmental Psychology, 10,* 146–154.

Cohen, T. F., & Dolgin, K. G. (1997, November 9). *Both sides now: A two-generational assessment of emotional and psychological dimensions of father involvement.* Paper presented at the National Council on Family Relations, Arlington, VA.

Coltrane, S. (1996). *Family man: Fatherhood, housework and gender equity.* New York: Oxford University Press.

Cowan, P. A. (1991). Individual and family life transitions: A proposal for a new definition. In P. A. Cowan and M. Hetherington (Eds.), *Family transitions.* Hillsdale, NJ: Lawrence Erlbaum Associates.

Daniels, P., & Weingarten, K. (1988). The fatherhood click: The timing of parenthood in men's lives. In P. Bronstein and C. P. Cowan (Eds.), *Fatherhood today: Men's changing role in the family* (pp. 36–52). New York: Wiley.

Doherty, W. J., Kouneski, E. F., & Erickson, M. F. (1998). Responsible fathering: An overview and conceptual framework. *Journal of Marriage and the Family, 60,* 277–292.

Dollahite, D. C., Hawkins, A. J., & Brotherson, S. E. (1997). Fatherwork: A conceptual ethic of fathering as generative work. In A. J. Hawkins & D. C. Dollahite (Eds.), *Generative fathering: Beyond deficit perspectives* (pp. 17–35). Thousand Oaks, CA: Sage.

Erikson, E. (1963). *Childhood and society.* New York: W. W. Norton.

Field, T. (1978). Interaction behaviors of primary versus secondary caretaker fathers. *Developmental Psychology, 14,* 183–84.

Furstenberg, F. F., Jr. (1988). Good dads-bad dads: Two faces of fatherhood. In A. J. Cherlin (Ed.), *The changing American family and public policy* (pp. 193–218). Washington, DC: Urban Institute Press.

Garbarino, J., (2000). The soul of fatherhood. *Marriage and Family Review, 29,* 11–21.

Hareven, T. K. (2000). *Families, history and social change: Life-course and cross-cultural perspectives.* Boulder, CO: Westview Press.

Haas, L. (1993). Nurturing fathers and working mothers: Changing gender roles in Sweden. In J. C. Hood (Ed.), *Men, work and family* (pp. 238–261). Newbury Park, CA: Sage.

Hawkins, A. J., Bradford, K. P., Christiansen, S. L., Palkovitz, R., Call, V. R. A., & Day, R. D. (1999, November). *The inventory of father involvement: A pilot study of a new measure of father involvement.* Paper presented at the National Council on Family Relations, Irvine, CA.

Hawkins, A. J., & Dollahite, D. C. (1997). Beyond the role-inadequacy perspective of fathering. In A. J. Hawkins & D. C. Dollahite (Eds.), *Generative fathering: Beyond deficit perspectives* (pp. 3–16). Thousand Oaks, CA: Sage.

Hawkins, A. J., & Palkovitz, R. (1999). Beyond ticks and clicks: The need for more diverse and broader conceptualizations and measures of father involvement. *Journal of Men's Studies, 8,* 11–32.

Hewlett, B. S. (2000). Culture, history and sex: Anthropological contributions to conceptualizing father involvement. *Marriage and Family Review, 29,* 59–73.

Ihinger-Tallman, M., Pasley, K., & Buehler, C. (1993). Developing a middle-range theory of father involvement postdivorce. *Journal of Family Issues, 15,* 550–571.

Kail, R. V., & Cavanaugh, J. C. (2000). *Human development: A lifespan view* (2nd ed.). Belmont, CA: Wadsworth.

King, P. M., & Kitchener, K. S. (1994). *Developing reflective judgment: Understanding and promoting intellectual growth and critical thinking in adolescents and adults.* San Francisco: Jossey-Bass.

Kotelchuck, M. (1976). The infant's relationship to the father: Experimental evidence. In M. E. Lamb (Ed.), *The role of the father in child development* (pp. 329–344). New York: Wiley.

Lamb, M. E. (1997). Fathers and child development: An introductory overview. In M. E. Lamb (Ed.), *The role of the father in child development* (3rd ed., pp. 1–18). New York: Wiley.

Lamb, M. E. (2000). The history of research on father involvement: An overview. *Marriage and Family Review, 29,* 23–42.

Lamb, M. E., Pleck, J. H., Charnov, E. L., & Levine, J. A. (1985). Paternal behavior in humans. *American Zoologist, 25,* 883–894.

Lamb, M. E., Pleck, J. H., Charnov, E. L., & Levine, J. A. (1987). A biosocial perspective on paternal behavior and involvement. In J. B. Lancaster, J. Altmann, A. Rossi, & L. R. Sherrod (Eds.), *Parenting across the lifespan: Biosocial dimensions* (pp. 111–142). New York: Aldine de Gruyter.

Lamb, M. E., & Sherrod, L. R. (Eds.). (1981). *Infant social cognition: Empirical and theoretical considerations.* Hillsdale, NJ: Lawrence Erlbaum Associates.

LaRossa, R. (1988). Fatherhood and social change. *Family Relations, 37,* 451–457.

MacDonald, K., & Parke, R. D. (1986). Parent–child physical play: The effects of sex and age of children and parents. *Sex Roles, 7–8,* 367–379.

Magnusson, D., & Cairns, R. B. (1996). Developmental science: Toward a unified framework. In R. B. Cairns, G. H. Elder, & E. J. Costello (Eds.), *Developmental science* (pp. 1–22). Cambridge: Cambridge University Press.

Marsiglio, W. (1991). Paternal engagement activities with minor children. *Journal of Marriage and the Family, 53,* 973–986.

Marsiglio, W., Day, R. D. & Lamb, M. E. (2000). Exploring fatherhood diversity: Implications for conceptualizing father involvement. *Marriage and Family Review, 29,* 269–293.

McBride, B. A. (1990). The effects of a parent education/play group program on father involvement in child rearing. *Family Relations, 39,* 250–256.

McBride, B. A., & Mills, G. (1993). A comparison of mother and father involvement with their pre school age children. *Early Childhood Education Quarterly, 8,* 457–477.

McKeown, K., Ferguson, H., & Rooney, D. (1998). *Changing fathers?* Cork, Ireland: Collins Press.

Minton, C., & Pasley, K. (1996). Fathers' parenting role identity and father involvement: A comparison of nondivorced and divorced nonresident fathers. *Journal of Family Issues, 17,* 26–45.

Nash, S. C., & Feldman, S. S. (1981). Sex role and sex-related attributions: Constancy and change across the family life cycle. In M. E. Lamb & A. L. Brown (Eds.), *Advances in developmental psychology* (Vol. 1, pp. 1–35). Hillsdale, NJ: Lawrence Erlbaum Associates.

Palkovitz, R. (1980). Predictors of involvement in first-time fathers. *Dissertation Abstracts International, 40,* 3603B-3604B. (University Microforms No. 8105035)

Palkovitz, R. (1987). Consistency and stability in the family microsystem environment. In D. L. Peters & S. Kontos (Eds.), *Annual advances in applied developmental psychology* (Vol. II, pp. 40–67). New York: Ablex.

Palkovitz, R. (1994, November). *Rethinking "involvement": Fathers and families in flux.* Paper presented at the meeting of the National Council on Family Relations, Minneapolis, MN.

Palkovitz, R. (1996). Parenting as a generator of adult development: Conceptual issues and implications. *Journal of Social and Personal Relationships, 13,* 571–592.

Palkovitz, R. (1997). Reconstructing "involvement": Expanding conceptualizations of men's caring in contemporary families. In A. J. Hawkins & D. C. Dollahite (Eds.), *Generative fathering: Beyond deficit perspectives* (pp. 200–216). Thousand Oaks, CA: Sage.

Palkovitz, R. (2000, November). *The bottom line: Men's perceptions of costs and benefits of active fathering.* National Council on Family Relations, Minneapolis, MN.

Palm, G. (1985, March). *Quality time: The search for intimacy.* International Symposium on the Future of Parenting. International Society for Research in Parenting, Chicago.

Palm, G. (1993). Involved fatherhood: A second chance. *Journal of Men's Studies, 2,* 139–155.

Parke, R. D. (2000). Father involvement: A developmental perspective. *Marriage and Family Review, 29,* 43–58.

Parke, R. D., & Brott, A. A. (1999). *Throwaway dads: The myths and barriers that keep men from being the fathers they want to be.* Boston: Houghton Mifflin Company.

Pedersen, F. A., Rubenstein, J. L., & Yarrow, L. J. (1979). Infant development in father-absent fami-
    lies. *Journal of Genetic Psychology, 135,* 51–61.
Peters, H. E., & Day, R. D. (2000). Editor's introduction. *Marriage and Family Review, 29,* 1–9.
Peterson, G. W., & Steinmetz, S. K. (2000). The diversity of fatherhood: Change, constancy and con-
    tradiction. *Marriage and Family Review, 29,* 3115–322.
Pleck, J. H. (1997). Paternal involvement: Levels, sources, and consequences. In M. E. Lamb (Ed.),
    The role of the father in child development (3rd ed., pp. 66–103). New York: Wiley.
Popenoe, D. (1993). American family decline, 1960–1990: A review and appraisal. *Journal of Mar-
    riage and the Family, 55,* 527–542.
Pruett, K. (1983). Infants of primary nurturing fathers. *Psychoanalytic Study of the Child, 38,*
    257–277.
Radin, N. (1982). Primary care-giving and role-sharing fathers. In M. Lamb (Ed.), *Non-traditional
    families: Parenting and child development* (pp. 173–204). Hillsdale, NJ: Lawrence Erlbaum Asso-
    ciates.
Radin, N. (1994). Primary care-giving fathers in intact families. In A. Gottfried & A. Gottfried (Eds.),
    Redefining families: Implications for children's development (pp. 11–54). New York: Plenum.
Rebelsky, F. G., & Hanks, C. (1971). Fathers' verbal interaction with infants in the first three months
    of life. *Child Development, 42,* 63–68.
Snarey, J. (1993). *How fathers care for the next generation: A four decade study.* Cambridge, MA:
    Harvard University Press.
Tamis-LeMonda, C., & Cabrera, N. (1999). Perspectives on father involvement: Research and policy.
    Social Policy Report 13(2), 1–26.
U.S. Census Bureau (1987, September). Child support and alimony: 1985 (advance data from
    March–April 1986 current population surveys). *Current Population Reports,* Series P-23, No. 9, 38.

6

Fathers' Contributions to Children's Peer Relationships

Ross D. Parke
David J. McDowell
Mina Kim
Colleen Killian
Jessica Dennis
Mary L. Flyr
Margaret N. Wild
University of California, Riverside

Families have traditionally been viewed as the major socialization agency for the development of children's social behavior, but our definition of family has undergone considerable revision in the last three decades. First, our view of the mother–child dyad as the central unit has been replaced by a view of the family as a social system in which fathers, siblings, and the marital relationship are all important in children's socialization. Second, it is increasingly recognized that social development is best understood as a contextual process in which extended families, adult mentors, children's peers, and friends play a role as well. There is no doubt that children's relationships with their peers play a significant role in children's later adjustment. Early problems with peers have been linked to elevated feelings of loneliness and depression in childhood (Asher, Parkhurst, Hymel, & Williams, 1990; Boivin, Poulin, & Vitaro, 1994) as well as higher rates of school dropout, delinquency, and adult criminality (Parker & Asher, 1987). The aim of this chapter is to articulate the links between families, especially fathers, and children's relationships with peers.

Several perspectives on the nature of the relation between families and peers as well as the relative importance of family and peers in childhood socialization are available. In his classic formulation of this issue, Hartup (1979) noted that children's relationships with peers are viewed as either independent of family ties or interdependent social systems. Advocates of the "independent view" argue that family and peer systems develop separately, and each perform unique functions in the socialization process (e.g., Harlow, 1958). More recently, some writers (e.g., Harris, 1995, 1998) have extended the independence argument and proposed that parents have little influence on children's behavior beyond a biological or genetic contribution, especially during adolescence. Instead, Harris argues that the peer group is largely responsible for socialization of children's social behavior. In contrast to the independent view, others argue that family and peer systems mutually influence each other in the course of socialization (Parke, Simpkins, et al. in press a). Most recent accounts, and the viewpoint that guides this chapter, suggest that families and peers both play important roles in children's social development and recognize the interdependence between these two social systems.

It is further assumed that fathers and mothers play unique as well as overlapping roles in the family. Fathers are best understood through the lens of a family systems theoretical perspective, which assumes that individual family members are influenced by sets of relationships (father–child, mother–father, mother–father–child) formed with other family members (chap. 4; Parke, 1996). Similarly, peer relationships are best appreciated from a social systems viewpoint that recognizes that children form a variety of types of relationships—acquaintanceships, close dyadic friendships, and peer group relationships—and that these relationship types are both distinctive and mutually influence each other (Rubin, Bukowski, & Parker, 1998; Parke, Simpkins, et al., in press a). Moreover, it is assumed that there are unique and similar links for fathers and mothers with their children's peer relationships. Finally, the nature of family–peer relationships vary across developmental periods as well as across different family types and ecological, historical, and cultural contexts. Our goal is to provide a contemporary perspective on the roles played by fathers as part of the family system in the development of children's peer relationships.

The chapter is organized around several themes. First, a three-pathway model is outlined that suggests fathers influence their children's peer relationships by (a) the nature of the father–child relationship, (b) the type of direct advice and supervision fathers provide concerning peer relationships, and (c) the opportunities fathers provide their children for peer contact. Second, fathers impact their children's peer relationships through the marital relationship. Direct and indirect models of marital influence will be discussed. Third, the unique and cumulative roles of mothers and fathers in their development of peer relationships will be noted. Finally, future directions in the study of fathers' roles in peer relationships will be discussed.

FATHER–PEER RELATIONSHIPS: A THREE-PATHWAY MODEL

There are many ways in which fathers influence their children's relationships with peers. We propose that there are three different paths that lead to variations in children's peer relationships. These three paths include lessons learned in the context of the father–child relationship, fathers' direct advice concerning peer relationships, and father's regulation of access to peers and peer-related activity. Although our focus is on fathers, it is important to recognize that mothers play these roles as well. To the extent that the literature permits, we will note the ways in which mothers and fathers differ in how they influence their children's peer relationships.

Pathway One: The Father–Child Relationship and Peer Relationships

In considering the first pathway, two approaches have been taken: namely, studying the effects of father's absence and direct assessment of the father–child relationship.

Father Absence and Peer Relationships.   Evidence that fathers matter for children's peer relationships came initially from studies of father absence. Although these studies have been criticized (Hetherington & Deur, 1972; Pedersen, 1976), they provide suggestive evidence and merit brief discussion. Stolz (1954) studied children who were infants during World War II, when many of their fathers were away at war. When the children were 4 to 8 years old, Stolz found that those whose fathers had been absent during their infancy had poorer peer relationships. Studies of the sons of Norwegian sailors, who are away for many months at a time, pointed to the same conclusion: The boys whose fathers are often absent are less popular and have less-satisfying peer-group relationships than boys whose fathers who are regularly available (Lynn & Sawyer, 1959). Possibly boys who grow up without their fathers have less chance to learn the behaviors that other boys in their culture value. They may, for example, tend to be shy, timid, and reluctant to play rough games—traits that are correlated with poor peer relationships (Rubin et al., 1998).

More recent and more compelling evidence of the potential detrimental impact of fathers' absence on children's social adjustment comes from the National Longitudinal Survey of Youth (Mott, 1994). This study involved a large national sample of mothers and children who were between 5 and 9 years of age when they were assessed. The data from this sample of children and their mothers confirm that children in homes where the father is absent are at higher risk for school and peer problems. But the gender and race of the child qualify the picture. White boys from father-absent homes were affected most severely in contrast to white boys from homes where a father was in residence. Only 9% of the White boys from father-present homes were rated by their mothers as "not liked by their peers," whereas over 25% of the White boys from father-absent homes were unpopular with their age-mates. Similarly, there is some evidence that White girls from father-absent homes are at a behavioral disadvantage in comparison with White girls in a home with a father. The effects on White girls are much less than on White boys, however, and the problems are different. As is often found, boys tend to act out or externalize whereas girls tend to display an internalizing pattern. Girls exhibit cheating

and lying and low remorse after misbehavior—relatively passive behavior problems. They also tend to become overly dependent and have difficulty paying attention but unlike boys do not get into trouble at school. Similar to boys, however,
White girls from father-absent homes have more trouble getting along with other
children than girls from father-present families. For African-American boys or girls,
there is very little evidence of adverse behavior associated with a father's absence.
The patterns for the White children are not due to the early effects of maternal and
family background (for example, a mother's education, income, or health) that are
present before the father leaves the home. The effects are reduced, however, when
factors linked with the disruption of the father's departure—such as family income
or long-term maternal health—are taken into account.

Mott (1994) suggests that the reason for these racial differences may lie in the
pattern of the father's absence in Black and White homes:

> Black fathers are much more likely to have been absent from the home very early in
> the child's life. In contrast . . . white fathers are more likely to leave in the preschool
> and early school ages and in all likelihood, are more likely to keep leaving in the
> years ahead. For Black children, the biological father, if he is going to leave, is
> probably gone. For white children, the father leaving process will represent a con-
> tinuing drama throughout the children's early and mid-school years . . . the depar-
> ture of parents when children are at the school ages probably represents a greater
> potential for ongoing psychological damage than does father-leaving at very early
> ages. (p. 207)

In addition, although there are nearly three times as many Black children as
White children without father or father figure present, Black fathers are more
likely to continue to maintain contact with their offspring than white fathers
(Mott, 1994). The traditional reliance of Black families on extended kin networks
for support may be a further factor in accounting for the lessened impact of
fathers' absence on Black children.

In summary, father absence is linked with decrements in peer relationships,
although this effect varies with the race and gender of the child. However, these
studies leave unanswered central questions about the causes of the effects of
father absence on children's peer competence, such as the specific aspects of the
fathers' attitudes and behaviors that may lead to poorer peer relationships. At the
same time, progress is being made in eliminating alternative explanations, such as
maternal stress and reduced income, which are often associated with father
absence (McLanahan, 1997). This work more clearly implicates father absence as
the probable cause of these outcomes. To better understand the specific aspects of
the father–child relationship that may be important in explaining these
father–peer links, next we examine the evidence concerning the effects of variation in father–child relationships in father-present families on children's relationships with peers.

The Quality of the Father–Child Relationship

Researchers have examined the impact of the quality of the father–child relationship on children's relationships with their peers from two perspectives. First, those in the attachment tradition have explored the connection between the infant–father attachment and social adaptation in the peer group. The second tradition focuses on the links between the quality of father–child interaction, especially in play, and children's peer relationships.

Attachment and children's social adaptation. An impressive amount of research suggests that the quality of the child–mother attachment is related to children's later social and emotional development—in preschool, in middle childhood, and even in adolescence. A secure attachment is likely to lead to better social and emotional adjustment. Children are better liked by others, have higher self-esteem, and are more socially skilled (Thompson, 1998). Does the quality of the infant's or child's attachment to the father matter? Suess, Grossman, and Sroufe (1992) suggest that the quality of the infant–father relationship at 12 and 18 months is related to children's later behavior with their preschool age-mates. In this German study, children with more-secure infant–father attachments showed fewer negative emotional reactions during play, showed less tension in their interactions with other children, and managed to solve conflicts by themselves rather seeking the teacher's assistance in settling their disputes with classmates. Mothers, of course, were important as well; the infant–mother attachment relationship was an even stronger predictor than the infant–father attachment of children's social adjustment. (See chap. 4 for a review of infant–father attachment issues.)

Father–child interaction and children's social adaptation. In contrast to the attachment tradition, researchers in the cognitive social learning tradition assume that face-to-face interactions between children and fathers may afford children the opportunity to learn social skills that are necessary for successful peer relationships (see Parke & O'Neil, 1997, for a fuller description). This research has shown that controlling parent interactional styles is related to negative social outcomes for children, and that warm interactional styles are related to positive social outcomes. In addition, these studies suggest that fathers' ability as a play partner is positively linked to children's social competence with peers. In an early study, MacDonald and Parke (1984) observed fathers and their 3- and 4-year-old boys and girls in 20 minutes of structured play in their homes. Teachers ranked these children in terms of their popularity among their preschool classmates. For both boys and girls, fathers who exhibited high levels of physical play with their children and elicited high levels of positive feelings during the play sessions had children who received the highest peer popularity ratings. For boys, however, this pattern was qualified by the fathers' level of directiveness. Boys whose fathers were both highly physical and low in directiveness received the highest popularity ratings, and the boys whose fathers were highly directive received lower popularity scores. Girls whose teachers rated them as popular had physically playful and feeling-eliciting but nondirective fathers and directive mothers. Later studies confirm this general pattern. Popular children have fathers who are able to sustain physical play for longer periods and use less directive or coercive tactics (See Parke, Cassidy, Burks, Carson, & Boyum, 1992; Parke, Burks, Carson, Neville, & Boyum, 1994). Barth and Parke (1993) found that fathers who were more effective play partners had children who made a more successful transition to elementary school. Other researchers report that the style of father–child play is important as well. Lindsey, Moffett, Clausen, and Mize (1994) have found that preschool children whose play with their fathers was characterized by mutuality or balance in making play suggestions and following partners' suggestions were less aggressive and more competent and were better liked by their peers. Children's friendships are also influenced by their relationship with their fathers. Youngblade and Belsky (1992) found that a positive father–child relationship at age 3 was associated with less-negative and less-asynchronous friendships at age 5, whereas more-negative father–child relationships forecast less-satisfactory friendships.

The quality of the emotions displayed by fathers and children during play is a further important predictor of social competence with other children as well. Perhaps children model their parents' emotional expressions; children rejected by their peers may have learned to settle their problems in an angry and sometimes aggressive fashion. Emulating their parents' negative and angry tactics and emotions can lead to maladaptive behavior for children with their peers and friends. Carson and Parke (1996) found that preschool-age children whose fathers showed more anger were more likely to be rejected by their peers than children of fathers who show less anger. In addition, when fathers were more likely to engage in reciprocal exchanges of negative feelings with their children, teachers rated these children as aggressive and low in sharing. In contrast, when parents responded to children's positive expressions with positive reactions of their own their children were more popular with their peers (Carson & Parke, 1996; Isley, O'Neil, Clatfelter, & Parke, 1999). A similar pattern is evident in observations of families at dinner. Boyum and Parke (1995) found that kindergarten -age children whose fathers displayed less anger themselves were better accepted by their peers. Finally, Isley, O'Neil, and Parke (1996) found that fathers' negative emotions expressed during play with their sons not only was related to how well their 5-year-old boys were accepted by their classmates concurrently but also was associated with their sons' social acceptance 1 year later. Although there is often overlap between mothers and fathers, this study showed that fathers make a unique contribution independent of the mothers' contribution to their children's social development.

MEDIATING PROCESSES THAT LINK FATHER–CHILD INTERACTION AND PEER OUTCOMES

A variety of processes have been hypothesized as mediators between parent–child interaction and peer outcomes. These include affect management skills such as emotion encoding and decoding skills, emotion regulatory abilities, cognitive representations, attributions and beliefs, problem-solving skills, and attention-regulation abilities (Ladd, 1992; Parke et al., 1994). It is assumed that these abilities or beliefs are acquired in the course of parent–child interchanges over the course of development and, in turn, guide the nature of children's behavior with their peers. It is also assumed that these styles of interacting with peers may, in turn, determine children's level of acceptance by their peers. In this chapter, we focus on the three sets of processes that seem particularly promising candidates for mediator status, namely, affect management skills, cognitive representational processes, and attention-regulation skills.

Affect Management: A Mediator Between Parents and Peers

It is not only the quality of emotions that fathers display that matters to children's social development, but also how children and their fathers deal with emotional displays. What do children learn from playing with their fathers? Being able to read a play partner's emotional signals and to send clear emotional cues is critical for successfully maintaining ongoing play activities. These skills allow partners to modulate their playful behavior so that neither becomes overly aroused or too understimulated, and play continues at an optimal level of excitement for both. Children learn to recognize others' emotions, improve their own emotional skills, and regulate their emotions in the context of parent–child play (Parke et al., 1992). Father–child play may be a particularly important context, because its range of excitement and arousal is higher than in the more-modulated play of mothers and children.

Are they accepting and helpful when children become distressed, angry, or sad, or are they dismissing and rejecting? Several researchers have found that fathers' comforting and acceptance of their children's emotional distress is linked with more positive peer relationships (Roberts, 1994). For example, Gottman, Katz, and Hooven (1997) found that fathers' acceptance of and assistance with their children's sadness and anger at 5 years of age was related to the children's social competence with their peers 3 years later. Girls were less negative with a friend and boys were less aggressive. Mothers' management of children's emotions, in contrast, was generally a less-significant predictor of children's later social behavior. Other findings suggest that the strategies parents employ to manage children's negative emotion are associated with children's emotional reactivity, coping, and social competence (O'Neil, Parke, Isley, & Sosa, 1997). Fathers who reported being more distressed by their child's expressions of negative affect had children who were more likely to report using anger and other negative emotions to cope with distressing events. When fathers reported using strategies to minimize distressing circumstances, children were more likely to report using reasoning to cope with a distressing situation. Fathers who reported emotion- and problem-focused reactions to the expression of negative emotions had children who were described by teachers as less aggressive/disruptive (see Parke, & O'Neil, 1997, for further details and the mother's role in this process). This work highlights the role of fathers in learning about relationships, especially in learning the emotion regulatory aspects of relationships. Fathers provide a unique opportunity to teach children about emotion in the context of relationships due to the wide range of intensity of affect that father's display and the unpredictable character of their playful exchanges with their children (Parke, 1995, 1996; Parke & Brott, 1999).

During early and middle childhood, children acquire and begin to use rules for the socially appropriate expression of emotion. A few studies have examined links between display rule knowledge and social competence. Underwood, Coie, and Herbsman (1992), for example, found that aggressive children have more difficulty understanding display rules. Recently, we have explored the relations between children's use of socially appropriate rules for displaying negative emotions and social competence with peers (McDowell, O'Neil, & Parke, 2000). We employed Saarni's (1984) "disappointing gift paradigm," which enables us to assess children's ability to mask negative emotions in the face of disappointment. Our data indicate that, among fourth graders, children, especially girls, who display positive affect/behavior following the presentation of a disappointing gift (thus, using display rules) are rated more socially competent by teachers and peers.

Only recently have researchers begun to examine links between children's experiences with parents and their ability to use display rules. Garner and Power (1996), studying a preschool sample, found that children's negative emotional displays in a disappointment situation were inversely related to observed maternal positive emotion. More recently, McDowell and Parke (2000) found that both fathers and mothers who were highly controlling of their children's emotional expressiveness, especially boys, demonstrated less knowledge about appropriate display rule use. Finally, Jones, Abbey, and Cumberland (1998) reported a further link between family emotional climate and display rule knowledge. These investigators found that maternal reports of negative emotional family expressiveness were related to self-protective display rules and negatively to prosocial display rules. However, much remains to be understood regarding the intergenerational continuity between parents' and children's display rule use.

Together, these studies suggest that various aspects of emotional development—encoding, decoding, cognitive understanding, and emotion regulation—play important roles in accounting for variation in peer competence. Our argument is that these aspects of emotion may be learned in the context of family interaction including father–child interaction and serve as mediators between the parents and peers. Accumulating support for this view suggests that this is an important direction for future research.

Cognitive Representational Models: Another Possible Mediator Between Parents and Peers

One of the major problems facing the area of family–peer relations is how children transfer the strategies that they acquire in the family context to their peer relationships. A variety of theories assume that individuals possess internal mental representations that guide their social behavior. Attachment theorists offer working model notions (Bowlby, 1969), whereas social and cognitive psychologists have provided an account involving scripts or cognitive maps that could serve as a guide for social action (Bugental & Goodnow, 1998). Researchers within the attachment tradition have examined attachment-related representations and found support for Bowlby's argument that representations vary as a function of child–parent attachment history (Main, Kaplan, & Cassidy, 1985). For example, children who had been securely attached infants were more likely to represent their family in their drawings in a coherent manner, with a balance between individuality and connection, than children who had been insecurely attached. As noted previously, securely attached children have better peer relationships as well (Thompson, 1998).

Research in a social interactional tradition reveals links between parent and child cognitive representations of social relationships (Burks & Parke, 1996). Moreover, parents of children of different sociometric status differ in their cognitive models of social relationships. Several aspects of cognitive models including attributions, perceptions, values, goals, and strategies have been explored (see Bugental & Goodnow, 1998; Mills & Rubin, 1993). Several studies will illustrate this line of research. Pettit, Dodge, and Brown (1988) found that mothers' attributional biases concerning their children's behavior (e.g., the extent to which they view an ambiguous provocation as hostile or benign) and the endorsement of aggression as a solution to interpersonal problems were related to children's interpersonal problem-solving skills that, in turn, were related to their social competence. We have also explored the links between parent and child cognitive representations of social relationships (McDowell, Parke, & Spitzer, in press). In this study, parents and their children responded to a series of vignettes reflecting interpersonal dilemmas by indicating how they might react in each situation. Open-ended responses were coded for goals, causes, strategies, and advice. The cognitive representations of social behavior of both fathers and mothers were related to their children's representations. Moreover, both mothers' and fathers' cognitive models of relationships were linked to children's social acceptance. Mothers who were low in their use of relational and prosocial strategies had children with high levels of peer-nominated aggression. Similarly, mothers who provided specific and socially skilled advice had more-popular children. Fathers' strategies that were rated high on confrontation and instrumental qualities were associated with low teacher ratings of children's prosocial behavior and high teacher ratings of physical and verbal aggression, avoidance, and being disliked. Fathers with relational goals had children who were less-often nominated as aggressive by their peers and rated by teachers as more liked and less disliked.

Research in the attachment tradition of cognitive working models provides additional support for the role of cognitive representational processes in exploring the link between family and peer systems. Cassidy, Kirsh, Scolton, and Parke (1996) found that children of varying attachment relationships responded differently to hypothetical scenarios involving ambiguous negative events. Securely attached children had more-positive representations about peer intent in ambiguous situations than did insecurely attached children. Moreover, Cassidy et al. (1996) found that the link between attachment and relationships with close friends is mediated partly by representations of peer relationships. This finding is supportive of our general argument and of Sroufe and Fleeson's proposition "that relationships are not constructed afresh, nor are new relationships based on the simple transfer of particular responses from old relationships. Rather it is assumed that previous relationships exert their influence through the attitudes, expectations and understanding of roles which they leave with the individual" (1986, p. 59). Together, this set of studies suggests that cognitive models of relationships may be transmitted across generations and these models, in turn, may serve as mediators between family contexts and children's relationships with others outside of the family.

Attentional Regulation: A Third Potential Mediator Between Parents and Peers

In concert with emotion regulation and social cognitive representations, attentional regulatory processes have come to be viewed as an additional mechanism through which familial socialization experiences might influence the development of children's social competence. These processes include the ability to attend to relevant cues, to sustain attention, to refocus attention through such processes as cognitive distraction and cognitive restructuring, and other efforts to purposefully reduce the level of emotional arousal in a situation that is appraised as stressful (Lazarus & Folkman, 1984). Attentional processes are thought to organize experience and to play a central role in cognitive and social development beginning early in infancy (Rothbart & Bates, 1998). Thus, Wilson (1999) aptly considers attention-regulatory processes as a "shuttle" linking emotion regulation and social cognitive processes because attentional processes organize both cognitions and emotional responses and, thus, influence the socialization of relationship competence. In support of direct influences, Eisenberg et al. (1993) found that children who were low in attentional regulation were also low in social competence. Other recent work suggests that attentional control and emotional negativity may interact when predicting social competence. Attention-regulatory skills appear to be more critical among children who experience higher levels of emotional negativity. Eisenberg argues that when children are not prone to experience intense negative emotions, attention-regulatory processes may be less essential to positive social functioning. In contrast, the social functioning of children who experience anger and other negative emotions may only be undermined when these children do not have the ability to use attention-regulatory processes, such as cognitive restructuring and other forms of emotion-focused coping.

Other work (O'Neil & Parke, 2000) suggests, in addition, that attentional processes may work in tandem with emotion-regulatory abilities to enhance social functioning. Parenting style may be an important antecedent of children's ability to refocus attention away from emotionally distressing events. Data from fifth graders in our study indicated that when mothers adopted a negative, controlling parenting style in a problem-solving discussion, children were less likely to use cognitive decision making as a coping strategy. In addition, children were more likely to report greater difficulty in controlling negative affect when distressed. Lower levels of cognitive decision making and higher levels of negative affect, in turn, were associated with more problem behaviors and higher levels of negative interactions with classmates (as reported by teachers). Similarly, when fathers adopted a negative, controlling style, children were more likely to use avoidance as a mechanism for managing negative affect. In addition, fathers who reported expressing more negative dominant emotions such as anger and criticism in everyday interactions had children who reported greater difficulty controlling negative emotions. Avoidant coping and negative emotionality, in turn, were related to higher levels of parent-reported problem behaviors. In summary, the ability to regulate attention is a further important mediating pathway through which paternal behavior may influence children's peer functioning.

Intergenerational Influences on Paternal Behavior

Fathers' own recollections of their early relationship with their own mother and father can help us better understand the impact of fathers on their children's overall behavior as well. As Bowlby (1973) commented: "Because children tend unwittingly to identify with parents and therefore to adopt, when they become parents, the same patterns of behavior towards children that they themselves have experienced during their own childhood, patterns of interaction are transmitted, more or less faithfully, from one generation to the next" (p. 137). Main and her coworkers developed an interview to tap mothers' recollections of their relationships with their own mothers during infancy and childhood (Main, Kaplan, & Cassidy, 1985). Interestingly, mothers' patterns of memories related to the quality of their current attachment relationships with their own infants. Mothers who had developed secure attachment relationships with their infants revealed in their interviews that they valued close relationships with their parents and others, but at the same time were objective and tended not to idealize their own parents—thus displaying a relatively clear understanding of this important relationship. In contrast, mothers with poor relationships with their infants had different sets of memories; some dismissed and devalued their relationship with their parents or claimed they couldn't recall. Others idealized their parents: "I had the world's best mom." Other mothers with poor attachment relationships with their children tended to recall many conflict-ridden incidents from childhood but could not organize them in a coherent pattern.

Do fathers show similar carryover effects of early memories? In a German longitudinal study, researchers found that a father's recollections of his own childhood relationship with his parents was indeed linked to his relationship with his own children (Grossman & Fremmer-Bombik, 1994). Fathers who viewed their own attachment relationship with their parents as secure were more likely to develop a secure attachment relationship with their own infants, were more likely to be present at birth, participated more in infant care, and were more supportive of their wives than men with insecure attachments. Moreover, fathers who remembered their childhood attachment experiences, including both positive and negative feelings, and who were open and nondefensive about their recollections continued to be better fathers as their children developed. They were better play partners to their toddlers. By the time their children reached age 6, these fathers served as more-sensitive guides during a teaching task and continued to be engaging and tender play partners. Later, when their offspring were age 10, these men were more accepting of their children's daily concerns and problems. Remembering both the good and the bad aspects of his own childhood makes a father more sensitive to the needs and feelings of his own child. An American study confirmed these European observations. Cowan and his colleagues (Cowan, Cohn, Cowan, & Pearson, 1996) found that fathers who recalled an earlier attachment relationship with their parents characterized as low in loving and high in expression of anger had children who tended to be rated as more externalizing (e.g., aggressive and hyperactive) in kindergarten.

Although fathers' involvement in infancy and childhood is quantitatively less than mothers' involvement, the data suggest that fathers nevertheless have an important impact on their offspring's development. Just as earlier research indicated that quality rather than quantity of mother–child interaction was the important predictor of cognitive and social development, a similar assumption appears to hold for fathers. Together, these recent findings lead to a revision in traditional thinking about the ways that mothers and fathers influence their children's development. According to the sociologist Talcott Parsons (Parsons & Bales, 1955), mothers were the emotional brokers in the family, and the fathers' role was an instrumental one. Instead, this recent work suggests that fathers play a much larger role in the socialization of children's emotions. And it is through the management of their own emotions and their reactions to their children's emotions that fathers may have the greatest impact on their children's social relations with peers and friends.

Pathway Two: Fathers as Advisers and Social Guides

Learning about relationships through interaction with parents can be viewed as an indirect pathway because the goal is often not explicitly to influence children's social relationships with extrafamilial partners such as peers. In contrast, parents influence children's relationships directly in their roles as direct instructors, educators, or advisers. In this role, parents explicitly set out to educate their children concerning the appropriate manner of initiating and maintaining social relationships. Research that emerged over the last 10 years suggests that young children in preschool and early elementary school gain competence with peers when parents supervise and facilitate their experiences, whereas among older children (middle school and beyond), great supervision and guidance on the part of parents of children's peer relationships may function more as a remediatory effort (Parke & O'Neil, 1997, 2000).

In a study of parental supervision, Bhavnagri and Parke (1991) found that 2- to 5-year-old children, especially the 2- to 3-year-olds, exhibited more cooperation and turn taking and had long play bouts when assisted by an adult than when playing without assistance. Although both fathers and mothers were effective facilitators of their children's play with peers, under natural conditions, mothers are more likely to play this supervisory and facilitory role than are fathers (Bhavnagri & Parke, 1991; Ladd & Golter, 1988).

As children develop, the forms of management shift from direct involvement or supervision of the ongoing activities of children and their peers to a less-public form of management, involving advice or consultation concerning appropriate ways of handling peer problems. This form of direct parental management has been termed consultation (Lollis, Ross, & Tate, 1992). Russell and Finnie (1990) found that the quality of advice that mothers provided their children prior to entry into an ongoing play dyad varied as a function of children's sociometric status. Mothers of well-accepted preschool-age children were more specific and helpful in the quality of advice that they provided. In contrast, mothers of poorly accepted children provided relatively ineffective kinds of verbal guidance, such as "have fun," or "stay out of trouble." The advice was too general to be of value to the children in their subsequent interactions.

Other evidence offers further support for the role of both fathers' as well as mothers' advice giving and the development of children's social acceptance and competence with peers. In one study (O'Neil, Garcia, Zavala, & Wang, 1995), parents were asked to read short stories to their third-grade child that described common social themes (e.g., group entry, ambiguous provocation, and relational aggression) and to advise the child about the best way to handle each situation. High-quality advice was considered to be advice that promoted a positive, outgoing, social orientation on the part of the child rather than avoidance or aggressive responses. The findings varied as a function of parent and child gender. Among father–son dyads and mother–daughter dyads, parental advice that was more appropriate and more structured was associated with less loneliness and greater social competence among children. Interestingly, among father–daughter and mother–son dyads, higher-quality advice about how to handle social conflict was associated with poorer teacher-rated social competence. Perhaps parents are more aware of the social problems of their opposite-gender children and make efforts to provide remedial advice. In contrast to the gender-specific findings for the content of parental advice, the quality of parent–child interactions during the advice-giving session were positively related to children's social competence. Interestingly, other results from our study, based on a triadic advice-giving session in which mothers, fathers, and their third grader discussed how to handle problems that their child had when interacting with peers, indicated that parental style of interaction appeared to be a better predictor of children's social competence than the actual solution quality generated in the advice-giving session (Wang & McDowell, 1996). Specifically, the controlling nature of fathers' style and the warmth and support expressed by mothers during the advice-giving task were significant predictors of both teacher and peer ratings of children's social competence.

The direction of effects in each of these studies, of course, is difficult to determine, and future models that explain links between parental management strategies and children's social development need to examine the potential of bidirectional relations. Under some circumstances, parents may be making proactive efforts to provide assistance to their children's social efforts, whereas under other circumstances, parents may be providing advice in response to children's social difficulties (see also Ladd & Golter, 1988; Mize, Pettit, & Brown, 1995). Highly involved parents, for example, may simply be responding to their children's poor social abilities. In turn, high levels of control may inhibit children's efforts to develop their own strategies for dealing with peer relations (Cohen, 1989).

Nevertheless, the bulk of the evidence suggests that direct parental influence in the form of supervision and advice giving can significantly increase the interactive competence of young children and illustrates the utility of examining direct parent strategies as a way of teaching children about social relationships. Finally, more attention needs to be given to the developmental aspects of this issue, so that we have a fuller understanding of how the impact of this direct form of influence changes across development.

Pathway Three: Fathers as Sources of Social Opportunities

Fathers (and mothers) also play an important role in the facilitation of their children's peer relationships by initiating informal contact between their own children and potential play partners, especially among young children (Parke & Bhavnagri, 1989). A series of studies by Ladd and his colleagues (see Ladd & Le Sieur, 1995) suggests that parents' role as social activity arranger may play a facilitory part in the development of their children's friendships. Ladd and Golter (1988) found that children of parents who tended to arrange peer contacts had a larger range of playmates and more-frequent play companions outside of school than children of parents who were less active in initiating peer contacts. When children entered kindergarten, boys, but not girls, with parents who initiated peer contacts were better liked and less rejected by their classmates than were boys with noninitiating parents. Other evidence (Ladd, Hart, Wadsworth, & Golter, 1988) suggests that parents' peer management (initiating peer contacts; purchasing toys with social applications) of younger preschool children prior to enrollment in preschool was, in turn, linked to the time that children spent in peers' homes.

Parents also influence their children's social relations by providing them with the opportunity to participate in more-formal afterschool activities such as team sports, Brownies, and Cub Scouts. Participating in these institutions can allow children access to a wider range of activities than more-informal play situations and can contribute to their social and cognitive development. For example, Bryant (1985) found that participation in formal activities for 10-year-olds was associated with better perspective taking. Although some studies have found that mothers are more involved in the interface between the children and social institutions and view these settings as being more important for children's development of social skills than do fathers, few studies have investigated father's participation in formal afterschool activities with their children (Bhavnagri, 1987). Although many fathers may serve as coaches of their children's sports team or lead their scout groups, little is known about the effects of these interactions on their relationships with their children or on their children's social development.

Parents' own social networks also may enhance children's social development and adjustment. Cochran and Niego (1995) suggested several ways that parents' own networks may influence children's social competence. First, the structure of parents' networks influence the exposure children have to possible social interactive partners (e.g., the offspring of adult network members). Second, the extent to which children observe the social interactions of parents with members of their networks may influence the children's own styles of social interaction. Third, parents in supportive social networks may have enhanced well-being that, in turn, may improve parents' relationships with their children.

Evidence suggests that structural characteristics of parents' networks such as network size are associated with social adjustment in young children. Homel, Burns, and Goodnow (1987), for example, found that the number of friends in parents' social networks was related to the social adjustment of 9- to 11-year-olds. Recently, this work was extended by showing relationships among characteristics of parents' networks, parents' attitudes toward their social networks, and children's social competence in kindergarten and first grade (Simpkins, O'Neil, Lee, Parke, & Wang, 2000). When mothers reported more closeness and enjoyment from their networks, they reported greater efficacy in managing their own relationships and felt more efficacious in assisting their children in forming social relationships. Fathers whose networks contained more nonkin members and were a source of more age-mates for their children reported feeling more efficacious in their personal relationships. When mothers viewed their social networks as sources of closeness and enjoyment, their children were described by teachers and peers as better accepted by classmates. Similarly, when fathers described their network relationships in a more positive light, children were rated by teachers as better accepted and less aggressive. When mothers' nonkin network provided the study child with more age-mates, children were rated by peers as better accepted. Similarly, when fathers reported a larger network of kin members and when fathers' network of nonkin afforded their children more age-mates, children tended to be rated by peers as better accepted. Although the specific mechanisms that account for these relationships remain to be determined, these findings suggest that parents' social networks may provide children with both better models of social relationships as well as more opportunities to interact with same-aged peers and refine developing social skills.

Finally, the quality of the relationship that adults develop with friends in their social network is an important correlate of their children's friendship quality. Doyle and Markiewicz (1996) found that mothers who reported having supportive friends had children who experienced more closeness with their best friend. Conversely, if mothers felt less secure about their best friendship or rated their friends as interesting, their own children were more likely to have a best friend. The findings concerning the links between lack of mothers' security about their friendships is consistent with earlier work on maternal recollections of their childhood peer experiences. In this work, Putallaz, Costanzo, and Smith (1991) found that mothers who had anxious peer relations as children had children who were more socially competent, which supports a compensatory model of parenting. More recently, Simpkins and Parke (2001) found that the quality of both maternal and paternal friendships was related to children's friendship quality. However, the quality of the parents' best friendship was a better predictor of daughters' friendships, while both the quality of the parents' best friendship and the breadth of their social network were predictive of sons' friendships. As these studies illustrate, the quality and scope of adult friendships and social networks are important correlates not just of children's peer competence but of their friendship qualities as well.

BEYOND THE FATHER–CHILD RELATIONSHIP: THE MARITAL DYAD AS A CONTRIBUTOR TO CHILDREN'S PEER RELATIONSHIPS

Another way in which fathers influence their children's peer relationships is through their marital relationships (Parke, Kim, et al., 2001). Two perspectives have been offered to explain these possible links between marital relationships and children's peer relationships. First, some propose a direct model, which means that exposure to marital conflict may directly alter children's capacity to function effectively in other social contexts (Cummings & O'Reilly, 1997). Others propose an indirect model whereby marital relationships alter parent–child relationships, which, in turn, affect children's outcomes (Fauber & Long, 1991).

Direct Model of the Links Between Marital Relationships and Peer Relationships

Recent work has focused on the specific processes by which the marital relationship itself directly influences children's immediate functioning and long-term adjustment. More-frequent interparental conflict and more intense or violent forms of conflict are not only particularly disturbing to children but are also associated with externalizing and internalizing problems. Grych, Seid, and Fincham (1992) found that children who were exposed to an audiotaped analog of marital interaction responded with distress, shame, and self-blame to angry adult exchanges. Exposure to unresolved conflict is associated with negative affect and poor coping responses in children (Cummings, Ballard, El-Sheikh, & Lake, 1991). In addition, Katz and Gottman (1993) found that couples who exhibited a hostile style of resolving conflict had children who tended to be described by teachers as exhibiting antisocial characteristics. When husbands were angry and emotionally distant while resolving marital conflict, children were described by teachers as anxious and socially withdrawn.

To date, few of these studies have focused explicitly on children's social competence with peers. Recent evidence from our lab has focused specifically on the links between marital conflict, interparental communication styles, and the peer relationships of sixth-grade children (O'Neil, Flyr, Wild, & Parke, 1999). Marital communication and conflict management style were observed during a couple "problem-solving" session. More negative paternal problem-solving strategies were associated with greater peer-rated avoidance and lower teacher-rated acceptance. Similarly, when mothers exhibited better problem-solving skills, adolescents were rated as less avoidant by peers. Poorer maternal problem-solving and communication strategies were linked to teacher ratings of less social engagement. These findings confirm our anticipated link between marital conflict and children's peer relationships.

Although the links between conflict and peer relations are clear, this represents only the first step. To assess factors that may be possible mediators between parental conflict and peer competence, two assessments were made, children's perceptions of marital conflict and children's emotional regulatory abilities. First, we examined the relation between indices of marital conflict and children's perception of interparental conflict (Kim, Parke, & O'Neil, 1999). Children's perceptions of marital conflict correlated with parents' reports of marital conflict in both grades 5 and 6. In other analyses, O'Neil et al. (1999) examined the relations between observations of marital communication and conflict management and children's perceptions of interparental conflict. When fathers expressed more negative affect during discussion of a marital disagreement, sixth graders reported more-frequent and intense interparental conflict. When fathers used more negative problem-solving strategies (e.g., hostility, denial, disruptive process), adolescents reported more-intense interparental conflict. In contrast, when fathers used better problem-solving strategies (e.g., negotiation, listener responsiveness), adolescents reported less-frequent and less-intense conflict. Mothers' observed communication and conflict management strategies were virtually unrelated to adolescents' perceptions of interparental conflict. Together, these two sets of analyses suggest a reliable relation between both self-report and observed indices of parental marital conflict and children's perceptions of marital conflict.

Next, we examined the relation between children's perceptions of marital conflict and children's competence with peers. Kim et al. (1999) found that teacher ratings of disruptive behavior, shyness, and sadness were associated with frequent parental conflict whereas children's self-blame was associated with teacher ratings of verbal and physical aggression. Children's self-blame was negatively associated with peer ratings of friendliness and peer and teacher ratings of prosocial behavior. In sum, there are clear relations among parental reports of marital conflict, children's perception of marital conflict, and children's peer competence.

Children who perceive high levels of marital conflict may have more difficulty in their self-regulation of emotion, which is a correlate of children's peer competence (Parke & O'Neil, 1997; Eisenberg & Fabes, 1994). Moreover, Cummings and Davies (1994) suggest that emotional reactivity in response to conflict may mediate the links between marital conflict and child outcomes. In a direct test of the model, Davies and Cummings (1998) assessed the links among children's emotional security, level of destructive and constructive marital functioning, and children's internalizing and externalizing behaviors. As predicted by the emotional security model, the links between marital discord and children's internalizing symptoms were mediated by measures of emotional security.

O'Neil et al. (1999) found further support for the links between marital conflict and children's emotional regulation. Children's emotional regulatory ability was measured by a self-report index of emotional reactivity and strategies for coping with emotional upset. We found several linkages between marital communication and conflict management style and children's emotional regulation.

Fathers' listener responsiveness, positive mood, and involvement in problem solving with their spouse were inversely related to a child's report of displayed anger. In addition, a child's calm response to a stressful situation was positively related to the rate of a father's verbal engagement with his spouse. Similarly, mothers' verbal and listening behaviors with their spouse were inversely related to children's reports of displayed anger. Finally, a child's calm response to situations related to a less-intrusive maternal communication style in the marriage. These data are consistent with earlier work that suggests that fathers' as well as mothers' styles of dealing with marital conflict were related to children's emotional regulatory abilities (Katz & Gottman, 1993). In turn, these emotional competence skills are linked to social competence with peers (Denham, 1998; Eisenberg & Fabes, 1994; Parke, 1994). Children who are less emotionally reactive and who respond with less anger and more positive coping strategies are more socially competent.

Conflict is inevitable in most parent relationships and is not detrimental to children's functioning under all circumstances. Disagreements that are extremely intense and involve a threat to the child are likely to be more disturbing to the child. When conflict is expressed constructively, is moderate in degree, is expressed in the context of a warm and supportive family environment, and shows evidence of resolution, children may learn valuable lessons regarding how to negotiate conflict and resolve disagreements (Davies & Cummings, 1994).

Indirect Model of the Link Between Marital Relationship and Children's Peer Relationships

Poor parenting and poor marriages often go together, and some father effects are best understood by recognizing this link between parenting and marriage. Gottman and Katz (1989) found that a poor parenting style, characterized as cold, unresponsive, angry, and low in limit setting and structuring, was linked to higher levels of anger and noncompliance on the part of 5-year-old children when interacting with their parents. This style was especially likely to be seen in couples with troubled marriages. This combination led to poor peer outcomes: Children from such homes have lower levels of positive play with peers, have more negative peer exchanges, and even have poorer physical health. Moreover, marital conflict has lasting effects on children's development. In a follow-up to their study, Katz and Gottman (1994) obtained teachers' ratings of internalizing (depression, withdrawal) and externalizing (aggression, disruption) behavior 3 years later. Couples who in the first study used a mutually hostile style of conflict resolution—one characterized by contempt and belligerence toward each other—had children who exhibited higher levels of externalizing behavior three years later. Families in which the husband exhibited an angry and withdrawn style in resolving marital disputes had children who were higher in internalizing behavior. It is not only the level of conflict in marriages that matters, but how conflict is managed that is critical, too.

Similarly, Cowan, Cowan, Schulz, and Hemming (1994) examined the influence of marital quality on children's social adaptation to kindergarten with results suggesting evidence of both direct and indirect links to children's social adjustment. Interestingly, internalizing difficulties (e.g., shy/withdrawn qualities) were predicted by the influences of marital functioning on parenting quality, whereas externalizing difficulties (e.g., aggressive/antisocial qualities) were predicted directly by qualities of marital interaction.

Further support for the role of parental behavior as a mediator between marital conflict and peer competence comes from a recent study by Stocker and Young-blade (1999). These investigations found that the paternal, but not maternal, hostility served as the mediator between marital conflict and problematic peer relationships. A variety of possible mechanisms may be involved to account for their outcome, including shifts in the affective interactions between fathers and children, which, in turn, would impair their affect management skills (Parke et al., 1992; Parke et al., 1998; Parke & McDowell, 1998).

Family systems theory suggests that not only does marital discord interfere with dimensions of the mother–child or father–child relationship, it also may impair qualities of the mother–father–child triadic relationship by interfering with the effectiveness of how the mother and father work together with the child. In an examination of marital adjustment and the effectiveness of joint mother–father supportiveness, Westerman and Schonholtz (1993) found that fathers', but not mothers', reports of marital disharmony and disaffection were significantly related to the effectiveness of joint parental support toward their children's problem-solving efforts. Joint parental support was, in turn, related to fathers' and teachers' reports of children's behavior problems. Men's lack of involvement in the triadic family process could account for these findings, because women tend to engage and confront, whereas men tend to withdraw, in the face of marital disharmony (Gottman, 1994).

In summary, as expected from a family systems perspective, to fully understand the father's influence on children's peer relationships the quality of the marital relationship needs to be recognized. Specfically, the literature suggests that the marital relationship, especially marital conflict, has both direct effects on children's peer relationships as well as indirect effects; marital conflict alters the parent–child relationship, which, in turn, influences children's social competence with peers. More attention to the impact of both the level of marital conflict and how parents manage their conflict on children's peer relationships is clearly warranted.

TOWARD A MORE COMPREHENSIVE PORTRAIT

Recollections often combine with current conditions—such as the quality of the marriage and parenting competence—to alter children's development. Although fathers' own attachment memories are important, an even better understanding of children's behavior with peers emerges when contemporary family relationships are considered as well. Fathers with poor attachment histories were often in marriages characterized by high conflict and low satisfaction, and in turn, these men were ineffective parents (low in warmth, responsiveness, and structuring) (Cowan et al., 1996). In combination, these three factors—prior attachment history, current marital relationship, and parenting competence—predicted externalizing behavior 2 years later when the children were in kindergarten nearly twice as well as the fathers' attachment history alone. Most important, this combination predicted externalizing behavior 2 times better than these same indices for mothers. Mothers' poor prior attachment history tended to be predictive of children's internalizing behavior in kindergarten. Again, internalizing behavior is better understood when mothers' current marriage and parenting are also considered. The combination of these factors with mothers' recollections was twice as good a predictor of children's internalizing behavior as fathers' scores. The authors note: "Given the fact that men are more implicated in problems of aggression and women in problems of depression, it may not be surprising that fathers and mothers make different contributions to young children's externalizing and internalizing behavior" (Cowan et al., 1996, p. 11). Not only are both fathers and mothers important to understanding children's development, but each also makes distinct contributions to children's social developmental outcomes.

REMAINING ISSUES AND FUTURE TRENDS

Several issues remain to be explored in future research. First, the impact of cultural and historical variations need more attention. In terms of cultural issues, we know that fathers play different roles in different cultural contexts (Parke, Coltrane, Powers, Adams, Braver, Fabricius, & Saenz, in press b), but little is known about the impact of these variations on children's social competence. It is necessary to move beyond descriptive studies of fathers in other cultures and examine the impact of variations in fathering—both in terms of interactive style and in amount of daily interaction—on children's social development with peers.

In terms of historical issues, we are witnessing a clear but modest shift in the extent to which fathers are active caregivers and participants in the lives of children (Parke & Brott, 1999; Parke & Stearns, 1993; Pleck, 1997), but we know much less about how these shifts, in turn, alter children's social competence. Many men are becoming fathers at older ages—not only for the first time but also some men are experiencing repeated fatherhood in middle or old age as a result of remarriage (Parke, 1996). The impact of this shift in timing in the onset of first-time or repeated fatherhood on father–child interaction patterns and, in turn, on their children's social competence with peers remains unclear. Some evidence (Neville & Parke, 1997) suggests that older fathers engage in less-vigorous physical play and instead focus on more cognitively oriented activities than on-time fathers. In light of the importance of this type of playful interchange between fathers and children for their social development (Parke et al., 1992; Parke, 1994), one could speculate that more peer-related difficulties may emerge for offspring of these older fathers. Alternatively, perhaps older fathers contribute in different but still effective ways to their children's social competence by increasing their investment in advice-giving activities and by encouraging and facilitating opportunities for peer-related interactions (Parke, 1995).

Another issue that is not well understood concerns the unique contributions of fathers to children's peer relationships. Although fathers' physical play style has been suggested as a unique way in which fathers influence their children's social adaptation, as argued in this chapter, this is clearly not the only way in which fathers influence their children's peer relationships. To date, however, the relative importance of fathers as interactive agent, adviser, or manager of social opportunities is not clearly understood. Similarly, the relative impact of these different influence pathways for fathers versus mothers is not well charted, although it appears that mothers play a more prominent role as a social manager than fathers (Coltrane, 1996). It is clear that more effort needs to be devoted to parceling out the relative contributions across different aspects of the father role as well as differences across mother and father roles. (See chap. 5.)

It is assumed that the father's role changes across development, but more specification of these changes are needed. As other work suggests (Collins & Russell, 1991; Larson & Richards, 1994) the direction of influence between parent and child becomes more balanced across development as issues of autonomy become of more central importance, especially during adolescence. Fathers are increasingly emotionally distant during adolescence, which, in turn, may increase their offspring's autonomy achievement and increase their non-family-based involvements (Shulman & Seiffge-Krenke, 1997). Detailed assessments of how changes in the father–adolescent relationship alter peer relationships would clearly be worthwhile.

Finally, the role of nonresidential fathers in children's peer relationships needs to be better understood. Although it is clear that father absence is linked with poorer social adjustment (McLanahan, 1997), less is known about the patterns of contact and the quality of relationships between children and nonresidential fathers that may contribute positively to these social outcomes. For too long, researchers have focused on the social deficits associated with nonresidential fathers, and more attention needs to be devoted to the constructive ways in which these men can contribute to their children's social lives. (See chap. 4.)

Through a more-textured understanding of the father's role in children's peer relationships, we will be in a better position to develop more-effective guidelines for preventive and interventive efforts on behalf of children who experience peer problems.

ACKNOWLEDGMENTS

Preparation of this chapter and our research program was supported by a National Science Foundation Grant BNS8919391 to Ross D. Parke, an NICHD grant, HT 32391, to Ross D. Parke and Robin O'Neil and NIMH grant 5RO1MH54154. Thanks to Mary Ann Stewart for her assistance in the preparation of the manuscript.

REFERENCES

Asher, S. R., Parkhurst, J. T., Hymel, S., & Williams, G. A. (1990). Peer rejection and loneliness in childhood. In S. R. Asher & J. D. Coie (Eds.), *Peer rejection in childhood.* New York: Cambridge University Press.

Barth, J., & Parke, R. D. (1993). Parent–child relationship influences on children's transition to school. *Merrill-Palmer Quarterly, 39,* 173–195.

Bhavnagri, N. (1987). *Parents as facilitators of preschool children's peer relationships.* Unpublished doctoral dissertation, University of Illinois at Champaign-Urbana.

Bhavnagri, N., & Parke, R. D. (1991). Parents as direct facilitators of children's peer relationships: Effects of age of child and sex of parent. *Journal of Personal and Social Relationships, 8,* 423–440.

Boivin, M., Poulin, F., & Vitaro, F. (1994). Depressed mood and peer rejection in childhood. *Development and Psychopathology, 6,* 483–498.

Bowlby, J. (1969). *Attachment and Loss: Vol. 1. Attachment.* New York: Basic Books.

Bowlby, J. (1973). *Separation and Loss.* New York: Basic Books.

Boyum, L. A., & Parke, R. D. (1995). The role of family emotional expressiveness in the development of children's social competence. *Journal of Marriage and the Family, 57,* 593–608.

Bryant, B. K. (1985). The neighborhood walk: Sources of support in middle childhood. *Monographs of the Society for Research in Child Development, 50*(3, Serial No. 210).

Bugental, D., & Goodnow, J. (1998). Socialization processes. In W. Damon & N. Eisenberg (Eds.), *Handbook of child psychology: Vol. 3. Social, emotional and personality development,* (pp. 389–462). New York: Wiley.

Burks, V. S., & Parke, R. D. (1996). Parent and child representations of social relationships: Linkages between families and peers. *Merrill-Palmer Quarterly, 42,* 358–378.

Carson, J. L., & Parke, R. D. (1996). Reciprocal negative affect in parent–child interactions and children's peer competency. *Child Development, 67,* 2217–2226.

Cassidy, J., Kirsh, S. J., Scolton, K. L., & Parke, R. D. (1996). Attachment and representations of peer relationships. *Developmental Psychology, 32,* 892–904.

Cochran, M., & Niegro, S. (1995). Parenting and social networks. In M. Bornstein (Ed.), *Handbook of parenting: Vol. 3. Status and social conditions of parenting.* Mahwah, NJ: Lawrence Erlbaum Associates.

Cohen, J. S. (1989). *Maternal involvement in children's peer relationships during middle childhood.* Unpublished doctoral dissertation, University of Waterloo, Ontario, Canada.

Collins, W. A., & Russell, A. (1991). Mother–child and father–child relationships in middle childhood: A developmental analysis. *Developmental Review, 11,* 99–136.

Coltrane, S. (1996). *Family man.* New York: Oxford University Press.

Cowan, P. A., Cohn, D. A., Cowan, C. P., & Pearson, J. L. (1996). Parents' attachment histories and children's externalizing and internalizing behaviors: Exploring family systems models of linkage. *Journal of Consulting and Clinical Psychology, 64,* 53–63.

Cowan, P. A., Cowan, C. P., Schulz, M. S., & Hemming, G. (1994). Prebirth to preschool family factors in children's adaptation to kindergarten. In R. D. Parke & S. G. Kellam (Eds.), *Exploring family relationships with other social contexts.* Hillsdale, NJ: Lawrence Erlbaum Associates.

Cummings, E. M., Ballard, M. El-Sheikh, M., & Lake, M. (1991). Resolutions and children's responses to interadult anger. *Psychological Bulletin, 116,* 387–411.

Cummings, E. M., & Davies, P. T. (1994). *Children and marital conflict: The impact of family dispute and resolution.* New York: Guilford.

Cummings, E. M., & O'Reilly, A. W. (1997). Fathers in family context: Effects of marital quality on child adjustment. In M. E. Lamb (Ed.), *The father's role in child development* (3rd ed.) New York: Wiley.

Davies, P. T., & Cummings, E. M. (1994). Marital conflict and child adjustment: An emotional security hypothesis. *Psychological Bulletin, 116,* 387–411.

Davies, P. T., & Cummings, E. M. (1998). Exploring children's emotional security as a mediator of the link between marital relations and child adjustment. *Child Development, 69,* 124–139.

Denham, S. A. (1998). *Emotional development in young children.* New York: Guilford.

Doyle, A. B., & Markiewicz, D. (1996). Parents' interpersonal relationships and children's friendships. In W. Bukowski, A. Newcomb, & W. Hartup (Eds.), *The company they keep: Friendship in childhood and adolescence.* New York: Cambridge University Press.

Eisenberg, N., & Fabes, R. (1994). Emotion, regulation and the development of social competence. In M. Clark (Ed.), *Review of personality and social psychology.* Newbury Park, CA: Sage.

Eisenberg, N., Fabes, R., Bernzweig, J, Karbon, M., Poulin, R., & Hanish, L. (1993). The relations of emotionality and regulation to preschoolers' social skills and sociometric status. *Child Development, 64,* 1418–1438.

Fauber R. L., & Long, N. (1991). Children in context: The role of the family in child psychotherapy. *Journal of Consulting and Clinical Psychology, 59,* 813–820.

Garner, P. W., & Power, T. G. (1996). Preschoolers' emotional control in the disappointment paradigm and its relation to temperament, emotional knowledge, and family expressiveness. *Child Development, 67,* 1406–1419.

Gottman, J. M. (1994).*What predicts divorce?* Hillsdale, NJ: Lawrence Erlbaum Associates.

Gottman, J. M., & Katz, L. F. (1989). Effects of marital discord on young children's peer interaction and health. *Developmental Psychology, 25,* 373–381.

Gottman, J. M., Katz, L. F., & Hooven, C. (1997). *Meta-emotion: How families communicate emotionally.* Mahwah, NJ: Lawrence Erlbaum Associates.

Grossman, F. K., & Fremmer-Bombik, E. (1994, June). *Fathers' attachment representations and quality of their interactions with their children in infancy.* Poster presentation at the meeting for International Society for the Study of Behavioral Development, Amsterdam.

Grych, J. M., Seid, M., & Fincham, F. D. (1992). Assessing marital conflict from the child's perspective: The Children's Perception of Interparental Conflict Scale. *Child Development, 63,* 558–572.

Harlow, H. F. (1958). The nature of love. *American Psychologist, 13,* 673–685.

Harris, J. R. (1995). Where is the child's environment? A group socialization theory of development. *Psychological Review, 102,* 458–489.

Harris, J. R. (1998). *The nurture assumption.* New York: Free Press.

Hartup, W. W. (1979). The social worlds of childhood. *American Psychologist, 34,* 944–949.

Hetherington, E. M., & Deur, J. (1972). The effects of father's absence on child development. In W. W. Hartup (Ed.), *The young child.* Vol. 2. Washington, DC: NAEYC.

Homel, R., Burns, A., & Goodnow, J. (1987). Parental social networks and child development. *Journal of Social and Personal Relationships, 4,* 159–177.

Isley, S., O'Neil, R., Clatfelter, D., & Parke, R. D. (1999). Parent and child expressed affect and children's social competence: Modeling direct and indirect pathways. *Developmental Psychology, 35,* 547–560.

Isley, S., O'Neil, R., & Parke, R. D. (1996). The relation of parental affect and control behaviors to children's classroom acceptance: A concurrent and predictive analysis. *Early Education and Development, 7,* 7–23.

Jones, D. C., Abbey, B. B., & Cumberland, A. (1998). The development of display rule knowledge: Linkages with family expressiveness and social competence. *Child Development, 69,* 1209–1222.

6. FATHERS' CONTRIBUTIONS TO PEER RELATIONSHIPS 165

Katz, L. F., & Gottman, J. M. (1993). Patterns of marital conflict predict children's internalizing and externalizing behavior. *Developmental Psychology, 29,* 940–950.

Katz, L. F., & Gottman, J. M. (1994). Patterns of marital interaction and children's emotional development. In R. D. Parke & S. Kellam (Eds.), *Exploring family relationships with other contexts* (pp. 49–74). Hillsdale, NJ: Lawrence Erlbaum Associates.

Kim, M., Parke, R. D., & O'Neil, R. (1999, April). *Marital conflict and children's social competence: Concurrent and predictive analyses.* Poster presented at the annual meeting of the Western Psychological Association, Irvine, CA.

Ladd, G. W. (1992). Themes and theories; Perspective on processes in family–peer relationships. In R. D. Parke & G. W. Ladd (Eds.), *Family-peer relationships: Modes of linkage.* Hillsdale, NJ: Lawrence Erlbaum Associates.

Ladd, G. W., & Golter, B. S. (1988). Parents' management of preschoolers' peer relations: Is it related to children's social competence? *Developmental Psychology, 24,* 109–117.

Ladd, G. W., Hart, C. H., Wadsworth, E. M., & Golter, B. S. (1988). Preschoolers' peer network in nonschool settings: Relationship to family characteristics and school adjustment. In S. Salzinger, J. Antrobus, & M. Hammer (Eds.), *Social networks of children, adolescents, and college students* (pp. 61–92). Hillsdale, NJ: Lawrence Erlbaum Associates.

Ladd, G. W., & Le Sieur, K. D. (1995). Parents and children's peer relationships. In M. H. Bornstein (Ed.), *Handbook of parenting: Vol. 4, Applied and practical parenting* (pp. 377–409). Hillsdale, NJ: Lawrence Erlbaum Associates.

Larson, R., & Richards, M. (1994). *Divergent realities.* New York: Basic Books.

Lazarus, S., & Folkman, S. (1984). *Stress, appraisal, and coping.* New York: Springer.

Lindsey, E. W., Moffett, D., Clausen, M., & Mize, J. (1994, April). *Father–child play and children's competence.* Paper presented at the biennial meeting of the Southwestern Society for Research in Human Development, Austin, TX.

Lollis, S. P., Ross, H. S., & Tate, E. (1992). Parents' regulation of children's peer interactions: Direct influences. In R. Parke & G. Ladd (Eds.), *Family–peer relationships: Modes of linkage* (pp. 255–281). Hillsdale, NJ: Lawrence Erlbaum Associates.

Lynn, D. B., & Sawyer, W. L. (1959). The effects of father absence on Norwegian boys and girls. *Journal of Abnormal and Social Psychology, 59,* 258–262.

MacDonald, K., & Parke, R. D. (1984). Bridging the gap: Parent–child play interaction and peer interactive competence. *Child Development, 55,* 1265–1277.

Main, M., Kaplan, N., & Cassidy, J. (1985). Security in infancy, childhood and adulthood: A move to the level of representation. In I. Bretherton & E. Waters (Eds.), *Growing points in attachment theory and research. Monographs of the Society for Research in Child Development, 50,* 1–2. Serial No. 209.

McDowell, D. J., O'Neil, R., & Parke, R. D. (2000). Display rule application in a disappointing situation and children's emotional reactivity: Relations with social competence. *Merrill-Palmer Quarterly, 46,* 306–324.

McDowell, D. J., & Parke, R. D. (2000). Differential knowledge of display rules for positive and negative emotions: Influence from parents, influences on peers. *Social Development, 9,* 415–432.

McDowell, D. J., Parke, R. D., & Spitzer, S. (in press). *Parent and child cognitive representations of social situations and children's social competence. Social Development.*

McLanahan, S. S. (1997). Paternal absence or poverty: Which matters more? In G. Duncan & J. Brooks-Gunn (Eds.), *Consequences of growing up poor.* New York: Russell Sage Foundation.

Mills, R. S., & Rubin, K. H. (1993). Parental ideas as influences on children's social competence. In S. Duck (Ed.), *Learning about relationships.* Vol. 2. Newbury Park, CA: Sage.

Mize, J., Pettit, G. S., & Brown, E.G. (1995). Mothers' supervisions of their children's peer play—Relations with beliefs, perceptions, and knowledge. *Developmental Psychology, 31,* 311–321.

Mott, F. L. (1994). Sons, daughters and fathers' absence: Differentials in father-leaving probabilities and in home environments. *Journal of Family Issues, 15,* 97–128.

Neville, B., & Parke, R. D. (1997). Waiting for paternity: Interpersonal and contextual implications of the timing of fatherhood. *Sex Roles, 37,* 45–59.

O'Neil, R., Flyr, M. L., Wild, M. N., & Parke, R. D. (1999, April). *Early adolescents exposure to marital conflict: Links to relationships with parents and peers.* Paper presented at the biennial meeting of the Society for Research in Child Development, Albuquerque, NM.

O'Neil, R., Garcia, J., Zavala, A., & Wang, S. (1995, April). *Parental advice giving and children's competence with peers: A content and stylistic analysis.* Paper presented at the biennial meeting of the Society for Research in Child Development, Indianapolis, IN.

O'Neil, R., & Parke, R. D. (2000). Family-peer relationships: The role of emotion regulation, cognitive understanding, and attentional processes as mediating processes. In K. Kerns, J. Contreras, & A. Neal-Barnett (Eds.), *Family and peers: Linking two social worlds* (pp. 195–225). Westport, Connecticut: Praeger.

O'Neil, R., Parke, R. D., Isley, S., & Sosa, R. (1997). *Parental influences on children's emotion regulation in middle childhood.* Paper presented at the biennial meeting of the Society for Research in Child Development, Washington, DC.

Parke, R. D. (1994). Progress, paradigms, and unresolved problems: A commentary on recent advances in our understanding of children's emotions. *Merrill-Palmer Quarterly, 40,* 157–169.

Parke, R. D. (1995). Fathers and families. In M. H. Bornstein (Ed.), *Handbook of Parenting* (Vol. 3, pp. 27–63). Hillsdale, NJ: Lawrence Erlbaum Associates.

Parke, R. D. (1996). *Fatherhood.* Cambridge, MA: Harvard University Press.

Parke, R. D., & Bhavnagri, N. (1989). Parents as managers of children's social networks. In D. Belle (Ed.), *Children's social networks and social supports* (pp. 241–259). New York: Wiley.

Parke, R. D., & Brott, A. (1999). *Throwaway dads: The myths and barriers that keep men from being the fathers they want to be.* Boston: Houghton Mifflin.

Parke, R. D., Burks, V. M., Carson, J. L., Neville, B., & Boyum, L. A. (1994). Family–peer relationships: A tripartite model. In R. D. Parke & S. G. Kellam (Eds.), *Exploring family relationships with other social contexts* (pp. 115–145). Hillsdale, NJ: Lawrence Erlbaum Associates.

Parke, R. D., Cassidy, J., Burks, V. M., Carson, J. L., and Boyum, L. (1992). Family contribution to peer competence among young children: The role of interactive and affective processes. In R. Parke & G. Ladd (Eds.), *Family–peer relationships: Modes of linkage* (pp. 107–134). Hillsdale, NJ: Lawrence Erlbaum Associates.

Parke, R. D., Coltrane, S., Powers, J., Adams, M., Fabricius, W., Braver, S., & Saenz, D. (in press b). Measurement of father involvement in Mexican-American families. In R. Day & M. E. Lamb (Eds.), *Reconceptualizing and measuring father involvement.* Mahwah, NJ: Lawrence Erlbaum Associates.

Parke, R. D., Kim, M., Flyr, M. L., McDowell, D. J., Simpkins, S. D., Killian, C., & Wild, M. (2001). Managing marital conflict: Links with children's peer relationships. In J. Grych & F. Fincham (Eds.), *Child development and interparental conflict* (pp. 291–314). New York: Cambridge University Press.

Parke, R. D., & McDowell, D. J. (1998). Toward an expanded model of emotion socialization: New people, new pathways. *Psychological Inquiry, 9,* 303–307.

Parke, R. D., & O'Neil, R. (1997). The influence of significant others on learning about relationships. In S. Duck (Ed.), *The handbook of personal relationships* (2nd ed., pp. 29–60). New York: Wiley.

Parke, R. D., & O'Neil, R. (2000). The influence of significant others on learning about relationships: From family to friends. In R. Mills & S. Duck (Eds.), *The developmental psychology of personal relationships* (pp. 15–47). New York: Wiley.

Parke, R. D., O'Neil, R., Isley, S., Spitzer, S., Welsh, M., Wang, S., Flyr, M., Simpkins, S., Strand, C., & Morales, M. (1998). Family–peer relationships: Cognitive, emotional, and ecological determinants. In M. Lewis & C. Feiring (Eds.), *Families, Risk, and Competence* (pp. 89–112). Mahwah, NJ: Lawrence Erlbaum Associates.

Parke, R. D., Simpkins, S., McDowell, D. J., Kim, M., Killian, C., Dennis, J., Flyr, M. L., Wild, M. N., & Rah, Y. (in press a). Relative contributions of families and peers to children's social development. In P. K. Smith & C. Hart (Eds.), *Handbook of social development.* London: Blackwell.

Parke, R. D., & Stearns, P. N. (1993). Fathers and child rearing. In G. Elder, J. Modell, & R. Parke (Eds.), *Children in time and place: Developmental and historical insights.* New York: Cambridge University Press.

Parker, J. G., & Asher, S. R. (1987). Peer relations and later personal adustment: Are low-accepted children at risk? *Psychological Bulletin, 102,* 357–389.

Parsons,T., & Bales, R. F. (1955). *Family, socialization, and interaction process.* Glencoe, IL: Free Press.

Pedersen, F. A. (1976). Does research on children reared in father-absent families yield information on father influences? *Family Coordinator, 25,* 457–464.

Pettit, G. S., Dodge, K. A., & Brown, M. M. (1988). Early family experience, social problem solving patterns, and children's social competence. *Child Development, 59,* 107–120.

Pleck, J. (1997). Paternal involvement: Levels, sources, and consequences. In M. Lamb (Ed.), *The role of the father in child development* (3rd ed., pp. 67–103). New York: Wiley.

Putallaz, M., Costanzo, P. R., & Smith R. (1991). Maternal recollections of childhood peer relationships: Implications for their children's social competence. *Journal of Social and Personal Relationships, 8,* 403–422.

Roberts, W. (June, 1994). The socialization of emotional expression: Relations with competence in preschool. Paper presented at the meeting of the *Canadian Psychological Association,* Penticton, British Columbia.

Rothbart, M., & Bates, J. (1998). Temperament. In W. Damon & N. Eisenberg (Eds.), *Handbook of child psychology: Vol. 3. Social, emotional, and personality development* (pp. 105–176). New York: Wiley.

Rubin, K., Bukowski, W. & Parker, J. (1998). Peer interaction, relationships and groups. In W. Damon & N. Eisenberg (Eds.), *Handbook of child psychology: Vol. 3. Social, emotional, and personality development* (pp. 619–700). New York: Wiley.

Russell, A., & Finnie, V. (1990). Preschool children's social status and maternal instructions to assist group entry. *Developmental Psychology, 26,* 603–611.

Saarni, C. (1984). An observational study of children's attempt to monitor their expressive behavior. *Child Development, 55,* 1504–1513.

Shulman S., & Seiffge-Krenke, I. (1997). *Fathers and adolescents.* New York: Routledge

Simpkins, S., O'Neil, R., Lee, J., Parke, R. D., & Wang, S. J. (2000). *The relation between parent and children's social networks and children's peer acceptance.* Unpublished manuscript, University of California, Riverside.

Simpkins, S., & Parke, R. D. (2001). The relations between parental and child friendships. *Child Development, 72,* 569–582.

Stocker, C. M., & Youngblade, L. (1999). Marital conflict and parental hostility: Links with children's sibling and peer relationships. *Journal of Family Psychology, 13,* 598–609.

Stolz, L. M. (1954). *Father relations of war-born children.* Stanford, CA: Stanford University Press.

Suess, G. J., Grossman, L. A., & Sroufe, L. A. (1992). Effects of infant attachment to mother and father on quality of adaptation to preschool: From dyadic to individual oganization of self. *International Journal of Behavioral Development, 15,* 43–65.

Thompson, R. A. (1998). Early sociopersonality development. In W. Damon (Ed.), *Handbook of Child Psychology* (5th ed, Vol. 3, pp. 25–104). New York: Wiley.

Underwood, M. K., Coie, J. D., & Herbsman, C. R. (1992). Display rules for anger and aggression in school-age children. *Child Development, 63,* 366–380.

Wang, S. J., & McDowell, D. J. (1996). *Parental advice-giving: Relations to child social competence and psychosocial functioning.* Poster session presented at the annual meeting of the Western Psychological Association, San Jose, CA.

Westerman, M. A., & Schonholtz, J. (1993). Marital adjustment, joint parental support in a triadic problem-solving task, and child behavior problems. *Journal of Clinical Child Psychology, 22,* 97–106.

Wilson, B. J. (1999). Entry behavior and emotion regulation abilities of developmentally delayed boys. *Developmental Psychology, 35,* 214–223.

Youngblade, L., & Belsky, J. (1992). Parent-child antecedents of five-year-olds' close friendships: A longtitudinal analysis. *Developmental Psychology, 28,* 700–713.

7

Nonresidential Fathers and Their Children

Michael E. Lamb
National Institute of Child Health and Human Development

Although the rates of divorce have leveled recently, it remains the case that about half of the children in the United States will experience the separation of their parents before they reach adulthood. Children are no longer stigmatized by their parents' divorce as they were in earlier decades, but divorce is still not a victimless experience, and the adverse effects on children have attracted the attention of many researchers and clinicians. Recognition of these adverse effects, along with increased awareness of the vast number of children affected by divorce, have fueled efforts to both understand and minimize the effects. A discussion of these issues is at the heart of this chapter.

At the dawn of the 21st century, divorce is typically followed in the United States by a period of time in which children live with their mothers, visiting their fathers on specified occasions. Many, perhaps most, fathers visit their children less and less frequently as time passes, and father absence is frequently presented as the root cause of the children's difficulties and subsequent maladjustment. This conclusion has been controversial, but the identification of fatherlessness as the worst consequence of divorce has spawned a series of questions about the extent to which the adverse effects on children are inversely correlated with measures of the extent to which nonresident fathers maintain relationships with their children. Assuming these are related, how can nonresident fathers be encouraged to continue seeing their children? Why do so many fathers agree to arrangements that afford them few opportunities to be with their children? We cannot answer all these questions in this brief chapter, particularly as the relevant evidence, for the most part, is not yet available. My more modest goal is to explore the role that residential fathers play and might play in the lives of their children. It is important to recognize, however, that nonresidential fathers do not operate in a vacuum; their roles, responsibilities, and behavior are influenced by social expectations and practices that cannot be ignored.

THE REDISCOVERY OF FATHERHOOD

The contemporary concern with nonresidential fathers emerged in response to rapid increases in the rate of divorce and an increased emphasis on the formative importance of father involvement by social scientists, mental health professionals, and the public at large beginning nearly three decades ago (Lamb, 1975, 1976; Levine, 1976). More recently, books like David Blankenhorn's *Fatherless America* (1995), David Popenoe's *Life Without Father* (1996) and Adrienne Burgess' *Fatherhood Reclaimed* (1997), as well as popular articles like that by Barbara Dafoe Whitehead (1993), have proclaimed and recounted the exceptional importance of fathers. Among those with a special interest in social policy, however, the focus has fallen not on fatherhood but on the number of children handicapped because they do not have fathers involved in their lives. As Blankenhorn (1995) argued:

> . . . the key for men is to be fathers. The key for children is to have fathers. The key for society is to create fathers. For society, the primary results of fatherhood are right-doing males and better outcomes for children. Conversely, the primary consequences of fatherlessness are rising male violence and declining child well-being. In the United States at the close of the twentieth century, paternal disinvestment has become the major source of our most important social problems, especially those rooted in violence. (p. 26)

In his book, Blankenhorn acknowledges that fatherlessness has many different origins, and it is important to remember that many of the children growing up in fatherless families were born to single mothers and never experienced the separation or divorce of their parents (Smith, Morgan, & Koropeckyj-Cox, 1996). The distinction may be important (Zill, 1996): Single-parent families created by divorce as opposed to nonmarital childbirth at minimum differ with respect to racial background (those created by divorce are more likely to be White) and socioeconomic circumstances (unmarried mothers tend to be worse off). From the perspectives of the individuals themselves, furthermore, experiencing the disruption of a relationship is quite different psychologically than never having had such a relationship. On the other hand, differences between the groups are increasingly blurred, as the numbers of unmarried mothers grow, and many of their children have some connection to their fathers, at least temporarily. As a result, I consider the effects of both divorce and non-divorce-related fatherlessness in this chapter.

In the next section, I briefly review evidence regarding the effects of divorce and fatherlessness on children's development. The literature has been reviewed comprehensively elsewhere, and I thus highlight key points and direct readers to more extended reviews for further details. I then turn attention to the implications of these findings for those making decisions about the amount and type of contact children are permitted to have with their nonresident parents. My explicit thesis is that the modal child experiencing his or her parents' separation would benefit from arrangements that facilitated greater paternal participation. Unfortunately, many contemporary time distribution plans wittingly or unwittingly restrict the quality of father–child relationships, and may drive fathers away from rather than help them draw closer to their children.

THE EFFECTS OF FATHER ABSENCE

Although interpretation of the findings has been controversial for three decades, there is substantial consensus that children are better off psychologically and developmentally in two- rather than single-parent families (see reviews by Amato, 1993, 2000; Amato & Keith, 1991; Amato, Loomis, & Booth, 1995; Cooksey, 1997; Downey, 1994; Goodman, Emery, & Haugaard, 1998; Hetherington & Stanley-Hagan, 1997; Hines, 1997; McLanahan, 1999; McLanahan & Sandefur, 1994; McLanahan & Teitler, 1999; Seltzer, 1994; Thomson, Hanson, & McLanahan, 1994) and that the effects of father loss due to the voluntary separation of the parents are more profound and reliable than the effects of father absence due to paternal death (Amato & Keith, 1991; Maier & Lachman, 2000). The now-voluminous literature reveals a number of developmental domains in which children growing up in fatherless families are disadvantaged relative to peers growing up in two-parent families. Specifically, the research literature is replete with studies focused on psychosocial adjustment, behavior and achievement at school, educational attainment, employment trajectories, income generation, involvement in antisocial and even criminal behavior, and the ability to establish and maintain intimate relationships. Such findings are evident in both small-scale studies as well as large representative surveys, and this permits confidence in the reliability of the associations. Unfortunately, survey data tend to be quite superficial and poorly suited for analyses of causal patterns; as a result, much remains to be learned about the ways in which limitations on father–child contact affect child adjustment. There is widespread consensus that the magnitude of the simple or bivariate associations between father absence/contact and child outcomes is much weaker than many commentators would have us believe. My aim here is thus to probe these associations further in an effort both to explain why the effects of postdivorce father–child contact may sometimes appear small and to articulate the implications for legal and judicial practice.

Along with social scientists such as Biller (1981, 1993), Blankenhorn offered a simple and straightforward interpretation of the association between fatherlessness and its effects, proposing that father absence affects children not because their households are poorer or their mothers are stressed, but because they lack a father figure—a model, a disciplinarian, and a male figure—in their lives. Many social scientists have questioned this interpretation because it fails to acknowledge the many salient and often traumatic events experienced by children when their parents do not live together (e.g., Lamb, 1999). Typically, for example, divorce disrupts one of the child's most important and enduring relationships, that with his or her father. Second, single-parent families are more economically stressed than two-parent families, and economic stresses also appear to account for a substantial portion of the impact of single parenthood on children (McLanahan, 1999). Third, because single mothers need to work more extensively outside the home than married mothers do, adults are less likely to be present, and the supervision and guidance of children is less intensive and reliable in single-parent families than in two-parent families (McLanahan, 1999). Fourth, conflict between the parents commonly precedes, emerges, or increases during the separation and divorce processes and often continues beyond them. Fifth, single parenthood is associated with a variety of social and financial stresses with which individuals must cope, largely on their own. Many of these factors (the disruption of parent–child relationships, parent–parent conflict, stress, economic hardship, and undersupervision) adversely affect the status of children with both single and divorcing mothers, and it is thus not surprising to find that father absence has deleterious consequences for children. Less clear are the specific processes by which these effects are mediated, yet an understanding of how divorce and custody arrangements affect child development is absolutely crucial if we as a society are to minimize or reverse the adverse effects of custody arrangements on children. Stepparenthood and remarriage further complicate efforts to understand the effects of diverse custody arrangements on child well-being (Hanson, McLanahan, & Thomson, 1996; Hetherington & Henderson, 1997; Isaacs & Leon, 1988).

As Amato (1993; Amato & Gilbreth, 1999) has shown with particular clarity, the bivariate associations between father absence and children's adjustment are much weaker than one might expect. Indeed, Amato and Gilbreth's (1999) recent meta-analysis revealed no significant association between the frequency of father–child contact and child outcomes, and similar conclusions have been reached by several other reviewers of the literature (Amato, 1993; Furstenberg & Cherlin, 1991; Furstenberg, Morgan, & Allison, 1987; McLanahan & Sandefur, 1994; Seltzer, 1994). In part, this may well reflect variation in the exposure to other pathogenic circumstances (e.g., changing family economic status, stress, marital conflict) as well as data sets with distributional properties that can obscure statistical associations (e.g., the inclusion of many children who never or very seldom saw their fathers and few whose nonresident fathers were involved), but it likely reflects in addition the diverse types of "involved" father–child relationships represented in the samples studied. Specifically, abusive, incompetent, or disinterested fathers are likely to have much different effects than devoted, committed, and sensitive fathers, and high-quality contacts between fathers and children are surely more beneficial than encounters that lack breadth and intensity. In addition, children whose parents are locked in high levels of conflict may be better adjusted when they do not have substantial contact with their nonresident fathers (Amato & Rezac, 1994). Consistent with this, Amato and Gilbreth (1999) reported that children's well-being was significantly enhanced when their relationships with nonresidential fathers were positive and when the nonresidential fathers engaged in "active parenting." Simons (1996); Hetherington, Bridges, and Insabella (1998); and Clarke-Stewart and Hayward (1996) likewise reported that children benefited when their nonresident fathers were actively involved in routine everyday activities. Similarly, data from the National Center for Education Statistics (*Father Times*, 1997) show that both resident and nonresident fathers enhance their children's adjustment when they are involved in the children's schooling. The clear implication is that postdivorce arrangements should specifically seek to maximize positive and meaningful paternal involvement rather than simply specify minimal amounts of contact between fathers and children. Such postdivorce arrangements would focus on the needs of the children concerned and would make no effort to "reward" or "punish" the parents differentially depending on their relative parental involvement prior to divorce. These implications are pursued more fully in the next section.

INDIVIDUAL DIFFERENCES IN POSTDIVORCE ADJUSTMENT

Divorce and the extent of postdivorce father–child contact do not affect all children similarly. This variability is important, inasmuch as it underscores the complexity of the processes mediating the associations between contact and adjustment and the fact that children vary with respect to the pathogenic circumstances they encounter as well as the buffering or protective factors that reduce their vulnerabilities.

As suggested in the previous section, five factors are particularly important when considering and seeking to predict the effects of divorce on children: (a) the level of involvement and quality of relationships between residential or custodial parents and their children; (b) the level of involvement and quality of the relationships between nonresidential parents and their children; (c) the amount of conflict between the two parents; (d) the amount of conflict between the children and their parents; and (e) the socioeconomic circumstances in which the children reside. Social scientists may argue about the relative importance of these factors, but such debates are not particularly fruitful because these factors are all highly interrelated, and this precludes research that could untangle and quantitatively evaluate the magnitude of independent effects. Although we can play statistical games, selectively partialing out the effects of individual factors or groups of factors, we need to remember that these statistical exercises cannot truly estimate relative importance when measurement is poor and the factors themselves are inextricably linked in the real world.

On the issue of measurement, we note controversy about the validity of varying measures of adjustment and continuing debates about the divergent perspectives of differing informants (Dremen & Ronen-Eliav, 1997; Sternberg, Lamb, & Dawud-Noursi, 1998). Overt behavior problems can be measured reliably, but how well do they index the "psychological pain" experienced by children affected by divorce (Emery, 1994)? Possible measures of socioeconomic circumstances abound, but their intercorrelations are far from perfect, and few take into account such crucial factors as the discrepancy between pre- and postdivorce circumstances, the qualitative consequences (e.g., residential moves within or to other school districts and neighborhoods), the availability and quality of noneconomic and economic support from relatives and friends, or even the timing of economic deprivation, which now appears quite important (e.g., Duncan & Brooks-Gunn, 1997). Conflict is almost ubiquitous in modern divorces; how much and what types of conflict are tolerable and how much is pathogenic (Cummings & Davies, 1994; Cummings & O'Reilly, 1997)? Both pre- and postdivorce conflict can be harmful to children, and Kelly (2000) has argued persuasively that some of the "effects of divorce" are better viewed as the effects of preseparation marital conflict. In addition, most experts agree that conflict localized around the time of litigation and divorce is of less concern than conflict that was and remains an intrinsic and unresolved part of the parents' relationship and continues after their divorce (Cummings & Davies, 1994). Similarly, "encapsulated conflict," from which children are shielded, also does not appear to affect their adjustment (Hetherington et al., 1998), whereas conflict that includes physical violence is more pathogenic than high conflict without violence (Jouriles, Norwood, McDonald, Vincent, & Mahoney, 1996; McNeal & Amato, 1998). Reports of and perspectives on paternal responsibility, conflict, and violence differ; which reports should be used by researchers attempting to measure conflict? How should researchers judge subjective (and competing) conceptions of severity, the frequency of contact, or the reliability of child support payments (Braver, Wolchik, Sandler, Fogas, & Zvetina, 1991; Sternberg & Lamb, 1999; Sternberg et al., 1998)? Stress is usually measured by assessing exposure to stress-inducing events, but these measures typically ignore potentially important differences in reactivity and coping styles. Can stress be measured in ways that capture its phenomenological significance?

Setting aside important measurement problems such as these, consider the interrelations among important constructs. Child adjustment is correlated with the quality of the relationships that children have with both their custodial and noncustodial parents (e.g., Amato & Gilbreth, 1999; Simons, 1996; Thompson & Laible, 1999). Child adjustment is also correlated quite consistently with the amount of child support received (Amato & Gilbreth, 1999; Furstenberg & Cherlin, 1991; McLanahan & Sandefur, 1994; Seltzer, 1994), however, and in at least some circumstances, it is associated with the amount of contact children have with their noncustodial parents (Amato & Gilbreth, 1999). The amount of child support is greater when there is joint custody, when fathers are more involved in decision making, and when fathers see their children more often (e.g., Braver et al., 1993; Seltzer, 1991, 1998; U.S. Census Bureau, 1997; Zill & Nord, 1996). Although the extent of visitation affects the opportunities for parental conflict, joint custody is not associated with increased levels of conflict (Pearson & Thoennes, 1990). Indeed, Gunnoe and Braver (in press) reported that joint custody was associated with more frequent father–child contact and better child adjustment, independent of the extent of predivorce conflict, although their sample likely excluded families characterized by high levels of conflict. Exposure to violence between the parents can be harmful, but significant numbers of children have warm and supportive relationships with parents who have violent relationships with one another, so we must be careful when reports of parental conflict are allowed to influence decisions about parent–child contact (Holden, Geffner, & Jouriles, 1998; Sternberg & Lamb, 1999). According to Appel and Holden (1998), 40% of the children whose parents were violent with one another were themselves victims of physical child abuse, suggesting that decision makers need to assess the relationships with the parents directly and not simply assume that the child must have been abused because the parents were violent with one another.

In sum, whether the associations are large or small in magnitude, the existing data suggest that the factors influencing child well-being work together in ways that make it impossible to design simple and universal decision rules that ignore individual circumstances. Although it is possible that increased child support may foster visitation and thereby enhance child adjustment (Zill & Nord, 1996), for example, it is also plausible that adequate contact makes nonresident fathers feel more involved and thus more willing to make child support payments that in turn enhance child well-being. And well-adjusted, happy children may simply make nonresidential parents want to be with and support them financially. Clearly, we have a constellation of correlated factors, and in the absence of intensive and reliable longitudinal data, it is difficult either to discern casual relationships definitively and unambiguously or to establish the relative importance of different factors.

In addition, the statistical associations are surely not linear, and the factors may operate together in complex ways. Voluntary child support may have more reliable associations with visitation frequency and child well-being than court-ordered support (Argys, Peters, Brooks-Gunn, & Smith, 1997; Zill & Nord, 1996), for example, and when there is substantial conflict between the parents, contact with nonresident parents may not have the same positive effect on children that it is does when levels of conflict are lower (Johnston, Kline, & Tschann, 1989). Unfortunately, our adversarial legal system has a way of promoting conflict around the time of divorce and as a result most divorcing families experience at least some conflict. Anger-based marital conflict is associated with filial aggression and externalizing behavior problems (Jenkins, 2000), perhaps because they have difficulty regulating negative affect themselves (Katz & Gottman, 1993).

When Should Access to Nonresidential Parents Be Restricted?

According to Maccoby and Mnookin (1992), somewhere around a quarter of divorcing families experience high levels of conflict around the time of divorce, and perhaps 10% of them may have conflict that is sufficiently severe and sufficiently intractable that it is probably not beneficial for the children concerned to have contact with their noncustodial parents (Johnston, 1994; personal communication). These statistics obviously represent selective samples, and we do not have access to more representative data concerning the incidence of high conflict in the broader population of divorcing couples, although Johnston has made especially careful efforts to differentiate among types of conflictful families, noting that conflict is intrinsically harmful to children in a minority of conflictful families. Litigation-related conflict and conflict triggered by the high levels of stress around the time of divorce do not appear to have enduring consequences for children and should not be confused by mental health professionals, custody evaluators, and judicial decision makers with conflict and violence that is endemic to the parents' relationships. Unfortunately, however, mere allegations of conflict or even marital violence can be powerful tools in our adversarial system, frequently resulting in reduced levels of court-approved contacts between fathers and children (Sternberg, 1997). Only a very small proportion of the divorcing families in America appear to experience parental conflict sufficiently severe and prolonged that contact between children and their noncustodial parents should be restricted.

The quality of the relationships between nonresidential parents and their children is also crucial. There are some families in which noncustodial fathers and children have sufficiently poor relationships that maintenance of interaction or involvement may not be of any benefit to the children, but we do not know how many relationships are like this. Unrepresentative data sets, such as those collected by Greif (1997) in the course of research designed to study fathers and mothers who lose (and frequently avoid) contact with their children after divorce, suggest that perhaps 10% to 15% of parents do not have either the commitment or individual capacities to establish and maintain supportive and enriching relationships with their children following divorce. Taken together, Johnston's and Greif's estimates suggest that, at most, 15% to 25% of the children who experience their parents' divorce might not benefit—indeed might perhaps be harmed—by regular and extended contact with their noncustodial parents. Stated differently, of course, this suggests that more than three quarters of the children experiencing their parents' divorce *could* benefit from (and at least not be hurt by) having and maintaining relationships with their noncustodial parents, although the benefits could be obscured if researchers did not distinguish between these types of families when studying the effects of postdivorce contact.

Fostering Relationships with Nonresidential Parents

Unfortunately, most contemporary custody and visitation decrees do not foster the maintenance of relationships between children and their noncustodial parents. For example, analysis of custody awards in two California counties, San Mateo and Santa Clara, revealed that a quarter of the children were permitted essentially no contact with their noncustodial fathers; we can only hope that the majority of these children were in fact those who were unlikely to benefit from continual contact, not simply those whose interests were poorly protected by the legal system (Maccoby, 1995; Maccoby & Mnookin, 1992; Peters, 1997). In addition, a substantial number of children were allowed by the courts to have very limited contact with their non-custodial parents; only a third of the total were allowed to spend three or more nights per 2-week period with their fathers, and some of these were allowed to spend two or fewer nights with their noncustodial mothers, further increasing the number of children apparently deemed unlikely to benefit from relationships with their non-custodial parents. Overall, then, 25% to 35% of the children in this large sample were allowed to spend little time with their noncustodial parents (with 40% to 50% spending no overnights with these parents). There are, unfortunately, no nationally representative data, but anecdotal and journalistic accounts suggest that the custody decrees in these two California counties are not atypically insensitive to children's needs for opportunities to maintain relationships with both of their parents.

The available data further suggest that the situation that exists around the time of separation or divorce is about "as good as it gets." Even when the amount of contact between children and noncustodial parents is as little as in these Califor-nia families, it typically declines over time, with increasing numbers of children having less and less contact with their noncustodial parents as time goes by (Furstenberg & Cherlin, 1991; Furstenberg, Nord, Peterson, & Zill, 1983). The families studied by Furstenberg and his colleagues divorced more than a quarter century ago, however, and more recent studies show that there have been secular decreases in the proportion of children who have little or no contact with their noncustodial fathers after divorce (Braver, 1998; Maccoby & Mnookin, 1992; Seltzer, 1991, 1998). To the extent that contact is beneficial, of course, such data suggest that many children continue to be placed at risk by the gradual (and some-times less-gradual) withdrawal of their noncustodial fathers.

Factors Affecting the Involvement of Nonresidential Fathers

What might account for the behavior of these men? Many fathers, most fathers' rights activists, and some scholars point to the fact that even when children do see their fathers regularly, these men are unable to play parental roles. These critics argue that many fathers drift away from their children after divorce because they are deprived of the opportunity to be parents rather than visitors. Most noncusto-dial parents are awarded "visitation" and they function as visitors, taking their children to the zoo, to movies, to dinner, and to other special activities in much the same way that grandparents or uncles and aunts might do. Children may well enjoy these excursions and may not regret the respite from arguments about getting homework done, getting their rooms cleaned up, behaving politely, getting their hair cut (or colored!), going to bed on time, getting ready for school, and respecting their siblings' property and their parents' limited resources, but the exclusion of fathers from these everyday tribulations is crucial, ultimately transforming the fathers' roles and making these men increasingly irrelevant to their children's lives, socialization, and development. Many men describe this as a sufficiently painful experience that they feel excluded from and pushed out of their children's lives (Clark & McKenry, 1997). Among the experts who drafted a recent consensus statement on the effects of divorce and custody arrangements on children's welfare and adjustment, there was agreement that parents not only need to spend adequate amounts of time with their children, but also need to be involved in a diverse array of activities with their children.

> To maintain high-quality relationships with their children, parents need to have sufficiently extensive and regular interactions with them, but the amount of time involved is usually less important than the quality of the interaction that it fosters. Time distribution arrangements that ensure the involvement of both parents in important aspects of their children's everyday lives and routines . . . are likely to keep nonresidential parents playing psychologically important and central roles in the lives of their children. (Lamb, Sternberg, & Thompson, 1997, p. 400)

If noncustodial parents are to maintain and strengthen relationships with their children, in other words, they need to participate in a range of everyday activities that allow them to function as parents rather than simply as regular, genial visitors. Kelly and Lamb (2000) showed that this need for extended, regular participation in diverse aspects of everyday socialization reflects accumulated professional understanding of how parent–child relationships are established and maintained, whether or not the parents live together. Both Kelly and Lamb (2000) and Warshak (2000) point out that overnight visits often play a crucial role in facilitating the types of parental responsibility and parent–child interactions that strengthen relationships and promote children's adjustment. When the levels of conflict between the parents are high, however, clinicians recommend that overnights with the noncustodial parent can be unusually stressful for very young children (Johnston & Roseby, 1997; Stahl, 1999). In such circumstances, time-distribution patterns that mimic the preseparation patterns of contact with the parents appear most suitable. Unfortunately, however, those constructing custody and visitation awards do not always appear to understand what sort of interaction is needed to consolidate and maintain parent–child relationships, and as a result, their decisions seldom ensure either sufficient amounts of time or adequate distributions of that time (overnight and across both school and nonschool days) to

promote healthy parent–child relationships. The statistics popularized by Furstenberg and Cherlin (1991) may show fathers drifting away largely because they no
longer have the opportunities to function as fathers in relation to their children.

> This pattern of visitation actually overstates the involvement of nonresidential
> fathers in raising their children. Even . . . where children are seeing their fathers
> regularly, the dads assume a minimal role in the day-to-day care and supervision of
> their children . . . most outside fathers behaved more like close relatives than par-
> ents . . . [R]outine parent–child activities were [un]common. (Furstenberg & Cher-
> lin, 1991, p. 36)

CONCLUSION

The issues discussed help explain the unexpectedly small and somewhat unreli-
able associations between various measures of child development and the amount
of contact between children and their noncustodial fathers. Evidently, contact
between a minority of children and their noncustodial parents may be harmful, so
the quality of the relationships needs to be taken into account when making decisions about the amount of interaction to encourage. Furthermore, it appears that
most children do not simply need more contact, but rather contact of an extent and
type sufficient to potentiate rich and multifaceted parent–child relationships.
When nonresidential fathers are fully and richly integrated into their children's
lives, they appear more likely to contribute economically to their children's support, and this too is associated with benefits for children. The concrete implications for custody evaluators and decision makers are clear. First, they should
determine whether the relationships between noncustodial parents and their children are worthy of support and protection; sadly, some (few) adults are incapable
even of mediocre parenting. Second, they should determine whether the conflict
between the parents is sufficiently intense, overt, and likely to continue indefi-
nitely. In some such cases, even minimal visitation may be undesirable. Third,
when contact is not contraindicated, evaluators should ensure that noncustodial
parents are able to participate in a broad range of everyday activities with their
children, particularly those demanding chores and contexts that "visiting" parents
often avoid. Fourth, custody evaluators should aim for voluntary agreements and
ensure that the actual custody orders both specify transitions and blocks of time in
detail and anticipate changes in the joint parenting plan as children's developmental needs change (Zill & Nord, 1996). Fifth, when voluntary agreements cannot be
reached, evaluators must avoid misinterpreting failure to compromise as a symp-
tom of severe underlying conflict too intense to permit coparenting. As long as
evaluators continue to make this mistake, they will continue to encourage mothers
who feel they have the upper hand to avoid meaningful compromises, relying
instead on allegations of conflict to help them "win" custody. Sixth, custody

awards should promote children's best interests; they should not reward or punish parents for real or alleged histories of involvement or noninvolvement, and they should not confuse "justice" for the parents with the children's best interests.

Just as it is relatively easy to conclude that abusive and incompetent fathers would likely harm rather than benefit their children and should thus not be granted unsupervised access, so is it easy to conclude that fathers who have assumed regular responsibility and have positive relationships with their children should be allowed to maintain and develop these relationships after divorce. The tougher decisions concern those fathers who have spent little time with their children, although they have been committed breadwinners, working additional hours so that their partners can afford to work less. The limited evidence available to us suggests that those who have developed positive relationships and want to remain involved in their children's lives should be encouraged to do so, even when the postdivorce plans demand different types of parental commitment (including more extensive hands-on parenting) than the predivorce history discloses (Amato & Gilbreth, 1999). Indeed, positive paternal involvement appears beneficial whether or not parents divorce, and social reformers should thus focus their attention on the division of responsibilities in two-parent families as well (Amato & Gilbreth, 1999; Lamb, 1997, 1999; Pleck, 1997).

Overall, there is substantial reason to believe that most (though not all) children would benefit following divorce from the opportunity to build and maintain relationships with both their noncustodial and custodial parents. Unfortunately, most custody decrees today permit limited and restricted opportunities for children to spend time with their noncustodial parents; these parents are thus peripheralized and their relationships weakened. In this way, time-distribution plans wittingly or unwittingly lead many noncustodial fathers to drift away from and out of the lives of their children. These trends might well be ameliorated by changing the typical postdivorce time-distribution plans, ensuring that they facilitate involvement by both parents. The proportion of families and children likely to benefit from more thoughtful time-distribution plans will also increase as secular changes in maternal and paternal roles continue. Even when direct responsibility for child care and socialization has been unequally divided between the parents, however, most children would benefit from time-distribution arrangements that permit and encourage both parents to become or remain active participants in their children's lives.

REFERENCES

Amato, P. R. (1993). Children's adjustment to divorce: Theories, hypotheses, and empirical support. *Journal of Marriage and the Family, 55,* 23–38.
Amato, P. R. (2000). The consequences of divorce for adults and children. *Journal of Marriage and the Family, 62,* 1269–1287.
Amato, P. R., & Gilbreth, J. G. (1999). Nonresident fathers and children's well-being: A meta-analysis. *Journal of Marriage and the Family, 61,* 557–573.
Amato, P. R., & Keith, B. (1991). Parental divorce and the well-being of children: A meta-analysis. *Psychological Bulletin, 110,* 26–46.

Amato, P. R., Loomis, L. S., & Booth, A. (1995). Parental divorce, marital conflict, and offspring well-being during early adulthood. *Social Forces, 73,* 896–916.

Amato, P. R., & Rezac, S. J. (1994). Contact with nonresidential parents, interparental conflict, and children's behavior. *Journal of Family Issues, 15,* 191–207.

Appel, A. E., & Holden, G. W. (1998). The co-occurrence of spouse and physical child abuse: A review and appraisal. *Journal of Family Psychology, 12,* 578–599.

Argys, L. M., Peters, H. E., Brooks-Gunn, J., & Smith, J. R. (1997). *Contributions of absent fathers to child well-being: The impact of child support dollars and father–child contact.* Unpublished manuscript, Department of Economics, University of Colorado, Denver.

Biller, H. B. (1981). Father absence, divorce, and personality development. In M. E. Lamb (Ed.), *The role of the father in child development* (rev. ed., pp. 489–551). New York: Wiley.

Biller, H. B. (1993). *Fathers and families: Paternal factors in child development.* Westport, CT: Auburn House.

Blankenhorn, D. (1995). *Fatherless America.* New York: Basic Books.

Braver, S. L. (1998). *Divorced dads: Shattering the myths.* New York: Putnam.

Braver, S. H., Wolchik, S. A., Sandler, I. N., Fogas, B. S., & Zvetina, D. (1991). Frequency of visitation by divorced fathers: Differences in reports by fathers and mothers. *American Journal of Orthopsychiatry, 61,* 448–454.

Braver, S. H., Wolchik, J. A., Sandler, I. N., Sheets, V. L., Fogas, B. S., & Bay, R. C. (1993). A longitudinal study of noncustodial parents: Parents without children. *Journal of Family Psychology, 7,* 9–23.

Burgess, A. (1997). *Fatherhood reclaimed: The making of the modern father.* London: Vermilion Press.

Clark, K., & McKenry, P. C. (1997). *Unheard voices: Divorced fathers without custody.* Unpublished manuscript, Department of Family Relations and Human Development, Ohio State University, Columbus.

Clarke-Stewart, K. A., & Hayward, C. (1996). Advantages of father custody and contact for the psychological well-being of school-age children. *Journal of Applied Developmental Psychology, 17,* 239–270.

Cooksey, E. C. (1997). Consequences of young mothers' marital histories for children's cognitive development. *Journal of Marriage and the Family, 59,* 245–261.

Cummings, E. M., & Davies, P. (1994). *Children and marital conflict: The impact of family dispute and resolution.* New York: Guilford.

Cummings, E. M., & O'Reilly, A. W. (1997). Fathers in family context: Effects of marital quality on child adjustment. In M. E. Lamb (Ed.), *The role of the father in child development* (3rd ed., pp. 49–65, 318–325). New York: Wiley.

Downey, D. B. (1994). The school performance of children from single-mother and single-father families: Economic or interpersonal deprivation. *Journal of Family Issues, 15,* 129–147.

Dremen, S., & Ronen-Eliav, H. (1997). The relation of divorced mothers' perceptions of family cohesion and adaptability to behavior problems in children. *Journal of Marriage and the Family, 59,* 324–331.

Duncan, G. J., & Brooks-Gunn, J. (Eds.). (1997). *Consequences of growing up poor.* New York: Russell Sage Foundation.

Emery, R. E. (1994). *Renegotiating family relationships: Divorce, child custody, and mediation.* New York: Guilford.

Fathers' involvement in their children's schools. (1997, winter). *Father Times, 6*(2), 1, 4–6.

Furstenberg, F. F. Jr., & Cherlin, A. J. (1991). *Divided families: What happens to children when parents part.* Cambridge, MA: Harvard University Press.

Furstenberg, F. F. Jr., Morgan, S. P., & Allison, P. D. (1987). Paternal participation and children well-being after marital dissolution. *American Sociological Review, 52,* 695–701.

Furstenberg, F. F. Jr., Nord, C. W., Peterson, J. L., & Zill, N. (1983). The life course of children of divorce. *American Psychological Review, 48,* 656–668.

Goodman, G. S., Emery, R. E., & Haugaard, J. J. (1998). Developmental psychology and law: The cases of divorce, child maltreatment, foster care, and adoption. In W. Damon, I. Sigel, & A. Renninger (Eds.), *Handbook of child psychology: Vol. 4. Child psychology in practice* (5th ed., pp. 775–874). New York: Wiley.

Greif, G. L. (1997). *Out of touch: When parents and children lose contact after divorce.* New York: Oxford University Press.

Gunnoe, M. L., & Braver, S. L. (in press). The effects of joint legal custody on mothers, fathers, and children controlling for factors that predispose a sole maternal vs. joint legal award. *Law and Human Behavior.*

Hanson, T. L., McLanahan, S. S., & Thomson, E. (1996). Double jeopardy: Parental conflict and stepfamily outcomes for children. *Journal of Marriage and the Family, 58,* 141–154.

Hetherington, E. M., Bridges, M., & Insabella, G. M. (1998). What matters? What does not? Five perspectives on the association between marital transition and children's adjustment. *American Psychologist, 53,* 167–184.

Hetherington, E. M., & Henderson, S. H. (1997). Fathers in stepfamilies. In M. E. Lamb (Ed.), *The role of the father in child development* (3rd ed., pp. 212–226, 369–373). New York: Wiley.

Hetherington, E. M., & Stanley-Hagan, M. M. (1997). The effects of divorce on fathers and their children. In M. E. Lamb (Ed.), *The role of the father in child development* (3rd ed., pp. 191–211). New York: Wiley.

Hines, A. M. (1997). Divorce-related transitions, adolescent development, and the role of the parent-child relationship: A review of the literature. *Journal of Marriage and the Family, 59,* 375–388.

Holden, G. W., Geffner, R., & Jouriles, E. N. (Eds.). (1998). *Children exposed to marital violence: Theory, research, and applied issues.* Washington, DC: American Psychological Association.

Isaacs, M. B., & Leon, G. H. (1988). Remarriage and its alternatives following divorce: Mother and child adjustment. *Journal of Marital and Family Therapy, 14,* 163–173.

Jenkins, J. M. (2000). Marital conflict and children's emotions: The development of an anger organization. *Journal of Marriage and the Family, 62,* 723–736.

Johnston, J. R. (1994). High-conflict divorce. *The Future of Children, 4,* 165–182.

Johnston, J. R., Kline, M., & Tschann, J. (1989). Ongoing postdivorce conflict in families contesting custody: Effects on children of joint custody and frequent access. *American Journal of Orthopsychiatry, 59,* 576–592.

Johnston, J. R., & Roseby, V. (1997). *In the name of the child.* New York: Free Press.

Jouriles, E. N., Norwood, W. D., McDonald, R., Vincent, J. P., & Mahoney, A. (1996). Physical violence and other forms of marital aggression: Links with children's behavior problems. *Journal of Family Psychology, 10,* 223–234.

Katz, L. F., & Gottman, J. M. (1993). Patterns of marital conflict predict children's internalizing and externalizing behaviors. *Developmental Psychology, 29,* 940–950.

Kelly, J. B. (2000). Children's adjustment in conflicted marriage and divorce: A decade review of research. *Journal of the American Academy of Child and Adolescent Psychiatry, 39,* 963–973.

Kelly, J. B., & Lamb, M. E. (2000). Using child development research to make appropriate custody and access decisions for young children. *Family and Conciliation Courts Review, 38,* 297–311.

Lamb, M. E. (1975). Fathers: Forgotten contributors to child development. *Human Development, 18,* 245–266.

Lamb, M. E. (Ed.). (1976). *The role of the father in child development.* New York: Wiley.

Lamb, M. E. (Ed.). (1997). *The role of the father in child development* (3rd ed.). New York: Wiley.

Lamb, M. E. (1999). Non-custodial fathers and their impact on the children of divorce. In R. A. Thompson & P. R. Amato (Eds.), *The post-divorce family: Research and policy issues* (pp. 105–125). Thousand Oaks, CA: Sage.

Lamb, M. E., Sternberg, K. J., & Thompson, R. A. (1997). The effects of divorce and custody arrangements on children's behavior, development, and adjustment. *Family and Conciliation Courts Review, 35,* 393–404.

Levine, J. A. (1976). *Who will raise the children?* Philadelphia: Lippincott.

Maccoby, E. E. (1995). Divorce and custody: The fights, needs, and obligations of mothers, fathers, and children. In G. B. Melton (Ed.), *The individual, the family, and social good: Personal fulfillment in times of change* (pp. 135–172). Lincoln: University of Nebraska Press.

Maccoby, E. E., & Mnookin, R. H. (1992). *Dividing the child: Social and legal dilemmas of custody.* Cambridge, MA: Harvard University Press.

Maier, E. H., & Lachman, M. E. (2000). Consequences of early parental loss and separation for health and well-being in midlife. *International Journal of Behavioral Development, 24,* 183–189.

McLanahan, S. S. (1999). Father absence and the welfare of children. In E. M. Hetherington (Ed.), *Coping with divorce, single parenting, and remarriage: A risk and resiliency perspective* (pp. 117–145). Mahwah, NJ: Lawrence Erlbaum Associates.

McLanahan, S. S., & Sandefur, G. (1994). *Growing up with a single parent: What hurts, what helps.* Cambridge, MA: Harvard University Press.

McLanahan, S. S., & Teitler, J. (1999). The consequences of father absence. In M. E. Lamb (Ed.), *Parenting and child development in "nontraditional" families.* Mahwah, NJ: Lawrence Erlbaum Associates.

McNeal, C., & Amato, P. R. (1998). Parents' marital violence: Long-term consequences for children. *Journal of Family Issues, 19,* 123–139.

Pearson, J., & Thoennes, N. (1990). Custody after divorce: Demographic and attitudinal patterns. *American Journal of Orthopsychiatry, 60,* 233–249,

Peters, H. E. (1997). *Child custody and monetary transfers in divorce negotiations: Reduced form and simulation results.* Unpublished manuscript, Department of Economics, Cornell University, Ithaca, NY.

Pleck, J. H. (1997). Paternal involvement: Levels, sources, and consequences. In M. E. Lamb (Ed.), *The role of the father in child development* (3rd ed., pp. 66–103). New York: Wiley.

Popenoe, D. (1996). *Life without father.* New York: Free Press.

Seltzer, J. (1991). Relationships between fathers and children who live apart: The father's role after separation. *Journal of Marriage and the Family, 53,* 79–101.

Seltzer, J. A. (1994). Consequences of marital dissolution for children. *American Review of Sociology, 20,* 235–266.

Seltzer, J. A. (1998). Father by law: Effects of joint legal custody on nonresident fathers' involvement with children. *Demography, 35,* 635–646.

Simons, R. L. (1996). *Understanding differences between divorced and intact families: Stress, interaction, and child outcome.* Thousand Oaks, CA: Sage.

Smith, H. L., Morgan, S. P., & Koropeckyj-Cox, T. (1996). A decomposition of trends in the nonmarital fertility ratios of Blacks and Whites in the United States. *Demography, 33,* 141–151.

Stahl, P. M. (1999). *Complex issues in child custody evaluation.* Thousand Oaks, CA: Sage.

Sternberg, K. J. (1997). Fathers, the missing parents in research on family violence. In M. E. Lamb (Ed.), *The role of the father in child development* (3rd ed., pp. 284–308). New York: Wiley.

Sternberg, K. J., & Lamb, M. E. (1999). Violent families. In M. E. Lamb (Ed.), *Parenting and child development in "nontraditional" families* (pp. 305–325). Mahwah, NJ: Lawrence Erlbaum Associates.

Sternberg, K. J., Lamb, M. E., & Dawud-Noursi, S. (1998). Understanding domestic violence and its effects: Making sense of divergent reports and perspectives. In G. W. Holden, R. Geffner, & E. W. Jouriles (Eds.), *Children exposed to family violence* (pp. 121–156). Washington, DC: American Psychological Association.

Thomson, E., Hanson, T. L., & McLanahan, S. (1994). Family structure and child well-being: Economic resources versus parental behaviors. *Social Forces, 73,* 221–242.

Thompson, R. A., & Laible, D. J. (1999). Noncustodial parents. In M. E. Lamb (Ed.), *Parenting and child development in "nontraditional" families* (pp. 103–123). Mahwah, NJ: Lawrence Erlbaum Associates.

U.S. Census Bureau. (1997). Child support for custodial mothers and fathers: 1997. (Report No. P60–212). Washington, DC: Author.

Warshak, R. A. (2000). Blanket restrictions: Overnight contact between parents and young children. *Family and Conciliation Courts Review, 38,* 422–445.

Whitehead, B. D. (1993). Dan Quayle was right. *Atlantic Monthly, 271,* 47–50.

Zill, N. (1996). Unmarried parenthood as a risk factor for children. *Testimony before Committee on Ways and Means, House of Representatives, March 12, 1996* (Serial 104–52, pp. 50–65). Washington, DC: U.S. Government Printing Office.

Zill, N., & Nord, C. W. (1996, November). *Causes and consequences of involvement by non-custodial parents in their children's lives: Evidence from a national longitudinal study.* Paper presented to the National Center on Fathers and Families Roundtable, New York.

III

Sociological and Anthropological Perspectives on Fatherhood: Traversing Lenses, Methods, and Invisible Men

Linda M. Burton

Pennsylvania State University

> I am an invisible man. No I am not a spook like those who haunted Edgar Allan Poe; nor am I one of your Hollywood movie ectoplasms. I am a man of substance, of flesh and bone, fiber, and liquids—and I might even be said to possess a mind. I am invisible, understand, simply because people refuse to see me. (Ellison, 1952, p. 3)

Over half a century ago, Ralph Ellison (1952), in his classic novel, *Invisible Man,* challenged us to consider the influences of social and cultural forces on the work and family lives of African-American men. In this novel, Ellison artfully chronicled the impact of nested contradictions in history, political ideologies, work, kinship relations, and personal development on one man's role in his family (Burton & Snyder, 1998). This man, who remained nameless throughout the novel, was two generations removed from slavery. Through his eyes, we witness his struggle to define, acquire, and maintain work and family roles during an era in U.S. history characterized by social and personal paradoxes concerning the place of minority men in the larger social order. This nameless man's family roles also implicitly reflected the interplay between visible and "invisible" social forces of the time. These forces included, but were not limited to, restrictive labor market opportunities for minority and economically disadvantaged males, and a general

185

public suspicion concerning whether these men served any purpose in their families and in society at large.

Ellison's *Invisible Man* offers an intriguing backdrop for the collection of chapters in this section of the book. Much like the work of Ellison, this collection of chapters inspires examination of social and cultural forces that shape the contemporary experiences of fathers in diverse racial and ethnic groups. Using demographic, sociological, and anthropological lenses, and survey, qualitative, and ethnographic methods, these chapters prod us to consider how different ways of thinking about and measuring fatherhood lead us to new levels of discovery about the complex nature of fathers' involvement in the lives of their children.

The metaphoric similarity between Ellison's work and this anthology of chapters is fortuitous. Ellison crafts the image of a nameless invisible man, much like some constituents in the current public discourse on "deadbeat, absent dads" have fostered images of fathers in America's disadvantaged families (Blankenhorn, 1995). In essence, the work presented here attempts to unpack and challenge popular notions of father involvement and absent dads, paying particular attention to the conceptual and methodological *opportunities* at our disposal for discerning what fathers contribute to the well-being of their children.

We begin our exploration of "not so invisible" fathers with a chapter authored by David Eggebeen. Eggebeen applies a demographic lense to the study of fatherhood, underscoring the critical role three social surveys—The National Survey of Children, the National Longitudinal Survey of Youth, and the National Survey of Families and Households—have played in advancing knowledge on fathers. Eggebeen informs us that, using surveys, social scientists have examined prevailing notions concerning nonresident fathers' involvement with their biological children, the level of support that nonresident and resident fathers provide to households in which their *biological* children live, distinctions between what comprises fathering as compared to mothering behaviors, and the relationship between aspects of fathering and traditional developmental outcomes for children. He also carefully articulates the limitations of surveys for addressing research and policy questions about fathers, implicitly noting that surveys cannot discern important subtle cultural and contextual features of fathering behaviors. One of the lingering questions that surveys have not been able to address is: How do biological fathers, inside and outside of the context of marriage, influence the well-being of children other than their own?

The chapter written by Robin Jarrett, Kevin Roy, and Linda Burton broaches this question and others about low-income, urban, African-American fathers. With an integrated sociological, developmental, and qualitative lens, Jarrett, Roy, and Burton provide an overview of the contributions qualitative and ethnographic studies have made to our understanding of fatherhood. Their focus on African-American men is an important one given that in various public and policy arenas, low-income African-American fathers have been implicitly designated a significant source of the "deadbeat dad" problem. This chapter takes us inside the lived experiences of urban African-American fathers, summarizing extant research in four areas: (1) the neighborhood context of fatherhood, (2) negotiations between fathers and mothers in a system of kin work, (3) the meaning of fatherhood and the social process of father involvement, and (4) the diverse set of father figures who fulfill a variety of flexible paternal role obligations.

In the chapter authored by Nicholas Townsend, the cultural anthropology lens is applied to the study of fatherhood. Townsend jettisons us into cross-cultural research on fathers, closely examining and comparing father involvement among two groups of men—one in the west coastal region of the United States and another in a village in the African country of Botswana. Drawing on intensive fieldwork conducted in both environments, Townsend describes the distinctive systems in which men in the United States and Botswana enact the role of fathers and the cultural meaning of fatherhood in the lives of children. Townsend's analysis leaves us with three points that challenge myopic views on fatherhood and that require further exploration: (a) fathers play important roles throughout their children's lives, not just when their children are young; (b) biological fathers are not the only men involved in the lives of children; and (c) different cultures have different norms about which men, at which stages of their lives, should be doing what for children.

The final chapter in this section, written by Jaipaul Roopnarine, provides another example of a finely focused cultural lens on fatherhood. Roopnarine explores father involvement practices among English-speaking Caribbean fathers from Guyana, Trinidad and Tobago, Jamaica, Grenada, Barbados, Dominica, St. Kitts, St. Lucia, St. Vincent, and Nevis and those who immigrated from these counties to North America. He questions the popular belief held by many that fatherhood in the Caribbean is "in crisis." Although he does not deny that the degree of father involvement varies within this culture, he contests the assumption that Caribbean fathers are uniformly uninvolved or "invisible." In this study, Roopnarine explores the context for father involvement through a discussion of the array of culturally approved marital and nonmarital unions prevalent in Carribean society. In addition, he examines cultural beliefs about manhood and fatherhood as well as assumptions about the nature of paternal roles and responsibilities.

Returning to the metaphor of Ellison's *Invisible Man*, using particular lenses and methods, these chapters collectively challenge social scientists to reevaluate prevailing notions of "invisible" fathers. At the very least, these chapters illustrate what sociological and anthropological paradigms and quantitative and qualitative methods have to offer concerning studies of fatherhood and child development. Fatherhood researchers have an array of conceptual and methodological tools to chose from in their work. These tools, when used appropriately, lead to novel discoveries about dads—discoveries that underscore the *visible* roles fathers often play in the lives of their's and other's children.

188 SECTION III: SOCIOLOGICAL PERSPECTIVES

REFERENCES

Blankenhorn, D. (1995). *Fatherless America: Confronting our most urgent social problem.* New York: Basic Books.

Burton, L. M., & Snyder, A. R. (1998). The invisible man revisited: Comments on the life course, history, and men's roles in American families. In A. Booth & A. C. Crouter (Eds.), *Men in families.* Hillsdale, NJ: Lawrence Erlbaum Associates.

Ellison, R. (1952). *Invisible man.* New York: Vintage Books.

8

Sociological Perspectives on Fatherhood: What Do We Know About Fathers from Social Surveys?

David J. Eggebeen
Pennsylvania State University

Social surveys are probably the most heavily used tool in the sociologist's tool bag. There are several good reasons for this. Much of what sociologists conceptualize as the important questions to be answered can be efficiently and effectively addressed with survey type questions. Most sociological research is quantitative; surveys are an effective mechanism to gather data best suited to quantitative research methods. Sociological approaches lean toward making generalizations. Generalizations are most comfortably made from analyses of data that are representative of the population of interest; surveys are an efficient means of obtaining a representative sample. Therefore, it is not surprising that the vast majority of research done on fathers and fathering from a sociological perspective has involved the use of social surveys. The purpose of this chapter is to examine the critical role in the scholarship on fathers played by three social surveys: the National Survey of Children (NSC), the National Longitudinal Survey of Youth (NLSY), and the National Survey of Families and Households (NSFH). I will argue that these surveys were the foundation for key empirical contributions to our knowledge about fathers through the 1980s and 1990s, challenged current thinking in ways that have lead to critical advances in our understanding about fathers, and each, in its own way, has set the stage for current and planned data collection efforts.

189

I will organize the discussion of these surveys around four questions: (a) Why choose these surveys? (b) What have we learned about fathers from these data? (c) What have we not learned (or avoided studying, if you will) about fathers from these surveys? And finally, (d) what lies ahead for using large, nationally representative surveys such as these three for addressing fathers and fatherhood?

WHY FOCUS ON THESE THREE SURVEYS?

There are several good reasons for limiting this review to empirical work based on the NSFH, the NLSY, and the NSC surveys. First, a number of good summaries and critiques of the scholarly literature on fatherhood have been published in the past five years (see Amato & Gilbreth, 1999; Cabrera, Tamis-LeMonda, Bradley, Hofferth, & Lamb, 2000; Lamb, 1997, 2000; Marsiglio, Amato, Day, & Lamb, 2000), and another encyclopedic review would add little beyond what has been already said. What has not been appreciated until very recently, however, is the emerging importance over the past two decades of major, nationally representative surveys for family scholarship in general and the study of fathers in particular. For example, of the 49 empirical articles published in Volume 42 (1980) of the *Journal of Marriage and the Family,* 12 used secondary data of this type (24%). By Volume 62 (2000), however, there were 18 articles based on secondary data sets out of a total of 44 empirical studies (41%). In particular, data for 10 of these 18 studies were drawn from the three surveys of interest here: the NSFH, the NLSY, and the NSC.

Indeed, the strategic importance of large, nationally representative surveys that cover a broad range of topics and issues pertinent to children, families, and fathers was clearly recognized in the series of conferences sponsored by the Federal Interagency Forum on Child and Family Statistics in 1996 and 1997. These meetings resulted in the publication of *Nurturing Fatherhood: Improving Data and Research on Male Fertility, Family Formation, and Fatherhood* in 1998. Within this document is a through review of "where we are now" in our data on fathers and a theoretical and conceptual framework for future data collection efforts, a "roadmap," if you will, for the kinds of data-collection efforts federal research dollars should be targeting.

It is my contention that three surveys—NSC, the NLSY, and NSFH—provided data for a series of studies of fatherhood that lead to a number of key findings. Analyses based on data from these surveys, for the first time, documented the amount of contact between nonresident fathers and their children. Our understanding of the interplay between child support and nonresident father involvement was greatly enhanced by studies using these data. These surveys provided initial estimates of the nature of nonresident father involvement beyond mere contact or visits. These surveys allowed researchers to begin to tease apart fathering into its various dimensions and examine systematically the linkage between these dimensions and developmental outcomes of children. Finally, studies based on these surveys began to challenge the prevailing notions that fathering is functionally equivalent to mothering, that the more time nonresident fathers spend with their children the better off they are, and that focusing on coresidential relationships will tell us most of what we need to know about fathers and fatherhood.

I was able to uncover 53 studies of some aspect of fatherhood that used data from one of these surveys. The NLSY surveys were used in 24 studies, the NSFH provided data for 21 articles, and I was able to find 8 empirical studies of fatherhood that used the NSC. I did not consider the plethora of studies that relied on these surveys to examine father absence per se, such as two- versus one-parent families or studies that address family structure as a determinant of child well-being (cf. McLanahan & Sandefur, 1994). Neither did I include the large number of unpublished works such as doctoral dissertations, conference papers, or working papers from research centers that have examined fathers using these surveys. These 53 studies were all published in referred journals or as book chapters, and all went beyond "father presence" to examine one of more component of fatherhood, as either an independent variable or as a dependent variable. A brief description of each of these social surveys follows.

National Survey of Children

The National Survey of Children (NSC) consists of three panels of data on a nationally representative sample of 2,301 children age 7 to 11 first interviewed in 1976 and subsequently reinterviewed in 1981 ($n = 1,423$) and in 1987 ($n = 1,147$). Detailed descriptions of the data can be found in several of the key studies using these data (Furstenberg, Morgan, & Allison, 1987; Furstenberg, Nord, Peterson, & Zill, 1983; Harris, Furstenberg, & Marmer, 1996). These data represent a pioneering effort to obtain nationally representative data on children that would provide a broad assessment of the social, physical, and psychological characteristics of children. The subsequent follow-up panel in 1981 on a subsample of the children allowed researchers to focus on the effects on children of marital conflict and divorce. The third wave of interviews in 1987 provided detailed information on the social, psychological, and economic circumstances of the children as they entered young adulthood.

A particularly innovative feature of these data was that information was obtained from a parent (usually the mother), the child, and a survey sent to the child's teacher. This use of multiple informants allowed researchers to check the validity of information gathered from any particular individual (cf. Smith & Morgan, 1994) and to avoid the problem of shared method variance (Marsiglio et al., 2000). What has made this survey valuable to researchers interested in fathers is the inclusion of a series of questions (in the 1981 and 1987 panels) directed at the amount of involvement and the emotional relationship the father had with the child. Because this information was obtained from the child or adolescent, researchers could, for the first time, document the nature and extent of nonresident father involvement in a nationally representative sample. These measures, then, combined with data on child or adolescent well-being, parallel questions about parenting directed at the child's mother, and the panel design gave researchers great potential to address questions that heretofore had either never been examined or had only been treated in an exploratory fashion with nonrepresentative data.

Taken together, these data represent one of the pioneering efforts to obtain a nationally representative sample of children, to measure the well-being of children with survey methods, and to follow children over time.

National Survey of Families and Households

In contrast to the NSC, the the National Survey of Families and Households (NSFH) was intentionally funded to be an omnibus survey of contemporary family life that would be made available to the research community almost immediately after the data collection was completed. This survey has had a profound effect on family scholarship. The NSFH Web site lists an incomplete research bibliography of nearly 373 articles, books, and theses that have used these data. Despite the fact that the second wave of data was released in 1992, studies based on this survey continue to appear in journals. For example, the *Journal of Marriage and the Family* alone published seven studies based on this survey in the year 2000.

For most readers, this survey needs little introduction. The 1987/88 wave consists of a nationally representative sample of 13,017 primary respondents ages 19 and older living in households (Sweet, Bumpass, & Call, 1988). The NSFH respondents consist of a main sample of 9,637 respondents, plus double samples of minorities (Blacks and Hispanics), single-parent families, families with stepchildren, cohabiting couples, and recently married couples. One of the most attractive features of this survey was the large amount of life history information that was collected, including the respondent's family living arrangements in childhood, the experience of leaving the parental home, marital and cohabitation experience, as well as education, fertility, and employment histories. The survey also obtained detailed descriptions of past and current living arrangements, marital and parenting relationships, kin contact, and economic and psychological well-being. A follow-up of this survey was conducted 5 years later on all surviving members of the original sample (10,007 respondents) (Sweet & Bumpass, 1996). In addition to updating the life history information and repeating questions from the first panel, additional data was collected via a number of specialized interviews with the current spouse or cohabiting partner of the respondent, the original spouse or partner in cases where the relationship had ended in the interval, a selected child who was age 13 to 18 in the original survey and who are age 18 to 23 by the second wave, a selected child who was originally age 5 to 12 at the time of the original survey and who are now age 10 to 17, a surviving spouse or other relative in cases where the original respondent has died or is too ill to interview, and a randomly selected parent of the main respondent.

This survey has proven to be invaluable to researchers interested in fatherhood. In particular, fathers were asked fairly detailed questions about the nature of their involvement with their children. For example, information was obtained about what activities they shared with their children, the kinds of monitoring performed, the nature of the affective relationship with child, the kinds and extent of conflicts and disagreements, and a series of questions about raising stepchildren (see Federal Interagency Forum on Child and Family Statistics, 1998, Appendix J for a more detailed description of questions relevant to father involvement). The NSFH went beyond the NSC by expanding the universe of children to include children of all ages up to age 19. The large sample size of the NSFH allowed for the examination of specific subpopulations that was not possible in the NSC. Finally, the NSFH offered an expanded set of questions of father involvement that permitted examination of nonresident fathers and fathers of adult children, as well as stepfathers.

The National Longitudinal Survey of Youth

The National Longitudinal Survey of Youth (NLSY) is really part of a family of surveys (the National Longitudinal Surveys), many of them still ongoing, funded by the U.S. Department of Labor, and maintained at the Center for Human Resources at Ohio State University. Detailed information about all the surveys, where the NLSY fits into the scheme of things, as well as extensive documentation about the publicly available data sets can be found at the following Web site: http://stats.bls.gov:80/nlshome.htm.

The NLSY began in 1979 as a nationally representative sample of 12,680 men and women age 14 to 22. Respondents have been interviewed yearly from 1979 to the present. In 1986, the women in the original cohort who had become mothers were given an additional interview, and fairly extensive information was gathered on 4,971 children, about 95% of eligible children. These special interviews and the child assessments have taken place every 2 years. At each reinterview, assessments were done on additional children born to the women, and previous children are reassessed. By the 1998 round, information was obtained on 7,067 children age 21 and younger born to these women. The 21 (and counting) waves of interviews on the adults and the 8 waves of data on the children have lead to an enormous amount of information and unique opportunities for researchers to address questions on the interconnected life courses of children and adults.

It is hard to overestimate the impact of this survey on social science research. The online bibliography database that is maintained (http://www.chrr.ohio-state.edu/nls-bib/) claims to list over 1,946 works that have used data from the main NLSY data sets and 467 scholarly papers that have used data from the mother–child data files. The NLSY has a much broader scope than the NSC or the NSFH surveys, which focused exclusively on families and children. In contrast to either the NSC or the NSFH, the NSYC is particularly useful for studies that reach beyond a narrow focus on family. For example, these data have been exploited to address important questions on the transition to adulthood, the interconnections of educational experiences and work, family and work, the economic returns to schooling, the consequences of early childbearing, and so on. The ongoing nature of this survey means that the data will only get better and that the potential to address new research questions will grow. For example, children who were first assessed in the 1986 wave (and were age 0 to about 14) have now entered young adulthood, opening up an unrivaled opportunity for researchers to examine a whole range of issues on the link between early life experiences and young adult transitions.

Ironically, the richness of these data on a range of individual and family dimensions does not extend to information on fathering. Relative to the NSC and the NSFH, the NLSY data contains fewer questions on father involvement. Although these data contain good information on the kinds and amounts of economic investments in children and the number and length of visits between nonresident fathers and children, the information on the nature and extent of shared activities is skimpy. Nevertheless, data from this survey has proven to be quite valuable to researchers interested in fatherhood, especially for those types of questions that play to the strengths of these data rather than its weaknesses.

WHAT HAVE WE LEARNED FROM THESE SURVEYS?

It is my contention that research based on these three surveys has provided strategic insights into fatherhood. Indeed, research using these data have been among the key works that have laid the empirical and conceptual foundations for our understanding of nonresident fatherhood, the nature of involvement among resident fathers, and the consequences of fatherhood for men. I begin with resident fathers.

Resident Fatherhood

The past decade has witnessed a golden age of research on fatherhood, especially on the topic of what kinds of behaviors fathers engage in and their meaning and significance for children (Marsiglio et al, 2000). Studies based on these three surveys have been central to this line of research and have made important contributions to our understanding of three domains of fathers' contributions to children: economic provision, child care, and various types of involvement.

Theoretically, it seems obvious that an important contribution that men could make to their child's well-being is economic support (cf. Amato, 1993; Amato &

Keith, 1991; McLanahan & Sandefur, 1994; Seltzer & Brandreth, 1994). However, attempts to determine what it is about the economic dimensions of men that affect children's well-being have received surprisingly little empirical attention. Several studies that have examined this angle have made use of the NLSY. Elizabeth Cooksey and her colleagues (1997) examined the importance of both parents' employment characteristics for young children's emotional well-being and behavior problems. They found that both maternal work characteristics, family characteristics, and to a lesser extent, fathers' work characteristics were independently related to child outcomes. Earlier work by Toby Parcel and Elizabeth Menaghan also found strong evidence for the importance of paternal working conditions in the NLSY. They found that the number of hours fathers worked had a significant impact on preschool-age children's behavior problems (Parcel & Menaghan, 1994). It is clear that we have a long way to go before we fully understand the independent influences of the varied ways fathers' economic contributions matter to children. However, these works clearly show the great potential of the NLSY to provide researchers with an opportunity to address empirically what we have long asserted theoretically—that we cannot fully understand the lives and circumstances of children until we view them as embedded in the ongoing lives of other members of their families.

Of course, researchers have also taken advantage of the NSC and the NSFH surveys to directly examine the parenting behavior of fathers in two-parent families. Indeed, specific questions in these surveys go beyond mere accounting for the amount of time fathers may have spent with children, to estimates of the quality of the relationship and the interaction and a reporting of the various kinds of activities that have been shared. Early work by Marsiglio (1991) using the NSFH documented the kinds of fathering activities of men and examined the determinants of father involvement. He found little evidence that characteristics of wives or partners were important determinants of father involvement. However, children's characteristics (e.g., age number, biological status, and gender composition) were strong and consistent predictors of fathers' engagement.

Two other studies use the NSFH data on fathering behavior to address the nature of the association between father involvement and child outcomes (Amato & Rivera, 1999; Cooksey & Fondell, 1996). Work by Cooksey and Fondell (1996) nicely details the differences in amounts and kinds of time spent with children for six different kinds of family arrangements of coresident dads. This work affirms what a considerable amount of other research shows—that the amount of time coresident fathers share with their children is good for the children. However, it also draws attention to the subtle but important differences that family circumstances (the ecology, if you will) make in both the time fathers spend with their children and the effect of this time on children's academic achievement.

Work by Amato and Rivera (1999) poses a slightly different question: Does father involvement make a unique contribution beyond mothers' involvement to children's behavior? Noting that most studies are plagued by same-source bias, these researchers take advantage of the use of multiple informants of the NSFH survey to avoid the problem of the same-respondent reporting on both father involvement and children's behavior. They find strong evidence that paternal involvement is negatively related to the extent of behavior problems reported by the mother. Furthermore, they found little difference in the effects of stepfather involvement relative to biological fathers on behavior problems—the beneficial effects of paternal involvement generalize beyond biology.

Finally, Harris and colleagues (1996) have used the three waves of data from the NSC to examine the quantity and quality of fathers' involvement over time, net of mothers' involvement, on the well-being of adolescents. This work highlights the variable nature of father involvement as children, and fathers, age— something virtually ignored in most other research on father involvement. This work is also notable for its attempt to look at the effects of both the level and course of involvement for the several pitfalls adolescents can experience in the transition to adulthood. In general, they find that fathers have an important effect on children's economic and educational achievement, children's social behavior, and their psychological well-being. These effects, however, are not as powerful as other aspects of the family environment of the adolescent.

Thus, we see that two of these surveys, the NSC and NSFH, have been used in key studies of the nature of resident father involvement. The nationally representative nature of these surveys has meant that findings from these studies can be generalized. The detailed questions on involvement of both parents have allowed for greater insight into the unique contributions of fathers to children's development. The detail on relationships with children, combined with the large-sample size opened the door for comparisons of different kinds of fathers. Finally, the longitudinal design was exploited by a number of studies to sort out causation, as well as to address the course of father involvement.

Nonresident Fathers

Research using data from these surveys have made four important contributions to our knowledge about nonresident fathers: (a) studies have demonstrated the dynamic nature of men's living arrangements with their children; (b) studies have documented the kinds and extent of contact between nonresident fathers and their children; (c) studies have documented the correlates and the conditions under which fathers contribute economically to their nonresident children; (d) studies have given scholars and policymakers a clearer picture of the interrelated nature of child support and involvement with the child; and (e) studies based on these surveys have shown which aspects of nonresident father involvement are important for children's well-being.

One of the more significant advances in our understanding of fatherhood in the past decade is the recognition that father presence or absence is too simplistic a frame for analysis of the role that men play in the lives of children (Marsiglio et al., 2000). Research using data from the NSFH and the NLSY have underscored the complexity and fluidity of fathers' connections to households where children reside. Much of this work is descriptive in nature, emphasizing the demography of living arrangements and their changes over time. Early work based on the NLSY documented, from the perspective of children, the experience of coresident adult males over the early life course (Eggebeen, Crockett, & Hawkins, 1990; Hawkins and Eggebeen, 1991; Mott, 1990). These descriptive analyses documented the considerable extent to which children had an adult male other than their biological father residing with them for at least part of their childhood, the demographic correlates of these relationships, and the highly unstable nature of these fatherlike relationships. Work based on the detailed marriage and living arrangement histories gathered in the NSFH survey has extended the preliminary descriptions of the early years of childhood based on NLSY data to that of documenting children's experiences of living with men through their entire childhood (Martinson & Wu, 1992; Wojtkiewicz, 1992; Wu, 1996; Wu & Martinson, 1993). The lesson learned from these analyses is clear: snapshot measures of family structure obscure more than illuminate the role men play in the lives of children. These attempts to view children's lives dynamically have opened our eyes to the multifaceted nature of fathers'—and other men's—ties to children. These studies demonstrate unequivocally that focusing exclusively on coresident, biological fathers excludes from analysis a host of relationships between men and children that may—or may not—be fatherlike. As a result of these studies, considerable contemporary work on fathers is focused on the relationships of cohabiting partners, stepfathers, nonresident fathers, and grandfathers with children (Marsiglio et al., 2000).

Concurrent with the work on the dynamics of living arrangements have been attempts to document the nature of the relationship between nonresident fathers and their children. These three surveys provided researchers with the first nationally representative data on the kinds and amounts of contact between nonresident fathers and their children. They also have given scholars the unique opportunity to address the consequences for children's well-being for different kinds of father involvement. One of the earliest and most cited works on nonresident father contact was a paper by Frank Furstenberg, Jr., and colleagues (Furstenberg et al., 1983) that used the NSC to document the consequences of divorce for the lives of children. Drawing on the 1976 and the follow-up 1981 panels, Furstenberg et al. (1983) found dramatically low levels of contact reported by the child's mother. One of the most-quoted statistics out of this paper was that more than half (51.8%) of children of divorced parents had little or no contact with their nonresident fathers. This finding of fathers "dropping off the map" was echoed in other work using the NLSY and the NSFH, and this work has extended Furstenberg's original analysis by examining race differences (King, 1994b; Mott, 1990); the kinds of contact and how they differ by gender (Stewart, 1999); the determinants of father visitation (Cooksey & Craig, 1998; King & Heard, 1999; Manning & Smock, 1999; McKenry, McKelvey, Leigh, & Wark, 1996); and the interrelationship between father contact and child support (Amato & Rezac, 1994; King, 1994a; Sorensen, 2000). Furthermore, a number of studies have taken advantage of the child assessments in the NLSY surveys and the child well-being indicators in the NSFH to address the fundamentally important question of whether father contact is related to child outcomes (Amato & Rezac, 1994; King 1994a; 1994b).

Research based on these surveys have been at the heart of our current understanding of the nature of nonresident fatherhood and its consequences for children. The emerging picture from these data is that father visitation and contact per se do not directly benefit children. In other words, the amount of time fathers spend with their children, independent of nature of the interactions between fathers and children, does not matter. These initial findings have challenged researchers to dig deeper into the nature of the tie between fathers and children who live apart by exploring the indirect effects of the variability in contact and by probing how fathers interact with their children.

One important avenue that has been explored with data from these surveys is that of the interconnection between child support, contact, and child well-being. A number of studies using the NSFH or the NLSY have documented the amount of child support (Seltzer, 1991; Veum, 1992); the potential of nonresident fathers to economically support their children (Brien & Willis, 1997b; Robertson, 1997; Veum, 1992); the link between visitation and economic support (Garfinkel & McLanahan, 1995; Seltzer, 1991; Veum, 1992, 1993); and the effect of fathers' economic support for children's well-being (Argys, Peters, Brooks-Gunn, & Smith, 1998; Baydar, & Brooks-Gunn, 1994; Furstenberg et al., 1987; Knox, 1996). These studies have demonstrated the importance of child support for children's well-being, behavior problems (Furstenberg et al., 1987), and academic success (Knox, 1996). Evidence for the interconnections between child support awards and father involvement are more mixed. Some evidence suggests that there is no relationship between the two (Veum, 1993), whereas other work points to findings in the data suggesting that fathers will spend more time with children as a result of increased child support payments, and this increased contact will benefit the children (Garfkinel & McLanahan, 1995).

To a lesser extent, researchers have examined the kinds of fathering behaviors of nonresident fathers. Research using the NSC and the NSFH has shown that nonresident fathers are significantly less likely to be engaged in instrumental kinds of tasks with their children like helping with homework or monitoring or supervising them and significantly more likely to be doing leisure activities (Furstenberg & Nord, 1985; Stewart, 1999). Other work using the NSC found little evidence that the quality of the relationship between the father and the child mattered for children's well-being (Furstenberg et al., 1987). Furthermore, there is evidence that nonresident fathers' relationships with their children tend to wane over time (Frustenberg & Harris, 1992). Of course, accurate data on what exactly fathers are doing with their children is a challenge. Data from the NSC and the NSFH have provided researchers a good opportunity to gauge the veracity of mothers', childrens', or fathers' reports of paternal involvement. In general, results from the NSFH show that fathers tend to report they are engaged in higher levels of participation with children than the child's mother reports (Seltzer & Brandreth, 1994). Data from the NSC show substantial disagreement between mother and child reports on the closeness of the child to his or her father (Smith & Morgan, 1994).

In sum, these surveys have been at the heart of research addressing the nature of nonresident fatherhood. They have provided researchers with unique opportunities to push beyond mere descriptions of contact, to investigations of the determinants of nonresident father involvement, their consequences for children's well-being, and examinations of the interconnections between father involvement and economic support. Of course, as many new questions have arisen from these investigations as have been answered, including questions about the nature of father involvement, how best to measure the multidimensional nature of fathers' impact on children, and what kinds of outcomes in children should be examined (Federal Interagency Forum on Child and Family Statistics,1998).

Consequences of Fatherhood for Men

Most research on fatherhood has concentrated on determining what men do, and whether and how these activities affect children. Comparatively ignored, despite our theoretical admonitions about the reciprocity of family relationships, have been attempts to determine the consequences of fatherhood for men. Data from the NSFH and the NLSY, however, have been instrumental in the two strands of research that have emerged around this question. One line of work examines the consequences of early timed fatherhood, whereas the other strand focuses on the social, psychological, and economic effects of normatively timed fatherhood.

The NLSY has proven to be an excellent data source for the examination of teenage fatherhood. Initial work focused on describing teen fathers (Elster, Lamb, & Tavare, 1987; Marsiglio, 1987; Pirog-Good, 1995). As one might expect, this work showed that teenage boys who father children are more likely to be African American, be from a lower socioeconomic background, and show evidence of academic, drug, and conduct problems (Elster et al., 1987; Pirog-Good, 1995). Work by Marsiglio (1987) shows that most premarital births to young males do not lead to marriage and only about half lived with their child shortly after the birth. More recent work has taken advantage of the longitudinal design of the NLSY to trace the short- and long-term consequences of early childbearing for men (Brien & Willis, 1997a; Nock, 1998). In general teenage childbearing, especially when it is premarital, is associated with poorer socioeconomic prospects. Men who become teen fathers may start out working more and seem to earn higher incomes than men of similar ages who do not become fathers, but by their late 20s teen fathers have accumulated fewer years of education, earn less money, and are more likely to have been repeatedly out of work (Brien & Willis, 1997a). Other work by Nock (1998) focuses on premarital fatherhood, finding similar socioeconomic consequences, as well as reduced chances of subsequent marriage.

Somewhat less common have been attempts to examine the consequences of normatively timed fatherhood for men. The most systematic treatment has been done by John Snarey (1993). Building on Eric Erikson's idea generativity, Snarey argues that men who are engaged fathers are more likely to be active participants in their communities, be mentors of younger men, and evidence greater concern for others. Using data from the NLSY, he finds evidence of greater social attachment among men who were fathers, as well as a more developed sense of responsibility. Work by Eggebeen and Knoester (2001) and Kaufman and Uhlenberg (2000) use data from the NSFH to further explore the nature of the consequences of fatherhood for men. Eggebeen and Knoester (2001) find that coresident fathers differed from other types of fathers in that they are more likely to have social relationships that involve connections to institutions and organizations that involve children (schools, churches, civic organizations like scouting, little league, etc.). Coresident fathers were also less likely to have experienced bouts of unemployment, and tended to work more hours. Kaufman and Uhlenberg (2000) focused more specifically on the relationship between parenthood and work. They found evidence of two distinct models of fatherhood: one built around the idea that good fathers are first and foremost "good providers" and one centered around the idea that a good father is someone who desires to be fully engaged in nurturing their children. Those men who view fatherhood fundamentally through the lens of being good providers tend to increase their time commitment to work with each additional child, whereas men who show evidence of a more "modern" view of fatherhood have precisely the opposite pattern: additional children are correlated with fewer hours of work per week (Kaufman & Uhlenberg, 2000). Of course, these correlations do not infer causation, and much work needs to be done to sort selection effects before we can argue confidently that fatherhood changes men.

This brief review does not do justice to detailed contributions of research using these three surveys to our understanding of fatherhood. As should be evident by this review, however, studies based on these surveys have been path breaking in a number of ways: They have provided conclusive answers to questions that could not be addressed because we did not have the data before. Studies based on these surveys have been instrumental in shattering previous certainties, thereby provoking new questions to be answered and revealing previously overlooked complexities. Finally, these surveys have been the "test beds" for the second generation of surveys that are just becoming available to researchers or are now in the field.

WHAT HAVE WE NOT LEARNED FROM THESE SURVEYS?

It has been easy to extol the virtues of these data for studying fatherhood. Yet, the high praise of the preceding paragraph must not cloud our sensitivity to a number of crucial weaknesses of these surveys. It is my contention that these shortcomings have limited our understanding of fatherhood in important, but often unappreciated, ways. I will discuss three significant weaknesses of these social surveys for studying fatherhood.

Coverage Problems

Ironically, one of the obvious strengths of these social surveys for studying fathers is also an important weakness—the claim of representativeness. There are two sources of error that threaten representativeness: an undercount of men in the survey design itself and the underreporting of fatherhood by men who are respondents in the survey. All three of these surveys begin with households as the basic sampling unit. This is a reasonable approach if the focus is on conventional families—where children live with their biological parents. When our attention shifts to fatherhood, however, we begin to run into problems. Rising divorce and non-marital childbearing have greatly increased the likelihood that fathers and their children no longer share the same dwelling. This problem could be managed within these surveys—provided that most men who were nonresident fathers remained in households. However, increasingly men who are nonresident fathers are likely to be in nonhousehold living arrangements such as military barracks or prisons. Over the course of the past 30 years, the number of incarcerated men has increased nearly sixfold (Pastore & Maguire, 2000), with a disproportionate share of the increase among African-American men, who showed a 271% increase from 1980 to 1993 (Bureau of Justice Statistics, 1995). A recent Bureau of Justice report (Mumola, 2000) estimated that nearly 1.4 million minor children had a father in state or federal prison by 1999. This number had grown 58% since 1991. Racial disparities are enormous, with Black children nine times more likely to have a parent in prison than White children. The consequences are clear: Studies that have attempted to use samples of men drawn from surveys such as the NSFH, the NSC, or the NLSY, based as they are on households, miss a consequential number of fathers. Even studies where fatherhood is indirectly ascertained by focusing on children or mother reports of nonresident father behavior are likely to be biased, because there is no attempt to distinguish the experience of fathers who are in prison and are by their circumstances limited to a very narrow range of fathering activities.

A second source of error is the missreporting of fatherhood by male respondents. That men are notoriously poor informants on family matters has been widely reported (see Cherlin, Griffith, & McCarthy, 1980). Men are significantly less likely than women to admit that they are parents. Even those men who admit to being fathers are likely to distort their experiences with children by overestimating the amount of time they are spending with children or the amount of child support they are giving (see Cherlin & Griffith, 1998, for a review of this literature).

In short, there is good reason to believe that when it comes to studying fathers, these three surveys will present data that has some biases. Furthermore, simply relying on men's reports of fathering behavior, or in the case of nonresident fathers, reports of contact, visits, or child support, is simply naive, as work based on the NSFH (Seltzer & Brandreth, 1994) has shown. Studies by Frank Furstenberg and his colleagues using the NSC data (Furstenberg, Morgan, & Allison, 1987; Furstenberg, Nord, Peterson, & Zill, 1983; Harris, Furstenberg, & Marmer, 1996) attempt to get around this issue by relying on children's or mother's reports of father behavior. Of course, mothers and children may have their own biases that affect the accuracy of what the father is doing. Furthermore, they may not be able to reliably report on the father's interactions with all his children.

Before we throw these surveys into the ash can, however, we need to keep several thoughts in mind. First, the biases of informants on father behavior are hardly unique. In reality, distorted reporting is ubiquitous in research on family behavior, making this concern a dilemma that needs to be addressed by all researchers. Nevertheless, there appears to be consistent evidence that men are especially likely to distort the record on some issues, and researchers should not simply ignore these observed tendencies and continue to rely exclusively on data drawn from men's reports on these domains as representing reality accurately. To be sure, both the NSFH and the NSC represent an advance over previous surveys in that they do contain some information drawn from multiple informants. Unfortunately, multiple reports are not available on some key issues (like father involvement in the NSFH, for instance), and only occasionally have researchers made full use of those that exist. Clearly, research is needed to gain a better sense of what kinds of information are more accurate if collected from informants or proxies rather than from fathers themselves. Findings from these studies would both guide research on existing data sets that have some information from multiple sources and be very helpful for future data collection efforts. Of course, techniques for analyzing multiple-source data also need to be refined, disseminated, and adopted. Finally, more discernment is needed to distinguish when it is important to try and measure reality as objectively as possible from those occasions when the fathers' perceptions of what is going on are important in their own right.

Lack of Diversity

A second closely related area of concern is that these surveys, although a big improvement over the more limited data previously available, still make it difficult to study the full range of fathers and fathering experiences of men. There are two issues here: social changes in cohabitation, marriage, divorce, remarriage, and nonmarital childbearing have made contemporary fatherhood a dramatically more complex enterprise—and these surveys were not specifically designed to deal with this complexity. Second, these studies are excellent for probing the fathering experiences of demographically dominant groups, such as middle-class Whites, but are less useful for examining the diverse experiences within socially important groups like African Americans, Hispanic groups, poor or working class men, and so forth.

The criticism that these surveys are not suited for examining the complexities of contemporary fatherhood is ironic, given they provided the data for the first wave of studies that pushed beyond an exclusive focus on coresident fathers. These efforts, however, raised more questions than answers, suggesting more complexity to the relationship between nonresident fathers and their children than these data could handle. For example, initial studies that sought to show that non-resident father contact was positively associated with child well-being were dis-appointing. Unfortunately, these surveys lacked the kinds of nuanced questions needed to determine just what kinds of activities and parenting nonresident fathers were engaged in. Neither were these surveys designed to allow researchers to carefully address the impact of the specific context within which these fathers are attempting to deal with their children, such as the ongoing relationship with the child's mother, the larger intergenerational family network, or any new intimate relationships that the father (or the child's mother) may have formed.

Both the NSFH and the NLSY are large enough for researchers to examine race, ethnic and social class differences, and many of the reviewed studies have been careful to either include race, ethnic, and class variables in their statistical models or to do some comparisons across subpopulations. These kinds of analyses are important for making generalizations for the entire U.S. population or for documenting the differences between various social groups. However, despite their large sample sizes and, in the case of the NLSY and the NSFH, oversamples for selected subpopulations such as Blacks, Hispanics, and the poor, these data remain inadequate for addressing within-group variation.

A simple example illustrates the problem. In a recent paper I sought to compare mens' experience of fatherhood across a variety of contexts using the NSFH (Eggebeen & Knoester, 2001). I distinguished four types of father statuses: living with biologically related or adopted children ($n = 1,726$); living with stepchildren only ($n = 191$); having only nonresident children who are less than 18 years of age ($n = 393$); and having only adult children ($n = 1,198$). The sample sizes of each status are for men of all races and ethnicity. It is clear from these numbers that even with the oversamples of minorities, the NSFH is not large enough to permit within-race analyses of at least two of these statuses for any group other than White Americans.

As a result of the inadequacy of these data for within-group analyses, we remain largely ignorant, for example, of how African-American men conduct themselves as fathers, as well the particular ways cultural forces, socioeconomic conditions, as well as fathers' own life experiences are implicated in the variable relationships between them and their children.

Measurement Limitations

A third weakness of these surveys is their neglect of important dimensions of fathering. All three of these surveys inquire about a variety of activities that may be ongoing between fathers and their children such as communication, teaching, monitoring, shared activities, emotional support, affection, and, in the case of the NSFH and the NSC, conflicts and harsh punishment. Although these measures are certainly valuable for understanding some of the concrete, behavioral manifestations of fatherhood, they are less helpful for examining some of the theoretical constructs that have emerged in recent years (Marsiglio et al., 2000). For example, the measures in these data do not allow for a systematic treatment of responsibility, which some scholars argue is one of the most critical components of fathering (Cabrera et al., 2000; Lamb, Pleck, Charnov, & Levine, 1987). We can learn, for example, from the NSFH data the extent to which fathers have helped their children with their homework, but what we cannot ascertain is the extent to which fathers have responsibility for overseeing their children's schoolwork.

These surveys are also somewhat limited in their potential to explore fathers' contributions to their children's welfare via fathers' social capital. The concept of social capital has received significant attention from sociologists in the past decade (see Coleman, 1988; Furstenberg & Hughes, 1995; Portes, 1998), with some scholars suggesting that this construct is particularly useful for understanding the contributions that fathers make to children's development (Marsiglio et al., 2000). A key component of social capital that these surveys are sorely deficient in measuring is the nature of fathers' connections to other individuals and key social organizations in the community. Fathers influence their children not only through their direct interactions, but also through the relationships they have with their children's friends, the parents of their children's friends, teachers, coaches, pastors, and neighbors (Marsiglio et al., 2000). Their participation in institutions that their children are involved in such as schools, churches, recreational sports teams, and so on can also have implications for children's development. Although the NSFH survey does have some questions on men's participation in a variety of community organizations, the ability to tie this information to their children's participation in these organizations is very limited.

In conclusion, the promise and the production from these surveys is a good example of the messy, fitful course of a scientific understanding human behavior. These data were strategic for addressing key unknowns; we have learned much about fathers and fatherhood from these surveys. Along with the "answers," however, came more questions. These questions spawned a reassessment of our conceptual approaches to fatherhood, unmasked the inadequacy of our sampling schemes, showed our initial questions to be somewhat naive, and pointed to new domains that we should be examining.

WHAT LIES AHEAD FOR SURVEY RESEARCH ON FATHERHOOD?

If these surveys are representative of our "best science" in survey approaches to studying fatherhood over the past decade, what should we expect from the new millennium? Already new data are available or will be shortly (see Federal Interagency Forum on Child and Family Statistics, 1998, for a review of new data collection efforts). It is my contention, however, that surveys targeting fatherhood must confront three challenges before they will have the potential for significantly advancing our understanding of fathers. They must address the growing complexity of contemporary family life in America; they must be designed to allow researchers to deal with race, ethnic, and class diversity; and they must play to the strengths—and away from the weaknesses—of survey approaches to studying social phenomena. Let me end this essay with a brief discussion of each.

It is obvious to most observers that families today are exceedingly diverse in form and structure. Unfortunately, our ability as social scientists to accommodate our conceptual and empirical models and data collection efforts to systematically address this diversity has been slow. Cross-sectional designs have been the mainstay of past survey research. This makes sense if the social phenomena under investigation is reasonably stable. One of the defining features of contemporary family life, however, is its fluidity. For us to understand contemporary fatherhood, we need data that is sensitive not only to the diverse settings of fatherhood, but also to its dynamic and constantly changing nature. Surveys are needed that will allow us to adequately capture the changing settings, the changing circumstances, the changing meanings associated with these new circumstances, and how each setting—and the accumulation of changes—affect children.

We have learned much about White, middle-class fatherhood. This not surprising, of course, because most researchers are studying what they "know best." Middle-class Whites are demographically dominant as well, making them the largest group in our samples. However, the growing recognition that it is naive to divorce the study of families from their social and cultural context, combined with the new demographic realities of American society, means that scholars of fatherhood can no longer ignore its racial, ethnic, and class context. This should not imply that the solution is surveys with larger sample sizes. What are needed are surveys targeting specific subpopulations with enough standard questions to not only encourage comparative work across groups, but also to contain questions that are sensitive to the unique circumstances, culture, and settings of the targeted group.

Finally, we must recognize the strengths, and limits, of survey approaches to studying fatherhood. Andrew Cherlin and Jeanne Griffith (1998) point out in their careful review of methodological issues in studying fathers that surveys are better at hypothesis testing than hypothesis generation. In the case of fatherhood, where a significant amount of conceptual development and exploratory work remains, surveys should not be the only tool in our arsenal. The challenge, then, in designing new surveys is not to just look to past surveys for what questions to include, but to draw on the insights and findings of new research that uses qualitative approaches, such as intensive observational methods, ethnography, focus groups, and so on, to inform the content domains, particular questions, question sequences, and settings for posing queries of sensitive topics (Cherlin & Griffith, 1998).

One of the central concerns of scholars studying families is making sense of the complexity and diversity of U.S. families at the dawn of the new millennium. Understanding the role of men as fathers is central to this enterprise. I have argued that the NLSY, the NSFH, and the NSC have been strategic in laying the foundations of our basic understandings of fatherhood over the course of the past two decades. Of course, the popularity of the NSC and the NSFH for studying fatherhood are likely to wain as they increasingly "show their age." Given the NSLY survey is an ongoing longitudinal data collection effort, it is likely to have some staying power. For the foreseeable future anyway, it is likely that social surveys like the these three will remain the basic data-gathering tool of sociologists who study fathers. However, the potential for social surveys to lead to important advances in our scientific understanding of fatherhood is predicated not only on their success in coping with the listed challenges, but also on their ability to accommodate to new challenges that arise from changing historical conditions and circumstances.

REFERENCES

Amato, P. R. (1993). Children's adjustment to divorce: Theories, hypotheses, and empirical support. *Journal of Marriage and the Family, 55,* 23–38.

Amato, P. R., & Gilbreth, J. G. (1999). Nonresident fathers and children's well-being: A meta-analysis. *Journal of Marriage and the Family, 61,* 557–573.

Amato, P. R., & Keith, B. (1991). Parental divorce and the well-being of children: A meta-analysis. *Psychological Bulletin, 110,* 26–46.

Amato, P. R., & Rezac, S. (1994). Contact with nonresidential parents, interpersonal conflict, and children's behavior. *Journal of Family Issues, 15,* 191–207.

Amato, P. R., & Rivera, F. (1999). Paternal involvement and children's behavior. *Journal of Marriage and the Family, 61,* 375–384.

Argys, L. M., Peters, H. E., Brooks-Gunn, J., & Smith J. R. (1998). The impact of child support on cognitive outcomes of young children. *Demography, 35,* 159–173.

Baydar, N., & Brooks-Gunn, J. (1994). The dynamics of child support and its consequences for children. In I. Garfinkel, S. S. McLanahan, & P. K. Robins (Eds.), *Child support and child well-being* (pp. 257–284). Washington, DC: Urban Institute Press.

Brien, M., & Willis, R. J. (1997b). The partners of welfare mothers. Potential earnings and child support. *The Future of Children, 7*(1), 65–73.

Brien, M., & Willis, R. J. (1997a). Costs and consequences for fathers. In R. Maynard (Ed.), *Kids having kids: Economic costs and social consequences of teen pregnancy*. Washington, DC: Urban Institute Press.

Bureau of Justice Statistics. (1995, August). *Prisoners in 1994*. NCJ-151651.

Cabrera, N. J., Tamis-LeMonda, C. S., Bradley, R. H., Hofferth, S., & Lamb, M. E. (2000). Fatherhood in the twenty-first century. *Child Development, 71*, 127–136.

Cherlin, A., & Griffith, J. (1998). Methodological Issues in Improving Data on Fathers: Chapter 5: Report of the Working Group on the Methodology of Studying Fathers. Federal Interagency Forum on Child and Family Statistics. *Nurturing Fatherhood: Improving Data and Research on Male Fertility, Family Formation, and Fatherhood*. Washington, DC.

Cherlin, A., Griffith, J., & McCarthy, J. (1980). A note on maritally-disrupted men's reports of child support in the June 1980 Current Population Survey. *Demography, 20*, 385–389.

Coleman, J. (1988). Social capital in the creation of human capital. *American Journal of Sociology, 94*, 95–120.

Cooksey, E. C., & Craig, P. H. (1998). Parenting from a distance: The effects of paternal characteristics on contact between nonresidential fathers and their children. *Demography, 35*, 187–200.

Cooksey, E. C., & Fondell, M. M. (1996). Spending time with his kids: Effects of family structure on fathers' and children's lives. *Journal of Marriage and the Family, 58*, 693–707.

Cooksey, E. C., Managhan, E. G., & Jekielek, S. M. (1997). Life course effects of work and family circumstances on children. *Social Forces, 76*, 637–667.

Eggebeen, D. J., Crockett, L. J., & Hawkins, A. J. (1990). Patterns of male co-residence for children of adolescent mothers. *Family Planning Perspectives, 22*, 219–223.

Eggebeen, D. J., & Knoester, C. (2001, May). Does fatherhood matter for men? *Journal of Marriage and the Family, 63*(2), 381–393.

Elster, A. B., Lamb, M. E., & Tavare, J. (1987). Association between behavioral and school problems and fatherhood in a national sample of adolescent youths. *Journal of Pediatrics, 111*, 932–936.

Federal Interagency Forum on Child and Family Statistics. (1998). *Nurturing fatherhood: Improving data and research on male fertility, family formation, and fatherhood*. Washington, DC: Author.

Furstenberg, F. F., Jr., & Harris, K. M. (1992). The disappearing American father? Divorce and the waning significance of biological parenthood. In S. J. South & S. E. Tolnay (Eds.), *The changing american family: Sociological and demographic perspectives*. Boulder, CO: Westview Press.

Furstenberg, F. F., Jr., & Hughes, M. (1995). Social capital and successful development among at-risk youth. *Journal of Marriage and the Family, 57*, 580–592.

Furstenberg, F. F., Jr., Morgan, S. P., & Allison, P. D. (1987). Paternal participation and children's well-being after marital dissolution. *American Sociological Review, 52*, 695–701.

Furstenberg, F. F., Jr., & Nord, C. W. (1985). Parenting apart: Patterns of childrearing after marital disruption. *Journal of Marriage and the Family, 47*, 893–904.

Furstenberg, F. F., Jr., Nord, C. W., Peterson, J. L., & Zill, N. (1983). The life course of children of divorce: Marital disruption and paternal contact. *American Sociological Review, 48*, 656–668.

Garfinkel, I., & McLanahan, S. (1995). The effects of child support reform on child well-being. In J. Brooks-Gunn, & P. Chase-Landsdale (Eds.), *Escape from poverty: What makes a difference for children?* New York: Cambridge University Press.

Harris, K. M., Furstenberg, F. F., Jr., & Marmer, J. K. (1996). Paternal involvement with adolescents in intact families: The influence of fathers over the life course. *Demography, 35*, 201–216.

Hawkins, A. J., & Eggebeen, D. J. (1991). Are fathers fungible? Patterns of co-resident adult men in maritally disrupted families and young children's well-being. *Journal of Marriage and the Family, 53*, 958–972.

Kaufman, G., & Uhlenberg, P. (2000). The influence of parenthood on work effort of married men and women. *Social Forces, 78*, 931–949.

King, V. (1994a). Nonresident father involvement and child well-being: Can dads make a difference? *Journal of Family Issues, 15,* 78–96.

King, V. (1994b). Variation in the consequences of nonresident father involvement for children's well-being. *Journal of Marriage and the Family, 56,* 963–972.

King, V., & Heard, H. E. (1999). Nonresident father visitation, parental conflict, and mother's satisfaction: What's best for child well-being? *Journal of Marriage and the Family, 61,* 385–396.

Knox, V. W. (1996). The effects of child support payments on developmental outcomes for elementary school-aged children. *Journal of Human Resources, 31,* 817–840.

Lamb, M. E. (1997). *The role of the father in child development* (3rd ed.). New York: Wiley.

Lamb, M. E. (2000). A history of research on father involvement: An overview. *Marriage and Family Review, 29*(2/3), 23–42.

Lamb, M. E., Pleck, J. H., Charnov, E. L., & Levine, J. A. (1987). A biosocial perspective on paternal behavior and involvement. In J. B. Lancaster, J. Altmann, A. S. Rossi, & L. R. Sherrod (Eds.), *Parenting across the lifespan: Biosocial dimensions* (pp. 11–142). New York: Aldine de Gruyter.

Manning, W. D., & Smock, P. J. (1999). New families and nonresident father–child visitation. *Social Forces, 78,* 87–116.

Marsiglio, W. (1987). Adolecent fathers in the United States: Their initial living arrangements, marital experience and educational outcomes. *Family Planning Perspectives, 19,* 240–251.

Marsiglio, W. (1991). Paternal engagement activities with minor children. *Journal of Marriage and the Family, 53,* 973–986.

Marsiglio, W., Amato, P. A., Day, R. D., & Lamb, M. E. (2000). Scholarship on fatherhood in the 1990s and beyond. *Journal of Marriage and the Family, 62,* 1173–1191.

Martinson, B.C., & Wu, L. L (1992). Parent histories: Patterns of change in early life. *Journal of Family Issues, 13,* 351–377.

McKenry, P. C., McKelvey, M. W., Leigh, D., & Wark, L. (1996). Nonresident father involvement: A comparison of divorced, separated, never married, and remarried fathers. *Journal of Divorce and Remarriage, 25,* 1–13.

McLanahan, S. S., & Sandefur, G. (1994). *Growing up with a single parent: What hurts, what helps.* Cambridge, MA: Harvard University Press.

Mott, F. L. (1990). When is a father really gone? Paternal–child contact in father-absent homes. *Demography, 27,* 499–517.

Mumola, C. J. (2000, August). Incarcerated parents and their children. *Bureau of Justice Statistics Special Report.* NCJ 182335.

Nock, S. L. (1998). The consequences of premarital fatherhood. *American Sociological Review, 63,* 250–263.

Parcel, T. L., & Menaghan, E. G. (1994). Early parental work, family social capital, and early childhood outcomes. *American Journal of Sociology, 99,* 972–1009.

Pastore, A. L., & Maguire, K. (2000). *Sourcebook of criminal justice statistics* Retrieved January 7, 2001 from http://www.albany.edu/sourcebook/.

Pirog-Good, M. A. (1995). The family background and attitudes of teen fathers. *Youth and Society, 26,* 351–376.

Portes, A. (1998). Social capital: Its origins and applications in modern sociology. *Annual Review of Sociology, 24,* 1–24.

Robertson, J. G. (1997). Young residential fathers have lower earnings: Implications for child support enforcement. *Social Work Research, 21,* 211–223.

Seltzer, J. A. (1991). Relationships between fathers and children who live apart: The father's role after separation. *Journal of Marriage and the Family, 53,* 79–101.

Seltzer, J. A., & Brandreth, Y. (1994). What fathers say about involvement with children after separation. *Journal of Family Issues, 15,* 49–77.

Smith, H. L., & Morgan, S. P. (1994). Children's closeness to father as reported by mothers, sons and daughters: Evaluating subjective assessments with the Rasch Model. *Journal of Family Issues, 5,* 3–29.

Snarey, J. (1993). *How fathers care for the next generation: A four decade study.* Cambridge, MA: Harvard University Press.

Sorensen, E. (2000). Father involvement with their nonmarital children: Patterns, determinants, and effects on their earnings. *Marriage and Family Review Special Issue: Fatherhood: Research, Interventions and Policies, 29,* 137–158.

Stewart, S. D. (1999). Disneyland dads, Disneyland moms? How nonresident parents spend time with absent children. *Journal of Family Issues, 20,* 539–556.

Sweet, J. A., & Bumpass, L. L. (1996). *The National Survey of Families and Households—Waves 1 and 2: Data description and documentation.* Madison: Center for Demography and Ecology, University of Wisconsin—Madison (http://www.ssc.wisc.edu/nsfh/home.htm).

Sweet, J. A., Bumpass, L. L., & Call, V. (1988). *The design and content of the National Survey of Families and Households.* Madison: Center for Demography and Ecology, University of Wisconsin–Madison. (NSFH Working Paper #1)

Veum, J. R. (1992). Interrelation of child support, visitation, and hours of work. *Monthly Labor Review, 115,* 40–47.

Veum, J. R. (1993). The relationship between child support and visitation: Evidence from longitudinal data. *Social Science Research, 22,* 229–244.

Wojtkiewicz, R. A. (1992). The counteracting influences of increased female headship and decreased number of children on inequality in economic well-being by age: 1960 to 1980. *Population Research and Policy Review, 11,* 263–279.

Wu, L. L. (1996). Effects of family instability, income, and income instability on the risk of a premarital birth. *American Sociological Review, 61,* 386–406.

Wu, L. L., & Martinson, B. C. (1993). Family structure and the risk of a premarital birth. *American Sociological Review, 58,* 210–232.

9

Fathers in the "Hood": Insights From Qualitative Research on Low-Income African-American Men

Robin L. Jarrett
University of Illinois, Urbana-Champaign

Kevin M. Roy
Purdue University

Linda M. Burton
Pennsylvania State University

> The oppressive fear that American society has held and continues to hold of African American males, and which tremendously distorts these men's ability to participate in family life, is a context often left unseen. Family studies in general have long been oriented toward examining women, not only because of reproductive concerns, but because of the social construction of the household as a "women's sphere" that is supported by men from the outside. Since this male role is restricted for African Americans, the men become invisible to household analysis. (Miller, 1993, pp. 266–267)

African-American fathers in low-income urban communities often have been characterized as invisible, irresponsible dads who are marginalized in their families and contribute little economically to the well-being of their children (Allen & Doherty, 1996; Burton & Snyder, 1998; Gadsen, 1999; Hamer, 1997; Marsiglio, Amato, Day, & Lamb, 2000). Over the past four decades, this perception of African-American fathers has been heatedly contested in academic, public, and policy arenas with both supporters and critics of this image framing their arguments in culture of poverty perspectives (Baca Zinn, 1989; Corcoran, Duncan, & Gurin, 1985; Ellwood & Bane, 1987; Moynihan, 1965; Rainwater, 1970), the underclass debate (Auletta, 1982; Darity & Meyers, 1984; Joe, 1984; Mead,

1986; Murray, 1984; Staples, 1985; Williams, 1978; Wilson, 1987; see also Jarrett, 1994, for an overview of the debate), and more recently, child support and
welfare reform policies (Garfinkel, McLanahan, Meyer, & Seltzer, 1998;
McLanahan & Sandefur, 1994; Mincy & Pouncy, 1997; Roy, 1999a). Further,
those involved in this discourse have supported their arguments with data from
nationally representative surveys (see Eggebeen, Chap. 8); journalistic accounts
of "ghetto" fathers (Dash, 1989; Kotlowitz, 1991; Lemann, 1986) and to a lesser
degree, qualitative and ethnographic studies on urban African-American family
life (Martin & Martin, 1978; Stack, 1974).

In this chapter, we consider the perspectives that qualitative studies provide
concerning the roles low-income, urban, African-American fathers play in the
lives of their families and children. Indeed, a rich tradition of qualitative studies
describes the lives of low-income, urban African-American families and fathers,
capturing the meaning of key parenting relationships and behaviors for men and
their children (for classic studies, see, for example, Hannerz, 1969; Liebow, 1967;
Martin & Martin, 1978; Rainwater, 1970; Schulz, 1969; Stack, 1974; Valentine,
1978; Williams, 1981; for contemporary studies, see, for example, Anderson,
1990, 1999; Edin & Lein, 1997; Furstenberg, 1992, 1995; MacLeod, 1987, 1995;
Newman, 1999; Sullivan, 1992; Williams & Kornblum, 1985, 1994).

Qualitative researchers have utilized traditional anthropological approaches—
participant observation and various forms of interviewing—to intimately understand the contextual, dynamic, and subjective aspects of African-American fathering
(see Becker, 1970; Bulmer, 1986; Burgess, 1982; Denzin, 1970; Denzin & Lincoln,
1994; Emerson, 1981; Fetterman, 1989). For example, the in situ nature of participant observation allows firsthand observation of the specific ecological conditions
that affect fathers and families (Burton & Graham, 1998; Jarrett, 1995). By sometimes living with and/or immersing themselves in the daily lives of African-
American fathers and significant others for extended periods of time, qualitative
researchers observe dynamic interchanges between people and local neighborhoods.
Moreover, participant observation allows the researcher to experience the everyday
routines and realities of men and significant others over time. It can provide detailed
descriptions of the roles that men play, as well as portrayals of household processes
and interhousehold linkages (Burton, 1995a; Jorgensen, 1989; Liebow, 1967; Stack,
1974; Sullivan, 1992; Williams, 1991; Williams & Kornblum, 1994).

In addition, the subjective nature of qualitative interviewing allows the
researcher to access individuals' personal interpretations of experiences and
activities that are not apparent from observation alone. By talking to African-
American fathers and their significant others, qualitative researchers come to
understand the meaning systems that undergird the paternal role, how meaning
systems are socially constructed, and how deeply held beliefs and values are
influenced by opportunities and constraints. More generally, qualitative methods
reveal microlevel individual, group, and neighborhood processes and patterns that
are missed or obscured by less-intensive methods (Furstenberg & Hughes, 1997;
Jarrett, 1992, 1994).

In this chapter, we draw on classic and contemporary qualitative studies to provide insights into the lives of low-income African-American fathers. The review concentrates on studies from the 1970s through the 1990s, although some earlier studies are included. The extended time period increases the number of cases available for review and provides an indication of change or continuity in men's roles.

The studies reviewed were primarily descriptive and use an array of qualitative data-collection strategies, including life-history, in-depth, retrospective, semistructured, open-ended, and group interviews, as well as various forms of ethnography, including focused ethnography, microethnography, participant observation, and community studies. Despite diverse substantive foci from the major fields of anthropology, education, human development, and sociology, the studies share an interest in men within the context of inner-city neighborhoods.

We begin our review by reporting on findings from qualitative studies that shed light on African-American men and the paternal role. Verbatim quotes from relevant studies are used to describe the intimate lives of inner-city fathers and their significant others. The qualitative findings are organized around four themes. These include: (a) the neighborhood context of fatherhood and the opportunities that they provide; (b) negotiations between fathers and mothers in a system of kin work; (c) the meaning of fatherhood and the social process of father involvement; and (d) the diverse set of father figures who fulfill a variety of flexible paternal role obligations. We consider each of these issues from the multiple perspectives of men, women, youth, and children. We conclude our review with a discussion of the implications of the qualitative findings for future policy development and research.

MEN AND JOBS: THE NEIGHBORHOOD CONTEXT OF FATHERING

It just gets to the point . . . where you can't tell your landlord I'm trying, or you can't tell a hungry child, I'm trying, wait a few more days until daddy gets his check, then he'll buy some food. . . . That money doesn't go for me, it goes for my children. (Achatz & MacAllum, 1994, p. 82)

Neighborhoods, by virtue of their institutional, economic, and social resources, shape opportunities for men and their families. In inner-city neighborhoods, key resources are quite limited. Such areas exhibit unstable institutions, low rates of education, high rates of unemployment, social problems, and the concentration of the most impoverished families (Burton, 1990; Newman, 1999; Sullivan, 1989; Wilson, 1987, 1996).

Lack of Job Opportunities

In particular, inner-city neighborhoods provide few jobs for men. Typical of many inner-city neighborhoods, a resident of the Projectville community in New York City describes its declining economic base (see also Burton, 1991; Valentine, 1978; White, 1999):

When I was little, there were lots of stores around the subway stop, and all the people in the stores knew all the little kids. I used to work for the newsstand on the corner, running little errands here and there. . . . Now, most of those stores, and the houses where we used to live too, are all burned down. (Sullivan, 1989, p. 75)

Other qualitative work echoes the loss of local jobs and limited opportunities for good-paying, steady employment (Kaplan, 1997; MacLeod, 1995; Williams, 1991). Dexter's discussion of job training programs succinctly underscores this point: "There ain't no jobs. What do I need training for when there ain't no jobs to go to?" (Williams & Kornblum, 1994, p. 152).

In addition to limited job opportunities for African-American men, educational systems in impoverished neighborhoods that prepare young men for work are deficient (Fine, 1985; Kaplan, 1997; Moore, 1969; Ogbu, 1974; Tatje, 1974). Consider the description of a typical high school that serves inner-city youth:

At Russell High it was estimated that the school had a forty percent failure rate; two of every five courses students took, they failed. Over . . . five years, the dropout rate exceeded fifty percent. . . . The average of math, reading, and language scores for Russell's 10th graders placed the school in the 24th percentile nationally, the lowest ranking among the state's forty-plus public high schools. (McQuillen, 1998, pp. 23, 78)

Most men understand that "your chances of getting a worthwhile job [are few] unless you have a high school diploma" (Johnson, 2000, p. 239; see also Clark, 1983; Fordham, 1996; Sullivan, 1989; Williams & Kornblum, 1994). However, critical factors discourage school completion. For Todd, a 21-year-old father, the disconnect between education and employment, as well as the pressures of family survival, outweigh the benefits of staying in school:

When I was going to school, we were not learning the skills I needed to get a job. I had a part-time job, and I was learning more in that job about work than I was in school. So I quit school because I had to help out my parents and younger sisters. My mother wanted me to stay in school but I could not see how it would help me. (Johnson, 2000, pp. 238–239)

Often African-American fathers begin their early work careers with errands for older local residents or publicly funded, neighborhood youth employment programs (Johnson, 2000; Sullivan, 1989; Williams & Kornblum, 1985; see also McLaughlin, Irby & Langman, 1994). It is unclear, however, if these local programs serve as conduits for young men into full-time jobs. Most adolescents find that few public jobs "look good when you apply for another job" (Williams & Kornblum, 1985, p. 35). At the very least, these programs provide temporary work experiences and income that keep youth engaged in the labor force (Williams & Kornblum, 1985).

Qualitative research identifies the range of economic opportunities available to inner-city adult men. Fathers are relegated to the most insecure jobs in the secondary labor market, such as car wash attendants; fast food clerks; grocery store stock and bag clerks; informal car repair; lawn work; street peddling; and street salvage (Jarrett, 1994). Men who work for cash in temporary day labor agencies and in seasonal, part-time jobs pass in and out of their jobs almost weekly (Roy, 1999b). If young fathers are employed at all, they typically work in several part-time, low-skilled positions (Kaplan, 1997; Rosier, 2000; Williams, 1991) and sometimes are put in the position of competing with their own fathers for the same jobs, as indicated in the comments of 16-year-old James:

> It's hard for a man to get a job here. Sometimes me and my friends go to apply for a job, and our fathers and grandfathers are trying for the same jobs, too! It's not fair! (Burton, Obeidallah, & Allison, 1996, p. 408)

Facing limited options in their local communities, some African-American fathers seek employment outside of the local neighborhood. Often, they are faced with discrimination in job hiring and practices (Reaves, 2000; Sullivan, 1992; White, 1999; Williams & Kornblum, 1985). For example, a young father in Grand Rapids, Michigan, confronted his supervisor about the lack of promotions for African-American workers:

> I've seen people come in there for six months, they put them in an office. . . . I finally went to [supervisor], . . . I've been with the company . . . for three years, whatever. I just really don't understand what is the problem with minorities getting into positions. I said, I've never seen anything like this in my life. I said, what do you as the owner have to say about this? (Johnson & Doolittle, 1996, p. 33)

Men also identify more subtle discriminatory factors that exclude African-American fathers from conventional jobs (Reaves, 2000; Williams & Kornblum, 1985). Theo, a 20-year-old father of two daughters, acknowledged a growing Chicago economy but also a new emphasis on "soft skills." Employers focus on skills such as appearance, language, and conventional lifestyles of workers that adversely impact many young African-American men:

> I think that there are more jobs out there than before. You have all those malls and stuff like that. But I think it's getting stricter now. You have to look a certain way, appearance, how you present yourself, how you keep your frame of mind. (Roy, 1999b, p. 83)

African-American men growing up in inner-city neighborhoods are further disadvantaged by the lack of well-developed job networks. Sullivan's study (1989) highlights the limits of kin sponsorship:

> Youths entered the period of work establishment with fewer personal connections to jobs. . . . [They were more] physically isolated. . . . Many of their parents had no jobs at all, and those parents who were employed tended to work in government jobs that recruited by bureaucratic means . . . instead of personal networks. (p. 80)

When job networks are available, they are typically linked to low-paying jobs. Typical of many males in the community, Jamal relies on a few key peer "acquaintances to hook [him] up" with job leads:

> Some of [Jamal's acquaintances] are local no-goods who live on his block, guys who deal drugs or guns for a living. But the others, the ones he depends upon when he needs to find work, have jobs in other fast food firms, small grocery stores in Queens, convalescent hospitals in the Bronx. (Newman, 1999, p. 162)

In other cases, even men with marginal jobs are unable to link their kin to low-paying jobs. Jasper, a father from Grand Rapids, explains: "It makes no sense. . . . I can't get my son a job, can't get my . . . nephew a job" (Johnson & Doolittle, 1996, p. 33). As qualitative data shows, inadequate education, limited job training, and discriminatory job practices keep many poor fathers out of the labor force (Newman, 1999; Young, 2000).

Alternatives to Formal Employment

Informal and underground economies, well-developed in impoverished inner-city neighborhoods, provide viable alternatives to limited conventional economies (Anderson, 1990; Burton 1991, Fine & Weis, 1998; Williams & Kornblum, 1985). A field-worker in New York observes how poor education and job options encourage involvement in alternative economies, particularly for young men:

> C. C. and Zero are among the countless youth who are on the streets because they have dropped out of school, cannot find jobs, or both. When they aren't hanging out at the candy store [a store for drug paraphernalia] or trying to kill each other, they spend their time stealing bicycles or engaging in petty hustles of various kinds, including doing favors for more successful hustlers. (Williams & Kornblum, 1985, p. 49)

The emergence of the "crack economy" in the inner city during the late 1980s offered impoverished men another source of income (Sullivan, 1989). Due to the difficulty of obtaining a good-paying job, some turn to dealing. Russell, a young custodial father in Chicago, details his situation:

> Getting a stable job like mine is not easy for Black men. We don't know anyone who can help us to get these jobs so we settle for what we can get. For a lot of friends, that means doing illegal things. But these guys are not criminals. At least, they don't set out to be criminals. They are just tryin' to make it in the world. (Johnson, 2000, p. 245)

Many fathers indicate that hustling is a way out of poverty, and they become involved at a young age (Hagedorn & Macon, 1988; MacLeod, 1995; Roy, 1999b). One young unwed father notes "[whenever I steal,] it's motivated by my child's needs for survival" (Achatz & MacAllum, 1994, p. 82). Richard, a young father in Buffalo, further underscores the point that men are "forced" into crime by economic deprivation:

> Because of the job situation, they are kind of forced into [crime], or led into it. You
> know, cause after a period of time . . . they don't want to work at McDonald's and
> make, I don't know, three something an hour. . . . They can make a couple of
> thousand [dollars] a week, you know, fourteen or fifteen years old. . . . You weigh
> that. . . . It's like, why not? (Fine & Weis, 1998, pp. 70–71)

As one teacher observes, "The boy makes more in one week than I make in
months. And I'm telling these kids to work at Popeye's or something" (White,
1999, p. 29; see also Anderson, 1990; Fine & Weis, 1998).

Although many families rely on resources from informal, and sometimes illegal, economies, in the most extreme cases street incomes cause problems for families. Wives and girlfriends sometimes view these activities as in conflict with
parenting roles (Hembry, 1988; Sullivan, 1992). For example, one mother, Jeannie, moved in with the father of her child, a man who is known as "Poison Pappa"
because he sells heroin and cocaine. Initially an involved father, his behavior
became erratic and dangerous as he began to use more of the drugs than he sells.
Eventually Jeannie and her child were forced to leave him altogether (Hembry,
1988, pp. 116–117).

The reality of hustling—high payoff but likely exposure to violence and
chance of incarceration—leads older fathers to "retire" from hustling. Alfred, a
father in his late thirties who retired from his hustling career, highlights this point:
"I refuse to go out on the corner and sell drugs. I am too old for that and I am not
going to jail for that. It's not a play thing" (Roy, 1999b, p. 92).

Despite low expectations and achievements in the labor market and forays into
the underground and informal economies, African-American fathers maintain a
traditional work ethic (Sullivan, 1992; Williams & Kornblum, 1994). Super, a
young father, has "completely conventional goals: to have a place of his own, get
married, and raise a family" (MacLeod, 1995, p. 231). Conrad, a young father in
Chicago, realizes that "I ain't just living for myself no more. I got my daughter
and son to live for, you know. . . . If I go, I want [them] to have something . . . to
collect something from me" (Young, 2000, p. 150). Asante, a 35-year-old unemployed father of a 2-year-old daughter in Chicago, asserts that:

> I want to work, I want to work so bad. It's time for money now, something with ben-
> efits that's stable. . . . I ain't fittin' to borrow, I have to do this for my daughter. . . .
> Something that will keep me physically busy. I couldn't sit at a desk. I love using
> my hands. I don't have a certificate or anything, but where are people at, what do
> they need? (Roy, 1999b, p. 80)

The availability of job opportunities often affects whether or not fathers are
actively involved in their children's lives. The following example telescopes how
job instability discourages active fathering:

> Charlie began to work less and less frequently at the car wash. The nice weather had
> begun. . . . Whenever the landlord came, Rose would explain that Charlie was respon-
> sible for paying the rent. . . . As an epilogue to these events, the economic strains per-

sisted in the lives of the Tower family until they separated after three years of marriage. Rose took the children and, Charlie took to the streets. (Williams, 1981, pp. 66–67)

Unable to provide financial support to their children and female companions, men become less involved with family life. This account, over 20 years old, continues to reflect the experiences of many contemporary fathers (see also Johnson, 2000; Johnson & Doolittle, 1996; Roy, 1999b). In a more recent account, a father from Harlem describes the impact of joblessness:

The jobs is what's wrong. They hire you for two weeks, get your hopes up, squeeze in a white boy. I don't want to go home and face her and the kids with no work. I don't want to go to jail. (Sullivan, 1992, p. 12)

Similarly, job stability buttresses family life and, relatedly, paternal role involvement. The following example of Lincoln Harrison illustrates the link between job stability and fathering in a Chicago family (see also Anderson, 1990; Williams & Kornblum, 1994):

Off and on . . . Lincoln has worked two (and sometimes three) jobs to support [his] family. He has always worked primarily as a cook, both in short order diners, and . . . in the kitchens of a well-known [local] restaurant The relationship between the children and Lincoln can best be described as "respectful". . . . Because of Lillie's constant references to his devotion . . . by working hard . . . they appreciate his efforts on their behalf. (Tatje, 1974, p. 180–181 & 195)

In more contemporary ethnographies, Alvin stands out as a father who stabilized his work career. After many years rotating from job to job, Alvin finally secures a solid job as a truck driver. He becomes a "constant presence in [his daughter] Latoya's life" and in the family household due to the stability of that job (Newman, 1999, p. 188).

In summary, the focus on neighborhood context identifies how the lack of economic and institutional resources influences men's job options. Inner-city neighborhoods offer only limited opportunities for stable employment. In the absence of these resources, alternatives to the formal labor market emerge in poor communities, often in the form of informal and underground economies. Both of these factors—limited opportunities and alternatives to formal employment—form the difficult context of men's family relationships.

FATHERS, MOTHERS, AND KIN: A PLACE IN THE FAMILY

I tell her now, it's not about me and her. It's about the kids. I'm not coming in her face telling her, look baby, you can trust me. . . . I show it by faithfully coming around and having something, not just taking all the time. If we don't buckle up and listen now, we're going to lose these kids to the streets or to [the Department of Family Services]. (Roy, 1999a, p. 448)

Shaped by the forces of the local job market and neighborhood context, men and women in low-income African-American communities look for ways to establish partnering relationships and parental commitment. These relationships often take nontraditional forms, outside of marriage and across multiple residences. Men and women, in turn, rely on the resources of kin networks to support their efforts to be involved partners and parents.

Normative Expectations of Marriage

Normatively defined life course models place fatherhood within the context of legal marriage, with parenting then following in sequence. Poor unmarried men and women aspire to conventional parenthood like other members of American society (Anderson, 1990; Jarrett, 1998). However, given the limited economic opportunities of poor African-American men, fatherhood and motherhood not only precede marriage, but often occur in the absence of marriage altogether. For example, Tisha had children before marriage and feels that she is "going backwards . . . somewhere along the line, I'm going to catch up with every[one] else" (Jarrett, 1994, p. 36). Men desire conventional roles associated with marriage as well (see also Roy 1999a, 1999b):

> I said no [to marriage]. It's not time. How could we? We're both living at home. We can't afford a place, there's just no way. It'd be crazy. But it would be nice, too, though. (MacLeod, 1995, p. 233)

Economic instability has direct consequences for marital trajectories (Aschenbrenner, 1975; Clark, 1983; Hembry, 1988; MacLeod, 1995; Merry, 1981; Williams, 1981). Fathers in inner-city neighborhoods describe how economic prospects depress marriage opportunities. As James professes his love for his girlfriend, he admits, "What kind of husband would I be? I need a job, man, I need a job" (MacLeod, 1995, p. 233). Leon, a 37-year-old father of two sons, is frustrated repeatedly by his partner's and his work and family trajectories being "off-time" and out of sync:

> We've been together since the seventh grade. I always say my wife, but we're not married. We just ain't really right. I'm not working, but she's working. When I was working, she wasn't working. So now we're hoping that both of us will be working and we can get the thing going right. (Roy, 1999b, p. 126)

Women also reflect on how their marriage prospects are delayed because of economic constraints (Hembry, 1988; Jarrett, 1998; Merry, 1981; Williams, 1991). Consider the following comment from Renee, a single mother, who describes the link between male economic marginality and marriage:

I could do bad by myself. . . . If we get married and he's working, then he lose his job, I'm going to stand by him and everything. I don't want to marry [any]body that don't have nothing going for themselves. . . . I don't see no future. . . . I could do bad by myself. (Jarrett, 1994, p. 38)

As men consider potential mates, they similarly consider women's economic contributions. Kevin, the father of a son from a previous marriage, finds secure high-paying employment, but is hesitant to commit to a long-term relationship with Kyesha because of her future economic prospects:

[Kevin] might feel differently if he thought Kyesha was going to make something . . . of herself over the long run—move up, maybe take a managerial job at Burger Barn. . . . But Kyesha doesn't seem inclined toward a job with much more responsibility that the one that she has. (Newman, 1999, p. 32)

To be sure, factors other than economic conditions come into play. Men and women both cite compatibility and personal preferences in the deliberations concerning marriage (Aschenbrenner, 1975). A single mother in Chicago expresses her view on compatibility: "I don't want to marry him 'cause me and him would never get along; but I like him. . . . Somehow our waves just won't click" (Jarrett, 1994, p. 35). Another father, who is proud of his ability to provide the basics, still loses his relationship due to his partner's preferences:

She said [that] I'm always working and when I'm not working I'm too tired and never wanna' do nothing with her. . . . I'm a good provider. . . . She said I was boring. . . . [But there's] a lot of mens out there that be tired and their women understand. (Achatz & MacAllum, 1994, p. 82)

Similarly, Duneier describes men's search for "finding the right woman. . . . Rather than being in the dominating position, many [men] are anguished by their inability to meet women who share their ideas and values" (Duneier, 1992, p. 41).

Dynamic Intimate Relationships

Despite the obstacles to marriage, some biological fathers marry the mothers of their children and live coresidentially. Married residential fathers play a positive role in the lives of inner-city children and teens. For example, ethnographies focusing on inner-city children and youth provide insight into the life of Marisa, one of the "Uptown kids," who lives with her mother and father in the Johnson projects (Williams & Kornblum, 1994); of Marc Gilliard, his married father, and two other teenage children (Williams & Kornblum, 1985); and of Kent, who lives with his mother, four younger siblings, and his father (Fordham, 1996). Earlier research notes Lincoln Harrison and his wife, Lillie, who have children ranging in age from 11 to 19 (Tatje, 1974; see also Aschenbrenner, 1975; Martin & Martin, 1978; Valentine, 1978).

Many of these fathers establish supportive and caring relationships with their wives and children. For example, Boyd Chivers is the primary breadwinner in his family and, along with his wife, is "oriented toward the goal of 'making it,' being a successful human being in society" (Clark, 1983, p. 39). Despite their residence in a deteriorating inner-city neighborhood in Philadelphia, Mr. and Mrs. James are "extremely gifted parents" in a "supportive and affectionate family" (Furstenberg, Cook, Eccles, Elder, & Sameroff, 1999, p. 105). Manny Ricky is married to Annette and the father of six young children. He holds several jobs to support his family and is a regular member at church (Rosier, 2000, p. 47).

The qualitative data also indicate that a number of informal relationships are established that result in children. Some of these nonmarital relationships are remarkably stable, considering the economic constraints that both women and men face. In Marissa's household, her son Jermaine's father, James Matthews, is described as "deeply involved with the family" (Rosier, 2000, p. 124). George and Renee remain committed to each other and their 1-year-old daughter, even with George's very sporadic work as a community organizer (Merry, 1981, p. 76). Another unmarried mother acknowledges her long-term partner's consistency and her affection for him:

> I'm not married. I got 3 kids. But their father is there with the kids. He been there since I was 16. . . . I been with the same guy since I was 16 years old and I'm still with him now. I only had really one man in my life. (Jarrett, 1994, p. 39)

Several factors shape the trajectories of intimate marital or nonmarital relationships. In addition to economic factors, some mothers and fathers live within the context of kin networks that may or may not have the resources to buttress relationships (Aschenbrenner, 1975; Burton, 1994; Jarrett, 1994; Jarrett & Burton, 1999; Stack, 1974). Also, relationships emerge at distinct life cycle stages for fathers. For example, older men may have more established work histories and developmental maturity that allow them to plan for relationships and families. Younger men, in contrast, often have more unstable work histories and are developmentally unprepared for the requirements of a relationship and family life.

Men's residence patterns play a significant part in relationships. As illustrated in previous examples, many fathers coreside and have strong relationships with their partners and children. However, a relationship can remain stable despite changes in residence, as men move in and out of the household (Williams, 1991). For example, Martin Davis, a "decent daddy" to both his biological son, Tommy, and his nonbiological son, Terry, spent many years living apart from his family before marrying his girlfriend, Jolene, and moving into the household (Anderson, 1999).

James' father has a positive relationship with his wife and exerts a positive influence on James. Yet James' father is not a continuous presence in the household: "He comes and he goes" (MacLeod, 1995, p. 54). Coresidence is not always an indicator of a solid relationship either (Clark, 1983). For example, Norris' parents are married but his father has no influence on him, and his mother runs the family household, virtually single-handedly (Fordham, 1996).

As previously discussed, job stability is central to consistent involvement in a family household. Successful fathers are committed to work that allows time for parenting as well. However, this is a rare situation, and poor fathers who frequently work multiple jobs to provide for their children find it difficult to remain actively involved in daily family life. For example, Mr. Gaines, father of 11 children, is "busy making money for the family" and is minimally involved in their lives (Clark, 1983, p. 151).

Related to job stability, men's access to and willingness to share scarce resources impacts household involvement. They can "stay" with their partners and children in a stable situation if they can hold down a job and, therefore, "pay" for the privilege (Edin & Lein, 1997; Newman, 1999). One father describes how his precarious job situation can lead to his exit from the household, and from his partner's and children's lives:

> You could say I work and pay my rent. I pay for where I stay at with my girl. My girl is my landlord, but nobody knows that. She does want money. I don't like to say this is my own bread, 'cause I don't like to be caught up in that "I'm gonna kick you out." So I always stay in contact with my family. . . . I'm on the edge when it comes to financial things. Cause if [I lose my job at Burger Barn], I'm off. (Newman, 1999, p. 202)

Men who are unable to contribute financially or emotionally to the household become increasingly isolated from family life (Achatz & MacAllum, 1994; Stack, 1974). Elliott's preoccupation with his job loss lead him to withdraw from his partner and children after less than a year of living together (see also Johnson 2000; Johnson & Doolittle, 1996; Roy, 1999b):

> For several months Julia and Elliott shared a small apartment and their relationship was strong. Elliott was very proud of his baby. On weekends he would spend an entire day carrying the baby around to his sister's [house] and would show it to his friends on the street. . . . After five months, Elliott was laid off from his job at the factory which hires seasonal help. . . . Elliott began spending more time with his friends at the local tavern and less time with Julia and [his] children. (Stack, 1974, p. 109)

Finally, men's expectations of intimate relationships and family life also influence the viability of involvement. Some men feel obligated to children and a long-term relationship with their partner, even in the absence of a legal contract. Derek, who lives with his common-law wife Maria and their children, is unable to save to buy a house and, as part of this inability to get ahead, has not pursued marriage either. His commitment is based on a notion of obligation to family:

I felt an obligation, a moral obligation [to be involved with kids]. . . . I provide for my kids. . . . I dunno', marriage, that's just not for me. But [my relationship with my kids is] working. (MacLeod, 1995, p. 235)

However, some men become fathers through short-lived relationships, as a result of sexual encounters or brief dating episodes (Anderson, 1990). Typically, their fathering a child does not result in father involvement. Susan met 17-year-old Joney at a party and became pregnant by him. Joney, who already has a 4-year-old son, assured her that "if you don't wanna' keep it, just give it up for adoption. Whatever you do, that's ok" (Kaplan, 1997, p. 46). In this instance, the young father placed the responsibility for the child solely on the young mother and failed to "step up" and provide any support for his child.

Some young fathers, developmentally and economically unprepared for long-term relationships, are unwilling to give up their nondomestic lifestyle despite demands from their partners. One father in Northton said that "if [my wife] had the baby, then she got me, you know. And that's the way she done me. [She] thought that's gon' trap me. That I'm all hers after she done have this baby" (Anderson, 1990, p. 121). After more than a year of a "good" relationship, another young father says that his girlfriend is "catching an attitude" and pressuring him to leave his peers behind in order to spend time together. He claims:

Then she started complainin' that I don't spend enough time with her and I only come in and come out when I want to. . . . She wanna' start keeping tabs on me . . . asking all kinds of questions like she was my mother. (Achatz & MacAllum, 1994, p. 41)

Conflicts surrounding control issues lead to relationship instability and sometimes dissolution (Hannerz, 1969; Liebow, 1967). A single mother in Chicago asserts: "I'm not married to him so I can do what I want to do. But when I get married, I can't do it at all. He says, 'I pay the bills.' But you don't get to boss me" (Jarrett, 1994, p. 35). In some instances, extreme conflicts around domestic control issues lead to emotional or physical abuse (Edin & Lein, 1997). Gloria, a mother from Buffalo, tells of how a violent relationship ended her husband's involvement with her and her children (see also Rosier, 2000):

My safety for my kids had to come first. He would want to be the controller. He wanted me to listen to him. He wanted me to bow down to his rules. He used to tell me, he used to make me believe that I was nothing. . . . My son walked into the room and he seen me get abused real bad, to the point where I went to the hospital and I was abused from the thigh down, from the back down, and my son was like, "Well, are you still going to let that man abuse you, Mommy?" . . . So I had made my decision for myself, on my own. I got rid of him; I left him. (Fine & Weis, 1998, pp. 170, 172)

As the examples illustrate, stable and unstable relationships exist among low-income African-American men and women, regardless of marital status. These intimate relationships are shaped by a variety of factors, including patterns of men's residence, economic stability and ability to share resources, and expectations for family life that include moral obligations, acceptance of domestic lifestyle, and coping with interpersonal conflict.

Negotiations Within Kin Systems

The context of kin obligations and family systems plays an important role in paternal involvement and relationships. Some fathers help to create and sustain interhousehold connections among networks of family members who provide flexible and interchangeable care for children (Aschenbrenner, 1975; Jarrett, 1994; Stack, 1974). For example, Asante, who provides money and resources sporadically for his daughter, turns to his kin when his resources are depleted:

> I might give you $200 at the end of the month, and I don't care if the courts know or not. The kids' mamas always know, I don't care how mad they are at me, they call me if they need something. . . . If I can't do it, and their mamas can't do it, they've got grandmamas and granddaddies. It's going to come together. (Roy, 1999a, p. 444)

Indeed, paternal relations and resources can play a formative role in children's lives, especially when the mother and her family are unable to provide housing and care (Hembry, 1988). Paternal involvement encourages some paternal kin to commit time and money toward children's well-being (Stack, 1974). Aaron, a 20-year-old father in New York, lives with his grandmother and 3-year-old son and is "one of those rarely talked about African American males who is taking care of his child" (Williams & Kornblum, 1994, p. 64). Similarly, Joe, a 40-year-old father in Chicago, leaves a substance abuse treatment program to return home to his young son, who lives with Joe's mother through informal custody arrangements:

> My son has been with my mom for three years—his mother is in a correctional institution. She knew what kind of people that my family were, and she felt safe since I was the father. . . . I let her know that I didn't have a job, so I couldn't really take care of the child, but I let her know that I would do my best. (Roy, 1999b, p. 142)

Some fathers negotiate with maternal kin in order to gain support for their involvement. Many of them are considered to be "renegade relatives" (Stack & Burton, 1993) by female kin, given their experiences with other men's prior lapses and absences from the family. Jordon, a father in Baltimore, can do little to prove his commitment to being a father to his partner's mother:

> All I know is that I was trying. Her mother wouldn't let me . . . take [my daughter]. "Well, you have to wait until Amy come home." So I left that day 'cause it happened to me twice. . . . I say, "Well, I'm her father." (Furstenberg, 1995, p. 131)

Sometimes kin members resist father involvement due to fathers' histories of irresponsible behavior and absence. Bird, a 20-year-old father and former gang member who had been incarcerated in Chicago, details how he is treated as a second-class parent. When his daughter's mother is absent from the household, Bird has to answer to her aunt, who questions his commitment:

> To see [my daughter] now, the auntie is straight about me seeing her, but she be acting like she doing me a favor by bringing mine through. . . . When she picks up the baby, she's like "Thank y'all for watching her." I be like, "Hold on, that's mine, you ain't got to thank me for taking care of mine. It's what I want to do." (Roy, 1999b, p. 143)

Both Jordon's and Bird's examples illustrate how frustrated efforts over time become obstacles to continued paternal involvement. In these instances, women believe that female kin are more reliable sources of child care and support (Burton, 1990; Newman, 1999; Stack, 1974).

Under certain circumstances, maternal kin support fathers' involvement. For example, Ricky, a 22-year-old father from Baltimore, has been consistently involved with his partner's family since childhood. As a result of this long-term history, his partner's mother encourages him to play the role of both biological and social father in the family:

> Ricky checks on us because my mother made him promise to make sure we OK. . . . She always know he always been around and be a big part of our lives. (Furstenberg, 1995, p. 127)

In summary, intimate relationships are shaped and sanctioned by kin networks. Paternal kin can enhance men's involvement through an extension of their resources for children's well-being. Maternal kin can also encourage men's involvement, although they often prove to be skeptical of male involvement due to unmet expectations from previous father figures. The complex extended family context suggests that low-income fathers must cope with a variety of social obligations and expectations in order to fulfill the role of parent.

FATHER INVOLVEMENT: SOCIAL PROCESSES OF PARENTING

> I was 18 years old at the time and I hardly had a commitment to myself. I just wasn't into taking care of someone else, not even my daughter that I truly love. . . . I do not have those crazy ideas now. I know what I must do for my newborn. (Johnson, 2000, p. 249)

Father involvement among low-income African-American men is a dynamic process. It entails negotiations around roles and responsibilities that are influenced by social and biological considerations. The meaning of a "good father" varies, based on men's (and significant others') beliefs about biological relationships and interpretations of their social roles. Men's involvement also changes qualitatively across the life cycle. With a consideration of dynamics over time, we are able to more clearly discern patterns and processes of involvement, as well as how social disadvantage accumulates and reemerges over many years.

Biology and Responsibility

Conversations with inner-city parents reveal the complex way in which they construct definitions of fatherhood. Sometimes this dichotomy is presented as a distinction between "fathers" and "daddies" (Furstenberg, 1992). The "father" is the actual progenitor of the child who is related by blood. The "daddy" is the man who actively assumes the rights and responsibilities associated with the role of the father, whether he is biologically related or not. Families assess men's parenting behaviors and, by assigning these terms, distinguish biological relations from actual involvement in children's lives (Aschenbrenner, 1975; Sullivan, 1993; Roy, 1999a).

One group of fathers believes that a biological relationship demands male involvement, because a father should not take it out on the child if he does not want responsibility. Bucky, a 24-year-old father from Trenton, works in a fast-food restaurant and supports his daughter and her disabled mother. He remarks that if fathers "do the crime," then they must "do the time" (Waller, in press).

Some men who link biological fatherhood to involvement are motivated to "be there" for their children because their own fathers were not involved with them (Allen & Doherty, 1996; Roy, 1999b; Sullivan, 1992). One young couple's histories with their own fathers shape their commitment to each other: "Jackie's absent father and her boyfriend's experience of being cut off from his first child motivated the couple to establish . . . intimacy and commitment" (Williams, 1991, p. 74). Another father states:

> My mom and my grandmother raised me. My dad? All I know is [what] his name was
> . . . . And when I was about [my] child's age, he left my mom. . . . I want to be a [cherished] memory [to my son]. I don't want to be like just a name. . . . I want to be part of his life. I want him to say, "My dad is right there." I want to take him to ball games, I want to keep him strong, I want to be [in] his life. (Allen & Doherty, 1996, p. 149)

For some fathers, a relationship with their children is a moral obligation that extends beyond any commitment to an intimate relationship with a partner. Their strident promises represent both a plan for future action and a social commitment to the role of "daddy" (Achatz & MacAllum, 1994; Johnson, 1998; Sullivan, 1992, 1993):

> Jordon promised his girlfriend Amy that she should "Do whatever you want to do, I'll do what I have to do." Amy explained that "He was going to take care of his daughter. He was going to be the father. Be the man he supposed to be and take care

of his responsibilities by taking care of the child. . . . He was going to be there for Nicole when [she] needed him, and he was going to be there even when she didn't need him. (Furstenberg, 1995, p. 124)

Some male peer groups in impoverished communities encourage men to "step off" and walk away from responsibility to their children and their partners (Anderson, 1990). Other community members, however, condemn such behavior: "[Fathers who neglect their kids] don't get no respect from me on that. I can understand if it happens, but it ain't nothing to brag about" (Sullivan, 1993, p. 59). A commitment to a child may set new social expectations in motion and prompt men to change their peer-oriented lifestyle. Ruben, a father of three boys in Chicago, "snapped out of his nonsense" with the birth of his first son. He realizes that fatherhood pulled him off the streets and may have saved his life (see also Sullivan, 1992):

[Her pregnancy] was about the only thing that slowed me down. I decided that you're going to have nobody to carry your name on, and there ain't no need to be going out anyway. (Roy, 1999a, p. 440)

Another group of fathers believe that the biological tie to children must be established, particularly if they are not in an established relationship with the mother of the child. These fathers typically look for physical resemblances with the child before they accept that the child is indeed their own (Anderson, 1990):

No one even told me I had a daughter until two weeks after she was born, and that just proved it more that she wasn't my child. . . . But [my mom and grandmom] matched up baby pictures . . . and said it was definitely my child. But I kept on denying the baby for a year. . . . It was [when] I held her for the first time and really looked at her. She had a lot of qualities just like me and I just started getting into her from that day on. (Achatz & MacAllum, 1994, p. 44)

Adolescent fathers and mothers in fragile relationships are involved in some of the most difficult negotiations around involvement. Young men express awe at the profound meaning a child brings to their lives, describing it as "an unexplainable feeling. . . . He looks at you and your body tingles. . . . It's almost like catching the Holy Ghost or something!" (Allen & Doherty, 1996, p.152). Many teen fathers, however, withdraw from their children's lives due to confusion, depression, and inability to approach fatherhood with maturity (Achatz & MacAllum, 1994; Allen & Doherty, 1996; Johnson, 2000; Kaplan, 1997). For example, John's confused attempts at providing for his child are dismissed by his girlfriend. He finally decides not to visit his son in the hospital because "I [didn't] have anything to take. . . . I asked my mother to help me out but she started 'sweating me' [giving a lecture]" (Johnson, 2000, p. 251).

A final group of fathers reject the children's mother or her influence (Achatz & MacAllum, 1994; Allen & Doherty, 1996; Roy 1999a; Sullivan, 1992). Despite efforts by the mother of his children, Kelvin, a father of three girls in Chicago, admits "I knew [the baby] was mine, but I denied it because I was living with another girl. . . . The second time I denied it again" (Roy, 1999a, p. 440). Another father directly links his poor relationship with his child's mother as the reason that he cannot be an involved "daddy":

> Like when me and [my partner] weren't fond of each other, it kept me and my son apart. She would always [say], "I don't want to see you today," or I would want to see my son, and me and her were fighting. I would say, "Well, I'm coming over" and she'd say "No, you don't" and leave. And I would come over and she'd be gone. (Allen & Doherty, 1996, p. 150)

Some men with children from different partners also have a difficult time being "daddies" for each child (Kaplan, 1997; MacLeod, 1995; Roy, 1999b; Sullivan, 1993). Denise, a young mother, says that her son's father does not visit or pay child support because "he has so many children that my son is just one more" (Kaplan, 1997, p. 103). Moreover, involvement can look qualitatively different for each child. For example, demands for financial support from two mothers sometimes conflict with the time that Juan has to spend with his two children:

> I really screwed up my life. Two children and two different mothers. Shit. . . . Now I've got to work every chance I get. Except Sundays, that's my day with my kids. . . . [My boss says I have to work], [and I say] "You need me here? My kids need me over there." You've got to put your kids first, that's how I look at it. I have no choice. (MacLeod, 1995, p. 234)

In other instances, mothers use men's contributions to their children to subsidize children of nonsupportive fathers, leading to ongoing couple conflict (Jeffers, 1967). Some mothers' current relationships threaten fathers, who see current boyfriends as potentially usurping their parenting role (Sullivan, 1993). Some fathers' current relationships also stand between fathers and children, such as when Ruby visits her father to pick up Easter shoes and encounters his new wife who "shook me and called me all kinds of low-down names and told me that I didn't have no father" (Stack, 1974, p. 13; see also Johnson, 2000).

The negotiation over linking biological "fathers" to the rights and responsibilities of social "daddies" suggests that low-income fatherhood is socially constructed between family members. Men may be biological fathers but unable or unwilling to perform the duties of an involved parent. Because there are many paths to paternity, many men and family members struggle with an appropriate definition of fatherhood.

The Meaning of the Good Father

Qualitative research clarifies how low-income parents give meaning to the content of involvement. Conventional expectations of father involvement typically equate "good fathers" with providing financial resources. Men know that "if you cannot take care of yourself, you cannot take care of your kids" (Sullivan, 1992, p. 9). Sean, who works two jobs, at Burger Barn and a security agency, sets high expectations for employment in order to be a responsible "daddy." He declares:

[People] come to me and say "I can't find a job. It's hard." I say, "Keep on trying. Don't give up." I know, believe me, I know how it feels to be down. To have to ask somebody for something, I know. You just keep trying, keep praying, have faith, and you'll be all right. (Newman, 1999, p. 212)

Both fathers' and mothers' conventional notions about providing sometimes discourage men's initial involvement with their children. Trane does not want his young son to live with him until he has a job; his son's mother does not allow Trane to visit until he can provide a home. Consequently, Trane has not seen his son for over three years and has only spoken on the phone to him a few times (Johnson & Doolittle, 1996). A young father from Harlem describes how his friend withdrew from his child's life because he cannot find a good job:

See, he didn't have a job, and maybe he didn't want to, you know, put his foot in his mouth and say he was gonna' do something even though he couldn't do it. Right now I'm quite sure he's regretting it, and I know he wants to see the baby. . . . [But] he has no visitation rights. (Sullivan, 1993, p. 60)

Men with unstable work often provide informal contributions to their children. Fathers with young children offer disposable diapers, baby clothes, or new shoes, as well as sporadic contributions of money when it is available (Furstenberg, 1995; Jarrett, 1992; Roy 1999b; Sullivan, 1992). These nonmonetary contributions serve as proxies for monetary support and are typically accepted by mothers as evidence of traditional involvement.

Some involved providers drop out of their family's lives when they transition out of the work role. One mother tries to predict the involvement of her child's father into the future, but realizes that "I shouldn't plan on depending on him, because [his job] can end at any time," due to job instability. She began to plan for his eventual absence because he is "hard pressed to provide any assistance" without a job (Edin & Lein, 1997, p. 165). Another father "thought that if I worked real hard, I could make it . . . get married, buy a little rundown house and fix it up real nice." His determination and motivation to get ahead eventually eroded with a court summons for child support. He is fired as his job performance slips, and his involvement with his children—defined as providing—ends (Achatz & MacAllum, 1994, p. 89).

"Daddies" revise traditional notions of the good provider role. For some families, responsible "daddies" give priority to time, not money. These fathers realize that "I don't need to have lots of money to be a good father the main thing that I need to give [my son] is love and spend a little time with him" (Achatz & MacAllum, 1994, p. 37). The emphasis on time reflects a different notion of men's commitment to children. Families use a common term to describe a commitment to responsible parenting: "being there" (Allen & Connor, 1997; Newman, 1999).

Some fathers realize that they hurt their children when they withdraw due to lack of finances. Andre, an 18-year-old father with a newborn daughter, illustrates this point:

> The main thing that people talk about is financially taking care of their child, providing good, clothing, shelter. And the second thing is just spending time with them. . . . The system takes away from the second thing, and they really just emphasize the first thing. And that really hurts the children. (Roy, 1999a, p. 447)

Isaiah is also adamant about the importance of time and nonmonetary commitment. To him, money does not provide the intangible support that involved fathers can provide:

> To me, that's the easy way out: give [the kids] some money and then run off. The money doesn't comfort them at night. They can't say, "Hey, Dollar Bill, I had a nightmare last night" and expect the Dollar Bill to rock them and hold them. Money is there because it's a necessity. But if you give a child love and attention, money is the last thing they are going to look for. (Roy, 1999a, p. 432)

Mothers often acknowledge the difficulty that men have finding employment. Consequently, women broaden their expectations of fathers to include alternative forms of support. One mother claims that "I wouldn't care if he didn't give [his son] nothing. . . . I would have paid child support if he would just spend a little more time with the children (Furstenberg, 1995, p. 125). Yvette acknowledges her child's father's economic limitations and seeks symbolic support instead. Yvette suggests that even a show of interest in her child is a positive sign of involvement—even though it means lowering expectations for a father:

> It's not what you do, it's how you do it. I don't expect him to buy my baby snowsuits and boots. . . . It's just the thought. When Keith's [my son's] birthday come around, [his father] ain't got to give him a quarter, he ain't got to send him a card. You could pick up the phone and wish him a happy birthday. . . . If they don't have it, they just don't have it. You can't get blood from a turnip. (Jarrett, 1994, p. 43)

Although financial contributions and fatherhood are tightly linked, many low-income families reject singular definitions of fatherhood based on men's economic abilities. Instead, they construct a notion of fatherhood that encompasses the time men spend with their children as well as other expressions of care and concern. Broader definitions of "the good father" allow men attainable measures of responsible fatherhood in the absence of economic markers.

Cycles of Engagement and Disengagement

Father involvement is a dynamic process that unfolds—and changes—over many months and years. Fathers and families move through distinct transition points. For example, the breakup/makeup of a relationship sometimes changes family structure and the meaning of involvement altogether. Consider the example of Tally, who over the course of the ebb and flow of his relationship with Bess becomes estranged from his son (see also Newman, 1999, for more recent examples):

> After the birth of [the] baby, . . . after she and Tally had stopped going out together, Bess came to the corner only on Tally's pay day, . . . sometimes bringing the child along, sometimes not. But as Bess and Tally rediscovered their attraction for each other, she began to bring the baby regularly, coming now on Friday or Saturday evenings and sleeping over with the baby in Tally's room until Sunday night or Monday morning. On these weekends, Tally sometimes took the boy into the carry-out shop for a soda or, on one occasion, marched up the street with the child on his shoulder, proudly announcing that Bess had "sent the men to get a loaf of bread." But after a few weeks, Tally and Bess had a fight. Bess stayed away from the neighborhood, and Tally's contacts with his son—dependent as they were on his relationship with Bess—ended abruptly. (Liebow, 1967, p. 90)

These transitions accumulate, resulting in rhythms or cycles of father involvement. Some cycles show patterns of consistent father involvement (Clark, 1983; Williams & Kornblum, 1985). For example, Vernon's persistence in his relationship with Tami keeps him attached to her and engaged with his children. He says, "Sometimes you get a little depressed, but we still stay together. . . . I can say that anything bad that happened between us in the past had made us strong" (Furstenberg, 1995, p. 141).

Other "blue moon" fathers move in and out of their children's lives in an inconsistent pattern over time (Kaplan, 1997; see also Furstenberg et al., 1999; Rosier, 2000). Eighteen-year-old Sheena lives with her grandmother and "saw her father only sporadically" (Williams & Kornblum, 1994, pp. 41–42). Reflecting a similar pattern, Lionel disappeared for six months after his partner Wanda became pregnant. When the baby was born, he reappeared and vowed "he will be with me one day, I'll see to that. . . . I want him to know that I am his father. . . . I'll do all I can for him" (Furstenberg, 1995, p. 126). However, even after having a second child with Wanda, Lionel is unemployed and does not pay child support. He has not seen either child in six months and attributes much of his absence to a "family misunderstanding," in which he refused to return his children after a scheduled visit.

As Lionel's pattern of involvement suggests, cycles are shaped by job stability. For example, numerous transitions between jobs lead Alvin, father of three daughters, into sporadic involvement over many years (Newman, 1999). He finally finds work as a truck driver, and the job alone solidifies his place in the household permanently. However, it is the fathers of his daughters' children who now cycle in and out of their children's lives. In this way, cycles of engagement and disengagement overlap across generations, shaped by the economy, individual stages of development, intergenerational relationships, and personal choices.

Reconnection between fathers and children is a common and, sometimes, problematic process (Furstenberg et al., 1999; Roy, 1999b; Williams, 1991). When children initiate reconnection, they run the risk of rejection. Salena queries relatives and finds her biological father after almost two decades. Her father is resistant to establishing a relationship, even calling into doubt his paternity (Zollar, 1985). Jackie's father "occasionally showed up and bought [her] things she wanted and didn't want" and she longed for him to be more involved in her life (Williams, 1991, p. 74). Absent fathers also run the risk of rejection from the family. For example, one mother is reluctant to allow her daughter's father back into her life because of past lapses. She says:

> When I was talking to him on the phone yesterday, it was the same thing. "You know I want you back. I've changed." I say, "Well, how can you prove to me that you've changed? You just last month told me you was gonna' take her Easter shopping. She did not see you." (Furstenberg, 1995, p. 137)

Despite their absence, fathers often make efforts to connect with their children across great distances and with gestures of affection (Roy, 1999b; Sullivan, 1993; Waller, in press). One young father's efforts to search for his son lead him far away from his job and home:

> I don't get to see my son since he moved away, but I think about him every day. . . . For a year, I sent him boxes of books, toys that he could put together himself, plastic tool sets. [His mother] never wrote back. . . . I have no way to know if he's even alive. I [left my job] and drove [1,500 miles], all day and night, to get out there. . . . I found out where she lived from a letter and . . . bought a map. (Achatz & MacAllum, 1994, p. 53)

Some fathers become involved during their children's teen years, a period when inner-city youth are seen as being particularly vulnerable to local risks and dangers (Aschenbrenner; 1975; Wilson, 1987; Zollar, 1985). Sometimes these first encounters are difficult for fathers and children, but as Dexter, a teen in Harlem who had talked to his father once when he was 9 years old, explains, "it ain't no mystery anymore" (Williams & Kornblum, 1994, p. 151). Other men reengage when they become grandfathers, and their children seek them out for guidance and support in the parenting role (Aschenbrenner, 1975; Williams, 1991).

Men may reach new levels of understanding about involvement as they age. They reflect on earlier decisions and see opportunities for "second chances" with children after a string of disappointments as students, workers, sons, and partners (Achatz & MacAllum, 1994; Allen & Doherty, 1996; Roy, 1999b). For example,

Hershey fought with his first partner about involvement and, several years later with other children and a new partner, takes a more responsible attitude. Over many years of struggling to be involved, he develops a new understanding that "having a child means taking care of her and for me, that means working to take care of her" (Johnson, 2000, p. 249).

In summary, fatherhood is a dynamic process, characterized by periods of involvement and absence. Several factors influence men's level of consistency or inconsistency in their children's lives. These include job status, male–female relations, and personal decisions. These transition points accumulate over time and emerge as cycles of engagement and disengagement. As men move in and out of their children's lives, reconnection may become problematic even though it proves significant to both children's and their fathers' development.

FLEXIBILITY AND VARIETY
OF FATHER FIGURES

> With him accepting and helping me out with her, that's all right. Most men they not going to do too much except maybe like buy her a little something, play with her and call it a day. But he accepts my daughter. And seeing that it is not his, I think that's a big responsibility. Because if I ask him for something for my daughter, he'll give it to me. So I figure that right there is a man. (Jarrett, 1994, p. 43)

With variable patterns of involvement for many biological fathers, low-income African-American families rely on a wide variety of men to fulfill the paternal role (Burton, 1995a; Jarrett 1994). The flexibility and interchangeability of the paternal role means that children receive care and concern from multiple individuals. In many instances, when the need arises for a father figure, men from both inside and outside the family are recruited.

Variety of Father Figures

Qualitative research points to a wide range of father figures who are found in the lives of poor children and youth.

Biological Fathers. In many instances, biological fathers assume the paternal role. The concern of this father is "to support the children that [he] brought into the world" (Schulz, 1969, p. 139). For example, a 25-year-old father assumes economic responsibility for his daughter and brings her into his relationship with his new family (Williams, 1991). Single biological fathers, like Steven, a 37-year-old father of three boys, also take care of their children (Burton, 1991).

Male Companions. When biological fathers do not or cannot act as "daddies," some mothers turn to their male companions to act as father figures

(Aschenbrenner, 1975; Liebow, 1967; Schulz, 1969). LaDawn finds that her new partner "accepts my daughter" and decides to remain involved because his personal commitment is matched by responsible behavior (Jarrett, 1994). A 16-year-old male in an ethnographic study of teenage pregnancy remarks:

> Tiffany (a pseudonym) is not my baby, but she needs a father. To be with her, I work in the day care center at school during my lunch hour. I feed her, change her diapers, and play with her. I buy her clothes when I can because I don't make much money. I keep her sometimes. Her mother and her family appreciate what I do and Tifffany loves me too. Every time she sees me she reaches for me and smiles. (Burton, 1995, p. 157)

In still another example, one father assumes responsibility for his partner's child, even though paternity is still unresolved (see also Roy, 1999a; Sullivan, 1992):

> When she told me she was pregnant, . . . I jumped at the opportunity to claim it. . . . I always knew that she was probably with other men and that the baby might not be mine. . . . He's three years old now, and I still don't know if he's mine biologically, but he's mine because I've always loved him and I'm the person he calls daddy. (Achatz & MacAllum, 1994, p. 30)

Stepfathers.   Stepfathers play important roles in children's lives. Sometimes they are second fathers to biological fathers, whereas at other times they supplant biological fathers altogether. For instance, Jimmie Martin is loved not only by his stepdaughter, Angela, but by her children and her cousins as well (Aschenbrenner, 1975). The Niles children in Chicago have come to regard their stepfather as their father once their mother lost contact with their biological father (Zollar, 1985). Tammy, a promising teen in Cleveland, has two supportive stepfathers. She gave them "cards on Fathers' Day and wished them a happy Fathers' Day" (Williams & Kornblum, 1985, pp. 21–22).

Foster Fathers.   Foster fathers provide yet another avenue to social fatherhood. Deacon Griffin, who lives in the Belmar neighborhood of Philadelphia, raised three foster children. Neighbors described them as "well-mannered and recognized as being different and distinctive from other children" (Williams, 1981, p. 54).

Uncles.   Some uncles become social fathers to children (Furstenberg et al., 1999; MacLeod, 1995). Harold provides an example. He suggests that his experience as a parental figure started early in life with his sister and her 2-year-old son, both of whom lived in the household when Harold was growing up (Sullivan, 1992). Another father in Baltimore "is the only steady male figure that's been there" for his nephews and nieces, who "call him daddy" (Furstenberg, 1995, p. 137). Yvette discovered that her uncle was not her real father when she was 14 years old, but the revelation "didn't stop me from thinking of him as my father":

He had done so much and just been there. He was always Daddy. . . . My father's also one of the people who helped me just to realize, "Yvette, you've got to make something of yourself. You see your cousins. They're not doing anything. . . ." So I guess my cousins got jealous that there was someone in my life who was actually paying my tuition to go to this school, who was actually picking me up from school every day, helping me do my homework. (Anderson, 1999, pp. 57–58)

Grandfathers.   Grandfathers can be called on for paternity help (Burton, 1992). In some instances women live coresidentially with their fathers, who assists them with child care. In other instances, grandfathers take full parenting responsibility for their grandchildren. One grandfather notes that:

Many more black grandfathers take care of babies and everybody than you think. We're just quiet about what we do. These babies love us too. Just look at how this one follows me around all the time. (Burton, 1995b, p. 94)

In addition, grandfathers offer advice to their grandchildren on how to progress in life. Benita tells of her grandfather's encouragement: "My granddaddy he want me to hit the sky. He want me to go to school for college, university—everything. He want me to do everything" (O'Connor, 2000, p. 113).

Older Brothers.   Older brothers who are often in the same households aid their mothers by caring and monitoring their siblings, as well as providing financial contributions. For example, Anthony Hayes mentions "[My brother] . . . took the place of my father" (Clark, 1983, p. 73). John Brown, father of four, plays a fathering role in his biological family: "[My father] left seven years ago . . . and I try to help my mom as much as I can. . . . I'm her oldest son. My brother is just a baby" (Anderson, 1990, p. 39).

Unrelated Family Friends and Mentors.   Nonromantic male friends of the family play an important father figure role as well (Rosier, 2000). Tyrone turns to Reggie Jones, his gymnastic coach, because "if you don't have no father, [Mr. Jones is] the guy to be with" (McLaughlin, 1993, p. 25). John, an academically promising youth, relies on father figures from his church. His unmarried mother, Pamela, "sought help from men in her church. . . . She hoped that these experiences would help him become a better citizen. . . . and a young man who would one day assume responsibility as a parent" (Furstenberg et al, 1999, p. 123). Sometimes, unrelated older men in the neighborhood serve as social fathers, or "old heads" (Anderson, 1990, 1999). These men promote mainstream values and serve as bridges to conventional developmental trajectories. As one young woman relates to an elder man, youth in inner-city neighborhoods look up to "ol' heads" as father figures:

I really love you. Me and my older sister used to pretend that you were our father. You were the father that we always wanted because you didn't drink; we never saw

you drunk. We never saw you staggering down the street. We never saw you messing with anybody. (Anderson, 1999, p. 184)

As these examples suggest, a wide variety of men are inducted into the paternal role. These men include a variety of partners of mothers, as well as family
members related to mothers. Friends and community members also become central to children's and youth's lives when they dedicate themselves to the paternal
role.

Paternal Roles and Activities

In many respects, poor African-American fathers, regardless of their marital status or biological relationship, perform common role activities. Some of the paternal role activities are traditional, such as playing with children, providing discipline, and serving as role models. Other activities are more nontraditional and
reflective of "new" or "nurturant" fathers, such as domestic work and primary
child care (LaRossa, 1993).

Recreation and Play.   Frequently fathers are involved in play activities.
Routine play activities serve multiple purposes. They enhance the development of
children and shape the attachment between children and fathers (Fordham, 1996;
Williams & Kornblum, 1985). One promising teen in his inner-city neighborhood
recounts his father's involvement in recreational activities, despite having limited
time:

> My Dad, he's busy, so we hook up, especially . . . on the weekends and stuff. And
> you know, go out, play sports, cause he's athletic. . . . And see, we're alike, so I play
> basketball a lot. We play chess, he taught me how to play chess. (Furstenberg et al.,
> 1999, p. 105)

Fathers like Robert monitor and comfort children during play activities. They
encourage communication and creative learning through their interaction with
boys and girls:

> When [the children] fell or were hit or had an object of value taken from them, they
> ran to Robert if he was there. He comforted them, laughed with them, and arbitrated
> their disputes. He painted pictures for them, made plywood cutouts of the Seven
> Dwarfs for them, and brought home storybooks. (Liebow, 1967, p. 84)

Play also alleviates some of the pain that men experience while failing to find
secure employment. One young father looks forward to play with his new baby
for this reason:

> Usually, my routine was I'd get up, go out and look for a job in the morning. . . .
> Then I would go over to my girl's house in the afternoon and see the baby, you
> know, play with her and stuff. . . . Seeing her smile always made me feel better 'cuz

I was steady downed by the fact that I couldn't find any job and everyday hearing about "oh, we ain't hiring" or "we need someone that's got so many years of experience" or "too bad, you should have been here last month." (Achatz & MacAllum, 1994, p. 50)

Domestic Work and Child Care.   Some men assume daily domestic chores associated with housework and child care. Although their contributions are less than children's mothers, men's involvement is significant to the household. Leroy, a mother's boyfriend, is involved in grooming as he "bathed the children, braided the girls' hair and washed their clothes at the 'Benedix' " (Liebow, 1967, p. 85). Sam is a 65-year-old retired factory worker who cares for his three nieces: "We gets ready really early in the morning. I comb the girls' hair, I dress and feed them. Then I take them to school" (Burton, 1991, p. 36).

Other fathers take on cooking duties, some on a regular daily basis, dependent on the employment status of the mother. Cory, a 27-year-old wrestler with three children, assumes key child care and domestic tasks, even though "usually the women stayed at home, but I reversed it. . . . [T]hat was my philosophy" (Roy, 1999a, p. 448). Isaiah does all of the shopping and cooking for his girlfriend's family:

She used to work nights, and I used to go home and cook to make sure her three girls had something to eat. I did all of the shopping. Her family made a joke about how I could take $60 for meat and stuff and make it last for four people over a month. (Roy, 1999b, p. 146)

Men sometimes focus on the health of their children as well. They realize that one parent cannot monitor and care for children's health as well as two or more parental figures. Calvin, for example, "played with the children during the day when they were well and stayed up with them at night when they were sick" (Liebow, 1967, pp. 84–85). GK, a teen father with a young son, visits his child and goes to "extraordinary lengths" to care for him:

My son was seven months old, and he had a bite mark on his face. I asked [my girl-friend] who did it, and she said she didn't know. I asked her, did she take him [to the emergency room], 'cause at the time she was staying [in] a place where cats and dogs was, and I figured, well, if a dog or somethin' bit him, he should go in for shots. [So I took him in for shots.] (Allen & Doherty, 1996, p. 150)

In some instances, fathers became primary parents. Even young fathers, such as 23-year-old Jelani, provide stable home environments for their children when mothers lose custody. They often rely on their own kin support networks to aid them in this responsibility. Jelani shares his story: "My son's mother, I don't know where she is. . . . I think she's in [a state prison]. I had been taking him on the weekends and summers, and she called me up and asked me to take him for three years" (Roy, 1999a, p. 448). Children are sometimes given to nonbiological fathers who express love, concern, and a desire to keep a child. Oliver Lucas, a 30-year-old resident of the Flats, asks to keep his ex-girlfriend's baby girl when they "quit."

> I asked if she would give the baby to me. She said fine, and my "daughter" has been living with me, my mother, my grandmother, my sisters and brothers ever since. My daughter is ten years old now. She sees her mother now and then, and her father takes her to church . . . sometimes, but our family is really the only family that she's ever had. (Stack, 1974, p. 66)

Role Models for Masculinity.   Fathers establish themselves as role models for proper masculine behavior. Darrell, a 15 year old, acknowledges that he "[hangs] with my old man. We is buds! I guess we both just men" (Burton, Allison, & Obeidallah, 1995). James insists that fathers' respectful behavior is needed to counter less-positive alternatives for their sons (see also Williams & Kornblum, 1994):

> I have a sixteen-year-old son, and my son have [to have respect for me]. And . . . your kids only do what they see you do. If you sit and smoke a cigarette or a joint on the porch, then that's what they're going to do . . . they'll think it's alright to do it because their daddy did it. . . . You feel it's alright to bring women in and out of your house, and you've got a son or daughter there, well . . . they think that's going to be alright when they . . . you know, well, you did it. So why can't I do it? (Fine & Weis, 1998, p. 77)

Other men provide youth with a roadmap and tips on how to "get ahead." One "ol' head" tells of his relationship with three of his "boys," who he steered into legitimate careers in the military, even supporting them with his own money:

> I got three of my boys in the [military] service right now, and another is on the way. Just the other day, a young boy comes up to me in the neighborhood and say he need 25 dollars to get some underwear and toiletries so he can get ready to leave for the army. We talked for awhile and then I reached into my pocket and come up with two tens and a five and handed it to him. (Anderson, 1990, p. 70)

Discipline, Protection, and Supervision.   Modeling masculinity also entails establishing fathers as authority figures and ensuring the safety and protection of children in the community. In the Northton community "certain fathers with domineering dispositions make territorial claims on a dwelling, informing their children's friends that this is my house, I pay the bills here, and all the activities occurring under its roof are my singular business" (Anderson, 1990, p. 122; see also 1999).

Men talk with their children "about how to behave" (Holloman & Lewis, 1978, p. 216; see also Zollar, 1985). At times, fathers' guidance keeps their sons from choosing a lifestyle of the streets. One mother in Chicago, who sent her son to live with his father in a Southern community, believes that under his father's supervision, her son will be protected from the hazards of street life:

> I have a thirteen-year-old. I sent him away when he was nine because the gangs was at him so tough, because he wouldn't join. . . . They took his gym shoes off his feet. They took his clothes . . . took his jacket off his back in subzero weather. . . . A boy pulled a gun to his head and told him, "If you don't join, next week you won't be here." I had to send him out of town. His father stayed out of town. [My son] came here last week for a week. He said, "Mom, I want to come home so bad." I said no. (Wilson, 1996, p. 4)

Men insist on teaching children "what is right and wrong," which often involves discipline. Some father figures administer discipline according to the age of the child. As Adam's father suggests:

> If [Adam] does not do what he should he knows that he will suffer some way or another. Not physically, you know, with beating or anything like that. You can discipline a child without beatings. If beatings are necessary, oh, he'll get that. . . . But at his age, I don't think beating is necessary. (Fordham, 1996, p. 152)

Socializing children involves monitoring their travels outside of the household, and even escorting them from place to place (Clark, 1983; Williams & Kornblum, 1994). Sade's father escorts her and her friends home from flag girl practice every week. He admits "we don't like the darkness to catch up with her. . . . You know, we try to emphasize being home before dark" (Fordham, 1996, p. 115; see also Davidson, 1996). Sam makes sure that his nieces are "in the house by three o'clock . . . [because] I don't want them to turn out like the low-life drugheads their mama and daddy are" (Burton, 1991).

Some men are particularly vigilant in screening youths' relationships with their peers (Anderson, 1999). Steven says that "I worry about [my sons]. . . . There is so much to get into. But I call my boys every hour and come home on my break" (Burton, 1991, p. 36). Men's monitoring of their teen daughters' relationships is particularly pronounced in qualitative studies (see also Patillo-McCoy, 2000). Dara feels that her father is "way overdone" in his need to protect her from potential boyfriends:

> You know, last week when we were in the mall and Paul came by and said, "What's up?", and Dad went off, saying that he was disrespectful [with the way that] he was acting. Now daddy's got my interest in mind, but why's he gotta do that? (White, 1999, p. 46)

Role Models for Achievement. Men are often strong role models for achievement (Clark, 1983; Davidson, 1996; Fordham, 1996). They promote education as integral to the advancement of their children. For example, Mr. Treppit recalls his conversations with his son:

This is what I'm trying to explain to James Earl, I want him to [succeed]. The only way he can do this is to be even smarter than I was because things is getting tougher. Now I told him he can get them on his own but he's gotta' get this here [schooling] finished. So I told him all you can do to survive actually is to have an education these days. (Clark, 1983, p. 57)

Marc Gilliard's father also sets clear educational priorities for his son: "School first, basketball second. . . . Marc [seemed] to think that he was right" (Williams & Kornblum, 1983, p. 15). Although fathers seldom model educational achievement based on their own academic success, they find in hindsight that schooling is necessary. James' father quit school, but nevertheless has high expectations for him. James asserts "he wanted me to be a lawyer when I was a little kid" (MacLeod, 1995, p. 58).

Men socialize their children to the realities of racism and discrimination. Anderson suggests that "ol' heads" socialize youth in an effort to defeat "racial apartheid" (1999, p. 181). This socialization is implicit in many men's messages to persevere despite educational and employment obstacles. Adam's father is supportive and encourages Adam to be pro-active:

I'd like the [people] that have done something with their education, sort of like to return it to the community—to the race. . . . I can look out and see things that we're not getting what the other races are getting, but I still say, hey, don't put your tail between your legs and whine about it. Go out and do something about it. Get your education. And then go out and make something of yourself, and then come back and help your fellow man. (Fordham, 1996, p. 182)

Conflict Over Father Role

As our examples to this point suggest, the expansion of the paternal role assures that poor children receive needed care and concern. Flexibility ensures that families tailor men's strengths to specific child-care and domestic needs. However, role flexibility can generate conflicts as well (Aschenbrenner, 1975). For example, when men and women establish new relationships through marriage or dating, it may be unclear who is the "daddy" (MacLeod, 1995; Roy, 1999b). In other circumstances, problems occur when men are asked to serve as "daddies" to children with uninvolved biological fathers. Violet demands that her first child's father treat all of her children as his own. One of the children becomes very upset when the man tells her "I ain't your daddy" (Stack, 1974, p. 80). Not all men accept the responsibility of serving as social fathers to nonbiological children. If they do play this role, there is the potential for exposing children and youth to personal danger. For instance, Mrs. Farland cites a series of childhood experiences with an incest-prone stepfather that figures heavily in her decision never to expose her children to another man living in the home (Clark, 1983, p. 104).

Men who do accept the role of father figure are potentially subjected to multiple, contradictory demands, particularly when they have children of their own. John, a 21-year-old with four children by three mothers, shuttles between a job at a pizza parlor, his children's homes, and his own mother's home. He questions his priorities: Are they to his young children or to his own mother and brother (Anderson, 1990)? Family demands are obstacles to success at school and work for Lamont, a father of a young daughter in Chicago. He says that "it's taking its toll, being a father figure for my nieces and nephews [as well as my own daughter]. . . . Just to know that I was going to be a husband, friend, big brother, uncle, father and employee all in the same boat" (Roy, 1999b, pp. 147–148). He is able to balance demands of his biological and nonbiological children, often relying on the mother of his child and her family to offer more support in difficult times. Lamont is adamant in not giving up on his nonbiological children, "like everyone else does, like the world does, or like them giving up on themselves" (p. 148).

Previous examples illustrate the variety of men who assume the paternal role and the nature of their relationships with children. To be sure, men vary in the level and quality of their participation, dependent on specific circumstances. However, the focus on roles and their performance provides an understanding of the ways in which men may or may not be involved in the lives of African-American children and youth, independent of marital, biological, or residential status.

DISCUSSION AND CONCLUSION

In this review of classic and contemporary research, we highlight the perspectives that qualitative studies offer concerning the roles low-income, urban, African-American fathers play in the lives of their families and children. The microlevel, in-depth, intensive nature of methods used in the studies we reviewed generated insights into the contextual, processural, and subjective aspects of African-American fathers' lives and those of their children. Through the work of qualitative researchers cited in this review, we were able to discern the informal, local systems of family support and the variety of contributions made by fathers in ways that less-intensive research methods cannot provide. Moreover, the studies document how fatherhood unfolds as a *process* over time among teenage, young-adult, midlife, and elderly dads and father figures. In particular, we find that qualitative research illustrates fathers' actual relations with their children over time, including how they feel about and interact with their children as infants, teens, and adults. Finally, the methods of participant observation and interviewing encourage a subjective understanding of fatherhood for low-income men, revealing a complex and humanistic portrait of men's lives.

We explored four themes that emerged in extant qualitative research on African-American fathers: (a) the neighborhood context of economic opportunities for fathers; (b) negotiations between fathers and mothers in a system of kin work; (c) the meaning of fatherhood and the social process of father involvement; and (d) the diverse set of father figures who fulfill a variety of flexible paternal role obligations. Overall, the qualitative research suggests that:

- Local economic opportunities shape the lives of poor African-American fathers at every juncture. Men aspire to conventional work values but cannot always find jobs. Men's inability to find good jobs and create a consistent job record harms their potential as involved parents. It also encourages marginal relationships with partners and family.
- Fatherhood is not a static relationship but a dynamic *process* over time. Important factors, such as past and present economic situations, relationship status, personal history, and developmental maturity influence men's movement in and out of children's lives.
- Negotiations within families allow fathers to tailor active roles in their children's lives. If they are not providers, then they can offer their time and other in-kind support. If they cannot commit to marital relationships, many enter nonmarital relationships.
- African-American families depend not only on biological fathers in parenting children, but on social fathers as well. Fatherhood is an active, *flexible* relationship in low-income African-American communities, and men other than children's biological fathers are often well suited to take on the responsibility of parenting.

We argue, with these considerations in mind, that assumptions embedded in contemporary public policy concerning poor fathers need to be closely reexamined. Current social policies, such as welfare reform, are predicated, *at least implicitly*, on the assumption that some men do not espouse a mainstream work ethic and need "paternal" or "supervisory" programs to modify their "responsible" behavior (Mead, 1997). Such policies will not address the lived experiences or motivation of low-income African-American men, who as our review suggests have conventional aspirations for work, for marriage, and for parenting and, in many instances, contribute in-kind support to their families and children (Achatz & MacAllum 1994; Edin & Lein, 1997; Jarrett, 2000; Johnson, 2000; Johnson & Doolittle, 1996; Roy, 1999a; Sullivan, 1992; Waller & Plotnick, 2001).

In order to more effectively address the needs of low-income African-American fathers, policymakers must move past current "public" assumptions concerning low-income fathers and craft policies with three goals in place. For example, appropriate fatherhood policies should take men's developmental stages into account. It is difficult to promote economic provision as a measure of responsibility for teen fathers; perhaps additionally policies can promote early attachment to their children. By the same token, older fathers have different concerns, particularly with problematic reentry into a child's life and the kin network.

In addition, public policy would benefit greatly from acknowledging the effective and informal family arrangements that are tailored for many father–child relationships. Policies must reflect an understanding of the degree of interdependence that exists even between children and their unmarried fathers who live outside the household. Such an acknowledgment would also recognize the importance of nonbiological social fathers in nurturing children, as well as nonmonetary contributions of time, material, and care.

It is problematic to tune policies finely enough to address only fathers. Broader mandates for policy changes at the neighborhood level, as qualitative evidence shows, would strongly shape men's involvement in the family. Initiatives to provide job training and placement would enhance opportunities for cohorts of low-income fathers who have never had stable employment histories. Education reform and innovative approaches to neighborhood safety would promote social and geographic mobility for poor families, diminishing other barriers that exist between parents and children.

To be sure, despite our consideration of extant qualitative research on African-American fathers and our ruminations about public policy, there are limits to the insights we have offered in this discussion. Indeed, more systematic studies of African-American men should be conducted giving attention to the informal roles that they play within the family, the various contributions that they make to children's well-being, and the multiple types of relationships that are formed with women and children. As we suggested previously, we encourage researchers to explore issues related to men's development in the context of family, work, and neighborhood. Further insights on the effects of development, age, and cohort on fatherhood are sorely needed as well.

Given the current renewed scientific interest in qualitative methods, mixed method studies that utilize complementary strengths of both qualitative and quantitative methods promise to provide new and unexpected insights on this topic. Combining some of the methods used in studies described in this review with contextually sensitive survey measures will offer coming generations of researchers both breadth and depth in understanding the "visible" place and roles of men in low-income families.

ACKNOWLEDGMENTS

Writing and research for this chapter were supported by a Hatch Award and University of Illinois Research Board Award to Robin L. Jarrett; grants from the Social Science Research Council's Program on the Urban Underclass to Robin L. Jarrett and Linda M. Burton; grants to Linda M. Burton from the National Institute of Mental Health (R29 MH46057-01, R01 MH49694-07); and a grant from the National Institute of Child Health and Human Development (R01 HD36093-02) to Andrew Cherlin, Ron Angel, Linda M. Burton, Lindsay Chase-Lansdale, Robert Moffitt, and William Julius Wilson.

REFERENCES

Achatz, M., & MacAllum, C. (1994, Spring). *Young unwed fathers: Report from the field.* Philadelphia: Public/Private Ventures.

Allen, W., & Connor, M. (1997). An African American perspective on generative fathering. In A. Hawkins & D. Dollahite (Eds.), *Generative fathering: Beyond deficit perspectives* (pp. 52–70). Thousand Oaks, CA: Sage.

Allen, W., & Doherty, W. (1996). The responsibilities of fatherhood as perceived by African American teenage fathers. *Families in Society: Journal of Contemporary Human Services, 79,* 142–155.

Anderson, E. (1990). *Streetwise: Race, class, and change in an urban community.* Chicago: University of Chicago Press.

Anderson, E. (1999). *Code of the street: Decency, violence, and the moral life of the inner city.* New York: W. W. Norton.

Aschenbrenner, J. (1975). *Lifelines: Black families in Chicago.* New York: Holt, Rinehart & Winston.

Auletta, K. (1982). *The underclass.* New York: Random House.

Baca Zinn, M. (1989). Family, race, and poverty in the eighties. *Signs: Journal of Women in Culture and Society, 14,* 856–874.

Becker, H. S. (1970). *Sociological work: Method and substance.* Chicago: Aldine.

Bulmer, M. (1986). The value of qualitative research. In M. Bulmer, K. G. Banting, S. Blume, M. Carley, & C. H. Weis (Eds.), *Social science and social policy* (pp. 180–204). London: Allen & Unwin.

Burgess, R. G. 1984. *In the field: An introduction to field research.* Boston: Allen and Unwin.

Burton, L. M. (1990). Teenage childbearing as an alternative life-course strategy in multigeneration black families. *Human Nature, 1*(2), 123–143.

Burton, L. M. (1991). Caring for children. *The American Enterprise, 2,* 34–37.

Burton, L. M. (1992). Black grandparents rearing children of drug-addicted parents: Stressors, outcomes, and social service needs. *The Gerontologist, 32*(6), 744–751.

Burton, L. M. (1994). Intergenerational legacies and intimate relationships. Perspectives on adolescent mothers and fathers. *ISSPR Bulletin, 10*(2), 2–5.

Burton, L. M. (1995a). Family structure and nonmarital fertility: Perspectives from ethnographic research. In Department of Health and Human Services, *Report to congress on out-of-wedlock childbearing* (pp. 147–165). Hyattsville, MD: Public Health Service. (Pub. No. (PHS) 95–1257)

Burton, L. M. (1995b). Intergenerational patterns of providing care in African-American families with teenage childbearers: Emergent patterns in an ethnographic study. In K. W. Schaie, V. L. Bengtson, & L. M. Burton (Eds.), *Intergenerational issues in aging* (pp. 79–96). New York: Springer.

Burton, L. M., Allison, K., & Obeidallah, D. (1995). Social context and adolescence: Perspectives on development among inner-city African American teens. In L. J. Crockett & A. C. Crouter (Eds.), *Pathways through adolescence: Individual development in relation to social contexts* (pp. 119–138). Hillsdale, NJ: Lawrence Erlbaum Associates.

Burton, L. M., & Graham, J. (1998). Neighborhood rhythms and the social activities of adolescent mothers. In R. Larson & A. C. Crouter (Eds.), *Temporal rhythms in adolescence: Clocks, calendars, and the coordination of daily life* (pp. 7–22). San Francisco: Jossey-Bass.

Burton, L. M., Obeidallah, D. A., & Allison, K. (1996). Ethnographic insights on social context and adolescent development among inner-city African-American teens. In R. Jessor, A. Colby, & R. Shweder (Eds.). *Ethnography and human development: Context and meaning in social inquiry* (pp. 395–418). Chicago: University of Chicago Press.

Burton, L. M., & Snyder, A. R. (1998). The invisible man revisited: Comments on the life course, history, and men's roles in American families. In A. Booth & A. C. Crouter (Eds.), *Men in families.* Mahwah, NJ: Lawrence Erlbaum Associates.

Clark, R. M. (1983). *Family life and school achievement: Why poor black children succeed or fail.* Chicago: University of Chicago Press.

Corcoran, M., Duncan, G. J., & Gurin, P. (1985). Myth and reality: The causes and persistence of poverty. *Journal of Policy Analysis and Management, 4,* 516–536.

Darity, W. A., & Meyers, S. L. (1984). Does welfare dependency cause female headship? The case of the black family. *Journal of Marriage and the Family, 46,* 765–779.

Davidson, A. L. (1996). *Making and molding identity in schools: Student narratives on race, gender, and academic engagement.* Albany: State University of New York Press.

Dash, L. (1989). *When children want children: An inside look at the crisis of teenage parenthood.* New York: Penguin Books.

Duneier, M. (1992). *Slim's table: Race, respectability, and masculinity.* Chicago: University of Chicago Press.

Denzin, N. K. (1970). *The research act: A theoretical introduction to sociological methods.* Chicago: Aldine.

Denzin, N. K., & Lincoln, Y. S. (1994). *Handbook of qualitative research.* Thousand Oaks, CA: Sage.

Edin, K., & Lein, L. (1997). *Making ends meet: How single mothers survive welfare and low-wage work.* New York: Russell Sage Foundation.

Ellwood, D., & Bane, M. (1987). The impact of AFDC on family structure and living arrangements. *Research in Economics, 7,* 137–207.

Emerson, R. M. (1981). Observational field work. *Annual Review of Sociology, 7,* 351–378.

Fetterman, D. M. (1989). *Ethnography: Step by step.* Newbury Park, CA: Sage.

Fine, M. (1985). Dropping out of high school: An inside look. *Social Policy, 16,* 43–50.

Fine, M., & Weis, L. (1998). *The unknown city: The lives of poor and working-class young adults.* Boston: Beacon Press.

Fordham, S. (1996). *Black out: Dilemmas of race, identity and success at Capital High.* Chicago: University of Chicago Press.

Furstenberg, F. F., Jr. (1992). Daddies and fathers: Men who do for their children and men who don't. In F. F. Furstenberg, Jr., K. E. Sherwood, & M. L. Sullivan (Eds.), *Caring and paying: What fathers and mothers say about child support* (pp. 34–56). New York: Manpower Demonstration Research Corporation.

Furstenberg, F. F., Jr. (1995). Fathering in the inner-city: Paternal participation and public policy. In W. Marsiglio (Ed.), *Fatherhood: Contemporary theory, research and social policy* (pp. 119–147). Thousand Oaks, CA: Sage.

Furstenberg, F. F., Jr., Cook, T. D., Eccles, J., Elder, G. H., & Sameroff, A. (1999). *Managing to make it: Urban families and adolescent success.* Chicago: University of Chicago Press.

Furstenberg, F. F., & Hughes, M. E. (1997). The influence of neighborhoods on children's development: A theoretical perspective and a research agenda. In J. Brooks-Gunn, G. Duncan, & J. L. Aber (Eds.). *Neighborhood poverty: Context and consequences for children* (pp. 23–47). New York: Russell Sage Foundation.

Gadsen, V. (1999). Black families in intergenerational and cultural perspective. In M. E. Lamb (Ed.), *Parenting and child development in "non-traditional" families.* Mahwah, NJ: Lawrence Erlbaum Associates.

Garfinkel, I., McLanahan, S., Meyer, D., & Seltzer, J. (1998). *Fathers under fire: The revolution of child support enforcement.* New York: Russell Sage Foundation.

Hagedorn, J., & Macon, P. (1988). *People and folks: Gangs and the underclass in a rustbelt city.* Chicago: Lake View Press.

Hamer, J. F. (1997) The fathers of "fatherless" black children. *Families in society: The Journal of Contemporary Human Services, 78,* 564–578.

Hannerz, U. (1969). *Soulside.* New York: Columbia University Press.

Hembry, K. F. (1988). *Little women: Repeat childbearing among black, never-married adolescent mothers.* Unpublished dissertation, University of California, Berkeley.

Holloman, R. E., & Lewis, F. E. (1978). The "clan": Case study of the black extended family in Chicago. In D. Shimkin, E. Shimkin & D. A. Frate (Eds.), *The extended family in black societies* (pp. 201–238). The Hague: Mouton.

Jarrett, R. L. (1992). A family case study: An examination of the underclass debate. In J. Gilgun, G. Handel, & K. Daley (Eds.), *Qualitative methods in family research* (pp. 172–197). Newbury Park, CA: Sage.

Jarrett, R. L. (1994). Living poor: Family life among single parent, African American women. *Social Problems, 41*, 30–49.

Jarrett, R. L. (1995). Growing up poor: The family experiences of socially mobile youth in low-income African American neighborhoods. *Journal of Adolescent Research, 10*, 111–135.

Jarrett, R. L. (1998). African American mothers and grandmothers in poverty: An adaptational perspective. *Journal of Comparative Family Studies, 29*, 388–396.

Jarrett, R. L. (2000). Voices from below: The use of ethnographic research for informing public policy. In J. M. Mercier, S. Garasky, & M. C. Shelley, II (Eds.), *Redefining family policy: Implications for the 21st century*. Ames: Iowa State University Press.

Jarrett, R. L., & Burton, L. M. (1999). Dynamic dimensions of family structure. *Journal of Comparative Family Studies, 30*, 177–187.

Jeffers, C. (1967). *Living poor: A participant observer study of choices and priorities*. Ann Arbor, MI: Ann Arbor Publishers.

Joe, T. (1984). *The "flip-side" of Black families headed by women: The economic status of men*. Washington, DC: Center for the Study of Social Policy.

Johnson, E., & Doolittle, F. (1996). *Low income parents and the Parents' Fair Share Demonstration: An early demographic look at low income non-custodial parents and how one policy initiative has attempted to improve their ability to pay child support*. New York: Manpower Demonstration Research Corporation.

Johnson, W. (1998, March). Paternal involvement in fragile, African American families: Implications for clinical social work practice. *Smith College Studies in Social Work, 68(2)*, 215–232.

Johnson, W. (2000). Work preparation and labor market experiences among urban, poor, non-resident fathers. In S. Danziger & A. Lin (Eds.), *Coping with poverty: The social contexts of neighborhood, work and family in the African American community* (pp. 224–261). Ann Arbor: University of Michigan Press.

Jorgensen, D. L. (1989). *Participant observation: A methodology for human studies*. Newbury Park, CA: Sage.

Kaplan, E. B. (1997). *Not our kind of girl: Unraveling the myths of black teenage motherhood*. Berkeley: University of California Press.

Kotlowitz, A. (1991). *There are no children here*. New York: Anchor Books.

La Rossa, R. (1993). Fatherhood and social change. *Family Relations, 37*, 451–457.

Lemann, N. (1986). The origins of the underclass. *Atlantic Monthly, 258*, 31–55.

Liebow, E. (1967). *Tally's corner: A study of Negro street corner men*. Boston: Little, Brown.

MacLeod, J. (1987). *Ain't no makin' it: Leveled aspirations in a low-income community*. Boulder, CO: Westview Press.

MacLeod, J. (1995). *Ain't no makin' it: Leveled aspirations in a low-income community* (2nd ed.). Boulder, CO: Westview Press.

Marsiglio, W., Amato, P., Day, R., & Lamb, M. (2000). Scholarship on fatherhood in the 1990s and beyond. *Journal of Marriage and the Family, 62(4)*, 1173–1191.

Martin, E., & Martin, J. (1978). *The Black extended family*. Chicago: University of Chicago Press.

McLanahan, S., & Sandefur, G. (1994). *Growing up with a single parent: What hurts, what helps*. Cambridge, MA: Harvard University Press.

McLaughlin, M. W. (1993). Embedded identities: Enabling balance in urban contexts. In S. B. Heath & M. W. McLaughlin (Eds.), *Identity and inner-city youth: Beyond ethnicity and gender* (pp. 36–68). New York: Teachers College Press.

McLaughlin, M. W., Irby, M. A., & Langman, J. (1994). *Urban sanctuaries: Neighborhood organizations in the lives and futures of inner-city youth*. San Francisco: Jossey-Bass.

McQuillen, P. J. (1998). *Educational opportunity in an urban American high school: A cultural analysis*. Albany: State University of New York Press.

Mead, L. (1997). *The new paternalism: Supervisory approaches to poverty*. Washington, DC: Brookings Institute.

Mead, L. (1986). *Beyond entitlement: The social obligations of citizenship*. New York: Free Press.

Merry, S. E. (1981). *Urban danger: Life in a neighborhood of strangers.* Philadelphia: Temple University Press.

Miller, A. (1993). Social science, social policy, and the heritage of African American families. In M. Katz (Ed.), *The "underclass" debate: Views from history* (pp. 254–289). Princeton, NJ: Princeton University Press.

Mincy, R., & Pouncy, H. (1997). Paternalism, child support, and fragile families. In L. Mead (Ed.), *The new paternalism: Supervisory approaches to poverty.* Washington, DC: Brookings Institute.

Moore, W., Jr. (1969). *The vertical ghetto: Everyday life in an urban project.* New York: Random House.

Moynihan, D. P. (1965). *The Negro family: The case for national action.* Washington, DC: Office of Policy Planning and Research, United States Department of Labor.

Murray, C. (1984). *Losing ground: American social policy, 1950–1980.* New York: Basic Books.

Newman, K. S. (1999). *No shame in my game: The working poor in the inner-city.* New York: Knopf and Russell Sage Foundation.

O'Connor, C. (2000). Dreamkeeping in the inner city: Diminishing the divide between aspirations and expectations. In S. Danziger & A. Lin (Eds.), *Coping with poverty: The social contexts of neighborhood, work, and family in the African American community* (pp. 105–140). Ann Arbor: University of Michigan Press.

Ogbu, J. U. (1974). *The next generation: An ethnography of education in an urban neighborhood.* New York: Academic Press.

Patillo-McCoy, M. (2000). Negotiating adolescence in a Black middle-class neighborhood. In S. Danziger & A. Lin (Eds.), *Coping with poverty: The social contexts of neighborhood, work, and family in the African American community* (pp. 77–101). Ann Arbor: University of Michigan Press.

Rainwater, L. (1970). *Behind ghetto walls: Black families in a federal slum.* Chicago: Aldine.

Reaves, A. (2000). Black male employment and self-sufficiency. In S. Danziger & A. Lin (Eds.), *Coping with poverty: The social contexts of neighborhood, work, and family in the African American community* (pp. 172–200). Ann Arbor: University of Michigan Press.

Rosier, K. B. (2000). *Mothering inner-city children: The early school years.* New Brunswick, NJ: Rutgers University Press.

Roy, K. (1999a). Low-income single fathers in an African American community and the requirements of welfare reform. *Journal of Family Issues, 20,* 432–457.

Roy, K. (1999b). *On the margins of family and work: Life course patterns of low-income single fathers in an African American community.* Unpublished dissertation, Northwestern University, Evanston, IL.

Schulz, D. (1969). *Coming up Black: Patterns of ghetto socialization.* Upper Saddle River, NJ: Prentice Hall.

Stack, C. B. (1974). *All our kin: Strategies for survival in a Black community.* New York: Harper and Row.

Stack, C. B., & Burton, L. (1993). Kinscripts. *Journal of Comparative Family Studies, 24,* 157–170.

Staples, R. (1985). Changes in black family structure: The conflict between family ideology and structural conditions. *Journal of Marriage and the Family, 47,* 1005–1013.

Sullivan, M. (1989). *Getting paid: Youth crime and work in the inner-city.* Ithaca, NY: Cornell University Press.

Sullivan, M. (1992). Non-custodial fathers' attitudes and behaviors. In F. Furstenberg, K. Sherwood, & M. Sullivan (Eds.), *Caring and paying: What mothers and fathers say about child support* (pp. 6–33). New York: Manpower Research Demonstration Corporation.

Sullivan, M. (1993). Young fathers and parenting in two inner city neighborhoods. In R. Lerman & T. Ooms (Eds.), *Young unwed fathers: Changing roles and emerging policies* (pp. 52–73). Philadelphia: Temple University Press.

Tatje, T. A. (1974). *Mother-daughter dyadic dominance in black American kinship.* Unpublished dissertation, Northwestern University, Evanston, IL.

Valentine, B. L. (1978). *Hustling and other hard work: Life styles of the ghetto.* New York: Free Press.

Waller, M. (in press). *My baby's father: Unmarried parents and paternal responsibility,* Ithaca, NY: Cornell University Press.

Waller, M., & Plotnick, R. (2001). Effective child support policy for low income families: Evidence from street level research. *Journal of Policy Analysis and Management, 20*(1), 89–110.

White, R. T. (1999). *Putting risk in perspective: Black teenage lives in the era of AIDS.* New York: Rowman & Littlefield.

Williams, C. W. (1991). *Black teen mothers: Pregnancy and child rearing from their perspective.* Lexington, MA: D. C. Heath & Company.

Williams, M. (1978). Childhood in an urban black ghetto: Two life histories. *Umoja, 2,* 169–182.

Williams, M. (1981). *On the street where I lived.* New York: Holt, Rinehart & Winston.

Williams, T., & Kornblum, W. (1985). *Growing up poor.* Lexington, MA: Lexington Books.

Williams, T., & Kornblum, W. (1994) *The Uptown kids: Struggle and hope in the projects.* New York: G. P. Putnam.

Wilson, W. J. (1987). *The truly disadvantaged: The inner city, the underclass, and public policy.* Chicago: University of Chicago Press.

Wilson, W. J. (1996). *When work disappears: The world of the new urban poor.* New York: Knopf.

Young, A. (2000). On the outside looking in: Low-income Black men's conceptions of work opportunity and the good job. In S. Danziger & A. Lin (Eds.), *Coping with poverty: The social contexts of neighborhood, work, and family in the African American community* (pp. 141–171). Ann Arbor: University of Michigan Press.

Zollar, A. C. (1985). *A member of the family: Strategies for Black family continuity.* Chicago: Nelson Hall.

10

Cultural Contexts of Father Involvement

Nicholas Townsend
Brown University

Definitions of good fatherhood and expectations of men's involvement with their children differ from one culture to another. I draw on intensive fieldwork among two groups of men, one in the San Francisco Bay region of northern California, the other in a village in the southern African country of Botswana, to illustrate this variation. Most of this chapter is devoted to a descriptive analysis of two systems of cultural expectations about the appropriate behavior of men and about what fathers are supposed to do for their children. In order to contextualize these cultural analyses, I first discuss four elements of an anthropological approach: (a) the meaning of cultural interpretation, (b) the particularism of anthropological method, (c) the nature of comparison, and (d) the concept of dominant cultural values. Then I consider the cultural specificity of parenthood and the theoretical development of the idea that children develop within a cultural context.

In the first of my two examples, I present an analysis of the way that men from California described the place of fatherhood in their lives, drawing out their assumptions about the life course, work, gender, and fathers' responsibilities. The pattern of these assumptions will be familiar to most readers and may be taken for granted by many of them. But I then turn to an extended analysis of the life story of a man from Botswana and illustrate that his lifelong involvement with his children has been guided by very different assumptions about what men should do to be successful fathers, sons, and husbands. In my conclusion, I make explicit some of the points of contrast between these two sets of cultural values and suggest some implications for considering the impact of fathers' involvement on the development and well-being of children.

INTERPRETATION AND PARTICULARISM

Outsiders to the discipline frequently think of anthropologists (when they think of them at all) as spending long periods of time living in remote and uncomfortable settings where, through the exercise of participant observation and ethnographic method, they arrive at an understanding of "the native's point of view" that is inaccessible to others. In interdisciplinary discussions, the contribution of anthropologists to the understanding of a topic is often expected to be through the application or communication of this method. Anthropologists have not always resisted this characterization. Faced with the difficulty of describing what we do, we sometimes fall back on what George Stocking, the most prominent historian of the discipline, has referred to ironically as "the ethnographer's magic" (Stocking, 1992).

The debate about the nature, desirability, and even possibility of doing fieldwork in such a way as to gain a greater understanding of the point of view and cultural meanings of others has been voluminous and sometimes acrimonious. My discussion of comparison and cultural models is not intended as a contribution to this debate, but as a clarification of my project, which is neither an empirical report of patterns of behavior nor in any way magical. Two points are particularly important to my discussion: the approach of cultural anthropology is interpretive and it is particularistic.

By interpretive, I mean that the objective is to reach an understanding of the ways that people make sense of their own actions and of the social world within which they live. It is important to stress that this enterprise is very different from an attempt to discover the underlying motives or internal causes of human action. The anthropologists Dorothy Holland and Margaret Eisenhart made this distinction in their analysis of the role of cultural models in the education of college women and their socialization as adult women. They stress that the cultural model "is first and foremost an interpretive structure, a meaning system, not a set of prescriptive rules. Actual relationships are not dictated or determined by the model, but rather experience is anticipated, interpreted, and evaluated in light of it" (Holland & Eisenhart, 1992, p. 95). Holland and Eisenhart go on to explore the many ways that romance can depart from the model and the ways in which women then deploy other cultural models to make sense of these departures. The French anthropologist Pierre Bourdieu (1977) has formulated an influential theory of human action as the practice of people who are operating within a set of potentially contradictory explanatory principles rather than following a set of rigid rules.

By saying that anthropological method is particularistic, I mean that it focuses on detailed examinations of the actions and meanings of particular people in specific situations. As Clifford Geertz points out in his much cited essay on "thick description": "anthropologists don't study villages . . . they study *in* villages" (1973, p. 22). In my case, I did not study a suburb, but I studied the meanings of fatherhood to a group of men who had been raised in a suburban community. The point is that topics such as "the meaning of fatherhood" cannot be studied in general; they must be the meanings of fatherhood to particular people who find themselves in particular circumstances. The interpretive project is, first, to grasp those meanings, and then to make "small facts speak to large issues" (Geertz, 1973, p. 23).

COMPARISON OF TWO SETTINGS

In attempting to make the "small facts" incorporated in the words and lives of a few men in northern California and southern Africa speak to the "large issues" of father involvement, I am comparing two systems of meanings about fatherhood and two sets of expectations about how men should meet their responsibilities over the course of their lives. This comparison should most emphatically not be read as one between modern and traditional models of fatherhood. Nor should it be seen only as a comparison of the varied and complex behavior of fathers in the two settings. In general terms, fathers certainly act differently in California and in Botswana, but my focus is on the cultural models that fathers use to judge themselves and that children, wives, mothers, and others use to judge fathers in two settings.

My studies of the two settings took different forms and produced different kinds of data and different presentations. In California I was concerned with investigating the place of fatherhood in men's lives because the great bulk of research attention to childbearing intentions and decisions had been directed at women. I relied heavily on in-depth interviews with men who shared many background characteristics in order to be able to identify their shared cultural orientation. These were men who both accepted the values of their culture and were in the social and economic situation of being able to achieve success in that culture's terms. My presentation of the place of fatherhood in their lives makes extensive use of their own words (Townsend, 1992, 2001, 2002). In Botswana, on the other hand, I was concerned with investigating the connections men had with children in a society where official statistics reported a very high percentage of female-headed households and out-of-wedlock births. In that situation, my research was directed at the disjuncture between the categories embodied in official data and the lived experience of the people being reported on (Garey & Townsend, 1996; Townsend, 1997, 1999). My research in Botswana concentrated on collecting information about the social connections and economic activity of a group of men over their lives, and my presentation takes the form of narrative and comparative discussion of those life courses.

I do not use these two examples because they are polar opposites or represent the extremes of cultural variation, but because I have studied both and can discuss them in detail. However, there is one great advantage to using these two examples: the California group typifies the hegemonic Western picture of the male life course and of paternal responsibility that is taken for granted by most Americans and many family researchers, whereas the Botswana group represents a contrast in economic situation, institutional context, and cultural norms that can work to denaturalize the Western picture. It is very easy to take some institutionalized pattern with which we are familiar, such as marriage between spouses of similar ages, and to assume that it is a universal, necessary, or natural state of affairs. Cross-cultural comparison undermines this assumption and opens the range of human arrangements and experience to our analyses.

Dominant Cultural Values

As I have indicated, cultural models and cultural systems of meaning are not monolithic: all cultural systems incorporate variation and alternatives. The particularistic approach of cultural anthropology focuses minutely on specific instances and expressions of cultural systems, each one of which is inevitably unique and idiosyncratic. But the enterprise of analyzing cultural patterns does not degenerate into an endless catalog of idiosyncrasy because each particular expression is a manifestation of general models and meanings

Audre Lorde's incisive invocations of differences among women were decisive contributions to the development of feminist theory because they demolished assumptions of the universality of white, Western, women's experience. Lorde wrote and spoke passionately about the ways that difference is used to divide and exclude. She was adamant that feminists, and anyone who wants "to define and seek a world in which we can all flourish," must recognize our differences and see them as a source of strength not of division. What all oppressed groups have in common, Lorde said, was that they were excluded and made to feel inferior. The oppressed groups in American society, "Black and Third World people, working-class people, older people, and women" (1984, p. 114), "stand outside the circle of this society's definition" (1984, p. 112). They depart from what Lorde called a "mythical norm" "defined as white, thin, male, young, heterosexual, christian, and financially secure" (1984, p. 116). Lorde's emphasis on difference was part of a program to build a better world on the basis of our real differences rather than to compare ourselves to the "mythical norm." Lorde's point, of course, was that the norm had enormous impact on the living situations and inner consciousness of all of us, even though it is "mythical," precisely because it is not a description of the majority but a standard by which all are judged.

Sociologist Erving Goffman, analyzing the ways in which we handle stigma in daily life, argued that "in an important sense there is only one complete unblushing male in America" and went on to describe this norm in terms very similar to Lorde's: "young, married, white, urban, northern, heterosexual Protestant father of college education, fully employed, of good complexion, weight and height, and a recent record in sports" (Goffman, 1963, p. 128). Goffman's norm is no more common or representative than Lorde's. Indeed, Goffman argued that "the general identity-values of a society may be fully entrenched nowhere," but he clearly described the impact of this norm on men's interactions and self-image: "Every American male tends to look out upon the world from this perspective. . . . Any male who fails to qualify in any of these ways is likely to view himself—during moments at least—as unworthy, incomplete, and inferior" (1963, p. 128).

Dorothy Smith, a sociologist whose theoretical work on the sociology of knowledge has its empirical roots in her research on single motherhood, has described the impact of a norm of family life, which she describes as the "Standard North American Family" characterized as: "a legally married couple sharing a household. The adult male is in paid employment; his earnings provide the economic basis of the family-household. The adult female may also earn an income, but her primary responsibility is to the care of husband, household, and children. The adult male and female may be parents . . . of children also resident in the household" (Smith, 1999, p. 159). Smith does not, it should be clear, make any claim that such a family form is either morally desirable or statistically dominant, and her analysis of this norm is an element of her research on single mothers. What she does claim is that this picture of the family operates as an "ideological code" that informs a great deal of research and policy in such a way as to denigrate or distort any other ways of organizing family life. Smith argues, for example, that the behavior of children is judged and treated very differently according to the kind of family they come from.[1]

I cite these three very different authors with very similar descriptions of dominant norms to make two points: first, that an analysis of a cultural norm is something very different than a description of majority experience, and second, that examining dominant norms is not a way to exclude or conceal people who cannot meet, or who resist, those dominant norms but is a necessary part of the project of describing the situations of their lives. To see the dominant values of society clearly is to understand what the members of that society must confront in their daily lives. My approach to this task has been to examine the lives and words of people who accept the dominant values, who judge themselves by those standards, and who occupy social positions that enable them to realize those values to an extent that they can find acceptable. It is in the sense that their lives and values represent the dominant cultural norms that I would describe the men I talked

---

[1]The great diversity of mothers who do not fit the cultural norm, and the condemnation they face as a result, is documented in the collection *Mothering Against the Odds* (García Coll, Surrey, & Weingarten, 1998). This collection describes both the variety of ways of being a mother and the way that all varieties are judged against dominant cultural values.

to as "typical." It is worth noting that, for men in the United States who were born in 1950, over 90% have married, almost 90% of their wives have had at least one child, and 95% of them are in the labor force at the end of the 20th century. For men in rural Botswana, the experience of labor migration has been similarly universal.

Cultural Specificity, Perception, and Father Involvement

In a review of studies on father love and its influence on children's well-being, the conclusion of study after study is that *perceived* paternal warmth and acceptance is an important and significant factor in explaining a whole range of adult children's characteristics, outcomes, and attitudes (Rohner & Veneziano, 2000).[2] Amato (1994), for instance, found that young adults' *perceived* closeness to their fathers made a unique contribution to their level of psychological distress, whereas Barrera and Garrison-Jones (1992) conclude that it is adolescents' degree of *satisfaction or dissatisfaction* with the support they get from their fathers that is related to their depression. Rohner and Veneziano multiply the examples in their review, and the tenor of their conclusions is supported by the recent summary statements of longtime researchers of fatherhood. Both Joseph Pleck (1997) and Michael Lamb (1997), for example, conclude that it is the *perceived quality* of paternal relationships, rather than the more easily observed amount of time that fathers spent with children, that matters to children's outcomes.

The critical feature of these conclusions is that what is important about father involvement is how it is *perceived* by children, and that this perception is necessarily culturally mediated. In order to be *unsatisfied* with their fathers' support, children must have a sense of what would be satisfactory—a sense that can come only from cultural norms about appropriate parenting or from comparison with a socially constructed or imagined reference group. In order to talk about the *quality* of the relationship they have with their fathers, children must have cultural knowledge about father–child relationships and the criteria that may legitimately be applied to those relationships and the understanding that some criteria are simply inapplicable. What matters in children's judgments of the quality of their relationships with their parents is *whether they think they got what they had a right to expect.*

Of course, children, both while they are young and when they are adult, may not recognize the significant consequences of their fathers' involvement with them, and because of this we must modify to some extent this emphasis on per-

---

[2]"Children" in this context are *adult* children, as they are in many places in this chapter and as they are in studies of "outcomes." To call people "children" is to call attention to their relationship with others, rather than to their chronological age.

ception. The level of child support provided by fathers after divorce, for instance, has a real impact on the standard of living and life chances of their children that is independent of whether the children appreciate this contribution, take it for granted but resent their father's "desertion," or forgive their fathers' failure to provide and emphasize their continuing love. Similarly, the impact of paternal affection or abuse can be very real, whether or not it is perceived by children. In my analysis of the ways in which adult men come to terms with their memories of their own fathers, for instance, I describe how they come to understand their fathers' absence at work through a greater appreciation of their fathers' roles as providers. Nearly all the men I talked to started their discussions of their fathers by complaining that they had not experienced emotional closeness and open communication with their fathers and insisted that they wanted to be closer to their children than their fathers were to them. But over the course of my interviews, these same men came to emphasize also the material responsibilities of fatherhood and said that, now that they were themselves fathers, they understood their own fathers and their commitment to work in new ways and appreciated employment and providing as an expression of paternal affection.

What these examples indicate is that although culture determines our expectations and perceptions, it does not impose a single and uniform pattern. Every culture gives its members, not an unbending program or set of directions, but what has been variously described as a "system of dispositions" (Bourdieu, 1977), a "vocabulary of motives" (Mills, 1940), and a "normative repertoire" (Comaroff & Roberts, 1981). In the case of fatherhood, any culture provides a range or repertoire of ways to be a successful father, and fathers and children may collaborate or compete in defining their relationship in appropriate terms. A father, for example, may claim that discouraging his son from dropping out of business school to become an actor was motivated by a proper paternal concern for his son's long-term happiness, whereas the son may argue that proper fatherly love should have led his father to support him in what he wanted to do. Within a culture, being a successful father, then, may take a variety of forms. But no culture allows free rein or permits the full range of potential fatherhoods. In one setting, arranging a very young daughter's marriage to a wealthy business associate in expectation of future profit may be laudable; in another it may be morally reprehensible or illegal. Or the actions required in one culture as part of a father's duty in sponsoring a son's initiation into adulthood would in another be seen as absence of every paternal feeling and gross abuse.

The cultural specificity of parenting and of the normatively approved life course has been a central interest of sociocultural anthropology since Margaret Mead's pioneering work in the South Pacific (1930, 1949). Some of the range of children's experience and of parent–child relations was systematically documented in the Six Cultures project directed by Beatrice and John Whiting (Whiting, 1963; Whiting & Whiting, 1975), which revealed that children in the United States were at a comparative extreme in the amount of time they spent alone with their mothers. Compared to children in other cultures, children in the United

States spend very little time in the presence of adult men. Subsequent anthropological work on parenting and human development, much of it conducted by researchers originally affiliated with the Six Cultures project, has built on this foundation and has elaborated the notion of socialization from one of simply absorbing a culture to a depiction of the interrelationships between individual development, cultural norms, and social institutions.

The Cultural Context of Child Development

Robert LeVine and his colleagues (LeVine et al., 1994), in a comparative study of Gusii (in western Kenya) and American childrearing, argue that population-level patterns (economic and kinship systems, language, and cultural norms about communication and behavior) must be considered in research on parenting, which should not move immediately between the poles of universal human patterns and individual variation. They demonstrate that these population-level, or cultural, systems have profound impacts on what are culturally defined as appropriate life courses of men and women. Among the Gusii, for example, women must marry by the age of 15 or 16 or suffer social stigma, whereas men marry when they can afford to, which may not be until they are over age 30. The consequences of this marital system, which combines gendered life courses with polygyny, include the fact that children are born into a variety of marital and residential family arrangements and that "fathers are distant socially as well as physically from some, if not all, of their children" (LeVine et al., 1994, p. 30). Crucially for a consideration of father involvement, LeVine and colleagues point out that the Gusii reproductive system includes cultural norms about fatherhood that are shared by all children, including "the expectation that the father will take another wife, the sense that it is legitimate for him to do so, and the understanding that it will enhance his prestige and status in the community while posing a threat to the position of their mother and the security of their inheritance" (LeVine et al., 1994, pp. 30–31). Within this family and reproductive system, the *expected* parameters of fathers' involvement in their children's lives are very different from those in the American middle class.

Thinking about the ways that cultural expectations shape development, Charles Super and Sara Harkness (1986), on the basis of their studies of Kipsigis parents and childrearing (also in Kenya), argue that parents construct a "developmental niche" for their children. This niche, bounded by physical, social, and cultural constraints, provides the space for children to grow and develop in ways that are compatible with adult needs and activities and that ensure that children acquire culturally appropriate values, abilities, and ways of acting. Super and Harkness make the point that the developmental niche is culturally specific and varies from culture to culture within the broad bounds imposed by the need to produce competent, functioning adults. What we should notice is that development within the niche produces, in most cases, adults with culturally appropriate ways of behaving who will, in looking back at their own childhoods, report that they were treated in ways that strike them as culturally appropriate. The developmental niche also provides them with the cultural resources and terms of reference to construct for themselves culturally comprehensible life stories. That is, it produces people who find themselves to be appropriately human and who feel that their parents were appropriately involved in their childhoods.

Thomas Weisner, another anthropologist who has studied childrearing in East Africa, has developed a similar view of development, which he refers to as an "ecocultural project" and in which he stresses the importance of daily routines and familiar settings in making children participants in the activities that are valued by their culture (1997, pp. 182–183). Development is a culturally situated project of parents and families following normatively prescribed patterns of behavior. Fathers, of course, are among the cast of characters following the cultural script of development and they are, therefore, expected to follow life courses that fit within the bounds of what the culture allows and expects of them (Townsend, 2002).

It is within this theoretical framework that a comparison of culturally appropriate male life courses, and of the place of fatherhood in those life courses, sheds light on the complex, lifelong, and situation-specific nature of father involvement.

FATHER INVOLVEMENT IN NUCLEAR FAMILIES IN THE UNITED STATES: THE DOMINANT CULTURAL IMAGE

The picture of fatherhood in a "father breadwinner, mother homemaker" nuclear family in which the married couple takes exclusive responsibility for the material and emotional well-being of their children has been rightly criticized as class- and ethnic-specific and historically outdated (Baca Zinn, 1994; Coontz, 1992; Dill, 1994; Stacey, 1990), but in the arena of Western cultural images it remains dominant. This image of the father as mainly involved in the public sphere of paid employment and physically absent from the domestic (and female) sphere of day-to-day or minute-to-minute child care and child raising continues to dominate, sometimes implicitly, public and private discussion of family life in the United States. High rates of divorce, single parenting, remarriage and stepparenting, and relatively uncommon but highly visible social phenomena such as same-sex couples parenting or stay-at-home dads provide alternative practices and alternative images of the role of father, but have made relatively little impact on cultural attitudes (Arendell, 1995; Coltrane, 1996; LaRossa, 1997; Walzer, 1998). This is not to assert that expressed attitudes are unchanging or that fathers are not changing their behavior as mothers' employment becomes the norm, but it is to point to the persistence of dominant cultural standards of judgment. Some men now take parental leave, for example, but those who do continue to face the criticism of their peers, and many others are deterred from doing so by their knowledge that such criticism will be forthcoming.

Two findings from the national survey of workers in the United States conducted by the Families and Work Institute give an indication of both change and persistence in the division of labor between parents. The first finding is about time spent with children on a routine basis. In 1997, employed fathers spent an average of 2.3 hours caring for and doing things with their children each workday. This was an increase of half an hour each day since 1977, but remained almost an hour per day less than employed mothers spent on the same tasks. The second finding is about the responsibility of parents: "When one member of a dual-earner couple has to care for a sick child or attend to other needs of children when both are supposed to be at their jobs, 83% of employed mothers say they are more likely than their partners to take time off, compared with only 22% of fathers who make this claim" (Bond, Galinsky, & Swanberg, 1998).

The dearth of quality child care responding to the needs of working parents, the way that public school schedules willfully ignore parents' work schedules, and employers' consistent demands for workers to put in long and inflexible hours at work all testify to the way that workers are expected to have no other obligations than those to their employers whereas children are expected to have parents with no responsibilities besides those children (Schor, 1991; Williams, 1999). A man's inability to provide financially for his children is seen as making him unsuitable for fatherhood; his unwillingness to do so makes him irresponsible. The culture's ideal worker is male; its ideal male is a worker. We all know about "working mothers" and take the term for granted, whereas the expression "working father" is used only to make a point by the explicit juxtaposition of two terms that are usually assumed to go together. In all these ways and many others, the cultural norm of the gendered division of labor remains a dominant force in our definitions of fatherhood and father involvement.[3]

It was certainly so in the accounts American men gave me of the place of fatherhood in their lives. I conducted in-depth, open-ended interviews with a group of men who had graduated from the same high school in northern California in the early 1970s and were in their late 30s when I spoke with them. These men's fathers had held blue-collar jobs in construction and manufacturing and had bought homes in one of the new suburban communities that were developed after the Second World War. The men themselves had ridden the boom of the 1970s and 1980s and, although they varied in education, occupa-

---

[3]It is a feature of the cultural pattern I am describing that the biological and social father are assumed to be the same person. Adoptive fathers, especially of infants, can assume all the elements of the role, but stepfathers are in a difficult position because they are not biologically related to their (step)children.

tion, income, and ethnic background, all considered themselves solidly middle class.[4]

Fatherhood, for these men, is an element of what I call a "package deal" that also includes marriage, having a job, and owning a home (Townsend, 2002). This means that men's plans and projects are directed toward a composite goal, that their decisions about one element will take into account their situation with regard to the other elements, and that their judgment of their own success will be multidimensional. The elements of the package deal are not simply combined or balanced against one another, but interact with each other. For instance, it is not simply the case that men want some number of children but settle for the number they can afford, reconciling a preexisting desired number of children against an income constraint. Rather, their idea of the ideal number of children becomes defined as the number they can support in an appropriate lifestyle.

Research on fatherhood too often separates it from the rest of men's lives and treats decisions about marriage, children, and work as if they were independent. The general concentration on fatherhood as the nurturing of young children is not just an oversimplification; it obscures and distorts our view of some complex patterns of behavior and sometimes makes men appear merely incomprehensible and "irresponsible." A too-narrow view of fatherhood does not help us to understand such phenomena as men's devotion to work at the expense of time with their children, the glacial pace with which they seem to be picking up the labor of the "second shift," or the limited contact between men and their children after divorce. To comprehend these and other aspects of men's behavior involves appreciating how fatherhood interacts with, and is influenced by, other elements of their lives. Making men's behavior more comprehensible is made particularly difficult by the continuity between the basic premises of academic research and very generally shared cultural assumptions about fatherhood. The congruence of the categories of academic analysis and those of the dominant culture does not, however, guarantee either their accuracy or their adequacy (Smith, 1987). Quite the contrary, this seeming congruence is an invitation to examine the disjuncture between a hegemonic view of fatherhood and the experience of fathers. Careful attention to the words and lives of men reveals the complexities and contradictions of their narratives and the strains imposed by their attempts to reconcile those contradictions. Fatherhood is not restricted to the care or nurturing of young children, but is a complex and pervasive feature of men's identities and lives.

Although fatherhood pervades men's identities, their involvement with children is primarily concentrated in a single phase of their lives. One of the men I

---

[4]The sample and study are described in detail in Townsend (1998, 2002). The "mediating" role of women in men's relationships with their children is analyzed in Townsend (2001).

interviewed gave a succinct account of the timing of fatherhood in his own life that illustrates this concentration.[5] Greg and his wife, Maggie, have been married for 8 years, having lived together for a year before that, and have two daughters, ages 3 and 5. Both Greg and Maggie are high school graduates, but neither of them, nor any of their parents, have a college degree. He works in aerospace manufacturing, she in personnel. They own a three-bedroom house in the community in which they grew up.

> I was twenty-nine when I got married. And I waited. Kind of got everything out of my system before I got married. And then, when I did get married I wanted it to be forever, as they say, and I was ready to have kids. When I got married I was ready to have kids. I think you just get to a certain age and you just kind of know that you want to settle down. And I didn't want to be forty years old and start a family because I didn't want to be real old when my kids were growing up.

Greg's idea of a suitable life course clearly included time as a young man neither involved with nor responsible for children As he went on to say about having children: "Once they're here it's almost like your life stops at that point and you start a new life and you kind of forget a life before." But life with children is not lifelong; they will grow up and leave home. Greg anticipated that: "That's going to be a hard day to have your children leave your home, but if you have the right attitude toward life you can start anew—almost like another section of your life that you and your wife can pick up." In Greg's view, which reflects his culture's blueprint, there comes an end to a father's involvement in his children:

> And then, "Hey I don't have the kids here, we can go to the Bahamas or something." Hopefully then you'll have money and stuff and you can do that kind of stuff, you know, and kind of start another new section of your life, and go have fun for us. You know we've spent eighteen or twenty years raising these girls and we've put all of our time and effort into them and, like I said, we still have a life of our own, and someday once we get our children raised I want to be able to take my wife and have fun. We may be fifty years old, but you know, I still don't consider that too old to go out and have fun, do a lot of fun things.

Father involvement is restricted to a period of "18 or 20 years," after which a man's time and money are once again primarily his own.

Although the cultural image of a successful adult man and good father is made up of closely linked elements, for the men I talked to, the most important element is that of financial provider. Sociologist Jessie Bernard (1981) analyzed the emergence of "the good provider role" as a central element of masculine identity in the 20th-century United States—an emergence that depended on jobs for men that

---

[5]The quotations from fathers are taken from my interview transcripts.

paid a "family wage" that would support both parents and children on one person's income (Potuchek, 1997). Providing remains a central element of paternal involvement, though one that is "not readily acknowledged in contemporary fatherhood literature" (Christiansen & Palkovitz, in press). The idea that our material support should derive from earnings paid to us by an employer is very basic in the United States and around the world. Even in rural Botswana, where people still plant crops for their own consumption and graze their cattle and goats on the common land from which they also collect firewood and building materials, the unvarying answer to the question of what people most needed was "water and jobs."

The role of provider remains central even in the face of major economic and social changes. In the last 40 years in the United States, women, mothers, and particularly mothers of young children have entered the labor force in huge numbers. This trend has been of enormous social significance and has attracted a vast amount of comment and attention. The importance of this trend should not, however, obscure another social fact that shapes U.S. society and the life experiences of Americans: almost *all* men are in the labor force throughout their adult lives. When the men I talked to were children, over 97% of the men of their fathers' generation were in the labor force. In 1990, when they themselves were in their late 30s, over 94% of their contemporaries were in the labor force.[6] Fathers of young children are not simply employed; many of them are working very long hours, on weekends, and at second jobs. According to Juliet Schor: "Thirty percent of men with children under fourteen report working fifty or more hours a week. . . . Thirty percent of them work Saturdays and/or Sundays at their regular employment. And many others use the weekends for taking on a second job" (1991, p. 21). That virtually every man spends his adult life in the labor force is a central feature of our society that we easily take for granted, but that has profound implications for fathers' involvement with their children.

For most of the men I talked to, work was central to being a man, and work was what men did as fathers for their families (cf. Cowan & Cowan, 2000; Christiansen & Palkovitz, in press). Skip, married with two children, put it this way:

> Everybody has a purpose in life. It's the same basic, mundane thing: you get up, you go to work, you come home. Your purpose is to provide for your family. Obviously when you have children, you have more of an incentive for that, to get up and go to work.

The identification of work with having children, and the further identification of having children and marriage, constitute part of the package deal of successful

---

[6]Labor force participation rates for men ages 25 to 44 were over 97% from 1945 to 1970, when they started a slow decline to about 93% in 1995 (U.S. Census Bureau, 1975, Series D 29–41, pp. 130–131; U.S. Census Bureau, 1996, Table 615, p. 393).

male adulthood. Skip's description of the package deal was typical in the way that it went beyond marriage, work, and children to include the gendered division of labor, ideals of child development, mortgage payments, commuting, and the scheduling of everyday life in his composite picture of how life should be. "We decided the best thing for her to do was to spend time with the children and to raise the children so they don't grow up in a babysitter environment." Skip made it clear that the decision that faced him and his wife was whether she would quit work to stay home with the children. Being a "stay-at-home dad" or full-time homemaker was not an option that had occurred to him or his wife. If only one of them was going to work, it would be him. Other men presented the decision about who was to work and who was to stay home with the children as a much more open choice, even though their "choices" resulted in the same outcome. In this case, as in so many others, the language of choice and decision conceals the social processes that produce social facts from individual action.[7]

Although my interviews elicited a coherent vision of the successful male life, they also revealed tensions and contradictions in these men's accounts of father-hood. Men consistently told me that they wanted to "be closer to" and "spend more time with" their children than their fathers did with them, but also that they felt rushed and were away from home more than they wanted to be. The tension was created by the continuing centrality of being good providers, which required that they be gone from home and children for long hours. In fact, their hours away were frequently longer than their fathers' had been. Instead of unionized jobs with 8-hour shifts and overtime pay, many of them were in salaried positions with employers who made open-ended demands on their time. In addition, the explosion of real estate prices had pushed them to distant suburbs and away from the neighborhoods near work where they had been raised. Their commutes were consistently much longer than their fathers' had been, sometimes as long as 2 hours in each direction.

The resolution of these contradictions and tensions, or at least a liveable accommodation with them, could only be achieved with difficulty and a great deal of "cultural work" (Townsend, 2002). Working long hours and devoting energy to being a good provider detract from time and energy directly applied to being emotionally close to children. A cultural redefinition of work as an expression of paternal love is one form of cultural work to deal with this tension (cf. Cowan & Cowan, 2000). Another form is the claim that a man's employment, by enabling his wife to spend time with the children, contributes to parental closeness—though of course the parent who is actually close is the mother and not the father. These resolutions of the contradictions between elements of the successful adult male life may meet the expectations of fathers, but will not necessarily sat-

---

[7]See Williams (1999) for a particularly clear discussion of "choice" and the gendered division of paid employment.

isfy the expectations of their children. I found that adult men had to do further cultural work, for instance by coming to recognize that they "did their best," to redefine their own fathers.

Beneath both the coherence and the contradictions of men's attitudes were a set of assumptions about family life. These assumptions are so widely accepted that they are frequently taken for granted, but cross-cultural comparison and recognition of variation within a setting show that they are, indeed, cultural assumptions and not facts of nature. The assumptions included: (a) if a couple is to live on one income, it will be that of the husband; (b) the first years of a child's life are crucial;[8] (c) a mother's influence on her children may be consciously directed; (d) events in a life course are the result of conscious decisions; (e) the married couple constitutes an autonomous unit; and (f) the responsibility for the care of children belongs to the couple acting alone and not, for instance, to the children's grandmothers or other senior women.

The sequence of life events described to me as both an expectation and an achieved reality for men will be familiar to most people in the United States. These men had an image of the male life course that is very generally held and that applies to the great majority of men of their generation (Buchmann, 1989; Cooney & Hogan, 1991; Hogan, 1981). The basic stages or events in this life course, in their appropriate order, are: to complete their education, to move out of one's parents' home and live independently, to get a job, to date a number of women, to meet the woman you want to marry, to spend time as a couple, to set up a home together, to buy a house, and to have children.

We need to remember that the morally approved sequences of life events varies from society to society and from class to class within the United States. And we need to remember that successfully achieving this particular sequence of events depends on a combination of circumstances. Getting a job and becoming financially independent as a young man, for instance, depends on living in an economy that is generating enough good jobs, just as buying the home you want depends on the state of the real estate market. The men I studied in California were following a life script that had enough flexibility and had a sufficient range of terms and values to use in describing their behavior that considerable variation in life course could be justified and reconciled. But there are limits to the flexibility and, compared to the range of cross-cultural variation, those limits are quite narrow. There was, for instance, no room for polygamy or polyandry, for long-term extended family coresidence, for many more than three children, or for very large age differences between husband and wife, all

---

[8]The first years of life may not be as critical for development as is often assumed (Kagan, 1998, pp. 83–150). Alternative views would be that the personality or character of the child is determined at birth, so experience is only a minimal influence, or that what determines a child's success and happiness is the quality of early social relationships, patronage, and connections negotiated for it by its parents (Riesman, 1992).

of which have been elements of other systems of family and reproduction and elements of other male scripts.[9]

One striking aspect of the life script of the men I interviewed was the relatively narrow span of age in while they feel it is appropriate for men to become fathers: old enough to be ready, but not too old to be able to have fun with their children or to be elderly when their children are grown. This position was expressed with remarkable uniformity by men from a range of backgrounds and with a variety of actual life experiences. Some emphasized a reasonable delay: "I knew I wouldn't be able to get married at a young age because I was too into playing sports and too into having fun." Other men stressed the importance of not waiting too long: "I didn't want to be forty years old and start a family because I didn't want to be real old when my kids were growing up." In every case, the contrast between the responsibility of raising children and "having fun" was clearly drawn. Children marked the beginning of responsibility, and when they get to be age 18 or 20, they are expected to leave home: "We still have a life of our own, and someday once we get our children raised I want to be able to take my wife and have fun. We may be fifty years old, but you know, I still don't consider that too old to go out and have fun." Their norm is born out in practice. It is physically possible for men to father children at any age from puberty onward, but in fact most children in the United States are born to men in a restricted part of their life span: over one third of American babies are born to men from 25 to 29 years of age, 60% to men in their 20s, and 82% to men between ages 20 to 35. Less than 4% of births are to fathers under age 20, less than 5% to fathers over age 40, and only 0.5% to fathers over age 50 (National Center for Health Statistics, 1986, p. 95). When men, following the script, start having children in their 20s and stop in their early 30s, they contribute to a society in which fathers are, in general, 28 years older than their children. When the men look around them, they see this age difference, and their sense that it is appropriate is reinforced by their perception that it is universal.[10]

The men whose cultural norms about fatherhood I have sketched here are living in a social and economic system that both provides them with opportunities and constrains their options. Within this context, "father involvement," the culturally appropriate way for men to be engaged in the lives of children, is highly con-

---

[9]Bohannan and Middleton (1968) and Hansen and Garey (1998) have edited accessible collections covering some of the range of marriage and family forms cross culturally and in the United States, respectively.

[10]This process, whereby a social pattern is created and reinforced by, and also normalizes, individual actions that the participants think of as choices, is a feature of social life. Goffman's "Arrangement Between the Sexes" (1977) lucidly describes how social ideas about women and men are constructed through interaction, a process further analyzed in West and Zimmerman's much-cited Article, "Doing Gender" (1987). Brodkin describes the same process driving the ethnic segregation of work (1998, pp. 58–59).

centrated in three respects. First, it is on the father that responsibility is focused. Fathers are expected to be married to their children's mothers and to live with their children, they are expected to be the only adult men living in the house, and with their wives, they are expected to care for, provide for, and protect their children. Second, although fathers are held responsible for their own children, they are not expected to be deeply involved with other children: grandchildren and uncles may have close relationships with children, but in the United States their roles are not culturally central or even clearly defined. Third, men's involvement with children is concentrated on young children and adolescents. Although relationships between adults and their parents are expected to be emotionally close, there is a strong cultural norm that young adults should be "on their own," to be self-supporting, and to make their own decisions.

Turning from northern California to southern Africa provides a contrast in the ages at which men are expected to be involved in the lives of children, in the number of men who are significantly involved in the life of a child, and in the cultural expectations of men as fathers.

FATHER INVOLVEMENT IN A LIFETIME OF RESPONSIBILITIES: MEN IN BOTSWANA

In comparison, I will use the example of one man's family life in Botswana to illustrate a different set of expectations about father involvement. This story also provides examples of the involvement of men with children who are not their own biological or social offspring, but for whom they perform many of the functions that in the "West" or "North" would be considered paternal. Above all, this brief account of a life shows how profoundly a man's fatherhood is embedded in his cultural and social situation. For the man I am describing, fulfilling his paternal responsibilities and being involved in the lives of his children required prolonged and culturally approved absences from them when they were young, just as it now requires intimate involvement in the lives of his young grandchildren.

In 1994, I lived next to the family I describe here during 11 months of fieldwork concentrated on a village of 5,500 people located about 40 kilometers west of Botswana's capital city of Gaborone.[11] The village had primary and junior secondary schools, a clinic, several shops, and piped water to 18 communal faucets. There was no telephone or electric service in the village, though power lines were being extended to the schools and other public sites in 1994. In 1991, the village

---

[11] I am indebted to Anita Garey, who conducted fieldwork on child-care arrangements in the village while I was doing my own research there, for sharing her data, observations, and conclusions with me.

was linked to the capital city of Gaborone by tarred road, and access to urban employment, services, and supplies was made much easier. The villagers maintained cattle and flocks of goats, but crops from arable farming had been minimal because of drought. Economically, the community has depended for decades on income from migrant labor. At an earlier period this was almost exclusively migrant labor of men in the mines of South Africa, but since independence in 1966, the rapid growth of the capital has provided employment opportunities in Botswana for many men and women from the village.

The life histories of men from the village demonstrate both the importance of migration and the changing destinations of migrant streams. Seventy percent of the men between the ages of 20 and 40 were living away from the village, and half of those who were living *in* the village were commuting to jobs in the city. The absolute centrality of work in the mines in the male life course had ended, but the experience of migrant labor remained dominant.

Traditional Tswana marriage is a process rather than a single event and does not necessarily involve the establishing of a separate household or even coresidence between husband and wife. These marriages are arrangements between families, and marriages tie families progressively closer through ceremony, negotiation, exchange, and obligation (Schapera, 1950, 1971; Comaroff & Comaroff, 1981). A primary function of marriage, however, is to provide a social position for children. A Tswana man can claim his wife's children as his legitimate heirs only after he has made a payment of bridewealth cattle (*bogadi*) to her family, something he may wait to do until the children are grown or which he may not do at all. When he does pay bridewealth, however, a man will incorporate all his wife's children, regardless of who their biological father is, into his lineage. That the connection between marriage and childbirth is differently defined in Botswana than in the United States is indicated by the fact that in 1981 only 53% of women ages 25 to 29 had ever been married (Botswana Government, 1983, Table 24), but 88% of them had borne at least one child (Botswana Government, 1983, Table 23).[12]

There is no provision in the traditional culture or in tribal law for men to directly support their biological children outside marriage (Molokomme, 1991). The customary pattern is that when a young woman becomes pregnant, the man whom she names as father is under an obligation to initiate marriage arrangements or to pay compensation in the form of cattle to the woman's parents. The one-time payment concludes his, and his family's, obligation. The child's social position and family membership remain with the mother's family and lineage,

---

[12]The cultural rules about appropriate motherhood in Botswana do not require marriage. Although marriage is generally, but by no means universally, preferred to lifelong single motherhood, there is no stigma attached to children whose mothers are not married, nor to women who have children out of wedlock. In fact, most women have at least their first child before they are married. Social disapproval is directed at births to very young women, who are not, for example, allowed to remain in school when they are pregnant.

and the cattle paid by the father provide both symbolic and material guarantees of the child's rights (Garey & Townsend, 1996).

The centrality of social paternity established through marriage, and the absence of a socially recognized biological paternity separated from marriage, finds expression in Tswana men's reports of their own fatherhood. In 1993, only 2 of the 34 men in the ward under age 30 had acknowledged children, though we would expect that more of them would be biological fathers. In 1973, for men whose life histories I knew, the figure had been 1 of 10. In 1993, even the two men who were divorced from women who had had children with them, and the man who had four children with the same woman to whom he was neither married nor engaged, did not report themselves as the fathers of those children. Conversely, men who reported themselves as fathers always reported themselves as married, even when the marriage was at the stage of intention or negotiation and did not involve cohabitation of the spouses. This pattern of reporting was not individual evasion of responsibility, for their biological fatherhood was well known, but an accurate representation of the fact that these men were not acknowledged as the social fathers of these children.

Mowetsi Motlamedi[13] was, in 1993, a vital man of 58, involved in the discussions and negotiations that make up the political and jural life of the village, acting as head of his *lolwapa* and frequently as spokesman for his ward, and attempting to coordinate the lives of his children, as well as working at a government warehouse in the capital, a job to which he commuted daily. Residing with his wife, two of his younger sons, and two of his younger daughter's children in his own household, he presents a picture of the male position in which economic support and coresidence with children coincide in a male-headed extended nuclear family. He was the very picture of involved fatherhood, but a life course perspective reveals a pattern of relationships and responsibilities that have changed over time. Mowetsi Motlamedi's fatherhood has been meshed in the other aspects of his life course and has overlapped with paternal relationships in both ascending and descending generations.

The youngest of nine children (seven of whom survived into adulthood), he attended primary school for five years and, at the age of 18, became a migrant worker in the mines of South Africa. His five years of formal schooling were the only schooling for any of his parents' male children and were an example of a common pattern, repeated for his own sons, of more years of schooling for younger sons. Because sibling order correlates with the economic position of the parents, with the composition of the domestic group, and with the demand and supply of labor in the family, education and birth order are frequently connected. Fathers do not produce interchangeable children, but rather a sequence of social beings whose life chances and circumstances differ markedly.

---

[13]Both are fictitious names, and neither is the name of any Motswana that I know of. Mowetsi, "one who finishes something," is, however, appropriate for a last born. Motlamedi means "one who cares for others."

Of Mowetsi's four older brothers, one had died before establishing his own household; one had married a woman from South Africa, had established his home in the capital, and had then moved to South Africa with his wife and children; and two had established their own households adjoining their parents' compound. Mowetsi's parents had died, and as the youngest sibling, he now occupied their compound. The creation of a cooperating band of brothers was the ideal of traditional Tswana men, though the centrifugal forces of competition also operated. The row of compounds occupied by Mowetsi and his brothers, now extended at both ends by households established by the next generation, was a central feature of the physical and social neighborhood. The group of kin in these adjacent compounds visited back and forth constantly and cooperated on a variety of tasks, and the children formed a large care and play group.

Mowetsi departed for the mines one year before the birth of his first child. At age 19, he was young to be father of an acknowledged child. Mowetsi was not unusual, however, in his domestic arrangements after the child's birth. No man under age 40 lived in his own home in the village with his own children in either 1993 or 1973 (Townsend, 1997), and Mowetsi's life followed this pattern, as the mother of his child continued to live in her parent's *lolwapa* while he continued to work at the mines. The couple were married in 1957, which was the year of the birth of their second child, when Mowetsi was 22 and his wife was 18. Over the next 18 years, they had five more children, and his wife had three additional pregnancies, which ended in miscarriage, stillbirth, or infant death. During this entire period, Mowetsi continued to work at the mines in South Africa, away from the village for months at a time, and his wife continued to live with her parents. In 1977, after 24 years as a miner and at age 42, Mowetsi left the mines and returned to live full-time in the village. His own parents were still alive, and he lived in the compound of his wife's parents for 10 years while working in the capital city.

Because Mowetsi was the youngest, he was in line to take over his parents' compound on their death, but this succession did not take place until he was age 52, 12 years after the birth of his youngest child and 3 years after the birth of his first grandchild. Mowetsi was older than most men when he became head of his own household, but he is typical in that his current position as household head and economic support of his coresident wife and children is a stage, and a late stage at that, of his fatherhood.

To summarize Mowetsi's paternal involvement by saying that he fathered seven surviving children over a period of 21 years is to obscure as much as it illuminates.[14] As an economic provider and as a coresident male, his fatherhood is widely and complexly distributed. Mowetsi's earnings have gone to the support of

---

[14]I am assuming, in this discussion, that Mowetsi is the biological father of all the children borne by his wife, all of whom are presented and claimed as his children. I am also assuming that he has not fathered any other biological children. If he has, they are not acknowledged as his social children.

his parents' household and, for most of his adult life, to the support of the household of his wife's parents—a household that included other children besides his own. His migrant labor meant that he was a physically absent father for 23 years of his oldest child's life, but for only 2 years of his youngest child's life. He is now the male head of household for two young grandchildren, whose parents live and work in the capital, as well as for his own three youngest children.

The importance of grandfathers for children's well-being can scarcely be exaggerated. All of Mowetsi's children were born into a household headed by their maternal grandfather, and his eldest daughter bore her own son into that household. Mowetsi's younger daughter bore her children in his compound, and the children continue to live there. I did not come across any firstborn children in the village who were *not* born into the house of their mother's parents. For married women in the village, the mean length of time between first giving birth and moving to their own households was 12 years, so that, in general, children born in the 12 years after their mother's first birth are born into their maternal grandparents' household (Garey & Townsend, 1996). Women who do not eventually marry usually bear all their children in their parents' home. In these cases, it is usually through the grandfather that children become members of the ward or lineage and acquire their rights to land, jural standing, and social position.

Sometimes the grandfather not only becomes the social father in this restricted sense, but fulfills the role of father more generally. "We call him father because he raised us" was how a set of siblings explained why they had named their mother's father when I had asked them who their father was. Grandpaternal claims of paternity are not simply a matter of default. In general, grandfathers would rather their grandchildren be firmly situated in their homes and lineages than ambiguously associated with a biological father who was not intending to marry the mother (Garey & Townsend, 1996).

A woman's first children, born into the household of their mother's father, develop their first important relationships with adult males with their maternal grandfather and maternal uncles. Their first relationships with peers are with their own siblings and with the children of their mother's sisters. These relationships, enduring over a lifetime, cut across the formal patrilineal social organization that groups together the children of brothers. Mowetsi's own children were born into a household headed by their maternal grandfather, in which their mother's brothers were also vital male presences and important emotional and economic supports for their sister and her children. One of a woman's brothers (or if she has no brothers, another man from her natal lineage) is designated as the "linked" mother's brother (*malome*) of her children. This mother's brother occupies a crucial social position as a link between the lineages or extended families of husband and wife. His social structural importance is made clear in Tswana practice. The linked mother's brother is a key figure in the discussions and negotiations that lead up to the marriages of his sisters' children. He is expected to contribute to his sisters' sons' bridewealth, and he has a claim to a portion of the bridewealth paid at the marriage of his sisters' daughters. He is also expected to contribute to the round of meals that accompany these weddings.

Moreover, the ritual and social structural elements of the relationship of a child and his or her maternal uncle coincide with the potential for emotional closeness. Mowetsi's younger sons lived with, played with, bathed, and supervised their sister's children (Mowetsi's grandchildren). The uncle, attached to his sister by enduring bonds of sentiment and interest, may well be a more stable figure in a child's life than the father (Fox, 1993). Economic and social changes that reduce the likelihood and stability of marriages increase the importance of brothers as supports of their sisters' children. This development has also been noted in areas of South Africa dependent on migrant labor (Niehaus, 1994; Sharp & Spiegel, 1990). For men, a sister's children are people with lifetime connections and mutual claims.

Mowetsi's children illustrate the common Tswana pattern of interrelationship and mutual aid between siblings. Mowetsi's two married daughters and his oldest son had each taken on the responsibility for educating one of his three youngest sons, who continued to live with Mowetsi. In the generation of Mowetsi's children, the three married couples had, in fact, taken on what Westerners might naturally consider to be "parental" roles with regard to Mowetsi's youngest children. But of Mowetsi's five grandchildren, only one lived with both his parents. One of the others lived with her maternal grandparents and other kin while her parents live and work in the city; another lived with his mother and her parents while his father (Mowetsi's son) works at the mines; and two lived with Mowetsi, their mother's father, his wife, and their youngest children.

One life cannot be taken as representative of the variety of experiences of the men in the ward. Mowetsi was younger than average when he married and had social children of his own and older when he established his own household. On the other hand, he was typical in the sequencing of herding, migrant labor, return to the village, and subsequent work in Gaborone. And at this point in his life course Mowetsi has reached a position that, in terms of residence, marriage, and relation to his children and grandchildren, is typical. The most important sense in which Mowetsi is typical of men in his culture is that he has moved through a culturally prescribed sequence of situations in which providing for and living with children has been one element of responsible adulthood and fatherhood. Following this culturally prescribed sequence gives a man claims on children, gives others the position from which to make claims on him, and provides clearly defined social positions and living situations for his children and grandchildren.

The family system I have described has many strengths of adaptability and flexibility, distributing rights and responsibilities relatively broadly so that no person's fate rests exclusively on any single other person or relationship. The system does not, however, always work perfectly. It is susceptible to outside forces and to individual failures and shortcomings. Children are not necessarily disadvantaged by the absence of their father, but they *are* disadvantaged when they belong to a household without access to the social position, labor, and financial support that is provided by men. A woman who does not have a competent father or reliable brothers and who cannot mobilize other kinsmen faces real difficulties. If she can get a secure, well-paying job, she may attain financial stability, but she remains at a social disadvantage. Such jobs are rare and are nonexistent for women who have not had the family support to gain education and qualifications. In its present form, the system of distributed rights and responsibilities depends on a male monopoly of wage-earning jobs, just as the traditional system depended on the control older men had over land and cattle. For women, under both systems, security and well-being are associated with relationships to men. For children, well-being is the result of being part of a complex web of interconnections that allow a variety of men to provide the material, social, and emotional benefits we usually associate with involved fatherhood.

What the system expects of men is that they be economically productive and that they be socially connected in ways that spread the fruits of their productivity to others, particularly to women and children, but not necessarily to their own wives and biological children. No man can meet all the claims that are made on him, but he is expected to meet some of them in ways that are both socially acceptable and practically useful to the claimants.

As domestic groups move through their cycles of new establishment, growth, and fission, they provide for men a sequence of competing, but also complementary, relationships with children. In the normative Western nuclear family, a child's claims to succession, inheritance, coresidence, economic support, nurturance, and emotional closeness are all bundled into a single paternal relationship. This concentration of roles in a single person is contingent rather than necessary. When the elements of the "paternal" role are distributed among different people, we must consider the developmental consequences of father involvement within the framework of a whole set of relationships.

Mowetsi himself, as I have illustrated, is helping to coordinate the lives of his adult children so that their work, parenthood, education, and residence patterns complement each other. Mowetsi and his wife are also in a directly "parental" position as coresident, supporting, and caretaking adults to their own youngest children and two young grandchildren (born in 1988 and 1992). The varying relationships men have with members of subsequent generations influence the lives of their sons and daughters and the life chances of their grandchildren. Father involvement may continue to the end of a lifetime and ties together the lives of men and women across generations.

CONCLUSION: COMPARING CULTURAL EXPECTATIONS OF PATERNAL RESPONSIBILITY AND INVOLVEMENT

As I have illustrated, the order of life events is culturally variable and variably evaluated. In rural Botswana a young man who followed the dominant cultural script of appropriate behavior for the United States would be considered totally irresponsible and would be described as "lost" by his parents.[15] According to this script, the young man in the United States is expected to set up a household with his wife before they have children. He and his wife are expected to be self-supporting and to support their own children. Mother and father are expected to divide the labor of supporting and caring for their children and are not expected to support or care for other people's children. In Botswana, this "responsible" and "involved" parenting would be condemned as an evasion of responsibility and a foolish turning away from the essential involvement of other people. This condemnation is not simply an expression of conflict between generations, but is voiced widely by men and women of all ages (Garey & Townsend, 1996) and reflects a view of the distribution of responsibility over a man's life (Townsend, 1999). A young man in Botswana is not expected to support only himself, nor is he expected to be self-supporting. The expected course of his life reflects an evaluation of the needs and capacities of people of different ages and of the pattern of responsibility for children fundamentally different from that in the United States.

In the United States, the responsibility for children, and the cultural expectation for emotional involvement in their lives, is concentrated almost exclusively on the young adults who are their parents. Roger, a California man who had been carried by the regional economic boom to a management position, a swimming pool, a boat, and a large house for his wife and three young children, summarized this vision of family life, parental responsibility, and his own contribution as a father:

> We wanted to be financially stable enough that we could survive on one income, for that five or ten year span, depending on how many children we decided to have. And that was the main concern with having children. We felt that was important: to bring up our own kids, not somebody else. That's a responsibility that I think the parents have; to bring their kids up. We wanted to raise our own children.

Wanting "to raise our own children" means that the couple is the decision-making and childrearing unit. Roger is expressing a cultural norm and expectation that he has thoroughly internalized and made his own. It is the *couple* who makes decisions about when to have children and how many to have and the couple who divides employment and child care so that they can support children financially, care for them physically, and be involved with them emotionally. In this picture, the father is the exclusive male figure in his children's life. The manifold potential relationships between men and children are concentrated in him

---

[15]Among the educated elite, a Western (or, more accurately, Northern) evaluation of the life course is common. A shift from land to capital (economic and human) as the critical factor of production, so that financial independence depends on individual employment rather than access to land, has been associated with a more individuated economic life and a greater emphasis on the nuclear family for some Batswana. It would be a mistake, however, to assume that this process is necessarily either universal or inevitable in southern Africa. Here I am describing a set of values about family life that was widespread and dominant in a rural community in the 1990s (Garey & Townsend, 1996; Townsend, 1997, 1999). The AIDS epidemic must throw any predictions about developments in African family forms into doubt.

alone, and he is not expected to have more than peripheral involvement in the lives of children other than his own. Father involvement, in this cultural version of family life, is concentrated on the father as exclusive male involved in his children's lives, on his children as the exclusive targets of his involvement, and because of low fertility and an emphasis on fathering as involvement with young children, on a relatively short period of the father's life course.

In the Tswana cultural model, all this concentration is replaced with distributed paternal involvement. Men are involved in the lives of a variety of children: grandchildren, nieces and nephews, as well as their own offspring. Correspondingly, children have many men involved in their lives as economic, social, and emotional supports. And men's involvement in children's lives endures vitally over their lifetimes as they pass through a sequence of culturally prescribed roles and relationships. The differences in paternal involvement in the two cultures may be seen very clearly when we consider what men are expected to do for their children when they become parents.

Roger, for instance, expects to support his children on his own, but he also expects them to be self-sufficient when they become parents in their turn. This is not to say that parents in the United States are not involved in their adult children's lives. Many provide homes for their adult children in times of hardship and crisis, and even more help with child care, grandchildren's schooling, and buying a family home (Townsend, 2002). But when these grandparental involvements go beyond help to the next generation of couples, when they become a direct responsibility for and daily participation in the lives of grandchildren, they are seen as departures from the expected. In Botswana, on the other hand, Mowetsi's involvement in the lives of his children extends to providing his daughters with the home in which they bear their children and in which those children then live while their mother is away working. Mowetsi does not do all this as a *departure* from expectations, but as part of what a man is expected to do for his children. Being a father to daughters entails intimate involvement with their children as well.

These very different cultural visions of father involvement are embedded in strikingly different political, economic, and demographic regimes. The Tswana pattern allows for stable family life in a situation of economic poverty, where no good jobs can be found where people live, where unemployment and uncertainty are high, and where well-being depends on the coordinated contributions of a number of people with varied attributes and abilities. The U.S. pattern, by contrast, works only when jobs are abundant and well paying, for it is dependent on the earnings of one or two people to maintain the family. The impacts of divorce and economic decline on nuclear families are evident, even though the United States has not experienced a major economic decline in recent history.[16]

---

[16]The economic boom in the United States has not, however, distributed its benefits equally. Large sections of the population remain in poverty, middle-class incomes are virtually stagnant in the face of great disparities in wealth and income, and some families are experiencing downward mobility (Hernandez, 1993; Newman, 1989; Stacey, 1990; Wilson, 1996).

For children, however, one of the absolutely crucial characteristics of both systems is that they provide predictable patterns of relationships and expectations of support and involvement that are generally shared and internalized. There can be no doubt that the involvement of adults is vital to children's well-being. The cross-cultural evidence, of which I have given only a glimpse, demonstrates that this involvement may take a variety of forms and that the involvement of fathers in particular, and men in general, with children takes place within family systems that are themselves part of social, economic, and cultural contexts.

As we turn our attention to the study of fathers in the United States, the cross-cultural evidence suggests that we should broaden the scope of our inquiry beyond the involvement of fathers in the lives of their young children. Three observations are crucial in this respect: (a) fathers play important roles throughout their children's lives, not just when their children are young; (b) fathers are not the only men involved in the lives of children; and (c) different cultures have different norms about which men, at which stages of their lives, should be doing what for children. Taken together, these observations suggest that we should always bear in mind that fathers are not the only men who have an impact on children's development. We often ask what fathers do with children. We also need to ask what else fathers do that may contribute to children's well-being. And we need to ask what other men do with children. Sometimes this question is only asked when fathers are absent, and we as researchers or children's advocates are interested in "father substitutes." Comparison with other family systems, however, suggests that the things we tend to expect from fathers may be routinely provided by others and that the proper context for the study of child development is the entire web of social relationships into which children are born and within which they live.

REFERENCES

Amato, P. R. (1994). Father–child relations, mother–child relations and offspring psychological well-being in adulthood. *Journal of Marriage and the Family, 56,* 1031–1042.

Arendell, T. (1995). *Fathers and divorce.* Thousand Oaks, CA: Sage.

Baca Zinn, M. (1994). Feminist rethinking from racial–ethnic families. In M. Baca Zinn & B. T. Dill (Eds.), *Women of color in U.S. society* (pp. 303–314). Philadelphia: Temple University Press.

Barrera, M., & Garrison-Jones, G. (1992). Family and peer social support as specific correlates of adolescent depressive symptoms. *Journal of Abnormal Child Psychology, 20,* 1–16.

Bernard, J. S. (1981). The good-provider role: Its rise and fall. *American Psychologist, 36,* 1–12.

Bohannan, P., & J. Middleton (Eds.). (1968). *Marriage, family, and residence.* Garden City, NY: Natural History Press.

Bond, J. T., Galinsky, E., & Swanberg, J. E. (1998). *The 1997 national study of the changing workforce.* New York: Families and Work Institute.

Botswana Government. (1983). *1981 population and housing census: Census administrative/ technical report and national statistical tables.* Gaborone, Botswana: Central Statistics Office.

Bourdieu, P. (1977). *Outline of a theory of practice.* New York: Cambridge University Press.

Brodkin, K. (1998). *How Jews became white folks and what that says about race in America.* New Brunswick, NJ: Rutgers University Press.

Buchmann, M. (1989). *The script of life in modern society: Entry into adulthood in a changing world.* Chicago: University of Chicago Press.

Christiansen, S. L., & Palkovitz R. (in press). Providing as a form of paternal involvement: Why the "good provider" role still matters. *Journal of Family Issues.*

Coltrane, S. (1996). *Family man: Fatherhood, housework, and gender equity.* New York: Oxford University Press.

Comaroff, J. L., & Comaroff, J. (1981). The management of marriage in a Tswana chiefdom. In E. J. Krige and J. L. Comaroff (Eds.), *Essays on African marriage in Southern Africa* (pp. 29–49). Cape Town, RSA: Juta.

Comaroff, J. L., & Roberts, S. A. (1981). *Rules and processes: The cultural logic of dispute in an African context.* Chicago: University of Chicago Press.

Cooney, T. M., & Hogan, D. P. (1991). Marriage in an institutionalized life course: First marriage among American men in the twentieth century. *Journal of Marriage and the Family, 53,* 178–190.

Coontz, S. (1992). *The way we never were: American families and the nostalgia trap.* New York: Basic Books.

Cowan, C. P., & Cowan, P. A. (2000 [1992]). *When partners become parents: The big life change for couples.* Mahwah, NJ: Lawrence Erlbaum Associates.

Dill, B. T. (1994). Fictive kin, paper sons, and *compadrazgo*: Women of color and the struggle for family survival. In M. Baca Zinn & B. T. Dill (Eds.), *Women of color in U.S. society* (pp. 149–170). Philadelphia: Temple University Press.

Fox, R. (1993). *Reproduction and succession: Studies in anthropology, law, and society.* New Brunswick, NJ: Transaction.

Garcia Coll, C., Surrey, J. L., & Weingarten, K. (1998). *Mothering against the odds: Diverse voices of contemporary mothers.* New York: Guilford Press.

Garey, A. I., & Townsend, N. W. (1996). Kinship, courtship, and child maintenance in Botswana. *Journal of Family and Economic Issues, 17,* 189–203.

Geertz, C. (1973). *The interpretation of cultures.* New York: Basic Books.

Goffman, E. (1963). *Stigma: Notes on the management of spoiled identity.* Upper Saddle River, NJ: Prentice Hall.

Goffman, E. (1977). The arrangement between the sexes. *Theory and Society, 4,* 301–336.

Hansen, K. V., & Garey A. I. (Eds.). (1998). *Families in the U.S.: Kinship and domestic politics.* Philadelphia: Temple University Press.

Hernandez, D. J. (1993). *America's children: Resources from family, government, and the economy.* New York: Russell Sage Foundation.

Hogan, D. P. (1981). *Transitions and social change: The early lives of American men.* New York: Academic Press.

Holland, D. C., & Eisenhart, M. A. (1992). *Educated in romance: Women, achievement, and college culture.* Chicago: University of Chicago Press.

Kagan, J. (1998). *Three seductive ideas.* Cambridge, MA: Harvard University Press.

Lamb, M. E. (1997). *Fathers and child development: An introductory overview and guide.* In M. E. Lamb (Ed.), *The role of the father in child development* (3rd ed.). New York: Wiley.

LaRossa, R. (1997). *The modernization of fatherhood: A social and political history.* Chicago: Chicago University Press.

LeVine, R. A., Dixon, S., LeVine, S., Richman, A., Leiderman, P. H., Keefer, C. H., & Brazelton, T. B. (1994). *Child care and culture: Lessons from Africa.* New York: Cambridge University Press.

Lorde, A. (1984). *Sister outsider: Essays and speeches.* Freedom, CA: Crossing Press.

Mead, M. (1930). *Growing up in New Guinea.* New York: William Morrow.

Mead, M. (1949). *Coming of age in Samoa: A psychological study of primitive youth for Western civilization.* New York: New American Library.

Mills, C. W. (1940). Situated actions and vocabularies of motive. *American Sociological Review 5*, 904–913.

Molokomme, A. (1991). *Children of the fence: The maintenance of extramarital children under law and practice in Botswana.* Research report 46. Leiden, The Netherlands: African Studies Center.

National Center for Health Statistics. (1986). *Vital statistics of the United States. 1982: Volume 1. Natality.* Hyattsville, MD: U.S. Department of Health and Human Services.

Newman, K. S. (1989). *Falling from grace: The experience of downward mobility in the American middle class.* New York: Vintage.

Niehaus, I. (1994). Disharmonious spouses and harmonious siblings: conceptualizing household formation among urban residents in Qwaqwa. *African Studies, 53,* 115–135.

Pleck, J. H. (1997). Paternal involvement: Level, sources, and consequences. In M. E. Lamb (Ed.), *The role of the father in child development* (3rd ed., pp. 66–103). New York: Wiley.

Potuchek, J. L. (1997). *Who supports the family? Gender and breadwinning in dual-earner marriages.* Stanford, CA: Stanford University Press.

Riesman, P. (1992). *First find your child a good mother: The construction of self in two African communities.* New Brunswick, NJ: Rutgers University Press.

Rohner, R. P., &. Veneziano, R. A. (2001). *The importance of father love: History and contemporary evidence. Review of General Psychology, 5*(4), 382–405.

Schapera, I. (1950). Kinship and marriage among the Tswana. In D. Forde & A. R. Radcliffe-Brown (Eds.), *African systems of kinship and marriage* (pp. 140–165). London: Oxford University Press.

Schapera, I. (1971). *Married life in an African tribe.* Harmondsworth: Penguin.

Schor, J. B. (1991). *The overworked American: The unexpected decline of leisure.* New York: Basic Books.

Sharp, J., & Spiegel, A. (1990). Women and wages: Gender and the control of income in farm and Bantustan households. *Journal of Southern African Studies, 16,* 527–549.

Smith, D. E. (1987). *The everyday world as problematic: A feminist sociology.* Boston: Northeastern University Press.

Smith, D. E. (1999). The standard North American family: SNAF as an ideological code. In D. E. Smith, *Writing the social: Critique, theory, and investigations* (pp. 157–171). Toronto: University of Toronto.

Stacey, J. (1990). *Brave new families: Stories of domestic upheaval in late twentieth century America.* New York: Basic Books.

Stocking, G. W. (1992). *The ethnographer's magic and other essays in the history of anthropology.* Madison: University of Wisconsin Press.

Super, C. M., & Harkness, S. (1986). The developmental niche: A conceptualization at the interface of child and culture. *International Journal of Behavioral Development, 9,* 1–25.

Townsend, N. W. (1992). *Paternity attitudes of a cohort of men in the United States: Cultural values and demographic implications.* Ph.D. dissertation, University of California–Berkeley.

Townsend, N. W. (1997). Men, migration, and households in Botswana: An exploration of connections over time and space. *Journal of Southern African Studies, 23,* 405–420.

Townsend, N. W. (1998). Fathers and sons: Men's experience and the reproduction of fatherhood. In K. V. Hansen & A. I. Garey (Eds.), *Families in the U.S.: Kinship and domestic politics* (pp. 363–376). Philadelphia: Temple University Press.

Townsend, N. W. (1999). Male fertility as a lifetime of relationships: Contextualizing men's biological reproduction in Botswana. In C. Bledsoe, J. Guyer, & S. Lerner (Eds.), *Fertility and the male life cycle* (pp. 483–513). New York: Oxford University Press.

Townsend, N. W. (2001). Fatherhood and the mediating role of women. In C. Brettell & C. Sargent (Eds.), *Gender in cross-cultural perspective* (3rd ed., pp. 120–134). Upper Saddle River, NJ: Prentice Hall.

Townsend, N. W. (2002). *The package deal: Marriage, work, and fatherhood in men's lives.* Philadelphia: Temple University Press.

U.S. Census Bureau. (1975). *Historical statistics of the United States: Colonial times to 1970.* Washington, DC: U.S. Census Bureau.

U.S. Census Bureau. (1996). *Statistical abstract of the United States: 1996.* Washington DC: Department of Commerce.

Walzer, S. (1998). *Thinking about the baby: Gender and transitions into parenthood.* Philadelphia: Temple University Press.

Weisner, T. S. (1997). The ecocultural project of human development: Why ethnography and its findings matter. *Ethos, 25,* 177–190.

West, C., & Zimmerman, D. H. (1987). Doing gender. *Gender & Society, 1,* 125–151.

Whiting, B. B. (Ed.). (1963). *Six cultures: Studies of child rearing.* New York: Wiley.

Whiting, B. B., & Whiting, J. W. M. (1975). *Children of six cultures.* Cambridge, MA: Harvard University Press.

Williams, J. (1999). *Unbending gender: Why family and work conflict and what to do about it.* New York: Oxford University Press.

Wilson, W. J. (1996). *When work disappears: The world of the new urban poor.* New York: Knopf.

11

Father Involvement
in English-Speaking
Caribbean Families

Jaipaul L. Roopnarine
Syracuse University

Over the past two decades there has been increased interest in understanding the degree of men's different commitments to the welfare of the family or mating union and to father–child relationships in diverse cultures around the world (see volumes by Hewlett, 1992; Lamb, 1987, 1997; Parke, 1996). Guided by theoretical principles rooted in the functions of the family (Popenoe, 1988), hierarchical parental goals (LeVine, 1974), the developmental niche (Harkness & Super, 1996), reciprocal altruism (Alexrod & Hamilton, 1981), evolutionary biology (Trivers, 1972), the social organization of work (Johnson & Johnson, 1975), and the culture's "maintenance systems" (Whiting, 1977) among others, anthropologists, sociologists, and psychologists have begun to document men's investment in biological and nonbiological offspring in different cultural systems. Collectively, this body of work has pointed to the extreme variations in male investment in children across societies (Hewlett, 1992) and to the wide range of economic, social, and cultural factors that may account for such variations. Yet, in the face of such data, there has been the practice of labeling fatherhood in some developing areas of the world as being in "crisis." Nowhere is this more apparent than in discussions of the roles and responsibilities of fathers in the Caribbean (Roopnarine & Brown, 1997). This is not to say that all Caribbean fathers are exemplars of good parents, but they are not uniformly uninvolved with children either.

This chapter provides an overview of what we know about fathers in the Caribbean and Caribbean immigrant fathers in North America. Emphasis is on men from the Anglophone Caribbean, namely Guyana, Trinidad and Tobago, Jamaica, Grenada, Barbados, Dominica, St. Kitts, St. Lucia, St. Vincent, and Nevis and on those who immigrated from these countries to North America (e.g., Indo-Caribbean and African-Caribbean families). The family context for bearing and rearing children in the English-speaking Caribbean is different from those in other parts of the world. The sociocultural practices of progressive mating and childbearing in multiple unions and child-shifting help define Caribbean men's differing commitments and abilities in meeting the diverse obligations within a family (e.g., provider, partner/spouse, protector, models) and the level and quality of their involvement with biological and nonbiological children. Understanding these practices along with men's conceptions of "manhood" and "fatherhood" and the degree to which they are modified by immigration to postindustrialized societies have overarching implications for the development of secure, sensitive, and enduring relationships between fathers and their children and for designing interventions for fathers that are culturally appropriate (Roopnarine, Shin, & Lewis, 2001).

Following the rich work of anthropologists and cultural psychologists (Garcia Coll et al., 1996; Harwood, Miller, & Irizarray, 1995; Ogbu, 1991; Schweder et al., 1998; Super & Harkness, 1997; Whiting & Whiting, 1963), attention is given to (a) the complex and dynamic mating/marital unions within which fatherhood is realized and father–child relationships begin to take shape; (b) cultural beliefs systems about "manhood," "fatherhood," and the roles and responsibilities of men; (c) factors that may conspire against successful fathering; and (d) levels and quality of father involvement and their consequences for childhood development.

A FEW PRECAUTIONARY REMARKS

In the past, there has been an obsession with the dysfunctional aspects of different family structures in the Caribbean, aberrant parenting behaviors (e.g., excessive use of physical punishment), the unequal distribution of male–female family roles, and male marginality (Roopnarine, 2000). Today, there is a growing body of research on normative patterns of father involvement in Caribbean families. However, the studies have focused primarily on African-Caribbean and Indo-Caribbean families. As a result, far less is known about father involvement in mixed-ethnic, Chinese-Caribbean, Amerindians, Portuguese-Caribbean, and Black Carib families. Nor is there much data on Caribbean immigrant fathers in North America and Europe, despite their salience in these geographic locations. A majority of the studies have used large-scale surveys, face-to-face interviews, or ethnographic accounts of family life during group discussions to assess levels of paternal involvement (Brown, Newland, Anderson, & Chevannes, 1997), and only two actually observed the quality of adult–child interactions as they unfolded (Flinn, 1992; Munroe & Munroe, 1992). Acknowledging up front that these studies have various limitations (see Pleck, 1997, for a discussion of the limitations of father involvement studies), an attempt is made to weave together an understanding of the significance of Caribbean and Caribbean immigrant fathers' levels of involvement with children.

THE COMPLEX AND DYNAMIC MATING/MARITAL UNIONS

Typically, childbearing and father–child relationships in the English-speaking Caribbean occur in different family/mating unions: visiting/friending, common law, marital, and single parent (Senior, 1991). Nonlegal family unions have been in existence in the Caribbean for over 150 years, and anthropologists (e.g., Chevannes, 1993) have argued that in some ethnic groups (e.g., African-Caribbean), family/mating patterns progress from the structurally unstable to the structurally stable. That is, marriage may occur after progressive mating and child-bearing in several nonlegal unions (mate-shifting). Bearing this in mind, a man's family(ies) and his responsibilities to and the nature of his relationships with his children and partner/spouse must be viewed in the context of multiple unions and at different points in his "marital careers" (Rodman, 1971). The diverse family prototypes within which fatherhood is exercised and father–child relationships evolve are discussed next. The possible consequences to childhood development of being raised in these different family configurations are discussed later.

Visiting/Friending Relationships

It is common for Caribbean men to begin sexual relationships and biological and social fatherhood in visiting unions. This type of union constitutes approximately 25% of mating relationships in the Caribbean and are more characteristic of African-Caribbean than Indo-Caribbean or Chinese-Caribbean men (only 2.7% of Indo-Caribbean vs. 17.4% of rural African-Caribbean Jamaican families are classified as visiting unions). In these relationships, men and women do not share a residence but meet at a prearranged location for sexual and social relationships. Women tend to be younger, whereas the age of the male partner varies quite a bit. For example, statistics gathered over a 25-year period by the government of Trinidad and Tobago showed that for mothers between ages 15 and 19, a signifi-cant number of the fathers of their children were over age 25 (reported in Sharpe, 1997). Due to the tenuous nature of visiting relationships, the roles and responsi-bilities of men toward their partner(s) and offspring are not well defined, and women often see the union as transitory (Powell, 1986; Senior, 1991). There is lit-tle legal protection offered to women in visiting relationships when it comes to child support and the ownership of property.

Common-Law Relationships

Unlike visiting unions, there is greater commitment by couples to common-law relationships, as they usually cohabit and share responsibilities for maintaining a household. Men and women in these unions are generally older and may have several offspring from previous relationships. Women assume primary responsibility for maintaining a household, whereas men are expected to be breadwinners. Men may provide financial support for nonbiological children in the current union, but their relationships with them can be antagonistic (Flinn, 1992). Financial support to and social contacts with biological children from previous unions are sporadic at best. About 20% of the unions in the Caribbean are common law. As was the case with visiting unions, common-law relationships are less evident among Indo-Caribbean and Chinese-Caribbean people (8.9% in Indo-Guyanese vs. 20.7% in rural African-Caribbean families in Jamaica) (Smith, 1996).

Marital Unions

Marriage eventuates after progressive mating and offspring from several nonlegal unions. Sociodemographic data collected in the *Contribution of Caribbean Men to the Family Study* (Brown et al., 1997) provide support for such a claim. Of fathers under age 30, 9.35% were married, 41.3% were in common-law unions, and 44.9% were in visiting unions. If we consider men who were over age 50 and who had engaged in progressive mating, 54.3% were married, 24.2% were in common-law unions, and only 8.9% were in visiting unions. As men acquire better economic resources, they are more likely to get married and to have fewer "outside" children (Brown, Anderson, & Chevannes, 1993). Having said that, couples do not see marriage as the only route to personal happiness, and there is an inclination toward "partnerships." By contrast, because of more conservative beliefs about sexual activity and greater conformity to traditional patterns of marital norms and the sexual division of labor (Roopnarine et al., 1997) among Indo-Caribbean couples, marriage rates tend to be high (88.4%) (Smith, 1996; Wilson, 1989).

Single Parents

In the Caribbean, the single parent is more likely to reflect union than marital status. More than 50% of Caribbean women ages 56 to 64 are single. They may be abandoning or be abandoned in a relationship, widowed, or divorced (Senior, 1991). Caribbean women as the de facto head of household is not a new phenomenon. Surveys of family life in the Caribbean (Massiah, 1982; Powell, 1986; Smith, 1996) indicate that 22.4% of women in Guyana, 27% in Trinidad and Tobago, 33.8% in Jamaica, 42.9% in Barbados, and 45.3% in Grenada are the head of their households. Indo-Caribbean women who are single parents are more likely to be widows. Because men often rely on their female partners/spouses and other adult females to care for children, corresponding data on the number of men who are single-parent fathers are not readily available.

What emerges from the aforementioned discussion is the tendency in the Caribbean for fatherhood and fathering to occur in family systems that are diverse and sometimes ephemeral. Clearly, progressive mating is more characteristic of low-income families. With better economic resources and stable employment, Caribbean men are more likely to be in a marriage and less likely to have "outside" children (Brown et al., 1997). This perhaps suggests that poor economic conditions may act to destabilize the father's role in the family, a point made repeatedly regarding fathers in other parts of the world (see Ahmeduzzaman & Roopnarine, 1991; Silverstein, 1993).

The proclivity toward the diverse family archetypes among Caribbean immigrant families in North America and Europe is not fully known. Meager statistics suggest that the marriage rates among Indo-Caribbean families remain high (Roopnarine, 1999) and that 33% of the households among Jamaican immigrants in five counties in the New York City area were female headed, a figure that is almost exactly the same as that reported for the island of Jamaica (34%) (Grasmuck & Grosfoguel, 1997). Additionally, data provided by Millette (1999) seem to indicate that outside sexual partners were evident in his sample of Caribbean immigrant families living in the United States, perhaps suggesting the presence of multiple-mating situations in some family arrangements.

CULTURAL BELIEFS SYSTEMS ABOUT "MANHOOD" AND "FATHERHOOD"

In spite of recent challenges to the concept of the "essential father" (Silverstein & Auerbach, 1999), whether the progenitor or not, some form of the father role exists in every society studied to date. In different societies, fathers' and mothers' culture-specific ideas or cognitions about paternal roles may guide the assumption of child-care responsibilities. Recent theoretical propositions (Harkness & Super, 1996) and research suggest that parental cognitions about child care and education influence daily socialization practices (Goodnow & Collins, 1990; Sigel, 1985) and may affect child development outcomes (Darling & Steinberg, 1993). Therefore, laying bare men's cognitions about manhood, fatherhood, and parental responsibilities across cultures can prove fruitful in interpreting what drives their level and quality of involvement with children. This is particularly useful in the case of Caribbean men, who have maintained deep-seated beliefs about male dominance and engage in childbearing in several nonmarital unions, despite movement toward less-sex-stereotyped roles in other societies (Lamb, 1997).

Manhood

It has been suggested that across socioeconomic and cultural groups in the Caribbean, the internal working models of what constitutes "manhood" are often connected to and govern men's construction of an understanding of fatherhood and the responsibilities that accompany it (Brown et al., 1997; Roopnarine, 1997). Not unlike men in more traditional patriarchal societies (e.g., India, China), religious beliefs and cultural ascriptions help define Caribbean manhood. Banking on varied interpretations of Christian and/or Rastafarian religious ideologies, African-Caribbean men define manhood through headship and sexuality. According to Brown et al. (1997), there are three essential components to the definition of manhood: prolific heterosexuality and number of offspring, financial responsibility for one's family, and being the head of the family. In theory, manhood is conferred by first engaging in rampant sexual activity followed by financial responsibility and protection of one's family. Seemingly, these then lay down the justifications for African-Caribbean men to be the head of their households.

Indo-Caribbean men, too, lean heavily on religious edicts to guide their conceptions of manhood and subsequently fatherhood. Borrowing from principles laid out in ancient Sanskrit texts and epics (e.g., Ramayana) about the largely demarcated roles and responsibilities of men and women (e.g., *Laws of Manu*), Indo-Caribbean men view manhood in the context of *pativarata*—female subservience and male dominance. Men are the head of the family, and women and children are expected to cater to their wishes and concerns within and external to the family (Roopnarine et al., 1997). As with African-Caribbean men, child care is purportedly the domain of women whereas the provider and headship roles are coveted by men. In short, patriarchy is the cornerstone to the Indo-Caribbean man's celebration of manhood.

Fatherhood

Although Caribbean women have a long history of providing economic support for their families, a firmly entrenched cultural belief of most men and women throughout the Caribbean is that the primary function of fathers is to provide economic support to "mind" family members. For instance, when asked during a face-to-face interview situation what they thought the role of the father is, 96% of low-income single-earner and 74% of low-income dual-earner Jamaican fathers in common-law unions indicated that fathers should be breadwinners and the head of the household (94% and 72%, respectively, for mothers). None of the 88 men mentioned that fathers should be primary caregivers (Roopnarine et al., 1995). Basically, the same beliefs were offered by men in 10 communities in Jamaica, Guyana, and Dominica (Brown et al., 1997) and by men in Barbados (Dann, 1986). Not surprisingly, a popular view in the Caribbean is that a man who cannot support his family financially falls short of being a "man," even though this may be difficult to achieve for men with offspring from several partners in the economically strapped countries of the Caribbean. The economic viability of fathers to family members is embraced in several other cultures as well (Hewlett, 1992; Lamb, 1987, 1997).

Underlying these beliefs regarding the provider role is the currency that Caribbean men derive through biological fatherhood. Being a father provides a sense of self-definition and is seen as a necessary process toward personal maturity. Children born to African-Caribbean men early in life enhance their status in the community and, simultaneously, are seen as tangible proof of their sexual prowess (Brown et al., 1993). Among Indo-Caribbean men, having children means fulfilling family expectations about continuing the lineage, especially if the offspring is male (see Kakar, 1992 for a discussion of Indian childbearing). Unfortunately, the belief in personal maturity is not always accompanied by concerns about the emotional and intellectual responsibilities of fathers toward children. Although some men in the Caribbean appear cognizant about the psychological aspects of fatherhood, others remain ignorant about their social and intellectual responsibilities toward children (Brown et al., 1997).

The dispositions in beliefs about manhood and fatherhood laid out previously appear fairly robust in Caribbean immigrant families in the United States, despite the demands of wives that husbands/partners change their beliefs about male responsibilities in the family. In a fairly comprehensive survey of male–female relationships among Caribbean immigrants in New York, New Jersey, Pennsylvania, Delaware, and Washington, D.C., women showed disdain toward traditional role responsibilities by men and expected their husband to change their "West Indian way of life." But men were largely reluctant to heed their wife's/partner's appeals; a synthesis of men's responses suggested strong allegiance to a double standard in husband–wife/partner relationships (Millette, 1998). Additional support for a traditional view of the father's role in the family was obvious in the findings of a study of a group of Caribbean families who recently immigrated to the New York City area (Roopnarine, 1999). Like their counterparts in the Caribbean, a majority of the men designated the provider role to the father.

Why do Caribbean immigrant men hold on so steadfastly to traditional beliefs about the role of the father? It has been suggested that the acculturation process is shaped by a multitude of forces within and external to immigrant families: personal psychological resources, religious affiliation, language, racism and discrimination, political and economic climate, and so on (Berry, 1998; Cohen, 1997). Caribbean families who immigrated within the last two decades tend to live in neighborhoods that are populated by other immigrants from the Caribbean, and they travel frequently to the Caribbean developing social affiliations in the Caribbean and the United States. Within their own ethnic enclaves in the United States and in communities in the Caribbean, the "prepackaged" traditional male concepts are reinforced through alliances with other men and are rarely, if ever, challenged.

Falling in line with those of men in some African (Nsamenang, 1987) and Asian societies (Jankowiak, 1992; Suppal, Roopnarine, Buesig, & Bennett, 1996), the beliefs of Caribbean men and Caribbean immigrant men in the United States provide a template of the socially and culturally constructed schemas of fatherhood and fathering. Long before they become etched into the Caribbean male's psyche, there are ample opportunities for these cultural schemas to be shaped and reshaped through the personal acts of living and witnessing how diverse male roles are carried out and reinforced in Caribbean society. Boys are often encouraged to engage in sexual activity early in their lives to win parental approval of manhood and to simultaneously thwart any suspicions of homosexuality. This transpires in the absence of profound knowledge of other aspects of parental responsibilities and the social and economic factors that may impede being a successful father. At the moment, beyond providing for children economically, there is little consensus on what constitutes a "good father" among Caribbean men.

FACTORS THAT MAY CONSPIRE AGAINST SUCCESSFUL FATHERING

Scattered data suggest that economic factors (Ahmeduzzaman & Roopnarine, 1991; Brown et al., 1997; McLloyd, 1989), residential patterns (Flinn, 1992; Hetherington & Stanley-Hagan, 1997), cooperative interactions during work (Hewlett, 1992), and employment-related variables (Pleck, 1997) can affect the level and nature of paternal involvement with children in diverse societies. Among the more plausible factors that could undermine significant levels of involvement between Caribbean men and their children, four were judged important for the present discourse: (a) mate-shifting and child-shifting, (b) economic conditions, (c) adequate knowledge about parenting, and (d) internal and external migration. Because the importance of each of these factors in influencing paternal involvement has not been determined fully, they are considered in global terms.

Mate-Shifting/Child-Shifting

The patterns of mate-shifting among Caribbean families have already received attention earlier. The focus here is on its sequalae, child-shifting. During the "marital career" process, as Caribbean men move on to new partners and relationships, children are left behind with their mothers or are shifted to other kinship members and sometimes to neighbors. Reliable data on rates of child-shifting by each parent and the eventual destinations of children are not easily available. In two different estimates, 15% of men in Barbados were raised by neither a mother nor a father (Dann, 1987), and approximately 15% of Jamaicans under age 14 were shifted to other residences (Roberts & Sinclair, 1978). Higher rates of child-shifting (24%) were observed among a group of young mothers in Barbados (Russell-Brown, Norville, & Griffith, 1997), and in 1600 households surveyed in three Eastern Caribbean countries by the *Women in the Caribbean Project*, more than 50% of the children were raised by female relatives, mainly grandmothers and siblings. It is highly unlikely for children to be shifted to their father's residence even, when fathers and other kinship members are involved in the decision-making process (Russell-Brown et al., 1997).

Probably a vestige from slavery, a time when children were treated as communal property (Sharpe, 1997), currently the practice of child-shifting is exercised when the child is a perceived threat to the existing or a new relationship, when parents migrate in search of better economic and professional opportunities, and when parents' economic responsibilities toward children become overwhelming. An obvious drawback of this practice is that the father–child relationship is compromised on several fronts due to a lack of social contacts with children. There is the possibility that children who are shifted suffer multiple losses to biological and nonbiological attachment figures (Sharpe, 1997). The emotive quality of children's interactions with adults may be undermined further because children who reside in nonresidential father households are exposed to less-caring interactions that can be harsh (Flinn, 1992). The links between unstable or insecure attachment figures, sustained poor parent–child interactions, and later psychological risks are well established (Ainsworth, 1989; Baumrind, 1996).

Knowledge About Parenting

In their conceptual framework on father involvement, Lamb, Pleck, Charnov, and Levine (1987) identified the importance of parenting skills, self-confidence, and parental motivation in men's engagement with children. Existing research on knowledge about parenting and parenting practices among Caribbean adults indicate some disturbing trends. There is confirmation that young, low-income parents seem unaware that children need to play with materials, as few offered children toys or played with them. Parents rarely dispense praise or reward to children, are less likely to support their intellectual curiosity, and had unreasonable developmental expectations of children (Leo-Rhynie, 1997; Payne & Furnham, 1992; Wint & Brown, 1988). Findings specific to fathers indicated that they were less emotionally expressive and encouraging to children than mothers (Payne & Furnham, 1992). Generally, across socioeconomic and ethnic groups, Caribbean parents favor stricter, more severe forms of discipline that are embedded in a mixture of authoritarian/punitive control and indulgence (Grant, Leo-Rhynie, & Alexander, 1983). These practices are steeped in religious doctrines and are widely endorsed throughout the Caribbean. Not unlike the findings in other cultural groups (e.g., Baumrind, 1996; Rohner, Bourque, & Elordi, 1996), qualitative and quantitative studies (Evans & Davies, 1997; Leo-Rhynie, 1997) have pointed to associations between harsh, insensitive care and negative child development outcomes in Caribbean children.

Economics

There is reasonable consensus that the economic realities and modes of production in different cultures influence patterns of fathering. Some economic systems of production (e.g., hunting/gathering) require less time for food production and thus permit greater opportunities for fathers to be with children, whereas in others (e.g., horticultural), the father may be required to spend considerable time away from children (Hewlett, 1992). Not discounting distance and time, economic resources appear crucial to paternal involvement for men in both the developed and developing societies (Silverstein, 1993). In the United States, economic stability is linked to higher levels of involvement with children in African-American families (Ahmeduzzaman & Roopnarine, 1991; Furstenberg, 1991), to the likelihood of being in a marriage (Glick, 1988), and of having a happier family life (Ball & Robins, 1986). Almost identical patterns of associations were determined in Caribbean families (Brown et al., 1997). But Caribbean men without jobs or adequate economic resources face a formidable obstacle. They run the risk of being thrown out of the household by their partners/spouses because their likelihood of provisioning for the family is severely diminished. This scenario is captured best in a popular Caribbean song: "There Is No Romance Without Finance."

Internal and External Migration

Population movement in and out of the Caribbean has a fairly lengthy history. Historically, Caribbean men migrated alone in search of better economic opportunities. However, patterns of migration during the last half of the 20th century were more varied: serial patterns (one spouse moves, establishes a household, and then sends for other family members), families immigrating as a unit, or male sojourners. Some Caribbean families migrate internally within the Caribbean; others move to Europe and North America. Yet others move back and forth from the industrialized countries of the North and the Caribbean—the phenomenon of transmigration that is witnessed increasingly among immigrants who have political, social, and economic affiliations in more than one society.

For Caribbean families, serial patterns of migration meant that children were left behind for as long as 5 years in the case of immigrants to England (Arnold, 1997). These children often mourned the loss of parental figures, and both parents and children experienced difficulties in reestablishing a close emotional bond with one another (Arnold, 1997; daCosta, 1985). There is some indication that partner/spousal relationships are also strained due to exposure to the cultural norms of more industrialized societies (Nsamenang, 1987). Apart from this, a large number of Caribbean male immigrants enter the developed countries with few skills and low educational attainment—factors that may hinder their chances of economic mobility postimmigration. When the benefits of immigration fall below expectations, Caribbean men may experience anger, resentment, and depression (Baptiste et al., 1997), all of which could undermine effective parenting, which in turn could affect child well-being.

Finally, Caribbean parenting practices migrate with mothers and fathers to North America and Europe. Much to the consternation of parents, some Caribbean parenting practices (e.g., harsh discipline) not only collide with those espoused in their new societies, but have also been implicated in causing alienation between fathers and children (Arnold, 1997). Caribbean fathers perceive parenting practices that are less authority driven as a threat to their parental rights to stricter forms of discipline (Baptiste et al., 1997).

LEVELS AND QUALITY OF FATHER INVOLVEMENT AND THEIR CONSEQUENCES FOR CHILDHOOD DEVELOPMENT

Fathers in the Caribbean

Across various cultures women assume most of the responsibility for early child care (Barry & Paxson, 1971), a trend that is conspicuously patent even in societies where fathers show heavy investment in childcare (e.g., the Batek and Aka, Endicott, 1992; Hewlett, 1987). In examining father involvement in Caribbean and in Caribbean immigrant families, the goal here is to analyze the level and quality of father–child relationships and their importance for the development of social and cognitive skills in children, not to figure out whether fathers are equally as capable of engaging in the basic care of young children as mothers. Men's ability to care for young children has been articulated in several reviews (see volumes by Lamb, 1997; Parke, 1995). Because basic care (e.g., feeding, cleaning/washing, holding and playing, having sole responsibility for child) and educational activities (stimulating child, reading, taking children to school, modeling, and so on) reflect direct investment in children and these areas have received the most research attention, the overview of paternal involvement that follows is largely focused on these modes of caregiving.

For some time now, social scientists, literary figures, journalists, reggae and calypso musicians, and government officials across different Caribbean countries have called attention to the marginal role of Caribbean men in family life. For instance, the seminal work of Edith Clarke, the Jamaican anthropologist, titled *My Mother Who Fathered Me* (Clarke, 1957), a controversial book, *Men at Risk,* written by Errol Miller (Miller, 1991), and popular calypso and reggae songs, all decry the minimal or peripheral role of Caribbean fathers. To add to this negative portrait of men is a body of research that paints all Caribbean families as poverty stricken, largely female headed, and dysfunctional (Roopnarine, 2000). As is clear in the following discussion, a consideration of a limited number of studies that span four decades suggest that Caribbean men are far from being marginally involved in their children's lives. In this segment, the level and quality of paternal involvement is laid out before their meaning for childhood development is addressed.

Beginning with studies from a few decades ago, father involvement and societal expectations of fathers were gleaned from the opinions of women in Jamaica (Blake, 1961; Roberts & Sinclair, 1978; Stycos & Back, 1964), from ethnographic accounts of Amerindian families in coastal Guyana (Sanders, 1973), and the Black Caribs in Dominica (Layng, 1983). These early studies were not very informative because they revealed little about men's actual responsibilities and the levels and quality of direct involvement with children. The childrearing research from the 1980s did not clarify fathers' involvement with children much further beyond suggesting that Jamaican and Barbadian fathers were responsible for the discipline and the moral education of children (Chevannes, 1985; Dann, 1987), and Barbadian men believed in sharing responsibilities with spouses/partners when making decisions about school-related activities (Dann, 1986). One exception was a large-scale survey conducted on a sample of Indo- and African-Caribbean families residing in Georgetown, Guyana (Wilson, 1989). Fathers' levels of involvement with infants on basic caregiving activities were measured on a Likert-type scale. Fully 72% of fathers reported changing diapers and bathing the infant, 70% prepared food/fed the baby, and 64% got up at night to attend to the baby "sometimes" or "often." This level of investment was also seen in how often fathers played with and cuddled the infant (only 2.9% of fathers reported not ever cuddling or playing with the infant). No significant ethnic differences were found in levels of involvement with infants, but Indo-Guyanese fathers reported higher levels of involvement with older children than African-Caribbean Guyanese fathers. Contrary to expectations, there was an inverse relationship between paternal involvement in basic care and nurturance and income status. Fathers in low-income households showed more sustained involvement with young children than their brethren at higher-income levels.

Efforts to catalog levels of Caribbean father involvement with children continued in the 1990s with more systematic investigations of men's roles in different communities. A study of 88 common-law, low-income single- and dual-earner Jamaican families living in the Whitfield township area of Kingston mapped fathers' time investment in feeding, cleaning, and playing with 1-year-old infants (Roopnarine et al., 1995). Fathers across the two groups spent on average .94 of an hour feeding infants, .52 of an hour cleaning/bathing infants, and 2.75 hours playing with them each day. These estimates are close to those calculated for father involvement with infants in other societies (e.g., Hossain & Roopnarine, 1994). Fathers' greater time commitment to play, above other activities, lends credence to Lamb's (1997) claim that fathers mainly avail themselves as play partners to young children.

In assessing paternal care on the northern coast of Trinidad, Flinn (1992) used a "behavioral observation route instantaneous scan sample" technique to record the care interactions of 342 inhabitants. Of a total of 24,577 observations made of the villagers, 5,343 constituted interactions of parents and offspring. From the latter, it was determined that during the infancy and early childhood period, the care of children was distributed across several individuals: mothers assumed 44.2%, fathers 10.3%, siblings 16.3%, grandparents 17.6%, aunts and uncles 4.5%, and distant kin and nonrelatives 7.2%. Genetic parent–offspring interactions accounted for 35.6% of observed care overtures, with mothers assuming more responsibility for care during infancy (average for coresident mothers = 31.9%, Range 14–67%; average for fathers = 3.3%, Range 0–9%) and early childhood (average for coresident mothers = 22.9%, Range 8–36%; average for fathers = 4.2%, Range 0–17%). Care interactions were more prevalent across caregivers in resident–father households than nonresident–father households, with far fewer interactions occurring between nonbiological fathers and children than between biological fathers and children. The interactions between nonbiological fathers and children were characteristically more agonistic than those between biological fathers and children.

Two projects, The *Contribution of Caribbean Men to the Family* and the *Caribbean Gender Socialization Project* launched at the Caribbean Child Development Centre, at the University of the West Indies in Jamaica, employed interview and ethnographic methodologies to examine male parenting in primarily low-income, working-class men in four communities in the Kingston, Jamaica, area and in six communities in Jamaica, Guyana, and Dominica (Brown et al., 1993; Brown et al., 1997). Despite their extensive nature, these projects were more concerned with men's conceptions of fatherhood and male–female roles rather than levels of father involvement. Nevertheless, different portions of data confirm that a majority of the 700 Caribbean men surveyed in four communities around Kingston, Jamaica, showed active involvement in caring for children and in assisting them with homework. No involvement data were available for the other six communities. Nearly 50% of fathers in the Jamaican samples reported that they were doing an adequate job raising children.

Two ethnographic studies of Indo-Caribbean families from different socioeconomic backgrounds (Jayawardena, 1963; Roopnarine et al., 1997) revealed some interesting trends in male parenting among fathers in Guyana. From both accounts, East Indian men who were fathers in the 1950s and 1960s maintained some distance from children and caregiving in general; this was done in order to avoid the encouragement of feelings of familiarity between parent and offspring that may encourage challenges to paternal authority (Jayawardena, 1963). But changes in patterns of basic caregiving were noticeable in more contemporary third-generation East Indian men, the offspring of indentured servants who had been brought to British Guiana from India (Roopnarine et al., 1997). Specifically, fathers with better educational attainment were more likely to embrace early care-giving activities than their predecessors, perhaps signaling a break in cultural continuity in patriarchal modes of paternal involvement.

In a comparative analysis of paternal involvement in four cultures (Newars, Logli, Black Caribs, and Samoans), further evidence was provided on the tremen-dous variability in men's social contacts with children (Munroe & Munroe, 1992). Information was gathered on father presence/absence and father surrogates present in the homes, and spot observations were made of infants (3- to 18-month-olds) and young children (3- to 9-year-olds) and caregivers. Of primary concern here are the data on the Black Carib community sample. Nineteen percent of the Black Carib households had surrogate fathers (individuals designated by household members to fill the social role of father), a figure that is higher than among the Newars of Nepal (0%) and Logoli of Kenya (4%), but lower than among Samoans (31%). Black Carib fathers were present in the infant's social environments only 11% of the time, engaged in no caretaking activities, and did not hold the infant at all. This pattern of care remained after rates were recomputed for those infants with resident fathers only. For children between ages 3 and 9, fathers were present in 48% of the homes. Black Carib fathers were present 3% of the time in the imme-diate social environments of 3- to 9-year-old children, a trend toward physical dis-tance from children that is within the range of father availability (3–14%) in other societies (Munroe & Munroe, 1992; Whiting & Whiting, 1975).

Caribbean Immigrant Fathers

Possibly out of concern for adjustment patterns in the new cultural environment, research on Caribbean immigrant families has focused on mental health issues (see Roopnarine & Shin, in press), the process of children's reunification with parents after long periods of separation due to immigration to Europe and North America (Arnold, 1997), husband–wife relationships (Millette, 1998), sources of stress and conflict (Baptiste, Hardy, & Lewis, 1997), ethnic/cultural identity (Arnold, 1997; Maxime, 1986), parenting styles (Deyoung & Zigler, 1994), and multicultural edu-cation and counseling (Gopaul-McNicol, 1993). Thus, father involvement among immigrant families as a topic of research lags behind these other areas of inquiry.

A recent study by Roopnarine (1999) provides some of the first clues on levels and quality of paternal involvement among Caribbean immigrants in the United States. Primary caregiving and educational activities were examined in 60 fami-lies with prekindergarten and kindergarten-age children from different ethnic backgrounds. At the time of the study, the families had immigrated to the New York City area on average 13 years previous (Roopnarine, 1999). All but three couples were married. Drawing on mothers' time estimates of the distribution of primary caregiving responsibilities during a typical weekday, it was calculated that on average mothers spent 6.3 hours and fathers 3.3 hours (fathers' own esti-mates = 4.2 hours) in caring for children. Although fathers' time investment with children rose (to an average of 8.6 hours) on weekends, so did mothers' (13.6 hours). These rates are proportionally higher than for weekday involvement. Turning to involvement in educational activities, from mothers' estimates, fathers spent 4.3 hours (fathers' own estimates = 6.8 hours per week) on average a week reading to children and assisting them with homework, compared to 8.1 hours for mothers. Again, there were diverse individuals who engaged in educational activities with children: grandparents, aunts, uncles, and kinship caregivers. The fathers' share of responsibility amounted to 25% (own estimate 32%) of the total time all individuals spent in educational activities with children.

Summary

Several prominent psychologists (e.g., Lamb, 1997) have argued that more so than individual characteristics and levels of involvement are the secure, supportive, and sensitive relationships that fathers have with their children that are so crucial for healthy psychological development. The small and disparate group of studies reviewed offer more insights into levels rather than the sensitive and caring aspects of father–child relationships in the different family arrangements in the Caribbean. The central question remains: Given economic and other constraints on family life, what levels and patterns of engagement between fathers and children are considered optimal for childhood development across cultures?

The levels of paternal involvement noted for Caribbean and Caribbean immigrant fathers match the individual, socioeconomic, and intracultural and intercultural variability in caregiving noted for men in industrialized and preindustrial societies (see Hewlett, 1992; Lamb, 1987). In his review of the literature on paternal involvement among European-American, African-American, and Puerto-Rican men in North America, Pleck (1997) reported that in the 1990s, fathers' proportional engagement with children was over two fifths of mothers'. Fathers spent roughly 1.9 hours on weekdays and 6.5 hours on Sundays with children. Even though Caribbean father involvement was exceedingly low in some groups overall, the time estimate, survey, and interaction data obtained showed that fathers' levels of engagement with young children were not far below those of men in other cultures. And, the findings from a study on Caribbean immigrant fathers suggest levels of involvement in primary caregiving and educational activities with children that are, in the very least, encouraging.

But what do these levels of involvement mean for Caribbean children's social and economic welfare? No one would dispute Lamb's (1997) assertion about the importance of sensitive and nurturing father–child relationships for positive childhood development. Remember, though, that fathers assume multiple, interconnected roles, with the likelihood of each role taking on a different meaning in different cultures. In the economically impoverished countries of the Caribbean, the biological father's presence alone might mean better provisioning for the family and hence better nutritional status for the child and the reduced likelihood that the child will be abandoned or forced to engage in the street economy early or be abused (see Leo-Rhynie, 1997; Sharpe, 1997). Obviously, when the father does not provision for the family or is abusive, his presence places the welfare of the child in jeopardy.

SIGNIFICANCE OF PATERNAL INVOLVEMENT FOR CHILDREN

It is a daunting task to speak of "father effects" in Caribbean families (see Phares & Compass, 1992; Phares, 1997) without experimental and longitudinal studies on paternal involvement. Nevertheless, studies on father presence/absence and the extent of social contacts with children permit some liberty in discussing the significance of father involvement in Caribbean families. Given the mating/family patterns in the Caribbean, there has been overwhelming concern over the impact of unstable male figures and family structural arrangements on children's healthy development. Anthropologists (Draper & Harpending, 1982) working in the tradition of evolutionary biology have proposed that in societies, such as the Caribbean where father absence/minimal presence is normative, young males confronted with unstable paternalism "will be more interested in and learn more easily interpersonal and competitive skills and face to face dominance striving, but not always physical aggressive violence," whereas "father-absent females will perceive that male parental effort is not crucial to reproduction and will be less coy and reticent, will engage in sexual activity earlier and with less discrimination, and will form less stable pair bonds" (p. 239). Broaching the significance of father absence/minimal presence from this perspective, the research covered is grouped into two broad categories: social-psychological and educational.

Social-Psychological

The psychological risks to children of father absence or minimal father contacts and the poor quality of the father as role model have been determined in some studies. By examining the life conditions of children in homes without fathers, the Trinidadian psychiatrist Jacqueline Sharpe concluded that children are at greater risk for poor nutrition, developmental delays, running away from home, engaging in petty crime, and experiencing physical and sexual abuse (Sharpe, 1997). Further, a pattern of early sexual activity and teenage parenting in nonlegal unions in men and women in the Caribbean provide partial support for the paternal unstability hypothesis discussed by anthropologists (Draper & Harpending, 1982). Fifty percent of Jamaican males were sexually active by age 14, and male dominance is expressed openly (Brown et al., 1997; Millette, 1998). Likewise, Trinidadian teenage mothers experienced severe interpersonal family difficulties prior to their pregnancies (Sharpe, 1997), and between 47% and 59% of

Caribbean mothers had their first child during the teenage years (Powell, 1986), a significant number in nonlegal unions. But not all of these young mothers are prone to experiencing difficulties as parents. As Garcia Coll and Garcia (1996) argued so cogently, interpersonal difficulties among young parents remain low in sociocultural contexts that are accepting and supportive of teenage parenting. Under these circumstances, teenage parenting takes on adaptive significance in that motherhood is embraced, and young mothers receive a wide range of instrumental and emotional support from family members.

Attempts to find more direct associations between father absence and social outcomes are reflected in two studies on Jamaican youth. Working with a sample of 169 undergraduate students who were seen over a 3½-year period at the Mental Health Division of the Health Service at the University of the West Indies in Jamaica, Allen (1985) was able to draw connections between passive-dependency in his patients and unsatisfactory relationships with their parents and the absence of one or both parents during childhood (35.7% of dependents vs. 22.2% of non-dependents had parents absent during childhood). Reverting to his clinical practice, Allen (1985) opined that the passive-dependency in his patients had their origins in poor parental bonding and lack of strong male figures. A similar argument was made regarding Barbadian children who grew up without fathers (Dann, 1987).

A somewhat parallel approach was undertaken to understand the role of family structure variables in contributing to psychological difficulties in another group of Jamaican children. Crawford-Brown (1997) compared the family histories and social contacts with parental figures in 69 adolescent with conduct disorder and 55 without conduct disorder. Surprisingly, there was a significant difference between the two groups in the number of mothers but not fathers who were absent from the child's life (53% of the children with conduct disorder vs. 49% in the control had absent fathers, respectively). Children with conduct disorder had far fewer contacts with mothers, were more likely to be exposed to poor parental role models (70% of the poor models were fathers), and were more likely to change living arrangements frequently (91.7% of the study group children vs. 8.3% of controls were shifted between two and six times) than controls. These results suggest that father absence in and of itself may not be a good predictor of problem behaviors in Caribbean children.

Educational Outcomes

As was stated in a previous paper (Roopnarine, 1997), the relationships between father absence/presence and children's school achievement have been surmised from comparisons of children in two-parent patriarchal families and single-mother Caribbean families. Based on limited work on Barbadian and Jamaican children, a few Caribbean scholars (e.g., Miller, 1991) have summarily argued that father absence may not be linked to the poor school performance of children. Of course,

such a conclusion ignores the problems Caribbean boys manifest in the educational system. For example, in comparison to males, females enter school earlier,
attend school more regularly, stay in school for longer durations, are less likely to
drop out, perform better on high school entrance and other examinations, and
enroll in greater numbers at Teachers' Training Colleges and the University of the
West Indies. Similarly, young boys are more likely to have poorer nutritional and
health status (Miller, 1991), an outcome observed in children in general in the
Dominican Republic (Brown, 1973), in Africa and Latin America (Desai, 1991),
and in hunting–gathering societies when the father dies (Hutardo & Hill, 1992). Is
it possible that Caribbean mothers are spending more time with and offer more
resources to daughters than sons when fathers are not residing in the household?
More importantly, could father absence place Caribbean boys at greater risk for
educational failure?

Returning to the two studies conducted by Brown and her colleagues for a
moment (Brown et al., 1993; 1997), a few of their findings indicated that
Caribbean girls are offered more protection and monitored more closely, restricted from moving about the neighborhood, encouraged to engage in domestic and
school activities, and perceived to be easier to raise than boys. On the other hand,
boys are given more latitude to roam about and to gain societal and economic
skills "on the road" and in the company of men in the neighborhood (Brown et al.,
1997). Inasmuch as boys do come into contact with other adult males in their
immediate environment, whether the father is present or not, these social contacts
may be of questionable quality to have compensatory value in warding off the
pernicious effects attributed to the biological fathers' absence or residential nonbiological fathers' lowered interest and antagonism toward children. It is highly
probable that the protection and guidance that girls receive from mothers and
other female figures help insulate them from these consequences. By comparison,
the greater freedom that is permitted to boys may predispose them to engagement
in noneducational, risk-taking activities that are encouraged in so many ways by
the male subculture.

Departing from the tendency to focus on the impact of the father's absence on
children's intellectual functioning, Roopnarine (2000) examined the associations
between Caribbean immigrant parenting practices (attending school functions,
regular monitoring of school progress and behaviors, ongoing support for education), parenting styles as conceived by Baumrind (1967), and prekindergarten and
kindergarten children's scores on the Kaufman Scales of Early Academic Performance. Based on propositions of alternative ways in which parenting styles can
influence academic achievement (Darling & Steinberg, 1993), three models were
tested: (a) the relationship between fathers' parenting styles and children's early
academic performance as mediated through fathers' parenting practices; (b) the
role of fathers' parenting styles as a moderating influence on the relationships
between fathers' parenting practices and children's early academic performance;
and (c) an additive model assessing the role of fathers' parenting practices and

fathers' parenting styles in children's academic performance. The role of parenting styles as a mediator or moderator of early academic performance was not supported. Analysis suggested the unique and direct role of parenting practices in children's early intellectual functioning. Over parenting styles, Caribbean immigrant fathers' involvement in attending school functions, close monitoring of children's behaviors and performance at school, and broad support for education may help to promote value conformity and educational success in their young children.

In closing this section, it is probably fair to say that research on the impact of father absence/presence and the quality of father–child relationships in Caribbean and Caribbean-American children has produced some findings that are similar to those outlined for children in the more industrialized countries of the world (see Biller, 1993; Biller & Kimpton, 1997). It is prudent to mention that father absence in the Caribbean is a normative phenomenon. Although the existing data suggest that children may be at psychological and educational risk due to low levels of involvement and poor father–child relationships, the impact of being raised in different family unions must be viewed in terms of adequate economic resources, appropriate knowledge about parenting, good parenting skills, and broad support for childrearing from kinship and nonkinship members. It is highly unlikely that living in a visiting or common-law union alone would account for maladjustment and educational deficiencies in childhood.

CONCLUSION

A major goal of this chapter was to explore the sociocultural context of fatherhood and fathering and the significance of paternal involvement for childhood development in Caribbean and Caribbean immigrant families in North America. There are a few cultural practices that appear unique to Caribbean families: progressive mating that may eventually lead to marriage when men become more economically stable and child-shifting. For a large number of Caribbean families, male parenting is realized in different mating unions over an extended period of time and appears driven by cultural schemas about roles and responsibilities intertwined in the concepts of "manhood" and "fatherhood." Broadly speaking, the impact of father absence and poor father–child relationships on childhood development are not dramatically different from what has been found for other cultural groups. However, the level and quality of father–child relationships must be considered within economic conditions, mate-shifting and child-shifting, migratory patterns and acculturative stress, multiple caregiving, and knowledge about parenting before we can begin to better understand the role(s) of the father in Caribbean and Caribbean immigrant families and be able to design culturally appropriate intervention strategies to increase sensitive and enduring relationships between fathers and children.

REFERENCES

Ahmeduzzaman, M., & Roopnarine, J. L. (1992). Sociodemographic factors, functioning style, social support, and fathers' involvement with preschoolers in African-American families. *Journal of Marriage and the Family, 54,* 699–707.

Ainsworth, M. (1989). Attachments beyond infancy. *American Psychologist, 44,* 709–717.

Allen, A. (1985). Psychological dependency among students in a "cross-roads" culture. *West Indian Medical Journal, 34,* 123–127.

Arnold, E. (1997). Issues in re-unification of migrant West Indian children in the United Kingdom. In J. L. Roopnarine & J. Brown (Eds.), *Caribbean families: Diversity among ethnic groups* (pp. 243–258). Norwood, NJ: Ablex.

Axelrod, R., & Hamilton, W. D. (1981). The evolution of cooperation. *Science, 211,* 1390–1396.

Ball, R. E., & Robins, L. (1986). Black husbands' satisfaction with their families. *Journal of Marriage and the Family, 48,* 849–855.

Baptiste, D., Hardy, K., & Lewis, L. (1997). Clinical practice with Caribbean immigrant families in the United States. The intersection of emigration, immigration, culture, and race. In J. L. Roopnarine & J. Brown (Eds.), *Caribbean families: Diversity among ethnic groups* (pp. 275–303). Greenwich, CT: Ablex.

Barry, H., III, & Paxson, L. M. (1971). Infancy and early childhood: Cross-cultural codes 2. *Ethnology, 10,* 466–508.

Baumrind, D. (1967). Child care practices anteceding three patterns of preschool behavior. *Genetic Psychology Monographs, 75,* 43–88.

Baumrind, D. (1996). The discipline controversy revisited. *Family Relations, 45,* 405–414.

Berry, J. W. (1998). Acculturation and health: Theory and research. In S. S. Kazarian & D. R. Evans (Eds.), *Cultural clinical psychology: Theory, research and practice* (pp. 39–57). New York: Oxford University Press.

Biller, H. (1993). *Fathers and families.* Westport, CT: Auburn House.

Biller, H., & Kimpton, J. L. (1997). The father and the school-aged child. In M. E. Lamb (Ed.), *The role of the father in child development* (3rd ed., pp. 143–161). New York: Wiley.

Blake, J. (1961). *Family structure in Jamaica.* New York: Free Press.

Brown, J. L. (1973). Coping and poverty in the Dominican Republic: Women and their mates. *Current Anthropology, 14,* 555.

Brown, J., Anderson, P., & Chevannes, B. (1993). *The contribution of Caribbean men to the family.* Report for the International Development Centre, Canada, Caribbean Child Development Centre, Mona: University of the West Indies.

Brown, J., Newland, A., Anderson, P., & Chevannes, B. (1997). In J. L. Roopnarine & J. Brown (Eds.), *Caribbean families: Diversity among ethnic groups* (pp. 85–113). Norwood, NJ: Ablex.

Chevannes, B. (1985). *Jamaican men: Sexual attitudes and beliefs.* Unpublished report, National Planning Board. Kingston: Jamaica.

Chevannes, B. (1993). *Stresses and strains: Situation analysis of the Caribbean family.* Regional meeting Prepatory to International Year of the Family, United Nations Economic Commission for Latin America and the Caribbean. Cartagena: Colombia.

Clarke, E. (1957). *My mother who fathered me: A study of family in three selected communities in Jamaica.* London: George Allen & Unwin.

Cohen, R. (1997). *Global diasporas: An introduction.* Seattle, WA: University of Washington Press.

Crawford-Brown, C. (1997). The impact of parent–child socialization on the development of conduct disorder in Jamaican male adolescents. In J. L. Roopnarine & J. Brown (Eds.), *Caribbean families: Diversity among ethnic groups* (pp. 205–222). Norwood, NJ: Ablex.

daCosta, E. (1985). *Reunion after long-term disruption of the parent–child bond in older children: Clinical features and psychodynamic issues.* Toronto: Clark Institute of Psychiatry.

Dann, G. (1987). *The Barbadian male: Sexual beliefs and attitudes.* London and Bassingstoke: Macmillan.

Dann, G. (1986). *"Getting outta hand: Men's view of woemn in Barbados.* Paper presented to the ISER/UNESCO seminar on *Changing family patterns and women's role in the Caribbean.* Cave Hill, Barbados: University of the West Indies.

Darling, N., & Steinberg, L. (1993). Parenting style as context: An integrative model. *Psychological Bulletin, 113,* 487–496.

Desai, S. (1991). *Children at risk: The role of family structure in Latin America and West Africa.* New York: Population Council Working Papers No. 28.

Deyoung, Y., & Zigler, E. F. (1994). Machismo in two cultures: Relation to punitive child-rearing practices. *American Journal of Orthopsychiatry, 64,* 386–395.

Draper, P., & Harpending, H. (1982). Father absence and reproductive strategy: An evolutionary perspective. *Journal of Anthropological Research, 38,* 255–273.

Endicott, K. (1992). Fathering in an egalitarian society. In B. Hewlett (Ed.), *Father–child relations: Cultural and biosocial contexts* (pp. 281–295). New York: Aldine de Gruyter.

Evans, H., & Davies, R. (1997). Overview of issues in childhood socialization in the Caribbean. In J. L. Roopnarine & J. Brown (Eds.), *Caribbean families: Diversity among ethnic groups* (pp. 1–24). Greenwich, CT: Ablex.

Flinn, M. (1992). Paternal care in a Caribbean village. In B. Hewlett (Ed.), *Father–child relations: Cultural and biosocial contexts* (pp. 57–84). New York: Aldine de Gruyter.

Furstenburg, F. (1991). As the pendulum swings: Teenage childbearing and social concern. *Family Relations, 40,* 127–138.

Garcia Coll, C., & Garcia, H. A. V. (1996). Definitions of competence in adolescence: Lessons from Puerto Rican adolescent mothers. In D. Cicchetti & S. L. Toth (Eds), *Adolescence: opportunities and challenges. Rochester symposium on developmental psychopathology* (Vol. 7, pp. 283–308). Rochester, NY: University of Rochester Press.

Garcia Coll, C., Lamberty, G., Jenkins, R., McAdoo, H., Crnic, K., Wasik, B., & Garcia, H. (1996). An integrative model for the study of developmental competencies in minority children. *Child Development, 67,* 1891–1914.

Glick, P. (1988). Demographic pictures of Black families. In H. P. McAdoo (Ed.), *Black families* (pp. 111–132). Beverly Hills, CA: Sage.

Goodnow, J., & Collins, W. A. (1990). *Development according to parents.* Hillsdale, NJ: Lawrence Erlbaum Associates.

Gopaul-McNicol, S. (1993). *Working with West Indian families.* New York: Guilford Press.

Grant, D. B. R., Leo-Rhynie, E., & Alexander, G. (1983). *Life style study: Children of the lesser world in the English speaking Caribbean: Vol 5. Household structures and settings.* Kingston: Bernard Van Leer Foundation–Centre for Early Childhood Education.

Grasmuck, S., & Grosfoguel, R. (1997). Geopolitics, economic niches, and gendered social capital among recent Caribbean immigrants in New York City. *Sociological Perspectives, 40,* 339–363.

Harkness, S., & Super, S. (Eds.). (1996). *Parental cultural belief systems: Their origins, expressions, and consequences.* New York: Guilford Press.

Harwood, R., Miller, J., & Irizarray, N. (1995). *Culture and attachment.* New York: Guilford Press.

Hetherington, E. M., & Stanley-Hagan, M. (1997). The effects of divorce on fathers and their children. In M. E. Lamb (Ed.), *The role of the father in child development* (3rd ed., pp. 191–226). New York: Wiley.

Hewlett, B. (Ed.). (1992). *Father–child relations: Cultural and biosocial contexts.* New York: Aldine de Gruyter.

Hewlett, B. (1987). Intimate fathers: Patterns of paternal holding among Aka Pygmies. In M. E. Lamb (Ed.), *The father's role: Cross-cultural perspectives* (pp. 295–330). Hillsdale, NJ: Lawrence Erlbaum Associates.

Hossain, Z., & Roopnarine, J. L. (1994). African-American fathers' involvement with infants: Relationship to their functioning style, support, education, and income. *Infant Behavior and Development, 17,* 175–184.

Hutardo, A. M., & Hill, K. (1992). Paternal effect on offspring survivorship among Ache and Hiwi hunter-gatherers: Implications for modeling pair-bond stability. In B. Hewlett (Ed.), *Father-child relations: Cultural and biosocial contexts* (pp. 31–55). New York: Aldine de Gruyter.

Jankowiak, W. (1992). Father–child relations in urban China. In B. Hewlett (Ed.), *Father–child relations: Cultural and biosocial contexts* (pp. 345–363). New York: Aldine de Gruyter.

Jayawardena, C. (1963). *Conflict and solidarity in a Guianese plantation.* London: University of London, Athlone.

Johnson, O. R., & Johnson, A. (1975). Male/female relations and the organization of work in a Machiguenga community. *American Ethnologist, 2,* 634–638.

Kakar, S. (1992). *The inner world.* New Delhi, India: Oxford University Press.

Lamb, M. (1997). Fathers and child development: An introductory overview and guide. In M. E. Lamb (Ed.), *The role of the father in child development* (3rd ed., pp. 1–18). New York: Wiley.

Lamb, M. E. (Ed). (1987). *The father's role: Cross-cultural perspectives.* Hillsdale, NJ: Lawrence Erlbaum Associates.

Lamb, M. E., Pleck, J. H., Charnov, E. L., & Levine, J. A. (1987). A biosocial perspective on paternal behavior and involvement. In J. B. Lancaster, J. Altman, A. Rossi, & L. R. Sherrod (Eds.), *Parenting across the lifespan: Biosocial perspectives* (pp. 11–42). New York: Academic Press.

Lamming, G. (1970). *In the castle of my skin.* Harlow, UK: Longman.

Layng, A. (1983). *The Carib reserve: Identity and security in the West Indies.* Washington, DC: University Press of America.

Leo-Rhynie, E. (1997). Class, race, and gender issues in child rearing in the Caribbean. In J. L. Roopnarine & J. Brown (Eds.), *Caribbean families: Diversity among ethnic groups* (pp. 25–55). Norwood, NJ: Ablex.

LeVine, R. (1974). Parental goals: A cross-cultural view. *Teachers College Record, 76,* 226–239.

Massiah, J. (1982). *Women who head households.* Cave Hill, Barbados: Institute for Social and Social Research, UWI, WICP.

Maxime, J. (1986). Some psychological models of Black concept. In S. Ahmed, J. Cheetham, & J. Small (Eds.), *Social work with Black children and their families* (pp. 100–116). London: Batsford Press.

McLloyd, V. (1989). Socialization and development in a changing economy: The effects of paternal job and income loss on children. *American Psychologist, 44,* 293–302.

Miller, E. (1991). *Men at risk.* Kingston: Jamaica Publishing House.

Millette, R. (1998). West Indian families in the United States. In R. Taylor (Ed.), *Minority families in the United States: A multicultural perspective* (2nd ed. pp. 46–59). Upper Saddle River, NJ: Prentice Hall.

Munroe, R., & Munroe, R. (1992). Fathers in children's environments: A four culture study. In B. Hewlett (Ed.), *Father-child relations: Cultural and biosocial contexts* (pp. 213–229). New York: Aldine de Gruyter.

Nsamenang, A. B. (1987). Fathers: A West African perspective. In M. E. Lamb (Ed.), *The father's role: Cross-cultural perspectives* (pp. 273–293). Hillsdale, NJ: Lawrence Erlbaum Associates.

Ogbu, J. (1991). Immigrant and involuntary minorities in comparative perspective. In M. Gibson & J. Ogbu (Eds.), *Minority status and schooling.* (pp. 3–33). New York: Garland.

Parke, R. (1995). *Fatherhood.* Cambridge, MA: Harvard University Press.

Parke, R. (1996). *Fathers and families.* Cambridge, MA: Harvard University Press.

Payne, M., & Furnham, A. (1992). Parental self-reports of childrearing practices in the Caribbean. *Journal of Black Psychology, 18,* 19–36.

Phares, V. (1997). Psychological adjustment, maladjustment, and father–child relationships. In M. E. Lamb (Ed.), *The role of the father in child development* (3rd ed., pp. 262–283). New York: Wiley.

Phares, V., & Compas, B. (1992). The role of the father in child and adolescent psychopathology: Make room for daddy. *Psychological Bulletin, 111,* 387–412.

Pleck, J. (1997). Paternal involvement: Levels, sources, and consequences. In M. E. Lamb (Ed.), *The role of the father in child development* (3rd ed., pp. 66–103). New York: Wiley.

Popenoe, D. (1988). *Disturbing the nest: Family change and decline in modern societies.* New York: Aldine de Gruyter.

Powell, D. (1986). Caribbean women and their responses to familial experience. *Social and Economic Studies, 35,* 83–130.

Roberts, G., & Sinclair, S. (1978). *Women in Jamaica.* New York: KTO Press.

Rodman, H. (1971). *Lower-class families: The culture of poverty in Negro Trinidad.* New York: Oxford University Press.

Rohner, R., Bourque, S., & Elordi, C. (1996). Children's perceptions of corporal punishment, caretaker acceptance, and psychological adjustment in a poor, biracial community. *Journal of Marriage and the Family, 58,* 842–852.

Roopnarine, J. L. (1997). Fathers in the English-speaking Caribbean: Not so marginal. *World Psychology, 3,* 191–210.

Roopnarine, J. L. (1999, April). *Father involvement and parenting styles in Caribbean immigrant families.* Paper presented at the American Educational Research Association meetings, Montreal, Canada.

Roopnarine, J. L. (2000). *Paternal involvement, ethnotheories about development, parenting styles, and early academic achievement in Caribbean-American children.* Paper presented in the Department of Applied Psychology, New York University.

Roopnarine, J. L., & Brown, J. (Eds.). (1997). *Caribbean families: Diversity among ethnic groups.* Norwood, NJ: Ablex.

Roopnarine, J., Brown, J., Snell-White, P., Riegraf, N. B., Crossley, D., Hossain, Z., & Webb, W. (1995). Father involvement in child care and household work in common-law dual-earner and single-earner families. *Journal of Applied Developmental Psychology, 16,* 35–52.

Roopnarine, J., & Shin, M. (in press). Caribbean immigrants from English-speaking countries: Socio-historical forces, migratory patterns, and psychological issues in family functioning. In L. L. Adler & U. P. Gielen (Eds.), *Migration, immigration and emigration in international perspectives.*

Roopnarine, J. L., Shin, M., & Lewis, T. Y. (2001). English-speaking Caribbean immigrant father: The task of unpacking the cultural pathways to intervention. In J. Fagan & A. Hawkins (Eds.), *Clinical and educational interventions with fathers* (pp. 235–255). New York: Haworth Press.

Roopnarine, J., Snell-White, P., Riegraf, N., Wolfsenberger, J., Hossain, Z., & Mathur, S. (1997). Family socialization in an East Indian village in Guyana: A focus on fathers. In J. L. Roopnarine & J. Brown (Eds.), *Caribbean families: Diversity among ethnic groups* (pp. 57–83). Norwood, NJ: Ablex.

Russell-Brown, P., Norville, B., & Griffith, C. (1997). Child shifting: A survival strategy for teenage mothers. In J. L. Roopnarine & J. Brown (Eds.), *Caribbean families: Diversity among ethnic groups* (pp. 223–242). Norwood, NJ: Ablex.

Sanders, A. (1973). Family structure and domestic organization among coastal Amerindians in Guyana. *Social and Economic Studies, 22,* 440–478.

Schweder, R., Goodnow, J., Hatano, G., LeVine, R., Markus, H., & Miller, P. (1998). The cultural psychology of development: One mind, many mentalities. In R. Lerner (Ed.), *Theoretical models of human development: Vol. 1. Handbook of child psychology* (pp. 865–937). New York: Wiley.

Senior, O. (1991). *Working miracles: Women's lives in the English-speaking Caribbean.* Bloomington: Indiana University Press.

Sharpe, J. (1997). Mental health issues and family socialization in the Caribbean. In J. L. Roopnarine & J. Brown (Eds.), *Caribbean families: Diversity among ethnic groups* (pp. 259–273). Norwood, NJ: Ablex.

Sigel, I. (1985). A conceptual analysis of beliefs. In I. Sigel, A. McGillicuddy-DeLisi, & J. Goodnow (Eds.), *Parental belief systems: The psychological consequences for children* (2nd ed., pp. 345–371). Hillsdale, NJ: Lawrence Erlbaum Associates.

Silverstein, L. (1993). Primate research, family politics, and social policy: Transforming "CADS" into "DADS." *Journal of Family Psychology, 7,* 267–282.

Silverstein, L., & Auerbach, C. F. (1999). Deconstructing the essential father. *American Psychologist, 54,* 397–407.

Smith, R. T. (1996). *The matrifocal family: Power, pluralism, and politics.* London: Routledge.

Stycos, J. M., & Back, K. W. (1964). *The control of human fertility in Jamaica.* Ithaca, NY: Cornell University Press.

Super, C., & Harkness, S. (1997). The cultural structuring of child development. In J. Berry, P. Dasen, & T. S. Saraswathi (Eds.), *Handbook of cross-cultural psychology: Basic processes and human development* (pp. 1–39). Needham, MA: Allyn & Bacon.

Suppal, P., Roopnarine, J. L., Buesig, T., & Bennett, A. (1996). Ideological beliefs about family practices: Contemporary perspectives among north Indian families. *International Journal of Psychology, 31,* 29–37.

Trivers, R. (1972). Parental investment and sexual selection. In B. Campbell (Ed.), *Sexual selection and the descent of man: 1871–1971* (pp. 136–179). Chicago: Aldine.

Whiting, B. B., & Whiting, J. W. M. (1975). *Children of six cultures: A psycho-cultural analysis.* Cambridge, MA: Harvard University Press.

Wilson, L. C. (1989). *Family and structure and dynamics in the Caribbean: An examination of residential and relational matrifocality in Guyana.* Unpublished doctoral dissertation, University of Michigan, Ann Arbor.

Wint, E., & Brown, J. (1987). Promoting effective parenting: A study of two methods in Kingston, Jamaica. *Child Welfare, 66,* 507–516.

IV

Father Involvement: Evolutionary Perspectives

Frank Marlowe
Peabody Museum at Harvard University

The three chapters in this section represent the field of human behavioral ecology, which emphasizes the influence of ecological constraints on behavior. Natural selection favors those who leave the most descendents (more precisely, genes better at making copies of themselves), which depends both on the number produced and the number surviving. Because parents have a limited budget to invest and the more they invest in one offspring means the less they have to invest in another, there is a trade-off between quantity and quality of offspring. Males often favor quantity over quality because the quantity they can produce is potentially so great. Because of this trade-off, it is impossible to divorce parenting behavior from mating behavior. Darwin (1871) noted differences between the sexes in secondary sexual characteristics and behavior and linked these to competition for mates, though he left unexplained exactly why competition for mates should be so different for males and females. To present the current view of why there are differences, I briefly discuss four factors that influence paternal investment: (a) anisogamy, (b) potential reproductive rate, (c) operational sex ratio, and (d) paternity confidence. This should provide some useful background for the chapters in this section. Afterward, I discuss direct and indirect care. Finally, I comment on the chapters.

Parental investment begins with the gametes (sex cells). Because eggs are much larger than sperm (anisogamy), as Bateman (1948) noted, female contribution is greater than male contribution. Small, plentiful sperm seek out larger, less-plentiful, energy-rich, highly prized eggs to exploit, and the two sexes tend to reflect the strategy of their gametes. However, despite this fundamental asymmetry there are numerous species in which the roles are reversed, showing that anisogamy cannot be the whole story. Trivers (1972) extended Bateman's logic beyond the gametes to postzygotic and postnatal investment, noting that because the reproductive success of the lower-investing sex is constrained mainly by access to mates, that sex tends to compete more vigorously for mates whereas the higher-investing sex tends to be choosier.

Among mammals, gestation and lactation are costly and time consuming, which means that the potential reproductive rate of females is much lower than males, who can potentially produce an offspring with only a few minutes of investment (Clutton-Brock & Parker, 1992). Most species of mammals are effectively polygynous (Clutton-Brock, 1991), meaning there is greater variance in male than female reproductive success, and females provide more care than males. When offspring need more care than one parent can provide, as in many species of birds, there will be selection for biparental care and monogamy (Black, 1996). However, it still may pay one sex more than the other to desert and seek additional mates (Maynard Smith, 1977). Because of their higher potential reproductive rate, males usually stand to gain more by desertion if that helps them find other mates. Males thus face a trade-off between investing more in parenting or seeking additional mates, between being dads or cads (Draper & Harpending, 1982). These alternative strategies have been the inspiration for research on father absence versus father presence.

Whether it will pay males to desert and look for other mates depends on the operational sex ratio (OSR), which is the ratio of reproductive-aged females to reproductive-aged males, taking into account the number of copulations per conception, which reflects the number of days females are fertilizable (Mitani, Gros-Louis, & Richards, 1996). This influences the bargaining position of each sex and thus the mating system, which in turn influences how much care each sex provides. Among Hadza hunter-gatherers of Tanzania with whom I work, men gave less care to their children when they lived in camps with more reproductive-age women per reproductive-age man (Marlowe, 1999). OSR also appears to be a better predictor of marital stability than the effect of father presence or absence on offspring survivorship among human foragers (Blurton Jones, Marlowe, Hawkes, & O'Connell, 2000).

In species with internal fertilization like mammals, paternity confidence is always lower than maternity confidence. Because males stand to gain more from investing in their own offspring, paternity confidence (PC) should influence the level of male care. In experiments designed to test this, some species of birds altered their level of care in response to cues of manipulated PC whereas others did not (Wright, 1998). Males might provide care even to offspring that are not their own either because they cannot gauge PC or because they are simply hardwired to care. However, it can also pay males to provide care to young not their own in order to gain sexual access to mates (Smuts & Gubernick, 1992). In other words, care itself can be a form of mating effort, which it must be in the case of men who care for their stepchildren. Nevertheless, I found Hadza men provided less care to their stepchildren than their biological children, as expected if paternity and PC matters (Marlowe, 1999).

Parental investment is usually divided into the two broad categories of direct care, such as holding, carrying, or grooming, and indirect care, such as provisioning, defending a territory, or building a nest (Kleiman & Malcolm, 1981). Often there will be a trade-off between direct and indirect care. For example, males who spend more time acquiring resources will have less time for holding infants. These two types of care vary greatly across human societies, especially in relation to the mode of subsistence. Direct care appears to be highest among foragers and lowest among pastoralists, where male resource contribution is highest (Marlowe, 2000). However, overall paternal investment (direct and indirect care combined) can also vary cross culturally. Where men invest heavily, we can expect female–female competition for such men to increase, resulting in greater monogamy, which is precisely what a cross-cultural analysis reveals (Marlowe, 2000).

The chapters in this section look at very different societies, the multiethnic Okavango Delta peoples of Botswana, the Maya of Belize and Ache foragers of Paraguay, and 19th century Mormons. They use a variety of methods from demography, time allocation and parenting orientation surveys, income measures, behavioral observations, anthropometry, and skill measurements. All three chapters explore the factors responsible for paternal investment as well as the consequences for children. Two chapters assess the effects of father presence and absence, whereas the third assesses the effect of monogamy and polygyny. All three examine men's mating strategies.

Bock and Johnson use embodied capital theory to analyze the effect of father presence and absence on children. Contrary to normal expectations, they found that father absence led to better growth of children because absent fathers were sending home wages. Children without fathers present therefore performed better on skills that depend more on size or strength than learning. Bock and Johnson's results show how the effect of father presence or absence can hinge on the benefits of direct versus indirect care.

Waynforth tests for the effects of father presence or absence on age at first reproduction and mating strategy among the Maya and Ache. Contrary to the expectations of the psychosocial stress model (Belsky, Steinberg, & Draper, 1991), which posits that less father involvement leads to earlier reproduction and more promiscuous mating by children, he found that father-absent Ache females and Maya males reproduced later. Waynforth takes a novel approach, arguing that the effects of father absence may best be explained by inclusive fitness theory and lower nepotistic cooperation. His results show that the effects of father presence and absence can vary from one society to another because the gains from mating effort and family orientation can vary.

Josephson uses historical demographic records on 19th century Mormons to look at the impact of a father's marital status—monogamy or polygyny—on survivorship and reproductive success of children. He found that polygynous men helped their children marry better and more often, possibly at the expense of survival. He also found some support for the Trivers-Willard hypothesis (Trivers & Willard, 1973), which predicts differential investment in sons and daughters depending on resources available, because he found that poorer monogamous men tended to help their daughters more. Josephson refines our understanding of the ways in which fathers may benefit their children. His results show that a short-term focus can miss an important part of the story.

These three chapters contribute to our understanding of father involvement in response to ecological variation such as whether men are foragers, subsistence farmers, or wage laborers. All three chapters challenge orthodoxy to some extent and therefore provide suggestions for future research. To better understand father involvement, we need to attend more to proximate mechanisms, whether hormones, cues of paternity, resource variation, OSR, or genetic qualities of men, and attend more to the local returns to direct and indirect care.

REFERENCES

Bateman, A. J. (1948). Intrasexual selection in Drosophila. *Heredity, 2,* 349–68.

Belsky, J., Steinberg, L., & Draper, P. (1991). Childhood experience, interpersonal development, and reproductive strategy: An evolutionary interpretation. *Child Development, 62,* 647–670.

Black, J. M. (Ed.). (1996). *Partnerships in birds.* Oxford: Oxford University Press.

Blurton Jones, N. G., Marlowe, F., Hawkes, K., & O'Connell, J. F. (2000). Paternal investment and hunter-gather divorce rates. In L. Cronk, N. Chagnon, & W. Irons (Eds.), *Human behavior and adaptation: An anthropological perspective* (pp. 65–86). New York: Elsevier.

Clutton-Brock, T. H. (1991). *The evolution of parental care.* Princeton: Princeton University Press.

Clutton-Brock, T. H., & Parker, G.A. (1992). Potential reproductive rates and the operation of sexual selection. *Quarterly Review of Biology, 67,* 437–456.

Darwin, C. (1871). *Descent of Man and Selection in Relation to Sex.* Princeton, NJ: Princeton University Press.

Draper, P., & Harpending, H. (1982). Father absence and reproductive strategy: An evolutionary perspective. *Journal of Anthropological Research, 38,* 255–273.

Kleiman, D. G., & Malcolm, J. R. (1981). The evolution of male parental investment in mammals. In D. J. Gubernick & P. H. Klopfer (Eds.), *Parental care in mammals* (pp. 347–387). New York: Plenum Press.

Marlowe, F. (1999). Male care and mating effort among Hadza foragers. *Behavioral Ecology and Sociobiology, 46,* 57–64.

Marlowe, F. (2000). Paternal investment and the human mating system. *Behavioural Processes, 51,* 45–61.

Maynard Smith, J. (1977). Parental investment: A prospective analysis. *Animal Behaviour, 25,* 1–9.

Mitani, J. C., Gros-Louis, J., & Richards, A.F. (1996). Sexual dimorphism, the operational sex-ratio, and the intensity of male competition in polygynous primates. *American Naturalist, 147,* 966–980.

Smuts, B. B., & Gubernick, D. J. (1992). Male–infant relationships in nonhuman primates: Paternal investment or mating effort? In B. Hewlett (Ed.), *Father–child relations: Cultural and biosocial contexts* (pp. 1–30). New York: Aldine.

Trivers, R. L. (1972). Parental investment and sexual selection. In B. Campbell (Ed.), *Sexual selection and the descent of man 1871–1971* (pp. 136–179). Chicago: Aldine.

Trivers, R. L., & Willard, D. E. (1973). Natural selection of parental ability to vary the sex ratio of offspring. *Science, 179,* 90–92.

Wright, J. 1998. Paternity and paternal investment. In T. R. Birkhead & A. P. Moller (Eds.), *Sperm competition and sexual selection* (pp. 117–139). San Diego: Academic Press.

12

Male Migration, Remittances, and Child Outcome Among the Okavango Delta Peoples of Botswana

John Bock
California State University, Fullerton

Sara E. Johnson
California State University, Fullerton

In this chapter, we examine the ways in which remittances by fathers engaged in migratory labor can impact children's growth and development among the Okavango Delta peoples of Botswana. The chapter begins with a presentation of the tripartite model of father involvement originally proposed by Lamb, Pleck, Charnov, and Levine. This is followed by an overview of embodied capital theory, a relatively recent integration of human capital theory from economics with life history theory from evolutionary biology. We then contrast growth-based and experience-based embodied capital as conduits for parental investment by fathers and examine the potential effects of parental investment in developing economies. This is followed by a description of the study community and further explication of the hypotheses to be tested. Following the hypotheses is a description of the data collection and analysis methods. We then present the results of the study, which are followed by a discussion of these results including their implications for our understanding of the effects of male parental investment in this community and broader implications for theoretical development and future research.

The effect of investment of time and resources by fathers on child outcome has been the subject of substantial investigation (see Lamb, 1997; Pleck, 1997 for reviews). Many studies have found gendered effects on children's psychosocial development whereas others have found that the timing of fathers' attention is crit-

ical in assessing the impacts of their investment in offspring. Differential investment of resources by fathers has also been implicated in variation in children's
growth in traditional societies (Sellen 1999) and in some measures of development
in nontraditional societies (Anderson, Kaplan, Lam, & Lancaster, 1999). In this
paper we use an evolutionary approach based in the embodied capital theory of
human life history evolution to examine the effects of father involvement among
the Okavango Delta peoples of Botswana. In this study, the effect of male parental
investment in a traditional society is evaluated using a model that incorporates
both effects on physical growth as well as on cognitive development.

THE TRIPARTITE MODEL
OF FATHER INVOLVEMENT

Lamb, Pleck, Charnov, and Levine (1985, 1987) proposed a model of paternal
behavior and involvement that was among the first to formalize the hypothetical
direction and intensity of effects of father involvement in several domains related to
child outcome. The model specifies three dimensions through which father involvement may impact child outcome: paternal engagement, paternal accessibility, and
paternal responsibility. Engagement refers to interaction between father and offspring, accessibility refers to the availability of the father, and responsibility refers to
the father's ability to recognize offspring needs and procure resources and/or provisioning for his offspring. Numerous studies in both Western and non-Western contexts have attempted to quantify or refine these dimensions (see Palkovitz, 1997),
though most studies have focused on the first two dimensions (Doherty, Kouneski, &
Erickson, 1998) due to the difficulty of operationalizing paternal responsibility.

   For those interested in an evolutionary perspective, the Lamb, Pleck, Charnov,
and Levine model is important in three respects. First, at its heart, it is an evolutionary framework that attempts to explain variation in fathering through an
understanding of the effects of parental investment on fathers' fitness (Lamb et
al., 1985). Second, although since its emergence this model has arguably been the
most influential (in both positive and negative attention) in recent studies of the
effects of father involvement on child outcome, very little of the additional theoretical development related to this model has had an explicitly evolutionary focus.
Third, the basic components of the model, especially with regard to the effects of
direct care and investment of resources, have much in common with recent theoretical developments in our understanding of human life history evolution.

THE EMBODIED CAPITAL THEORY
OF HUMAN LIFE HISTORY EVOLUTION

Kaplan and associates (Kaplan, Lancaster, Bock, & Johnson, 1995; Kaplan, 1996;
Kaplan, Lancaster, Hill, & Hurtado, 2000; Kaplan and Bock, 2001) have pro-

posed a theory of human life history evolution based on returns to investment in embodied capital. This theory integrates human capital theory in economics with life history theory from evolutionary biology by treating the processes of growth, development, and maintenance as somatic investments. Investment in embodied capital has two aspects, the physical and functional. The physical payoff to investment in embodied capital is the actual tissue involved. The functional payoff to investment in embodied capital is manifested in qualities such as strength, immune function, coordination, skill, knowledge and other abilities, which are based in organized somatic tissue (see Kaplan et al., 2000 for a complete treatment). The total of both the physical and functional aspects of embodied capital can be viewed in relation to the capacity to be a competent adult.

Growth-Based and Experience-Based Embodied Capital

We can further distinguish embodied capital into growth-based forms and experience-based forms (Bock, in press). Growth-based forms of embodied capital are attributes like body size, strength, balance, and general coordination. Experience-based forms of embodied capital are attributes such as cognitive function, memory function, task-specific skills, learned knowledge, endurance, and specific coordination. Growth-based forms tend to be more related to general competency, whereas experience-based forms tend to be more related to specific competency. The ability to perform any task is comprised of a suite of both growth-based and experience-based embodied capital. Depending on the physical demands and complexity of the task, we can imagine the gamut from those heavily weighted toward growth-based embodied capital to those nearly entirely dependent on experience-based embodied capital, with many tasks requiring hefty portions of both.

For complex tasks there is a threshold of ability that must be reached before we can consider someone able to perform a task. It is possible for a person to have one or two of the necessary forms of embodied capital but still be unable to perform a task. One must achieve a certain level at each of these components before the threshold of ability is crossed. Even after one is able to perform the task at a rudimentary level, depending on the difficulty of the task, there may be considerable opportunity for improvement.

THE EFFECTS OF PATERNAL INVESTMENT IN DEVELOPING ECONOMIES

This formulation can be used to frame the effects of paternal investment of time and resources on child outcome in terms of the different forms of embodied capital just outlined. In different subsistence ecologies and across different tasks, the amount of investment in growth that would bring a return in learning will vary (Bock, in press). In essence, as growth-based embodied capital constrains the payoff to investment in experience-based embodied capital, there will be diminishing returns to investment in learning. The degree to which growth constrains learning will vary as a function not only of subsistence ecology but also of the economics of production and may be strongly influenced by the value of labor and the opportunity cost to alternative activities. In foraging economies as in all others, the variety of tasks performed can be expected to reflect a number of different levels of growth constraints on payoffs to learning. Investment of resources and time by men in their offspring can be used to build growth-based embodied capital or it can be used to develop experience-based embodied capital. The optimal solution to the trade-off between investment in growth- and experience-based embodied capital is expected to be dependent on the societal based gender- and age-patterning of production, on the specific labor needs of the household, and on the reproductive interests of parents.

A second trade-off in a developing economy is that between traditional and school-based systems of learning and knowledge (Bock 1998, 1999, 2002; Bock & Johnson, 2002; Caldwell, 1980; Lancy, 1996; Akabayashi & Psacharopolous, 1999). Fathers can invest time and resources in developing children's skills and knowledge appropriate to traditional economic pursuits or use those resources to develop children's school curriculum-based skills and knowledge appropriate to a market-incorporated economy. Again, the optimal solution to this trade-off in the forms of experience-based embodied capital is expected to be based on the payoffs to investment in these different forms based on a child's age, gender, and features of the household economy.

When a father is faced with these allocation decisions across a number of offspring, determining the optimal solution quickly becomes a complicated endeavor. In a situation where only one child is involved, assessing the costs and benefits of investment in different forms of embodied capital is relatively clear cut from a theoretical standpoint. With each additional child, this assessment becomes more complex with the addition of opportunity costs and multiple time frames. A parent's reproductive interests are not necessarily congruent with a beneficial outcome to any one child (Blurton Jones, 1993; Bock, 1995, 1999, 2002, in press; Worthman, 2000). Rather, an evolutionary perspective leads us to believe that a parent should be concerned with the totality of his or her reproductive interests and should be willing to act to the detriment of a child if doing so benefits the parent.

The Study Community

These issues are examined using data collected in a multiethnic community of approximately 400 people in the Okavango Delta of northwestern Botswana (for a detailed description of the study community, see Bock, 1995, 1998; Bock &

Johnson, 2002). Several aspects of social and economic organization in this remote rural community made it particularly suited for a study of the impacts of male parental investment on child health, growth, and development. Historically, there have been relatively high levels of male labor migration coupled with very low levels of market incorporation. As a result, at the time of the study there was little cash economy within the community, and almost all residents were deeply involved in traditional economic pursuits. Men who had migrated for labor purposes, however, were able to remit cash to family members residing in the study community. This cash influx distinguished recipients from those without access to cash through the ability to purchase food and other supplies and thus buffer themselves from cyclical perturbations due to variation in rainfall, which heavily impact traditional economic activities such as foraging, farming, fishing, and herding. The low level of market incorporation and cash-based economic activities also made it possible to acquire accurate measures of household productivity, although it should be stated here that it was often difficult to apportion productivity or consumption on the individual level.

School attendance in the community was low. The nearest primary school was in the next community, approximately 30 km away, and children needed to board while attending school. Although there are no school fees in Botswana, the cost of boarding, uniforms, and books, as well as the lost labor, made school costly to parents. At any one time, approximately 25% of the children in the community attended primary or secondary school. Those attending secondary school boarded at communities at least 100 km away. Due to the lack of vehicles and roads, children attending school returned home only sporadically. The low rate of school attendance, however, meant that most children could be observed, allowing for exploration of their role in household and family economy.

Lastly, the community was extremely diverse with regard to traditional economic pursuits. Community members engaged in a wide variety of activities ranging from foraging and fishing to farming to herding, or some combination thereof. The economic diversity meant that children's and adults' time allocation, as well as parental investment in the embodied capital of offspring, could be examined across a number of traditional economic pursuits.

Five ethnic groups are represented: Hambukushu, Dxeriku, Wayeyi, Xanekwe, and Bugakwe. Hambukushu, Dxeriku, and Wayeyi people are Bantus who inhabit the Okavango River drainage from Angola through the Caprivi Strip of Namibia into northern Botswana. Historically, they have participated in mixed economies of farming; fishing, hunting, and the collection of wild plant foods; and pastoralism. Xanekwe and Bugakwe people are San speakers who inhabit the Okavango drainage in Namibia and Botswana. Xanekwe have historically had a riverine orientation in their foraging, whereas Bugakwe have been savanna foragers. The Xanekwe living in the study community practice a mixed economy, but farm at a much less intensive level than the Bantus. Moreover, among 50 Xanekwe, there are only four head of cattle, whereas a typical Bantu homestead of 20 people has an average of 12 head. Bugakwe in this community are largely oriented toward fishing, hunting, and the collection of wild plant foods. None own cattle, and their agricultural fields are very small.

People from all of the ethnic groups live in extended family homesteads based on patrilocal organization. Among the Bantus, polygyny is common, with 45% of the men over age 35 participating in polygynous relationships at any one time. Polygyny is rare among the San speakers. Marriage and reproductive unions, however, are fluid among all the ethnic groups. Multipartnered sexuality is commonplace, and disputes over paternity and child support are common in the tribal court. For all the ethnic groups the norm is for men to marry and become fathers in their 30s.

Most men of all ethnic groups over the age of 35 had worked in migratory labor, usually in the mines of South Africa, for an average of 5 years. Many of the Xanekwe and Bugakwe men over the age of 25 had been soldiers in the South African Defence Force during the bush wars of the 1970s and 1980s. Few women, however, had ventured beyond the next community 30 km away. There was no school, clinic, or borehole, with water drawn from a river source.

Historically, the Bantus represented in this community have all had some degree of matrilineality in their social organization with a tradition of the avunculate (Larson, 1970). In particular, this implies that in earlier times a boy's strongest male influence would not be from his father but from his mother's eldest brother. Both Bugakwe and Xanekwe were strongly influenced by Bantus over at least the last 100 years and also have some degree of matrilineality and the avunculate. The situation is not clear cut, however, because all ethnic groups in the study community have been under strong political and social influence of Tswana-speaking tribes for at least 200 years. The Tswana have a strong tradition of patrilineality, and their social organization and customs regarding marriage, the family, and childrearing have been codified as Botswana's Customary Law. All disputes are settled using this legal code regardless of the ethnic origin of the litigants, and this has had a profound impact on the maintenance of social organization and tradition by non-Tswana groups.

Work in this community began in 1992 as part of a dissertation project focusing on the determinants of children's activities, which in turn was planned to integrate with data collected by Henry Harpending and Jeffrey Kurland on Herero families and children in another part of northern Botswana. It soon became clear that anthropometric measurements were critical as both a factor influencing children's activity profile and as an effect of variation in children's workloads. Measures of household productivity also were integral to the research design both as possible predictors of children's activity profiles and as outcomes of variation in children's work levels. Before work began, every family in the community was visited, and the aims of the project were explained through an interpreter and any questions or comments were addressed. Additionally, the local headman and Village Development Committee planned a *kgotla* (community meeting). This is a traditional means in Botswana of achieving consensus regarding serious issues facing a community. Several days prior to the *kgotla,* messengers were sent to every household and to all outlying areas inviting residents to the meeting. The local councilor and Member of Parliament also attended the *kgotla* meeting. At that time, the goals and methods of the project were explained, and community members had the opportunity to comment and ask questions. Many people availed themselves of this opportunity, and when there were no further questions, a vote was taken. The project was approved, and at that point individual households were approached to gain their consent to participate in data collection. As part of the informed consent process, the goals of the project and data collection methods were again explained to all individuals, and it was made clear to individuals that their participation was entirely voluntary and they could choose to end participation at any time. A subset of eight households was selected to participate in the behavioral observation component of the study. This subset was chosen to represent the diversity of the community but was small enough to allow sufficient repeat measures of individual time allocation.

There was a process of several months of piloting data collection methods, studying the local *lingua franca,* Thimbukushu, and becoming familiar with daily life in the community. We made every effort to be active community members, to participate in community events, and to offer aid and assistance whenever possible. People by then had become aware of the collaborative and participatory nature of the data collection and that a principle aim of the project was to provide information to improve the health and welfare of children in this community. It was only after this period that parents were asked to allow their children to participate. Parents voiced their concerns that participation in data collection would in no way cause risk to their children. As a result, small children were always escorted to and from data collection sites, food and water were always available to children participating, and parents were always welcome to observe and/or participate in measurement. In addition, the involvement of parents and other community members had a very positive influence in setting the tone for communitywide data collection events, resulting in them taking on the characteristics of a school field day or picnic.

There was an additional field session in this community covering most of 1994, and there have been frequent subsequent visits, with the latest occurring in 2001. A second community that was far more market incorporated was included in the study beginning in 1996, with two years of data collection ending in 1997. Again, there have been frequent subsequent visits to this community. Future research in these and other communities will focus on the effects of the HIV/AIDS epidemic on the family and child development in Botswana, which has one of the highest HIV prevalence rates in the world (approximately 36% of adults).

The collaborative and participatory nature of the consent process and of the data collection regime was critical in allowing the collection of multiple forms of data, some of which, such as behavioral observation and household productivity assessment, were quite intrusive. People in the study community came to realize that our intention was that there would be mutual benefits. As one elderly gentleman said to a visitor who asked about our presence, *"Ghana keya ku kukuhonga diko dya ghaghuva popa. Nyanyi ghene kuhuka kukweto gho ku kayenda ghe karanganga ku kuchanga mambapera ku ghagheya ghaghuva she ku mutongora tua karire."* "They have come to learn about our culture and our ways. They will return to where they live far away to write a letter to all the people in the world to tell them that once we were here."

TESTABLE HYPOTHESES

A central theoretical proposition intrinsic to this research is that men face a number of trade-offs in the investment of their time and resources in their children's embodied capital. In essence, men can use time and resources to invest in experience-based or growth-based embodied capital. Paternal investment in the form of time is expected to have its greatest effect on child outcome through learning. In the context of this developing economy, learning is expected to constitute traditional forms of skills and knowledge. Therefore, we expect that paternal investment in the form of time spend will have an effect on the amount of experience-based embodied capital in an offspring. Paternal investment in the form of resources can be used for the achievement of growth-based embodied capital in offspring. We expect that with economic provisioning fathers can affect the growth of their children through access to nutrition and health care. That growth-based embodied capital can be measured both as body size and as strength, skill, coordination, and other growth-based forms of embodied capital. Lastly, paternal investment in the form of resources can be used to acquire experience-based embodied capital in the form of schooling.

In the study community, there are two possible avenues through which the effects of differential paternal investment can be examined. Throughout the developing world male labor migrants send remittances home (Lucas & Stark, 1985). These remittances represent an influx of cash resources that give the remitter far more flexibility in investment decisions than traditional resources, because cash can be dispersed at a controlled rate, focused on specific individuals, or equitably distributed across many individuals. Children of these migrants will face a reduction in the amount of time fathers spend with them, with potential reduction in learning of traditional skills and knowledge. These children, however, will face a potential increase in resource influx and paternal investment that could be used for the acquisition of growth-based embodied capital and experience-based embodied capital in the form of schooling. We expect, therefore, that children of economic migrants will show deficits in traditional skills and knowledge, but will show advantages in growth-based forms of embodied capital. These same children should also be more likely to attend school.

The second avenue is through polygynous marriage. Although the potential for biased investment by fathers has long been acknowledged (Brabin, 1984; Isaac & Freinberg, 1982), detecting these biases has proven elusive (Sellen, 1999). In the context under consideration here, the first, or senior, wife is in a controlling position of some resources (Bock, 1995; Larson, 1970), thereby potentiating any bias in paternal investment. This leads to the expectation that children of senior wives should have advantages in dimensions of both growth- and experience-based embodied capital.

These hypotheses led to a set of predictions regarding the effect of fathers' migratory labor and mothers' polygynous marital status on children's acquisition of different forms of embodied capital. Children of men who are not resident in the community are expected to have lower ability in traditional tasks to the extent that time investment in men is spent in learning those tasks. Given the strong gendered division of labor in this community, these effects should be stronger in boys because they are in the process of acquiring skills and knowledge specific to male roles. This effect should also be related to the skills required to perform a task (see Bock, in press for a review of the relationship between growth- and experience-based embodied capital and the performance of specific tasks). Boys of nonresident fathers, then, should show deficits in performance of skill-intensive tasks.

Those men who are engaged in migratory labor have less time available for their children but greater resources in the form of cash. Therefore, children of men not resident in the community are also expected to have higher levels of paternal investment of resources. This should lead to higher levels of growth-based embodied capital measured as body size, strength, and general physical ability. In terms of task performance, we expect these children to have advantages in the performance of tasks that are less skill dependent and more dependent on body size and strength. The higher level of paternal investment in terms of resources can also be used to acquire experience-based embodied capital through schooling, and children of men not resident in the community should have higher levels of school attendance. Children of senior wives are expected to show advantages on every dimension, receiving higher levels of both resource and time investment from fathers.

Methods

In this analysis, five types of data are used: behavioral observation, anthropometric measurements, tests of performance ability, household demographic data, and household economic data.

Behavioral Observation. The behavioral observation data were used to construct activity profiles for all individuals including children's school attendance. These data consist of instantaneous scan samples collected over the course of 11 months in 1992. Extended family homesteads were sampled on a rotating basis repeatedly over three 4-hour periods, 0600–1000, 1000–1400, and 1400–1800 that roughly correspond to the daylight hours. On an hourly time point, the activity, location, and interactants of all residents of the homestead were noted. For residents who were not present, other residents were asked for that person's activity and location, and this information was verified with the focal subject either on his or her return or later. In addition, the commodity, amount, producer or collector, and recipient of all food brought into the homestead was recorded.

The "Field Days." Anthropometric measurements and tests of general performance ability were collected from 54 girls and 74 boys on three days in 1994—August 28, August 29, and October 8. The first two dates comprised a weekend. In this way, both children who attend school away from the community and those who do not were included. The third date was a "makeup" date that allowed us to measure any child not previously captured. The tests of general performance ability included: throwing for distance, running, and an arm pull on a 25 kg spring balance. Each test was set up as a station, and the children were rotated through the stations in the same order. These test days were organized along the lines of a field day. The community was divided into three parts. Shortly after dawn, the three researchers, each equipped with a list of children ages 3 to 18 from each homestead, ventured into a different part of the community, visiting homesteads and meeting with the most senior person available. Researchers asked permission to test the children in that homestead in a series of throwing, running, and carrying tests as well as to measure the height and weight of the children. Permission was invariably granted. The children were then called together and told to proceed to the researchers' house at a certain time indicated by the position of the sun. These times were staggered to facilitate data collection.

At the end of each of the first two days, we noted which children were absent. The following test day, a special effort was made to impress on those children and responsible adult caretakers that the participation of all children would be of great help to the researchers. At the completion of testing, children were provided with soft drinks, popcorn, and other snacks, and as always, were allowed to use any recreational equipment they desired such as soccer balls, Frisbees, and ball and bat.

Measures of Growth-Based Embodied Capital. Arm pull strength was obtained in order to estimate the effect of strength on task performance. A 25 kg or 50 kg Homs hanging spring balance was attached to a tree trunk. An individual would then sit cross-legged in the sand at such a distance from the tree that the person's arm was fully extended when grabbing the hook on the balance, but not so far that he or she needed to lean forward. A researcher sat or squatted behind the person so that his or her back remained perpendicular to the ground during the test. The participant was instructed to grab the hook with whichever arm was stronger and to pull the hook toward him or her using only the arm, not the back, shoulders, or legs. If a person was using these other body parts, the test was begun again after further instruction. A researcher watched the scale on the spring balance to determine the maximum value that the individual could sustain, rather than a peak value resulting from a quick pull or jerk on the hook. This value was recorded to the nearest kg.

After the arm pull, children were weighed on an Ohaus D10L-M digital scale. Weight was recorded to the nearest tenth kg. Heights were measured using a standard stadiometer attached to a leveling head. These were recorded to the nearest cm. To examine the predicted effect of investment in growth-based embodied capital on body size, children's BMI was calculated (kg/m^2). BMI is a measure of weight for height, or general leanness/plumpness, but controls for greater variation in height than weight and has become a preferred anthropometric tool for evaluating children's growth (McMurray, 1996).

Running speed was tested on the same 50 meter by 5 meter lane used for the throw for distance. The time from a stationary start to the finish line was measured to the hundredth second.

Measures of Skill for Traditionally Male Activities. Experimental return data were collected in 1994 for a number of productive activities. For log cutting, 10 logs approximately 3 meters long and 8 to 9 cm in diameter were obtained. The logs were all from the same variety of hardwood tree. Stripes were painted at 20-cm intervals down the length of each log using white paint. Two axes were procured from local sources. Both these axes had a narrow blade made of spring steel and a handle made from the root bulb of a small tree. One axe was designed for adult men, whereas the other was designed for use by adolescent boys and women. Participants were shown a stripe and were asked to cut the log at that point. People were given the choice of axe. The time taken to cut through the log was measured to the nearest hundredth second using a digital stopwatch, and the diameter of the log at the cut was measured to the nearest mm. If the log had not been severed at 2 minutes, the person was stopped, and the deepest part of the cut measured to the nearest mm. The time limit was for safety reasons, because people who are not skilled at cutting become tired and lose a great deal of accuracy. For children under age 7 the time limit was 1 minute, because children tended to become tired more quickly.

Throw for distance was measured along a 50-meter-by-5 meter lane. Throwing sticks were obtained from a 14-year-old boy, who was asked to cut five sticks of excellent quality. These sticks were nearly identical in weight and length, each being about 30 cm long and weighing between 350 and 450 g. Each child was given three consecutive tries and was told to aim at the tree and throw as far as possible. Distances were measured in meters by pacing from the divot mark the stick left in the sand to the nearest flag.

Measures of Skill for Traditionally Female Activities.   For the mongongo nut processing return rate experiments, a sack of mongongo nuts was bartered
in return for transporting a group to a mongongo tree patch. A woman was then
enlisted to perform the first stage of processing, leaving the nuts with their outer
shell exposed ready to process. For the processing rate experiment, an individual
was given 500 g of whole nuts in the outer shell. These were also counted. The
individual was instructed to process them as if he or she was at home, and the digital timer started. After 15 minutes the individual was told to stop and the number
of nuts processed was counted. The remaining nuts were weighed, as were the
product. In addition, the number of intact inner-shelled nuts was counted, and it is
this quantity that is used in the analysis.

Water-carrying ability was assessed by having the child carry a 1-liter bowl
(measured using a graduated cup) full of water along a 9-meter-by-2-meter lane
marked by surveying flags. At the end of the lane was a pole. The child then
either placed the bowl on his or her head or asked a researcher, sibling, or friend
to place it. Children with recently shaved heads were allowed to use a scarf as a
head wrap, but were not allowed to use it as a donut-shaped support for the bowl.
The children were instructed to walk down the lane to the pole, go around the
pole, and return, while spilling as little water as possible. The children were
instructed not to run. If a child spilled the entire contents of the bowl, the location was marked and measured from the pole to the nearest 10 cm, and it was
noted whether the child had as yet rounded the pole. If a child made it around the
pole and back to the starting line, the water was emptied from the bowl into
the graduated cup, and the amount of water remaining was recorded to the nearest 5 ml.

Measures of Fishing Skill for Both Males and Females.   Fishing return
rates were collected throughout both planned and opportunistic observation of
children between ages 3 and 18 during the period from January to November
1992. Focal follows of individuals were undertaken 12 times a week. Homesteads
were sampled on a rotating basis, as were children within homesteads. The follows lasted 2 hours and consisted of point samples every 10 minutes. At the point
sample, the activity in which the child was engaged, the location, and identity of
coparticipants was recorded. In addition, the time of any resource acquisition was
noted, as well as the type, amount of resource, and method of acquisition.
Weights were obtained using Homs hanging spring balances. A second type of
data collection regarding the fishing return rates was opportunistic in nature.
Most fishing activity either took place or originated at a beach on the central
lagoon. In addition, fishing had a periodicity with respect to the time of day. Most
fishing took place in the midmorning to midafternoon. On selected days this area
was visited prior to the usual start of fishing. All children were offered a hook and
a length of line, including children who would usually be considered too young to
fish. The start and stop times of fishing, the location of the fishing, the time of any

resource acquisition, and the weight of each fish caught were recorded for each child until all children had ceased fishing.

Four types of fishing by children were observed: hook and line from shore and hook and line from a dugout canoe, basin, or basket. There is a sexual difference with respect to these methods. Hook and line fishing from a boat is nearly exclusively a male activity. Younger boys, some girls, and some older boys who cannot find a boat at the time they wish to fish usually do hook and line fishing from shore. Basin and basket fishing are exclusively female activities.

Demography. Interviews regarding household and family demography and economy were conducted in 1992 and 1994. An initial census was conducted asking who resided in each house within each homestead. In addition, data were collected on people who were occasional residents or who were considered residents but were currently elsewhere. The head of the household was then asked how each of these people was related to him or her. Also, reproductive histories were collected for all men over age 20 and all women over age 16, and these data were cross-checked with the census data. Both the census and reproductive history data have been regularly updated since 1992.

Economic Resource Assessment. On a monthly basis, each head of household was asked about nonmonetary and monetary resource flow into the household. He or she was asked what resources, including cattle, were acquired, by whom, and from whom. These data, when combined with the acquisition data collected during the homestead instantaneous scans, give an accurate picture of resource flow. To establish the level of storable resources, a cattle census was conducted for each homestead in 1992, as well as measurement of the entire harvest production for each household in 1992.

Results

The results begin with a discussion of BMI as a function of fathers' migrant status and mothers' polygynous marital status. They continue with a discussion of the impact of fathers' community residential and mothers' polygynous marital status on task performance. The last set of results is concerned with the effects of fathers' migrant status and mothers' polygynous marital status on children's school attendance. For all analyses there are statistical controls for children's age and gender.

Body size. As predicted, father's migrant labor had significant positive effects on body size for both boys and girls (see FIG. 12.1 and FIG. 12.2).

For boys, this effect was focused before age 8 and after age 14. For girls, the effect was consistent for all ages. Over all children, the effect was positive controlling for age and gender (see Table 12.1).

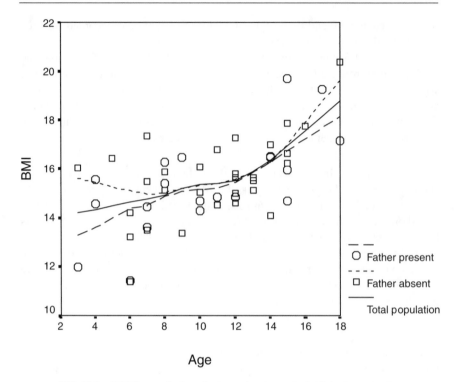

FIG. 12.1.   BMI for age for boys in the study community by father's community
residence status. Boys whose fathers are away from the community have higher
BMI before age 8 and after age 15. The open squares represent boys whose fathers
are not resident in the community, predominantly because they are labor migrants.
Open circles represent boys whose fathers are resident in the community. The
dashed line is a lowess curve fit to the data from boys whose fathers are resident in
the community, whereas the dotted line is a lowess curve fit to the data from boys
whose fathers are not resident in the community. Compare this to the lowess curve
for the total population of boys ages 18 and under represented by the solid line. See
Table 12.2 for results from a general linear model.

As predicted, an independent positive effect was also seen for mothers' polygynous marital status. Controlling for age and gender, children of senior wives had
significantly higher BMI than those of nonsenior wives (see Table 12.2).

Task performance.   Both fathers' community residential status and mothers' polygynous marital status had little effect on task performance in boys in
terms of growth- or experience-based embodied capital (see Table 12.3).

The most strength-intensive tasks, running, throwing for distance, and arm
pull, showed no significant effects. For the most skill-intensive tasks, throwing
for accuracy, fishing, and log cutting, fathers' community residential status only

had significant effects on log cutting. Contrary to expectation, boys of fathers engaged in migrant labor showed higher ability. This result is questionable, how-ever, because the sample size for log cutting is small, and the effect was concen-trated in one 18-year-old. Surprisingly, father absence had no effect on arguably the most skill intensive task, fishing (see FIG. 12.3). A possible explanation for this is that, given the tradition of matrilineality and avunculate in this community, the primary male influence on boys' skill acquisition is not their father but rather their mother's brother. A direction for future research is to analyze these effects.

Mothers' polygynous marital status also showed significant effects only in log cutting, and this finding is questionable for the same reason.

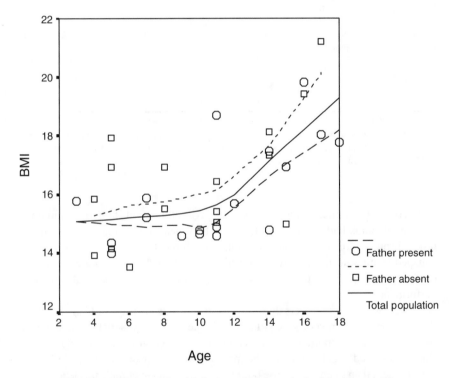

FIG. 12.2.   BMI for age for girls in the study community by father's community residence status. Girls whose fathers are away from the community have consis-tently higher BMI at each age. The open squares represent girls whose fathers are not resident in the community, predominantly because they are labor migrants. Open circles represent girls whose fathers are resident in the community. The dashed line is a lowess curve fit to the data from girls whose fathers are resident in the community, whereas the dotted line is a lowess curve fit to the data from girls whose fathers are not resident in the community. Compare this to the lowess curve for the total population of girls ages 18 and under represented by the solid line. See Table 12.2 for results from a general linear model.

TABLE 12.1
General Linear Model ANOVA of the Effect of Father's Community
Residential Status on Child's BMI

Source	Type III Sum of Squares	df	Mean Square	F	Sig.
Corrected model	219.858	47	4.678	2.703	.001
Intercept	15717.357	1	15717.357	9081.903	.000
Father migrant labor	8.065	1	8.065	4.660	.037
Age	142.076	15	9.472	5.473	.000
Gender	2.715	1	2.715	1.569	.218
Interaction of father migrant labor*Age	31.435	13	2.418	1.397	.206
Interaction of father migrant labor*Gender	.0776	1	.0776	.045	.833
Interaction of age*Gender	16.224	13	1.248	.721	.731
Interaction of father migrant labor*Age*Gender	5.672	2	2.836	1.639	.208
Error	65.764	38	1.731		
Total	21787.117	86			
Corrected total	285.622	85			

Father's status is coded as "Father migrant labor" = 1 if the father is nonresidential in the community and 0 if he is in residence in the community. Results show that, controlling for age, children of non-residential fathers have higher achieved BMI than children of residential fathers. Gender of child had no significant effect.

In contrast to fathers' presence and male skill attainment, fathers' community residential status had significant effects on two measures of girls' growth-based tasks, throwing for distance and arm pull (see Table 12.4). Daughters of fathers engaged in migrant labor were advanced over other girls. There were no significant effects of mothers' polygynous marital status on any measures of girls' task performance.

Daughters of absent fathers threw greater distances at each age until age 10. After that age, the pattern reverses (see FIG. 12.4). One possibility is that strength advantages become less important as girls become more experienced in throwing. Further study is required to determine if father presence is more critical to girls' skill-based development than to boys' because boys have a wider range of male influence due to persisting traditions regarding avuncular relationships with mother's brother.

Girls whose fathers were not resident in the community showed greater arm strength at every age than girls whose fathers were resident (see FIG. 12.5). This suggests that other factors in addition to arm strength influenced girls' performance in the throw for distance.

There was also a significant effect on log-cutting speed, but it was in the opposite direction as expected (see FIG. 12.6). In this community, girls' log-cutting ability was substantially less developed than that of boys because this was an

TABLE 12.2
General Linear Model ANOVA of the Effect of Mother's
Polygynous Status on Child's BMI

Source	Type III Sum of Squares	df	Mean Square	F	Sig.
Corrected model	210.457	47	4.478	2.209	.007
Intercept	15591.174	1	15591.174	7692.317	.000
Age	119.673	15	7.978	3.936	.000
Mother's marital order	10.616	1	10.616	5.238	.028
Gender	1.359	1	1.359	.671	.418
Interaction of age*Mother's marital order	20.736	12	1.728	.853	.599
Interaction of age*Gender	15.155	13	1.166	.575	.858
Interaction of mother's marital order*Gender	.483	1	.483	.238	.628
Interaction of age*Mother's marital order*Gender	3.852	3	1.284	.633	.598
Error	74.993	37	2.027		
Total	21549.965	85			
Corrected total	285.450	84			

Mother's status is coded as "Mother's marital order" = 1 if the mother is the senior wife in a polygynous marriage and 0 if she is not. Results show that, controlling for age, children of senior wives have higher achieved BMI than children of junior wives. Gender of child had no significant effect.

TABLE 12.3
Results of General Linear Model ANOVAs of the Effect of Father's
Community Residential Status and Mother's Polygynous Status
on Boys' Task Performance Ability

Ability	Father Residential	Mother Is Senior Wife
Distance throw	$F = 0.072$, 1 df, ns	$F = 0.403$, 1 df, ns
Running	$F = 0.314$, 1 df, ns	$F = 0.018$, 1 df, ns
Accuracy throw	$F = 0.157$, 1 df, ns	$F = 0.030$, 1 df, ns
Arm pull	$F = 0.418$, 1 df, ns	$F = 0.013$, 1 df, ns
Fishing from boat	$F = 0.268$, 1 df, ns	$F = 0.695$, 1 df, ns
Fishing from shore	$F = 12.117$, 1 df, ns	$F = 0.669$, 1 df, ns
Log-cutting depth	$F = 4.374$, 1 df, ns	$F = 16.651$, 1 df, $p = 0.055$
Log-cutting speed	$F = 41.705$, 1 df, $p = 0.098$	$F = 100.470$, 1 df, $0 = 0.010$

$N = 30$; for log cutting $N = 8$) Controlling for age, boys whose fathers were not residential in the community had greater log-cutting ability, as measured by the depth per cut, than other boys. Father's community residential status had no significant effects on any other ability. Mother's polygynous status had significant effects on both measures of log cutting. Controlling for age, sons of senior wives exhibited significantly greater ability in log cutting.

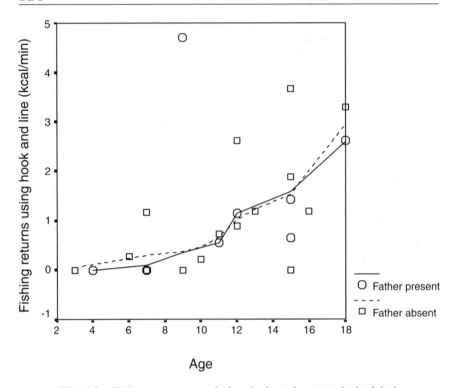

FIG. 12.3.   Fishing returns per age for boys in the study community by father's community residence status. There are no significant differences in return rates at any age. The open squares represent boys whose fathers are not resident in the community, predominantly because they are labor migrants. Open circles represent boys whose fathers are resident in the community. The dashed line is a lowess curve fit to the data from boys whose fathers are resident in the community, whereas the dotted line is a lowess curve fit to the data from boys whose fathers are not resident in the community. See Table 12.3 for results from a general linear model.

activity infrequently performed by girls and women (Bock, in press). For girls, log-cutting proficiency may be more related to strength than skill. The two measures of log-cutting ability can be used to examine this assumption, because log-cutting depth is a measure of accuracy and log-cutting speed is more of a measure of endurance. On the other hand, if this is due to benefits in traditional skill due to father presence, this is an important direction for further investigation. As with the boys' log-cutting experiment small sample size may also be an issue.

School attendance.   Fathers' community residential status had no effect on the probability of a child attending school controlling for age and gender (see Table 12.5), contrary to expectation. This suggests that although remittances have an apparent effect on children's growth, there is no comparable effect on educational attainment. Mothers' polygynous marital status, however, had significant effects on children's school attendance, with children of senior wives substantially more likely to attend school than children of nonsenior wives. This effect was significant for both boys and girls.

Overall, the results provide support for the hypothesis that children of migrant labor fathers will have greater access to resources used for growth. There was a gender difference in the effects of fathers' time on the acquisition of experience-based embodied capital as measured by skill acquisition. In general, there was little effect on boys' skill attainment, whereas there were some effects on girls'. Fathers' migrant labor status had no effect on school attendance, indicating that remittances were not used to further educational attainment. In addition, there is evidence that there was differential allocation of resources across children of different wives in polygynous marriages. Children of the first wife attained greater body size at every age and were also more likely to attend school.

Discussion

In this paper the effect of investment of time and resources by fathers was examined using a model of embodied capital investment. In this model, fathers can impact their children's outcome through investment in either growth- or experience-based embodied capital. Viewed across men, investment can vary due to the availability of men's time and resources. Those men who are engaged in migratory labor have less time available for their children but greater resources in the form of cash. It is expected, then, that children of men who are working away from the community will show deficits in the acquisition of traditional skills and

TABLE 12.4

Results of General Linear Model ANOVAs of the Effect of Father's
Community Residential Status and Mother's Polygynous Status
on Girls' Task Performance Ability

Ability	Father Residential	Mother Is Senior Wife
Distance throw	$F = 11.765, 1\ df, p = 0.006$	$F = 2.185, 1\ df, ns$
Running	$F = 0.266, 1\ df, ns$	$F = 1.363, 1\ df, ns$
Accuracy throw	$F = 0.183, 1\ df, ns$	$F = 0.296, 1\ df, ns$
Arm pull	$F = 7.925, 1\ df, p = 0.017$	$F = 0.562, 1\ df, ns$
Water carrying	$F = 1.059, 1\ df, ns$	$F = 2.433, 1\ df, ns$
Mongongo nut processing	$F = 0.045, 1\ df, ns$	$F = 0.162, 1\ df, ns$
Log cutting depth	$F = 0.668, 1\ df, ns$	$F = 0.992, 1\ df, ns$
Log cutting speed	$F = 11.568, 1\ df, p = 0.077$	$F = 4.978, 1\ df, ns$

$N = 33$; for log cutting and mongongo processing $N = 8$. Controlling for age, girls whose fathers were not residential in the community had greater log-cutting ability, arm pull, and distance throw. Father's community residential status had no significant effects on any other ability. Mother's polygynous status had no significant effects.

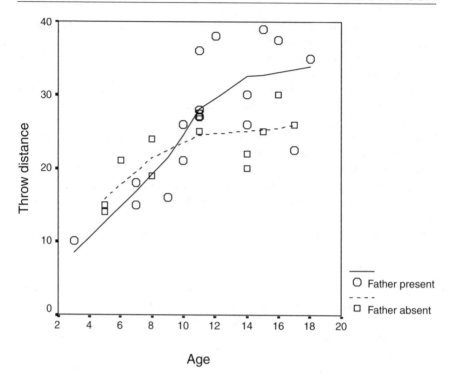

FIG. 12.4.   Throw distance for age for girls in the study community by father's community residence status. Girls whose fathers are away from the community have longer distance throws at earlier ages, but the pattern reverses for ages 9 and above. The open squares represent girls whose fathers are not resident in the community, predominantly because they are labor migrants. Open circles represent girls whose fathers are resident in the community. The dashed line is a lowess curve fit to the data from girls whose fathers are resident in the community, whereas the dotted line is a lowess curve fit to the data from girls whose fathers are not resident in the community. See Table 12.4 for results from a general linear model.

knowledge gained from interaction with fathers, and that in this community with strong gender roles and a gendered division of labor, this will impact boys at greater rates. It is also expected that children of men engaged in migratory labor will show advantages in growth-based embodied capital due to the greater availability of resources. These children are also expected to show higher levels of investment in experience-based embodied capital in the form of schooling due to this higher resource level.

The study found that

- Both sons and daughters of men engaged in migratory labor had greater body size for age.

- Sons show no effect of fathers' absence from the community in task performance related to either strength or traditional skills and knowledge.
- Daughters show mixed effects of fathers' absence, apparently due to higher strength levels of girls whose fathers are engaged in migratory labor.
- There is no effect of male migratory labor on children's school attendance.

It is also hypothesized that differential investment patterns can occur with an individual man, and that these patterns can be seen through polygynous marital contexts. In this community, senior wives have some supposed advantages in resource distribution. Remittances are therefore hypothesized to have greater positive impacts on the children of senior wives.

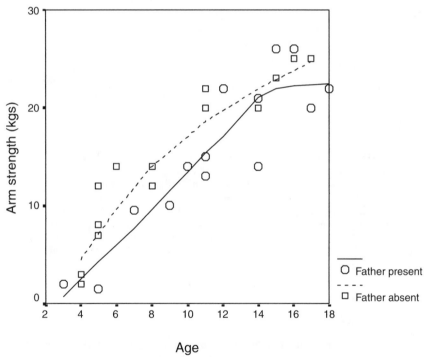

Age

FIG. 12.5. Arm strength for age for girls in the study community by father's community residence status. Girls whose fathers are away from the community have consistently higher strength at each age. The open squares represent girls whose fathers are not resident in the community, predominantly because they are labor migrants. Open circles represent girls whose fathers are resident in the community. The dashed line is a lowess curve fit to the data from girls whose fathers are resident in the community, whereas the dotted line is a lowess curve fit to the data from girls whose fathers are not resident in the community. See Table 12.4 for results from a general linear model.

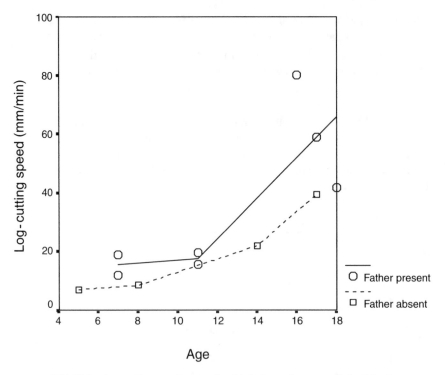

FIG. 12.6.   Log-cutting speed per age for girls in the study community by father's community residence status. Girls whose fathers are resident in the community have consistently higher ability at each age. The open squares represent girls whose fathers are not resident in the community, predominantly because they are labor migrants. Open circles represent girls whose fathers are resident in the community. The dashed line is a lowess curve fit to the data from girls whose fathers are resident in the community, whereas the dotted line is a lowess curve fit to the data from girls whose fathers are not resident in the community. See Table 12.4 for results from a general linear model.

Results show that

- Both sons and daughters of senior wives have greater body size for age.
- There are no effects of mothers' polygynous marital status on task perform-ance.
- Both sons and daughters of senior wives are more likely to attend school.

These results show that in this community male migratory labor and remit-tances can affect child outcome in a number of dimensions. The embodied capital model is useful in understanding the multiple pathways and trade-offs in play. This model also assists us in seeing potential interfaces with other theoretical per-spectives that may benefit our understanding of these processes in the future.

Perhaps the most striking implication of these results is that paternal invest-ment in this community has profound effects on the acquisition of growth-based embodied capital but has more limited effects on the acquisition of experience-based embodied capital. The acquisition of experience-based embodied capital through schooling is, like growth-based embodied capital, a function of paternal resources but not time. The implication of this study is that fathers' material

TABLE 12.5
General Linear Model ANOVA of the Effect of Father's Community Residential
Status and Mother's Polygynous Status on Child's School Attendance

Source	Type III Sum of Squares	df	Mean Square	F	Sig.
Corrected model	1459.315	89	16.397	1.672	.021
Intercept	211.130	1	211.130	21.531	.000
Age	198.191	17	11.658	1.189	.304
Mother's marital order	72.952	1	72.952	7.439	.009
Gender	.804	1	.804	.082	.776
Father migrant labor	.026	1	.026	.003	.959
Interaction of age*Mother's marital order	213.002	14	15.214	1.552	.124
Interaction of age*Gender	151.162	16	9.448	.963	.507
Interaction of mother's marital order*Gender	1.220	1	1.220	.124	.726
Interaction of age*Mother's marital order*Gender	291.513	6	48.586	4.955	.000
Interaction of age*Father migrant labor	132.695	13	10.207	1.041	.428
Interaction of father migrant labor*Mother's marital order	12.907	1	12.907	1.316	.256
Interaction of age*Mother's marital order*Father migrant labor	115.457	4	28.864	2.944	.028
Interaction of gender*Father migrant labor	1.613	1	1.613	.164	.687
Interaction of age*Gender*Father migrant labor	171.237	5	34.247	3.492	.008
Interaction of mother's marital order*Gender*Father migrant labor	.019	1	.019	.002	.965
Interaction of age*Mother's marital order*Gender*Father migrant labor	.019	1	.019	.002	.965
Error	539.333	55	9.806		
Total	2245.000	145			
Corrected total	1998.648	144			

Father's status is coded as "Father migrant labor" = 1 if the father is nonresidential in the communi-ty and 0 if he is in residence in the community. Mother's status is coded as "Mother's marital order" = 1 if the mother is the senior wife in a polygynous marriage and 0 if she is not. Results show that, control-ling for age and gender, children of senior wives have a significantly higher probability of attending school. Father's residential status had no significant effect, nor did child's age or gender. There were sig-nificant interactions, however, between child age, gender, and mother's polygynous status, and between child age, gender, and father's residential status. In the reduced model, these are not significant.

resources impact the measures of child outcome used in this study whereas fathers' time has little or no impact.

These results also, however, need to be situated within the cultural context of the study community. The gender differences in the effect of fathers' presence on children's skill development raises the question, "When are fathers the primary or even a significant male influence on skill acquisition?" Clearly, further investigation will help to understand the effects of male investment from a wider range of potential actors. We must also be cognizant of the action of other individuals in the allocation of remitted funds. Fathers are not remitting directly to children but rather to others, usually wives. An important further step is to analyze the pathway by which money and other resources reaches children and to develop a theoretical framework that accounts for the potential commonality and conflicts of interest among interested parties (see Bock, 1999 for a review of this issue). We hypothesize that remittances from male migrant laborers are resulting in differential access to resources among children, yet we have no direct measures of this. The results of this study support this hypothesis, but direct measures would provide stronger and more detailed evidence and are an important direction for future research.

These findings support many studies in the United States and the developed world, which find that fathers' financial support of children has major positive effects on children's educational attainment and well-being (Argys, Peters, Brooks-Gunn, & Smith, 1998; Baydar & Brooks-Gunn, 1994; King, 1994; Knox, 1996). The Lamb, Pleck, Charnov, and Levine model, however, illustrates the perceived importance of father involvement to children's psychosocial and emotional well being (Black, Dubowitz, & Starr, 1999; Blankenhorn, 1995; Cooley, 1998; Crockett, Eggebeen, & Hawkins, 1993; Harper, 1996; Lamb, 1995; Popenoe, 1996; Pruett, 1998). There have been many attempts to understand cultural construction of normative development in relation to cross-cultural variation in paternal style and involvement, especially in the African context (Engel & Breaux, 1998; Harkness & Super, 1992; Hewlett, 1991; LeVine et al., 1994; Nsamenang, 1987). Although this study does not directly measure children's psychosocial and emotional development in the context of a Euro-American industrial paradigm, this study raises the question of how we should conceptualize these aspects of development in the context of this community. It may well be the case that in communities such as this, the impact of investment is greatest on growth-based embodied capital because access to nutrition and health care is often marginal. Yet, in other contexts, such as Euro-American industrial communities, basic needs are nearly universally met, and as a result investment has much greater impact on psychosocial and emotional development.

According to Weisner's ecocultural concept, culture is the framework in which adaptation and development occur (Weisner, 1997). We must then be especially careful in choosing measures of human development that address the individual's changing adaptation over the life course in the progress from child to adulthood

(Lancy, 1996). We would argue that this means beginning with a conceptualization of the constituents of adult competency in a given cultural context, and then relating features of child development to achieving adult competency in several domains. The role of father involvement, then, becomes related to cultural context and moves us away from a more rigid normative approach. Our current understanding of the evolution of the human life course leads us to the conclusion that humans have a great deal of developmental flexibility in their responses to environmental variation, and that flexibility itself is the result of natural selection (Potts, 1998; Worthman, 2000).

In the cultural and socioecological context of rural Botswana in the 1990s, one might argue that the most lasting positive effect of a father's involvement in a child's psychosocial and emotional development was to have ensured the child had a full belly, received medical care when he or she was sick, and had some symbols of contact with the urban life. In this context, the trade-off between time and resources might always favor resources. It is essential that we firmly ground studies of child development in the reality of specific time and place. This is not to say that Lamb and colleagues might not be right, but only to illuminate the complexity of determining the optimal kinds and degrees of father involvement in cross-cultural contexts.

REFERENCES

Akabayashi, H., & Psacharaopoulos, G. (1999). The trade-off between child labour and human capital formation: A Tanzanian case study. *Journal of Development Studies, 35,* 120–140.

Anderson, K. G., Kaplan, H. S., Lam, D., & Lancaster, J. B. (1999). Paternal care by genetic fathers and stepfathers II: Reports by Xhosa high school students. *Evolution and Human Behavior, 20,* 433–451.

Argys, L. M., Peters, H. E., Brooks-Gunn, J., & Smith, J. R. (1998). The impact of child support on cognitive outcomes of young children. *Demography, 35,* 159–173.

Baydar, N., & Brooks-Gunn, J. (1994). The dynamics of child support and its consequences for children. In I. Garfinkel, S. S. McLanahan, & P. K. Robins (Eds.), *Child support and child well-being* (pp. 257–279). Washington: Urban Institute Press.

Black, M. M., Dubowitz, H., & Starr, R. H. (1999). African American fathers in low income, urban families: Development, behavior, and home environment of their three-year-old children. *Child Development, 70,* 967–978.

Blurton Jones, N. (1993). The lives of hunter-gather children: Effects of parental behavior and parental reproductive strategy. In M. E. Pereira and L. A. Fairbanks, (Eds.), *Juvenile Primates* (pp. 309–326), New York: Oxford University Press.

Blankenhorn, D. (1995). *Fatherless America.* New York: Basic Books.

Bock, J. (2002). Evolutionary demography and intrahousehold time allocation: Schooling and children's labor among the Okavango Delta peoples of Botswana. *American Journal of Human Biology 14*(2):206–221.

Bock, J. (in press). Learning, life history, and productivity: Children's lives in the Okavango Delta, Botswana. *Human Nature.*

Bock, J. (1999). Evolutionary approaches to population: Implications for research and policy. *Population and Environment, 21,* 193–222.

Bock, J. (1998). Economic development and cultural change among the Okavango Delta peoples of Botswana. *Botswana Notes and Records, 30,* 27–44.

Bock, J. (1995). *The determinants of variation in children's activities in a southern African community.* Unpublished Ph.D. dissertation, University of New Mexico, Albuquerque.

Bock, J., & Johnson, S. E. (2002). The Okavango Delta Peoples of Botswana. In R. K. Hitchcock & A. J. Osborn (Eds.), *Endangered peoples of Africa and the Middle East.* New York: Greenwood.

Brabin, L. (1984). Polygyny: An indicator of nutritional stress in African agricultural societies. *Africa, 54,* 31–45.

Caldwell, J. C. (1980). Mass education as a determinant of the timing of fertility decline. *Population and Development Review, 6,* 225–255.

Cooley, R. L. (1998). Children's socialization experiences and functioning in single-mother households: The importance of fathers and other men. *Child Development, 69,* 219–230.

Crockett, L. J., Eggebeen, D. J., & Hawkins, A. J. (1993). Fathers' presence and young children's behavioral and cognitive adjustment. *Journal of Family Issues, 14,* 355–377.

Doherty, W. J., Kouneski, E. F., & Erickson, M. F. (1998). Responsible fathering: An overview and conceptual framework. *Journal of Marriage and the Family, 60,* 277–292.

Engel, P., & Breaux, C. (1998). Fathers' involvement with children: Perspectives from developing countries. *Social Policy Report, 12,* 1–23.

Harkness, S., & Super, C. M. (1992). Shared child care in East Africa: Sociocultural origins and developmental consequences. In M. Lamb, K. Sternberg, C.-P. Hwang, & A. Broberg (Eds.), *Child care in context: Cross-cultural perspectives* (pp. 441–459). Hillsdale, NJ: Lawrence Erlbaum Associates.

Harper, C. C. (1996). *From playpen to federal pen: Family instability and youth crime.* Unpublished Ph.D. dissertation, Princeton University.

Hewlett, B. S. (1991). *Intimate fathers: The nature and context of Aka Pygmy paternal infant care.* Ann Arbor: University of Michigan Press.

Isaac, B., & Freinberg, W. (1982). Marital form and infant survival among the Mende of rural upper Barbara kingdom, Sierra Leone. *Human Biology, 54,* 627–634.

Kaplan, H. S. (1996). A theory of fertility and parental investment in traditional and modern human societies. *Yearbook of Physical Anthropology, 39,* 91–135.

Kaplan, H. S., & Bock, J. (2001). The embodied capital of human life history evolution. In J. M. Hoem (Ed.), *International encyclopedia of the social and behavioral sciences: Demography* (pp. 5561–5568). (Editors-in-chief N. J. Smelser and P. B. Baltes). New York: Elsevier.

Kaplan, H. S., J. B. Lancaster, J. Bock, & S. E. Johnson. (1995). Does observed fertility maximize fitness among New Mexican men? A test of an optimality model and a new theory of parental investment in the embodied capital of offspring. *Human Nature, 6,* 325–360.

Kaplan, H. S., J. B. Lancaster, K. Hill, & A. M. Hurtado. (2000). A theory of human life history evolution: Diet, intelligence, and longevity. *Evolutionary Anthropology, 9,* 156–185.

King, V. (1994). Nonresident father involvement and child well-being: Can dads make a difference? *Journal of Family Issues, 15,* 78–96.

Knox, V. W. (1996). The effects of child support payments on developmental outcomes for elementary school-age children. *Journal of Human Resources, 31,* 817–840.

Lamb, M. E. (1997). Fathers and child development: An introductory overview and guide. In M. E. Lamb (Ed.), *The role of the father in child development* (3rd ed., pp. 1–18). New York: Wiley.

Lamb, M. E. (1995). Paternal influences on child development. In M. van Dongen, G. Frinking, & M. Jacobs (Eds.), *Changing fatherhood: A multidisciplinary perspective* (pp. 145–157). Amsterdam: Thesis.

Lamb, M. E., Pleck, J. H., Charnov, E. L., & Levine, J. A. (1987). A biosocial perspective on paternal behavior and involvement. In J. B. Lancaster, J. Altmann, A. S. Rossi, & L. R. Sherrod (Eds.), *Parenting across the life span: Biosocial dimensions* (pp. 111–142). New York: Aldine de Gruyter.

Lamb, M. E., Pleck, J. H., Charnov, E. L., & Levine, J. A. (1985). Paternal behavior in humans. *American Zoologist, 25,* 883–894.

Lancy, D. F. (1996). *Playing on the mother ground: Cultural routines for children's development*. New York: Guilford Press.

Larson, T. J. (1970). The Hambukushu of Ngamiland. *Botswana Notes and Records, 2,* 29–44.

LeVine, R. A., Dixon, S., LeVine, S., Richman, A., Leiderman, P. H., Keefer, C. H., & Brazelton, T. B. (1994). *Child care and culture: Lessons from Africa*. New York: Cambridge University Press.

Lucas, R. E., & Stark, O. (1985). Motivations to remit: Evidence from Botswana. *Journal of Political Economy, 93,* 901–918.

McMurray, C. (1996). Cross-sectional anthropometry: What can it tell us about the health of young children? *Health Transition Review, 6,* 147–168.

Nsamenang, B. A. (1987). A West-African perspective. In M. E. Lamb (Ed.), *The father's role: Cross-cultural perspectives* (pp. 273–293). Hillsdale, NJ: Lawrence Erlbaum Associates.

Palkovitz, R. (1997). Reconstructing "involvement": Expanding conceptualizations of men's caring in contemporary families. In A. J. Hawkins, & D. C. Dollahite (Eds.), *Generative fathering: Beyond deficit perspectives* (pp. 200–216). Thousand Oaks, CA: Sage.

Pleck, J. H. (1997). Paternal involvement: Levels, sources, and consequences. In M. E. Lamb (Ed.), *The role of the father in child development* (3rd ed., pp. 66–103). New York: Wiley.

Popenoe, D. (1996). *Life without father*. New York: Free Press.

Potts, R. (1998). Variability selection in hominid evolution. *Evolutionary Anthropology, 7,* 81–96.

Pruett, K. D. (1988). Father's influence in the development of infant's relationships. *Acta Paediatrica Scandanavia, 344,* 43–53.

Sellen, D. W. (1999). Polygyny and child growth in a traditional pastoral society: The case of the Datoga of Tanzania. *Human Nature, 10,* 329–371.

Weisner, T. S. (1997). The ecocultural project of human development: Why ethnography and its findings matter. *Ethos, 25,* 177–190.

Worthman, C. M. (2000). Evolutionary perspectives on the onset of puberty. In W. R. Trevathan, J. J. McKenna, & E. O. Smith (Eds.), *Evolutionary Medicine* (pp. 134–164). New York: Oxford University Press.

13

Evolutionary Theory and Reproductive Responses to Father Absence: Implications of Kin Selection and the Reproductive Returns to Mating and Parenting Effort

David Waynforth
University of New Mexico

Evolutionary theorists are in the business of seeking ultimate explanations for behavior. Ultimate explanations concern why a behavior or trait would have evolved by Darwinian natural or sexual selection and would therefore be adaptive in particular environments. This is in contrast to what is termed *proximate explanation,* which is usually about more immediate types of motivation, an example being understanding the hormonal underpinnings of a behavior. The topic of father absence due to divorce has not escaped the attention of evolutionary theorists seeking ultimate explanation for its patterns and effects. Many readers may initially pose the question, "Why apply evolutionary theory to father absence?" One answer is that evolutionary theorists were bound to find father absence interesting because reproductive life-history parameters of children from father-absent homes tend to be affected. Variation in life-history parameters, such as age at first reproduction, are known to be major determinants of lifetime reproductive output and of genetic fitness (genetic contribution to future generations). Hence, father absence appears to be associated with the very traits that are the fundamental focus of study for evolutionary research, and due to this, it is likely that researchers working in evolutionary psychology, anthropology, and human biology will continue to try to understand it from an evolutionary perspective.

The first part of this chapter focuses on a particularly influential ultimate explanation for the pattern of events that appear to be typically associated with father-
absent household structure in industrialized countries and its link to attachment theory in psychology. Utilizing data drawn from a hunter–gatherer group (Ache) and a
largely subsistence-level horticulturalist population (Maya), I then examine whether
being raised father-absent appears to have similar consequences in traditional societies. This includes tests of being raised father-absent and the timing of first birth,
paternal orientation, and testosterone cues in Mayan men. After concluding that the
existing evolutionary framework for interpreting reproductive strategies that result
from being raised father-absent is not consistent with some findings from the Maya
and Ache, an evolutionary ecological approach is offered. Instead of being focused
on attachment and child development, attention is given to how reproductive payoffs
for different categories of behavior (mating effort, parenting, and nepotism) differ
for men raised with their father absent as opposed to those raised father-present. Following this, some attention is given to another aspect of evolutionary theory that
could be applied to the topic of father absence, involving life-history theory and relationships between risk and reproductive strategies. Given the chapter's focus on
men, women's reproductive strategies as a function of father-absent rearing are then
given some consideration, followed by a summary and conclusions.

A THEORY OF CHILDHOOD
ENVIRONMENT AND REPRODUCTIVE
STRATEGY

Patricia Draper and Henry Harpending sparked the genesis of much of the work
on evolution and father-absent household structure that has been published since
the 1980s. Their 1982 paper posited that children are sensitive to being raised in
father-absent versus present family structure, and that this feature of early environment kicks off a sequence of developmental effects. The developmental trajec-
tory of those raised in homes with father absence due to divorce culminates in
early maturation, sexuality, and first reproduction. This empirical pattern had
already been observed (e.g., Whiting, 1965), but Draper and Harpending's contribution was to attach evolutionary logic to why the pattern should exist. Their
argument can be summarized for male reproductive strategies as follows: males
who perceive during childhood that the environmentally appropriate reproductive
strategy does not involve forming stable unions will develop behavioral strategies
suited to low male parental care mating systems, including intense direct
male–male competition for access to females and aggression. On the other hand,
males growing up in mating systems in which they receive and perceive high levels of male parental involvement will correspondingly develop a high paternal
care strategy and be more interested in being able to secure resources in the long
term for sustained parental investment. The corresponding female strategy in high

male care systems is to very carefully choose an investing male, being careful not to reproduce in a short-term union. In high male investment systems, both sexes pay mate searching time costs, because all or most reproductive effort will be tied up in a single mate. This is likely to delay first reproduction. When females do not perceive a need for high paternal investment from their mate, there is no need to pay the costs associated with establishing a long-term sexual union, and early maturation and reproduction may proceed at an early age.

Draper and Harpending refined their model in 1988, but the next major advance for their idea came with the assimilation of attachment theory to their model of developmental strategies. Attachment theory offered a mechanism through which father-absent household structure could act on behavior to produce the adaptive outcomes that Draper and Harpending had originally proposed. In a 1991 paper, Jay Belsky, Laurence Steinberg, and Patricia Draper introduced the idea of psychological attachment as a key mediator between father absence and reproductive strategy. In their model, family context, including father-absent or father-present status, was theorized to cause differences in childrearing styles. In families with single parenthood, the concomitant stress involved in this situation was expected to lead to harsh and inconsistent parenting. This would lead to insecurely attached children, who in turn would mature rapidly and engage in early sexual activity in short-term unions. The concept of attachment and its definition had been laid out previously by Bowlby (1969) and others: insecurely attached individuals display aggressive behavior, particularly if male, tend to be anxious and depressed, particularly if female, and see others as uncaring and untrustworthy. As a consequence, insecurely attached individuals experience difficulty in establishing long-term relationships. Belsky's proposition was that the attachment process appropriately prepares children for the existing "mating environment" of short-term unions with little paternal investment or long-term unions with significant male investment and willingness to delay reproduction until a suitable mate can be located. Belsky et al. (1991) thus incorporated existing research in psychology to the general argument for adaptive reproductive strategies as a function of family context put forward by Draper and Harpending (1982, 1988). Belsky et al. backed up their theory of incipient mating strategies with an impressive number of studies linking the pieces of their argument: that family context is associated with particular childrearing styles and that these variables tend to predict attachment and behaviors indicative of reproductive strategy. Readers interested in these studies should refer to Belsky et al.'s (1991) paper.

In 1997 I included variables relevant to testing the Draper and Harpending and Belsky, Steinberg, and Draper model (which I shall refer to as the "psychosocial stress" model) in field research on mating strategies of male Maya horticulturalists living in Belize, Central America. I felt that it was key that variables such as father absence should be associated with reproductive variables not only in industrialized nations but also in traditional societies with predemographic transition fertility regimes. To test evolutionary hypotheses in traditional societies is one way to get closer to looking at humans living in conditions that would have prevailed during the bulk of human evolution. There was evidence, for example, that father absence leads to early first reproduction in North America and Australia, but it had not, and still has not absolutely, been established that this very fundamental link in the Draper and Harpending and Belsky, Steinberg, and Draper models holds in traditional societies. Thus, the research question that I wished to answer in Belize was whether father absence and attachment have similar reproductive consequences under conditions more similar in important ways to our environment of evolutionary adaptedness (typically abbreviated as EEA). I also had at my disposal some relevant data collected in more than 20 years of research on the lives of Ache hunter–gatherers in Eastern Paraguay by Kim Hill and Magdalena Hurtado. Of course, information gathered from a few modern nonindustrialized societies will give us a less-than-perfect window to our EEA, but the Ache in particular subsist as hunter–gatherers much like the humans that existed up until the spread of agriculture.

FATHER ABSENCE AND REPRODUCTIVE STRATEGY IN THE MAYA AND ACHE

Those studying evolution and human behavior often assume for the sake of convenience that we evolved in a *single* environment type, or EEA. The Ache and Maya environments, if they represent something approximating our EEA, are dramatically different social environments in many ways. Although they both have fertility regimes typical of societies that have not undergone industrialization, as well as relatively high morbidity and child mortality rates, they differ substantially in marital patterns. Ache marriages, which are almost always monogamous, tend not to be enduring. On average, Ache men marry nine times in their lifetime (Hill & Hurtado, 1996). In contrast, in the Mayan sample, few men married more than once. Both the Ache and Maya have experienced change due to contact with other groups. The Ache, since contact with the outside world during the 1970s, have ceased existing solely as hunter–gatherers and are now settled on permanent reservations. The Maya of Western Belize have been in contact with other groups for well over 100 years. Many inhabitants of my study site are descendants of refugees from the Yucatan in Mexico or from highland Guatemala and still maintain their separate Mayan languages. Both the Ache and Maya have had sustained contact with Christian missionaries. In Belize, evangelical missionaries from North America have been particularly persistent in their attempts to convert Maya. The effect of efforts of missionaries on Ache and Mayan mating systems is difficult to determine. Ache marriages, since settlement on reservations, have become more enduring (Hill & Hurtado, 1996). It is unlikely that the Mayan general pattern of lifetime monogamous marriage represents a recent change. Whatever changes have occurred in the Ache and Maya in recent decades, for the Maya there is a high social value placed on father involvement with their children and on stable family relations. The Ache data analyzed here show a high rate of father-absent household structure, and the social importance of father presence is almost certainly much lower than in the Maya.

Father Absence and Age at First Reproduction in the Maya and Ache

Analysis of Ache and Mayan men's age at first reproduction was initially report-ed in Waynforth, Hurtado, and Hill (1998). The analyses presented here include these results and expand on them. Data on the age at first birth of Ache women and their father-absence status (due to marital separation) have not previously been reported. These data are included to back up the data on men and to make a general case for the effect that father absence will tend to have on the timing of first reproduction: women's reproductive strategies will not be considered in detail in this chapter. This is not because they are not interesting, but because there are differences in the implications of father absence on female reproductive strategies that deserve a paper in their own right.

Father absence had to be measured quite differently for the two populations. For the Maya, it was collected through interviews as the number of years that the subject's biological father resided in the subject's household, up until age 18. Cases in which the father was not present due to his death were omitted from all analyses, because the effects of father absence due to death may not be the same as for father absence due to marital dissolution (e.g., Hetherington, 1972). For the Ache, the data consisted of the number of children men and women had in each marriage, making it impossible to obtain the number of years of father presence in the same way. Instead, the proportion of children that the father had with the sub-ject's mother was calculated for male subjects. For example, if the father only had children with the subject's mother, the proportion equals 1, and lower values indi-cate that the father had children with more women. For female subjects, the pro-portion of the mother's children that she had with the subject's father was used. The resulting variable represents not only whether the subject was raised in the absence of their biological father, but also indicates the reproductive strategy of the subject's same-sex parent (i.e., it gives a measure of how many of the same sex parent's marriages ended, not just whether the marriage to the subject's other bio-logical parent ended). So it turns out that this limitation in the Ache database with regard to measuring father absence can be viewed as a particularly interesting test of the psychosocial stress theory, because it comes closer to testing whether chil-dren respond closely to the reproductive strategies of their same-sex parents.

Calculating ages at first birth for Ache was also methodologically problematic. Birth dates are known for all Ache born after 1976, but prior to Hill and Hurtado's record keeping, ages had to be determined by using relative age lists (for a detailed description of this method and of the difficulties involved in achieving accurate age estimates in an illiterate population, see Hill & Hurtado 1996, p. 120). A system of birth records and certificates for the Maya was originally established by British colonial authorities, and most men in the Mayan sample had records of and/or knew the year in which they and their children were born, although by no means are all births recorded by the government.

As originally reported in Waynforth, Hurtado, and Hill (1998), for Mayan men, the number of years of father presence in the subject's household was significantly negatively associated with age at first birth, with birth year controlled for in the time-to-event statistical model (Gamma LIFEREG estimate $= -0.012$, Chi-squared $= 4.46$, $df = 1$, $p = 0.03$, $n = 50$). The statistical test used took account for the fact that not everyone in the sample had experienced the outcome variable of first birth or fatherhood. For a detailed description of time-to-event modeling and when it is appropriate to apply it, see Collett (1994). This result was counter to the prediction, which was that father absence would lead to early first reproduction. For Ache men, the result was nonsignificant in the same direction (estimate $= -0.08$, Chi-squared $= 1.56$, $df = 1$, $p = 0.21$, $n = 272$). Again, birth year was controlled for in the regression model to partial out any shifts through time in age at first reproduction. To avoid bias toward fathers with fewer children appearing to have more stable marriages simply because they had fewer children, the total number of children that the father had was also controlled for in the statistical model of Ache age at first reproduction.

For Ache women, a similar pattern emerged: the more men that female subjects' mothers had children with, the later the subject tended to have her first child (LIFEREG estimate $= -0.16$, Chi-squared $= 12.00$, $df = 1$, $p = 0.0005$). The statistical model included three control variables: the total number of children that the mother had, the subject's birth year (see previous discussion for explanations), and the mother's age at first birth, as an attempt to partial out genetically heritable effects. Figure 13.1 graphically displays the tendency for father-absent women to have later ages at first birth. To produce this graph, women whose mothers never had children with men other than the subject's father were compared with those whose mother had children with two or more men. What Fig. 13.1 shows is that a higher proportion of father-present women experience first birth in their teens and early 20s. By age 24, equal proportions of father-absent and father-present women have had a child. The SAS LIFETEST analysis used to generate Fig. 13.1 revealed that the difference between the two groups is statistically significant over the early reproductive years (Wilcoxon Chi-squared $= 6.33$, $df = 1$, $p = 0.02$, $n = 199$).

Also of interest in the model of Ache women's first birth, women's ages at first birth were not significantly associated with their mothers' ages at first birth (LIFEREG estimate $= -0.01$, Chi-squared $= 0.27$, $df = 1$, $p = 0.61$). It has been argued that most of the variance in age at first reproduction can be explained by genetic factors. In the Ache case, genetic influences appear to have no effect.

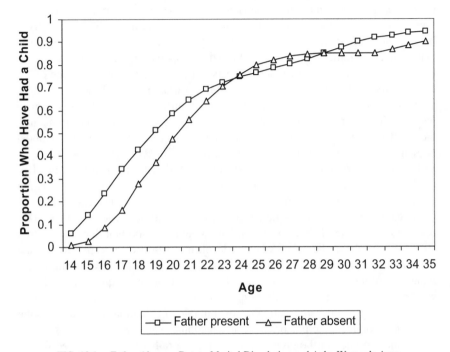

FIG. 13.1.   Father Absence Due to Marital Dissolution and Ache Women's Ages at First Birth. Data stratified by whether or not women's mothers ever had children with more than one man.

FATHER ABSENCE, MATING, AND PARENTAL ORIENTATION IN MAYAN MEN

Father absence, although not showing an association with early first reproduction, was consistent with the psychosocial stress model when data on Mayan men's self-reported willingness to maintain sexual relationships were analyzed (Waynforth, Hurtado, & Hill, 1998). Before going on to further discussion of the preceding findings on the timing of first reproduction, I will present this and other analyses of Mayan men's reproductive strategies that are associated with father-absent rearing, so that the entire pattern of findings can be evaluated together.

The sample of Mayan men was asked to rate their own performance of a number of activities related to the maintenance of sexual relationships with women. Because the psychosocial stress model predicts that father-absent individuals will show preference for short-term sexual unions without extensive continued paternal support of children, the prediction was that men would show a lack of effort toward maintenance of marriage or sexual relationships with women in general. The variables contributing to the self-rated measure were constructed using responses to the following statements about men's behavior in relationships: I frequently promise commitment or marriage; I try to be sensitive to her needs; I stay home to care for her when she is ill; I sacrifice spending time with my friends to be with her; I frequently run errands for my partner; I frequently do what she wants me to do rather than what I want to do. Responses were given on a Likert-type scale according to how much subjects felt that they actually did each of the things listed and were collapsed into a single variable using Principal Components Analysis (for more detail, see Waynforth, Hurtado, & Hill, 1998). Men who had experienced more years of father absence assessed their relationship maintenance effort as being lower than that of father-present men (in a regression model with age controlled for, beta $= 0.19$, $T = 2.50$, $p = 0.02$).

In order to expand on the analyses shown in Waynforth, Hurtado, and Hill (1998), similar methods to those applied were used to assess men's orientation toward paternal care, in both its financial and direct-care forms. The statements presented to men were: I stay home to be with my children whenever I can; I do not go to work when I have a sick child at home; it is important that my children attend school above the primary school level; it is worthwhile to pay for private schooling. Again, responses to these statements were recorded on a 7-point Likert scale according to how strongly the subject felt about each question, and they were reduced to a single variable using Principal Components Analysis. The first Principal Component, representing the overall rate of performance or rating of the importance of the paternal orientation questions, was significantly associated with father absence in the predicted way in a one-tailed test: men raised father-absent reported less orientation toward valuing paternal contribution (in an age-controlled linear regression model, Beta $= 0.12$, $T = 1.69$, $p = 0.04$, $n = 50$).

FATHER ABSENCE AND FACIAL TESTOSTERONE CUES IN MAYAN MEN

The success of father absence as a predictor of self-rated lack of orientation toward paternal care and relationship maintenance led me to seek corroborative evidence from the Mayan men's database. Testosterone appears to be associated, among other things, with many of the male behaviors predicted to be causally related to father-absent rearing in the psychosocial stress model. Booth and Dabbs (1993) found that men with higher testosterone levels were more likely to separate and divorce their wives. High testosterone levels are also associated with indicators of high mating effort, such as more frequent thoughts about sex (Udry, 1988) and more sex partners (Udry, 1988; Dabbs & Morris, 1990).

Several masculine features of male faces indicate the presence of testosterone during development. Evidence of the link between testosterone and masculine facial architecture can be seen in a particularly interesting experimental study, which used boys who showed no signs of puberty at age 14 or older. The boys were assigned to a treatment group or a control group. The treatment group was given regular low doses of testosterone. At the end of the experiment, the boys who had received testosterone showed more masculinized facial architecture than the control group (Verdonck, Gaethofs, Carels, & de Zegher, 1999). For the Mayan sample of men, two masculine features that can be easily measured from frontal facial photographs—cheekbone prominence and mandibular robusticity— were recorded and added together to create a measure of facial testosterone. Cheekbone prominence was measured as the width of the face at its widest point minus the width of the face at the mouth, divided by face height. Mandibular robusticity was measured as chin length: the distance from the bottom of the lower lip and the tip of the chin, again, divided by face height. All distances were measured in pixels using Scion Image software.

The result of the analysis of Mayan men's facial testosterone cues were consistent with the self-rated relationship maintenance and paternal orientation patterns: men raised father-absent had significantly larger facial testosterone cues (in an age-controlled regression model, Beta $= -0.004$, $T = -2.10$, $p = 0.041$).

AN EVALUATION OF THE PSYCHOSOCIAL STRESS MODEL

To summarize so far, we found that counter to expectations, in Mayan men and Ache women, father absence was associated with later, rather than earlier, reproduction. Yet, consistent with the psychosocial stress model, father-absent Mayan men were less oriented toward maintaining their sexual relationships and parenting and had larger facial testosterone cues.

In industrialized societies, father-absent household structure or family stress usually results in early ages at first birth and/or early reproductive maturation (e.g., Kim, Smith, & Palermiti, 1997; Surbey, 1990; Moffitt, Caspi, & Belsky, 1992; Jones, Leeton, McLeod, & Wood, 1972). However, the Ache and Mayan findings on father absence strongly suggest that in conditions more like those in which humans evolved, early maturation and reproduction cannot be an adaptive response to father absence, because the pattern simply appears not to exist in small-scale nonindustrialized groups.

For Mayan men, the disadvantage of late first fatherhood leads to lower lifetime reproductive success: in a statistical model predicting offspring number (with age and age squared controlled for), age at first fatherhood was strongly associated with lower fertility (Beta $= -0.28$, $T = -7.00$, $p = 0.0001$).

The findings regarding the timing of first reproduction seem to suggest that the psychosocial stress model is inadequate. Indeed, recent research indicates a move away from this model and a focus instead on attachment rather than father absence (e.g., Belsky, 1997; Chisholm, 1999a). This may be because father absence can be viewed as a predictor of attachment, rather than an important causal variable in its own right. Whether or not father absence can be viewed as a root cause of incipient reproductive strategies, any theory that predicts reproductive strategies as mechanistic responses to rearing conditions faces a problem. The problem is simply this: individuals that can respond reproductively to the current conditions that they face would outreproduce individuals tracked from childhood (through experience) to model their reproductive strategy on that of their parents. To maximize reproductive success, individuals should determine their reproductive strategy using their own personal situation or characteristics. Associations between father-absent rearing and reproductive strategy may only occur because father absence creates a common or typical situation that these individuals face when formulating their reproductive strategies. The question then becomes, what exactly constitutes this particular situation, and what would be the fitness-maximizing approach to it? In the next sections of this chapter, these questions are considered.

AN EVOLUTIONARY ECOLOGICAL APPROACH TO FATHER ABSENCE

The psychosocial stress model assumed that being oriented toward short-term mating produces the highest fitness returns in environments with low-existing pair-bond stability. Evolutionary ecologists typically pay a great deal of attention to theoretical and actual fitness consequences of behavior, and I will use this approach to pay careful attention to how fitness and mating strategies might vary according to father-absence status.

Questions relevant to reproductive strategy decisions and father absence have in the past been addressed as mate desertion versus parental care problems (e.g., Hurtado & Hill, 1992; Parker & McNair, 1978; Trivers, 1972). This body of theory generally predicts that male reproductive decisions should be governed by the fitness payoffs to parental care and mating effort. If men receive high fitness returns to paternal care (in the form of improved offspring survival and competitiveness at maturity) and at the same time low benefits to attempting to seek new mating opportunities, then marital stability should be high. Conversely, when the male parenting contribution makes little difference to offspring survival, and new mating opportunities are relatively easy to attain, marital stability should tend to be low (Hurtado & Hill, 1992). However, even if the returns to male parental investment are very high (as they appear to be in the Ache) the optimal male mating strategy can still involve a high emphasis on mating effort and, as a consequence, marital instability, if the returns to mating effort are also high (i.e., sexual access to new partners is relatively easy) (Hurtado & Hill, 1992). The important message from this is that to predict mating strategy, the returns to other opportunities have to be considered simultaneously.

To apply a simple evolutionary ecological theoretical approach to the decisions of offspring who are the product of stable or unstable (father-absent) unions, the conditions created by father-absent rearing that are relevant to offspring repro-ductive decisions need to be considered. Here, I focus on two likely conditions: that the children of father-absent homes face the mating market with fewer eco-nomic resources on average than children from father-present homes and that father-absent children tend to be raised in homes in which they are less closely genetically related to the other family members in the home. As in the preceding models, the fitness returns to two types of behavior will be considered: mating effort and parenting effort, but one additional route to increasing fitness will be added, which is investment in existing genetic kin.

FATHER ABSENCE AND INVESTMENT IN KIN

For humans living in the industrialized world, in which extended kin networks tend to be broken up geographically due to migration patterns, it can be difficult to even imagine the importance that kin can play in the lives of those living in less-mobile, small-scale societies. In the Maya, there is a tendency for male sib groups to maintain close relationships during adulthood, and it is common to find them setting up households in close proximity to one another and helping each other with agricultural tasks. Perhaps not surprisingly, the number of brothers that a man has positively influences fertility. Figure 13.2 shows the relationship between number of brothers and offspring number for the sample of 56 Mayan men. Because age and age squared have a large influence on fitness in any model predicting offspring number using men age 18 and up, Fig. 13.2 displays off-spring number with age and age squared effects partialled out. This creates a vari-able that includes negative numbers (standardized residuals). The wide age range of the subjects additionally produced a nonnormal distribution for offspring num-ber, which was modeled statistically by fitting a Poisson model. In a regression model predicting offspring number with age, age squared, and number of broth-ers, the estimate for number of brothers was 0.08 (Chi-squared $= 4.01$, $p = 0.046$).

Divorce or male desertion in Mayan households tends to result in one of three outcomes: (a) the mother will remarry, particularly if she is still young; (b) the mother will remain unmarried and attach herself to a male-headed household (almost always a parent or other relative); or (c) less commonly, she will adopt out her children to increase her chances of remarriage. All of these situations tend to mean that father-absent children are raised in homes in which they are less closely genetically related to others in their household. This reduces the benefits to cooperating with household members, as cooperating with stepbrothers or sis-ters, half sibs, or cousins will have lower or no genetic benefit. Thus, the potential for contributing to inclusive fitness through relatives (Hamilton, 1964) cannot be fully realized for individuals raised father-absent, and on top of this, fewer close

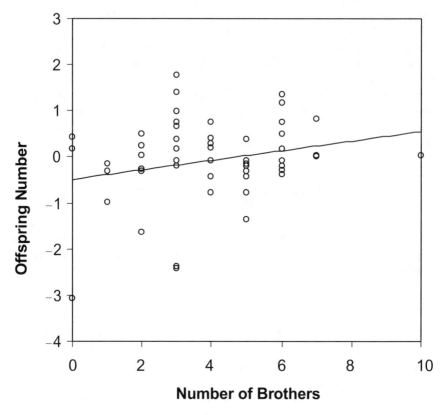

FIG. 13.2. Number of Brothers and Offspring Number for 56 Mayan Men. Offspring number is expressed as standardized residuals to partial out age and age-
squared effects. Line is a least-squares regression line.

kin will be present to help contribute to the fitness of those who are father-absent.
As a consequence, it may be optimal for father-absent individuals to be less oriented to investing in family and more oriented toward being independent from the
family group that raised them.

There is some evidence that the degree of genetic relatedness within households has some importance. Jankowiak and Diderich (2000) studied family solidarity in a polygamous Mormon community in the United States. Polygamy created a predominance of households containing both full and half siblings. Within
these households, full siblings reported that they felt more affectual solidarity,
were more likely to state willingness to lend money to full siblings over half siblings, and preferred full siblings to half siblings as baby-sitters to infants.

A prediction testable with the Mayan men's database is whether men raised
father-absent spend more time away from the individuals in the family home in
which they were raised, as well as the children of all those with whom they were

raised as siblings (i.e., their nephews and nieces). The time-use data for Mayan men were collected retrospectively from interviews. Men were asked to remember in detail the last day when they did not work. Nonworking days were chosen to maximize the amount of choice that men would be able to exert over their time-use decisions. Some men had not recently taken a day off at the time of interview and were asked instead to recall their time-use on the day within the previous two weeks on which they worked the least. Men were asked to report in 1-hour blocks, both their activity and who they were with, beginning with times for which they were the most certain of their activity.

Retrospectively gathered time-use data are convenient to collect, but less than ideal to analyze due to the problem of recall bias. This was minimized by never asking men to remember activities more than 2 weeks prior to interview. A second problem with the methods employed is that time-use on only 1 day was recorded. These methodological deficiencies are likely to decrease the probability of finding any significant statistical relationship between time-use and any predictor, although these time-use data confirmed a predicted negative association between Mayan men's physical attractiveness and time spent with family (Waynforth, 1999).

The maximum reported amount of time spent with kin was 15 hours (out of a 24-hour period), and the minimum and mode was zero. In a Poisson regression model, father presence (recorded as number of years of father presence in the home) was significantly associated with time spent with kin: Estimate $= 0.06$, Chi-squared $= 4.77$, $df = 1$, $p = 0.03$, $n = 50$. Number of siblings was controlled for in the model, although men raised father-absent did not grow up with fewer siblings (defined as full, half, and stepsiblings) on average. The regression estimate for sibling number was 0.09, Chi-squared $= 25.55$, $df = 1$, $p = 0.0001$, $n = 50$. It is difficult to know how much of this effect is driven by the fact that men who had more siblings were simply more likely to encounter a sibling, and hence spend time with them.

Those from father-absent homes were predicted to not spend as much time with kin, as on average, they are less related to those individuals with whom they were raised. Father-absent Mayan men's time use appears to be optimal in that it reflects an orientation away from kin, but the question of what exactly men raised father-absent should be doing with their time instead remains. Next, mating and parental effort will be considered.

FATHER ABSENCE, MATING, AND PARENTING EFFORT

Mating effort should, in part, be based on the availability of mating opportunities. These can come in the form of short-term sexual relationships in which no extended resource flow to the woman is expected or long-term relationships with extended paternal care. The fitness returns to seeking short-term relationships may not differ greatly between men who were raised father-absent and those raised father-present if women tend not to be seeking resources from short-term mates. This is because it is more likely that women's greatest gain from short-term mating comes in the form of high-quality male genetic contribution to offspring. Genetic quality may be read by women via physically attractive facial and body characteristics, and there is evidence that the physical attractiveness of potential mates is of primary importance to women in the short-term mating context (Buss & Schmitt, 1993; Gangestad & Simpson, 1990). The utility of mating with physically attractive men may be that offspring produced will have superior disease resistance. Consistent with this, research by Gangestad (1993) showed a tendency cross-culturally for physical attractiveness to be more important in mate choice in pathogen-prevalent regions of the world.

There appears to be no evidence linking low physical attractiveness and father absence. In the Mayan sample, men raised father-absent did not have fewer (or more) lifetime sex partners than father-present men (Waynforth, Hurtado, & Hill, 1998), and they also did not differ in facial attractiveness ratings or another component of male physical attractiveness, fluctuating asymmetry (for facial attractiveness, in an age-controlled model, Beta $= 0.02$, $T = 0.05$, $p = 0.60$; for fluctuating asymmetry, Beta $= -0.00$, $T = -0.02$, $p = 0.99$). However, as shown earlier, men raised father-absent did differ in the degree of testosterone influence on their facial structure. Some researchers have found that men with highly developed facial testosterone cues are preferred by women (Cunningham, Barbee, & Pike, 1990), whereas others have found a preference for the opposite (i.e., feminized male faces) (e.g., Perrett et al., 1998; Rhodes, Hickford, & Jeffery, 2000). At this point, it cannot be concluded that large facial testosterone cues are either particularly attractive or unattractive to women. One unresolved problem is that although Perrett et al. (1998) and Rhodes (2000) found that women rated computer-manipulated photos of men with masculine facial features less attractive, it is not known whether women would in practice mate with these men and perhaps seek long-term relationships with men with feminized features (who might provide more paternal care). For the present argument, it appears that men raised father-absent will face little disadvantage in the context of accessing short-term mates, and what disadvantage they might have could be compensated for if their adult testosterone levels are also higher, leading them to be motivated to seek more short-term sex partners (see previous argument).

In seeking long-term sexual relationships, there is substantial evidence that women focus extensively on male resource provisioning ability (e.g., Buss, 1989; Waynforth & Dunbar, 1995; Weiderman, 1993). At the same time, there is firm evidence that those from father-absent homes have worse economic outcomes, including school performance (e.g., Keith & Finlay, 1988). Levels of direct and financial paternal involvement, which are lower in father-absent households, are generally associated with lowered educational attainment (e.g., Amato, 1998). It therefore can be concluded that men raised father-absent will have less to offer women in the context of long-term mating; indeed, men raised father-absent may often have difficulty finding a long-term mate at all. In the Mayan data, there is a marginally statistically significant association between current income and whether men have ever been married (Logistic regression, 1-tailed $p = 0.035$). Given that the income data consist of income in only the year prior to interview, any effect is surprising. Current income was not significantly associated with extramarital sex partner number (in an age-controlled Poisson regression model, estimate $= 0.04$, Chi-squared $= 2.28$, $df = 1$, $p = 0.14$). Income was associated with offspring number (see Fig. 13.3): (in an age- and age-squared-controlled Poisson regression model, estimate $= 0.05$, Chi-squared $= 8.55$, $df = 1$, $p = 0.004$). These results are consistent with income having a greater impact on fitness in long-term relationships than in short-term relationships, as well as possible difficulty in marrying without resources to offer. The highly significant effect of

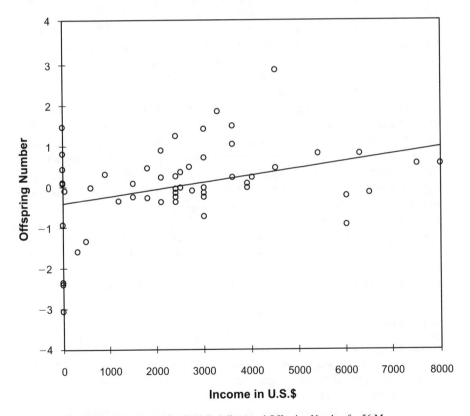

FIG. 13.3.   Income in 1996 (in U.S. dollars) and Offspring Number for 56 Mayan Men. Offspring number is expressed as standardized residuals to partial out age and age-squared effects. Line is a least-squares regression line.

resources on fertility may stem from early marriage for wealthier men, as well as marriage to women with greater reproductive potential. The missing link in the Mayan data is between father absence and income: income in a single year was not associated with father absence (Waynforth et al., 1998). Father absence probably has a stronger effect on income for young men, and the Mayan data unfortunately do not provide enough cases to show this. Nevertheless, as evidenced by late first reproduction in father-absent Mayan men and research in other societies consistently showing economic and educational disadvantages to those from father-absent homes, father absence implies disadvantages in mate acquisition and ability to produce competitive offspring through long-term paternal care.

This argument contends that men from father-absent homes may not get the chance to choose a strategy that involves focusing on paternal care of their children. When they do get the chance, their reduced education and earning capacity may reduce the fitness returns to high investment in their offspring, relative to the potential gains to seeking new mating opportunities. A problem with the idea that father-absent, resource-poor men should focus more on short-term mating than father-present men, because men raised father-absent receive lower returns to paternal care, is that it assumes that men with resources will maximize their fitness through parenting effort, as appears to be the case for the Maya. This is not necessarily true for all societies: in the Ache it appears that resources have a larger effect on fitness via mating effort than via paternal care (Hill & Hurtado, 1996). It is therefore unlikely that there is a universally valid fitness-maximizing response to father-absent rearing, and the conditions particular to every society will have to be considered to make a prediction in each context. A second issue is that women may assess male genetic quality partly through their resource acquisition ability. Indeed, resource acquisition ability and other markers of genetic quality may typically be positively correlated with one another. In the Mayan sample, fluctuating asymmetry was correlated with income in the expected direction despite the availability of only a single year's data on income (Pearson $r = -0.15$, $p = 0.26$). However, father absence may constitute a special case in which resource level and attractiveness do not correlate strongly. As I have argued, father absence restricts the resource acquisition ability of young men without affecting their physical attractiveness (i.e., these men are not poor because they carry "bad" genes).

Summary

In attempting to clarify the likely returns to important fitness-influencing behavior in men (kin investment, mating, and parenting), we have seen how father-absent men's optimal strategy might be to focus on short-term mating, because they get lower returns to nepotistic effort and lower returns to paternal investment if they can access a woman for a long-term relationship, but probably not lower returns to short-term mating effort. This argument is consistent with father-absent Mayan men's orientation toward mating effort and away from spending time with their kin group. Their larger testosterone cues may reflect preparation for a strategy consisting largely of mating effort, and the fact that they reproduce later on average than father-present men could just reflect disadvantage in competing for access to long-term mates. Because almost all of men's reported children came from long-term unions, it is hardly surprising that the data would show late ages at first fatherhood for men raised father-absent.

RISK AND FATHER-ABSENT REPRODUCTIVE STRATEGIES

I have tried to show how father absence can affect the relative fitness returns to men's set of behavioral options and in turn affect their optimal reproductive strategy. There are additional possible evolutionary adaptations that may simultaneously operate on reproductive timing decisions and be related to father absence. Chisholm (1999a; 1999b) has explored the possibility that mortality hazard influences the decision about whether to reproduce now versus later. Life-history theorists have studied the effects of survivorship on the timing of first reproduction in animals. For example, if chemicals produced by predators are introduced into a tank containing *Daphnia* (a freshwater invertebrate), they will reproduce earlier (Stibor, 1992). This is because in high mortality conditions, early reproduction tends to be favored by natural selection, because any benefits of waiting to reproduce have to be weighed against the probability of survival to reproductive age (for a concise explanation of life-history theory and first reproduction, see Hill & Hurtado, 1996, p. 27). Some aspects of human reproduction seem to be consistent with this life-history theoretical perspective: In industrialized nations, mortality rates tend to vary by neighborhood. Analysis of Chicago neighborhoods showed high rates of early childbearing in neighborhoods with high mortality (Wilson & Daly, 1997). Chisholm (1999a) found that female university students who believed that they would die young had earlier ages at first sex. Father absence may become involved as an issue because early reproduction might also entail not waiting to obtain a long-term mate.

There are, however, problems with this line of research that need addressing in future work. For example, it is not known whether individuals at risk of dying young or who believe that they will die young are in this mortality risk category because they selected a mating strategy that puts them at risk or because mortality hazard drove their mating decisions.

FATHER ABSENCE AND OPTIMAL FEMALE REPRODUCTIVE STRATEGIES

I have focused on optimal male reproductive strategies here, in part because the Mayan men's database allowed a number of qualitative tests of male optimal reproductive strategy under father-absent versus father-present conditions. For women, some of the same predictions should hold: women from father-absent homes should, like men, be less oriented toward nepotistic effort and should become oriented away from the home in which they were raised in favor of their own reproductive effort. For women, however, focusing on achieving successive short-term matings cannot have the same degree of reproductive benefit, because women are constrained by high minimal time and energy costs for each child that they produce (Bateman, 1948). Father absence may in some ways put women into situations in which they cannot secure long-term male investment. This can be easily envisioned in industrialized societies, in which the economic disadvantages of father absence might put young women into a neighborhood or mating pool with few men who plan on long-term parental investment. In this scenario, women need not pay the time and energy costs associated with seeking out a long-term mate and would tend to reproduce early, much as Draper and Harpending (1982) originally theorized. In traditional societies, the resource disadvantage from father absence may lead to nutritional and other social stress that could delay menarche and first reproduction. The result reported here for Ache women's first reproduction may be explained as stress-induced reproductive suppression.

SUMMARY AND CONCLUSIONS

The development of the psychosocial stress model of father absence and the timing of first reproduction marked the beginning of the application of evolutionary theory to father absence in humans and became very influential, particularly in the field of evolutionary psychology. The results reported here suggest that patterns in age at first reproduction in traditional societies do not fit the model (for another criticism of the psychosocial stress model, see Geary, 2000), but instead, father absence may simply create a difficult set of conditions for fitness maximization that individuals try to overcome through adjusting the allocation of their reproductive effort. By examining potential consequences from father absence for three components of fitness—kin help, mating effort, and parenting effort—more realistic predictions about fitness maximization as a function of father absence than had been identified in the psychosocial stress model could be made. Because individuals in households that have split up due to marital dissolution tend to be less closely genetically related to each other, it was predicted that father-absent individuals would be less oriented toward those reared with them and would focus instead on their own reproductive effort. The time use of Mayan men was consistent with this prediction: men from father-absent homes spent less time with the family in which they were raised.

The Belizean Mayan mating system is one in which long-term sexual relationships predominate, and short-term partners are also obtainable, although not to the extent that they are in many other societies (the Ache, for example). Resources had a large effect on marital fertility, but less of an effect on the number of sex partners that men reported outside of marriage. Because raising children successfully entails long-term commitment of resources, it seemed plausible that long-term mating effort with paternal care might yield lower net fitness gain for men raised father-absent, as these men will likely have received lower parental investment and be disadvantaged in their ability to acquire resources. Due to the fact that father absence might not affect the returns to short-term mating effort as much as it does long-term mating effort (or by aiding existing genetic kin), men raised father-absent were hypothesized to focus on short-term mating effort. In Mayan men, this appeared to be the case: men raised father-absent self-reported less orientation toward the maintenance of sexual relationships and less paternal orientation. They also had larger facial testosterone cues, suggesting physiological adaptedness to short-term mating.

Despite father-absent Mayan men's orientation toward short-term mating appearing to be optimal, the optimal allocation of effort is likely to depend on aspects of the environment in any given society. For example, father-present men's optimal strategy could be to focus on mating effort if resources do not affect offspring survival or competitiveness to a great extent. This makes universal predictions about reproductive strategies as function of father absence impossible.

The inadequacy of the psychosocial stress model for predicting reproductive strategies as a function of father absence does not preclude an important role for psychosocial stress as a concept relevant to reproductive decisions, and it may genuinely be causally related to early first reproduction in modern conditions. Volatile family relations and inconsistent parenting might indicate limited parental investment and force children to focus away from the nuclear family and toward their own reproductive choices. Future studies that take into account the fitness consequences of mating strategies as a function of psychosocial stress may provide a more fruitful approach to the study of evolution and stress-induced mating strategies.

REFERENCES

Amato, P. (1998). More than money? Men's contributions to their children's lives. In A. Booth & A. Crouter (Eds.), *Men in families: When do they get involved? What difference does it make?* Mahwah, NJ: Lawrence Erlbaum Associates

Bateman, A. (1948). Intra-sexual selection. *Drosophila. Heredity, 2,* 349–368.

Belsky, J., Steinberg, L., & Draper, P. (1991). Childhood experience, interpersonal development, and reproductive strategy: An evolutionary theory of socialization. *Child Development, 62,* 647–670.

Belsky, J. (1997). Attachment, mating, and parenting: An evolutionary interpretation. *Human Nature, 8,* 361–381.

Booth, A., & Dabbs, J. (1993). Testosterone and men's marriages. *Social Forces, 72,* 463–477.

Bowlby, J. (1969). *Attachment and Loss*: Vol. 1. *Attachment*. New York: Basic Books.

Buss, D. (1989). Sex differences in human mate preferences: Evolutionary hypotheses tested in 37 cultures. *Behavioral and Brain Sciences, 12,* 1–49.

Buss, D., & Schmitt, D. (1993). Sexual strategies theory: And evolutionary perspective on human mating. *Psychological Review, 100,* 204–232.

Chisholm, J. (1999a). Attachment and time preference: Relations between early stress and sexual behavior in a sample of American university women. *Human Nature, 10,* 51–83.

Chisholm, J. (1999b). *Death, hope and sex: Steps to an evolutionary ecology of mind and morality.* Cambridge: Cambridge University Press.

Collett, D. (1994). *Modelling Survival Data in Medical Research.* London: Chapman and Hall.

Cunningham, M. R., Barbee, A. P., Pike, C. L. (1990). What do women want? Facialmetric assessment of multiple motives in the perception of male facial physical attractiveness. *Journal of Personality and Social Psychology, 59*(1), 61–72.

Dabbs, J., & Morris, R. (1990). Testosterone, social class and antisocial behavior in a sample of 4,462 men. *Psychological Science, 1,* 209–211.

Draper, P., & Harpending, H. (1982). Father absence and reproductive strategy: An evolutionary perspective. *Journal of Anthropological Research, 38,* 255–279.

Draper, P., & Harpending, H. (1988). A sociobiological perspective on the development of human reproductive strategies. In K. McDonald (Ed.), *Sociobiological perspectives on human development* (pp. 340–372). New York: Springer-Verlag.

Gangestad, S. (1993). Sexual selection and physical attractiveness: Implications for mating dynamics. *Human Nature, 4,* 205–235.

Gangestad, S., & Simpson, J. (1990). Toward an evolutionary history of female sociosexual variation. *Journal of Personality, 58,* 69–96.

Geary, D. (2000). Evolution and proximate expression of human paternal investment. *Psychological Bulletin, 126,* 55–77.

Hamilton, W. (1964). The genetical evolution of social behaviour. *Journal of Theoretical Biology, 7,* 1–52.

Hetherington, E. (1972). Effects of father absence on personality development in adolescent daughters. *Developmental Psychology, 7,* 313–326.

Hill, K., & Hurtado, M. (1996). *Ache life history: The ecology and demography of a foraging people.* New York: Aldine de Gruyter.

Hurtado, M., & Hill, K. (1992). Paternal effect on offspring survivorship among Ache and Hiwi hunter-gatherers: Implications for modeling pair bond stability. In B. Hewlett (Ed.), *Father-child relations: Cultural and biosocial contexts* (pp. 31–56). New York: Aldine de Gruyter.

Jankowiak, W., & Diderich, M. (2000). Sibling solidarity in a polygamous community in the USA: Unpacking inclusive fitness. *Evolution and Human Behavior, 21,* 125–139.

Jones, B., Leeton, J., McLeod, I., & Wood, C. (1972). Factors influencing the age at menarche in a lower socio-economic group in Melbourne. *Medical Journal of Australia, 2,* 533–535.

Keith, V., & Finlay, B. (1988). The impact of parental divorce on children's educational attainment, marital timing, and the likelihood of divorce. *Journal of Marriage and the Family, 50,* 797–809.

Kim, K., Smith, P., & Palermiti, A. (1997). Conflict in childhood and reproductive development. *Evolution and Human Behavior, 18,* 109–142.

Moffitt, T., Caspi, A., & Belsky, J. (1992). Childhood experience and the onset of menarche: A test of a sociobiological model. *Child Development, 63,* 47–58.

Parker, G., & McNair, M. (1978). Models of parent-offspring conflict. I. Monogamy. *Animal Behaviour, 26,* 97–110.

Perrett, D., Lee, K., Penton-Voak, I., Rowland, D., Yoshikawa, S., Burt, D., Henzi, S., Castles, D., & Akamatsu, S. (1998). Effects of sexual dimorphism on facial attractiveness. *Nature, 394,* 884–887.

Rhodes, G., Hickford, C., & Jeffery, L. (2000). Sex-typicality and attractiveness: Are supermale and superfemale faces super-attractive? *British Journal of Psychology, 91*(1), 125–140.

Stibor, H. (1992). Predator induced life-history shifts in a freshwater cladoceran. *Oecologia, 92,* 162–165.

Surbey, M. (1990). Family composition, stress, and the timing of human menarche. In T. Zeigler & F. Bercovitch (Eds.), *Socioendocrinology of Primate Reproduction* (pp. 11–32). New York: Wiley-Liss.

Trivers, R. (1972). Parental investment and sexual selection. In B. Campbell (Ed.), *Sexual Selection and the Descent of Man 1871–1971* (pp. 136–179). London: Heinemann.

Udry, J. (1988). Biological predispositions and social control in adolescent sexual behavior. *American Sociological Review, 53,* 709–722.

Verdonck, A., Gaethofs, M., Carels, C., & de Zegher, F. (1999). Effects of low dose testosterone treatment on craniofacial growth in boys with delayed puberty. *European Journal of Orthodontics, 21,* 137–143.

Waynforth, D., & Dunbar, R. (1995). Conditional mate choice strategies in humans: Evidence from "lonely hearts" advertisements. *Behaviour, 132,* 755–779.

Waynforth, D., Hurtado, M., & Hill, K. (1998). Environmentally contingent reproductive strategies in Mayan and Ache males. *Evolution and Human Behavior, 19,* 369–85.

Waynforth, D. (1999). Differences in time use for mating and nepotistic effort as a function of male attractiveness in rural Belize. *Evolution and Human Behavior, 20,* 19–28.

Weiderman, M. (1993). Evolved gender differences in mate preferences: Evidence from personal advertisements. *Ethology and Sociobiology, 14,* 331–352.

Whiting, J. (1965). Menarcheal age and infant stress in humans. In F. Beach (Ed.), *Sex and Behavior* (pp. 221–233). New York: Wiley.

Wilson, M., & Daly, M. (1997). Life expectancy, economic inequality, homicide, and reproductive timing in Chicago neighborhoods. *British Medical Journal, 314,* 1271–1274.

14

Fathering as Reproductive Investment

Steven C. Josephson
University of Utah

This chapter examines how men's reproductive strategies impact their children's lives. In the first section, I will review Darwinian theory on mating and parenting, asking how we should expect men to spend their time and energy given the options open to them. In the next section, "Nineteenth-century Utah Mormons," I will describe a sample of men's reproductive histories that contains both men who had several wives and men who had only one wife. I will then examine aspects of their children's life histories (fertility, survivorship, marriages, divorces, and widowhood) to discern the effects of their fathers' investment. I will finish with "Fathering as a Reproductive Strategy," discussing monogamy and polygyny as reproductive strategies and how they affect the way men invest as fathers. In this sample, fathers with few resources seem to have invested more in their children's survival, whereas fathers with more resources helped their children marry. To see the logic behind this, we need to look at fathering not as a given, but as merely one component of men's reproductive strategies (Clutton-Brock, 1991).

Evolutionary theory is predicated on the assumption that individuals act to maximize their own Darwinian "fitness," or genetic contribution to future generations. Once they reach adulthood, organisms spend their resources in two, often conflicting, ways; they can invest in their children or they can invest in finding mates. We call the first parental investment, and the second mating investment, and usually treat them as different ways of expending effort (Trivers, 1972). In practice, however, it can be difficult to separate the two (Maynard Smith, 1977). This may be especially true with human fathering because paternal effort and mating effort may overlap in surprising ways and to an unusual degree (Josephson, 2000).

For males in all species, mating and parenting usually compete for the same limited resources. The reason stems from a simple fact of biology; males are the sex that need not invest more than their genes in their offspring (Andersson, 1994; Williams, 1966, 1975). This leaves males free to invest in their offspring or to invest in seeking mates with whom to have more offspring. It is different for females, who have a much higher obligate investment in their children. Females are likely to have the same number of offspring no matter how many mates they have, so they are far less motivated to seek extra mates (Krebs & Davies, 1991; Low, 2000). The result is that males in most species tend to specialize in mating, and females tend to specialize in parental investment, seeking resources that they can put into children (Krebs & Davies, 1991; Vehrencamp & Bradbury, 1984).

This produces conflict between parents about how resources should be allocated to children. This happens in virtually all sexually reproducing organisms, yet most anthropologists and psychologists are not used to thinking about how this conflict has shaped human behavior. Humans are no doubt aware of the conflicts that arise with gender differences, but we remain largely unaware of the adaptive purpose these differences may serve. Yet our psychological tendencies have likely been shaped by selection, although we need not be consciously aware of our attitudes in order for them to serve an adaptive goal (Borgerhoff Mulder, 1991). I mention this to avoid unnecessary confusion, as, by using language that seems to imply conscious intent in this essay, I do not mean to suggest that humans consider the adaptive consequences of their actions. I will simply assume that the attitudes that guide our reproductive decisions have been shaped by selection, an assumption that has gained substantial empirical support in the past 25 years (Essock-Vitale, 1984; Flinn, 1986; Irons, 1975).

One of the primary conflicts in human reproduction arises over the investment men make in their children. By mammalian standards, human males are attentive fathers, although there is considerable variation in this regard (Clutton-Brock, 1991; Woodroffe & Vincent, 1994). Because the minimum investment in offspring is simply gametes and the effort necessary to place them in close proximity to female gametes, men are faced with an interesting trade-off. They can continue to invest parentally, which is something their wives and children might prefer them to do. They can, however, also divert time and energy into seeking additional mates, something that would not benefit their previous wife and children. This is one of the central trade-offs for male animals, and it has a strong influence on how and how much men invest in their offspring (Borgerhoff Mulder, 1988; Searcy & Yasukawa, 1989).

Paternal investment helps children and indirectly fathers themselves, but this does not mean that fathers will always do what is best for their offspring (Veherencamp & Bradbury, 1984). Investing in offspring may interfere with men's attempts to seek extra mates and have more children, something that would benefit men themselves but not necessarily their families. Where the benefit of seeking mates outweighs the benefit of investing in children, men may invest little or nothing in parenting (Trivers, 1972). Even when men's children stand to gain substantially from their investment, it is men's own interests that determine whether they actually invest. We should expect men to invest more when the indirect net benefit they get is greater than the benefit they could get from some other use of their time and energy. This can be hard to see, though, because there are many ways men can invest parentally.

Fathering is not a single behavior but many, following from a series of specific decisions. Once a father has decided to invest, there are a number of ways they can do so. The most basic investment comes earliest, namely, helping children survive long enough to have children of their own (Lack, 1966, 1968; Smith & Kunz 1976; Strassman, 1997; Woodroffe & Vincent, 1994). Once they reach adulthood, fathers can invest by helping their children attract mates (Cronk, 1991; Hartung, 1982; Josephson, 1993), attract better mates (Andersson, 1994; Flinn, 1986; Smith & Kunz, 1976), or find extra spouses (Borgerhoff Mulder, 1988; Josephson, 2000). Extra spouses can take the form of polygynous marriages, but they can also be a remedy for an unforeseen calamity such as widowhood or divorce (Josephson, 2000; Mineau, 1988). All of these can have a substantial impact on their children's reproductive success, which may in fact be very limited without parental investment (Clutton-Brock, 1991).

Even when men choose to invest parentally, they may do so in some ways but not others. From a father's perspective, some types of parental investment may be less desirable because they interfere with his other plans. Men might be less inclined to help their sons find wives if it comes at the cost of finding additional wives for themselves (Borgerhoff Mulder, 1988). Similarly, the effect of providing a dowry for a daughter would have to be substantial for it to outweigh the benefit to men themselves of keeping the money and having more children. This may explain why men often relinquish their wealth only at death, when their chance of using it themselves disappears (Judge, 1995). The timing of paternal investment can be a good indicator that men invest as a way of helping themselves, sometimes by helping their children, sometimes not. Where paternal investment comes into conflict with mating investment, it can be hard to anticipate what men will do.

On the other hand, some types of paternal investment may help men attract wives. All else equal, women should prefer to have children with men who can increase their children's fertility, ensuring lots of grandchildren. This is probably why women are so picky about whom they marry, preferring wealthy, socially successful men (Low, 2000). Women may even be willing to pay a price to have children with preferable men, even to the point of sharing a husband with other women (Borgerhoff Mulder, 1988). The cost women incur would have to be balanced by some benefit, but this benefit need not accrue to women directly. It is not difficult to see that men can have a substantial effect on their children's reproductive success, and benefit to a woman's offspring is indirectly beneficial to her

(Searcy & Yasukawa, 1989). This creates the possibility that men may be helped, rather than hindered, in their mating efforts by being good fathers (Grafen, 1991; Krebs & Davies, 1991). Wealth and influence may put men in a better position to help their children, which may explain why men everywhere are so concerned with these issues. Men could benefit both in the short run by having more wives (who are attracted to them because of their ability to invest in children) and in the long run by having children who have augmented fertility (Josephson, in press). Such paternal investment would also function as mating investment if men can make this work. All men may compete for wealth and status, but only a few will be able to integrate their mating and parenting.

This would only work for men who are in a position to invest more than other men. Like as not, all men invest in their children to some extent, so a given amount of investment may not be much of an indicator of men's quality. It is a *relatively* high ability that sets some men apart, meaning that men who want to use paternal investment as mating investment must not only be able to help their children, but they must also be better able than other men. This opens the possibility that men with less to invest may do so in other ways (Hewlett, 1992; Kaplan, 1996; Trivers & Willard, 1973). To explore these possibilities, we need to examine the long-term effects of different reproductive strategies.

NINETEENTH-CENTURY UTAH MORMONS

To examine how a man's resources and reproductive strategy influence his allocation to fathering, it is best to look at men who have already completed their reproductive careers. Such data can be gathered by looking at historic records, although using them raises a number of problems, most of which concern the resolution of the data. The information people tend to record is never as fine grained as that derived from the usual methods of cultural anthropology, such as interviewing living subjects and participant observation. Historical demographic data is often limited to the most basic facts of life—births, deaths, marriages, and divorces. Because of this, it is difficult to address many of the questions we are usually interested in asking, such as the influence of culture on reproductive decisions. The loss in resolution is, however, made up for by excellent time depth, unmatched even by the longest studies of living populations. Even basic demographic information can tell us a great deal about the long-term effects of different reproductive strategies, some of which may take a generation to fully manifest (Josephson, 1993). This information simply cannot be derived in any other way, and the results from one group can be compared with other groups because reproductive issues are common to all humans.

For men, the trade-off between mating and parenting is easier to document in a polygynous group than in a monogamous one. Although virtually all cultures allow some form of polygyny such as serial monogamy, many modern groups including our own limit men to one wife at a time (Essock-Vitale, 1984; Fox,

1993). Still, even in monogamous groups, men trade off parental investment for mating investment, choosing whether to invest in their children or to divorce and start a second family. The problem is that groups where men divorce and remarry make for complicated analyses because we would need to know the causes of specific divorces. Husbands or wives might initiate a divorce for their own reasons, so it can be hard to know whose reproductive interests are likely to be served in any particular case. The situation is much simpler for men in polygynous groups, as these men need not dissolve their first marriage in order to contract a second. They need only convince another woman to marry them, a dicey proposition given that women are usually suspicious of sharing a husband.

For these reasons, I chose to use a sample of reproductive histories of polygynous and monogamous men from 19th-century Utah Mormons. The Mormon Church began to allow plural marriages in the 1840s, even though such marriages were forbidden under federal law (Brodie, 1945; Ivins, 1956; May, 1992). For the next half century, polygynous marriages were locally recognized, although most marriages were still monogamous. Women were encouraged to find polygynous marriage acceptable, but lurid popular accounts aside, there is little evidence that they were forced to marry polygynously against their will (Ivins, 1956). Polygyny remained popular until the 1890s, when the church officially renounced "plural marriage" under pressure from the federal government (Brodie, 1945).

The sample consists of the complete reproductive histories of 83 men who married in Utah in the 1840s and 1850s. It includes information about 43 monogamous and 40 polygynous men, their 251 wives, plus their approximately 1,100 children and 8,000 grandchildren (Josephson, 2000). All of the men in this sample spent some portion of their lives living in Utah, although most immigrated there during and after the Mormon diaspora in the late 1840s (May, 1992; Mineau, Bean, & Skolnick, 1979). The sample is unusually large and complete for a polygynous group, and for most individuals I was able to record date of birth, marriage, and death for themselves and two generations of descendents. Because most polygynous marriages were not officially recorded, I also used these dates to infer whether marriages were monogamous or polygynous.

I divided the sample into two groups based on men's marital history. Men were defined as "polygynous" if they were married to two or more women at the same time during their reproductive careers. Generally polygynous men married for the first time in their early 20s, then again in their mid to late 30s. Those who married subsequent wives usually did so every 4 years on average, and a few continued to add wives well into their 60s, a few beyond. Thus, the reproductive careers of polygynous men were much longer than those of monogamous men, as polygynous men usually married women who were much younger than themselves.

Monogamous men were married to only one woman at a time, although a few remarried after their spouse died or divorced. These men too married for the first time in their early 20s, although a few married in their 30s. Their reproductive careers were short compared to polygynous men because, after their wife reached the age of 50, the chance of having children with her was essentially zero. Although monogamous men were usually men of more modest means, this is not reflected in the number of children they had with their one wife. On average, monogamous women in this sample had more children than polygynous women (Josephson, 2000).

There is also strong evidence that the incidence of polygynous marriage was directly related to wealth and status in men. Several studies of this group have concluded that men with many wives were both of higher status in the church and wealthier than monogamous men (Mealey, 1985; Smith & Kunz, 1976). This agrees well with numerous studies from other polygynous groups, which have shown that polygyny is invariably the prerogative of wealthy, socially successful men (Borgerhoff Mulder, 1988; Betzig, 1986; Dickemann, 1979; Irons, 1975, 1983; Voland & Dunbar, 1995). The connection between wealth and polygyny in Mormons is strengthened by the fact that permission to take a second wife was restricted by the church itself (Brodie, 1945; Smith & Kunz, 1976). I will assume that polygynous men had more resources over their life span to invest in mating and parenting than monogamous men. I would have preferred to measure men's wealth directly, but this is difficult to do reliably using historic records (see Josephson, 2000, for discussion).

Although historic circumstances are hard to reconstruct, monogamous and polygynous men likely varied greatly in resources and opportunity to invest. If number of wives is any indication, the men in the sample varied in the resources they had to attract mates. Monogamous men, of course, had only one wife, whereas the number of wives for polygynous men varied greatly, from 2 to 16. There also seems to have been ample opportunity for men to affect the lives of their children. The average fertility of women in this population was very high, approximating natural fertility levels (Bean & Mineau, 1986). There was also a great deal of childhood mortality, as approximately 25% of these men's children died before the age of 5. Even among the children who lived long enough to have children of their own, there was substantial variation in reproductive success, with many children having a dozen or more offspring whereas others had none (Josephson, 2000). It is this variation that is important, as not all children were equally likely to experience reproductive bankruptcy. Even at first glance, it is obvious that the children of polygynous men fared very differently than the children of monogamous men.

Fertility of Children

By any measure, the children of polygynous men enjoyed a tremendous reproductive advantage over the children of monogamous men. The sons and daughters of polygynous men had two more children on average than the sons and daughters of monogamous men (Josephson, 1993, 2000). We see this difference in both sexes, although the disparity is greater in sons than in daughters. This difference is interesting in and of itself, but it is the way that this happened that suggests the influence of paternal investment. Polygynous men's children benefited preferentially in many, but not all, ways over the children of monogamous men. The pattern of this investment suggests that polygynous men, with more resources to invest, allocated them differently than poorer monogamous men. The patterns also suggest that all

men allocated resources to fathering in ways that ultimately serve their own reproductive purposes, sometimes at their own children's expense.

Survivorship

The most essential type of paternal investment is helping offspring live long
enough to reproduce (cf. Strassman, 1997). Although it is not known how fathers
in this group influenced their children's survivorship, there was certainly the
potential for a powerful influence. The high level of infant mortality in this group
meant that a great deal of time and energy went into babies who died without issue.
The simplest way to examine childhood survivorship is to look at the mean age at
death for the sons and daughters of monogamous and polygynous men (Fig. 14.1)

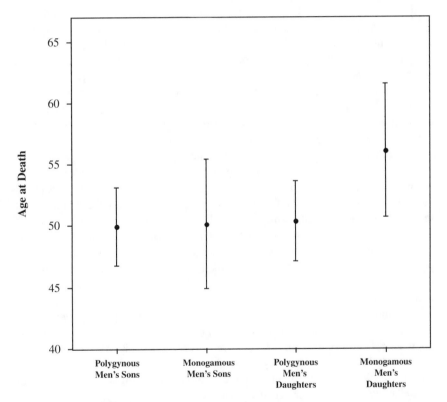

FIG. 14.1.   Average age at death ($\pm$ 2 standard error) for sons and daughters of
polygynous and monogamous men. The sons of polygynous men lived on average
for the same number of years as the sons of monogamous men (49.97 ± 3.60, $n =$
434, vs. 50.13 ± 5.27, $n = 157$, $p = 0.9596$). The daughters of polygynous men
died at an earlier age than the daughters of monogamous men, although the difference is not significant at the $\alpha = 0.05$ level (50.33 ± 3.27, $n = 387$, vs. $56.11 \pm$
5.40, $n = 139$, $p = 0.0690$).

Even at this level of analysis, some interesting patterns are evident. The sons of monogamous and polygynous men show no difference in average age at death, indicating that they were equally likely to survive. The daughters of monogamous men, however, died at a slightly older age, although this difference just misses significance at the $\alpha = 0.05$ level. From this figure alone, it is difficult to speculate why there is a difference in daughters or why this difference did not appear in sons. We do not know why these children died, or even if there is some significance to the fact that monogamous men's daughters seem to be more likely to survive. Although few of the records that comprise this sample included information about cause of death, nevertheless, the age at which these children died might tell us something about why they did.

We see more if we plot the age at which children died by cumulative percent in 5-year groups (Fig. 14.2). Even at this level, the sons of polygynous and monogamous men seem equally likely to survive at all ages. The daughters, however, show an interesting pattern: The infant daughters of monogamous men were less likely to die young than the young daughters of polygynous men. The difference between daughters approaches significance for ages 0 to 5, although it becomes less so at older ages. It is this early period that is responsible for the lower average age at death for the daughters of monogamous men, although it is still not clear why this happened. How this happened is suggested by a more in-depth analysis; the daughters of monogamous men may have received preferential care (Josephson, 2000). Why they may have done so is a matter we will return to later.

Regardless, this result is somewhat surprising. We might have expected polygynous men to help their children preferentially survive if they had more to invest, but this does not seem to be the case. If anything, the daughters of polygynous men are slightly *less* likely to survive early childhood than the daughters of monogamous men (see Strassman, 1997). This seems odd—if monogamous men had fewer resources to invest than polygynous men, why didn't polygynous men's daughters survive at least as well as monogamous men's daughters? If polygynous men's daughters were less likely to survive to adulthood, how did they (and their brothers) end up having more offspring than the children of monogamous men?

It would be tempting to conclude that polygynous men simply spread their paternal investment over a greater number of children to the detriment of investing in each. This would seem to be incorrect, as there is evidence that polygynous men simply invested in other ways than survivorship. Their children may not have been more likely to survive but once they had survived to marry, the benefits of having a polygynous father began to manifest.

Marriage

The children of polygynous men benefited socially from having a wealthy, high-status father, and they benefited reproductively as well. There is evidence, for instance, that polygynous men's children married more preferable mates (Joseph-

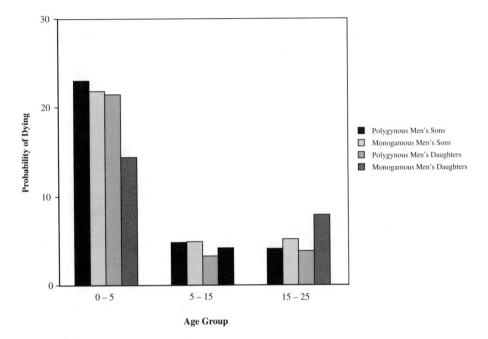

FIG. 14.2.   The probability of survivorship for the sons and daughters of polygynous and monogamous men. The age categories are from 0 to <5, 5 to <15, and
15 to <25. There were no differences in the percentage of sons dead at any age or
any difference between the sons and the daughters of polygynous men. The daughters of monogamous men are somewhat more likely to survive in the interval from
0–5, although the difference was only significant at the $\alpha = 0.10$ level (likelihood
$\chi^2 = 3.450$, $p = 0.0633$) and greater than 0.10 thereafter (ages 5–15, $p = 0.1310$;
ages 15–25, $p = 0.1324$).

son, 2000; Quinn 1976; Smith & Kunz, 1976). The sons of polygynous men,
although no younger themselves at marriage than the sons of monogamous men,
married women who were a few years younger (Josephson, 2000). Polygynous
men's sons were also much more likely to marry polygynously themselves: 12%
managed to attract an extra wife or two, whereas only 1% of monogamous men's
sons became polygynous (see Josephson, 2000). This reproductive advantage
appears in daughters as well, but in different ways and to a different degree. The
daughters of polygynous men also had more children than the daughters of
monogamous men, although the difference in daughters is less than the difference
in sons. Even so, the advantage for polygynous men's daughters is present in
almost every aspect of reproductive history we care to examine. Daughters of
polygynous men were, for instance, more likely to marry high-status men and
have more children as a result (Josephson, 2000).

   Overall, the influence of having a polygynous father was strong once children
reached adulthood and married, but their influence continued during their children's lifetime in surprising ways. Although the strongest effect came when

children married, having a polygynous father even helped later when unexpected crises arose. A reproductive career can be interrupted or even terminated by divorce or death of a spouse, either of which can have severe reproductive consequences. The adverse effects can be somewhat ameliorated by remarriage, as this allows reproductive careers to resume. This only if a new spouse can be found, but there is strong evidence that the children of polygynous and monogamous men fared differently in this regard.

Divorce

Divorce was somewhat rare in 19th-century America, yet it was at least as common in Utah as elsewhere. Although the average divorce rate nationally was in the range of 4%, the rate among children in this sample was approximately 6% (see also Mineau, 1988). Although rare, divorce could still spell trouble, so it would behoove men to help their children remarry if they could. A father's ability to do this is likely mediated by social factors, so it is not surprising that high-status, polygynous men were better able to help their children.

It can be hard to discriminate between divorce and polygyny in historical records. Divorce was a tender subject, and so they were often not officially recorded along with other vital information. Without this, divorce can be hard to discriminate from polygyny if there is no record that the husband and wife remarried other people. It is important to make this distinction because divorce is very different from polygynous marriage as polygyny raises a host of other issues (Josephson, 2000). Before we can see a clearer picture of what happened to the children who remarried, we must first remove the effect of polygynous marriages. I did this by eliminating from the sample at this point all children who married polygynously, leaving only those married monogamously.

There is also the problem that divorces can be difficult to distinguish from the death of a spouse. Although these records were remarkably complete overall, some information was missing. The records for some individuals lacked dates of death, making it hard to be sure if their spouse had remarried because of divorce or death. Death and divorce are very different because, with divorces, we don't know who initiated the breakup. Deaths are simpler in this regard, as the death of a spouse is unlikely to be part of a reproductive strategy. They were instead a crisis to be dealt with as best as one could, although the resolution of this crisis probably did reflect something about an individual's desirability as a mate.

For a first pass, let us consider all children who married more than once, whether due to divorce or the death of a spouse. This is a larger subset of remarried children because we need not discriminate between divorce and death, nor need we exclude ambiguous cases. At this level, the similarities between the children of monogamous and polygynous men seem to outweigh the differences (Fig 14.3).

Having married once, the sons and daughters of polygynous men were no more likely to marry again. Although the sons of polygynous men seem more likely to remarry than the sons of monogamous men, the difference between them is small and not statistically significant. The daughters of these men were even more similar than their brothers, with virtually no difference in their likelihood of remarriage.

For some of these sons and daughters, the records indicated why they remarried. Some divorced, which we know because a few records included this information. Other divorces were not recorded as such, but we can infer that a couple divorced if records show that the husband and wife were still alive but married to other people. If we consider only those marriages we know ended in divorce, we begin to see an interesting pattern.

Although divorces are fairly rare, there is some indication that the children of polygynous men were more likely to divorce than the children of monogamous

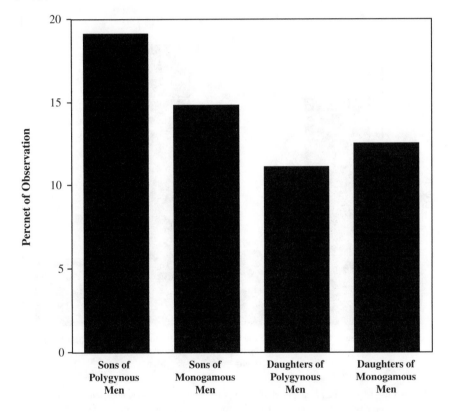

FIG. 14.3.   Percent of children who married and later remarried for polygynous and monogamous men. The sons of polygynous fathers were no more likely to marry than were the sons of monogamous fathers (57 of 298, vs. 14 of 94, likelihood ratio $\chi^2 = 0.8942$, $p = 0.3443$). The daughters of polygynous men were also no more likely to marry more than once than were the daughters of monogamous men (32 of 288, vs. 13 of 104, likelihood ratio $\chi^2 = 0.1428$, $p = 0.7055$).

men (Fig. 14.4). Neither the difference in sons nor the difference in daughters is statistically significant, likely owing to the very small number of divorces in the children of monogamous men. It is hard to interpret this because it is hard to know whose reproductive goals are served by divorce, or if anyone's interests are actually served. Nevertheless, if the children of polygynous or monogamous men who divorced had more children, it might suggest that this was part of a reproductive strategy.

There is little reason to believe this is so, as we see little effect of divorce on reproductive success. If anyone stood to gain reproductively from divorce we might expect it to be men, as divorce and remarriage may offer a kind of polyg-

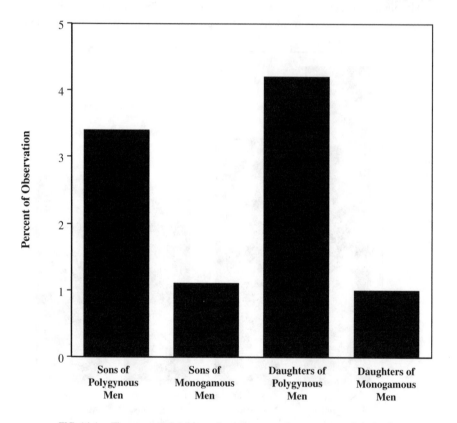

FIG. 14.4.   The percent of children of polygynous and monogamous fathers who divorced at least once in their lives. The sons of polygynous fathers were more likely to experience divorce during their reproductive careers, although this difference is not significant at $\alpha = 0.05$ (10 of 298, vs. 1 of 94, $p = 0.4719$, Fisher's exact test, two-tailed). The daughters of polygynous men were similarly more likely to divorce than were the daughters of polygynous men, although again this difference is not significant at $\alpha = 0.05$ (12 of 288, vs. 1 of 108, $p = 0.1983$, Fisher's exact test, two-tailed).

yny, namely serial-monogamy polygyny. This does not seem to be the case, as divorced and never-divorced sons of monogamous and polygynous men had roughly equal numbers of children (Fig. 14.5). This may be an artifact of analysis, as the rarity of divorced children presents analytical problems for a sample this small. There was only one divorced son of a monogamous father in this sample, so it was not possible to derive statistical comparisons using this group.

The daughters of polygynous and monogamous men show a similar pattern. For women, divorce is time out of a reproductive career that they cannot make up by marrying a young spouse as men can. This would make divorce less likely to be part of a female reproductive strategy, as the cost of lost time is high for women. Although again the sample size for divorced daughters of monogamous men is too

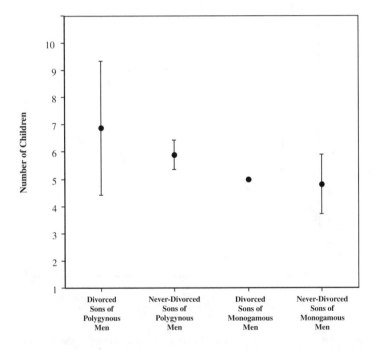

FIG. 14.5.   The average number of children ($\pm$ 2 standard error) by the divorced and never-divorced sons of polygynous and monogamous men. The divorced sons of polygynous men had as many children as their never-divorced brothers (6.88 ± 2.46, $n = 8$, vs. 5.89 ± 0.54, $n = 252$, $p = 0.5185$). The never-divorced sons of polygynous men had more children than the never-divorced sons of monogamous men, although this difference was not significant at the $\alpha = 0.05$ level (5.89 ± 0.54, $n = 252$, vs. 4.81 ± 1.08, $n = 78$, $p = 0.0579$). It was impossible to make comparisons with the divorced sons of monogamous men because of their rarity ($n = 1$).

small for statistical tests, the fertility of divorced daughters of polygynous men looks roughly equal to that of their never-divorced counterparts (Fig. 14.6).

Divorce itself seems to have no consistent effect on reproductive success, but there is a pattern worth noting. There seems to be a difference in reproductive success between the children of different types of fathers once we remove the effects of divorce. There is a substantial difference in the average fertility of never-divorced children of polygynous men compared to the never-divorced children of monogamous men. The never-divorced sons of polygynous men averaged more children than the never-divorced sons of monogamous men (see Fig. 14.5). There is also the suggestion that the never-divorced daughters of polygynous men had more children than the never-divorced daughters of monogamous men, although this difference just misses statistical significance. It seems likely that divorce sim-

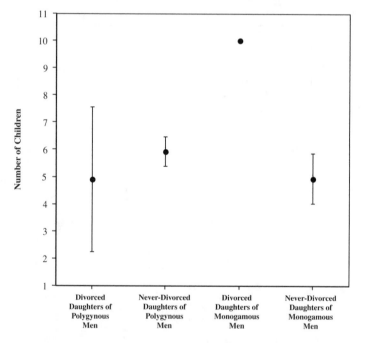

FIG. 14.6.   The average number of children (± 2 standard error) by the divorced and never-divorced daughters of polygynous and monogamous men. The divorced daughters of polygynous men had as many children as their never-divorced sisters (4.90 ± 2.67, $n = 10$, vs. 5.93 ± 0.54, $n = 230$, $p = 0.4346$). The never-divorced daughters of polygynous men had more children than the never-divorced daughters of monogamous men, although this difference was not significant at the $\alpha = 0.05$ level (5.93 ± 0.54, $n = 230$, vs. 4.94 ± 0.92, $n = 100$, $p = 0.0519$). It was impossible to make comparisons with the divorced sons of monogamous men because they are rare ($n = 1$).

ply adds noise to the problem of discerning differences between the children of polygynous and monogamous men.

Widowhood

The other way that monogamous and polygynous men's children end up married more than once is because their spouse died. Death of a spouse is far more common than divorce in this sample, as a fair percentage of these children ended up widows and widowers (Fig. 14.7). Oddly, the sons of polygynous men were much more likely to become widowers at some point in their reproductive careers than the sons of monogamous men. Evidently the wives of polygynous men's sons were at greater risk of death than the wives of monogamous men's sons, although it is not clear why (Josephson, 2000). Whatever the reason, this could have had a strong impact on their reproductive careers.

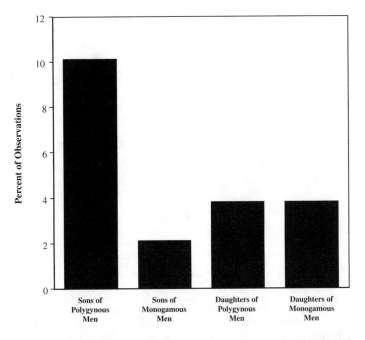

FIG. 14.7.   The percent of children who were widowed at some time in their reproductive careers for polygynous and monogamous fathers. The sons of polygynous fathers were more likely to become widowers than were the sons of monogamous men (30 of 298, vs. 2 of 94, $p = 0.0056$, Fisher's exact test, two-tailed). The daughters of polygynous men were no more likely to be widowed than were the daughters of monogamous men (11 of 288, vs. 4 of 104, $p = 1.000$, Fisher's exact test, two-tailed).

And so it did, but not in the way we might have expected. Having a wife die puts the sons of polygynous men at risk of having shortened reproductive careers, so we might expect them to have had fewer children (Mineau, 1988). Surprisingly, we find just the opposite (Fig. 14.8). The widowed sons of polygynous men had far more children on average than their never-widowed brothers. The same cannot be said of the widowed sons of monogamous men, who had no more children on average than their never-widowed brothers. Although it is hard to believe that having their wives die was part of a reproductive strategy, the widowed sons of polygynous men were able to make the best of a bad situation, even though they were no more likely to have remarried than the sons of monogamous men.

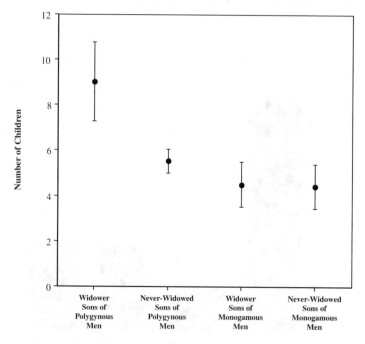

FIG. 14.8.   The average number of children ($\pm$ 2 standard error) of the widower and never-widower sons of polygynous and monogamous men. The widower sons of polygynous men had more children than their never-widower brothers (9.03 ± 1.73, $n = 29$, vs. 5.53 ± 0.53, $n = 231$, $p < 0.0000$). Conversely, the widower sons of monogamous men had no more children than their brothers who were never widowers (4.50 ± 1.0, $n = 2$, vs. 4.43 ± 0.98, $n = 90$, $p = 0.9840$). The widower sons of polygynous men had more children than the widower sons of monogamous men, although this difference was not significant at the $\alpha = 0.05$ level (9.03 ± 1.73, $n = 29$, vs. 4.50 ± 1.0, $n = 2$, $p = 0.1865$). The never-widower sons of polygynous men had more children than the never-widower sons of monogamous men (5.53 ± 0.53, $n = 231$, vs. 4.43 ± 0.98, $n = 90$, $p = 0.0375$).

The picture is somewhat different for daughters. Recall that the daughters of polygynous and monogamous men, unlike their brothers, were equally likely to be widowed before the age of 50 (Fig. 14.7). The effect of widowhood on the reproductive success of daughters is also different (Fig. 14.9). Becoming a widow seems to have little effect on number of children for the daughters of polygynous men compared to their never-widowed sisters, as is true for the daughters of monogamous men. This is likely a reflection of how remarriage affects women's and men's reproductive careers differently. Widows who remarry were unable to extend their reproductive careers past the age of 50, unlike widowers who can continue having children if they remarry a younger woman. Also, many of the husbands who died did so after their wives had nearly finished their reproductive

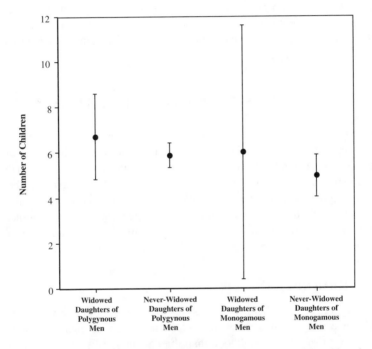

FIG. 14.9.   The average number of children ($\pm$ 2 standard error) of the widowed and never-widowed daughters of polygynous and monogamous men. The widowed daughters of polygynous men had as many children as their never-widowed sisters (6.70 $\pm$ 1.89, n = 10, vs. 5.86 $\pm$ 0.54, n = 230, p = 0.5243), also true for the daughters of monogamous men (6.00 $\pm$ 5.60, n = 4, vs. 4.95 $\pm$ 0.93, n = 97, p = 0.6577). The widowed daughters of polygynous men had as many children as the widowed daughters of monogamous men (6.70 $\pm$ 1.89, n = 10, vs. 6.00 $\pm$ 5.60, n = 4, p = 0.7614). The never-widowed daughters of polygynous men had more children than the never-widowed daughters of monogamous men, although this difference was not significant at the α = 0.05 level (5.86 $\pm$ 0.54, n = 230, vs. 4.95 $\pm$ 0.93, n = 97, p = 0.0804).

careers, so the effect of their death on their wife's reproductive success was reduced. For those who were widowed at younger ages, the high rate of remarriage tended to mitigate the adverse effects of widowhood, regardless of whom their father was (Josephson, 2000; Mineau, 1988).

Yet again, we see that the sons and daughters of polygynous men had more children, even when we remove the effects of remarriage. The nonpolygynous, once-married sons and daughters of polygynous men had more children overall than the sons and daughters of monogamous men. The absolute difference was greater in sons than in daughters, but there is a significant effect in both sexes. This implies that the fecundity of these marriages was higher in some way not captured by the number of marriages (Josephson, 2000). Nevertheless, the effect of having a polygynous, high-status father is clearly higher fertility for his children. Although this no doubt increased the long-term reproductive success of polygynous men themselves, it may also explain other things, such as how these men got to be polygynous in the first place and why monogamous men invested in their daughters' survivorship.

FATHERING AS REPRODUCTIVE STRATEGY

At the broadest level, these results suggest that men follow different paternal investment strategies depending on their level of resources. For men with fewer resources, it may have been better to invest in their children's survivorship or at least in the survival of their daughters. For men with more resources, it may have been better to invest in helping their children marry. We've seen some indication how this happened, but we still don't know *why* it happened. The reason may be that men allocate resources to fathering in ways that maximize their own reproductive success, contingent on whether or not they were able to attract one wife or several.

Monogamous Men

For monogamous men, there are two issues to address, both likely related. First, the evidence suggests that the daughters of monogamous men were somewhat more likely to survive to adulthood than the daughters of polygynous men, and even more likely to survive than their own brothers. Second, although monogamous men's sons and daughters had lower fertility than the children of polygynous men, monogamous men's sons fared far worse than their sisters. How might these two issues be related and what does this tell us about the way monogamous men allocated resources to fathering?

The simplest explanation turns on the idea that monogamous men probably had fewer resources to invest overall. Monogamous men may have wanted to augment their children's fertility as polygynous men did, if only as a way of increasing their own long-term reproductive success. But whatever it was that polygynous men did to help their children marry, monogamous men may simply have been less able to do it. This would explain why the sons and daughters of monogamous men had fewer children on average, even when we restrict attention to children who married only once. It also brings us back to the issue of why monogamous men's sons had fewer children than monogamous men's daughters.

It may all come back to the fact that this was a group that allowed polygynous marriage. If there are roughly equal numbers of men and women in a group, two wives for one man means no wife for another. This is especially a problem in polygynous groups, where men can have more than one wife at the same time. This could only increase the competition for spouses among men, although it may ease the competition among women. Women can almost always marry in a group where every man is a bachelor, meaning that the variance in reproductive success will likely be lower in women than in men. With such keen competition for mates, sons who receive greater assistance from their fathers can have a real advantage over those who receive less. Monogamous men may not have been able to help their sons be competitive with polygynous men's sons, but even a poorly supplied daughter might be at less of a disadvantage. Given their sons' dismal prospects, monogamous men may have preferentially helped their daughters marry, although still not enough to bring them equal to polygynous men's daughters.

This also suggests an explanation for why the daughters of monogamous men showed higher survivorship. If monogamous men are trying to maximize their own long-term reproductive success, they might be more inclined to invest in their daughter's survivorship rather than their son's. If monogamous men "know" (in an evolutionary sense, if not consciously) that they will be unable to make their sons competitive with the sons of polygynous men, this may have affected their parental investment from the start (Trivers & Willard, 1973). It is easy to see why they might want to invest more in daughters, as we know that monogamous men's daughters had far more children than monogamous men's sons. It may seem hard to imagine that monogamous men would be able to anticipate so far into the future that their daughters would be a better bet than their sons. Yet such biased investment is exactly what we might expect when parental resources are limited and parents are forced to make trade-offs (Trivers & Willard, 1973). Given limited resources and a highly competitive environment, we might expect monogamous men to invest less in their sons, because they lack the resources to make sons competitive with the sons of polygynous men. Given that daughters are likely to have more children, we might also expect monogamous men to channel their investment to where it would do themselves the most good, helping daughters survive into adulthood and to have children of their own.

Polygynous Men

The investment in fathering by polygynous men is also contingent on their own reproductive interests. Polygynous men may have had more resources to expend than monogamous men, but this does not mean that they invested indiscriminately. They did not, for instance, preferentially invest in their children's survivorship, even though there is some suggestion that they might have been able to do so. As we saw, polygynous men's daughters, at least, were actually less likely to survive to adulthood than the daughters of monogamous men. If monogamous men could do it, why didn't polygynous men do it as well? The sons and daughters of polygynous men did benefit greatly once they had lived long enough to marry and have children of their own, but this happened much later. If these patterns reflect investment by polygynous men, we have to wonder why they invested later but not earlier in their children's lives.

The reason may be that polygynous men, like monogamous men, used paternal investment to maximize their own reproductive success. This may seem an odd explanation because increasing the survivorship of their children could only have increased polygynous men's own long-term reproductive success. Yet even if these men had more resources than monogamous men, this does not mean that they were not also forced to make trade-offs. Investing early in their children's lives may have meant having less to invest later. Even more interesting, investing later in their children's lives may have helped men become polygynous, the price of which could be increased risk to their children.

Polygynous marriages seem to have a bad effect on the survivorship of children, in this group and elsewhere. In several groups where data is available, the children of polygynous men have a somewhat lower rate of survivorship than the children of monogamous men, although it is still unclear why this happens (Chojnacka, 1980; Josephson, 2000; Strassman, 1997). Whatever the reason, the decrease in survivorship is a serious cost from the perspective of polygynous men. We have to wonder why polygynous men would allow such a thing to happen if they could prevent it. If, however, reduced survivorship in children is an inescapable price of polygynous marriage, then this may not be so mysterious after all (see Josephson, in press). Men may be willing to expose their children to increased risk if they themselves derived some benefit from doing so.

For men, the positive effect of marrying several wives was far greater than the negative effects of increased child mortality. The lower survivorship for polygynous men's daughters is not great, implying that polygynous men's loss by not investing more in his children's survivorship was small. On the other hand, polygynous men with even one extra wife had far more children and grandchildren. In this sample, each new wife meant an extra 22 grandchildren, equal to the number of grandchildren monogamous men could expect from their one wife (Josephson, 2000). Given these circumstances, we might expect men to opt for polygyny whenever they could, even if this increased the risk of death for his children (Josephson, 1999).

Interestingly, the reason polygynous men were able to become polygynous may have been their investment as fathers. Absent coercion, the only way to get women into polygynous marriage is to get them to agree to it. This may be difficult, as women even in polygynous cultures are often suspicious of polygynous marriage (Borgerhoff Mulder, 1988, 1991). And well they might be, as in this group and most others, polygynous women had substantially fewer children on average than monogamous women (Bean & Mineau, 1986; see review in Josephson, 2000). This cost would have to be offset by some benefit, otherwise women should avoid polygyny whenever possible (Searcy & Yasukawa, 1989; Josephson, 2000). In this group at least, the benefit women received from polygyny was having high-fertility children, which exactly offset their own reduced fertility. This meant that polygynous women ended up with the same number of grandchildren as they might have had they married monogamously. Thus, polygynous men's investment in fathering may explain why women are sometimes willing to marry polygynously and why polygyny is invariably the prerogative of socially successful men.

Polygynous men seem to have used paternal investment to maximize their own reproductive success, in the short run and the long run. In the short run, these men used their resources not so much to help their children survive but to gain social status, positioning themselves to be able to help their children in the future. They gained from this immediately by attracting extra wives, women who were willing to share these men in order to have his highly successful children. Polygynous men also gained in the long run because their influence helped their children have high fertility, again increasing their own long-term reproductive success. For polygynous men, helping their children marry may have been simply the best route to help themselves (Josephson, 1999).

CONCLUSION

All of this suggests that the effort men put into fathering is subject to a number of conflicting interests. Regardless of how much men have to invest in fathering, how much they actually will invest depends on their own reproductive interests. This has implications not only for other polygynous groups, but for ostensibly monogamous groups as well. Wherever men can divert resources away from their children and into seeking additional mates, we should not be surprised that some do so. The fact that this is not best for their children is less important than whether or not men themselves benefit. The way men invest in fathering and the psychology that underlies this depends on men's overall reproductive strategy and may, in fact, be difficult to understand outside this context.

REFERENCES

Andersson, M. (1994). *Sexual selection.* Princeton, NJ: Princeton University Press.

Bean, L. L., & Mineau, G. P. (1986). The polygyny-fertility hypothesis: A reevaluation. *Population Studies, 40,* 67–81.

Betzig, L. L. (1986). *Despotism and differential reproduction: A Darwinian view of history.* New York: Aldine de Gruyter.

Borgerhoff Mulder, M. (1988). Is the polygyny threshold model relevant to humans? In C. G. N. Mascie-Taylor & A. J. Boyce (Eds.), *Mating patterns.* (pp. 209–230). Cambridge: Cambridge University Press.

Borgerhoff Mulder, M. (1991). Behavioral ecology of humans. In J. Krebs & N. Davies (Eds.), *Behavioral ecology: An evolutionary approach* (3rd ed., pp. 69–98). Oxford: Blackwell Scientific Publications.

Brodie, F. M. (1945). *No man knows my history: The life of Joseph Smith the Mormon prophet.* New York: Alfred Knopf.

Chojnacka, H. (1980). Polygyny and the rate of population growth. *Population Studies, 34,* 91–107.

Clutton-Brock, T. H. (1991). *The evolution of parental care.* Princeton, NJ: Princeton University Press.

Cronk, L. (1991). Wealth, status, and reproductive success among the Mukogodo of Kenya. *American Anthropologist, 93,* 414–429.

Dickemann, M. (1979). Female infanticide, reproductive strategies and social stratification: A preliminary model. In N. A. Chagnon & W. Irons (Eds.), *Evolutionary biology and human social behavior: An anthropological perspective,* (pp. 321–367). North Sinuate, MA: Duxbury Press.

Essock-Vitale, S. M. (1984). The reproductive success of wealthy Americans. *Ethology and Sociobiology, 5,* 45–49.

Flinn, M. V. (1986). Correlates of reproductive success in a Caribbean village. *Human Ecology, 14,* 225–243.

Fox, R. (1993). *Reproduction and succession: Studies in anthropology, law, and society.* New Brunswick, NJ: Transaction.

Grafen, A. (1991). Modeling in behavioral ecology. In J. R. Krebs & N. B. Davies (Eds.), *Behavioral ecology: An evolutionary approach* (3rd ed., pp. 5–31). Oxford: Blackwell Scientific Publications.

Hartung, J. (1982). Polygyny and the inheritance of wealth. *Current Anthropology, 23,* 1–12.

Hewett, B. S. (Ed.). (1992). *Father-child relations: Cultural and biosocial contexts.* New York: Aldine de Gruyter.

Irons, W. (1975). *The Yomut Turkmen: A study of social organization among a central Asian Turkic speaking population.* Ann Arbor: Museum of Anthropology, University of Michigan.

Irons, W. (1983). Human reproductive strategies. In S. K. Wasser (Ed.), *Social behavior of female vertebrates.* New York: Academic Press (pp. 169–213).

Ivins, S. (1956). Notes on Mormon polygamy. *Western Humanities Review, 10,* 229–239.

Josephson, S. C. (1993). Status, reproductive success, and marrying polygynously. *Ethology and Sociobiology, 14,* 391–396.

Josephson, S. C. (1998a, December). *An evolutionary perspective on the "polygyny-fertility" hypothesis.* American Anthropological Association Meeting, Philadelphia, PA.

Josephson, S. C. (1998b, July). *Polygyny and paternal investment.* Human Behavior and Evolution Society Meeting, University of California–Davis.

Josephson, S. C. (1999). *The grandfather effect.* Human Behavior and Evolution Society Meeting, Salt Lake City, UT.

Josephson, S. C. (2000). *Polygyny, fertility, and human reproductive strategies.* Ph.D. dissertation, University of Utah, Salt Lake City.

Josephson, S. C. (in press). Does polygyny reduce fertility? *American Journal of Human Biology.*

Judge, D. S. (1995). American legacies and the variable life history of women and men. *Human Nature, 6,* 291–323.

Kaplan, H. (1996). A theory of fertility and parental investment in traditional and modern human societies. *Yearbook of Physical Anthropology, 39,* 91–135.

Krebs, J. R., & Davies, N. B. (1991). *Behavioral ecology: An evolutionary approach.* Oxford: Blackwell Scientific Publications.

Lack, D. (1966). *Population studies of birds.* Oxford, UK: Clarendon Press.

Lack, D. (1968). *Ecological adaptations for breeding in birds.* London: Chapman & Hall.

Low, B. S. (2000). *Why sex matters: A Darwinian look at human behavior.* Princeton, NJ: Princeton University Press.

May, D. (1992). A demographic portrait of the Mormons, 1830–1980. In D. M. Quinn (Ed.), *The new Mormon history.* (pp. 121–136) Salt Lake City, UT: Signature Books.

Maynard Smith, J. (1977). Parental investment—a prospective analysis. *Animal Behavior, 25,* 1–9.

Mealey, L. (1995). The relation between social status and biological success: A case study of the Mormon religious hierarchy. *Ethology and Sociobiology, 6,* 249–257.

Mineau, G. P. (1988). Utah widowhood: A demographic profile. In A. Scadron (Ed.), *On their own: Widows and widowhood in the American southwest 1848–1939* (pp. 129–154). Urbana: University of Illinois.

Mineau, G. P., Bean, L. L., & Skolnick, M. (1979). Mormon demographic history, II: The family life cycle and natural fertility. *Population Studies, 33,* 429–446.

Quinn, M. (1976). *The Mormon hierarchy, 1832–1932.* Unpublished Ph.D. dissertation, Yale University.

Searcy, W. A., & Yasukawa, K. (1989). Alternative models of territorial polygyny in birds. *American Naturalist, 134,* 323–343.

Smith, J. E., & Kunz, P. R. (1976). Polygyny and fertility in nineteenth century America. *Population Studies, 30,* 465–480.

Strassman, B. I. (1997). Polygyny as a risk factor for child mortality among the Dogon of Mali. *Current Anthropology, 38,* 688–695.

Trivers, R. L. (1972). Parental investment and sexual selection. In B. Campbell (Ed.), *Sexual selection and the descent of man* (pp. 136–179). Chicago: Aldine.

Trivers, R. L., Willard, D. E. (1972). Natural selection of paternal ability to vary the sex ratio of offspring. *Science, 179,* 90–92

Vehrencamp, S. L., & Bradbury, J. W. (1984). Mating systems and ecology. In J. R. Krebs & N. B. Davies (Eds.), *Behavioral ecology: An evolutionary approach* (pp. 251–278). Oxford: Blackwell Scientific Publications.

Voland, E., & Dunbar, R. I. M. (1995). Resource competition and reproduction: The relationship between economic and parental strategies in the Krummhorn population (1720–1874). *Human Nature, 6,* 33–49.

Williams, G. C. (1966). Natural selection, the costs of reproduction and a refinement of Lack's principal. *American Naturalist, 100,* 687–690.

Williams, G. C. (1975). *Sex and Evolution.* Princeton, NJ: Princeton University Press.

Woodroffe, R., & Vincent, A. (1994). Mother's little helpers: Patterns of male care in mammals. *TREE, 9,* 294–297.

V

Father Involvement: Economic Perspectives

Irwin Garfinkel
Columbia University

The three chapters in this section approach the question of fathers' involvement with their children from an economic perspective. All three examine both the predictions derived from economic theories and empirical evidence. All also examine the effects of social policies, especially welfare and child support policies. The first chapter, "Involving Dads: Parental Bargaining and Family Well-Being," by Paula England and Nancy Folbre, explores the relationship between parental involvement and bargaining among both married coresident parents and nonmarried noncohabiting parents. Parenting, like all human activities, involves costs as well as benefits. One cost, borne disproportionately by mothers, is that the time put into parenthood reduces earnings. The partner with lower earnings has less bargaining power. Direct caregivers often find themselves in a weak position not only because they have lower earnings and less economic independence, but also because they have become more emotionally attached to the child they are caring for. Thus, parents who specialize in primary caregiving (usually mothers) have less bargaining power than parents who specialize in contributing financial support.

Less gender specialization in the form of parental involvement could lead to improved outcomes for children by improving mothers' economic position and by strengthening emotional connections between fathers and children. Imposing standardized monetary obligations through strict enforcement of child support probably raises the bargaining power of married and divorced mothers. But, in some situations, it can have adverse consequences for both mothers and children. Standardized child support guidelines can also reduce mothers' informal bargaining power over both forms and levels of father involvement. Inflexible and coercive rules imposed on families receiving public assistance have negative effects, undermining the sense of emotional connection and intrinsic pleasure of parenting that is the best guarantee of father involvement. England and Folbre conclude that there are better ways to improve the relative bargaining power of mothers and the well-being of children.

"The Effects of Welfare, Child Support, and Labor Markets on Father Involvement" by Sigle-Rushton and Garfinkel, assumes that father investments of time and money in their children promote good child outcomes. Economic theory predicts that marriage promotes these kinds of father–child involvement. Theory also predicts that welfare and child support policies and labor market conditions effect marriage. Thus, the chapter reviews the economic literature on the effects of welfare, child support enforcement, and labor markets on father noninvolvement with their children due to divorce, separation, and nonmarital births.

Economic theory predicts that welfare programs like AFDC/TANF that are limited to unmarried parents and/or are steeply income tested will discourage marriage. More universal programs like child allowances, or the EITC, may encourage or discourage marriage. Child support enforcement may either discourage or encourage divorce among families who would not be reliant on welfare but is likely to discourage divorce and nonmarital births among families who would be reliant on welfare. Increases in labor market opportunities for men promote marriage, whereas increases in labor market opportunities for women may either promote or discourage marriage.

Empirical research mostly confirms the theoretical predictions. Fathers who live with their children invest substantially more time and money in their children than do nonresident fathers. High AFDC/TANF benefits are associated with more divorce and, more questionably, with more nonmarital births. Strong child support enforcement deters divorce and nonmarital births. Higher wages and greater employment for males are associated with higher marriage rates. Greater employment of women is associated with more divorce, but the effects of wage rates are more ambiguous and appear to differ by education and race. But, most studies find that the effects of welfare, or child support, or labor market opportunities are, by themselves, small.

"Nonresident Fathers and Their Children: Child Support and Visitation from an Economic Perspective," by Graham and Beller, reviews recent economic theories that help explain why nonresident fathers may fail to either pay much child support or spend much time with their children. The chapter summarizes empirical evidence on fathers' involvement with their children, examines the ability of fathers to pay support, reviews new programs designed to help low-income fathers pay support, and looks at the consequences of child support payments and visitation for the well-being of children and the behavior of fathers.

The authors found that most nonresident fathers pay little or no child support and also spend little or no time with their children. Although most nonresident fathers could pay more child support, there is a large group of very poor nonresident fathers who can pay very little child support. These fathers need help in meeting their child support obligations, but child support enforcement has only recently turned its attention in this direction, and we know very little about how to assist such fathers. Moreover, there is a strong deterrent for low-income fathers to pay child support for his children on welfare because, under current welfare rules, little or no child support actually gets passed through to his children.

There is abundant evidence that higher child support payments are associated with higher academic achievement of children. Whether there is a causal relationship is less clear. Furthermore, forcing nonresident fathers to comply with the child support system may result in increased conflict between the parents, which could offset, or more than offset, the beneficial effects of the additional income.

15

Involving Dads: Parental Bargaining and Family Well-Being

Paula England
Northwestern University

Nancy Folbre
University of Massachusetts

Some fathers are more involved with their children than others, but few do as much caregiving as mothers. How does the degree of father involvement affect the relative bargaining power of parents with each other? And, reversing the causal arrow, how does the relative bargaining power of parents affect how involved fathers will be with their children? To what extent are these dynamics affected by whether the two parents are (or ever were) a married or cohabiting couple? What does a concern for both gender equality and the well-being of children suggest for public policies related to fathers' involvement with children?

These questions converge from two distinct but related academic literatures, one motivated by a concern for women and the other by a concern for children. Even among married coresident parents, paternal involvement generally takes the form of economic support rather than direct child care. Feminists interested in gender equality have long advocated more equal sharing of direct responsibility between mothers and fathers in order to equalize career opportunities between men and women. Specialization in child care, they argue, is economically risky for women and lowers their relative bargaining power within marriage.

In this chapter we develop an interdisciplinary analysis of negotiations over different forms as well as levels of parental involvement. Parenting requires inputs of time and emotional care, for which money cannot always buy substitutes. Furthermore, the form of parental involvement has important implications for the development of emotional ties, which in turn influence the goals of bargaining itself. Although married, cohabiting, and noncohabiting parents are in very different situations, all are likely to be affected by the relationship between bargaining power and parental involvement.

Although our analysis is conceptual and exploratory, it generates some hypotheses relevant to both empirical research and policy debate. The first section of this chapter delineates different forms of parental involvement and explains the basic logic of bargaining models. The second section explores links between parental involvement and the relative bargaining power of mothers and fathers among married or cohabiting parents. The third section provides a parallel analysis of noncoresident parents. In a concluding section focused on policy implications, we emphasize the need to think carefully about the ways in which specific laws and rules may affect intrafamily dynamics.

PARENTAL INVOLVEMENT AND BARGAINING

Academic research on parental involvement has been characterized by a rather strict disciplinary division of labor: Psychologists focus on emotional dimensions, economists on transfers of income and wealth, and sociologists on the effects of family structure and social norms. We believe that bargaining models offer a way of developing a more integrated, interdisciplinary approach.

Parental Involvement

The most visible aspects of parental involvement are inputs of money and time. Parents who choose not to contribute either of these inputs are generally considered uninvolved "deadbeats." Within a certain range, money and time are substitutes. For instance, noncustodial parents are expected to contribute money, but less time than a custodial parent. But a parent who spends absolutely no time—and has no personal contact with their child—would seldom be considered "involved." Indeed, the importance of personal contact suggests that the effects of both money and time are greater when they are combined with emotional care—a combination of altruism, effort, and skill—that affects the extent to which the child feels loved, listened to, and supported—in short, "parented."

Therefore, we focus on three dimensions of parental involvement—money, time, and emotional care—all of which contribute to children's well-being.[1] In

---

[1] Our typology of types of parental involvement overlaps with that of Michael Lamb (1986), who examines involvement in terms of interaction, accessibility, and responsibility. Despite our different terminology, it is clear that his categories of interaction and accessibility relate to our category of inputs of time, and his category of responsibility to our notion of emotional effort.

some families, both parents make substantial contributions along all three dimensions. A more traditional arrangement is a gender-based division of labor in which mothers provide time and emotional care and fathers provide money. Among single-parent households, it is not unusual for mothers to provide virtually 100% of all parental contributions.

Recognition of the limits to substitutability among money, time, and care should be accompanied by appreciation of their complementarity. Although it is hard to know which way causality flows, there is some evidence that each form of involvement encourages others. Parents who spend more time with their children tend to develop stronger emotional relationships with them, so giving inputs of time and emotional care tend to go together. High paternal involvement prior to divorce is associated with a higher likelihood of later making child support payments (Peters et al., 1993). Divorced fathers who do not want contact with their children tend to be those who were less involved within marriage (Greif, 1995). Fathers with joint legal custody tend to have more contact with their children, even controlling for the quality of family relationships prior to divorce (Seltzer, McLanahan, & Hanson, 1998). Payment of child support leads to good outcomes for children independent of increases in income (Baydar & Brooks-Gunn, 1994). These findings suggest that stricter enforcement of child support could increase other dimensions of paternal involvement. However, if enforcement is seen by fathers as coercive and involuntary, it may elicit a compensatory reduction in time and emotional care, or even a kind of emotional backlash (McLanahan, Seltzer, Hanson, & Thomson, 1994; Seltzer et al., 1998).

Custody itself is probably the biggest factor determining the level of parental involvement among parents who do not live together, because of its long-run effects on the level of emotional effort, care, and connection. In some families, noncustodial parents visit frequently and consistently. This is especially true immediately after children are born to unmarried parents who are romantically involved. However, these relationships tend to either turn into cohabitation or marriage or break up within a year or two. When parents are divorced or were never married and are no longer romantically involved, fathers' involvement with children is often minimal and sporadic. Among a significant minority of such families, paternal visitation tapers off to nothing or nearly nothing within a few years (Furstenberg, Nord, Peterson, & Zill, 1983; Nord and Zill, 1996).

Noncustodial parents tend to disengage emotionally for several reasons, whether as a result of relationship atrophy ("out of sight out of mind"), emotional avoidance ("it's just too painful to see my kids under these conditions"), or over-reliance on the custodial parent ("she'll take good care of the kids no matter what I do"). Custodial parents may want to avoid contact with their previous partners at all costs. Emotional disengagement may contribute to financial disengagement, or vice versa. In any case, the effects are cumulative: The more emotionally disengaged the noncustodial parent becomes, the less implicit bargaining power the custodial parent has to increase either payment or time inputs. If the noncustodial

parent feels little connection to—and wants no contact with—the child, the custodial parent is less able to successfully use an appeal to the needs of the child or a
threat to make visitation or contact more difficult as a bargaining strategy. Furthermore, the less emotionally engaged the noncustodial parent becomes, the less
the custodial parent and child have to gain from personal contact with him (or
her). Thus, disengagement of one type breeds further disengagement.

Most parents want to increase their children's well-being. But the ways they
want to do so are shaped not merely by their perceptions of children's needs but
also by their own preferences—how they weigh their children's and fellow-
parent's well-being relative to their own. A father may feel less need to be
involved in direct parenting if a mother is already providing substantial effort, and
vice versa. Both levels and forms of parental involvement are subject to negotiation and bargaining. For instance, one parent might want the other parent to spend
more time or money or simply give more personal attention to a child. That parent
might offer something in return, as in, "If you'll put the children to bed, I'll do the
dishes."

Parents don't negotiate over every detail of their lives. Many aspects of the
division of labor in parenting are determined by social norms or prior agreement.
Traditionally, we expect fathers to provide more income and mothers to provide
more direct care for children. But in periods of time when both social norms and
individual economic opportunities are rapidly changing, the scope for individual
bargaining probably increases. For instance, a mother who has high earnings
potential or who is committed to her career is likely to bargain with the father to
increase his direct involvement in child care (Mahoney, 1995).

Such negotiations are necessarily complex. Parental involvement is a not a
simple "product" but a process that requires emotional effort as well as time and
money. It imposes costs, but it also confers benefits. Therefore, we cannot assume
that parents always want to minimize it or to maximize it—rather they probably
seek some level of involvement that is determined both by their perceptions of
what children need, their own preferences, and what they believe the other parent
should and could provide. It is important to remember, however, that some circu-
larity comes into play; for example, a parent's bargaining power may affect how
much the other parent is involved with the child, but that involvement may in turn
affect the parents' relative bargaining power.

Bargaining Models

Bargaining models reject the assumption that families can be described as a unit
with common preferences and call attention to the fact that individuals maneuver
to get what they want. The fundamental idea is that the more one has access to a
resource that he or she is sharing with the other, but could withhold and use for
oneself, the greater one's bargaining power. What can one use bargaining power
for? For any of the things that family members negotiate—where they will live,
how many children they will have, what their joint social life will be, what each

partner will do with their time, how they will treat each other, what they will buy with their money, and many other issues.

In our discussion of bargaining models, we will distinguish between two kinds of resources on which bargaining power can be based: economic and noneconomic resources. Economic resources refer to money that a person has through inheritance, earnings, or rights to governmental transfers. Noneconomic resources include other things such as one's personal attractiveness or being in a situation to control the other parent's access to time or the affections of a child. How do resources affect one parent's power in bargaining with the other? Economists answer this question with the concept of "threat points" (Lundberg & Pollak 1996; McElroy, 1990; McElroy & Horney, 1981). Sociologists applying exchange theory use similar logic (Molm & Cook, 1995; Heer, 1963; Scanzoni, 1979.)

"External threat point" models emphasize that bargaining within marriage is conducted in the shadow of the possibility of divorce. (For cohabitants, the analogue to divorce is breaking up the cohabitational arrangement.) An individual's "threat point" is what they have to fall back on if the marriage (or cohabitation) dissolves. The individual's well-being if the marriage dissolves is affected by their economic resources—their earnings and access to other income (e.g., from child support or the state)—because this is what they would have to live on in the event of a divorce. Well-being after a breakup would also be affected by how individuals would fare on the remarriage market and on whether they could have custody of and support for their children. Optimizing individuals will choose whether or not to stay in the marriage by comparing the utility they experience in the marriage to what they anticipate if they leave the marriage.

"Internal threat point" models focus on what one spouse can withhold from the other without leaving the marriage (Lundberg & Pollak, 1993, 1996). In the absence of explicit negotiation, the partners will rely on a rule or a social norm regarding the allocation of household resources. However, they may negotiate, or bargain over, reallocations that leave them both better off. For instance, one partner might agree to provide more money to the household in return for more assistance with care responsibilities. As in external threat point models, resources need not have pecuniary value to yield bargaining power. Contributions of nonmarket work or emotional care can be a source of power, if the contributor can credibly threaten to withhold them.

Both married and cohabiting couples need to manage shared resources and responsibilities on a daily basis. Marriage may signal greater emotional commitment to the relationship and is often accompanied by a greater commingling of economic resources, making dissolution of the relationship more costly to both parties. With the advent of no-fault divorce rules, however, the differences between marriage and cohabitation have diminished, suggesting that the basic dynamics of bargaining are similar in both married and cohabiting couples. Among noncohabiting parents, the scope of bargaining is more limited to arrangements concerning the care of children.

Broadening Bargaining Models

In defining bargaining power, it is tempting to consider only resources and pay-offs that can be easily quantified, such as money or hours of work. Such a definition implies that individuals are primarily motivated by a desire to maximize their personal consumption or leisure time. But in families, people are not simply trying to maximize their material consumption or leisure; they are also hoping for love, affection, trust, respect, and reciprocity. If we could assume that everyone in the family loved each other in perfectly equal ways, feelings and levels of concern for one another would not impinge on bargaining.

In fact, however, some family members (e.g., children) may have a greater need for love than others, and some family members may be more skilled than others at providing the emotional aspects of care and connection in families (women are often credited with this skill). Furthermore, these feelings are not simply given from the outset, nor do they remain unchanged. In some respects, these feelings are actively produced by the efforts of family members to maintain and strengthen their family relationships. Promising or withholding emotional access—either directly, or through contact with children—can play an important, if difficult to assess, role in parental bargaining.

Another shortcoming of traditional approaches to bargaining is that they assume that people immediately recognize opportunities for striking deals that will make everybody better off. In technical terms, it is traditionally assumed that bargaining is "efficient." As any family therapist will point out, however, many families are not very good at negotiating solutions that make everybody better off. For example, people are often too proud to ask for emotional nurturance, wishing that their partners would perceive when it is needed and provide it without them having to feel the vulnerability that comes of asking. But as a result, a partner willing to provide support may never know when it is wanted.

It is important, therefore, to think about factors that might affect the process rather than simply the outcomes of bargaining (Folbre, 2000). Emotional skills of various sorts may be important. Thus, we recommend considering all relevant resources, economic and noneconomic, that affect bargaining. We also think it important to remember that power struggles in the family (and probably elsewhere) are not just over payoffs such as being able to spend money on what you want, but also include emotional rewards.

MARRIED CORESIDENT PARENTS

The influence of fallback positions on bargaining means that all families with children—including those that remain intact—are affected by the consequences of separation or divorce. Married coresident couples are on one side of that divide, nonmarried noncoresident parents are on the other. Almost by definition, married coresident couples have much more to bargain over—their division of labor in parenting, as well as the many decisions affecting a common household. Therefore, the causal arrow that runs from parental involvement to bargaining seems especially important for them.

Effects of Parental Involvement on Bargaining

Married or Cohabiting Couples.   Fathers in married or cohabiting couples exhibit a wide range of levels and forms of involvement with children. In traditional, specialized "breadwinner/homemaker" households, paternal involvement largely takes the form of contributions of income rather than time. Constraints on fathers' time come not only from their hours of market work but also from gendered norms that designate tasks such as bathing, feeding, dressing, and emotionally soothing children as "women's work," even during the hours the dad is at home.

One alternative to the traditional pattern is the "equal participation" dad, who provides close to one half of the direct care that children receive (Mahoney, 1995; Deutsch, 1999). This is most likely to occur where spouses both have jobs, so we might expect closer to equal earnings in these couples. Equal participation by mothers and fathers can be achieved in two very different ways—by reducing maternal participation or by increasing paternal participation. For example, parents who both have very demanding careers may purchase child care and many related services as substitutes for their own time. On the other hand, both spouses may reduce their hours of market work, or work different shifts, in order to spend more time with their children.

What do the bargaining theories considered above have to say about how these ideal-typical families would differ in terms of the relative bargaining power of fathers and mothers? The implications for bargaining power that flows from the economic resource of earnings are clear, because specialization in the direct care of children almost always entails a loss of earnings. While mothers are at home taking care of children, they are not employed, or reduce their employment to part-time, and thus earn less. Apart from the immediate reduction in earnings there are indirect effects on job tenure and experience that reduce future earnings. More subtle negative effects of parenting time on earnings may operate via productivity, such as being affected by exhaustion on the job from parenthood (Waldfogel, 1997; Budig & England, 2001).

Some mothers seem aware of the ways in which specialization in direct care may increase their economic vulnerability. An interesting illustration of this awareness comes from a comparison of the labor force participation rates of mothers in states with and without no-fault divorce rules. When either partner can easily obtain divorce without the consent of the other, neither partner can threaten to block the divorce. When divorce requires mutual consent, on the other hand, the partner least eager to divorce can threaten to withhold consent unless more generous property division or child support agreements are offered. In states with no-fault divorce, mothers tend to increase their labor force participation in the years preceding divorce, perhaps because they anticipate greater economic vulnerability (Peters, 1986). If specialization in direct care increases women's vulnerability to poverty after a divorce, it must surely reduce their bargaining power in marriage, according to the logic of bargaining theory.

The implications of specializing in caregiving for noneconomic dimensions of bargaining power are less clear. One could argue that a woman who provides such services could gain power from them: She could potentially withdraw her inputs of time and emotional care just as he could withdraw his earnings. However, women don't typically stop giving time and emotional caring to their children on divorce; rather, they get custody of the children and continue caring for them. Indeed, most mothers feel so much emotional connection to and altruism toward their children that they would not consider withdrawing their mothering services as a bargaining ploy with the father. Maternal altruism may be greater than paternal altruism, partly for biological reasons, although this is hotly debated. (See Hrdy, 1999, for a nuanced consideration of evolution and maternal altruism.) Whatever the cause, women's commitment to care for their children, although probably good for children's well-being, virtually eliminates the extent to which they can use the noneconomic resource of childrearing to get things for themselves in bargaining with fathers (England & Farkas, 1986; England & Kilbourne, 1990).

Fathers' relatively lower level of emotional connection to children reduces the extent to which a threat of maternal withdrawal, even if credible, would change their behavior. All this suggests that, although giving time and emotional care to children undoubtedly offers rich rewards, it does not lend itself to use as a resource in bargaining. Fathers know that mothers are likely to take care of the children no matter what they do. In this respect, we might call mothers "prisoners of love."

Mothers may derive some bargaining advantage from a credible threat to deprive the father of regular contact with the child. If a man can only live with his children and their mother by remaining married, and he wants to do so, the threat of divorce gives his wife some bargaining power. However, being able to leave a marriage and take the children is a hollow victory less conducive to the woman's or child's well-being if she can't be sure she will get custody of the children *and* continued economic support from the father. This makes us doubt how much bargaining power women get from this threat. In any case, it suggests that the legal realities of custody and child support both affect men's and women's threat points and thus their bargaining power within marriage. We turn to a consideration of these issues now.

Noncohabiting parents.   In practice, custody arrangements vary along a continuum from sole custody with no visitation rights to sole custody with visitation rights, joint legal custody, and joint physical custody. Most families lie in the mid-

dle of this continuum. In 1995, three quarters of custodial mothers reported having
either a visitation or a joint custody agreement (Peters, 2000, p. 7). Many observers
suggest that we are seeing a trend toward an increase in joint legal custody
(Garfinkel & Huang, 2000) As in the preceding analysis, which parent this benefits
the most depends both on their preferences and on their relative economic positions.

Rules about custody and support interact in ways that illustrate the interplay of
nonpecuniary and economic benefits. Child custody is psychologically important
to parents, especially to primary caregivers whose involvement is time and care
intensive. They may feel that custody is necessary in order to provide greater continuity for themselves or the child; furthermore, as primary caregivers, they may
be more emotionally attached to the child. As we discussed, this means that most
mothers cannot make a credible threat to stop taking care of the child within the
marriage or in the event of divorce (to leave the child with the father); thus, their
ability to use the fact that they are providing child care as a bargaining chip with
the father is limited, and it is limited even more if the father's empathy for the
child is low because he has been less emotionally involved.

On the other hand, child custody is economically burdensome, particularly
when child support from the noncustodial parents is set at low levels or is poorly
enforced, as has typically been the case in the United States (Beller & Graham,
1993; Garfinkel, McLanahan, Meyer, & Seltzer, 1998). Partly as a result, single-
parent families are highly susceptible to poverty, with negative consequences for
children. Economist Victor Fuchs argues that high rates of poverty among single
mothers are a reflection of high maternal altruism: women are willing to pay a
high price for the pleasures of living with and directly caring for their own children (1988). This can be interpreted as a bargaining problem: mothers seem to
have a difficult time obtaining both custody and generous child support.

Figure 15.1 illustrates the interaction between sole custody and child support
in a two-way table. Assume, for the time being that fathers and mothers have identical preferences for child custody. The columns compare policy regimes that generally assume maternal custody versus those that use less-gender specific criteria
and thereby increase the risk to a mother that she will not obtain custody. The
rows compare legal regimes that provide high levels and high probability of child
support collection versus those that do not. The combination that affords mothers
the greatest bargaining power within marriage is one in which the probability of

FIG. 15.1.   Effects of Custody and Enforcement Policies on Maternal Bargaining
Power

| | | Presumption of maternal custody | |
		Strong	*Weak*
	High	High maternal	Intermediate maternal
Probability of		Bargaining power	Bargaining power
effective child	*Low*	Intermediate maternal	Low maternal
support enforcement		Bargaining power	Bargaining power

generous child support and sole child custody is high. In this situation, mothers' threat point situation is most advantageous. The combination that affords mothers the least bargaining power is one in which she can neither be confident of custody nor of economic support. Which of the other two cells is most attractive to mothers depends on how they weigh the nonpecuniary benefits against the economic costs and risks of custody.

Now, drop the assumption of equal preference for sole custody. Whichever parent wants sole custody the most would see his or her bargaining power weakened the most by a rule that lowers their probability of gaining that custody. However, the parent who wants sole custody the most will be in a weaker position regarding child support obligations. If mothers have a stronger preference than fathers for sole custody, then rules choosing the custodial parent by some gender-neutral criterion, or encouraging joint or shared custody, have an ambiguous effect on mothers. Again, the outcome depends on how they weigh the nonpecuniary benefits of sole custody against the economic costs.

The intensification of child support enforcement efforts over the past 10 years has provoked tremendous controversy. Although success has been uneven, more divorced fathers are paying children support (Garfinkel et al., 1998). This, together with the growing cultural stigmatization of "deadbeat dads" has almost certainly increased the bargaining power of mothers relative to fathers within marriage as well as among noncohabiting parents. Mothers' external threat points are higher as a result. Men can withdraw some of their earnings by divorce, but the amount of withdrawal is reduced by the amount of child support mandated by the state. Not surprisingly, some men have responded to this trend by demanding greater consideration as potential custodians in the event of divorce. In most states today the presumption of legal custody is no longer gender specific, but rests instead on what the court deems best for the child. Relatively few fathers try to convince judges that they are the better custodial parent, and even fewer succeed. But the number of men who seek and get custody or joint physical custody is rising.

Thus, the legal environment has produced two changes in recent decades. Mothers' confidence that they will get child support if they divorce has increased, but they can be less sure than before that they will get custody. What is the net effect of this change on bargaining power likely to be? One could argue that two changes cancel each other out in their effect on maternal bargaining power—that is, mothers gain a higher probability of effective child support enforcement at the cost of a higher risk of losing sole custody and so there is no effect on their bargaining power. It is hard to say.[2]

---

[2]The matter is further complicated by the fact that sole custody may become a less-important goal for mothers if they believe that fathers will improve their participation in direct care both within marriage and in the event of divorce. If fathers' participation in direct care increases their emotional attachment to their children, children in both intact and divorced families will benefit. Mothers, recognizing this benefit, are likely to welcome it.

Overall, then, we conclude that specializing in the care of children generally reduces married or cohabiting women's bargaining power with the father. If men were more involved in directly providing the hands-on inputs of time and emotional care, they would likely form stronger connections with their children. If women and men shared both the economic provision and the direct care aspects of parental involvement, their relative bargaining power would tend toward greater equality.

Effects of Bargaining Power on Parental Involvement

We have been discussing the ways in which parental involvement affects bargaining power when parents are married. But we should also examine instances in which causality seems to run the other way, with bargaining power affecting parental involvement. One interesting research tradition examines whether women's access to economic resources affects a particular kind of parental involvement—their ability to divert material resources to children. We suggested earlier that, for biological and/or social reasons, women are likely to be more altruistic toward their children than men. If this is the case, we would expect increases in mothers' bargaining power to improve outcomes for children. Many empirical studies in developing countries offer some support for this "good mother" hypothesis (Benería & Roldan, 1987; Chant, 1991). Income that is controlled by women is more likely to be spent on children's health and nutrition and less likely to be spent on alcohol (Dwyer & Bruce, 1988; Hoddinott, Alderman, & Haddad, 1998).

Evidence for the developed countries is harder to come by. However, there is evidence that a shift in the payment of family allowances from fathers to mothers in Great Britain was associated with an increase in expenditures on children's clothing (Lundberg, Pollak, & Wales, 1997). Mothers are significantly less likely than fathers to neglect their children, and their ability to leave an abusive partner is key to their ability to protect against paternal abuse (Kurz, 1995). These are all reasons why we might expect an increase in the relative bargaining power of mothers to have positive effects on children.

However, there is another pathway through which increasing women's bargaining power may harm children. Women's increased bargaining power may be reflected in either "voice" or "exit." Increased freedom to exit was undoubtedly a factor in the increase in divorce rates between 1960 and 1980 (Cherlin, 1999b). It is difficult to assess the impact of divorce on children, because it is misleading simply to compare those who experienced divorce with those who did not. Parents who undergo divorce presumably have less-satisfying and more-conflictual marriages than those remain together. Divorce may be better for children than continued coresidence with unhappy parents. Still, evidence suggests that divorce has some negative effects (Cherlin, 1999a; McLanahan & Sandefur, 1994).

Thus, it is unclear what the net effect of women's increased bargaining power on children is—it may be positive through getting more resources to children within marriage and negative through leading more to divorce, which leads fathers to reduce their economic provision. This suggests that if we could find ways to increase women's ability to bargain with their increased earnings without ending the marriage—encouraging "voice" rather than "exit," children would benefit. Fathers' resistance to taking more responsibility for direct care of children may make it harder for mothers to get the bargain they want.

Another limiting factor is U.S. common law, which dictates that agreements between married couples—beyond the basic stipulation of mutual support—are not enforceable by law (Silbaugh, 1996, p. 54). Married parents cannot appeal to courts to enforce an agreement that one parent will provide X level of time to the child only if the other parent devotes Y level of time or money. Mothers who take substantial time away from paid employment when the child is young in expectation that the father will assume more responsibility for care when the child is older suffer from a "first mover disadvantage" because they cannot enforce reciprocity. As a result of the risk that this most costly form of parental involvement will not be reciprocated, parents may "underinvest" in direct care of their children. Both parents work more hours in the labor market than they would prefer to in a world in which they could make a binding and enforceable agreement (Wells & Maher, 1996).

The process of negotiation over parental involvement is costly, especially if parents are not very good negotiators. Lack of agreement can lead to frustration, anger, and a spiraling deterioration of personal relationships. Both shared parenting and joint custody look better in theory than in reality precisely because they are more emotionally demanding. Still, one could argue that these activities may seem especially difficult now because they entail such an abrupt departure from traditional norms toward individual negotiation. Practice may not make perfect, but it often makes better. Individuals become more skilled at negotiating a greater variety of parental involvements. Furthermore, as they do so, new social norms of appropriate behavior may emerge, smoothing the coordination process.

NONMARRIED NONCOHABITING PARENTS

When parents are living separately and custodial arrangements are stable, individuals have little to bargain over except parental involvement itself. Any negotiation between nonmarried noncohabiting parents is even more strongly influenced by legal rules and social policies than negotiation between married parents for two reasons. First, and most obviously, parents who are living apart generally do so because they have been unable to reach a mutually satisfactory agreement for daily cooperation.[3]

Second, and more importantly, nonmarried parents are more susceptible to legal rules governing their mutual responsibilities. Divorced noncustodial parents are required to pay child support (provided there is a court order for it), and custodial parents are required to allow visitation by the other father. Furthermore, states limit the ability of unmarried parents to bargain by setting separate and independent rules regarding custody, visitation, and support. Failure to pay child support, for instance, cannot generally be used as a reason to deny a noncustodial parent contact with a child. Nor can failure to enjoy visitation easily be used as a reason not to pay child support. Only a few jurisdictions make modest provision for conditionality (Estin, 1995).[4] However, despite this, there is some room for bargaining, in part because state enforcement of stipulated rules is not very efficient. Recent efforts have been far more successful at establishing than enforcing awards: between 1985 and 1995 award rates grew by 140%, whereas receipt rates increased only 80% (Peters, 2000, p. 7). Both custodial and noncustodial parents can make physical threats, hide from each other, move to another jurisdiction, or simply make all transactions difficult (not keeping appointments, bouncing checks). Clearly, there is considerable room for individual maneuvering.

Although many unmarried parents, especially those that are romantically involved, are reluctant to involve the state, the likelihood of state intervention is greatest for low-income families receiving public assistance. Most states impose very strict requirements on establishment of paternity and child support agreements and aggressively prosecute noncompliance. In all these situations, parental involvement almost certainly affects bargaining power among parents, as well as vice versa.

Effects of Parental Involvement on Bargaining Power

Differences in levels of maternal and paternal involvement are likely to be greatest among parents who have never been married, rather than those who have undergone divorce or separation. Marriage usually, though not always, represents an implicit agreement to cooperate in raising children. Even if this agreement breaks down, its explicit nature carries some emotional weight. Many out-of-wedlock births are unplanned, and the definition of reproductive rights in the United States gives mothers, unlike fathers, the right to terminate a pregnancy. As a result, pregnant women can threaten to undergo an abortion if they are unable to

---

[3]An exception is couples with children who would like to live together but are constrained by factors such as inability to find employment in the same area or a common place to live.

[4]Some lawyers have argued that strict conditionality would offer better linkages between these two. It would certainly increase the scope for parental negotiation. See Estin, 1995.

extract a promise of commitment or cooperation from the father of their child. Many mothers do not make this threat or are unwilling to follow through on it precisely because they are sufficiently committed to motherhood to pursue it, even without a promise of assistance from the father.

In this situation, both fathers and mothers might prefer to opt out of any mutual obligation—fathers to avoid paying child support for a child they do not want, mothers to avoid contact with a father who has no desire to be a partner or father. Low-income parents are seriously constrained in their ability to strike such a "nonparticipation-of-the-father" bargain. Mothers are generally not eligible for public assistance unless they name the father of their child, and most states vigorously pursue and enforce child support in order to reduce public expenditures on assistance. Increased state efforts in recent years, combined with DNA testing, have made establishment of paternity far less optional than it once was.

Still, a high percentage of nonmarital births take place in a context in which both parents are eager to cooperate in childrearing. Preliminary findings of the Fragile Families Study, research on a nationally representative sample of nonmarital births, show that 82% of unmarried mothers and fathers are romantically involved at the time their child is born, and 44% are living together. Among those who are not romantically involved, about half of mothers say they are friends with the father. Virtually all the fathers interviewed reported that they wanted to be involved in raising their children, and 93% of unmarried mothers report that they want the father to be involved (Fragile Families Initiative, 2000).

Among nonmarital births, maternal custody is typical, and it both implies and contributes to a higher degree of maternal than paternal involvement. How does this affect women's bargaining power? The basic trade-off is similar to that described for married couples. The more mothers depend on money from fathers, the less power they have to negotiate for better paternal behavior. However, maternal power is increased if the father is paying child support informally but would be required to pay more if she "turned him in." However, as with married mothers, the mother's "prisoner of love" position limits her bargaining power; she cannot make a credible threat of withdrawing her childrearing services to get the father to do something she wants him to do. Whereas the married mother may derive some power from her credible threat to take the child away from living with the father, the unmarried mother is limited to threats not to let the father see the child. Overall, then, limited earning power and their involvement in care of the children mean that noncustodial mothers often have even less bargaining power with fathers of their children than do married mothers. This asymmetry is diminished among low-income families, because high rates of unemployment and incarceration among males and mothers' eligibility for public assistance reduce differences in male and female access to income.

The existence of a formal child support agreement is not a good indicator of the relative bargaining power of the custodial mother. Indeed, the absence of an agreement can reflect two extremes. It may reflect total noncooperation by the father. A man who wants absolutely no involvement with his child and has no affection for the mother can threaten to make their lives miserable if his paternity is revealed or any claim is made on his income. On the other hand, a father who can make a credible promise to provide consistent informal support may persuade a mother not to seek a formal child support agreement. This is particularly likely to be the case if the father, though unmarried, is living with the mother and child and helping pay for common expenses of rent and food as well as providing direct care for the child. In the United States today, about 40% of nonmarital births involve cohabiting parents (McLanahan, Garfinkel, Reichman, & Teitler, 2000). This suggests that conventional measures of child support enforcement are somewhat misleading in their focus on formal agreements as an indicator of paternal involvement in economic support. Public policy toward poor families seems to recognize only two options for paternal support: marriage or a formal child support order. Indeed, strict enforcement of formal child support agreement requirements among couples who are reluctant to marry may actually discourage their cooperative cohabitation (Achatz & MacAllum, 1994; Furstenberg, Sherwood, & Sullivan, 1992; Sorensen & Turner, 1997).

Effects of Bargaining Power on Parental Involvement

The most important thing that nonmarried parents bargain over are their respective levels and forms of parental involvement: custody and control as well as money, time, and emotional care. Issues range from big questions like what school the child should attend to little ones such as what kind of candy they should be allowed to eat. A number of public policies have an important impact on the relative bargaining power of custodial parents, which in turn affect parental involvement. Levels of public assistance, publically subsidized child care, and publically subsidized health services have profound effects on the cost of rearing children. Some states offer incentives, known as "Bridefare," to women on public assistance who marry.[5]

Most important, however, are state policies relevant to establishment and enforcement of formal child support agreements. These agreements occasionally include language regarding visitation rights, but they stop far short of covering all aspects of paternal involvement. Formal agreements almost always increase the bargaining power of the custodial parent with respect to obtaining child support payments. Equally important, there is evidence, reviewed earlier, that when men

---

[5]The net effects of such incentives are unclear, as they often result in blended families. With remarriage often come new responsibilities, including additional children, that compete for the money, time, and attention of first-round children. In general, remarriage of either parent is associated with a reduction in child support (Garasky, 1991).

pay child support, they usually spend more time with their children (Seltzer et al., 1998). If this relationship is causal, then child support enforcement may increase noncustodial fathers' provision of economic support and direct care to children.

However, in some cases, formal support orders can have paradoxically negative effects both on child support and other dimensions of paternal involvement, for two reasons. First, formal agreements can reduce discretionary power to negotiate trade-offs among different kinds of inputs away from the individual parents. They define the noncustodial parents' responsibility solely in terms of cash support and make it more difficult for that parent to offer inputs of time or emotional effort in their place, contributing to paternal disengagement. One could argue that such agreements give noncustodial parents a motive for greater involvement in order to more closely monitor how their money is spent. But this is true only if closer monitoring allows them to respond to what they see as poor expenditures by reducing their contribution. Indeed, they may not want to know more about something that they are powerless to change. Noncustodial parents (typically fathers) know that their financial contributions may simply improve the mothers' standard of living, rather than the child's (Weiss & Willis, 1985). They might be willing to devote more resources to the child if they were allowed to make a larger proportion of their contribution in the form of in-kind transfers or emotional effort.

Second, if formal agreements are imposed without any negotiation or voice, noncustodial parents are far less predisposed to cooperate with them. Many empirical studies show that voluntary agreements have higher compliance rates and greater flexibility in terms of modifications over time as the child matures (Peters, Argys, Maccoby, & Mnookin, 1993). Furthermore, the nature of the agreement may affect the form of paternal involvement. In their analysis of data from the National Longitudinal Study of Youth, Argys and Peters (1999) found that 24% of all fathers in court-ordered settlements subsequently had no contact with their children, compared to 13% of fathers who settled voluntarily. There is even evidence suggesting that voluntary awards are associated with higher levels of cognitive development for children (Argys, Peters, Brooks-Gunn, & Smith, 1997). It is difficult to tell if these associations are causal; their effects may simply reflect the fact that fathers who are more committed to their children are more likely to make voluntary agreements and to maintain contact with their children. But if they are causal, it suggests that, by alienating fathers, the legal system may discourage their participation and harm children.

One way to balance the need for public enforcement with the benefits of private negotiation is to design policies that encourage parents to reach their own agreements by threatening to impose a "fallback" agreement if they fail. This strategy, aptly termed "bargaining in the shadow of the law," is already in effect in states that publish official child support guidelines that will be applied to unmarried parents unless they reach a voluntary agreement (Mnookin & Kornhauser, 1979). In general, the bigger difference between potential levels of child support and those mandated and enforced by law, the more bargaining power the noncustodial parent will have to influence the decisions of the custodial parents. Likewise, the bigger the difference between the level and form of contact the noncustodial parent wants and what the custodial parent is legally required to concede, the more bargaining power the custodial parent will have. Both parents are constrained in their bargaining by their levels of concern for the well-being of the child. A number of states are experimenting with arbitration programs designed to help parents come to agreement (Garfinkel et al., 1998).

At the opposite extreme, most states impose child support requirements on families receiving public assistance that potentially amplify the adverse effects of formal enforcement. As aforementioned, mothers have an incentive to identify and impose support even on fathers who have expressed complete disinterest in childrearing. Support levels are set in ways that allow fathers—especially those who are unfamiliar with or fearful of the legal system—relatively little voice. Support levels are regressive, representing a much larger share of a poor father's than an affluent father's earnings. Support requirements are retroactive, leading to calculation of huge debt that is virtually impossible for many low-income fathers to pay off. Requirements are also unforgiving of economic circumstances such as unemployment or low earnings (Sorensen, 1999). Violators are subject to incarceration, which largely precludes paternal involvement with children.

In most states (Wisconsin is an exception), fathers' child support payments go directly into state coffers, rather than to the family itself, largely canceling out any positive effects on children themselves. This practice encourages parents to break the law and bargain on the side, with the noncustodial parent making an "under-the-table" payment that is less than what he would have officially paid, but more than what the mother would officially have received.

Ethnographic research suggests that such bargains are relatively common among low-income families. A sample of mothers receiving public assistance in several major cities showed that the percentage receiving informal child support was about equal to that receiving formal support. About one half of mothers reported misleading the welfare authorities on this point (Edin & Lein, 1998). This research also observed that fathers often prefer to make in-kind payments, such as milk, disposable diapers, or gifts for their children rather than simply providing cash (about one third of mothers on public assistance received such in-kind transfers from fathers). In addition to reducing the monitoring problem, in-kind transfers such as gifts, in particular, may contribute more directly to the development of an emotional relationship with the child than simple contributions to family income.

Failure to measure these informal transfers, like failure to estimate the number of unmarried parents without child support who are living together and sharing expenses, contributes to a tendency to underestimate the extent of paternal involvement within the low-income population. More importantly, it suggests that more stringent establishment and enforcement of formal child support orders can actually worsen the position of mothers and children by diminishing their flexibility in this informal bargaining process.

If the goal of our public policies in this area was to improve outcomes for poor children rather than to reduce welfare expenditures, it would take a very different form. Nonmarried parents could be urged to develop an agreement they consider mutually beneficial and practical, with administrative formulas applied only if they fail to agree. Kathryn Edin (1994) suggests a number of potential guidelines, such as basing father's child support obligations on their current earnings, using a progressive rather than a regressive formula. Furthermore, efforts could be made to provide more public support for paternal involvement, as mandated by the Fathers Count Act of 1999, passed by the House of Representatives, which makes federal grants available for this purpose. We could also offer more support for childrearing through universal programs such as publicly funded child care and health care.[6]

CONCLUSION AND POLICY IMPLICATIONS

What does paternal involvement have to do with bargaining between parents? As the second section of this chapter emphasized, parenthood has many rewards, but it also has costs. One of those costs is that the time put into parenthood reduces one's earnings, and in so doing, one's bargaining power relative to the other parent. Also, the actual process of caring for a child usually increases feelings of altruism and emotional responsibility for the child, making it difficult to credibly threaten withdrawal of care. One conclusion, therefore, is that primary caregivers (usually mothers) usually have less bargaining power than parents whose contributions simply take the form of financial support. Is this economic weakness fully compensated by the less-tangible, nonpecuniary resources that result from greater physical proximity and stronger emotional connection to the child? It is impossible to say. But high levels of poverty among families maintained by women alone in the United States suggest that the weak economic bargaining power of mothers takes a large toll on children's economic welfare.

Less gender specialization in the form of parental involvement could lead to improved outcomes for children not only by improving mothers' economic position but also by strengthening emotional connections between fathers and children. As the third section of the chapter emphasizes, the tendency to administratively impose standardized monetary obligations through strict enforcement of

---

[6]Recent proposals to let women and children on welfare keep all the money the state collects from the father, rather than passing through only $50/month as is common today, would seem to solve the problems we are concerned with here and would provide more income to low-income children, which is a point in their favor. However, this amounts to a law saying that fathers' economic contributions do not count toward eligibility for welfare or reduction in benefits if the father doesn't live with the child, but they do if he does live with the child (certainly if the couple is married). This seems unfair to families with fathers in residence and creates a disincentive to fathers living with their children.

child support probably raises the bargaining power of married and divorced mothers. But, in some situations, it can have adverse consequences for both mothers and children. Although such enforcement can increase the economic bargaining power of custodial parents, it can also reduce their informal bargaining power over both forms and levels of involvement. It seems quite likely that the inflexible and coercive rules imposed on families receiving public assistance have negative effects, undermining the sense of emotional connection and intrinsic pleasure of parenting that is the best guarantee of father involvement. There are better ways to improve the relative bargaining power of mothers and the well-being of children.

REFERENCES

Achatz, M., & MacAllum, C. A. (1994). *Young unwed fathers: Report from the field.* Philadelphia: Public/Private Ventures.

Argys, L. M., & Peters, H. E. (1999). *Can adequate child support be legislated? A model of responses to child support guidelines and enforcement efforts.* Department of Economics, University of Colorado at Denver.

Argys, L. M., Peters, H. E., Brooks-Gunn, J., & Smith, J. R. (1997, October). *The impact of child support dollars and father child contact.* Paper presented at NICHD Conference on Father Involvement, Bethesda, MD.

Baydar, N., & Brooks-Gunn, J. (1994). The dynamics of child support and its consequences for children. In I. Garfinkel, S. S. McLanahan, & P. K. Robins (Eds.), *Child support and child well-being* (pp. 257–284). Washington, DC: Urban Institute Press.

Beller, A. H., & Graham, J. W. (1993). *The economics of child support.* New Haven, CT: Yale University Press.

Benería, L., & Roldan, M. (1987). *The crossroads of class and gender.* Chicago: University of Chicago Press.

Budig, M. J., and England, P. (2001). The wage penalty for motherhood. *American Sociological Review, 66,* 204–225.

Chant, S. (1991). *Women and survival in Mexican cities: Perspectives on gender, labour markets and low-income households.* New York: Manchester University Press.

Cherlin, A. (1999a). Going to extremes: family structure, children's well-being, and social science. *Demography, 36,* 421–428.

Cherlin, A. (1999b). *Public and private families* (2d ed.) New York: McGraw-Hill.

Deutsch, F. M. (1999). *Halving it all: How equally shared parenting works.* Cambridge, MA: Harvard University Press.

Dwyer, D., & Bruce, J. (Eds.). (1988). *A home divided: Women and income in the third world.* Stanford, CA: Stanford University Press.

Edin, K. (1994). *Single mothers and absent fathers: The possibilities and limits of child support policy.* Center for Urban Policy Research Working Paper No. 68, Rutgers University.

Edin, K., & Lein, L. (1998). *Making ends meet: How single mothers survive welfare and low-wage work.* New York: Russell Sage Foundation.

England, P., & Farkas, G. 1986. *Households, employment and gender: A social, economic and demographic view.* New York: Aldine de Gruyter.

England, P., and Kilbourne, B. (1990). Feminist critiques of the separative model of the self: Implications for rational choice theory. *Rationality and Society, 2*(3), 517–525.

Estin, A. L. (1995, March). Love and obligation: Family law and the romance of economics. 36 *William and Mary Law Review 989.*

Folbre, N. (2000, June). *Bargaining for love*. Paper presented at the Meetings of the Canadian Economics Association, Vancouver, CA.

Fragile Families Initiative. (2000, May). *Fragile Families Research Brief, 1*.

Fuchs, V. (1988). *Women's quest for economic equality*. Cambridge, MA: Harvard University Press.

Furstenberg, F., Jr., Nord, C. W., Peterson, J. L., & Zill, N. (1983). The life course of children of divorce: Marital disruption and parental conflict. *American Sociological Review, 48*, 656–668.

Furstenberg, F., Jr., Sherwood, K., Sullivan, M. (1992). *Caring and paying: What fathers and mothers say about child support*. New York: MDRC.

Garasky, S. (1991). Child support and second families: Which children come first? Technical Analysis Paper No. 43, Washington, DC: U.S. Department of Health and Human Services.

Garfinkel, I., & Huang, C. 2000. Unpublished analysis of the April Child Support Supplement to the monthly CPS from 1979 to the present. New York: Columbia University School of Social Work.

Garfinkel, I., McLanahan, S. S., Meyer, D. R., & Seltzer, J. A., (1998). *Fathers under fire: The revolution in child support enforcement*. New York: Russell Sage Foundation.

Greif, G. (1995). When divorced fathers want no contact with their children. *Journal of Divorce and Remarriage, 23*,(1/2), 75–84.

Heer, D. (1963). The measurement and bases of family power: An overview. *Marriage and Family Living, 25*, 133–139.

Hoddinott, J., Alderman, H., & Haddad, L. (Eds.). (1998). *Intrahousehold resource allocation in developing countries: Methods, models and policy*. Baltimore: Johns Hopkins University Press.

Hrdy, S. B. (1999). *Mother nature. A history of mothers, infants, and natural selection*. New York: Pantheon Books.

Kurz, D. (1995). *For richer, for poorer: Mothers confront divorce*. New York: Routledge.

Lamb M. (1986). *The father's role: Applied perspectives*. New York: Wiley.

Lundberg, S., & Pollak, R. A. (1993). Separate spheres bargaining and the marriage market. *Journal of Political Economy, 101*(6), 988–1010.

Lundberg, S. & Pollak, R. A. (1996). Bargaining and distribution in marriage. *Journal of Economic Perspectives, 10*, 139–158.

Lundberg, S. J., Pollak, R. A., & Wales, T. J. (1997). Do husbands and wives pool their resources? Evidence from the United Kingdom child benefit. *Journal of Human Resources, 32*(3), 463–480.

Mahoney, R. (1995). *Kidding ourselves. Breadwinning, babies, and bargaining power*. New York: Basic Books.

McElroy, M. (1990). The empirical content of Nash-bargained household behavior. *Journal of Human Resources, 25*(4), 559–583.

McElroy, M. B., & Horney, M. J. (1981). Nash bargained household decisions: Toward a generalization of the theory of demand. *International Economic Review, 22*(2), 333–349.

McLanahan, S., Garfinkel, I., Reichman, N., & Teitler, J. (2000). Unpublished report from Fragile Families Study.

McLanahan, S., & Sandefur, G. (1994). *Growing up with a single parent: What hurts, what helps*. Cambridge, MA: Harvard University Press.

McLanahan, S., Seltzer, J., Hanson, T. L., & Thomson, E. (1994). Child support enforcement and child well-being: Greater security or greater conflict? In I. Garfinkel, S. McLanahan, & P. K. Robins (Eds.), *Child support and child well-being* (pp. 239–256).

Mnookin, R. H., & Kornhauser, L. (1979). Bargaining in the shadow of the law: The case of divorce. *Yale Law Journal, 88*(5), 950–977.

Molm, L., & Cook, K. (1995). Social exchange and exchange networks. In K. Cook, G. Fine, & J. House (Eds.), *Sociological Perspectives on Social Psychology* (pp. 209–235). New York: Allyn and Bacon.

Nord, C. W., & Zill, N. (1996). *Non-custodial parents' participation in their children's lives: Evidence from the survey of income and program participation, Volume II*. Washington, DC: Office of Assistant Secretary for Planning and Evaluation, U.S. Department of Health and Human Services.

Peters, E. (1986, June). Marriage and divorce: Informational constraints and private contracting. *American Economic Review, 76*(3), 437–454.

Peters, E., (2000, March–April). Can child support policies promote better father involvement? The role of coercive vs. supportive policies. *Poverty Research News, 4*(2), 7–9.

Peters, E., Argys, L. M., Maccoby, E. E., & Mnookin, R. H. (1993). Enforcing divorce settlements: Evidence from child support compliance and award modifications. *Demography, 30*(4), 719–735.

Scanzoni, J. (1979). A historical perspective on husband-wife bargaining power and marital dissolution. In G. Levinger & O. Moles (Eds.), *Divorce and separation* (pp. 10–36). New York: Basic Books.

Selzer, J. (1998). Father by law: Effects of joint legal custody on nonresident fathers' involvement with children. *Demography, 35*(2), 135–146.

Selzer, J. A., McLanahan, S. S., & Hanson, T. L. (1998). Will child support enforcement increase father-child contact and parental conflict after separation? In Garfinkel, S. McLanahan, D. Meyer, & J. Seltzer (Eds.). *Fathers under fire* (pp. 157–190). New York: Russell Sage Foundation.

Silbaugh, K. (1996). Turning labor into love: Housework and the law. *Northwestern University Law Review, 91*(1), 1–87.

Sorensen, E. (1999, March). *Obligating dads: Helping low-income noncustodial fathers do more for their children.* Research Brief, Washington, DC Urban Institute.

Sorensen, E., & Turner, M. (1997). Barriers to child support policy: A review of the literature. *National Center of Fathers and Families.* University of Pennsylvania, Philadelphia (*www.ncoff.gse.upenn.edu*).

Waldfogel, J. (1997). The effect of children on women's wages, *American Sociological Review, 62,* 209–217.

Weiss, Y., & Willis, R. J. (1985, July). Children as collective goods and divorce settlements. *Journal of Labor Economics, 3*(3), 268–292.

Wells, R., & Maher, M. (1996). *Time and surplus allocation within marriage.* Research Paper No. 1372, Graduate School of Business, Stanford University.

16

The Effects of Welfare, Child Support, and Labor Markets on Father Involvement

Wendy Sigle-Rushton
London School of Economics and Political Science

Irwin Garfinkel
Columbia University

This chapter assumes that greater investment of fathers' time and money in their children positively effects child well-being. Economic theory predicts that marriage promotes father–child involvement. Theory also predicts that welfare and child support policies and labor market conditions effect marriage. Thus, the chapter reviews the economic literature on the effects of welfare, child support enforcement, and labor markets on father noninvolvement with their children due to divorce, separation, and nonmarital births. We begin with an overview of the massive changes in household structure that have taken place in the past decades and the theoretical rationale for why household structure is related to father involvement. In subsequent sections on the effects of welfare, child support, and labor markets on marriage, we first explicate the predictions of economic theory and then examine the empirical evidence for and against the predictions of economic theory. The magnitude and the significance of relationships can provide information about whether policy tools can effectively manipulate family structures, and in the process, perhaps influence levels of father involvement and child well-being.

TRENDS AND CONSEQUENCES

Family patterns have changed dramatically since the 1960s when the majority of all births occurred within marriage, and most children could expect to be living in a household with both of their biological parents. Since that time, rates of female headship have increased steadily due to both divorce and nonmarital childbearing. Divorce rates began to rise steadily from the 1960s, and in less than 20 years, more than tripled. Although divorce rates declined somewhat after 1979 (Moffitt, 1992), estimates using 1985 Current Population Survey data suggest that between one half and two thirds of all marriages end in divorce. Rates of nonmarital childbearing, the other major source of changes in family structure, have also shown tremendous increases over the past 25 years. Between 1965 and 1997, the ratio of nonmarital births to total births increased from 8% (24% for Black Americans and 3.1% for White Americans) to over 30% (69% for Black Americans and 25.4% for White Americans) in the United States.

From a policy perspective, the increase in single-parent, predominantly female-headed households merits careful consideration. Single-parent households are more often impoverished, and the children raised within them do not fare as well as children who are brought up by both biological parents. But the decline in the two-parent family is not just a matter of greater female autonomy and income combined with an increased social acceptance of single mothers. It is also likely to be a story of men's retreat from the responsibilities and the rewards of parenting. A study of changes in household structure between 1960 and 1980 estimated that men between the ages of 20 and 40 were spending 15% less of their lifetimes married and coresident with children. As Goldschieder and Kaufman (1996) point out, however, this study does not differentiate between coresidence with own and nonbiological children. If men have less of a parental relationship with nonbiological children and nonresident own children, the number of years of active involvement would have likely seen a far greater decrease than years of coresidence. This last issue is extremely important because if mothers are unable to fill this parenting gap, it is likely that children are going to suffer as a result.

There are many reasons to believe that marriage or a marriagelike relationship promotes greater father investments of both time and money in their children. First of all, coresident fathers are able to spend more time with their children than most nonresident fathers. If involvement is a function of time spent together and not just time spent actively or exclusively parenting, fathers who do not live with their children are necessarily going to be less involved. From an economic perspective, this is because nonresident fathers have to use a greater level of resources to spend time with their children. Time spent with children can be priced at the opportunity cost of the father's time. More often for resident than for nonresident fathers, the opportunity cost of spending time with the child will be near zero because time spent with the child amounts to passive involvement. The child will be present when the father is engaging in normal everyday activities, such as showering, shaving, getting dressed, eating breakfast, and eating dinner. The cost might not be exactly zero, because the child may divert the father's attention away from accomplishing tasks. On the other hand, to the extent that the father enjoys the child's company, the costs could actually be negative—that is a benefit. The point is that just being present is an important part of parenting in which nonresident fathers do not engage except, perhaps, during visitation periods when the child lives with them. To spend time with their children, nonresident fathers also incur additional costs because they have to make arrangements to visit (which may include fairly high emotional costs depending on the relationship with the child's mother), incur travel expenses, and sometimes arrange a venue for the visit to take place. All these factors increase the cost of temporal involvement and result in a lower level of involvement for nonresident fathers.

Similar arguments apply to nonresident fathers' financial involvement, and their well-documented reluctance to provide child support. First of all, coresident fathers can provide more for their children because coresidence allows for shared consumption of many goods. Housing is a good example of such a public good. Nonresident fathers privately consume many items—such as housing—that would otherwise be collective goods, jointly consumed by the entire household, and the result is less money available to spend on the child. Both Willis and Weiss (1985) and Willis and Haaga (1996) discuss an additional explanation that focuses on the relationship between divorced or never married parents. They point out that nonresident fathers who care about their children can enjoy the benefits of the investments that women make in their children even when they do not contribute. If, in the absence of child support, the mother will provide for the child, the father can enjoy the benefits of her investment and reallocate what he would have spent on the child toward his own consumption. A related issue is the fact that as women's incomes increase—either by higher wages or more generous forms of public assistance—a father's optimum transfer should go down. Furthermore, they posit that any cost-sharing agreement between the two separated parents is not likely to be self-enforcing[1] because they will each have an incentive to raise their own consumption and let the other parent bear the burden of support.[2]

One further argument is discussed in Willis and Weiss (1985) and Del Boca and Flinn (1995). These authors point out that child support is paid by the father to the mother, and it is the mother who decides how to spend the money. When the mother treats child support income as her own income, she is effectively taxing a man's child support contributions. For instance, suppose the mother spends 50% of her child support income on herself and 50% on the child. The father will have to pay $2 in child support in order to see the impact of a $1 investment in the

---

[1]Agreements made within marriage are considered to be self-enforcing because proximity allows monitoring and because the relationship is assumed to be one based on trust and cooperation.

[2]There have, however, been some fairly recent attempts that show that if the interactions are repeated, a cost-sharing agreement may be viable even among noncoresident spouses (Flinn, 2000).

child, and this tax will cause the man to offer less child support than he otherwise might.

Taken together, these explanations provide convincing support for our assumption that children benefit from the highest level of father involvement when they live in households with both biological parents. Nonresidency—resulting from either divorce, separation, or nonmarriage—reduces the amount of time and money a father makes available for his children.

ECONOMIC THEORY OF FAMILY FORMATION

According to economic theories of marriage and divorce (Becker, 1973, 1974, 1981), individuals decide to marry because they expect they will be better off inside marriage than outside it. When deciding whether or not to divorce or separate, each individual compares the expected happiness from remaining together to that of becoming single again and possibly remarrying. Divorces occur because people were initially uncertain about the quality of the match (Becker et al., 1977). As new information becomes available, marital happiness or expected happiness outside marriage may change, and people may decide they want to dissolve the relationship. Increases in expected happiness outside marriage that leave marital happiness unaltered increase the probability of divorce and nonmarriage or nonmarital births.[3] Divorce or nonmarriage occurs when the sum total of utility to both partners of being unmarried exceeds the total utility of being in the partnership. In all other cases, the partners should be able to divide the marital happiness in such a way that both partners can be made better off by remaining together.[4] Although the application of economic theory is sometimes criticized for ignoring the complexity of human motives and behaviors, the predictions of economic theory do not require that all individuals act rationally all the time. So long as some individuals on the margin of choice weigh their options some of the time, the predictions will hold.

THE IMPACT OF WELFARE

Theoretical Predictions

Utilizing this basic model of family formation, we can explore the effects of welfare on divorce and nonmarital births. The impact of welfare programs on mar-

---

[3]Rosenzweig and Neal extend the basic model to allow for three choices for unmarried mothers— no child, child within marriage, child outside marriage.

[4]As Becker, Landes, and Michael (1977) and Peters (1986) discuss, this is simply an application of the Coase theorem and requires the assumption that couples can bargain at a zero or small cost.

riage depends on the rules of the program. Programs, like the old Aid to Families with Dependent Children (AFDC) program, that provide benefits only to (or primarily to) unmarried parents will decrease marriage because they increase the mother's well-being outside marriage but provide no increase within marriage. Programs that provide benefits to married as well as to unmarried parents could either increase or decrease marriage, depending on the gains available to the parents inside and outside marriage. Though the Temporary Assistance to Needy Families (TANF) program appears to be more available to married couples than the old AFDC program and should therefore do less to discourage marriage, most state TANF programs, like AFDC before them, reduce welfare benefits by one dollar for each dollar the father earns. Welfare programs with such steep income tests increase the well-being of mothers outside marriage more than they increase well-being inside marriage.

Although program eligibility requirements and income tests have discouraged marriage, they may have created an incentive for women to cohabit, at least in more recent years. Early on, many states withdrew benefits if it was discovered that a welfare recipient was living with an unrelated man. Officials would sometimes conduct surprise bedroom checks and other types of searches in order to establish that a welfare recipient was not cohabiting. After these "man in the house" laws were deemed unconstitutional, eligibility rules became more similar to those applied to married women. Nevertheless, it is easier to hide a cohabiting partner than a spouse, so it is possible that the stringency of the income testing created an incentive for women to cohabit rather than marry because it was easier for them to hide the income contributions and the existence of a more unofficial partner.

Given the rules surrounding welfare provision, economic theory implies that restrictions in welfare should reduce divorces by reducing the attractiveness of life outside of marriage, but only among those women likely to require assistance. When other alternatives dominate the welfare option, there should be no change in a woman's happiness outside of marriage[5] and, consequently, no change in the likelihood of divorce among those women. Although theory implies that more restrictive welfare policies would result in more resident fathers and increased involvement, it also implies that within the marriages of would-be recipients, restrictions in welfare should also result in a renegotiation of marital payoffs in favor of the husband.[6] If women prioritize the well-being of children to a greater

---

[5]There should be no change in expected happiness outside of marriage for women who do not expect to receive benefits unless the presence of welfare benefits carries an insurance value for those women who are unlikely to require aid. Although they do not expect to require assistance, they feel better knowing that there is a safety net.

[6]When welfare benefits are restricted, marriage becomes a better option for some women who are likely to require welfare. The difference in well-being between the marriage state and the best possible nonmarriage state represents what economists call a "quasi-rent." Spouses—in this example husbands—who recognize that their partner is benefiting from a quasi-rent can threaten divorce and extract the quasi-rents from their wives. The result of such opportunistic behavior would be a renegotiation of marital payoffs in favor of the husband.

extent than men, this shift in bargaining power could have important countervailing effects that need to be considered.

Within this simple framework, the current marital status of the decision maker is irrelevant. Both divorce and nonmarital childbearing can be thought of as decisions to opt out of marriage. In both instances, women simply compare their well-being within marriage to their well-being outside of marriage. A married woman who wants to obtain a divorce is making the same sort of choice that an unmarried, pregnant woman is making when she chooses to have a nonmarital birth. She is simply deciding that the single state is superior to the married one. Consequently, as outlined in the case of divorce, economic theory predicts that restrictions in AFDC/TANF should encourage marriage and reduce nonmarital births among would-be welfare recipients.

Empirical Evidence for Welfare Effects

There are many studies that look at the relationship between female headship and welfare generosity, but the dependent variable frequently groups together all routes into female headship and therefore does little to differentiate the variety of paths followed into female headship and father absence. Because our interest in this chapter involves an examination of the impact of policy variables on each of the different routes to lone parenthood, studies that do not distinguish between outcomes are not considered in the following sections. Interested readers can refer to Garfinkel and McLanahan (1986) or Moffitt (1992, 1998) for very thorough literature reviews on the relationship between welfare and all types of household structure. These reviews report mixed results. Most studies find small or no effects. Some even report counterintuitive results implying that high welfare benefits are associated with lower rates of female headship. All the reviews recognize, however, that the relationship, although small, appears to have strengthened over time due to either improved study designs or changing underlying behavior.

Before turning to more sophisticated statistical studies, it is perhaps instructive to look at more aggregate data to see if the relationships between changes in welfare generosity over time appear to explain the increases in divorce and nonmarital childbearing that have occurred in recent decades. Total welfare benefit levels began to increase during the mid-1950s, increased very rapidly in the decade following the War on Poverty in 1964, then fell from 1975 to 1988, and have leveled off or risen slightly since then. Rates of female headship began increasing in the mid-1960s and have continued to increase since that time. Although both female headedness and welfare benefits began to increase at the same time, if there were an underlying causal relationship, it is unclear why the fall in benefits did not cause a decline in female-headed households in the 1970s and 80s. Given the divergence of the trends, it would appear that other forces are dominating any welfare effects. Moffitt (2000b) shows that among lower-educated individuals, decreases in male wages and, to a lesser extent, increases in female wages during this period should have led to a larger increase in female headship than actually occurred. Thus, the decline in welfare benefits may have restrained divorce and nonmarital childbearing after all.

Cross-sectional studies do not compare trends but seek to utilize differences across space—differences in welfare generosity across states at a single point in time. These types of studies are meant to hold everything else fixed at one point in time and determine how a change in welfare benefits in one place—changing Michigan's levels of welfare to those of Alabama's, for instance—would change behavior there. The majority of studies on the effects of welfare have been of this type (Moffitt, 1998).

An important issue in these types of studies involves the fact that states differ, often dramatically, from one another, and these potentially unmeasured differences may be reflected in varying levels of welfare generosity as well as varying levels of divorce and nonmarital births (Pitt, Rosenzweig, & Gibbons, 1993; Rosenzweig, 1999). For instance, those states with more liberal welfare policies may also be states with more liberal attitudes toward nontraditional family types. It is possible that some states may have responded to liberal attitudes by increasing welfare generosity. If this were the case, we would find high rates of female headedness in states with higher welfare benefits, even if women were not responding to levels of generosity. Differences in attitudes across states would be responsible. It is also possible that state policies regarding welfare can respond to as well as result in observed outcomes. States that have a large number of unwed mothers may have lower benefits because they could not afford to maintain them at previous levels. If this is the case, it might appear that low benefit levels "cause" higher rates of divorce or lone parenthood when, in fact, the causation has run in the opposite direction. Either of these types of spurious correlation is potentially problematic. When efforts to control for this kind of spurious correlation weaken estimated relationships in otherwise similar models, there is reason to suspect that parameter estimates may be biased by unobserved differences across states.

Compared to the vast literature on nonmarital childbearing and general female headship, there are not a great deal of empirical studies in economics that focus on the relationship between welfare generosity and divorce. Across studies, the results generally demonstrate some relationship between AFDC benefits and divorce, but there is a good deal of variation in the way that benefits are measured and some variation in results when the models are estimated separately by race. The typical AFDC measure is the guarantee for a family of two or four, although one study by Hoffman and Duncan (1995) finds that a 5-year moving average is a better measure than the more typical AFDC guarantee at one point in time. This is perhaps because, as Rosenzweig (1999) points out, women may not respond to small temporal changes as much as to an expected benefit profile—the amount they expect to receive over some period of time. In general, most individual-level studies indicate, consistent with the predictions outlined, that higher state levels of AFDC are associated with higher levels of divorce (Ellwood & Bane, 1985;

Hoffman & Duncan, 1995; Nixon 1997[7])—but the size of the effect varies considerably across studies. For instance, Hoffman and Duncan (1995) find that a 25% increase in welfare benefits results in a less than a one percentage point change in the risk of divorce over 15 years. Using a different model and earlier data set, Ellwood and Bane (1985) estimate that a $100 increase in welfare benefits would increase the probability of divorce by 0.10 on average, with the strongest effects among younger, non-White samples. Estimated relationships generally strengthen when attempts are made to control for state specific unobservables or the likelihood of AFDC receipt in the event of a divorce. In contrast to the studies mentioned, which look at the probability that a particular individual with a particular group of characteristics obtains a divorce, models estimated on state level data often yield imprecise and even anomalous relationships. These types of models relate state level outcomes—the percentage of people currently divorced in each state, for instance—to the characteristics of the state populations. In these more aggregate studies, real welfare effects among individuals within the state populations may have been lost simply because welfare recipients are a minority of all women in each state.

As noted in previous literature reviews, the results from studies that assess the impact of AFDC benefits on nonmarital births yield somewhat mixed results, with earlier studies showing weaker, less significant relationships than later studies (Moffitt, 1992). Parameter estimates presented in more recent studies, however, tend to be small in magnitude even when they are significant. Although there is surprisingly little agreement across studies, some interesting generalities do emerge. Dividing the studies into those that utilize pre-1978 data and post-1978 data, it becomes obvious that earlier studies, those that, with the exception of one (Cutright, 1970), cover time periods from the 1960s up to the mid-1970s, were rarely carried out at an individual level. In fact, only one study (Ellwood & Bane, 1985), in part, considers individual-level data. State-level nonmarital birth rates were, by far, the most popular choice of dependent variable, although one study (Freshnock & Cutright, 1979) examines county-level data, and another (Janowitz, 1976) considers MSMAs with populations over 250,000. The parameter estimates reported from these studies are usually small and sometimes imply that higher levels of AFDC are associated with lower rather than higher rates of nonmarital childbearing—a result entirely at odds with theoretical predictions. Where positive relationships between AFDC generosity and nonmarital births do emerge, they tend to do so after the 1960s and to be more consistently identified for young, adult White women.[8] In the pre-1978 data, there appears to be only a

---

[7]Although Nixon does include AFDC benefits in her model, her focus is on child support enforcement rather than welfare benefits. When she estimates the models on subsamples more likely to receive benefits, she only presents the coefficients for her variables of interest.

[8]Because White women are less likely to end up on welfare than non-White women, this result is often explained by difference in sample size. Most data sets have far more observations for White women, so any effects are more likely to be estimated precisely in the larger sample.

very slight association between AFDC and nonmarital births for teenagers in general (Ellwood & Bane, 1985; Freshnock & Cutright, 1979).

In more recent studies, only two (Case, 1998; Garfinkel, Gaylin, Huang, & McLanahan, 2000) use aggregate measures; most carry out individual-level analyses. Similar to earlier studies, the aggregate-level analyses fail to find a robust relationship between measures of AFDC generosity and nonmarital births at a state level. Whether it is due to the different level of analysis or to underlying changes in behavior and attitudes over time, it is apparent that more-recent studies are more likely to find that teenage pregnancies are associated with welfare generosity, especially among Whites (Lundberg & Plotnick, 1990, 1995; Plotnick,1990). Although the relationships are more consistently in the anticipated direction (higher levels of welfare imply higher rates of nonmarital births), the size of the effect remains rather small. Lundberg and Plotnick (1990) report that a 25% increase in benefits increases the proportion of teenagers with a nonmarital birth by only 0.8 percentage points. Using a model that considers several marital status/fertility choices, Rosenzweig (1999) shows that compared to having no birth, average AFDC benefit levels[9] are positively related to nonmarital births for both teenagers and young adults. Moreover, when the model is estimated using samples of low-income (as measured by parental income) women, his is one of the few studies in which the results strengthen.[10] In his model, a 37% increase in the expected stream of welfare benefits increases the proportion with a nonmarital birth by 3 percentage points for the full sample and nearly 7 points for the low-income subsample—much larger than the results reported in previous papers. Replicating Rosezweig's results using a different data set, however, Hoffman and Foster (2000) found that these results were driven by the inclusion of women in their early 20s and were not robust to the specification of controls for state-level unobservables.

Finally, in those studies using data that span both the pre- and post-1978 periods, annual aggregates do not result in very strong relationships (Murray, 1993). Those studies often cover time periods in which the data are more heavily weighted toward the 1960s and 1970s. Similar to the early studies, where relationships are consistent with theoretical predictions, they are less likely to yield large relationships for teenagers, particularly Black teenagers (An, Haveman, & Wolfe, 1993; Duncan & Hoffman, 1990). Using a very careful modeling approach, An et al. (1993) report that a 20% increase in welfare benefits would increase the proportion of women with a nonmarital birth by 2 percentage points, but the coefficient shrinks when the model is estimated on a Black subsample. Duncan and

---

[9]Unlike most other cross-sectional studies presented here, this study does not measure cross-sectional variation in benefits at one point in time, but instead, differences in AFDC trends across space and time are the source of variation.

[10]Similar to previous studies, however, when Rosenzweig estimates his model for Black and White populations separately, the welfare coefficient for the Black sample has a counterintuitive, negative sign implying that high welfare benefit profiles are associated with a reduced probability of nonmarital births.

418

Hoffman (1990) estimated their model on a sample of Black teenagers and found similarly small effects of AFDC generosity on nonmarital teenage births.

Taken together, the results from these studies of welfare benefits and nonmarital births seem to be consistent with economic theory in that welfare restrictions appear most often to decrease the likelihood of nonmarital births. Although the estimated effects have strengthened over time, some questions linger. The hypothesis that effects should be strongest among those women most likely to require AFDC assistance receives inconsistent support among existing studies—often coefficient estimates from subsamples likely to require assistance are smaller than estimates that rely on the whole sample. Moreover, the inclusion of state-fixed effects, an attempt to control for unobserved differences across states, frequently tends to mitigate the relationship between welfare and nonmarital births indicating that the measured "effects" may be capturing, in part, differences in states that are not due to welfare generosity but some unmeasured, third variable. These issues make the hypothesized relationship between welfare benefits and nonmarital births the most weakly supported by existing evidence, particularly for teenaged subsamples.

THE IMPACT OF CHILD SUPPORT ENFORCEMENT

Theoretical Predictions

Increased child support enforcement should also have an impact on family formation. Increases in child support payments reduce the well-being of nonresident fathers (85% of nonresident parents are fathers) and increase the well-being of custodial mothers outside of marriage. Because stronger enforcement has opposite effects for mothers and fathers, the net effect on divorce is unclear. There are three possibilities. The first possibility is that changes in the expectation of happiness outside of marriage change such that the increases in mothers' well-being and decreases in fathers' well-being which result from stronger child support enforcement are exactly equal. In this case, the total value of happiness (the sum of the husband's and the wife's utility) within and outside marriage remain unchanged, and there are neither more nor less divorces than before the increased child support provision. The second possibility is that stronger enforcement increases the mother's expected well-being more than it decreases the father's expected well-being outside marriage. In this case, the total relative value of non-marriage to marriage increases, which leads to more divorce. The third possibility is that increased child support enforcement makes men more worse off than their partners are made better off outside marriage. In this case, increases in the expected amount of child support transferred lead to fewer divorces In any of these situations, because increased child support means that men will be made worse off (and women better off) if they are unmarried, we would expect a rene-gotiation of the payoffs within marriage in order to compensate women who would otherwise want a divorce because of changes in their expected happiness outside marriage.

Which possibility best matches reality? The answer differs depending on whether the mother would expect to rely on welfare if she were to become (or remain) unmarried. Because in most states, AFDC/TANF recipients receive only the first $50 of child support,[11] the most likely scenario for those couples in which the woman is likely to end up relying on welfare is that the father loses more than the mother gains from strengthened child support enforcement.[12] For those cou-ples in which the woman will not end up relying on welfare if she divorces, either the second or the third scenario is possible. Following a divorce, women are usu-ally worse off financially and men are usually better off financially. Thus, the wife is likely to place a higher value on the increase in her income than he places on the decrease in his income.[13] On the other hand, the stricter child support enforcement is, the more likely that nonresident fathers will be required to pay more than they would freely choose to provide, and the greater the probability that he places a higher value on his income loss than the mothers place on their income gain. Hav-ing to pay what they perceive to be too much child support might introduce some added level of disutility—the emotional cost resulting from resentment at what fathers think is "unfair." This basic economic model would therefore predict that increased child support enforcement should result in fewer divorces for couples who are likely to require AFDC/TANF assistance after divorce and either more or less divorces among those couples who are not likely to require assistance.

Understanding the relationship between nonmarital births and child support enforcement is similarly complicated by the fact that male and female incentives should work in opposite directions. Although increased child support enforce-ment increases the father's costs of childbearing, at the same time, it decreases the mother's costs of single parenthood. But of the competing concerns, whose is likely to dominate? A decrease in nonmarital births would only be likely to occur in those cases where the man has complete control over contraceptive decisions or where the increased child support enforcement has little impact on the woman's utility. Although the former case may be unlikely, the latter is very like-ly when the mother will have to rely on welfare as a single parent. As Nixon

---

[11]Except for the state of Wisconsin, changes brought forth under TANF are similar in their "tax-ing" of child support benefits and often leave the mother with even less than the first $50.

[12]Nixon (1997) also takes into account over- and under-the-table child support payments. If increased child support enforcement causes men to substitute over-the-table payments for what they were previously paying under the table, it is women on AFDC who will be made worse off because they will lose that income. The end result is the same—increased child support enforcement results in fewer efficient divorces among couples where the woman is likely to require AFDC assistance, but this time it is because the woman is made worse off.

[13]This follows from the assumption of declining marginal utility of income.

(1997) points out, women likely to require welfare benefits could actually see a decline in their well-being as a result of increased child support enforcement. If men who would otherwise provide informal, under-the-table support no longer do so because they have to make formal payments, the total support a woman receives would, in fact, decline. In this instance, both men and women would have an incentive to prevent a nonmarital birth.

Empirical Evidence for the Effects of Increased Child Support Enforcement

Unfortunately, there is much less research on the effects of child support enforcement than on the effects of welfare on family formation. In part, this is due to the fact that child support enforcement became a federal responsibility only in 1974. Furthermore, the largest changes in child support policy have occurred even more recently. There are only two recent studies that have attempted to explore the possibility of a relationship between increased child support enforcement and divorce. One study (Nixon, 1997) uses state policies to proxy for the likelihood and level of child support a woman would receive if she divorces. The author finds a negative relationship between increased child support enforcement and divorce for families with children, and no relationship for families without. Because women without children are not eligible for child support, this finding provides some additional evidence that the policy parameters are capturing real effects and not a spurious correlation. Estimating the models on subsamples of the population—those women who are more likely to require AFDC benefits in the event of a divorce—she finds even stronger negative effects. The latter result is most definitely consistent with the predictions of economic models whereas the former may or may not be. Recall that under typical utility assumptions, most models would predict that women not likely to receive welfare would be more likely to divorce. It is possible that the more impoverished subsample is driving the results and negating the positive response of other women. The author does not, however, attempt to determine whether women unlikely to receive welfare actually have a greater chance of divorce, so that question remains unanswered at present. Hoffman and Duncan (1995) attempt to capture variations in expected child support payments and find no effect at all. This study however, uses a sample of already divorced women to estimate the amount of child support a woman would receive if she were to divorce. In an environment with changing laws and procedures governing child support awards and amounts, this procedure is likely to introduce a good deal of measurement error, which may account for the weak relationship they find between child support and divorce.

There are two studies that attempt to relate state-level child support enforcement variables to nonmarital births. In an attempt to control for state-level unobservables that may bias parameter estimates, state-specific fixed effects are often introduced. In Garfinkel et al. (2000) the authors find a significant relationship between some child support enforcement variables and state-level nonmarital births. Their largest estimates imply that changes in child support enforcement were responsible for a 12% decline in nonmarital births over the period 1980–1996. Interestingly they found that changes in child support were much more important than changes in welfare benefits over the same time period. Case (1998) also looks at state-level rates of nonmarital childbearing, but attempts to control for the fact that cross-state variation in child support policy may be endogenous by using an instrumental variables technique. In both studies, with the preferred model specification that attempts to control for state-level unobservables, many of the parameter estimates increase in magnitude. This implies that the relationships are not in fact due to state-level unobservables and may be causal. Moreover, the most precisely estimated coefficients are consistent with the predictions of economic theory. Policies that increase the costs of parenthood by making child support obligations higher appear to decrease nonmarital births at the state level so that the male incentives dominate. The existing evidence, though sparse, seems at present to be consistent with the predictions of economic theory in that increased child support enforcement seems to be negatively related to nonmarital births. The additional implication that women should respond differently to increased child support enforcement depending on their expected welfare needs has not, at this point, been examined.

THE IMPACT OF LABOR MARKET OPPORTUNITIES

Theoretical Predictions

Finally, we turn to the effects of labor market opportunities on family formation. Most economic theories of marriage suggest that good employment opportunities for men strengthen marriage and poor employment opportunities weaken marriage. Becker extends the theory of comparative advantage to argue that specialization within marriage is optimal. Because fathers tend to specialize in income earning, an increase in their market wage will increase their gains from trade, and therefore stabilize marriage.[14] But these "price effects" are not the only possible source of marital gains. Financially, partners can act as an alternative source of credit. Think, for instance, of the woman who works to put her husband through medical school so that he has fewer high-interest loan payments on graduation.[15]

---

[14]Becker also shows that an unexpected high or low wage will increase divorce. Once married, increased labor market opportunities, if unexpected, may make the option of remarriage seem more attractive. Men or women who find themselves (their partners) with improved (weakened) labor market opportunities or higher (lower) than expected wages may feel that they want to exit from the current marriage and attempt to make a better match because they have experienced outcomes that are likely to be better than anticipated when the original marriage was contracted.

[15]This would represent a gain to marriage if we assume that there are imperfect credit markets. Assuming that partners have more information about the quality of the loan, this is not an unreasonable assumption.

Similarly, spouses can act as a buffer to risk. If one partner becomes ill or unemployed, the other partner can help to make ends meet (Moffitt, 2000a). Furthermore, so long as there are public (jointly consumed) goods, within marriage such as housing, the utility gains from marriage increase with income. These "income effects" mean that increased labor market opportunities for both men and women should stabilize marriage and decrease divorce. For men, both price and income effects should increase marriage, so the total effect of increased labor market opportunities should be positive.

Increased labor market opportunities for females reduce their comparative advantage in the home and may reduce marriage. They also enable women to purchase more privacy and independence resulting in less marriage. On the other hand, just as for men, higher wages for women increase the other types of gains from marriage. For women, increased labor market opportunities have negative price effects—resulting from decreased gains to specialization—and positive income effects because they can help out financially and purchase more public goods. The total effect on marriage is ambiguous and depends on which effect is stronger.

Search models of marriage focus on the costs of continuing to search for a more perfect partner. Individuals have in a mind a minimally acceptable quality of match.[16] Potential matches that appear to be below the minimum are not accepted, and the individual continues searching. These models also take into account uncertainty at the time of marriage regarding what the future outcomes of the marriage will be. For instance, women who encounter a young job entrant may not be as certain of his earning capacity as they are of a man who has worked for several years. Longer searches can decrease uncertainty and increase the chance of a high-quality match. In these models, increased labor market opportunities make men more desirable partners, but also allow them to fund longer searches designed to increase the quality of a match. In search models, it is possible for improved labor market opportunities to lead to less marriage for both men and women because higher minimum standards will mean that a larger share will never encounter an acceptable match. But among those individuals who do find mates, it also predicts longer-lasting matches and less divorce—an ambiguous total effect.

Finally, with respect to nonmarital births, what Willis (1999) calls an "underclass equilibrium" may occur if there is a shortage of men and if women's incomes are high relative to men's. When this is the case, low-income women may find that their best choice is to have children out of wedlock, and low-income men will optimally decide to father children out of wedlock with several different partners. The assumption is that women who cannot find suitable mates are

---

[16]Although most people acknowledge that there are a variety of factors that people consider when choosing a mate, few characteristics can be easily and accurately measured. For this reason, empirical estimates of search models frequently focus on female searches and use the man's earnings as a measure of quality.

unable or unwilling to marry, but may nonetheless become parents and contribute to the rise in nonmarital childbearing. By increasing the supply of marriageable men, women will marry rather than choose lone parenthood. In this way employment opportunities for men should decrease nonmarital childbearing by making the marriage option more attractive. Similar to Becker's model of divorce, one implication is that greater employment or income opportunities will have an asymmetric incentive effect for women and men. For women, greater opportunities will exacerbate the underlying problem—a shortage of "marriageable men"—and lead to more nonmarital births. However, this hinges on the assumption that marriage behavior is changing but fertility behavior is not. In other words, fertility decisions do not change as a result of new labor market opportunities. As Garfinkel et al. (2000) point out, better labor market opportunities for women should also decrease fertility. If fertility rates fall more than marriage rates, the result may, in fact, be a decline in nonmarital births even if women are choosing not to marry. Increasing the labor market opportunities of men will, however, lead to more "marriageable" men, and as a result of increased marriage, most models would predict fewer nonmarital births.

Empirical Evidence for the Effects of Labor Market Opportunities

Although their data are extremely limited and only use information on male earnings, Becker et al. (1977) find that any shocks to income—positive or negative—increase the likelihood of divorce. The authors explain their results by suggesting that high incomes likely increase marriage, but, once married, any deviations from expectations lead to a higher probability of divorce. Consistent with a search model of marriage, this may imply that positive shocks resulting from new labor market opportunities may result in more marital instability because individuals who have higher-than-anticipated earnings may try their luck in the remarriage market.

The coincident increases in female labor supply and female headship could imply that there is a relationship between female economic opportunities and divorce. Indeed, cross-sectional and time series studies indicate that higher female employment opportunities are associated with more nonmarriage (Blau, Kahn, & Waldfogel, 2000) and higher female headship through divorce. It could also be the case, however, that divorced women need to work in order to support themselves and their children. This brings into question the underlying causality (Haurin, 1989). In addition, women who believe they may divorce in the future are likely to want to invest in work experience "just in case," so the timing of work and divorce experiences is unlikely to imply a causal relationship (Johnson & Skinner, 1986; Peters, 1986).

Similar to what we observe in time trends, cross-sectional evidence regarding economic opportunities and divorce is usually consistent with theoretical predictions. Although a good deal of studies demonstrate a positive relationship between female earnings and divorce, there are some interesting counterpoints that need to be considered. Underlining the importance of the economic gains to marriage, South (1991) demonstrated that men would prefer their wife be employed. Similarly, Mare and Winship (1991) demonstrated that Black women with high education and earnings are more desired by potential husbands. These indicators would seem to imply that either the gains from specialization are or have become small relative to the income gains. More consistent with the predominance of gains due to comparative advantage, van der Klaaw (1996) found that higher female earnings and employment lead to increased divorce whereas higher male earnings have the opposite effect. Using the same data but a different model, Hoffman and Duncan (1995) found that both the husband's and the wife's earnings decrease the likelihood of divorce.[17]

Time series, cross-sectional, and longitudinal analyses all find that poor male employment opportunities are associated with low marriage and high nonmarital fertility. But causation flows not only from work to marriage but also from marriage to work, making it difficult to obtain unbiased estimates of the effects of employment opportunities on marriage. Furthermore, most studies indicate that changes in employment rates account for only a small portion of the changes in marriage. On the other hand, Moffitt (2000b) suggests that reductions in male wage rates account for a great deal of the increase in female headship among the low educated, but he stresses the importance of including both male and female wages, absolute and relative, in order to control, if only imperfectly, for both specialization and income effects (Moffitt, 2000a).

Time trends in labor market opportunities, at least for Black men, appear, at first glance, to explain some of the observed increase in female-headed households due to increased nonmarital births. Wilson (1987; Wilson & Neckerman, 1986) shows that the trend in his "male marriageable pool index" (MMPI)—the ratio of the number of employed men to women who are of similar age and the same race—turned downward for young Black men in the late 1960s through the early 1980s. This fall coincided with a rapid decline in marriage for this group, and as a consequence, appears to be a strong candidate for explaining the rise in Black, female-headed households over that time period. In addition, Smith, Morgan, and Koropeckyj-Cox (1996) demonstrate that increases in the Black nonmarital birth ratio between 1960 and 1992 were due almost entirely to changes in age-specific marital rates, making the retreat from marriage an attractive explanation. Examining the time trends more closely, researchers have found some interesting issues that need to be addressed by proponents of this theory, however.

If a lack of economic opportunities is the driving force in the retreat from marriage, as Lerman (1989) points out, theorists are going to have to explain why college-educated Black men also show declines in marriage. Theories of an underclass equilibrium would predict either no change or an increase in the marriage propensities of this "marriageable" group. Changing the focus from educa-

---

[17]The wife's wage coefficient becomes insignificant in the full model specification, however.

tion to employment, Ellwood and Crane (1990) find declines in marriage among employed as well as unemployed men. This kind of universal decline is not easily explained by the economic models presented that assume higher-quality men would continue to marry at the same or even higher rates.

Cross-sectional and longitudinal studies consistently find a relationship between employment status or earnings of males and family structure, particularly for Black families. The estimated effects, however, usually explain only a very small portion of the change—10% or smaller (Blau et al., 2000; Brien, 1997; Lichter, LeClere, & McLaughlin, 1991; Lloyd & South, 1996; Sampson, 1987; White, 1979). Mare and Winship (1991) use both employment and earnings to predict marriage within the past year. Their study uses measures of both current employment and previous year's earnings. The findings stand out from many others in that they find that declines in Black male employment explain about 20% of the decline in marriage. Their study fails to address adequately a very important problem however. Earnings and marriage are likely to be linked. Married men earn more than unmarried men, but it is not clear that low earnings cause low marriage or that low marriage causes low earnings. Estimates of the relationship may be biased upward if marriage makes men more productive. Most studies, therefore, do not control for the link between marriage and earnings, and their small estimated impacts are likely to be overestimated. Wood (1995) uses a variety of models in attempting to control for the link between marriage and earnings. He finds that there is a good deal of reverse causality, and that although income level provides a better indicator than the more traditional MMPI measure, less than 5% of the decline in marriage rates can be attributed to the decline in economic opportunities.

Olsen and Farkas (1990) use quasi-experimental data (labor market shocks generated by a social program to provide young men with work opportunities) to show that increased opportunities for Black men increased the likelihood of partnering (but not marriage) and had negative effect on nonmarital childbearing. Neal (2000) estimates the expected spousal earnings for women and finds that expected spousal earnings are not associated with family structure for White women. For Black women—those with the lowest education in particular— increased expected spousal earnings appear to increase marriage and decrease nonmarital childbearing. The estimated impact of even an additional $5,000 per year on these rates is somewhat modest, but he mentions that it would reduce the differential in single motherhood between Blacks and Whites by over 10%. Conversely, South and Lloyd (1992) find that although mate availability has a small effect on the nonmarital fertility of Whites and Blacks, male unemployment, contrary to the predictions of the underclass equilibrium, reduces nonmarital fertility rates. Furthermore, they conclude that the bulk of the racial differences in nonmarital childbearing cannot be attributed to differences in their respective marriage markets. Although it is an important factor, declines in employment opportunities for males, by reducing marriage, fail to explain the bulk of the increases in nonmarital births over the past few decades.

The relationship between economic opportunities for women and nonmarital childbearing is more complicated, however. Better opportunities allow women to opt out of marriage, but research also shows that better opportunities and expectations of opportunities reduce the desire to have a nonmarital birth. Empirical work provides support for both of these countervailing effects.

Moffitt (2000a) compares time trends in wages, relative wages, and marriage by race, cohort, and education level. His analysis shows that for more-educated, White couples, the income effect (measured as total income) seems to have dominated marriage incentives, whereas for less-educated women, the declines from reduced comparative advantage (measured as the ratio of male to female incomes) appear to be most important. That is, higher wages for White women led to more marriage among the highly educated and less marriage among the less educated. Among less-educated Black women decreases in comparative advantage appear to have dominated, resulting in less marriage. Neither changes in comparative advantage nor income effects can explain changes in marriage patterns among highly educated Black women.

Examining employment opportunities for Black females, Duncan and Hoffman (1990) find that increasing expected age-26 income by 25% would modestly reduce teenage childbearing (a 2 percentage point deduction in the proportion of teen births). More importantly, they report that if "black women could translate their backgrounds into age-26 incomes in the same way as white women, . . . the incidence of AFDC-related births would fall by one-fifth" (p. 531). Such an impressive reduction in AFDC-related births would require closing a substantial White-Black earnings gap and would imply a 75% increase in mean age-26 income for Black women. More realistic changes in earnings opportunities would nevertheless result in substantially fewer AFDC-related births. Thus, the role of employment opportunities for women may be worth further investigation.

CONCLUSION

Economists generally assume that father investments of time and money in their children will improve child outcomes. Economic theory predicts that marriage promotes these kinds of father–child involvement. Fathers who live apart from their children incur greater costs than resident fathers when sharing income or time with the child. The cost of housing a child or spending an hour or two with the child is much lower if the child and father live in the same household.

Economic theory also predicts that welfare programs like AFDC/TANF that are limited to unmarried parents and/or are steeply income tested will discourage marriage. More universal programs like child allowances, or the EITC, may encourage or discourage marriage. Child support enforcement may either discourage or encourage divorce among families who would not be reliant on welfare, but is likely to discourage divorce and nonmarital births amongst families who would be reliant on welfare. Increases in labor market opportunities for men promote marriage, whereas increases in labor market opportunities for women may either promote or discourage marriage.

Although there are some empirical studies that are inconsistent with these predictions and although there are shortcomings to even the best studies, on the whole, empirical research confirms the predictions. Fathers who live with their children invest substantially more time and money in their children than do nonresident fathers. High AFDC/TANF benefits are associated with more divorce, and although the evidence remains weak and questions remain unanswered, with more nonmarital births. Strong child support enforcement deters divorce and nonmarital births. Higher wages and greater employment for males are associated with higher marriage rates. Greater employment of women is associated with more divorce, but the effects of wage rates are more ambiguous and appear to differ by education and race.

Most studies find that the effects of welfare, child support, or labor market opportunities are, by themselves, small. None of these factors has changed enough to fully account for the large changes in U.S. family structure. Researchers may yet demonstrate, however, that taken together, changes in all of these factors explain a large proportion of the change.

REFERENCES

An, C., Haveman, R., & Wolfe, B. (1993). Teen out-of-wedlock births and welfare receipt: The role of childhood events and economic circumstance. *Review of Economics and Statistics, 75*(2), 195–208.

Becker, G. S. (1973). A theory of marriage, Part I. *Journal of Political Economy, 81*(4), 813–846.

Becker, G. S. (1974). A theory of marriage, Part II. *Journal of Political Economy, 82*(2), S11–S26.

Becker, G. S. (1981). *A treatise on family.* Cambridge, MA: Harvard University Press.

Becker, G. S., Landes E. M., & Michael, R. T. (1977). An economic analysis of marital instability. *Journal of Political Economy, 85*(6), 1141–1187.

Blau, F. D., Kahn, L. M., & Waldfogel, J. (2000). Understanding young women's marriage decisions: The role of labor and marriage market conditions. NBER Working Paper No. 7510.

Brien, M. J. (1997). Racial differences in marriage and the role of marriage markets. *Journal of Human Resources, 32*(4), 741–778.

Case, A. (1998). The effects of stronger child support enforcement on nonmarital fertility. In I. Garfinkel, S. McLanahan, D. Meyer, & J. Seltzer (Eds.), *Fathers under fire: The revolution in child support enforcement* (pp. 128–156). New York: Russell Sage Foundation.

Cutright, P. (1970). AFDC, family allowances, and illegitimacy. *Family Planning Perspectives, 2*(4), 4–9.

Del Boca, D., & Flinn, C. J. (1995). Rationalizing child-support decisions. *American Economic Review, 85*(5),1241–1262.

Duncan, G. J., & Hoffman, S. D. (1990). Welfare benefits, economic opportunities, and out-of-wedlock births among black teenage girls. *Demography, 27*(1), 16–35.

Ellwood, D., & Bane M. J. (1985). The impact of AFDC on family structure and living arrangements. In R. Ehrenberg (Ed.), *Research in Labor Economics* (Vol. 7, pp. 137–207). Greenwich, CT: JAI Press.

Ellwood, D., & Crane, J. (1990). Family change among black Americans: What do we know? *Journal of Economic Perspectives, 4*(4), 65–84.

Flinn, C. J. (2000). Modes of interaction between divorced parents. *International Economic Review, 41*(3), 545–578.

Freshnock, L., & Cutright, P. (1979). Models of illegitimacy: United States, 1969. *Demography, 16*(1), 37–47.

Garfinkel, I., Gaylin, D. S., Huang C. & McLanahan S. S. (2000). *The roles of child support enforcement and welfare in nonmarital childbearing.* Center for Research on Child Wellbeing Working Paper 00–06-FF. New York: Columbia University School of Social Work.

Garfinkel, I., & McLanahan, S. S. (1986) *Single mothers and their children* Washington DC: Urban Institute Press.

Goldscheider, F. K., & Kaufman, G. (1996). Fertility and commitment: Bringing men back in. *Population and Development Review, 22*(Issue Supplement: Fertility in the United States: New Patterns, New Theories), 87–99.

Haurin, D. R. (1989). Women's labor market reactions to family disruptions. *Review of Economics and Statistics, 71*(1), 54–61.

Hoffman S. D., & Duncan, G. J. (1995). The effect of incomes, wages, and AFDC benefits on marital disruption. *Journal of Human Resources, 30*(1), 19–41.

Hoffman, S. D., & Foster, M. E. (2000). AFDC benefits and nonmarital births to young women. *Journal of Human Resources, 35*(2), 376–391.

Janowitz, B. S. (1976). The impact of AFDC on illegitimate birth rates. *Journal of Marriage and the Family, 38*(3), 485–494.

Johnson, W. R., & Skinner, J. (1986). Labor supply and marital separation. *American Economic Review, 73*(3), 455–469.

Lerman, R. I. (1989). Employment opportunities of young men and family formation. *American Economic Review, 79*(2), 62–66.

Lichter, D., LeClere, F., & McLaughlin, D. (1991). Local marriage markets and the marital behavior of black and white women. *American Journal of Sociology, 96*(4), 843–867.

Lloyd, K. M., & South, S. J. (1996). Contextual influences on young men's transition to first marriage. *Social Forces, 74*(3), 1097–1119.

Lundberg, S., & Plotnick, R. (1990). Effects of state welfare , abortion, and planning policies on premarital childbearing among white adolescents. *Family Planning Perspectives, 22,* 246–275.

Lundberg, S., & Plotnick, R. (1995). Adolescent premarital childbearing: Do economic incentives matter? *Journal of Labor Economics, 13*(2), 177–200.

Mare, R., & Winship, C. (1991). Socioeconomic change and the decline of marriage for blacks and whites. In C. Jencks & P. Peterson (Eds.), *The urban underclass* (pp. 175–202). Washington: Brookings Institution.

Moffitt, R. (1992). Incentive effects of the U.S. welfare system: A review. *Journal of Economic Literature, 30*(1), 1–61.

Moffitt, R. (1998). The effect of welfare on marriage and fertility: What do we know and what do we need to know? In R. Moffitt (Ed.), *Welfare, the family, and reproductive behavior: Research perspectives* (pp. 50–97). Washington, DC: National Research Council.

Moffitt, R. (2000a). Female wages, male wages, and the economic model of marriage: The basic evidence. In L. Waite (Ed.), *The ties that bind: Perspectives on marriage and cohabitation* (pp. 302–319). New York: Aldine de Gruyter.

Moffitt, R. (2000b) Welfare benefits and female headship in U.S. time series. *American Economic Review, 90*(2), 373–377.

Murray, C. (1993). Welfare and the family: The U.S. experience. *Journal of Labor Economics, 11*(1), S226–S261.

Neal, D. (2000). *The economics of family structure.* Department of Economics, University of Wisconsin. Mimeo.

Nixon, L. A. (1997). The effect of child support enforcement on marital dissolution. *Journal of Human Resources, 32,* 159–181.

Olsen R., & Farkas, G. (1990). The effect of economic opportunity and family background on adolescent cohabitation and childbearing among low-income blacks. *Journal of Labor Economics, 8*(3), 341–362.

Peters, H. E. (1986). Marriage and divorce: Informational constraints and private contracting. *American Economic Review, 76*(3), 437–454.

Pitt, M., Rosenzweig, M. R., & Gibbons, D. (1993). The determinants and consequences of the placement of government programs: Child health and family planning interventions. *World Bank Economic Review, 7,* 319–348.

Plotnick, R. (1990). Welfare and out-of-wedlock childbearing: Evidence from the 1980s. *Journal of Marriage and the Family, 52,* 735–746.

Rosenzweig, M. R. (1999). Welfare, marital prospects, and nonmarital childbearing. *Journal of Political Economy, 107*(6), S3–S32.

Sampson, R. (1987). Urban black violence: The effect of male joblessness and family disruption. *American Journal of Sociology, 93*(2), 348–82.

South, S. J. (1991). Sociodemographic differentials in mate selection preferences. *Journal of Marriage and the Family, 53,* 920–940.

South, S. J., & Lloyd, K. M. (1992). Marriage markets and nonmarital fertility in the United States. *Demography, 29*(2), 247–264.

Smith, H. L., Morgan, S. P., & Koropeckyj-Cox, T. (1996). A decomposition of trends in the nonmarital fertility ratio of blacks and whites in the United States. *Demography, 33*(2), 141–151.

van der Klaauw, W. (1996). Female labor supply and marital status decisions: A life-cycle model. *Review of Economic Studies, 63*(2), 199–235.

White, L. K. (1979). The correlates of urban illegitimacy in the United States, 1960–1970. *Journal of Marriage and the Family, 41,* 715–726.

Willis, R. (1999). A theory of out-of-wedlock childbearing. *Journal of Political Economy, 107*(6), S33–S64.

Willis, R., & Haaga, J. G. (1996). Economic approaches to understanding nonmarital fertility. *Population and Development Review, 22*(Issue Supplement: Fertility in the United States: New Patterns, New Theories), 67–86.

Willis, R., & Weiss, Y. (1985). Children as collective goods and divorce settlements. *Journal of Labor Economics, 3*(3), 268–292.

Wilson, W. J. (1987). *The truly disadvantaged: The inner city, the underclass, and public policy.* Chicago: University of Chicago Press.

Wilson, W. J., & Neckerman, K. M. (1986). Poverty and family structure: The widening gap between evidence and public policy issues. In S. H. Danzinger & D. H. Weinberg (Eds.), *Fighting poverty: What works and what doesn't* (pp. 232–59). Cambridge, MA: Harvard University Press.

Wood, R. G. (1995). Marriage rates and marriageable men: A test of the Wilson hypothesis. *Journal of Human Resources, 30*(1), 163–193.

17

Nonresident Fathers and Their Children: Child Support and Visitation From an Economic Perspective

John W. Graham
Rutgers, The State University of New Jersey

Andrea H. Beller
University of Illinois at Urbana-Champaign

At the end of the 20th century, nearly 12 million American men were not living in the same household as their approximately 20 million (under age 21) children. They have been called absent fathers, noncustodial fathers, nonresident fathers, or sometimes deadbeat dads, and yet, as we will see, most of them are not entirely absent from their children's lives, some retain joint legal or physical custody, and many provide at least some financial assistance to their children. The number of nonresident fathers has been growing quickly, as a result of high rates of divorce and nonmarital fertility. Along with this growth has come the recognition that father absence can have severe and long-term consequences for children's well-being. The purpose of this chapter is to provide an economic perspective on the lives of nonresident fathers and their children.

After a brief introduction, the chapter reviews recent economic theories that help explain why nonresident fathers may fail to support their children or to provide as much support as resident fathers do. These theories also have implications for child custody, visitation, and the rise in nonmarital fertility. Next, the chapter summarizes empirical evidence on fathers' involvement with their children, looking at aggregate trends in and determinants of child support and visitation. It also assesses the ability of fathers—particularly poor fathers—to pay support. The chapter then looks at the consequences of child support and visitation for the well-being of children, especially their educational attainment, and the behavior of fathers, especially their labor supply and likelihood of remarriage. The chapter ends with some recommendations for future research.

IDENTIFYING AND CHARACTERIZING NONRESIDENT FATHERS

It has always been difficult to use household surveys to identify all nonresident fathers. Men tend to underreport their fertility (Cherlin, Griffith, & McCarthy, 1983), and surveys often miss men in the military or prison (Sorensen, 1997). As a result, the population of nonresident fathers may be best estimated by counting the number of custodial mothers, assuming the number of mothers and fathers to be roughly equal (Garfinkel & Oellerich, 1989). Since 1979, the U.S. Census Bureau has been surveying custodial mothers in a supplemental questionnaire appended every other year to its April Current Population Survey (CPS-CSS). As of 1996, there were 11.6 million custodial mothers (age 15 and over), up from 7.1 million (age 18 and over) in 1979.

The main disadvantage of the CPS-CSS is that it gathers no information from or about nonresident fathers. As a result, sketching a portrait of nonresident fathers is difficult at best. There have been some small-scale surveys of nonresident fathers, but these are likely not to be nationally representative (Sonenstein & Calhoun, 1990). A few recent studies have attempted to adjust national household surveys for underreporting of nonresident fathers (Garfinkel, McLanahan, & Hanson, 1998; Sorensen, 1997). They find that, compared with fathers who live with their children, nonresident fathers tend to be slightly younger and less healthy, have less education and lower incomes, and work fewer hours. About one third of nonresident fathers have new families to support.

Nonresident fathers have a legal and moral obligation to support their children, although data show that many fathers pay little or nothing, and many have little physical contact with their children. Only 37.4% of custodial mothers reported receiving any child support payments in 1995. The mean amount paid was $1,781 to ever-married (that is divorced or separated) and $469 to never-married mothers.[1] As of April 1996, 55% of nonresident fathers had visitation privileges, and 21% shared joint legal or physical custody. Still, almost one in four fathers had no legal right to see their children. Fathers who visited their children were more likely to pay child support: 47% who visited at least once in 1995 paid support, compared with just 29% who did not see their children.

---

[1]U.S. Census Bureau (1999). The expected payment is the percent of mothers awarded and due support times the percent due support that receive some times the mean amount received.

ECONOMIC THEORY OF NONRESIDENT FATHERS AND THEIR CHILDREN

Over the past 25 years, economists have shown that microeconomic theory can be applied to the study of family behavior, yielding useful insights about marriage, divorce, household production, fertility, and child development. According to one of its leading proponents, "the combined assumptions of maximizing behavior, market equilibrium, and stable preferences, used relentlessly and unflinchingly, form the heart of the economic approach" (Becker, 1976, p. 5). In this section, we look at some insights offered by this new theory for parents' behavior regarding child support and visitation (Becker, 1981; Del Boca & Flinn, 1994, 1995; Weiss & Willis, 1985, 1993; Willis, 1999).

Why Deadbeat Dads?

A key question addressed by this new theory is: Why do children, who are usually conceived in love and willingly supported when their parents live together, too often lose that support when their father lives elsewhere; or put more simply, why deadbeat dads? To start with, three possible reasons can be acknowledged, although none is central to this new theory. First, the "real income" of parents may simply be lower following divorce or separation, due in part to the costs of divorce per se, but also to the loss of economies of scale, shared (or public goods), and the division of labor that occur within marriage. Second, taxes and transfer programs (such as Aid to Families with Dependent Children, or AFDC) can create economic disincentives, particularly for low-income parents, to pay child support, as discussed more fully later in this section. Third, the emotional bonds that link fathers and children may be lessened over time when families do not live together, and ongoing conflicts between the parents are likely to exacerbate the situation.

Although acknowledging these factors, the theory sketched out in the following discussion emphasizes two other ideas—the so-called free-rider and principle-agent problems. The free-rider problem occurs whenever spending by one party on a shared or collective good allows another party to also benefit without paying; in our case, children are the collective good, and each parent tries to free ride on child spending by the other. The principle-agent problem refers to conflicts of interest that can occur when a principle needs to conduct business through an agent; in our case, the nonresident father is the principle who can only transfer income to his children through his agent, their mother. As a result of these problems, parental cooperation in maintaining high levels of spending on their children is difficult outside of marriage. Readers without a strong background in mathematics may want to skip ahead to the next subheading, "Child Support Payments."

An Economic Model

Following Weiss and Willis (1985), assume that parents act to maximize their own well-being (or utility) subject to certain constraints. Suppose the utility of each parent depends on their own level of consumption (C_f for fathers and C_m for mothers) and the consumption of the children (K), no matter where the children live. Consumption of the children, in turn, equals the total of what is spent on them by their father and mother ($K = K_f + K_m$). Thus, we can write the utility function of the father as $U_f(C_f, K)$ and the mother as $U_m(C_m, K)$. Because K enters both functions, it represents a so-called collective, shared, or public good, whereas C is a private good. In addition, each parent faces a budget constraint that limits their own spending choices, $K_f + C_f = I_f$ for the father, and $K_m + C_m = I_m$ for the mother, where I represents a given level of income. In general, it is difficult to characterize a parent's optimal choices of their own and children's consumption, because these depend in part on the (expected) behavior of the other parent. But, we can show that children's consumption will usually be higher when the parents are married rather than divorced, or if divorced, when cooperation and trust are greater.

To obtain an explicit solution, suppose utility functions are Cobb-Douglas; that is, $U_f = \ln(C_f) + a \ln(K)$, and $U_m = \ln(C_m) + a\ln(K)$, where ln is the natural log and a is the weight attached to children's consumption.[2] If the parents cooperated with each other (as a married couple might) and maximized their joint utility, then it can be shown that:

$$K^* = K_f + K_m = b\{I_f + I_m\}, \text{ where } b = a/(a+1). \tag{1}$$

If parents did not cooperate with each other, but maximized their own utility by taking spending by the other as given, then we can derive the following "reaction" curves:

$$K_f = b\{I_f - (1/a)K_m\} \text{ and} \tag{2}$$

$$K_m = b\{I_m - (1/a)K_f\}. \tag{3}$$

These reaction curves show that the father's spending on his children decreases as the mother spends more, and vice versa. Solving the equations simultaneously, we can find the level of spending by each parent that would be consistent with the observed spending level of the other. This is the so-called Cournot-Nash, or non-cooperative, equilibrium in which neither parent has any incentive to change his or her own spending on children, given the observed level of spending by the other. It can be shown that:

$$K^{**} = K_f + K_m = b'\{I_f + I_m\}, \text{ where } b' = a/(a+2). \tag{4}$$

---

[2]Del Boca and Flinn (1995) also assume Cobb-Douglas utility, but let a be parent specific, a_f and a_m. Our simplifying assumption is that likes marry likes, so $a_f = a_m$.

Finally, notice that because b' is less than b, K^{**} is less than K^*; that is, overall spending on children is less when parents do not cooperate with each other than when they do.

To see why it may be difficult to achieve cooperation, we can redo the preceding problem using the economic tools of game theory. We assume that $I_f = I_m = 30$, and $a = 2$.[3] In this case, the payoff matrix in Table 17.1 shows the utility and spending levels of mothers and fathers for relatively "high" and "low" spending levels on children. If mother and father act cooperatively, devoting a relatively high level of spending to their children (that is, $K_f = K_m = 20$, so $K^* = 40$), then each parent achieves a relatively high level of utility ($U_f = U_m = 9.68$), as shown in the upper left-hand corner of the payoff matrix. If they do not cooperate, the Cournot-Nash equilibrium is a relatively low level of spending on children ($K_f = Km = 15$, so $K^{**} = 30$), and each parent achieves a lower level of utility ($U_f = U_m = 9.51$), as shown in the lower right-hand corner. Even though both parents are better off by agreeing to maintain a high level of spending on children, this preferred outcome may not be achieved, because each can do better still by cheating on the agreement and reducing their own spending on children, assuming the other abides by the agreement of high spending [from equation (3), if $K_m = 20$, then $K_f = 13.33$, which increases the father's utility to $U_f = 9.83$, as shown in the lower left-hand corner]. This is the classic "prisoner's dilemma" in game theory, which shows that cooperation and trust may be hard to achieve. As a result, outside of marriage, when it is difficult to monitor the spending of the other parent, "low" spending on children is likely to be the outcome.

There is another possible outcome, known as the Stackelberg solution (or first-mover advantage), which may be particularly relevant given the nature of child support payments. In most cases, a nonresident father cannot make separate or independent expenditures on his children, but instead must transfer resources to them through the custodial mother. He knows that not all of what he transfers (K_f)

TABLE 17.1
Payoff Matrix for Parental Spending on Children

		Mother's Spending on Her Children			
		High		Low	
Father's Spending on His Children	High	$K_f = 20$ $C_f = 10$ $U_f = 9.68$	$K_m = 20$ $C_m = 10$ $U_m = 9.68$	$K_f = 20$ $C_f = 10$ $U_f = 9.32$	$K_m = 13.33$ $C_m = 16.67$ $U_m = 9.83$
	Low	$K_f = 13.33$ $C_f = 16.67$ $U_f = 9.83$	$K_m = 20$ $C_m = 10$ $U_m = 9.32$	$K_f = 15$ $C_f = 15$ $U_f = 9.51$	$K_m = 15$ $C_m = 15$ $U_m = 9.51$

[3]The assumption of equal incomes simply makes the payoff matrix symmetric.

will be spent on the children, as shown above by the mother's reaction curve (equation 3). If we assume that the father maximizes his own utility taking into account how the mother will react to his choice of K_f, it can be shown that his optimal transfer will be[4]

$$K_f = b\{I_f - (1/a)I_m\}. \tag{5}$$

Combining equations (5) and (3), total spending on children will now be

$$K^{***} = K_m + K_f = b^2\{I_f + I_m\}. \tag{6}$$

Recalling that $b = a/(a+1)$ is a fraction and comparing equations (6) and (1), it can readily be seen that total spending on children in this case will be less than under cooperation. In addition, comparing equations (6) and (4), spending on children will now be even less than under the noncooperative Cournot-Nash equilibrium (as long as $a > 1/2$). For example, if as before $I_f = I_m = 30$ and $a = 2$, then $K_f = 10$, $K_m = 16.67$ and $K^{***} = 26.67$.[5] In other words, the Stackelberg outcome generates lower total spending on children than cooperation ($K^* = 40$) and even lower than the noncooperative equilibrium ($K^{**} = 30$).

Child Support Payments

Equation (5) defines the nonresident father's *voluntary* child support payment.[6] (It should be noted that K_f is positive if and only if $a > I_m/I_f$.) K_f is an increasing function of the father's income and a decreasing function of the mother's income. These are testable hypotheses that we explore in the next section. In addition, K_f increases with the utility weight attached to children's consumption, which, although unobservable, is likely to be correlated with characteristics we can measure, such as the duration of the parents' marriage (if any) prior to separation and the number and ages of the children.

Although equation (5) defines the amount of support a nonresident father is *willing* to pay, it may be less than the amount he is *required* to pay. One reason for this is that the mother may have a strong incentive to compel him to pay more, if, as in our numerical example, his voluntary payment leaves her worse

---

[4]That is, given $C_f = I_f - K_f$, he maximizes $U_f = \ln(I_f - K_f) + a \ln(K_f + K_m)$, subject to $K_m = b\{I_m - (1/a)K_f\}$, where $b = a/(a+1)$. Substituting the expression for K_m into the utility function, he chooses K_f to maximize $U_f = \ln(I_f - K_f) + a \ln (b\{I_m + K_f\})$, which shows that children's consumption depends on the mother's income and his transfer to her. The solution is given by equation (5).

[5]It might also be noted that $C_f = 20$ and therefore $U_f = 9.56$, which means that the father is better off than under the Cournot-Nash equilibrium, which illustrates the first-mover advantage of the Stackelberg case. On the other hand, $C_m = 13.33$ and therefore $U_m = 9.157$, which leaves the mother even worse off.

[6]K_f and its determinants can also be illustrated graphically as in Hoffman (1990) or chapter 3 of Beller and Graham (1993).

off (see footnote 5). Even if this involves significant legal costs on her part, she may be better off by spending some of her income to compel him to spend more of his income on their child(ren). Another reason he could be forced to pay more is if his voluntary level of support falls short of that required by the state's guidelines. Since 1988, states have been required to use numeric guidelines in establishing awards; today, most states set award amounts either as a fraction of the nonresident father's income alone or as a share of both parent's income.

Finally, consider the impact of the welfare system on child support payments. Until 1996, AFDC offered poor mothers a basic income guarantee, which was reduced dollar for dollar by income from other sources, including child support (except for the first $50 per month of child support, which states were mandated to disregard). As a result, nonresident fathers had no incentive to pay support to mothers on AFDC (or to pay more than $50), and mothers had little incentive to seek payment from them. It is not surprising that, as a condition of eligibility for AFDC, mothers were required to assist the state in collecting child support on their behalf. Welfare reform in 1996 introduced new work requirements and lifetime limits on benefits, and eliminated the state mandate of a $50 child support disregard. By helping to cut the welfare rolls, the first two reforms have given low-income parents greater incentive to seek (or to pay) child support, but the loss of the $50 disregard (which has occurred in most states) has reduced the incentive.

Child Custody and Visitation

Economic theory has tended to focus more on child support payments than on nonmonetary involvement of nonresident fathers with their children, such as custody arrangements and visitation.[7] Nevertheless, game theory does suggest a possible role for visitation. One way a nonresident father can monitor the mother's child spending is through frequent contact with his children. As long as he sees her maintaining a high level of spending, he will too (called the "tit-for-tat" strategy), and the couple achieves the cooperative (high-high) outcome. In this case, theory predicts a positive correlation between child support payments and visitation—that is, they are said to be complements.

It is also possible to describe a theory in which child support and visitation are substitutes for each other. Suppose the father's utility function is $U_f = U(C_f, Q_f)$, where Q_f is his perception of children's "quality," which depends on their consumption of goods (K), and on the fraction of time he spends with them (T_f); that is, $Q_f = Q(K, T_f)$. Ignoring all other uses, time not spent with children is devoted

---

[7]Weiss and Willis (1985), examine why in most divorce settlements it is the wife who obtains custody of the children.

to earning income at the rate w; that is, $I_f = w(1 - T_f)$. All else equal, an increase in T_f increases Q_f and raises U_f. However, an increase in T_f decreases I_f, which in turn reduces K, decreases Q_f, and lowers U_f. Thus, he can either spend more time with his children or more income on them, but not both.[8]

Consequences for Children

The choices parents make regarding marriage, divorce, child custody, visitation, and child support have important consequences for the current and future well-being of their children. Unfortunately, even altruistic parents do not always make decisions that are "in the best interests of the child," as shown in the preceding bargaining model, where the "low-low" spending equilibrium is an all too likely outcome. Leibowitz (1974) offers a model of home investments in children, in which parents select the quantity and quality of both goods and time to devote to their children's development. These early home investments, in turn, affect children's own attainment, as measured by such indicators as their final schooling level and lifetime earnings. The resources that parents spend on children are determined by the parent's own attributes (abilities and education), income, and family structure. In recent years, economists have increasingly studied the impact family structure—particularly single parenthood—on children's attainment (Haveman & Wolfe, 1995).

A key question we focus on in our empirical work is how child support payments affect children's attainment. Specifically, would an increase in child support be expected to have a larger, smaller, or equal impact on children relative to other sources of income available to custodial mothers, and does it matter whether these payments are voluntary or not? Del Boca and Flinn (1994) specify conditions under which child support is more likely than other income to be used to purchase child-specific goods. In the context of our bargaining model, this is equivalent to forcing a nonresident father to spend more on his children so as to increase the likelihood of the "high-high" spending outcome, rather than simply raising the income of the mother (I_m). If fathers who pay more support also spend more time with their children (even if only to monitor the mother's spending), then total resources—money and time—invested in children will increase all the more.

EMPIRICAL EVIDENCE ON FATHER INVOLVEMENT

In this section we turn to evidence from survey data on nonresident fathers' involvement with their children. First we look at current levels and trends over time in child support and visitation, for both ever-married and never-married fathers. Next we summarize empirical findings on the determinants of child sup-

---

[8]In addition, Del Boca and Ribero (2001) develop a model in which mothers trade child's time (visits) for father's income.

port and visitation, focusing on the impact of father's and mother's characteristics and child support laws. Finally, we look at fathers' ability to pay and programs to help low-income fathers meet their obligations.

Trends in Child Support

The most widely cited evidence on how much nonresident fathers contribute to the financial support of their children come from the U.S. Census Bureau's biennial survey of custodial mothers (CPS-CSS), available from 1978–79 to 1995–96.[9] Assuming an equal number of custodial mothers and nonresident fathers, 61.2% of fathers were legally required to pay child support as of April 1996, up only slightly from 59.1% in 1979. Ever-married (that is, divorced or separated) fathers were much more likely than never-married fathers (more precisely, the fathers of children whose mothers were never married) to have a support obligation: 68.0 versus 44.1% as of 1996. The percent of fathers required to pay has remained roughly constant among ever-married men, but has risen sharply for never-married men (from just 10.6% in 1979), due in large part to higher rates of paternity establishment. Never-married men make up an increasing share of all nonresident fathers, rising from 19.4 to 28.4% between 1979 and 1996.

Not all those required to pay support actually do so: just 69.8% of fathers with an obligation paid any in 1995, down from 71.7% in 1978. Payment rates vary by marital status: 73.0% of ever-married versus 56.4% of never-married men paid some in 1995. Payment rates increased over time among ever-married men, but fell sharply among never-married men. Combining award and payment rates, 44% of all ever-married fathers paid child support in 1995 (up from 41.4% in 1978), compared with 20.6% of all never-married fathers (up from 6.3% in 1978).

How much child support are fathers paying? Among those who pay something, payments averaged $3,767 in 1995, up from $1,799 in 1978. Taking account of inflation, however, the *real* value of child support payment was actually 10% lower in 1995 compared with 1978, which mirrored an ever-larger decline in the real value of support due. On average, ever-married fathers paid $4,046; never-married fathers paid $2,271. Finally, taking into account the amount of support paid and the likelihood of payment, nonresident fathers, on average, contributed $1,409 in 1995, or about $70 per child per month; ever-married fathers contributed $1,781 and never-married fathers $469.[10]

Trends in Child Visitation

Information on the amount of time fathers spend with their children usually

---

[9]Sonenstein and Calhoun (1990), report that in the pilot study to the never-completed Survey of Absent Parents, fathers reported paying 30% more child support on average than mothers reported receiving. Unfortunately, their sample size was only 205 matched pairs of parents.

[10]This assumes an average of 1.7 children per father, as explained in Beller and Graham (2000).

comes from surveys of custodial mothers. Since 1992, the CPS-CSS has questioned mothers about visitation and custody arrangements and since 1994 about contact between fathers and children. In 1992, 42% of custodial mothers reported that the children's father had neither joint custody nor visitation privileges; by 1996 this figure had dropped to just 24%. Over the same time period, the percent of nonresident fathers with joint custody increased from 14 to 21%, and the percent with only visitation rights rose from 44 to 55%. Thirty-six percent of custodial mothers reported that their children had no contact with their father in 1995, down slightly from 39% in 1993.

There is more information about father–child contact in other surveys, although most are based on small samples and are not nationally representative. In the National Survey of Families and Households conducted in 1987–88, 71% of nonresident fathers reported seeing their children at least once in the previous year; among those who did, nearly 39% saw their children as often as once a week (Seltzer, McLanahan, & Hanson, 1998). In the 1981 National Survey of Children, among children ages 11 to 16 whose parents were divorced or separated, 23% of fathers had no contact with their children in the past 5 years, and another 20% had no contact in the previous year. Twenty-one percent of fathers spent 1 to 12 days with their children, 11% spent 13 to 24 days, and 26% spent at least 24 days (Furstenberg, Morgan, & Allison, 1987).

Determinants of Child Support

This section summarizes findings from more than 15 years of empirical research using various data sets to estimate the magnitude and significance of the determinants of child support payments. These studies use multivariate regression techniques to isolate the impact of specific characteristics of fathers, mothers, the parental relationship, and the legal environment on four outcome variables: whether or not the father has an award obligation, the value of the award, whether or not he pays anything, and how much he pays. Characteristics of the father include his income and other socioeconomic factors such as race, ethnicity, age, education, and marital status to capture his ability and desire to support his children. Mother's characteristics include her income and socioeconomic characteristics, as well as the number of children and the quality of the ongoing parental relationship. The legal environment includes state guidelines for setting awards and enforcement techniques to collect support due. Among the data sets used are the CPS-CSS, National Survey of Families and Households (NSFH), Survey of Income and Program Participation (SIPP), Panel Study of Income Dynamics (PSID), National Longitudinal Survey of Youth (NLSY), and Survey of Absent Parents (SOAP).

Consistent with economic theory, empirical studies find a positive association between fathers' income and child support payments. Unfortunately, not all data sets have fathers' income, and those that do are not always nationally representative. Using the 1987 NSFH adjusted for missing fathers, Garfinkel et al. (1998) report the mean income of nonresident fathers who pay no child support to be about half that of fathers who pay. They also estimate that between 30 and 40% of nonpayers had incomes below $6,500. Using the same data, Meyer (1998) observes a nonlinear relationship between income and child support, with fathers whose income is below $20,000 paying little or no support, and those above $20,000 paying about $900 more per year for each $10,000 increase in income. Using a small sample pilot study to SOAP, Sonenstein and Calhoun (1990) find an even stronger association: each additional $1,000 in father's income raised award amounts by $301 and the likelihood of paying by 1.5%. Teachman (1990, 1991), using NLSY data on divorced parents only, reports a statistically significant but small impact of fathers' income on both child support awards and receipts.

Several studies employ CPS-CSS data, despite the absence (after 1979) of income data on nonresident fathers. Using the 1979 sample in which about half of all custodial mothers did provide an estimate of father's current income, Beller and Graham (1986) found each additional $5,000 in his income raised awards by $219 and the probability of payment by 2.7%; but, controlling for the amount of support owed, his income had no effect on the amount of support paid. Hanson, Garfinkel, McLanahan, and Miller (1996) use six waves of data from 1979 to 1990 and estimate fathers' income based on a technique proposed by Garfinkel and Oellerich (1989). They found each additional $1,000 raised the probability of an award by 1.1% and the amount due by $80. Unlike Beller and Graham, they found that fathers' income is also positively associated with paying support: each $1,000 increase in income raised payments by $36.

In addition to fathers' income, most studies include other characteristics, such as race, ethnicity, and marital status. Among these, race plays the biggest role: Black men are just half as likely as other men to have an award obligation, owe about 15% less, and pay 10% less, even controlling for income (Hanson et al., 1996). Hispanics owe less than non-Hispanics, but are no less likely to pay support owed. Whether or not a father was married (and for how long) may capture his commitment to his children, and thus his desire to pay. Never-married fathers are much less likely to have an obligation and owe less support; but among those who do, they are more likely to pay. Among ever-married fathers, time since the marital disruption reduces both the likelihood of paying any support and the amount paid (Beller & Graham, 1986, 1993; Hanson et al., 1996).

An important policy question is how remarried fathers with second families to support treat their child support obligations to their first families. Garfinkel et al. (1998) report that 37% of fathers who pay child support have a second family, compared with just 28 to 33% of fathers who pay no support, but this association does not control for other differences between fathers. In a multivariate context, both Sonenstein and Calhoun (1990) and Teachman (1991) find remarried fathers are significantly more likely to pay support than single fathers, suggesting they may be more "family oriented."

Theory predicts that, all else equal, mothers' income should be negatively related to child support, but empirical evidence is less certain. On the one hand, Hanson et al. (1996) found mothers' income was negatively related to award amounts: each additional $1,000 in income reduces awards by $90. On the other hand, Teachman (1990, 1991) found mothers' income positively related to award rates, and Sonenstein and Calhoun (1990) report that each additional $1,000 in a mother's income raises awards by $84.

Empirical evidence is stronger and more consistent regarding other maternal characteristics. Compared with single mothers, remarried women are significantly less likely to receive support they are due. Mothers with more children are more likely to have awards and to have larger awards; but the impact of number of children on receipts is uncertain. Isolating the impact of AFDC status on child support is difficult because it is often impossible to disentangle cause and effect. Even still, Beller and Graham (1993) report award rates to be 40% lower and receipt rates 30% lower for AFDC mothers, and Sonenstein and Calhoun (1990) found mothers on AFDC received less support. Finally, regarding the parental relationship, voluntary (as opposed to court-ordered) child support awards are more likely to be paid (Beller & Graham, 1986), and the quality of the ongoing parental relationship has a positive influence (Sonenstein & Calhoun, 1990).

As federal and state child support enforcement spending has grown and new laws have multiplied, researchers have begun to study their impact on the behavior of custodial mothers and nonresident fathers. A full review of this literature (see Lerman & Sorensen, 2000) is beyond the scope of this chapter, but we do summarize a few significant results. Sorensen and Halpern (1999) estimate half of the increase in child support receipts among never-married mothers and one third of the increase among ever-married mothers can be attributed to the widespread adoption of a few specific child support policies: guidelines to set award levels, in-hospital programs to establish paternity, interception of tax refunds to collect overdue support, wage withholding to collect current support (for the ever-married), and the $50 disregard by AFDC (for the never-married).

Determinants of Visitations

Like child support, contact between a nonresident father and his children is a multidimensional concept that can be measured several ways, including whether or not visitation occurs, and if so, by its frequency, length, and quality. Employing many of the same data sets discussed earlier, researchers have investigated the socioeconomic determinants of visitations and the link between paying support and visiting. A limitation of this research is that few studies have estimated the impact of a father's income on his visitation behavior.

Seltzer (1991) uses NSFH data to estimate the effect of parental characteristics on visitations. She finds the likelihood of any father–child contact (within the previous year) to be higher among the ever-married and lower among the remarried. Older children are more likely to see their father. Mothers' education has a positive impact and remarriage a negative impact on visitation. Physical distance reduces contact, as does the amount of time since the father–child separation. In addition, Seltzer et al. (1998) found a negative association between "high" ongoing parental conflict and the frequency of visitation.

Most empirical research on visitation found a strong positive relationship between paying child support and paying visits (Furstenberg et al., 1987; Seltzer, 1991; Seltzer et al., 1998). But it is important to note this finding does not necessarily mean engaging in one (supporting or visiting) *causes* the other one to occur, as it is not clear which is cause and which effect, or whether both behaviors are the result of other factors. Seltzer et al. (1998) take account of observable and unobservable characteristics of fathers so as to isolate the impact of child support on the likelihood and frequency of visitations. All else equal, they find the likelihood of any visits to be 15% higher and the frequency 20% higher if a father pays any child support. The amount of support he pays, however, appears to be unrelated to either the likelihood or frequency of visitations.

How Much Support Can Fathers Pay?

From a public policy perspective, an important question is how much support a father can be expected to pay. This is because most states have adopted numeric guideline formulas to establish award amounts based in whole or in part on the fathers' income. (Some states also take into account the mothers' income, as well as family size.) Garfinkel et al. (1998) summarized estimates of the income of nonresident fathers from 15 different studies. Most of these studies focus on subsets of the population, but among the few nationally representative ones, two general approaches are followed: One (Garfinkel & Oellerich, 1989; Miller, Garfinkel, & McLanahan, 1997) uses CPS-CSS data to obtain indirect estimates of fathers' incomes using observed characteristics of mothers; the other (Garfinkel et al., 1998; Sorensen, 1997) uses actual survey data on fathers adjusted for widespread underrepresentation and misreporting. Both approaches yield remarkably similar estimates of mean annual incomes (in 1995 dollars), ranging from about $28,000–30,000, based on imputed CPS-CSS data, to $27,000–29,000, based on adjusted SIPP and NSFH data, or about 30% less than the mean for resident fathers. In terms of income distribution, Garfinkel et al. (1998) estimate that about 20% of nonresident fathers earn more than $40,000, 40% earn less than $20,000, and 20% less than $6,000.

Several studies employ these income estimates to assess fathers' abilities to pay child support based on existing guideline formulas. Using the Wisconsin formula, Miller et al. (1997) computed the average potential child support payment in 1990 to be $3,369 per father, which is three times the actual amount owed ($1,138) and more than four times the actual amount paid ($764). Judged by the same standard, Sorensen (1997) estimated that fathers could have paid between $37 and $51 billion in aggregate in 1996, whereas they actually paid $17 billion. Meyer (1998) estimates potential payments under six different guidelines, including the Wisconsin formula, one that imposes a minimum payment, one that exempts low-income fathers from payment, and three that adjust for the needs of remarried fathers. On average, potential orders (in 1995 dollars) ranged from $2,671 to $4,172, compared with $1,668 actually due and $584 paid. He estimates that fathers earning over $40,000 could be expected to pay about three times as much as they currently owe, fathers earning $10,000–$20,000 could pay twice as much, whereas fathers earning less than $10,000 already owe as much as they would under all but one formula.

Helping Low-Income Fathers Support Their Children

Mincy and Sorensen (1998) estimate that as many as 37% of young (age 18 to 34) nonresident fathers are poor, and most pay little or no support. It is becoming clear to researchers and policymakers that getting these men to support their children will involve more than simply increasing award amounts and enforcing payment. A new approach is needed, one that includes more flexible child support orders (that increase over time along with his earning capacity) as well as employment-based and other social support services for fathers that will enable them to meet their obligations in the future. One such program, begun is 1992, is Parents' Fair Share (PFS), enrolling parents (mostly fathers) not paying their child support obligations, who are under- or unemployed and whose children are receiving welfare. There are four components to PFS: child support enforcement (to reschedule payments), peer support and responsible fatherhood training, employment and job training, and family mediation to resolve disputes over access to children (Johnson, Levine, & Doolittle, 1999). PFS advocates a holistic approach to helping low-income fathers, recognizing they are likely to have both economic and social hurdles to overcome on their way to becoming responsible fathers. Evaluations of the effectiveness of projects like PFS are just beginning to emerge.

ECONOMIC CONSEQUENCES OF CHILD SUPPORT AND VISITATION

In this section, we focus on the economic consequences of child support and visitation for the well-being of children and the behavior of fathers. Concern for the well-being of children in families eligible for child support stems from many sources. A primary concern is the average level of incomes and other resources (e.g., parental time, school quality, and community services) available to many of them. In 1995, the median income of married-couple families with children was $50,052, compared with just $17,936 for mother-only families (U.S. Census Bureau, 1996a).[11] About one third of custodial mothers had incomes below the poverty line in 1995, whereas only 7.5% of married couple families with children and 14% of custodial fathers did (U.S. Census Bureau, 1996b, 1999).

Regular payment of child support can make a difference: Custodial mothers receiving child support had incomes that averaged almost $8,000 higher than mothers without a child support award. Consequently, they have lower poverty rates and are less likely to have to rely on welfare. In 1995, about 36% of custodial parents[12] without awards fell into poverty, whereas only 22% of the parents who received either some or all of their payment due fell into poverty.[13] Child support appears to have an even bigger impact on welfare dependency: 26% of custodial mothers without child support awards in 1995 received some AFDC payments, whereas only 14% of those who received any child support payments did (U.S. Census Bureau, 1999).

Overall, in 1995, total family income averaged $21,829 among all mothers who received any child support payment, $5,736 (or 36%) more than the average income of $16,093 among mothers who had awards but who received no payment. The average child support payments of $3,767 accounted for about 17% of total family income. Child support receipts comprise only two thirds of the total income differential between the two groups. Most of the remainder comes from the higher earnings of mothers who receive child support.[14] According to Beller and Graham (1993), mothers with child support were more likely to be employed and earned more when they were employed. In 1995, approximately 82% of mothers receiving child support were employed, compared with just 76% of those due support who received none and 69% of those without an award. Child support and mother's earnings are likely to become even more important sources of income as a result of recent changes in public assistance laws, which place lifetime limits on welfare payments and require most recipients to have a job.

---

[11]The income differential narrows somewhat when taxes and cash transfers are also taken into account: $45,605 versus $21,786. See Table F in U.S. Census Bureau (1996a).

[12]The percent of custodial mothers falling into poverty is higher, but the data is not available in the report (U.S. Census Bureau, 1999).

[13]Analyses by Institute for Women's Policy Research (IWPR) (1999) based on data from the U.S. Census Bureau Survey of Income and Program Participation in 1990 and 1991 show that the poverty rate for mothers receiving child support would have increased to 46% had they not received their child support.

[14]Even mothers on AFDC had higher earnings if they had a child support agreement than if they did not have one (IWPR, 1999).

Child Support and Children's Well-Being

In the last decade, public attention has been increasingly focused on the effects of various circumstances in children's families on their current and future well-being. From an economic perspective, we are most concerned with immediate outcomes such as academic achievement in the form of test scores or grade retention, long-run outcomes such as educational attainment (measured by years of school completed and college attendance), and ultimately labor market outcomes, especially employment and earnings. Related socioeconomic outcomes of interest include whether they later had teen births or as young adults became a single parent and went on welfare.

The limited resources available to single-parent families frequently force them to spend less on their children than do two-parent families. A significant body of literature shows that growing up in a single-parent family, usually headed by a woman, reduces children's well-being (see for example, Krein & Beller, 1988; McLanahan & Sandefur, 1994). The greatest number of such studies focus on educational attainment and find that children who spend time in a single-parent family complete fewer years of schooling, are less likely to graduate from high school, and are less likely to go on to college (e.g., Krein & Beller, 1988). McLanahan and Sandefur (1994) document adverse outcomes not only on educational attainment, but also on the labor force attachment of young men and the risk that daughters become teen mothers.

Higher income reduces the negative impacts of living in a single-parent family by increasing the resources available for investments in children. There is considerable evidence that child support income is at least as beneficial as other sources of income, but may have additional benefits known to result from greater contact with the nonresident parent. The question that remains to be answered is whether contact with nonresident fathers who have to be compelled to pay child support is as beneficial as contact with those who pay it voluntarily. For example, there may be differences in the extent of their commitment to their children's education. If so, the outcome, may not be as beneficial.

The earliest study of this question (Beller & Chung, 1988) found that child support increased educational attainment more than income from other sources. Subsequent studies confirmed this finding (e.g., Graham, Beller, & Hernandez, 1994; Peters & Mullis, 1997). Graham et al. (1994) showed that support helps children overcome about two thirds of the disadvantage in years of school completed and reduces high school dropout rates as well as the percentage of students who fall behind their age cohorts in high school. Recent studies have also found that the receipt of child support has a greater positive effect than other income on cognitive test scores of children (Argys, Peters, Brooks-Gunn, & Smith, 1998; Knox, 1996) and of adolescents (Peters & Mullis, 1997).

These studies did not, however, rule out the possibility that the larger effect of child support income was due to unobservable characteristics of the nonresident fathers who paid support (Argys et al., 1998; Graham et al., 1994; Knox & Bane, 1994). Hernandez, Beller, and Graham (1995, 1996) found that as more reluctant payers were added to the child support system by increasingly strong child support enforcement during the 1980s, the magnitude of the beneficial effect of child support on children's educational attainment declined, suggesting that the unobserved characteristics of fathers who paid voluntarily were at least in part responsible for the more favorable outcomes of their children.

Taking a different approach, Aughinbaugh (2001) suggests that noncustodial parents will use information about children's achievement as a signal of how well the custodial parent is caring for them and that thus provides an incentive for the custodial parent to invest more in the children than they would have otherwise. The results of this study show that a "child's current achievement has a significant, positive, and large impact on child support outcomes" (p. 7). The results seem to suggest that fathers pay more when they think their children are being better cared for, thus resulting in the extra large effect of child support compared with other income. Although there is no direct evidence concerning the effects of child support on pregnancies of unmarried teens, it reduces welfare receipts, which are associated with higher rates of childbearing among daughters (Haveman & Wolfe, 1995).

To date the evidence is mixed as to whether the benefits of child support extend beyond the teenage years. Gray, Beller, and Graham (1997) found that child support increases the earnings of young adults, not only indirectly through its positive effect on educational attainment, but also directly. However, other studies (Krein, 1986; Peters & Mullis, 1997) found no direct effect on work experience or earnings. This is an area that warrants further investigation.

Visitation and Children's Well-Being

As already reported, contact of nonresident fathers with their children tends to be infrequent and varies with the type of birth and current living arrangements of the child (Furstenberg et al., 1987; Seltzer, 1991). Fathers not married to the mother of the children when they were born tend to visit less (Seltzer, 1991). But out of this group, those for whom legal paternity has been established have higher levels of all types of involvement with their children (Argys & Peters, 2001; Seltzer, 2000). Despite its relatively low levels, visitation and other contact is often believed to be beneficial for children. There is, however, no convincing evidence that this is necessarily beneficial. According to Seltzer et al. (1998), studies based on small clinical samples find that contact with fathers improves children's adjustment to divorce, but studies based on national surveys find no direct relationship between visiting and children's well-being. Even so, greater contact with fathers tends to be associated with more child support being paid (Seltzer, 1991; Seltzer et al., 1998), and studies are unequivocal in showing the benefits of child support income for children's achievements.

As discussed previously, a number of studies have found a strong positive link between visitation and child support (e.g., Peters, Argys, Maccoby, & Mnookin, 1993; Seltzer, Schaeffer, & Charng, 1989); but Veum (1993) found changes in visitation to be independent of changes in levels of child support. The relationship may be causal, or both may be the result of other factors, either observable ones, such as demographic characteristics, or unobservable ones, such as fathers' degree of commitment to their children. Seltzer et al. (1989) conclude that although both outcomes have common observable demographic predictors such as positive effects from higher fathers' education or father residing in the same state as the child and negative effects such as length of time since the divorce, visiting and paying child support also tend to be complementary activities. If parents pay child support, they may feel uncomfortable about playing only part of the parental role and so they may visit as well. Seltzer (2000) finds that paying child support has a small direct effect on visiting. Parents who pay child support may also be the ones with more commitment to their children, and thus they visit more as well. This then could explain why child support has a stronger positive effect on children's achievements than other sources of income. Paying child support or paying more support may signal greater father involvement with children along the social dimension as well.

The nature of this relationship is important because it has implications for the effects of increased efforts to strengthen paternity establishment for children born outside of a marriage and child support enforcement designed to compel reluctant fathers to pay support, or a larger amount. It is possible that strictly limiting their discretion about paying may have the unintended effect of decreasing nonresident fathers' contact with their children (Del Boca & Ribero, 2001; Seltzer, 2000). Seltzer et al. (1998) found that stricter child support enforcement increased the amount of influence fathers had over their children. Together with the results of Seltzer (2000), this provides modest support to answer this question in the affirmative. Whether more frequent visits will be beneficial for children may depend in part on whether stronger child support enforcement also increases conflict between the parents, which would be expected to have detrimental effects for the children. This may well happen as a result of forced contact between parents who would prefer not to have any, or when a father expects to have more say because he pays more child support, and the mother resents it. Seltzer et al. (1998) found that greater child support does often increase conflict between parents, and such conflict is likely to diminish children's well-being. Whether and under what circumstances this increase in conflict could partially or wholly offset the beneficial effects of more child support being paid is an important question that has not been fully addressed.

Father's Behavior

It has only been relatively recently that researchers have turned their attention to the economic well-being of nonresident fathers and to how child support orders affect their behavior. As might be expected, this research is limited by the relative paucity of data on noncustodial fathers.

How much child support he owes and how the obligation is enforced may affect one of the primary economic decisions a father makes—how much to work in the labor market. Child support awards have both an income and substitution effect on hours worked. First, the obligation to pay child support acts like a lump-sum tax, and if leisure is a normal good, then according to the income effect, a child support award will increase hours of work (Bitler, 1998). But because child support payments are usually specified by state guidelines as a percentage of income, they also have a substitution effect. If he has to give up, say, 20% of his additional net income,[15] child support obligations act like a tax on his marginal earnings, reduces how much he gains from an additional hour of work, and discourages work effort.[16] If this latter effect were to dominate the former, it could undermine efforts to increase child support through stronger enforcement. Fortunately, recent evidence suggests a small positive effect of child support obligations on noncustodial fathers' hours of work and a somewhat larger effect of each additional dollar of child support paid (Bitler, 1998). Other findings suggest that stronger child support enforcement is not likely to reduce male labor supply and may even increase it among nonmarital fathers (Freeman & Waldfogel, 1998).

Child support obligations will also affect a noncustodial father's likelihood of remarrying and having and supporting additional children. Having children from an earlier relationship can reduce a man's attractiveness as a potential marriage partner because it may reduce the time he has for his new family as well as the amount of money he has for them, especially because state guidelines generally do not reduce child support obligations to accommodate second families. In fact, recent findings show that greater child support enforcement reduces (re)marriage rates, especially among low-income fathers (Bloom, Conrad, & Miller, 1998). Child support enforcement may also affect the likelihood that men will get divorced or father children out of wedlock in the first place, and at least one recent study finds that stronger enforcement of paternity establishment laws leads to moderately lower rates of nonmarital fertility (Case, 1998).

Among low-income fathers whose children are on welfare, there is some qualitative evidence that they have an incentive to collude with the child's mother to encourage her not to cooperate with the child support agency in identifying him, if paternity has not been established, and to pay her child support informally rather than formally if it has been established. This may benefit his children more when little or no child support is passed through to the child, but instead goes to reimburse the state for welfare paid (Edin & Lein, 1997; Johnson et al., 1999; Waller & Plotnick, 2000). Further, it is a legitimate concern that laws encouraging

---

[15]This would be the case in Illinois if he has one child living elsewhere.

[16]We all hear stories about men who give up high-paying jobs to avoid paying large amounts of child support.

mothers to identify their child's father as a condition of eligibility for welfare may promote domestic abuse, if the father is prone to violence against his children and/or their mother (Turetsky & Notar, in press).

SUMMARY AND CONCLUSIONS

In this chapter, we explored nonresident fathers' involvement with their children through payment of child support and visitation from an economic perspective. First, we considered economic theories that explain why fathers often fail to support their children financially. Then we examined the available empirical evidence. Much of what we know is by inference because there are so few surveys of nonresident fathers. To gain a better understanding of this population, it might be beneficial to mount a new survey, but high nonresponse rates on previous surveys of this group tend to militate against that.

In surveying the consequences of fathers' involvement for the well-being of their children and for their own behavior, we found some definitive work, but also many unresolved questions. There is an abundance of evidence supporting the beneficial effects of child support payment on the academic achievement of children, effects that are stronger than from any other source of income. But exactly what the reason for this stronger effect is remains unclear. One hypothesis is that the fathers who pay child support have unobservable characteristics that also promote better outcomes in their children, like greater commitment or dedication. There is some evidence that fathers who pay voluntarily are different, but it is not clear precisely how. We do not know to what extent it is the added visitation that often comes with child support, the specific use of child support, or the strategic behavior of the mother. Although conventional wisdom says that more visiting by fathers benefits children, studies fail to find consistent effects. Under some circumstances increased conflict appears to offset the beneficial effects of the additional income. Evidence is also unclear about whether the additional benefits from receiving child support extend beyond schooling and affect employment and earnings directly. This entire subject warrants further research.

Another subject that requires more research is what the best strategies are for getting low-income fathers, many of them unmarried, to support their children. One major problem is that when fathers of children who are on welfare pay support, this does little to increase their children's income. Also, to date we know little about the effects of the responsible fatherhood programs or what the long-term prognosis is for these men paying child support, especially if their incomes grow over time. We still need to learn how to raise paternity establishment rates and the rate of child support payments after paternity is established.

REFERENCES

Argys, L. M., & Peters, H. E. (2001). Interactions between unmarried fathers and their children: The role of paternity establishment and child support policies. *American Economic Review, Papers and Proceedings, 91*, 125–129.

Argys, L. M., Peters, H. E., Brooks-Gunn, J., & Smith, J. R. (1998). The impact of child support on cognitive outcomes of young children. *Demography, 35*, 159–173.

Aughinbaugh, A. (2001). Signals of child achievement as determinants of child support. *American Economic Review, Papers and Proceedings, 91*, 140–144.

Becker, G. S. (1976). *The economic approach to human behavior.* Chicago: University of Chicago Press.

Becker, G. S. (1981). *A treatise on the family.* Cambridge, MA: Harvard University Press.

Beller, A. H., & Chung, S. S. (1988, April). *The effect of child support payments on the educational attainment of children.* Paper presented at the Population Association of America Annual Meeting, New Orleans, LA.

Beller, A. H., & Graham, J. W. (1986). The determinants of child support income. *Social Science Quarterly, 67*, 353–364.

Beller, A. H., & Graham, J. W. (1993). *Small change: The economics of child support.* New Haven, CT: Yale University Press.

Beller, A. H., & Graham, J. W. (2000). The economics of child support. In S. Grossbard-Shectman (Ed.), *Marriage and the economy* (pp. 143–160). Cambridge, MA: Cambridge University Press.

Bitler, M. P. (1998). *The effect of child support enforcement on non-custodial parents' labor supply.* Unpublished paper. Washington, DC: U.S. Federal Trade Commission.

Bloom, D. E., Conrad, C., & Miller, C. (1998). Child Support and Fathers' Remarriage and Fertility. In I. Garfinkel, S. S. McLanahan, D. R. Meyer, & J. A. Seltzer (Eds.), *Fathers under fire: The revolution in child support enforcement* (pp. 128–156). New York: Russell Sage Foundation.

Case, A. (1998). The effects of stronger child support enforcement on nonmarital fertility. In I. Garfinkel, S. S. McLanahan, D. R. Meyer, & J. A. Seltzer (Eds.), *Fathers under fire: The revolution in child support enforcement* (pp. 191–215). New York: Russell Sage Foundation.

Cherlin, A., Griffith, J., & McCarthy, J. (1983). A note on maritally-disrupted men's reports of child support in the June 1980 Current Population Survey. *Demography, 20*, 385–389.

Del Boca, D., & Flinn, C. J. (1994). Expenditure decisions of divorced mothers and income composition. *Journal of Human Resources, 29*, 742–761.

Del Boca, D., & Flinn, C. J. (1995). Rationalizing child-support decisions. *American Economic Review, 85*, 1241–1262.

Del Boca, D., & Ribero, R. (2001). The effect of child support policies on visitations and transfers. *American Economic Review, Papers and Proceedings, 91*, 130–134.

Edin, K., & Lein, L. (1997). *Making ends meet: How single mothers survive welfare and low-wage work.* New York: Russell Sage Foundation.

Freeman, R. B., & Waldfogel, J. (1998). Does child support enforcement policy affect male labor supply? In I. Garfinkel, S. S. McLanahan, D. R. Meyer, & J. A. Seltzer (Eds.), *Fathers under fire: The revolution in child support enforcement* (pp. 94–127). New York: Russell Sage Foundation.

Furstenberg, F. F., Morgan, S. P., & Allison, P. D. (1987). Paternal participation and children's well-being after marital dissolution. *American Sociological Review, 52*, 695–701.

Garfinkel, I., McLanahan, S. S., & Hanson, T. L. (1998). A patchwork portrait of non-resident fathers. In I. Garfinkel, S. S. McLanahan, D. R. Meyer, & J. A. Seltzer (Eds.), *Fathers under fire: The revolution in child support enforcement* (pp. 31–60). New York: Russell Sage Foundation.

Garfinkel, I., & Oellerich, D. (1989). Noncustodial fathers' ability to pay child support. *Demography, 26*, 219–233.

Graham, J. W., Beller, A. H., & Hernandez, P. (1994). The effects of child support on educational attainment. In I. Garfinkel, S. S. McLanahan, & P. K. Robins (Eds.), *Child support and child well-being* (pp. 317–354). Washington, DC: Urban Institute Press.

Gray, J., Beller, A. H., & Graham, J. W. (1997, March). *Childhood family structure, child support, and socioeconomic outcomes of young men.* Paper presented at the Population Association of America Annual Meeting, Washington, DC.

Hanson, T. L., Garfinkel, I., McLanahan, S. S., & Miller, C. K. (1996). Trends in child support outcomes. *Demography, 33,* 483–496.

Haveman, R., & Wolfe, B. (1995). The determinants of children's attainments: A review of methods and findings. *Journal of Economic Literature, 33,* 1829–1878.

Hernandez, P., Beller, A. H., & Graham, J. W. (1995). Changes in the relationship between child support payments and educational attainment of offspring, 1979–1988. *Demography, 32,* 249–260.

Hernandez, P., Beller, A. H., & Graham, J. W. (1996). The Child Support Enforcement Amendments of 1984 and educational attainment of young adults in the United States. *Labour: Review of Labour Economics and Industrial Relations, 10,* 538–558.

Hoffman, S. D. (1990). *An economic model of child support payments.* Unpublished paper, University of Delaware, Newark.

Institute for Women's Policy Research (IWPR). (1999). *How much can child support provide? Welfare family income and child support* (Research-in-brief No. D435). Washington, DC: Institute for Women's Policy Research.

Johnson, E. S., Levine, A., & Doolittle, F. C. (1999). *Fathers' fair share: Helping poor men manage child support and fatherhood.* New York: Russell Sage Foundation.

Knox, V. W. (1996). The effects of child support payments on developmental outcomes for elementary school-age children. *Journal of Human Resources, 31,* 816–840.

Knox, V. W., & Bane, M. J. (1994). Child support and schooling. In I. Garfinkel, S. S. McLanahan, & P. K. Robins (Eds.), *Child support and child well-being* (pp. 285–316). Washington, DC: Urban Institute Press.

Krein, S. F. (1986). Growing up in a single parent family: The effect on education and earnings of young men. *Family Relations, 35,* 161–168.

Krein, S. F., & Beller, A. H. (1988). Educational attainment of children from single-parent families: Differences by exposure, gender, and race. *Demography, 25,* 221–234.

Leibowitz, A. (1974). Home investments in children. *Journal of Political Economy, 82,* S111–131.

Lerman, R., & Sorensen, E. (2000, May). *Child support: Interactions between private and public transfers.* Paper presented at the NBER Conference on Means-Tested Programs in the United States, Cambridge, MA.

McLanahan, S., & Sandefur, G. (1994). *Growing up with a single parent: What hurts, what helps.* Cambridge, MA: Harvard University Press.

Meyer, D. R. (1998). The effect of child support on the economic status of non-resident fathers. In I. Garfinkel, S. S. McLanahan, D. R. Meyer, & J. A. Seltzer (Eds.), *Fathers under fire: The revolution in child support enforcement* (pp. 67–93). New York: Russell Sage Foundation.

Miller, C., Garfinkel, I., & McLanahan, S. (1997). Child support in the United States: Can fathers afford to pay more? *Review of Income and Wealth, 43,* 261–281.

Mincy, R. B., & Sorensen, E. J. (1998). Deadbeats and turnips in child support reform. *Journal of Policy Analysis and Management, 17,* 44–51.

Peters, H. E., Argys, L. M., Maccoby, E. E., & Mnookin, R. H. (1993). Enforcing divorce settlements: Evidence from child support compliance and award modifications. *Demography, 30,* 719–735.

Peters, H. E., & Mullis, N. C. (1997). The role of family income and sources of income in adolescent achievement. In G. Duncan & J. Brooks-Gunn (Eds.), *Consequences of growing up poor* (pp. 340–381). New York: Russell Sage Foundation.

Seltzer, J. A. (1991). Relationships between fathers and children who live apart. *Journal of Marriage and the Family, 53,* 79–101.

Seltzer, J. A. (2000). Child support and child access: Experiences of divorced and nonmarital families. In J. T. Oldham & M. S. Melli (Eds.), *Child support: The next frontier* (pp. 69–87). Ann Arbor: University of Michigan Press.

Seltzer, J. A., McLanahan, S. S., & Hanson, T. L. (1998). Will child support enforcement increase father–child contact and parental conflict after separation? In I. Garfinkel, S. S. McLanahan, D. R. Meyer, & J. A. Seltzer (Eds.), *Fathers under fire: The revolution in child support enforcement* (pp. 157–190). New York: Russell Sage Foundation.

Seltzer, J. A., Schaeffer, N. C., & Charng, H.-W. (1989). Family ties after divorce: The relationship between visiting and paying child support. *Journal of Marriage and the Family, 51,* 1013–1031.

Sonenstein, F., & Calhoun, C. (1990). Determinants of child support: A pilot survey of absent parents. *Contemporary Policy Issues, 8*(1), 75–94.

Sorensen, E. (1997). A national profile of non-resident fathers and their ability to pay child support. *Journal of Marriage and the Family, 59,* 785–797.

Sorensen, E., & Halpern, A. (1999). *Child support enforcement is working better than we think* (New federalism: Issues and options for states, Series A, No. A-31). Washington, DC: Urban Institute.

Teachman, J. D. (1990). Socioeconomic resources of parents and award of child support in the United States: Some exploratory models. *Journal of Marriage and the Family, 52,* 689–699.

Teachman, J. D. (1991). Who pays? Receipt of child support in the United States. *Journal of Marriage and the Family, 53,* 759–772.

Turetsky, V., & Notar, S. (in press). Models for safe child support enforcement. *American University Journal of Gender, Social Policy and Law.*

U.S. Census Bureau. (1996a). *Money income in the United States: 1995* (Current population reports, Series P-60, No. 193). Washington, DC: U.S. Government Printing Office.

U.S. Census Bureau. (1996b). *Poverty in the United States: 1995* (Current population reports, Series P-60, No. 194). Washington, DC: U.S. Government Printing Office.

U.S. Census Bureau. (1999). *Child support for custodial mothers and fathers: 1995* (Current population reports, Series P-60, No. 196). Washington, DC: U.S. Government Printing Office.

Veum, J. R. (1993). The relationship between child support and visitation: Evidence from longitudinal data. *Social Science Research, 22,* 229–244.

Waller, M., & Plotnick, R. (2000). A failed relationship? Low-income families and the child support enforcement system. *Focus, 21,* 12–17.

Weiss, Y., & Willis, R. J. (1985). Children as collective goods and divorce settlements. *Journal of Labor Economics, 3,* 268–292.

Weiss, Y., & Willis, R. J. (1993). Transfers among divorced couples: Evidence and interpretation. *Journal of Labor Economics, 11,* 629–679.

Willis, R. J. (1999). A theory of out-of-wedlock childbearing. *Journal of Political Economy, 107,* S33–S64.

VI

Father Involvement: Social Policy and Intervention

Jeanne Brooks-Gunn
Columbia University

Sara S. McLanahan
Princeton University

The preceding sections of this book, for the most part, focus on the ways in which different social science disciplines conceptualize and study fathers. In contrast, this section takes a multidisciplinary look at how research informs practice and policy, or at least the implications of the various research perspectives for practice and policy. Issues related to risk, prevention, and policy are considered.

RISK

Our focus is on fathers at risk, in some way, for becoming disengaged from the mothers of their children as well as their offspring themselves. Two overlapping categories of fathers are of concern here—those who are poor or near poor and those who are not married. Fathers in the bottom two quintiles of the income distribution are most likely struggle to make ends meet and to provide for their children. These fathers, compared to more economically secure men, have lower levels of education, less-stable work experiences, and more mental health and substance use problems. And, they are less likely to be married to the mother of their children and to pay child support (given, in part, their lower and less-stable earnings). However, it is important to note that not all of these near-poor fathers are unmarried; many are married (but, we would argue, are still at risk for making ends meet and marital stability). Unwed fathers comprise the other category (which includes many poor and near-poor fathers). McLanahan, Mincy, and their colleagues call these fathers members of "fragile families," fragile because the relationships between mothers and fathers are in many cases unstable.

The four chapters in this section consider at-risk fathers in terms of the capacities and conditions that contribute to the sometimes tenuous nature of their relationships with mothers and children. Carlson and McLanahan focus on out-of-wedlock childbearing. They show that the proportion of children born outside marriage increased dramatically during the last half of the 20th century, growing from only 4% of children in 1940 to about one third of all children in 2000. Driven primarily by declines in marriage and increases in nonmarital birthrates, these trends have given rise to a new family form—the fragile family, defined as unmarried parents raising their children together (either through cohabitation, visitation, or infrequent contact). Using data from a new survey of unwed parents starting at the birth of their child (the Fragile Families and Child Wellbeing Study), they find that most unmarried parents have "high hopes" about their future at the time their child is born. Over 80% are romantically involved, nearly half are living together, and over two thirds expect to marry each other. Likewise, the vast majority of unmarried fathers want to be recognized as the child's father and expect to help raise the child in the future.

Despite their high hopes, unwed parents face many barriers to establishing a stable family life. As shown in this chapter as well as in chapter 19, by Cabrera, Brooks-Gunn, Moore, West, and Boller (which reviews three new national initiatives focusing on becoming a father and being a father in the early years of childhood), about one third of unwed couples have not completed high school and less than 5% have completed college. Unemployment rates are high among the fathers (about one fourth are not working when the baby is born). And both unwed mothers and fathers have relatively low wage rates, compared to married parents (making them poor or near poor). Furthermore, more unmarried than married fathers, especially those who are in a conflictual romantic relationship with the mother or who are no longer romantically involved, are likely to engage in substance use, domestic violence, or smoking or to be depressed or in poor health. Thus, despite high hopes, the capacities of many fragile families are low.

The chapter by Cabrera and colleagues further supports these findings, by reporting not only on the Fragile Families Study, but on the Early Head Start Fatherhood Initiative and on the just-begun Early Childhood Longitudinal Study—Birth Cohort. All three of these initiatives began after the federal Fatherhood Initiative was launched. Each focuses on a particular group of fathers: (the Fragile Families and Child Wellbeing Study, with almost 4,900 families, samples unwed couples with a comparison sample of married couples; the Early Head Start National Evaluation has about 2,500 Head Start eligible families (based on family income), one half of whom entered the Early Head Start program in 17 sites and one half of whom did not, via randomization; the Early Childhood Longitudinal Study—Birth Cohort will eventually sample almost 20,000 families in a representative sample, including both poor and near poor as well as wed and unwed couples). Together, these studies will provide information about at-risk fathers, both in terms of antecedents of their relationship status and the consequences for couple stability and child involvement. Current studies have so few unwed and/or poor fathers or have such poor response rates for these men that no detailed or vaguely representative picture of at-risk fathers exists today.

Chapter 20, by Nelson, Edin, and colleagues provides some nuance to these three new large national studies. Based on extensive, ethnographic interviews with fathers in three cities, the authors describe how poor and near-poor fathers who are not married manage to support themselves and provide, in a myriad of ways, for the well-being of their children. The portraits make clear that these fathers are deeply committed to their children, even though their earning capacity, as well as their emotional and physical health, constrain their choices with regard to support and involvement. The role of the mothers in managing the fathers' relationships with the children is also illustrated. One of the themes that reoccurs in these interviews is the importance that fathers attach to "being there" for their children (even when they are not living with the children). The emotional ties evoked by the term *being there* are also voiced in the Fragile Family Study and Early Head Start interviews.

PREVENTION

Mincy and Pouncy (chap. 21) provide a thorough and fascinating account of the rise of fatherhood programs in the last decade. They describe fatherhood organizations, some of which focus on preventing pregnancies, enforcing child support obligations, encouraging nurturance and care, and promoting marriage. They also examine the impact of these diverse organizations on men's behavior. The Early Head Start Study, described by Cabrera and colleagues, also looks at fatherhood programs, in this case those that are part of Early Head Start. Many Head Start programs are now offering services to fathers as their continuing emphasis on the family (rather than just the child or the child and the mother). Interviews with fathers who have participated in Early Head Start provide anecdotal evidence of impact, although relatively few fathers are, at present, participating in these programs. The question of what aspects of programs are both appealing and useful to fathers is raised in all four chapters.

According to Mincy and Pouncy, the first fatherhood demonstration project— Teen Fathers Collaboration—operated between 1983 and 1985. Although the original goal of the program was to prevent pregnancy, it pioneered activities such as job training and peer counseling and quickly expanded to include many of the ingredients found in more recent fatherhood initiatives (parenting classes, tutoring and educational assistance, individual and group counseling). However, at the present, the few evaluations that have been conducted report no evidence of the efficacy of such programs.

The chapters in this section provide clues as to why the programs to date have not been successful. Carlson and McLanahan argue that programs often start too late and focus on the wrong fathers. The largest federal demonstration—Parents' Fair Share—targeted fathers who had failed to pay child support and who had lost contact with their child. Not surprisingly, many of these men were not highly motivated to assume the role of "responsible father." The authors suggest that fatherhood programs are likely to be most successful if they target new unwed parents who are motivated to keep their fragile families together and if they work with couples as opposed to fathers alone.

POLICY

Mincy and Pouncy examine a series of policy initiatives and programs. One thrust has involved child support enforcement (also discussed in Section V). Programs have considered barriers to fathers' involvement with their children. These programs include "fathers' rights" groups, whose primary objectives are to work with divorced and separated fathers on custody and child visitation issues (these programs cut across the income spectrum). Also, some programs help low-income parents reconnect with their children and meet their financial obligations.

Other programs are focusing more on the culture of government, business, and schools, encouraging them to emphasize the importance of fathers in their children's lives. Recently, several fatherhood initiatives have joined forces with other organizations to promote marriage. These groups argue that the culture of government and business must be changed to become more "father friendly" (just as other groups have argued for more "family friendly" policies).

What policies have been most successful? Government policies have helped alter barriers to involved fatherhood, especially with regard to paternity establishment and child support. However, it is unclear that government or business policies are more "father friendly." Other government policies may have adverse effects. For example, the Earned Income Tax Credit (EITC) requires married couples to count the incomes of both mothers and fathers in order to determine the size of the earned tax credit. This policy encourages near-poor couples who are both working not to get married, as they would receive less EITC.

The chapter by Nelson and colleagues (chap. 20) also suggests that highly punitive policies may not enhance father involvement. In Charlestown, one of the cities in their ethnographic study, fathers who do not pay child support go to prison, even if they are unable to find jobs in order to comply with the law. Contact with children and mothers is severed during these spells of incarceration. Similarly, studies using the Fragile Families data, as reported in two chapters here, suggest that in a small proportion of cases, unwed mothers do not want the fathers involved because of fears of violence or drug dealing. Policies that do not take into account such factors may result in domestic violence and conflict.

These examples make clear that research needs to inform practice and policy, just as practice and policy need to guide the types of research that are conducted on fragile families.

18

Fragile Families, Father Involvement, and Public Policy

Marcia J. Carlson
Columbia University

Sara S. McLanahan
Princeton University

Nonmarital childbearing has increased dramatically during the past 40 years, with one third of births now occurring outside of marriage. Although this trend has received considerable attention from both researchers and policymakers as it relates to women and children, the role of unmarried fathers has been largely overlooked beyond their provision (or lack of provision) of financial support. Only recently—as new data have become available—have researchers begun to explore the nature of relationships between unmarried parents and the role of unmarried fathers in the lives of their children. This new research has yielded some surprising findings that deconstruct myths about "absent fathers" and point to ways that policymakers might strengthen fathers' involvement with their children. In this chapter, we describe trends in nonmarital childbearing since the mid-1900s. We define the concept of *fragile families* and describe relationships in these families. Then, we explain how father involvement is important for children. Finally, we discuss how public policies—welfare, child support, and fatherhood programs—affect father involvement in fragile families.

TRENDS IN NONMARITAL CHILDBEARING

The latter half of the 20th century witnessed a sharp rise in nonmarital child-bearing in the United States. In 1940, only 4% of all births occurred outside of marriage, whereas by 1999, fully one third were to unmarried parents (Ventura & Bachrach, 2000). The proportion of all births that occur outside marriage (sometimes called the nonmarital birth ratio) is affected by three proximate factors: the proportion of women in the population that are unmarried, birthrates among unmarried women, and birthrates among married women. We briefly describe trends in each of these areas, noting important group differences where they exist.

Because only unmarried women can give birth outside marriage, delays in marriage increase the risk of a nonmarital birth. Between 1964 and 1990, the median age at marriage rose from 21.4 in 1964 to 26.7 for women and from 23.6 and 28.7 for men (Clarke, 1995). The proportion of unmarried women ages 30 to 34 rose from 13.8% in 1950 to 31.3% in 1998 (Ventura & Bachrach, 2000).

Even with no other secular demographic changes, we would have expected nonmarital births to rise because of the greater pool of unmarried women in the population.[1] Yet, other changes did occur, which drove the nonmarital birth ratio even higher. Along with delays in marriage, the rate at which unmarried women were giving birth increased after midcentury. Recent estimates show that live births per 1,000 unmarried women ages 15 to 44 rose from 7.1 in 1940 to 43.9 in 1999, a more than sixfold increase (Ventura & Bachrach, 2000). The rate of increase, which was generally steady from 1940 to 1990, has leveled off since that time.

Finally, as fertility among unmarried women was rising, fertility among married women was declining, further exaggerating the growth in the proportion of all births that occur outside of marriage. Birthrates among married women ages 15 to 44 dropped sharply between 1960 and 1976 (from 156.6 to 91.6 live births per 1,000 married women). Since the mid 1970s, they have declined only slightly, to 87.3 births per 1,000 in 1999 (Ventura & Bachrach, 2000).

Whereas nonmarital childbearing has risen throughout the population, the magnitude of the rise and the current prevalence varies significantly by socio-demographic status. Data that differentiate Hispanics from non-Hispanic Whites are only available for the past two decades, but these data highlight important differences by race and ethnicity. In 1980, 9% of births among non-Hispanic White women occurred outside marriage, compared to 56% among Black

---

[1]The rising divorce rate has also increase the proportion of women at risk of a nonmarital birth. Indeed, about one third of births outside marriage in 1980–85 occurred to formerly married women (Bumpass & McLanahan, 1989).

women and 24% among Hispanic women. By 1999, the comparable figures were 22% among non-Hispanic Whites, 69% among Blacks and 42% among Hispanics (Ventura & Bachrach, 2000). Thus, Black women had a higher overall rate of nonmarital childbearing at midcentury, but the rate of increase between 1980 and 1999 was notably greater for Whites (144%) and Hispanics (75%) than for Blacks (23%).

Teen childbearing has also been a cause for concern among policymakers because of the greater economic disadvantage among and welfare use by teenage mothers. Nonmarital birth rates for teenagers (ages 15 to 19) rose steadily between 1940 and 1994 but have declined since that time; unmarried birthrates have fallen among teens of all races since 1994, but they have dropped the most for Black teenagers (Ventura & Bachrach, 2000). Overall, teen births as a proportion of all unmarried births have declined from 50% in 1970 to 29% in 1999, primarily due to rising birthrates among women ages 20 and older and increasing numbers of these women (Ventura & Bachrach, 2000). Still, births to teens are much more likely to occur outside of marriage (79%) than births to older women; only 48% of births to women in their early 20s occur outside marriage (Ventura & Bachrach, 2000). Moreover, births to unmarried teens account for about half of all *first* nonmarital births (Moore, 1995). Thus, teen childbearing remains an important aspect of nonmarital childbearing and family formation among unmarried parents.[2]

FRAGILE FAMILIES

"Traditional" family formation in the United States has typically followed a linear course—first dating, then marriage, and then childbearing, but the rise in nonmarital childbearing (along with concomitant changes in union formation) has yielded a range of complex and diverse family arrangements. Today, it is not uncommon for intercourse, conception, and/or cohabitation to occur outside marriage. The vast majority of unmarried women are sexually active: 77% of women ages 20 to 29 in 1995 reported engaging in sex during the previous year (Ventura & Bachrach, 2000). Also, most pregnancies among unmarried women are unintended, and most are not voluntarily terminated: 78% of pregnancies among never-

---

[2]It is important to note that teen birth data reflect mothers' fertility and do not provide information about fathers' fertility patterns. Although accurate estimates of male fertility are difficult to obtain, we do know that approximately 85% of children born to teen mothers are fathered by men in their teens or early 20s (contrary to earlier reports of large age differences between teen mothers and their partners) (Elo, Berkowitz, & Furstenberg, 1999). These young fathers (and mothers) may face additional challenges compared to their older counterparts that require particular types of policy or program interventions.

married women in 1994 were unintended (Henshaw, 1998), and 4 of every 10 pregnancies among unmarried women in 1995 ended in abortion (Ventura & Bachrach, 2000). Further, whereas in the 1950s and 1960s, 52 to 60% of first births conceived before marriage were "legitimized" by marriage prior to the birth, this was the case for only 23% of premaritally conceived first births in the period from 1990 to 1994 (Bachu, 1999). These facts about sexual activity and pregnancy resolution portend that the nonmarital birthrate is not likely to attenuate at any time in the near future.

Beyond major changes in the norms and practices related to sexuality and fertility, fundamental shifts have also been noted in union formation and marital behavior over the past 40 years. Marriage has become less central to the life course both because individuals are marrying later (or choosing not to marry at all) and divorcing more often. Unmarried cohabitation has arisen as a precursor to—or possible substitute for—legal marriage such that today over 50% of marriages are preceded by cohabitation, and nearly half of all women have cohabited by their late 30s (Bumpass & Lu, 2000; Smock, 2000). Further, many cohabiting households include children, and nearly 40% of nonmarital births occur to cohabiting couples. Indeed, much of the recent increase in nonmarital childbearing can be attributed to births to cohabiting couples (Bumpass & Lu, 2000; Smock, 2000).

The changes in family patterns described imply that many "single" mothers are not rearing their children alone and suggest the emergence of a new family type—the *fragile family,* composed of unmarried parents who are raising their child together. Some of these parents are cohabiting, whereas others are living apart but maintaining frequent contact (Mincy & Pouncy, 1997; Sorenson, Mincy, & Halpern, 2000). We denote these relationships as *families* to highlight the fact that the parents are raising their child(ren) together, and we call them *fragile* because of their high risk of poverty and union instability.[3]

Despite the recent rise in—and high prevalence of—nonmarital childbearing, surprisingly little is known about fragile families, especially about the fathers in these families. Typically, researchers and policymakers have focused solely on single mothers and their children, in part because of a concern over children's welfare and in part because data on fathers were not readily available. Furthermore, the information that exists about nonresident fathers typically comes either from studies that combine unwed fathers with divorced or separated fathers or from research based on small and/or unrepresentative samples (Garfinkel et al., 1998).

---

[3]Although we do not apply a strict economic criterion to the definition of *fragile families,* the vast majority of unmarried parents and their children are not economically advantaged (only 3% report household income of $75,000 or above), so the term broadly applies to this demographic group.

This situation is about to change with the launching of a new survey of *Fragile Families and Child Wellbeing*.[4] This new study, which is being conducted by a team of researchers at Princeton University and Columbia University, is following a birth cohort of approximately 3,700 nonmarital births in 20 large cities throughout the United States.[5] The new study is representative of nonmarital births in cities with populations of 200,000 and over and will provide a wealth of information on unwed mothers and fathers and the relationships between them.[6] In the Fragile Families Study, mothers are interviewed in person at the hospital within 48 hours of having given birth, and fathers are interviewed in person either in the hospital or shortly thereafter. Follow-up interviews are planned for when the children are 12, 30, and 48 months old. The survey focuses on four major questions:

- What are the characteristics and capabilities of unmarried parents, especially fathers?
- What is the nature of the relationships between unmarried parents, and what factors push them together or pull them apart?
- What are the consequences for children over time?
- How do public policies and labor market conditions affect parents' relationships and children's well-being?

Although it is too soon to know very much about the consequences for children born into fragile families or how policies affect parents' relationships over time, data from the baseline interviews highlight several key findings about the capabilities and relationships of unmarried parents at the time of their child's

---

[4]The *Fragile Families and Child Wellbeing Study* is funded by the National Institute of Child Health and Human Development (NICHD), the California HealthCare Foundation, the Commonwealth Fund, the Christian A. Johnson Endeavor Foundation, the Ford Foundation, the Foundation for Child Development, the Fund for New Jersey, the William T. Grant Foundation, the Healthcare Foundation of New Jersey, the William and Flora Hewlett Foundation, the Hogg Foundation for Mental Health, the Robert Wood Johnson Foundation, the Kronkosky Charitable Foundation, the Leon Lowenstein Foundation, the John D. and Catherine T. MacArthur Foundation, the A.L. Mailman Family Foundation, the Charles Stewart Mott Foundation, the National Science Foundation, the David and Lucile Packard Foundation, the Public Policy Institute of California, the St. David's Foundation, the St. Vincent Hospital and Health Services, and the U.S. Department of Health and Human Services (ACF and ASPE).

[5]The 20 cities are Oakland, CA; San Jose, CA; Jacksonville, FL; Chicago, IL; Indianapolis, IN; Boston, MA; Baltimore, MD; Detroit, MI; Newark, NJ; New York City, NY; Toledo, OH; Philadelphia, PA; Pittsburgh, PA; Nashville, TN; Austin, TX; Corpus Christi, TX; San Antonio, TX; Norfolk, VA; Richmond, VA; and Milwaukee, WI. For detailed information on the design of the Fragile Families Study, see Reichman et al., 2000.

[6]A comparison group of approximately 1,200 married parents from all 20 cities is also being followed.

birth. Some of this information is reported in Figure 18.1 and in Tables 18.1 through 18.3.[7]

Figure 18.1 depicts relationships between unmarried parents by (mother's) race/ethnicity around the time that their child is born. Most unmarried fathers are closely connected to the mother of their child at the time of birth. Overall, 83% of mothers report being romantically involved with the baby's father; 51% of couples are cohabiting, and another 32% are romantically involved but living separately (which we refer to as a "visiting" relationship).[8] About 8% of mothers report that they are "just friends" with the fathers, and only 9% report that have very little contact with the father.[9]

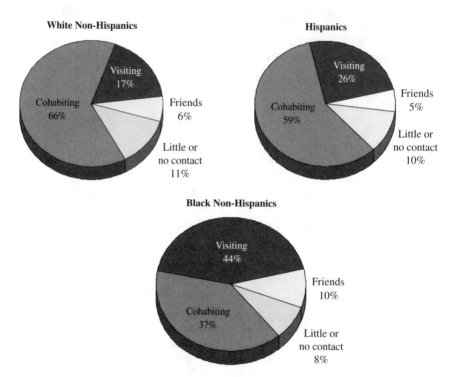

FIG. 18.1.   Relationship Status by Race/Ethnicity

[7]All frequencies presented are weighted by national sampling weights to adjust for selection probabilities and demographic characteristics. Therefore, the data are representative of all nonmarital births in the 77 U.S. cities with populations over 200,000.

[8]We use mothers' reports about parents' relationship and father involvement, as their reports provide information about *all* unmarried fathers; only 76% of fathers were interviewed.

[9]The proportions in various relationship types are remarkably similar across age groups, except that teenage mothers (less than age 20) are less likely to be cohabiting (43%) than older mothers (about 55% of whom are cohabiting).

The proportions of couples in any romantic relationship are similar across different racial and ethnic groups, but there is variation in the type of relationship. Non-Hispanic White and Hispanic parents are more likely to be coresiding (66 and 59%, respectively) than non-Hispanic Black parents (37%), whereas Black parents are more likely to be in a "visiting" relationship (44%) than either Whites (17%) or Hispanics (26%).

Most unmarried parents have positive expectations about marriage to the baby's father in the future. As shown in Table 18.1, about 58% of unmarried mothers think their chances of marriage to the father are "pretty good" or "almost certain," whereas 74% of unmarried fathers take this position with respect to the mothers. We would expect fathers in the Fragile Families sample to be somewhat more positive than mothers, because the 76% of fathers who participated in the study represent a select group that is likely more committed to their children than the average unwed father.

Assessments of marriage probabilities are higher among parents that are cohabiting, as compared to parents that are romantically involved but living apart ("visiting") and couples that are not romantically involved. The fact that 26% of fathers who are no longer romantically involved with their child's mother say that their chances of marriage are "pretty good" or "almost certain" (compared to only 3% of all mothers in this relationship type) underscores the fact that the fathers interviewed in the Fragile Families Study are more attached to their families (or desire attachment) than the fathers not interviewed.

Although somewhat less positive about marriage than married couples, most unmarried couples agree with the statement, "It is better for children if their parents are married." Positive views of marriage are slightly more common among cohabiting couples than among noncohabiting couples, but the difference is small. Even the majority of couples that are no longer romantically involved report that they believe children would be better off if their parents were married.

Table 18.1 also reports information on unmarried parents' trust of the opposite sex. Overall, the numbers suggest that distrust is more than twice as high among unmarried parents, as compared with married parents. Yet, a relatively small fraction of parents in both groups are likely to agree with the statement, "Women (men) cannot be trusted to be faithful." For parents in all relationship types, mothers are less trusting than fathers in the area of sexual fidelity.

Finally, Table 18.1 reports information on several aspects of the quality of parents' relationships in fragile families and on the incidence of physical violence. Most parents in fragile families report very positive relationships with their partners shortly after their child's birth. Cohabiting parents are very similar to married parents in terms of emotional support (represented by mothers' reports about fathers' affection and encouragement) and fathers' negative behaviors such as violence or insults/criticism. Couples that are not romantically involved at the time of the child's birth (about 17% of the sample) report

TABLE 18.1
Parents' Attitudes Toward Marriage and Relationship Quality[1]

	Married	Unmarried		
		Total	Cohabiting	Visiting	Other
Attitudes Toward Marriage					
Chances of marriage					
Mother—pretty good or almost certain	NA	57.9	80.5	49.6	2.5
Father—pretty good or almost certain	NA	73.9	85.7	63.5	26.2
Marriage attitudes—marriage is better for children					
Mother agrees or strongly agrees	84.5	64.1	67.5	60.9	59.6
Father agrees or strongly agrees	90.8	77.3	77.9	76.9	74.7
Gender attitudes					
Men cannot be trusted to be faithful	10.0	22.5	16.7	25.7	34.1
Women cannot be trusted to be faithful	3.9	13.0	10.6	16.6	17.4
Relationship Quality					
Potentially exploitative relationships (mothers' reports)					
Father is sometimes/often violent	2.7	4.0	2.2	3.1	11.7
Father often insults or criticizes	3.1	3.7	1.9	2.9	10.9
Father's supportiveness of mother (mothers' reports)					
Father often expresses affection or love	84.4	74.5	84.6	75.8	39.7
Father often encourages mother	77.0	69.8	81.0	70.5	32.5
Unweighted number of cases (n)	1,186	3,704	1,782	1,272	650

[1]All figures are weighted by national sampling weights.

much higher levels of abuse and notably lower levels of supportiveness in the relationship.

Most unwed fathers are highly involved with their families during the pregnancy and at the time of the child's birth. Table 18.2 reports information on fathers' recent contributions and future intentions toward the child. According to mothers' reports, over 80% of unwed fathers contributed financial support during the pregnancy, and three fourths visited the mother and baby in the hospital. Eighty percent of mothers say the baby will take the father's last name, and 84% say that the father will sign the birth certificate. Finally, over 90% of the mothers *want* the father to help raise the child.

Although new unwed parents clearly have high hopes for their relationship at the time of the child's birth, the Fragile Families data clearly show that the capabilities of these new parents are quite low. According to Table 18.3, 38% of unmarried mothers have less than a high school degree, and 34% of unmarried fathers have not finished high school. Less than 30% of new unwed parents have any college education, and only 3 to 5% obtained a bachelor's degree. The contrast with married parents is striking: married mothers and fathers are much less likely to have dropped out of high school and much more likely to have attended college; more than a third of married mothers—and 33% of fathers—have a bachelor's degree.

TABLE 18.2
Unmarried Father's Relationship With Child (Mothers' Reports)[1]

	Total	Cohabiting	Visiting	Other
Father contributed money during pregnancy	82.9	97.0	85.6	32.5
Father visited mother and baby in hospital	78.1	96.2	72.9	32.1
Baby will have father's last name	79.5	93.6	76.7	41.0
Father's name will be on birth certificate	83.9	95.5	82.8	50.3
Father plans to help raise child	91.5	99.7	95.6	56.4
Mother wants father involved	92.8	99.6	97.6	61.7
Unweighted number of cases (n)	3,704	1,782	1,272	650

[1]All figures are weighted by national sampling weights.

The picture for employment is less bleak, although again unmarried parents are not as well off as married parents. Whereas 92% of married fathers were working when their child was born, 80% of unmarried fathers were employed. Thirty-eight percent of all unmarried mothers had received welfare assistance during the past year, with a slightly lower proportion receiving welfare among mothers that were cohabiting compared to those that were visiting, or no longer romantically involved with the father. Because 46% of unmarried mothers are having their first child (and thus are less likely to be on welfare at the time of the birth), the proportion of mothers who received welfare in the year prior to the birth may underestimate the true level of need among this population. A more accurate estimate of the proportion of mothers who are likely to be eligible for welfare is 70%, which is the proportion of nonmarital births that were covered by Medicaid (figure not shown in table).

Table 18.3 also reports predicted hourly wage rates and predicted annual earnings for new parents in the Fragile Families Study. Married mothers are predicted to earn $14.74/hour and married fathers $17.44/hour. By contrast, unmarried mothers—regardless of relationship type—earn between $8.00 and $9.00/hour and unmarried fathers around $11.00/hour. If we multiply the fathers' wage rates by 2,000 hours (full-time work) and mothers' wage rates by 1,000 hours (half-time work), we can obtain an estimate of the annual earnings of these couples. These figures highlight the fact that unmarried couples are very different from married couples in terms of their human capital and earnings capacity, a difference that would not change if these couples were to legally marry. If fathers worked full-time and mothers worked half-time, the average unmarried couple would have income around $30,000, which is about three fifths of that of the average married couple ($50,000). Many unmarried couples face precarious economic circumstances and are likely to be affected by welfare and child support policies over time.

In sum, although the birth of a child may represent a "magic moment" of high attachment and expectations among unmarried parents, these couples face an uncertain future. Specifically for children, studies show that children born outside

TABLE 18.3
Unmarried Parents' Capabilities[1]

	Married	Unmarried			
		Total	Cohabiting	Visiting	Other
Mother's education					
Less than high school	15.4	38.3	36.2	37.3	46.9
High school or the equivalent	17.5	32.3	32.9	33.2	28.5
Some college	28.2	26.0	27.6	25.9	21.6
Bachelor's degree or higher	39.0	3.4	3.4	3.6	3.0
Father's education					
Less than high school	13.0	34.2	33.5	34.2	37.5
High school or the equivalent	22.3	39.0	39.4	39.8	35.2
Some college	32.1	22.2	22.8	22.8	18.5
Bachelor's degree or higher	32.7	4.6	4.4	3.3	8.9
Parents' Employment					
Father worked in last week[2]	92.0	79.5	85.9	72.1	67.6
Father worked in last year[2]	99.1	96.8	98.0	95.2	95.0
Mother worked in last year	73.4	74.2	75.3	71.0	76.9
Mother received welfare	10.2	38.0	34.4	42.2	40.9
Earnings					
Mother's predicted hourly wage	$14.74	$8.74	$8.92	$8.69	$8.30
Father's predicted hourly wage	$17.44	$10.80	$10.83	$10.49	$11.67
Predicted couple earnings[3]	$50,007	$30,316	$30,544	$29,502	$31,464
Unweighted number of cases (n)	1,886	3,704	1,782	1,272	650

[1]All figures are weighted by national sampling weights.

[2]Based on mothers' reports. While overall, information is missing for about 10% of fathers, a much higher fraction of cases are missing (about 40%) for fathers in the "Other" relationship category.

[3]Assuming mothers work half-time (1,000 hours/year) and fathers work full-time (2,000 hours/year).

of marriage are less likely to have contact with their fathers than their counterparts born within marriage; also, involvement by nonresident fathers (both divorced and never-married) typically diminishes over time (Lerman & Sorenson, 2000; Seltzer, 1991). Both of these findings suggest that there is cause for concern about the prospect that fathers in fragile families will remain highly involved in their children's lives in the long term.

THE IMPORTANCE OF FATHERS' INVOLVEMENT

A multitude of sociological studies have shown that children who live apart from their biological fathers do not fare as well on a range of outcomes as children who grow up with both biological parents (McLanahan & Sandefur, 1994). Children in single-parent families are often deprived of two types of resources from their fathers—economic (money) and relational (time) (McLanahan, 2000). The economic consequences can be most easily quantified: single-parent families with children have a significantly higher poverty rate (39% in 1998) than two-parent families with children (8% in 1998) (Committee on Ways and Means [CWM], 2000), and living in extreme poverty has adverse effects on child development and well-being (Duncan & Brooks-Gunn, 1997). Yet, children in single-parent families are also disadvantaged because they lack the parental attention and emotional support that a father can provide. Nonresident fathers see their children less often than resident fathers, and lack of interaction decreases the likelihood that a father and child will develop a close relationship (Seltzer, 1991; Shapiro & Lambert, 1999). Most of this research is based on divorced fathers, but we can assume that for unwed fathers the pattern would be the same if/when the parents' relationship ends.

The academic literature has consistently documented that fathers' involvement—at least economic involvement—can obviate some of the disadvantage of living in a single-parent family and positively affect child well-being. The provision of child support is associated with improved child outcomes, particularly in the domains of cognitive/academic and behavioral outcomes (Graham, Beller & Hernandez, 1994; Greene & Moore, 1996; King, 1994b; Knox & Bane, 1994; McLanahan & Sandefur, 1994). Child support is particularly beneficial for children when the relationship between mothers and fathers is amicable (Argys & Peters, 1996). Also, paying child support is correlated with direct involvement, so requiring fathers to pay child support may increase their interaction with their children as well (Seltzer, 1991, 2000).[10]

Although the benefits of fathers' economic contributions are clearly demonstrated by research, the benefits of fathers' relational involvement with their children are less well documented. In fact, studies of the frequency of contact between nonresidential fathers and their children do *not* demonstrate that greater father–child interaction has beneficial effects for children and adolescents (Crockett, Eggebeen, & Hawkins, 1993; Furstenberg, Morgan, & Allison, 1987; Hawkins & Eggebeen, 1991; Kandel, 1990; King, 1994a, 1994b; Simons, Whitbeck, Beaman, & Conger, 1994). This lack of effects of father–child contact exists regardless of the child's race and gender, mother's education, or marital status at birth (King, 1994b). It is important to note, however, that most of these studies are based on samples of divorced fathers rather than on samples of fragile families.

---

[10]Although some of the association between current child support and contact is explained by the frequency of fathers' visitation in an earlier time period and other family characteristics, Seltzer (2000) finds "modest support for claims that stricter child support enforcement will increase fathers' contact with children."

Several researchers have suggested that the *quality* of the father–child relationship may be more important than the quantity (Amato, 1998; Crockett et al., 1993; King, 1994b; Simons et al., 1994), and recent sociological research supports this argument (Amato & Rivera, 1999; Harris, Furstenberg, & Marmer, 1998; Harris & Marmer, 1996; Parke, in press; Zimmerman, Salem, & Maton, 1995). These findings are consistent with psychological research that has documented clear, beneficial effects of fathering for children (e.g., Lamb, 1997), and we would expect that future research with improved measures of the quality of father involvement will corroborate these results.[11] Again, these findings suggest that father involvement in fragile families, particularly when the relationship with the child's mother remains positive, is likely to have beneficial effects for children.

Many sociologists and psychologists have examined the nature of fathers' involvement with their children and what may be important antecedents of greater involvement. Although several well-known typologies of the predictors of father involvement have been developed (see Belsky, 1984, 1990; Lamb, Pleck, Charnov, & Levine, 1987; Pleck, Lamb, & Levine, 1986), we focus here on two key factors that public policy may be able to influence—fathers' capacity as economic providers, and the quality of the relationship between the father and mother.

The Father as Economic Provider

Cultural understandings of fathering have broadened beyond the provision of economic resources in recent decades, but breadwinning remains a central element of the father role in most segments of society (Lamb, 1997). Thus, all else being equal, we would expect fathers' employment status and earnings capacity to affect their contributions to children (Marsiglio & Cohan, 2000).[12] There are two primary ways that fathers' capability as an economic providers may affect their involvement. First, fathers who have higher incomes can simply afford to provide more economic resources to their children. Research shows that earnings capacity is strongly related to the amount of child support paid by nonresident fathers (Garfinkel, McLanahan, & Hanson, 1998).

A second (and less-obvious) way that fathers' economic capabilities affect involvement is that fathers with greater earnings capacity are more likely to per-

---

[11]Some research suggests that both the quantity and quality of father involvement are important for children, although the necessary "thresholds" of each are unclear (see chap. 5).

[12]Although Lerman & Sorenson (2000) find that higher earnings among unmarried fathers are associated with greater involvement one year later, they note that the causal relationship between fathers' earnings/employment and involvement could go in either direction. Because from a policy perspective, it is may be more feasible to influence fathers' human capital and earnings potential than to directly affect the quantity or quality of fathers' involvement with their children, we focus on the effects of socioeconomic status on involvement.

ceive themselves—and to be perceived by others—as having "rights" to their child. Fathers who cannot meet the expectations of the breadwinner role may disengage from their families out of a sense of shame or inadequacy (Liebow, 1967). Alternatively, fathers who are unemployed or otherwise unable to provide resources to the child may be "pushed out" of the family—or not be given access to the child—by mothers (Edin & Lein, 1997; Marsiglio & Cohan, 2000). Thus, the fathers' lack of economic stability may preclude them being able to stay engaged in their children's life, with the mothers (or grandmothers) serving as "gatekeeper" to the children.

Studies confirm that fathers of higher socioeconomic status (as measured by education and employment status) are more likely to live with their children and/or more likely to exhibit positive parenting behaviors than fathers of lower status (Coley & Chase-Lansdale, 1999; Cooksey & Craig, 1998; Landale & Oropesa, 2001; Woodworth, Belsky, & Crnic, 1996), although the evidence is not entirely consistent (Pleck, 1997; Garfinkel, McLanahan, & Hanson, 1998). Edin's ethnographic work confirms the importance of fathers' economic stability for mothers' acceptance of them as partners. She notes that many mothers maintain a "pay and stay" rule, such that men who are unemployed or not contributing to household expenses are neither welcome as cohabitors nor viewed as desirable marriage partners (Edin, 2000). Recent research from the Fragile Families Study also shows that unmarried fathers are more likely to be involved around the time of their child's birth if they are employed (Carlson & McLanahan, in press). Mincy and Dupree (2001) also find that among unmarried parents who have just had a child, the father's being employed positively affects both the mother's intentions and her actual behavior with respect to family formation.

The Father as Provider of Emotional Support

Bronfenbrenner argues that healthy child development depends on the presence of a primary caregiver who is committed to the welfare of the child plus another adult who provides support to the primary caregiver (Bronfenbrenner, 1986). Because the biological father is the most likely candidate for providing support to the mother (usually the primary caregiver), the nature of the father–mother relationship serves as a useful indicator of whether the mother has the support she needs.

Two (related) aspects of parents' relationship that are likely to be important for parenting are whether the parents live together and the quality of their relationship (regardless of coresidence). To some extent, unmarried parents' relationships can be viewed on a continuum, with cohabiting parents having the "best" relationships, followed by couples who are romantically involved but living separately, couples who are friends, and finally couples who are not in any kind of relationship. In some instances, relationship quality may be higher among visiting couples than among cohabiting couples, but on average, we would expect it to be higher among cohabitors.

In addition to supporting the mothers' parenting, there are at least three reasons why the mother–father relationship should affect father involvement. First, when fathers live with their children (and the mother, as most children still live with their mothers), they automatically share time and money with the child. Second, living with the child increases a father's information about—and empathy toward—the child which, in turn, may increase his altruism toward the child. Men's ties to their children are often mediated by their connection to the child's mother, with the sexual union (and the accompanying "pillow talk" by which mothers convey information to fathers about the child) playing an important role in fostering the father–child bond (Heimer & Staffen, 1998). This mechanism is relevant even if parents do not cohabit and/or no longer have any romantic connection between them; having an amicable (nonromantic) relationship with the child's mother is likely to encourage higher levels of fathers' involvement because fathers who can effectively communicate with the child's mother will have greater access to information about—and ultimately a greater understanding of—the child.

Third, when fathers live apart from their child, they cannot be sure that the money they contribute is actually being used to benefit the child, and thus, they are likely to contribute fewer resources (Weiss & Willis, 1985). For men who live apart from their child, the problem of monitoring is also related to the quality of the parents' relationship. If the father trusts the mother and believes that she has the interest of the child at heart, he is likely to contribute more money to the child, even if he is no longer romantically involved with the mother.

Previous research supports the notion that fathers are more likely to be involved with their children if the relationship with the child's mother, particularly within marriage, is positive and supportive (Belsky, Youngblade, & Rovine, 1991; Gottman, 1998). For unmarried parents, a conflicted relationship between the parents discourages positive father involvement, whereas an amicable relationship supports healthy father–child interaction (Coley & Chase-Lansdale, 1999; Danziger & Radin, 1990; Seltzer, 1991). Early results from the Fragile Families Study confirm the importance of the mother–father relationship for father involvement. Fathers who are cohabiting with the child's mother are much more likely to have been involved during the pregnancy and around the time of the birth (such as by giving money, providing help with chores or transportation, and visiting the mother in the hospital); further, regardless of the couples' relationship status, having a high level of commitment and trust between them is also associated with greater involvement (Carlson & McLanahan, in press).

PUBLIC POLICY AND FATHER
INVOLVEMENT

Assuming that fathers' participation in children's lives offers important benefits, public policy should encourage—or at a minimum, not undermine—father involvement. Unfortunately, many of the policies that were designed to help children in low-income families actually discourage fathers from being involved with their children.[13] The problem is due in part to the fact that most of the programs that are in place today were designed for children who had lost their father either because of death, divorce, or abandonment. Because the parents' romantic relationship was by definition dissolved in such cases, policymakers were not concerned that the programs they designed might undermine the relationship between the mother and father. On the contrary, the Fragile Families data tell us that many single mothers today are still in a romantic relationship with the father of their child, at least at the time of the child's birth; this means that policymakers need to reassess the logic behind many of the programs intended to help low-income families. In this section of the chapter, we discuss three types of policies affecting father involvement—welfare policy, child support policy, and fatherhood initiatives—and discuss ways to make these policies more family friendly.[14]

Welfare Programs

The fact that the United States relies primarily on means-tested programs to assist low-income families (as compared to most European nations, which utilize mostly universal programs) penalizes families that include two parents. The penalty occurs because income and asset eligibility tests are not adjusted for family size but are based on total family (or household) income. By this rule, two-parent families are less likely to qualify for benefits than single-parent families simply because there are two parents (at least potentially) contributing income. The major welfare program in the United States for aiding single mothers and their children is Temporary Assistance to Needy Families (TANF) (formerly Aid to Families with Dependent Children, AFDC). In both of these programs, benefits are reduced by one dollar for each additional dollar of family income. So even if a two-parent family were able to qualify for assistance, the family's benefit level would be reduced by the amount of income a cohabiting partner (or spouse) contributed. Thus, although single individuals in the general population who choose to cohabit or marry benefit from the economies of scale that come with coresi-

---

[13]See Cabrera & Evans (2000) for a discussion of issues surrounding welfare reform and father involvement.

[14]See chapter 16 for a discussion of the economic literature on how welfare and child support are linked to father involvement.

dence, families that receive welfare reap no such benefit. Consequently, there is little economic incentive to have the father around, and there may be a serious disincentive to live with him (and pool household resources).

Another problem with the original AFDC program was that its rules did not allow states to provide assistance to children in two-parent homes unless the second parent was incapacitated. In 1961, Congress amended the law so that families with an unemployed father could qualify for AFDC in what became known as the AFDC-Unemployed Parent (UP) program. Yet, the rules for AFDC-UP have always been more stringent than the rules for single-parent families, requiring previous attachment to the labor force and previous eligibility for unemployment insurance. These rules exclude many low-income parents. With the passage of the Personal Responsibility and Work Opportunity Reconciliation Act (PRWORA) in 1996, states were given the option to eliminate the work rules for two-parent families, and as of this writing, 33 states have taken advantage of this option, and 17 have maintained the more stringent requirements (State Policy Documentation Project, 2001). The work eligibility rules provide additional hurdles for two-parent families compared to single-parent families. Finally, under the old AFDC program, mothers cohabiting with a man who was *not* the child's father could qualify for the basic AFDC program, whereas mothers living with the child's father were required to enroll in the AFDC-UP program with its more stringent eligibility requirements (Moffitt, Reville, & Winkler, 1995). This distinction between biological and stepfathers provides an additional disincentive for unmarried mothers to maintain a relationship with the biological father.

Empirical Evidence on the Effects of Welfare on Father Involvement. There is a long history of concern in the United States that cash welfare benefits (now TANF) increase single parenthood, either by encouraging nonmarital births and/or by discouraging marriage. Economic theory (Becker, 1991) tells us that individuals take account of economic incentives in determining whether to marry and/or have children. Thus, providing transfer income to single mothers should increase mothers' ability to bear and rear children alone and reduce their need for marriage. A vast academic literature has investigated this topic, and several generations of findings have yielded somewhat different conclusions about the effects of welfare on family formation. Early research on the Seattle and Denver Income Maintenance Experiments (SIME/DIME) suggested that increases in guaranteed income were associated with greater marital dissolution (Hannan, Tuma, & Groeneveld, 1977, 1978), but this conclusion was later disputed when the same data were reanalyzed using a different sample and more sophisticated analytic techniques (Cain & Wissoker, 1990). During the 1970s and 1980s, researchers concluded that welfare has no effects on marriage and fertility (Bane & Jargowsky, 1988). More recently, a new consensus has emerged that holds that welfare benefits have small but significant positive effects on nonmarital childbearing (Moffitt, 1998). Although the "marriage penalty" may vary, depending on the combination of parents' earnings, welfare income, and other program benefits (Primus & Beeson, 2000), most researchers agree with Robert Moffitt when he states that ". . . the conventional perception of the U.S. welfare system as largely favoring single-parent families over two-parent families and childless couples and individuals is essentially correct" (Moffitt, 1998, p. 53).

What Can Be Done?   Not everyone would want public policy to explicitly favor legal marriage over other family statuses, but most people agree that policy should not discourage marriage and family formation, and that supporting parents who live together is appropriate. Eliminating all categorical distinctions for two-parent families has been suggested as an important first step in leveling the playing field for two-parent families (Garfinkel, 2001; Primus & Beeson, 2000). Also, raising the income test for eligibility for TANF for families with two adults in the household would counteract the bias toward single-parent families inherent in means-tested programs. Finally, it seems reasonable to not discriminate against the biological father as compared to other men with whom the mother may cohabit.

The recent evaluation of the Minnesota Family Investment Program (MFIP) provides evidence that easing the rules for two-parent families increases family formation and stability. The MFIP demonstration eliminated the work-history eligibility rules for two-parent families and increased benefits available to two-parent families; these features of the program are credited with significantly reducing divorce among two-parent married families who participated in the program (Knox, Miller, & Gennetian, 2000). At the same time, greater incentives for employment and flexibility in benefits for single-parent families, as well as the changes in rules for two-parent families, increased marriage rates (Knox, Miller, & Gennetian, 2000). These findings support the idea that individuals will respond to financial incentives surrounding marriage and that greater income (through a combination of earnings and welfare assistance) positively affects entry into and stability within marriage.

Other researchers argue that the best way to encourage marriage and/or cohabitation among unwed parents is to provide supports outside welfare, by which they mean assistance that is less income tested and more universal (Bernstein & Garfinkel, 1996). Examples of such programs include earnings subsidies, childcare subsidies, and health care subsidies. Although the 1996 welfare reform legislation garnered most of the attention of welfare analysts and advocates during the 1990s, the last decade also brought a virtual revolution in the levels of assistance provided *outside* of traditional welfare. Between 1984 and 1999, federal spending on low-income families not on welfare rose more than eightfold, from $6 billion to an estimated $52 billion (Ellwood, 1999). The biggest component of this growth was in the federal Earned Income Tax Credit (EITC), which now provides a refundable tax credit up to 40% of earnings to low-wage workers with children.

Although the EITC may discourage marriage in some instances, it is much more marriage friendly than welfare, particularly for low-income couples. Indeed, if a mother earns less than $8,000 per year and her partner earns $12,000 a year, the couple stands to gain $3,500 a year if they marry or cohabit.[15]

Child Support Enforcement

Another program that has had a dramatic effect on fragile families is the child support enforcement system. The federal child support enforcement (CSE) program was started in 1975 to ensure that nonresident fathers provided financial support to their children. Federal matching funds were provided to states for establishing paternity, establishing child support awards, and collecting child support payments. As initially structured, collections were used to offset welfare expenditures in the AFDC program, and child support paid by fathers of mothers on welfare was to be applied to recover welfare costs (and sometimes to recoup Medicaid payments for the medical costs related to the child's birth); this practice continues today. In 1980, the program was broadened to serve all children eligible for support regardless of income or welfare status, but historically and at the present time, the majority of cases in the federal child support enforcement system involve parents and children connected to the welfare system. From its inception, the child support enforcement system was charged solely with enforcing fathers' financial support of their children, whereas other aspects of fathers' involvement, including visitation and custody, were (and remain) governed by state laws.

Legislative reforms in the last two decades, most recently PRWORA, have increased the overall effectiveness of the CSE system. Rates of paternity establishment, child support orders in place, and amount of collections have all risen, closing the estimated $34 billion gap (in 1990) between the amount of child support owed and the amount actually paid (Sorenson, 1995). Yet, although policy has appropriately increased collections from fathers who failed to pay child support (the so-called deadbeat dads), new research suggests that stronger enforcement may be driving a significant subgroup of fathers away from their children (Garfinkel et al., 1998; Sorenson, 1995; Sorenson & Turner, 1996). For these fathers—typically the fathers of children on welfare—the child support enforcement system is not meeting their needs and may in fact be undermining their involvement with their children. As noted earlier, fathers may disengage from their children if they are not adequately fulfilling the provider role, and child support enforcement may be creating disincentives for fathers to provide for their children.

---

[15]The amount of the credit is based on the custodial parent's income if parents live apart and on parents' joint income if they are married. For cohabiting couples with a child in common, the benefit is based on the earnings of the parent with the higher earnings (Primus & Beeson, 2000).

As noted, child support payments by fathers of children on welfare are used to reimburse the welfare expenditures of the mother and child. Mothers on welfare must assign their rights to the receipt of child support to the government, and any child support paid by the father goes to repay welfare expenditures and not to increase family income. Historically, states were required to pass through the first $50 per month to mothers, which at least improved the family's well-being slightly. However, this requirement was eliminated with the 1996 welfare reform, and as of December 1998, 30 states and the District of Columbia had entirely eliminated any child support pass-through. This policy (of reimbursing state welfare costs) provides significant disincentives for fathers to pay their obligations, as their children are not economically better off from their payments (Garfinkel, Meyer, & McLanahan, 1998). Therefore, in such circumstances the father may avoid paying altogether.

Strong child support enforcement may also reduce fathers' in-kind contributions to their children. Qualitative research suggests that unmarried parents generally prefer informal support arrangements (Waller & Plotnick, 2001) because the money goes to the child rather than to the state. Moreover, unmarried fathers who are living with their child are already providing support insofar as they are sharing their incomes with their children. The child support enforcement system was developed to meet the needs of children whose fathers were not living with the mother. Yet, the situation for fragile families is vastly different because nearly half of these fathers are coresiding with the mother and child, at least at the time of the child's birth. For unmarried parents whose relationship has ended, it is reasonable to establish and collect child support obligations from fathers (who are typically the noncustodial parents). For parents whose relationship is more fluid, a formal child support agreement (whereby the father's contributions go directly to the state) is likely to discourage fathers' *informal* involvement and may drive the father away. Resources are finite, and low-income fathers can often not afford both to buy clothes or toys for the child at the same time that they are paying a substantial fraction of their income in child support payments. If the father is forced to pay formally, his in-kind contributions—that are more directly seen by both the child and the mother to benefit the child—will likely diminish. Consequently, the child support enforcement system may be decreasing the total support provided to children because money that would otherwise be used by fathers to improve their children's well-being is being paid instead to the state.[16]

A second way that the current child support enforcement system may discourage fathers' involvement is that child support orders are often not appropriately linked to fathers' economic status. Because many states have minimum orders (based on the assumption that the father is working full-time regardless of his

---

[16]Obviously, if a father is living with the child and not paying child support, his income would have to be counted in determining the TANF benefit.

actual employment status), low-income fathers may be forced to pay a much higher proportion of their income in child support than middle-income fathers (Sorenson, 1999). This policy affects fathers in fragile families more than it affects other families, because the former have lower wages and are much more likely to not work year-round. Finally, child support orders are not routinely adjusted for changes in the father's income. This can lead fathers to accumulate large debts that, according to the 1986 Bradley amendment, cannot be forgiven or adjusted. Further, failure to pay child support is often treated as a criminal act, so fathers delinquent in child support may be put in jail or prison, which further diminishes their long-term earnings potential (Western, 2000).

Empirical Evidence on the Effects of Child Support on Father Involvement. Economic theory is ambiguous about whether stronger child support enforcement will encourage or discourage father involvement. On the one hand, child support reduces the costs of nonmarital childbearing to women (assuming women actually receive some of the money paid by fathers). On the other hand, it increases the costs to men. The net effect is an empirical question. The research on this topic indicates that the negative effects of stronger enforcement on men appear to dominate, with strong child support enforcement leading to lower levels of both nonmarital childbearing (Case, 1998; Garfinkel, Huang, McLanahan, & Gaylin, in press) and divorce (Nixon, 1997). Thus, it appears that the effects of public and private transfers may go in opposite directions, with welfare benefits slightly discouraging the formation of families and strong child support enforcement, on balance, encouraging families to form or stay together (or couples not to have a child outside of marriage in the first place).

The effects of child support enforcement may be more complicated for low-income families who are receiving—or potentially eligible for—welfare. Although child support is increasingly effective, children born outside of marriage are less likely to have a child support established than children born within marriage. In part, this may be due to the fact that (as noted previously) unmarried parents prefer informal support arrangements and up until recently the government has largely ignored low-income fathers (Waller & Plotnick, 2001). If unmarried parents have an informal agreement between themselves such that he contributes money under the table or makes in-kind contributions, any welfare received by the mother is in addition to any support received by the father. Because economic stability is generally associated with marriage and family formation (a so-called income effect), in this case the additional income from welfare may *encourage* family formation because parents are better able to pool their resources (Mincy & Dupree, 2001).

Qualitative studies of low-income couples show that strict enforcement also increases tension between unmarried parents—the mother may perceive that the father is not doing enough to help her and her child(ren) (not realizing that child support is used to reimburse welfare costs), whereas the father may perceive that the mother is "going after him" (not realizing that she is required to cooperate in establishing paternity as a criterion for receiving welfare). The findings in the qualitative literature are supported by studies that show that stronger child support enforcement is associated with high conflict among low-income couples (Seltzer, McLanahan, & Hanson, 1998).

What Can Be Done? One solution would be to not require child support orders for fathers who are cohabiting with the mother and child (Garfinkel, 2001). Of course, the income of these fathers would have to be counted in the calculation of the welfare benefit, although hopefully with a higher disregard than is currently allowed (see previous discussion). This would provide an incentive for fathers to live with the mother and child.

Another proposal would be to change the rules for the child support enforcement program so that a significant proportion of child support payments (in particular) are disregarded for the purposes of TANF eligibility determination and benefit calculation. This would ensure that private support is received by the mother *in addition to* any public transfers for which she and the child would otherwise be eligible. A related suggestion—but distinct from TANF benefit rules per se—would be to pass through the full amount of child support paid to the mother, regardless of the family's welfare status. Thus, fathers' payments would directly benefit the custodial-parent family instead of being used to offset state welfare spending. Both of these changes—changing TANF eligibility/benefits rules and delinking child support and TANF cost recovery—would promote father involvement (by increasing his incentives to pay) and would thus improve the economic well-being of mothers and children.

A third policy reform would be to ensure that the child support rules are responsive to the circumstances of low-income fathers. This would mean setting orders as a percent of income, ensuring that orders are regularly updated when the father's income changes, and developing ways to help fathers overcome the burden of child support debts.

Finally, because child support orders should be linked to fathers' income *and* should reasonably reflect the actual costs of raising a child, particular supports could be instituted for the children of very low-income fathers. Child support incentive payments—in the form of government contributions to match actual child support payments by very low-income fathers—could augment the meager support that children would otherwise receive in such situations (Primus & Daugirdas, 2000). Also, a publicly funded minimum assured benefit could be made available to children in limited circumstances when paternity has been established and the custodial parent is fully cooperating with the child enforcement system, yet no child support is being collected (Garfinkel, 1992, 2001; Primus & Daugirdas, 2000). The incentive payments and assured benefit would ensure that *all* children receive some support, even if their father cannot pay a sufficient amount or is not able to pay at all.

Fatherhood Programs

Most people agree that father involvement is generally positive and that we should be doing more to encourage fathers' involvement with their children.[17] Thus, beyond TANF program rules and child support policies, there is an opportunity for public policy and programs to provide incentives and supports for fathers to be involved with their children, either by improving their earnings capacity or by increasing their skills for—or investment in—parenting.

Although the primary mission of the child support enforcement system has been collecting money from nonresidential parents, several demonstration projects linked to child support enforcement were undertaken in the 1980s and 1990s. These programs were explicitly designed to improve fathers' labor market outcomes and/or to strengthen fathers' connections to their children. The primary demonstration in this area was the Parents' Fair Share (PFS) program, which was designed to increase low-income noncustodial parents' earnings and ability to pay child support. The program, which was administered in seven sites around the country, drew its clientele primarily from fathers who were divorced, were unemployed, had fallen behind in their child support payments, and were disconnected from their children. Most of the men who participated in the program were ordered to do so in lieu of going to jail; therefore, their enrollment likely reflects their desire to avoid incarceration more than any intrinsic motivation to improve their labor market prospects and family relationships.

Evaluation of the program highlighted the difficulty and complexity of improving labor market outcomes for low-income men and the fact that child support and welfare programs are not equipped to adequately meet the needs of poor fathers (Johnson, Levine, & Doolittle, 1999). Although the PFS program did not increase earnings and employment for participants overall, it was able to increase earnings for men with greater barriers to employment such as low education and limited previous work experience (Martinez & Miller, 2000). Also, the program increased the proportion of fathers who provided any formal child support and slightly increased the average support amount paid by some fathers (Knox & Redcross, 2000). PFS did not, on average, increase the frequency of noncustodial fathers' visits with their children, although some positive effects were noted in sites with particularly low initial levels of father–child contact (Knox & Redcross, 2000).

---

[17]One caveat to this concerns the possibility that some fathers may be dangerous or violent, and encouraging their involvement may threaten mothers and/or children. Although violence is obviously a very serious problem for those who experience it, data from the Fragile Families Study indicate that only a small minority of unmarried fathers are physically violent toward the mothers (4.0%) or have problems due to drug or alcohol use (5.8%). Further, about 70% of mothers who report that the father is either physically violent or has a substance problem also report that they want the father involved in the child's life (authors' tabulations).

More recently, numerous small-scale programs have been developed to serve divorced fathers as well as fathers in fragile families; these programs diverge in their emphases but often intend to improve both fathers' parenting skills and their employment capabilities and to increase their connection to their children (see Mincy and Pouncy, chap. 21 for an overview of fatherhood programs). In March 2000, the U.S. Department of Health and Human Services (DHHS) approved 10 new state demonstration projects to "improve the opportunities of young, unmarried fathers to support their children both financially and emotionally" (U.S. Department of Health and Human Services, 2000). These demonstration programs, which developed out of the Partners for Fragile Families (PFF) programs, sponsored by the Ford Foundation in the 1990s, focus exclusively on low-income fathers and families. Their stated objective is to encourage team parenting among unwed parents and increase the earnings capacity of low-skilled fathers. These DHHS-sponsored demonstrations represent the first national effort to develop programs to better meet the needs of fathers in fragile families.

Based on the early findings from the Fragile Families Study, the new generation of fatherhood programs are likely to make a difference *if* they are targeted on the right men and *if* they are timed correctly. Practitioners who run employment programs for disadvantaged men say that motivation is important in determining whether these men can sustain their participation in these program long enough to reap their benefits. The Fragile Families data suggest that new fathers are likely to be highly motivated and to take advantage of the services that fatherhood programs may provide. Thus, fatherhood programs should start early—at the hospital if possible—and should target men who are still involved with their children and their child's mother. The disappointing results from the Parents' Fair Share program may have been due in large part to the fact that the intervention occurred too late. The program drew its clientele from men who had *already* fallen behind in their child support obligations, who were no longer involved with the mother, and who had limited contact with their child. Starting at the time of a new birth may provide greater momentum for strengthening fathers' own capabilities and their family attachments, given the optimism unmarried couples have about their future at that time.

Beyond starting early, programs should treat fathers both as individuals (recognizing their personal strengths, limitations, and needs) and as part of families (recognizing their familial commitments, responsibilities, and supports). Further, programs should be equipped to address multiple needs faced by both mothers and fathers; in particular, programs should assist parents with expanding their labor market skills and capabilities, developing parenting and relationship skills, and overcoming substance abuse or mental health problems. Finally, programs should provide education to both parents about the nature of program rules and the financial implications of their choices with respect to living arrangements and marital status.

CONCLUSION

In this chapter we have described the emergence of a new family form—the *fragile family*—defined as unmarried parents who are raising their child together. Fragile families are the fastest-growing family form in the United States today, and they account for about 80% of all nonmarital births. Although at birth, unmarried parents have high hopes for marriage and/or continued father involvement, the resources of these parents (in terms of human capital and employment stability) are relatively low. Thus, if these families are to meet their goal of raising their child together, they will likely need both public and private support. Insofar as most individuals believe that children would be better off if they were being raised by both biological parents and insofar as most parents in fragile families want to marry, a restructuring of social policy to strengthen fragile families would appear to have wide bipartisan support. Indeed, as we enter the 21st century, there is a growing move to fund programs that address exactly these aims. But the new fatherhood initiatives do not exist in a vacuum, and their success will depend in large part on how they interact with welfare policy (TANF) as well as child support enforcement policies. Thus, to be successful, all three policies and programs must work together, which, at present, is not the case. In this chapter, we have discussed some of the recommendations that have been proposed to make welfare and child support policies more family friendly so that they would enhance rather than undermine the efforts of fatherhood initiatives. Drawing on the insights from the Fragile Families and Child Wellbeing Study, we also highlight the fact that the birth of a new child represents a "magic moment" in the lives of poor parents that increases motivation and enhances the possibility for real change.

ACKNOWLEDGMENTS

This research was supported by grants from NICHD (Child Support and Fragile Families) and from the Bendheim-Thoman Center for Research on Child Wellbeing at Princeton University. We are grateful to Christina Norland and Cary Bodenheimer for research assistance, to Ofira Schwartz for data management and calculations of predicted wages.

REFERENCES

Amato, P. R. (1998). More than money? Men's contributions to their children's lives. In A. Booth & A. C. Crouter (Eds.), *Men in families: When do they get involved? What difference does it make?* (pp. 241–278). Mahwah, NJ: Lawrence Erlbaum Associates.

Amato, P. R. and Rivera, F. (1999). Paternal involvement and children's behavior problems. *Journal of Marriage and the Family, 61,* 372–384.

Argys, L. M., Peters, H. E., Brooks-Gunn, J., & Smith, J. R. (1996). *Contributions of absent fathers to child well-being: The impact of child support dollars and father-child contact.* Materials for NICHD conference on father involvement.

Bachu, A. (1999). Trends in premarital childbearing, 1930 to 1994. *U.S. Census Bureau: Current Population Reports, 23–197.*

Bane, M. J., & Jargowsky, P. A. (1988). The links between government policy and family structure: What matters and what doesn't. In A. J. Cherlin (Ed.), *The changing American family and public policy* (pp. 219–261). Washington, DC: Urban Institute Press.

Becker, G. S. (1991). *A treatise on the family.* Cambridge, MA: Harvard University Press.

Belsky, J. (1984). The determinants of parenting: A process model. *Child Development, 55,* 83–96.

Belsky, J. (1990). Parental and nonparental child care and children's socioemotional development: A decade in review. *Journal of Marriage and the Family, 52,* 885–903.

Belsky, J., Youngblade, L., & Rovine, M. (1991). Patterns of marital change and parent–child interaction. *Journal of Marriage and the Family, 53,* 487–498.

Bernstein, J., & Garfinkel, I. (1996). Welfare reform: Fixing the system inside and out. In T. Schafer & J. Faux (Eds.), *Reclaiming prosperity: A blueprint for progressive economic reform* (pp. 173–190). New York: Economic Policy Institute.

Bronfenbrenner, U. (1986). Ecology of the family as a context for human development. *Developmental Psychology, 22*(6), 723–742.

Bumpass, L., & Lu, H. (2000). Trends in cohabitation and implications for children's family contexts. *Population Studies, 54,* 29–41.

Bumpass, L., & McLanahan, S. (1989). Unmarried motherhood: Recent trends, composition and black–white differences. *Demography, 26*(2), 279–286.

Cabrera, N., & Evans, V. J. (2000). Wither fathers in welfare reform. *Poverty Research News, 4*(2), 3–5. Joint Center for Poverty Research, Northwestern University/University of Chicago.

Cain, G. G., & Wissoker, D. (1990). A reanalysis of marital stability in the Seattle-Denver income maintenance experiment. *American Journal of Sociology, 95,* 1235–1269.

Carlson, M., & McLanahan, S. (in press). Early father involvement in fragile families. In R. Day & M. Lamb (Eds.), *Measuring father involvement.* Mahwah, NJ: Lawrence Erlbaum Associates.

Case, A. (1998). The effects of stronger child support enforcement on nonmarital fertility. In I. Garfinkel, S. McLanahan, D. Meyer, & J. Seltzer (Eds.), *Fathers under fire: The revolution in child support enforcement* (pp. 67–93). New York: Russell Sage Foundation.

Clarke, S. C. (1995). Advance report of final marriage statistics, 1989 and 1990. *Monthly Vital Statistics Report, 43,12S.* Hyattsville, MD: Centers for Disease Control and Prevention, National Center for Health Statistics.

Coley, R. L., & Chase-Lansdale, P. L. (1999). Stability and change in paternal involvement among urban African American fathers. *Journal of Family Psychology, 13*(3), 416–435.

Committee on Ways and Means, U.S. House of Representatives. (2000). *2000 Green Book: Background material and data on programs within the jurisdiction of the Committee on Ways and Means.* Washington, DC: U.S. Government Printing Office.

Cooksey, E. C., & Craig, P. H. (1998). Parenting from a distance: The effects of paternal characteristics on contact between nonresidential fathers and their children. *Demography, 35*(2), 187–200.

Crockett, L. J., Eggebeen, D. J., & Hawkins, A. J. (1993). Father's presence and young children's behavioral and cognitive adjustment. *Journal of Family Issues, 14*(3), 355–377.

Danziger, S., & Radin, N. (1990). Absent does not equal uninvolved: Predictors of fathering in teen mother families. *Journal of Marriage and the Family, 52*(3), 636–642.

Duncan, G. J., & Brooks-Gunn, J. (Eds.). (1997). *Consequences of growing up poor.* New York: Russell Sage Foundation.

Edin, K. (2000). Few good men: Why poor mothers don't marry or remarry. *The American Prospect, 11*(4), 26–31.

Edin, K., & Lein, L. (1997). *Making ends meet: How single mothers survive welfare and low-wage work.* New York: Russell Sage Foundation.

Ellwood, D. T. (1999, November). The plight of the working poor. *Children's Roundtable, No. 2.* Washington, DC: Brookings Institution.

Elo, I. T., Berkowitz, R., & Furstenberg, F. F., Jr. (1999). Adolescent females: Their sexual partners and the fathers of their children. *Journal of Marriage and the Family, 61,* 74–84.

Furstenberg, F., Morgan, P., & Allison, P. (1987). Paternal participation and children's well-being after marital dissolution. *American Sociological Review, 52,* 695–701.

Garfinkel, I. (1992). *Assuring child support: An extension of Social Security.* New York: Russell Sage Foundation.

Garfinkel, I. (2001). *Assuring child support in the new world of welfare.* Paper presented at the conference on The New World of Welfare: Shaping a Post-TANF Agenda for Policy, Washington, DC.

Garfinkel, I., Huang, C., McLanahan, S. S., & Gaylin, D. S. (In press). Will child support enforcement reduce nonmarital childbearing? *Journal of Population Economics.*

Garfinkel, I., McLanahan, S., & Hanson, T. (1998). A patchwork portrait of nonresident fathers. In I. Garfinkel, S. McLanahan, D. Meyer, & J. Seltzer (Eds.), *Fathers under fire: The revolution in child support enforcement* (pp. 31–60). New York: Russell Sage Foundation.

Garfinkel, I., Meyer, D. R., & McLanahan, S. (1998). A brief history of child support policies in the United States. In I. Garfinkel, S. McLanahan, D. Meyer, & J. Seltzer (Eds.), *Fathers under fire: The revolution in child support enforcement* (pp. 14–30). New York: Russell Sage Foundation.

Gottman, J. M. (1998). Toward a process model of men in marriages and families. In A. Booth & A. C. Crouter (Eds.), *Men in families: When do they get involved? What difference does it make?* (pp.149–192). Mahwah, NJ: Lawrence Erlbaum Associates.

Graham, J. W., Beller, A. H., & Hernandez, P. M. (1994). The determinants of child support income. In I. Garfinkel, S. S. McLanahan, & P. K. Robins (Eds.), *Child support and child well-being* (pp. 317–333). Washington, D.C.: Urban Institute Press.

Greene, A., & Moore, K. (1996). Nonresident father involvement and child outcomes among young children in families on welfare. Paper presented at the Conference on Father Involvement, Bethesda, MD.

Hannan, M. T., Tuma, N., & Groeneveld, L. P. (1977). Income and marital events: Evidence from an income-maintenance experiment. *American Journal of Sociology, 82*(6), 1186–1211.

Hannan, M. T., Tuma, N., & Groeneveld, L. P. (1978). Income and independence effects on marital dissolution: Results from the Seattle and Denver income-maintenance experiments. *American Journal of Sociology, 84*(3), 611–633.

Harris, K. M., Furstenberg, F. F., Jr., and Marmer, J. K. (1998). Paternal involvement with adolescents in intact families: The influence of fathers over the life course. *Demography, 35*(2), 201–216.

Harris, K. M., & Marmer, J. K. (1996). Poverty, paternal involvement, and adolescent well-being. *Journal of Family Issues, 17*(5), 614–640.

Hawkins, A. J., & Eggebeen, D. J. (1991). Are fathers fungible?: Patterns of coresident adult men in maritally disrupted families and young children's well-being. *Journal of Marriage and the Family, 53,* 958–972.

Heimer, C. A., & Staffen, L. R.. (1998). *For the sake of the children: The social organization of responsibility in the hospital and the home.* Chicago: University of Chicago Press.

Henshaw, S. K. (1998). Unintended pregnancy in the United States. *Family Planning Perspectives, 30*(1), 24–29, 46.

Johnson, E., Levine, A., & Doolittle, F. (1999). *Fathers' fair share: Helping poor men manage child support and fatherhood.* New York: Russell Sage Foundation.

Kandel, D. B. (1990). Parenting styles, drug use, and children's adjustment in families of young adults. *Journal of Marriage and the Family, 52,* 183–196.

King, V. (1994a). Nonresident father involvement and child well-being: Can dads make a difference? *Journal of Family Issues, 15*(1), 78–96.

King, V. (1994b). Variation in the consequences of nonresident father involvement for children's well-being. *Journal of Marriage and the Family, 56,* 963–972.

Knox, V., & Bane, M. J. (1994). Child support and schooling. In I. Garfinkel, S. S. McLanahan, & P. K. Robins (Eds.), *Child support and child well-being* (pp. 285–310). Washington, D.C.: Urban Institute Press.

Knox, V., Miller, C., & Gennetian, L. A. (2000). *Reforming welfare and rewarding work: A summary of the final report on the Minnesota Family Investment Program.* New York: Manpower Demonstration Research Corporation.

Knox, V., & Redcross, C. (2000). *Parenting and providing: The impact of Parents' Fair Share on paternal involvement.* New York: Manpower Demonstration Research Corporation.

Lamb, M. (Ed.). (1997). *The role of the father in child development.* New York: Wiley.

Lamb, M., Pleck, J. Charnov, E., & Levine, J. (1987). A biosocial perspective on paternal behavior and involvement. In J. Lancaster, J. Altman, A. Rossi, & L. Sherrod (Eds.), *Parenting across the lifespan: Biosocial perspectives* (pp. 111–142). New York: Academic Press.

Landale, N. S., & Oropesa, R. S. (2001). Father involvement in the lives of mainland Puerto Rican children: Contributions of nonresident, cohabiting and married fathers. *Social Forces, 79,* 945–968.

Lerman, R., & Sorenson, E. (2000). Father involvement with their nonmarital children: Patterns, determinants, and effects on their earnings. *Marriage and Family Review, 29*(2/3), 137–158.

Liebow, Elliott. (1967). *Tally's Corner: A study of Negro street corner men.* Boston: Little Brown.

Marsiglio, J., & Cohen, M. (2000). Contextualizing father involvement and paternal influence: Sociological and qualitative themes. *Marriage and Family Review, 29*(2/3), 75–95.

Martinez, J., & Miller, C. (2000). *Working and earning: The impact of Parents' Fair Share on low-income fathers' employment.* New York: Manpower Demonstration Research Corporation.

McLanahan, S. (2000). Family, state, and child well-being. *Annual Review of Sociology, 26,* 703–706.

McLanahan, S., & Sandefur, G. (1994). *Growing up with a single parent: What hurts, what helps.* Cambridge, MA: Harvard University Press.

Mincy, R. B. & Dupree, A. T. (2001). Welfare, child support and family formation. *Children and Youth Services Review, 23*(6/7), 577–601.

Mincy, R., & Pouncy, H. (1997). Paternalism, child support enforcement, and fragile families. In L. Mead (Ed.), *The new paternalism* (pp. 130–160). Washington, DC: Brookings Institution.

Moffitt, R. A. (1998). The effect of welfare on marriage and fertility. In R. A. Moffitt (Ed.), *Welfare, the family, and reproductive behavior* (pp. 50–97). Washington, DC: National Academy Press.

Moffitt, R. A., Reville, R., & Winkler, A. E. (1995). *Regarding cohabitation and marriage: description and findings.* A telephone survey of state AFDC rules, special report #62. Madison: Institute for Research on Poverty, University of Wisconsin.

Moore, K. (1995). Nonmarital childbearing in the United States. In *U.S. Department of Health and Human Services report to Congress on out-of-wedlock childbearing* (pp. v–xxii). Hyattsville, MD: National Center for Health Statistics.

Nixon, L. (1997). The effect of child support enforcement on marital dissolution. *Journal of Human Resources, 32*(1), 159–181.

Parke, R. D. (in press). Fathers and families. In M. Bornstein (Ed.), *Handbook of Parenting.* Hillsdale, NJ: Lawrence Erlbaum Associates.

Pleck, J. H. (1997). Paternal involvement: Levels, sources, and consequences. In M. Lamb (Ed.), *The role of the father in child development* (pp. 66–103). New York: Wiley.

Pleck, J. H., Lamb, M. E., & Levine, J. A. (1986). Epilogue: Facilitating future changes in men's family roles. In R. A. Lewis & M. Sussman (Eds.), *Men's changing roles in the family* (pp. 11–16). New York: Haworth.

Primus, W. E., & Beeson, J. (2000). *Safety net programs, marriage and cohabitation.* Paper presented at the Pennsylvania State University 2000 Family Issues Symposium, Just Living Together: Implications of Cohabitation for Children, Families, and Social Policy, State College, PA.

Primus, W., & Daugirdas, K. (2000). *Improving child well-being by focusing on low-income noncustodial parents in Maryland.* Baltimore, MD: Abell Foundation.

Reichman, N., Teitler, J., Garfinkel, I., & McLanahan, S. (2001). Fragile Families: Sample and design. *Children and Youth Services Review, 23*(4/5), 303–326.

Seltzer, J. (1991). Relationships between fathers and children who live apart: The father's role after separation. *Journal of Marriage and the Family, 53,* 79–101.

Seltzer, J. (2000). Child support and child access: Experiences of divorced and nonmarital families. In T. Oldham, & M. Melli (Eds.), *Child support: The next frontier.* (pp. 69–87). Ann Arbor: University of Michigan Press.

Seltzer, J. A., McLanahan, S. S., & Hanson, T. L. (1998). Will child support enforcement increase father–child contact and parental conflict after separation? In I. Garfinkel, S. McLanahan, D. Meyer, & J. Seltzer (Eds.), *Fathers under fire: The revolution in child support enforcement* (pp. 157–190). New York: Russell Sage Foundation.

Shapiro, A., & Lambert, J. D. (1999). Longitudinal effects of divorce on the quality of the father–child relationship and on fathers' psychological well-being. *Journal of Marriage and the Family, 61,* 397–408.

Simons, R., Whitbeck, L., Beaman, J., & Conger, R. (1994). The impact of mothers' parenting, involvement by nonresidential fathers, and parental conflict on the adjustment of adolescent children. *Journal of Marriage and the Family, 56,* 356–374.

Smock, P. J. (2000). Cohabitation in the United States: An appraisal of research themes, findings, and implications. *Annual Review of Sociology, 26,* 1–20.

Sorenson, E. (1995). *Noncustodial fathers: Can they afford to pay more child support?* Washington, DC: Urban Institute.

Sorenson, E. (1999). *Obligating dads: Helping low-income noncustodial fathers do more for their children.* Washington, DC: Urban Institute.

Sorenson, E., Mincy, R., & A. Halpern. (2000). *Redirecting welfare policy toward building strong families.* Washington, DC: Urban Institute.

Sorenson, E., & Turner, M. (1996). *Barriers in child support policy: A review of the literature.* Prepared for the System Barriers Roundtable, sponsored by the National Center of Fathers and Families. Philadelphia, PA.

State Policy Documentation Project. (2001). Retrieved February 18, 2002, from http://www.spdp.org

U.S. Department of Health and Human Services. (2000, March 29). Press release, "HHS awards child support waivers to help promote responsible fatherhood." Washington, D.C.

Ventura, S. J., & Bachrach, C. A. (2000). Nonmarital childbearing in the United States, 1940–99. *National Vital Statistics Reports, 48*(16). Hyattsville, MD: National Center for Health Statistics.

Waller, M. R., & Plotnick, R. (2001). Effective child support policy for low-income families: Evidence from street level research. *Journal of Public Policy Analysis and Management, 20*(1), 89–110.

Weiss, Y., & Willis, R. J. (1985). Children as collective goods and divorce settlements. *Journal of Labor Economics, 3*(3), 268–292.

Western, B. (2000). *The Impact of Incarceration on Earnings and Inequality.* Paper presented at the annual meeting of the American Sociological Association, Washington, DC.

Woodworth, S., Belsky, J., & Crnic, K. (1996). The determinants of father involvement during the child's second and third years of life: A developmental analysis. *Journal of Marriage and the Family, 58,* 679–692.

Zimmerman, M. A., Salem, D. A., & Maton, K. I. (1995). Family structure and psychosocial correlates among urban African-American adolescent males. *Child Development, 66,* 1598–1613.

19

Bridging Research and Policy: Including Fathers of Young Children in National Studies

Natasha Cabrera
National Institute of Child Health and Human Development

Jeanne Brooks-Gunn
Columbia University

Kristin Moore
Child Trends, Inc.

Jerry West
National Center for Education Statistics

Kimberly Boller
Mathematica Policy Research, Inc.

Catherine S. Tamis-LeMonda
New York University

Interest in research on fatherhood and its impact on the economic, psychological, and social well-being of children and families surged in the last decade. The concern came from various economic, cultural, and social sources, as well as from a national collaborative effort that enjoyed both private and public support. This effort, entitled the Fatherhood Research Initiative, began the process of revisiting available information on fathers, the gaps in research, the inclusion of fathers in intervention programs, and possible directions for research and policy. In addition to raising the visibility of fathers' roles in families and in childrearing, the Fatherhood Research Initiative provided a blueprint for a renewed research agenda on fathers. One of the surprising research deficiencies highlighted was the scarcity of data on fathers, especially those who were low income, were not living with their children, or had never been married. Although public policies are often targeted to low-income families, how men in these families develop as adults and as fathers, let alone how their well-being intersects with and enhances their children, is not well studied (Burton & Snyder, 1998; Cabrera, Tamis-LeMonda, Bradley, Hofferth, & Lamb, 2000; Federal Interagency Forum on Child and Family Statistics, 1998; Tamis-LeMonda & Cabrera, 1999). Moreover, policies and programs have mainly focused on paternity establishment, marriage, and child support and have paid less attention to the types of noneconomic involvement that fathers have with their children (Amato & Gilbreth, 1999; Booth & Crouter, 1998; Eggebeen & Knoester, 2001; Marsiglio, 1995; Parke, 1995).

Not only may fathers be important to the social, emotional, and cognitive lives of their children, but they may also make unique contributions to child outcomes when compared to mothers (Lamb, 2000; Nord & West, 2001; Nord, Brimhall, & West, 1997; Parke, 1995). Fathers may interact with young children in significantly different ways and for different amounts of time than mothers; they may contribute to their child through financial support and stimulating activities; they may participate in the organization of routines in the child's daily life; they may make major decisions about the child (or take part in such decision making); and they may offer emotional support to the child's mother. They may also show love and affection through behaviors that are different from those of mothers, which might reflect gender expectations, family history, or perceptions about themselves as parents and what it means to be a parent.

The Fatherhood Research Initiative provided opportunities to change the knowledge base on fathers. At the same time this Initiative began (1996), three national studies or multisite evaluations were being developed that focused on the first several years of life (Fuligni & Brooks-Gunn, in press; Tamis-LeMonda & Cabrera, 1999). These are the Early Head Start Research and Evaluation Project (EHS), the Fragile Families and Child Wellbeing Study (FF), and the Early Childhood Longitudinal Study—Birth Cohort (ECLS-B). As a consequence of the Fatherhood Research Initiative, the three studies have formed a Developing a Daddy Survey (DADS) consortium, which meets regularly to select measures, discuss design, and consider the conceptual issues raised when thinking about how to measure fathers' roles in families. In this chapter, we (a) describe the Fatherhood Research Initiative and focus on the research questions and policy questions that emerged out of this effort; (b) describe the three ongoing father-oriented studies of very young children and their families; (c) discuss the conceptual, methodological, and measurement challenges and opportunities that emerged out of these studies; and (d) explore lessons learned across these studies. We close with an eye toward how the forthcoming findings can be linked to policies and programs.

THE FATHERHOOD RESEARCH
INITIATIVE

In 1995, Former President Clinton and Vice President Gore asked federal agencies to assume greater leadership in promoting father involvement by reviewing programs and policies to strengthen and highlight the importance of fathers in the lives of children, as well as to improve data collection on fathers (Federal Interagency Forum on Child and Family Statistics, 1998). Agencies were to review their activities in four areas:

- Ensure, where appropriate and consistent with program objectives, that programs seek to engage and include fathers.
- Modify those programs that were designed to serve primarily mothers and children where appropriate and consistent with program objectives to include fathers explicitly and to strengthen their involvement with their children.
- Include evidence of father involvement and participation, where appropriate, in measuring the success of programs.
- Incorporate fathers, where appropriate, in government-initiated research regarding children and their families. This goal was an impetus to collaborate broadly in examining data, theory, measures, analyses and data collection strategies regarding fathers as well as in synthesizing the research base.

Under the leadership of the Interagency Forum on Child and Family Statistics, a number of groups, including federal statistical agency staff, federal and state policymakers, and practitioners and scholars from the family and child policy research community, gathered to take stock of the research base on fertility, family formation, and fatherhood (Tamis-LeMonda & Cabrera, 1999). The result was a series of conferences held in 1996 and 1997 that came to be known as the Fatherhood Research Initiative. Although they confirmed the importance of fathers to children (and of children to fathers), these meetings highlighted major limitations of current research on fatherhood. These meetings were summarized in a report entitled *Nurturing Fatherhood: Improving Data and Research on Male Fertility, Family Formation and Fatherhood* (Federal Interagency Forum on Child and Family Statistics, 1998). This report presented a detailed analysis of the state of data collection and research on male fertility, family formation, and fathering and provided a foundation for additional data collection and research within both the public and private sectors.

The Fatherhood Research Initiative was part of the impetus for several large-scale studies of young children and families to highlight fathers. The Early Head Start Research and Evaluation Project Fatherhood Study (EHS), the Fragile Families and Child Wellbeing Study (FF), and the Early Childhood Longitudinal Study—Birth Cohort (ECLS-B) collect comprehensive information on *being a father* from the men themselves as well as from mothers. Although these studies vary in terms of their design, purpose, and population, the measures used to assess father involvement share commonalities of constructs and survey questions. This coordination of measures is the product of Developing a Dad Survey (DADS; Cabrera et al., 2000), which began in 1997 and focuses on improving the design and development of father involvement measures. The DADS consortium coordinates measurement across six surveys that focus on *being a father* and *becoming a father*—the three just mentioned examine the former and three others consider the latter (the National Longitudinal Survey of Youth 1997 Cohort, the National Survey of Family Growth, and the National Longitudinal Study of Adolescent Health). The goals of the DADS consortium are (a) to make constructs scientifically, methodologically, and theoretically comparable across father studies that examine the process of *being a father;* (b) to assemble survey items measuring father involvement into one document for comparative purposes; and (c) to establish validity and reliability for these measures.

THREE NATIONAL STUDIES ON BEING A FATHER OF YOUNG CHILDREN

Most research on fathers has mainly focused on middle-class fathers and resident fathers, has collected data from mothers as proxy for fathers, has used dichotomous definitions of father involvement, does not follow fathers over time, and is not nationally representative. The studies profiled here collect data from the fathers themselves; use multidimensional definitions of father involvement; include low-income, divorced, and never-married fathers; are nationally representative (or, in the case of EHS, are multisite); and follow fathers from the first year of life throughout the early childhood years (and perhaps into the middle childhood years, depending on future funding). Collectively, these studies will provide rich and previously unavailable information on the type, nature, and frequency of father involvement in the United States.

The Fragile Families Study of Child Well-Being

The Fragile Families and Child Wellbeing Study addresses three areas of great interest to policymakers and community leaders—nonmarital childbearing, welfare reform, and the role of fathers—and brings these three areas together in an innovative, integrated framework. More specifically, it addresses the following questions: (a) What are the conditions and capabilities of new unwed parents? (b) What is the nature of the relationship between unwed parents? (c) What factors push new unwed parents together? What factors pull them apart? In particular, how do public policies affect parents' behaviors and living arrangements? and (d) What are the long-term consequences for parents, children, and society of new welfare regulations, stronger paternity establishment, and stricter child support enforcement?

The study follows a birth cohort of mostly unwed parents and their children and provides previously unavailable information about the conditions and capabilities of new parents and the well-being of their children. Table 19.1

TABLE 19.1
The Fragile Families and Child Wellbeing Study

Design	Longitudinal design following a representative panel of children of unmarried and married parents (includes both mothers and fathers). Families drawn from 21 cities selected based on welfare and child support policies and labor market strength.
Sample	A hospital-based sampling procedure was used to enroll 4,800 families, including 3,675 unmarried couples and 1,125 married couples.
Measures	*Child:* Health, cognitive, language, social, and emotional development. *Mothers and Fathers:* Mothers' prenatal care; parental health, education, employment, knowledge about local policies, and community resources; mother–father relationship; attitudes about marriage and about fathers' rights and responsibilities; social support and extended kin. *Neighborhood:* Census data and information on community resources and institutions (schools, day-care facilities, churches, health and social services, neighborhood organizations).
Data Collection	In 1998–99, parents were interviewed at the birth of their first child. Follow-up interviews with both parents are scheduled for when the child is 12, 30, and 48 months old.
Principal Investigators & Funders	*Principal Investigators:* Sara McLanahan & Irwin Garfinkel; Jeanne Brooks-Gunn, Marta Tienda, Nancy Reichman, and Julien Teitler are coinvestigators. *Funders:* NICHD, the Ford Foundation, the Robert Wood Johnson Foundation, the William T. Grant Foundation, the Public Policy Institute of California, the California HealthCare Foundation, the Hogg Foundation, the St. David's Hospital Foundation, the Commonwealth Fund, the Fund for New Jersey, the Healthcare Foundation of New Jersey, the Foundation for Child Development, the David and Lucile Packard Foundation, the Kronkosky Charitable Foundation, the A.L. Mailman Foundation, St. Vincent Hospitals and Health Services, the Office of Population Research at Princeton University, the Center for Research on Religion and Urban Civil Society at the University of Pennsylvania, the William and Flora Hewlett Foundation, the Christian A. Johnson Endeavor Foundation, the Leon Lowenstein Foundation, the John D. and Catherine T. MacArthur Foundation, the Charles Stewart Mott Foundation, the National Science Foundation, and the U.S. Department of Health and Human Services.
Internet Site	http://crcw.princeton.edu/fragilefamilies/

(From Brooks-Gunn et al., 2000)

presents a brief description of the Fragile Families Study (taken from Brooks-Gunn, Berlin, Leventhal, & Fuligni, 2000). These new parents and their children are called "fragile families" because of the multiple risk factors associated with nonmarital childbearing and to signify the vulnerability of the relationships within these families. In addition to the main study, the Fragile Families Study includes an intensive study of 75 couples being conducted in conjunction with the main study. This substudy entails ethnographic interviews with mothers and fathers separately and together, repeatedly over the first three years of the child's life. This study examines the type of relationship these unwed couples have, with a special focus on conflict, cohesion, and bargaining.

The study employs a longitudinal design to follow 4,700 couples (1,100 marital and 3,600 nonmarital births) in 20 large American cities. The sample is nationally representative of nonmarital and marital births in cities with populations over 200,000. In-hospital baseline interviews with mothers and fathers began in 1998 and were completed in 2000; both mothers and fathers were interviewed separately immediately following the birth of their child. Follow-up interviews with both parents, including nonresident fathers, will occur when the child is ages 12, 30, and 48 months of age.

Prior to random selection, cities were stratified into nine cells. Cities were ranked in terms of (a) the strength of their labor markets, (b) the strictness of child support enforcement, and (c) the generosity of their welfare grants. Cities in the top or bottom third of all three distributions formed eight of the nine cells. Cities that fell in the middle on one or more dimension formed the ninth cell. One city was selected randomly from each of the eight extreme cells, and eight cities were selected randomly from the remaining cell (see Reichman, Teitler, Garfinkel, & McLanahan, 2001, in the appendix for a more detailed description of the sampling plans and specific procedures). Hospitals in each city were sampled to be representative of nonmarital births in that city. For the entire 20-city study, parents have been interviewed in 75 hospitals (see Reichman et al., 2001, for a list of the hospitals and cities). The IRB committees in two thirds of the hospitals did not allow Fragile Families researchers to interview parents younger than age 18. Table 19.2 provides information on the sample size and variations in generosity of TANF benefits, strictness of child support enforcement, and unemployment rates in the 16 national cities (Reichman et al., 2001).

Although the process of obtaining access to so many hospitals was labor intensive, the strategy of sampling births in hospitals was very successful. In nearly all of the cities, at least 75% of the unwed fathers have been interviewed. Not only will the data on unwed fathers be more complete than those from previous surveys (i.e., many fewer missing fathers), but it will also allow for a comparison of fathers who were not interviewed with fathers who were interviewed based on information provided by the mothers. Mothers reported on the fathers of their babies, so there will be information on fathers' characteristics, even when the mother has no current relationship with the father. The fathers (final sample was 4,700) who were not interviewed cut across type of relationship with the mother. The response rate is lowest for those fathers with whom the mothers reported they had no relationship at the time of the birth of the child. Response rates were high for unwed fathers who were cohabitating and for those who were still romantically involved with the mother. Of the 4,892

TABLE 19.2

Fragile Family Study National Cities with Information About Labor Market, Welfare Generosity, Child Support Enforcement, and Sample Size

	# Cases	Labor Market	Welfare Generosity	Child Support
Austin, TX	325	Strong	Low	Lenient
Boston, MA	100	Strong	High	Strict
Corpus Christi, TX	325	Weak	Low	Lenient
Indianapolis, IN	325	Strong	Low	Strict
New York City	325	Weak	High	Lenient
Richmond, VA	325	Weak	Low	Strict
San Jose, CA	325	Strong	High	Lenient
Toledo, OH	100	Weak	High	Strict
Baltimore, MD	325	Average	Moderate	Moderate
Chicago	100	Average	Moderate	Lenient
Jacksonville, FL	100	Strong	Moderate	Moderate
Nashville, TN	100	Average	Low	Moderate
Norfolk, VA	100	Strong	Moderate	Strict
Philadelphia, PA	325	Average	Moderate	Strict
Pittsburgh, PA	100	Average	High	Strict
San Antonio, TX	100	Average	Low	Lenient

(From Reichman et al., 2001)

mothers (final sample was 4,700) who were interviewed after the birth of their child, 78% of the fathers were interviewed—89% of the married fathers, 90% of the unmarried but cohabitating fathers, 73% of the unmarried nonresidential fathers who were in a romantic relationship with the mother, 52% of those fathers who were "just friends" with the mothers, and 40% of those fathers to whom the mother speaks infrequently. Almost all fathers in all groups except the No Relationship Group visited the mother and baby in the hospital (Wilson & Brooks-Gunn, 2001; Reichman et al., 2001).

The Early Head Start Research and Evaluation Project

The Early Head Start Research and Evaluation Project began in 1995 and includes a study of the Early Head Start program and a longitudinal study of infants and toddlers in low-income families (children in the study were born from 1996 to 1998; see Table 19.3). The EHS Fatherhood Study was funded by the National Institute of Child Health and Human Development (NICHD); the Administration on Children, Youth and Families (ACYF); the Office of the Assistant Secretary for Planning and Evaluation (ASPE); and the Ford Foundation. Mathematica Policy Research, Inc., and the Center for Children and Families at Teachers College, Columbia University, serve as the national evaluators in collaboration with a consortium of university-based researchers and their local program partners.

The Early Head Start Research and Evaluation Project includes approximately 3,000 families living in 16 diverse communities and in 15 states (17 sites total; 2 sites are in Denver, Colorado, and 2 sites are in the state of Washington). Table 19.3 presents a summary of the EHS project (taken from Brooks-Gunn et al., 2000). The strategies to recruit families into the EHS program include exchanging referrals with other community service providers, going door-to-door, posting fliers, and using other outreach methods. As part of the experimental research design, families who applied were randomly assigned to the Early Head Start treatment group and received program services or were assigned to the control group and received the services available in their communities. The EHS Evaluation Project includes measures of a broad range of child and family outcomes and extensive information about the programs and the individual families' experiences with them. Data on family demographics and service needs were collected prior to random assignment; families are interviewed 6, 15, and 26 months after random assignment and at program exit. Child assessments, parent interviews, and parent–child interaction assessments are conducted when the children were 14, 24, and 36 months old. The last 36-month child assessments and exit interviews were completed in July 2001.

EHS Evaluation Project mothers and their children were enrolled first, and fathers were recruited after mothers identified them. The EHS Fatherhood Workgroup, which begun after the EHS Project was in the field, expanded data collection in 12 of the 17 research sites to include interviews with fathers and, in 9 of 12 sites, father–child interactions were videotaped when the children were age 24 and 36 months. The EHS Fatherhood Studies are among the first to investigate involvement of low-income fathers in children's lives, together with mother involvement, in the context of an intervention program for infants and toddlers. Four strands are included in the EHS Fatherhood Studies: (a) Father Involvement with Toddlers Study (EHS-FITS); (b) Father and Child Interactions during Toddlerhood Study (EHS-FACITS); (c) Father and Newborn Study (EHS-FANS); and (d) Fatherhood Program Participation and Service Use Study (EHS-F-PASS). In addition, local research sites are investigating a wide range of other topics. Table 19.4 summarizes the design of these studies.

The EHS Father Involvement with Toddlers Study (EHS-FITS) is being conducted in 12 of the 17 EHS research sites when the children are age 24 and 36 months. In all of the Early Head Start sites, mothers were asked during their interviews about the child's biological father and his involvement with the child. If the biological father did not live with the mother and child, mothers were asked about any men in the child's life who might be "like a father" to the child. In the 12 EHS-FITS sites, at the end of the interview with the mother, the interviewer described the father study, reviewed the father interview section, and identified the man who is most involved with the child. Approximately 60% of the completed mother interviews when the children were age 24 months at the EHS-FITS sites yielded a viable father interview identification. Of the approximately 1,370

TABLE 19.3

Early Head Start (EHS) Research & Evaluation Project

Design	Seven-year, national study employing a randomized design with two conditions: EHS program group and a control group including eligible families who applied to EHS at one of the 17 research sites (control group does not receive an offer of EHS services but can receive any other community services). Design includes (a) implementation study, (b) impact evaluation, (c) local research studies, (d) policy studies, (e) father studies, and (f) continuous improvement activities.
Sample	Approximately 3,000 low-income families from 17 local EHS sites with children born between September 1995 and July 1998.
Measures	IMPACT EVALUATION: *Child:* Health, motor, cognitive, language, social, and emotional development, includes standardized assessments (e.g., Bayley Scales, PPVT-3, CDI, CBCL) and videotaped child–parent interactions (e.g., Nursing Child Assessment Teaching Scales). *Mothers:* Household demographic information, education, employment, work and family issues, mental and physical health, the home environment, family routines and conflict, stress, social support, parenting attitudes and knowledge about child development, discipline, child care, parent–child activities, the parent–child relationship, and verbal ability. *Fathers:* Fathers interviewed or interviewed and observed with the children in three substudies (Core Father Study, Fathers of Newborns Study, and Practitioners Study). *Parenting Behavior* (via videotaped child–parent interactions): Includes ratings of sensitivity, intrusiveness, detachment, mutuality. *Neighborhood:* Program coordination with other community service providers, parental perception of community services, qualitative descriptions of the community. *Child Care:* Observations and provider interview in formal and informal settings. IMPLEMENTATION STUDY: *Parent Services Interview:* Perceived needs and resources, employment, education, child care and home visits, health status/services, family support services. *Exit Interview:* Early Head Start Program experiences. *Early Head Start Ratings of Program Quality:* Quality of center-based care, aspects of home visits. *Early Head Start Ratings of Program Implementation:* Consensus-based ratings of early child development and health services, family partnerships, community partnerships, staff development and management systems and procedures.
Data Collection	From 1996 to 2001, children are being assessed and parents interviewed when children are 14, 24, and 36 months old; parents are also interviewed at 6, 15, and 26 months after enrollment and when they exit the program. A follow-up study of the children and families is being planned. Public use files will be available after the final project impact report has been submitted to Congress.
Principal Investigators & Funders	*Principal Investigators:* John Love, Ellen Kisker, and Jeanne Brooks-Gunn; Helen Raikes, Rachel Cohen, and Louisa Tarullo are the project monitors for the national research; Esther Kresh is the project monitor for the local research studies. *Funders:* Administration on Children, Youth, and Families (ACYF). ACYF, NICHD, Office of the Assistant Secretary for Planning and Evaluation, and the Ford Foundation for the father studies.
Internet Site	http://www.mathematica-mpr.com/

(From Brooks-Gunn et al., 2000)

TABLE 19.4
The Early Head Start (EHS) Research and Evaluation Project
(Fatherhood Component)

Purpose	Fathers added to the study to broaden understanding of the family context, learn about the role of fathers in the lives of low-income families, explore how fathers become involved in Early Head Start, and examine how Early Head Start programs work to involve fathers in the program and in the lives of infants and toddlers.
Design	For the Father Involvement with Toddlers Study (EHS-FITS), the man who is most involved with the child at the time of the mother interviews was recruited. Fathers in the study may be biological or father figures who live with the child or not. The study includes quantitative and qualitative components and videotaping of father–child interactions in seven sites (the Father and Child Interactions during Toddlerhood Study (EHS-FACITS). For the Father and Newborns Study (EHS-FANS), the biological father was recruited around the time of the child's birth and followed longitudinally. The study includes quantitative and qualitative components, videotaping of father–child interactions, mother interviews, and child assessments. For the Fatherhood Program Participation and Service Use Study (EHS-F-PASS), program staff members from the 17 research sites participated in the qualitative study components, including individual interviews, group interviews, and a single-site case study. All Early Head Start programs were recruited to participate in the survey of father involvement, which included a Web-based survey followed by mail.
Sample	For the EHS-FITS, approximately 800 fathers/father figures drawn from 12 of the 17 local sites. For the EHS-FACITS, approximately 300 fathers/father figures drawn from 7 of the 17 local sites. For the EHS-FANS, approximately 200 fathers, children, and mothers. For the EHS-F-PASS, staff members from the 17 research sites for the qualitative work and approximately 270 Early Head Start programs for the 1999 survey of father involvement.
Periodicity	For the EHS-FITS and EHS-FACITS, fathers are interviewed when the children are 24 and 36 months old. For the EHS-FANS, fathers are interviewed when the children are 1, 6, 14, and 24 months old. For the EHS-F-PASS, qualitative work was conducted from 1997 to 2000, and the survey of father involvement was conducted in 1999. A follow-up study of the fathers and programs is being planned. Public use files will be available after the final project impact report has been submitted to Congress.
Topics Covered/ Content	EHS-FITS and EHS-FACITS: *Father:* Education, employment, work and family issues, mental and physical health, family conflict, stress, social support, parenting attitudes and knowledge about child development, discipline, father–child activities, the father–child relationship, attitudes toward fathering and his experience with his father and mother.

(Continued)

TABLE 19.4
(Continued)

	Father Parenting Behavior (via videotaped child–father interactions): Includes ratings of sensitivity, intrusiveness, detachment, mutuality.
	Father Beliefs about Fathering (via audiotaped qualitative questions): Includes responses to questions about what being a good father means to them, expectations of fatherhood, relationship with their own father, perceived support needed to be a father, and what makes them proud of their child.
	EHS-FANS
	Unique contribution is early timing of interviews and videotaping of father–child interaction and ability to understand how father involvement changes over time. Includes all of the topics covered in the Fatherhood Study.
	EHS-F-PASS
	Qualitative Study: How programs develop and implement father involvement activities.
	Survey of Father Involvement: Program descriptive information, families with fathers/father figures, extent of father/father figure involvement in the program, successes and barriers to father involvement, ways program has worked to become "father friendly," and overall rating of stage in father involvement.
Limitations	EHS-FITS and EHS-FACITS
	Sample is not nationally representative, nor is it representative of all Early Head Start families in the study. Mother survey responses provide basis for drawing the father sample.
	EHS-FANS
	Small sample but provides in-depth view of father participation from child's birth.
	EHS-F-PASS
	Possible lack of generalizability of the qualitative work to the other 600 Early Head Start programs based on anecdotal evidence that the research interest in father activities may drive some of the program activities.
Internet Site and Contact Information	Contact Kimberly Boller at Mathematica for information about the father studies.

fathers identified, 820 twenty-four-month interviews were completed. Approximately half of the father interviews completed were conducted with fathers of children in the EHS treatment group and half were conducted with fathers of children in the control group.

The EHS Father and Child Interaction during Toddlerhood Study (EHS-FACITS), includes 9 of the 12 EHS Father Interview with Toddler Study (FITS) sites. Father–child interaction assessments were videotaped when the children were ages 24 and 36 months. Approximately 330 father–child interaction assessments were completed when the child was 24 months of age sites (of the 450 fathers interviewed in the 7 sites). So far, the number of videotaped interactions collected at age 36 months is about 240 (of the initial 330 collected at age 24 months). The father–child interaction assessment activities include (a) a Nursing Child Assessment Satellite Training Programs (NCAST) teaching task; (b) a task where fathers chose what they wanted to do; (c) a structured play task with toys in three bags brought by the interviewer; and (d) a clean-up task. The teaching and structured play activities are identical to the mother–child interaction assessments, except the actual materials used were changed so that children would not be bored. To help identify unique dimensions of father interaction with toddlers, the Father Studies Workgroup developed the "Your Choice" task for the father study that included asking the fathers to do something with their child that they normally would for 5 minutes. This task was added to the mother–child interaction protocol in some sites as well. Two father–child interaction assessments at age 24 months are coded—the father–child NCAST teaching task and the three-bag task (Berlin, Brady-Smith, & Brooks-Gunn, in press). At age 36 months, a problem-solving task with puzzles replaced the teaching task, and the cleanup task was dropped.

The EHS Father and Newborn Study (EHS-FANS) is a study of about 200 fathers, their infants, and partners. It addresses the following questions: (a) How do different degrees, timing, and intensity of father involvement influence infant/toddler development? (b) How do fathers interact with and become involved with their newborns? (c) How do fathers' relationships with their children's mothers relate to their children's development? and (d) How does early father involvement predict later parental involvement? Interviews are conducted when the children are ages 1, 3, 6, 14, and 24 months. Father–child interaction assessments are conducted when the children are ages 6, 14, and 24 months.

The EHS Fatherhood Program Participation and Service Use Study (EHS-F-PASS) describes how EHS program sites involve fathers, how fathers view their roles (and the support they would like to enhance their parenting), and for program-group fathers, how they feel supported by the EHS programs. During implementation study site visits to all 17 of the EHS programs, data were collected about program activities to engage fathers in the program and how successful programs were in involving fathers. Implementation of father program activities was rated based on the number of father-specific program activities sites were conducting as well as the relative proportion of fathers who participated. The F-PASS study also includes a qualitative investigation of the evolution of program approaches to father involvement across all 17 Early Head Start research sites (Raikes, 2000). This study includes group and individual interviews with program directors and fathers.

The Early Childhood Longitudinal Study— Birth Cohort

The Early Childhood Longitudinal Study—Birth Cohort (ECLS-B) is a component of the National Center for Education Statistics' Early Childhood Longitudinal Studies Program, which is comprised of two cohort studies—a birth cohort and a kindergarten cohort. Table 19.5 presents a description of ECLS-B (taken from Fuligni & Brooks-Gunn, in press). The kindergarten cohort follows children from the beginning of kindergarten through fifth grade and includes direct child assessments, parent interviews, classroom teacher and school administrator questionnaires, and special education teacher questionnaires. The structure of the ECLS-B is similar to that of the kindergarten cohort, as both studies are designed using a multiple source, multiple methods approach. The ECLS-B is funded by the U.S. Department of Education, National Center for Education Statistics (NCES) in collaboration with several health, education, and human services agencies (National Center for Health Statistics, the National Institutes of Health, the Administration for Children, Youth and Families, the U.S. Department of Agriculture, and the Maternal and Child Health Bureau).

The ECLS-B is the first study in the United States to track a nationally representative sample of children from infancy to the time they enter school. The sample will consist of 16,000 infants randomly selected from birth certificates in 2001 and 2002. It will include oversamples of important populations such as Asian and American Indian infants, moderately low and very low birth weight infants, and twins. Children whose mothers were younger than age 15 or children who were adopted at or near to birth are not included in the sample. Using multiple modes of data collection, the ECLS-B seeks to identify factors at various ecological levels that influence children's health status and development in domains that are critical for later school readiness and academic achievement. Of particular interest are how transitions (e.g., from parental to nonparental care or from preschool to kindergarten) affect children's development and how their background and characteristics influence their transition to kindergarten and first grade. Over time, the ECLS-B will provide information on relationship links between children's early care and education experiences and their growth in physical, emotional, cognitive, and social domains. (National Center for Education Statistics, 1999).

Data will be collected when the study children are ages 9, 18, 30, and 48 months and at entrance into kindergarten and first grade. The primary modes of data collection are in-person parent interviews and direct child assessments that occur during home visits. During the home visit, field staff conduct direct assessments of children's mental and motor development, take physical measures (e.g., length/height and weight), videotape mother–child interactions, and conduct a computer-assisted interview with the child's primary caregiver (usually the child's mother). At ages 18 and 48 months, children's child-care providers are identified and computer-assisted telephone interviews with the providers are conducted.

The father component of the ECLS-B provides information on men as fathers. Fathers are asked about their attitudes and behaviors and the quality and quantity of their involvement with their children. The ECLS-B father component includes fathers who live in the same household with the sampled children (resident fathers) and fathers who live elsewhere (nonresident fathers).

TABLE 19.5
Early Childhood Longitudinal Study—Birth Cohort (ECLS-B)

Design	The ECLS-B is a longitudinal study of 15,000 nationally representative children born in the year 2000. Children will be followed from birth through first grade in order to assess their school readiness, as well as their growth and development in multiple domains (health, physical, gross and fine motor, cognitive, language, and socioemotional). Data about children's homes, communities, health care, nonparental child care, early childhood programs, schools, classrooms, and teachers will be gathered.
Sample	Sample includes 15,000 nationally representative children identified through birth certificates. Asian and Pacific Islanders, moderately and very low birth weight infants, and twins will be oversampled.
Measures	*Child:* Physical growth, cognitive development, gross and fine motor skills, perceptual competencies, receptive and expressive language, temperament, behavior problems, behavioral self-control, attachment. *Mother:* Pregnancy and breastfeeding experiences, household demographics and composition, education, employment, ancestry, country of origin, language, family composition growing up, receipt of public assistance growing up, school experiences, marital history, quality of current marriage or partner relationship, knowledge of child development, educational aspirations for child development, home learning environment, parenting behaviors and attitudes, child-care arrangement, family health, neighborhood quality/safety, social support, community support, family routines, biological father information, public assistance, maternal teaching style. *Resident Father:* Activities with child, child's behavior and abilities, prenatal/neonatal experiences, knowledge about child development, discipline techniques, attitudes about *being a father*, separations from child, influence in child-care decision making, current marital/partner relationship, marital and childbearing history, demographics, education, employment, health, family background, social support. *Child-Care Provider:* Caregiver background, program characteristics (staffing, program services provided, licensing, fees), type of care (length, time), other children in care, caregiver–child relationship, parental involvement, caregiver beliefs and attitudes, learning environment, caregiver health, caregiver income.
Data Collection	Scheduled for 9 months (2000), 18 months (2001–2002), 30 months (2002–2003), 48 months (2004), kindergarten (2005–2006), and first grade (2006–2007).
Principal Investigators & Funders	*Principal Investigator:* U.S. Department of Education, National Center for Education Statistics *Funders:* National Center for Health Statistics, the National Institutes of Health (NIH), the U.S. Department of Agriculture, the Administration for Children, Youth and Families, the Office of Special Education Programs, the Division of Nutrition and Physical Activity/Centers for Disease Control and Prevention, the Administration for Children and Families, and the Office of Minority Health. Within NIH, funding comes from the National Institute of Child Health and Human Development, Office of the Director, the National Institute of Mental Health, the National Institute on Nursing Research, the National Institute on Aging, and the Office of Behavioral and Social Sciences Research.
Internet Site	http://nces.ed.gov/ecls/Birth/Birth.htm

(From Fuligni & Brooks-Gunn, in press)

The questions posed to these two groups of fathers differ somewhat from each other.

In combination with the main ECLS-B components, the father questionnaires can be used to address the following questions: (a) What role do fathers play in the early care and rearing of their children and how does this change over time? (b) How does father involvement with their children and families affect their children's development and school readiness? (c) What influences the type and amount of activities that fathers do with their children? and (d) What are fathers' perceptions of themselves as fathers and how do their perceptions change as their children grow older?

At each data collection point, resident fathers are asked to complete a 20-minute self-administered questionnaire. The resident father questionnaires cover a range of topics such as father activities with his child, prenatal/neonatal experiences, knowledge about child development, discipline and parental control, attitudes about *being a father,* separations from child, influence in child-care decision making, current marital/partner relationship, father's childbearing and marital and partner history, background information, education, cognitive ability, employment, health, family background, social support network, and for nonresident fathers, child support and frequency of contact with the study child closing statement and tracing information. Resident fathers are asked to fill out a questionnaire while the mother is completing the parent interview. If the father is not in the home during the home visit, the questionnaire is left with the mother to give to her spouse/partner and mail back in a self-addressed stamped envelope. Nonresident fathers are asked a shorter set of questions that take about 10 minutes to complete. These fathers either complete a self-administered questionnaire, if they are in regular contact with the child's mother, or are interviewed by telephone or in person. Items are included on child support, time spent with the child, relationship with the child's mother, feelings about self as a father, how he helps the family and child, education, employment, depression, and income.

Summary

Although fathers are the focus of all three studies, each has unique features. The Fragile Families Study follows mostly unwed parents from the time their child is born. It is a nationally representative sample of unwed and married parents in cities of 200,000 or more people, and the sample size is 4,892. The clustered design also makes the data representative of each of the 20 cities and allows for the analyses of possible effects of state and local policies and labor markets. The ECLS-B is a large nationally representative study of infants (16,000) born in 2001–2002 that will collect information from mothers, fathers, and children. It includes large samples of infants that are not usually included in large numbers in national surveys (e.g., Asian, Native American, moderately and very low birth weight children, and twins). In the EHS father studies, the father involvement questionnaire taps key dimensions of parenting and parent–child relationships using the same data collection procedures and measures used with mothers. This instrument goes beyond the "mother template" by assessing areas seen as unique to fathering. The quality of father–child interactions is examined during video-taped, semistructured play activities. In addition, qualitative measures will provide information about how fathers see the father role, their experiences with their own father, and the support they need to be a father.

CONCEPTUAL, METHODOLOGICAL, AND MEASUREMENT CHALLENGES AND OPPORTUNITIES

Identifying Fathers

Multiple studies indicate that the fathers most likely to be missed in national surveys are never-married fathers, divorced fathers, and minority fathers (Garfinkel, McLanahan, & Hanson, 1998; Cherlin & Griffith, 1998). In addition, men in the military, prisons, jails, or other institutions are also typically excluded from household surveys (Western & McLanahan, 2000). For example, in the National Survey of Families and Households (NSFH), which is considered to be the best national data set for studying families and households, Garfinkel and his colleagues (1998) identified 9.6 million mothers, as compared to 5.6 million fathers, who reported having a child with a nonresident parent. This means that as many as 4 million fathers are either not represented or not identified in the NSFH. The problem is most serious for low-income fathers and for men who were never married to the mothers of their children (see Sorensen, 1997). The problem of missing fathers may also be severe in longitudinal surveys among young men. For example, Robertson (1995) estimated that the National Longitudinal Survey of Youth underreports nonresident fathers by only 25 to 30%. This is still a large percentage that underreports the existence of such fathers. This underrepresentation of men has serious implications for public policy. Policymakers are particularly interested fathers' earning capabilities for welfare reform and child support enforcement. But most estimates of fathers' earnings and capabilities have been seriously limited because nonresident fathers are underrepresented in national and local surveys.

Mothers are typically asked about the father. However, their knowledge about a nonresident father is sometimes limited. In a few cases, women do not know who fathered their children, or knew him so briefly that they lack basic information on social and demographic characteristics. For example, in the Fragile Families Study, of the 4,892 mothers interviewed in the hospital, 27 indicated that they did not know who the father was. In other cases, women cannot or will not reveal the identity of the father because they were raped or are the victims of domestic abuse. It might also be the case that mothers who have had children through unwanted sex may not want the father to know about the child or to know they know he is the father. An unknown number of these mothers might provide some social and demographic information about these men. Other mothers, who fear that legal authorities will pursue the father for child support, may be reluctant to share the identify of the father (although given the requirement of many states to withhold TANF benefits unless paternity is established, this concern may be less relevant today than it was earlier). Locating fathers under these circumstances may antagonize the mother. Information probably cannot be obtained from these fathers (Greene, Halle, LeMenestrel, & Moore, 1998). In the Fragile Families Study, of the 4,892 mothers, 151 of them indicated that they never talk to the father.

Depending on the purpose of the study, it might be important to collect information from stepfathers who live with children over a substantial portion of the childhood years and/or from men who are living with infants and toddlers who are not the child's biological fathers. "Social fathers" such as grandfathers, boyfriends, and others may play an important role in the lives of young children. At the very least, collecting information from these men provides a more complete picture of extended kin networks and social supports to the mother (Garfinkel et al., 2001). Although the father might be the best respondent, the mother is the one who decides who is a father figure to the child and whether to identify him. In the case of unmarried mothers, the name of the father is often recorded on the birth certificate; if not, the name of the father can only be obtained from the mother (although, practically, most studies are unable to contact either the mother or the father via birth certificate information for reasons of confidentiality).

Obviously, locating men who became fathers under extremely harmful conditions, who refuse to acknowledge their children, or who do not know they fathered a child is difficult or possibly dangerous. Additionally, many nonresident fathers have serious problems related to their mental health status, abuse of drugs and alcohol, and/or physical abuse and violence. These fathers are probably overrepresented in those fathers who are missing from national studies. In the Fragile Families Study it is estimated about 10% of all new unwed fathers fall into one or more of these categories (of the fathers we interviewed). These fathers are much more likely to be identified as having no relationship with the mother. Also, this is the only group of unwed fathers with very low paternal response rates (i.e., about 35%; Wilson & Brooks-Gunn, 2001). In the EHS Project, mothers only provide information for contacting the father for the father interview study for about 50 to 60% of the children, even though close to 90% of the mothers report that there is some contact between the child and the father or father figure. In the Fragile Families Study, of the 3704 unwed mothers, about 10% did not provide information on locating the father. The EHS Fatherhood Workgroup is analyzing father identification and father contact reports by the mothers to help understand the gap between those two key components of the FITS response rates (i.e., who are the fathers with whom the mother and child have contact and who are those for whom she does not give permission to contact for the fatherhood study).

Defining Fathers

Fathers can be biological or social fathers, can reside with the child or not, and can be romantically involved with the mother or not. Which fathers are important to interview? If the study's goal is to learn about the biological fathers themselves, then data collection efforts focus on locating these men wherever they are. Only studies that will collect information on national samples of men such as the National Survey of Families Growth, the National Longitudinal Study of Youth 1997 Cohort, and the National Longitudinal Study of Adolescent Health allow for such identification. If the focus is on the child, the mothers identify fathers or father figures who will be part of the study. The Fragile Families Study collects data on biological fathers, the EHS Project on biological and social fathers, and the ECLS-B on biological fathers and social fathers, when the latter is a member of the sampled child's household and is the spouse/partner of the child's primary caregiver.

Enrolling and Locating Fathers

Each of the studies discussed employed a different method for enrolling fathers. During the initial phase of the Fragile Families Study, early pretests revealed that researchers could gain permission to interview new parents in hospitals, that unwed mothers would provide contact information on fathers, that many unwed fathers go to the hospital to see the baby, and that the majority of fathers agree to be interviewed. The results of a pilot study conducted in Philadelphia showed that the response rate was somewhat higher for the mothers in prenatal clinics than that for mothers in the hospital (90% vs. 80%), yet the proportion of mothers who identified the fathers was about the same in the two groups. However, the proportion of identified fathers who were located and interviewed in the pilot study was much higher in the hospital than the prenatal clinic sample (70% vs. 53%). The higher response rate of fathers from the hospitals was due to the fact that most of the fathers visited the mothers and babies in the hospital, and it was therefore relatively easy to locate and interview them (Garfinkel et al., 2001). In the Fragile Families Study, the percentage interviewed was higher then what was found in the pilot study, as reported earlier in this chapter.

In the EHS Project, if there is not a resident biological father, mothers are asked whether there is someone who is "like a father" to the child. Identified men included those who were not only romantic partners (some of whom were involved with the mother for only a short period of time), but also maternal and paternal relatives. The investment of these social fathers in the children tended to depend on their relationship with the mother. Although these men were not asked whether they felt like a father to the child, they were asked about many dimensions of their relationship with the child and about how involved they plan to be in the child's life in the future.

The ECLS-B sample of resident fathers is determined by responses to questions on the main parent interview during a home visit at each data collection wave. The preferred respondent for the main parent interview is the infant's mother, and the resident father is identified as the spouse or partner who is currently residing in the household. That person may be the biological father, a stepfather, an adopted father, or a social father. And the resident father and his relationship to the child may change over the multiple waves of data collection. The ECLS-B sample of nonresident fathers at age 9 months is always the biological father, but this may change over the life of the study. Field staff face a variety of problems when attempting to locate nonresident fathers based on the information that is provided to them by the study children's mothers. Mothers often do not have the biological fathers' current addresses and/or telephone numbers or give field staff inaccurate contacting information.

Retention and Response Rates

Strategies to increase fathers' participation include financial incentives for in-person interviews, explanation of the purpose of the study in a way that motivates participation, matching the demographic characteristics (gender and race) of the interviewer to the respondent, flexibility with arranging interviews, and dissociating the study from government child support efforts. Computer Assisted Personal Interview (CAPI), when used in addition to financial incentives, has also been found to increase the response rates for sensitive topics (Turner, Forsyth, Reilly, & Miller, 1996).

In the EHS-FITS and EHS-FANS, the interviewers attempt to be as flexible as possible about when and where to schedule the father interviews. Interviewers also work to establish rapport with the men, and interviewers report that that they use different rapport-building techniques with the fathers than they do with the mothers (more conversation about father-specific activities, sports, and work activities). Once interviewers are able to get the interview started, most of the fathers spontaneously express how much they enjoy talking about their child. Fathers also report that they rarely have the opportunity to reflect on their role as fathers and that they appreciate having that experience. Modest financial incentives are used to express appreciation to fathers for their time and effort.

For participation in the ECLS-B, financial incentives are used to acknowledge respondents' time and effort, help secure their cooperation, convey a sense of the importance of the study, and recognize the importance of the respondent's contribution. Interviewers are also trained to identify and address hesitations or concerns that fathers express about participating in the study. Where the child's mother and nonresident father are in frequent contact, the mother is asked to hand the nonresident father a packet containing the father questionnaire and a stamped, self-addressed envelope. There is some evidence from the ECLS-B 1999 field test that this approach may increase the likelihood that a father will participate. Field staff also encourage the mothers to serve as an advocate for the study. Mothers that encourage the fathers to participate and discuss the study may contribute to the likelihood of a completed father questionnaire. Both resident and nonresident fathers are also given attractive study materials that explain the study and present the purpose of wanting to know more about the important and unique contributions that fathers make to the lives of their children. In the Fragile Families Study, financial incentives are used to compensate respondents for their time and effort. A parent newsletter informing participants of general findings and policy relevance of the study is sent one month prior to each wave of interviews.

Defining Father Involvement

Scholars have struggled with the definition of an "involved father" (Cabrera, 1999). Research strategies include time-use diary data, interview questions on type of involvement, and observations of father–child interactions. Different conceptual models have been used to design items tapping father involvement. (Cabrera et al., 2000; Lamb, 2000; Parke, 1995). One well-known model proposes three dimensions of father involvement: *engagement, availability,* and *responsibility* (Lamb, Pleck, Charnov, & Levine, 1985). In the three studies, father involvement is loosely organized around this model. Table 19.6 lists many of the measures being collected by the studies profiled in this chapter.

LESSONS LEARNED

Because of their unique purpose, design, and population, each of the studies profiled here has important methodological, measurement, and design lessons to share with other researchers who study fathers. An important lesson from the Fragile Families Study is that sampling from hospitals is much more efficient and desirable than sampling from prenatal clinics. The latter strategy leads to fewer completed father interviews and is less representative of all nonmarital births. Almost all unwed fathers go to the hospitals to see the baby, and most agree to be interviewed. Levine and Bryant (1997) noted that the 1988 National and Maternal Infant Health Survey, which sampled from birth records, was able to locate and complete interviews with only 80% of the mothers. Presumably, the response rate was even lower for unmarried mothers. Clustering of mothers along with intensive interviewer coverage and availability in the hospitals allow researchers to attain even higher response rates among mothers. One could expect high response rates for fathers because so many came to visit the baby at the hospital. Additionally, interviewing in the hospital cost one third less than

TABLE 19.6
Matrix of Measures/Constructs Used in the EHS, ECLS-B,
and Fragile Families Studies (The DADS Binders)

Father Involvement Measures & Constructs	Early Head Start (Father Interview)		ECLS-Father Involvement	Fragile Families	
	1 month (FANS)	24 months (FITS)	9 months	Birth	12 months
Sociodemographics					
Bio or social father	X	X			
Residence (e.g., type of home, number of moves,	X	X	X	X	X
Household composition/ living situation	X	X	X	X	X
Marital/partner status	X	X	X	X	X
Number of biological children	X	X	X	X	X
Hispanic origin	X	X		X	
Race/ethnicity	X	X		X	
Age mth/yr born	X	X	X	X	
Country of origin, Citizenship/immigration*	X	X	X	X	
Language (including literacy)	X	X	X		
Employment status* (including off-the-books activities—FF)	X	X	X	X	X
Occupation	X	X	X	X	X
Work schedule	X	X	X	X	X
Satisfaction w/ income/job	X	X			
Income (including monthly expenses—FF)/Earnings	X	X	X	X	X
Education	X	X	X	X	X
Religion			X	X	X
Enrollment and training (including military service—FF)		X	X	X	X
Employment benefits			X		
Income & ownership					X
Family Background					
Family composition while growing up			X		

(Continued)

TABLE 19.6
(Continued)

Father Involvement Measures & Constructs	Early Head Start (Father Interview)		ECLS-Father Involvement	Fragile Families	
	1 month (FANS)	24 months (FITS)	9 months	Birth	12 months
Receipt of public assistance during childhood			X		
Educational attainment of father's parents			X		X
Whether father's parents are still living					
Parent's country of origin					X
Accessibility					
Lived with child since birth/last interview	X	X	X		
How long father lived in HH or child lived with father	X	X	X		
Since child born ever lived in same household	X	X	X	X	X
How old child when first met/ when did you start living w/child	X	X			
How many miles/minutes away does dad live	X	X	X		X
How do you get to child	X	X			
How often spent 1 or more hrs a day w/child since birth/or past month	X	X	X		
How many months able to see child on regular basis		X			
Separations from child and duration		X	X		X
How long since last contact with child			X		
In past 12 month/since birth/ past 30 days how often seen child			X		X
How often child's mother able to contact father when he's not at home					

(Continued)

TABLE 19.6
(Continued)

Father Involvement Measures & Constructs	Early Head Start (Father Interview)		ECLS-Father Involvement	Fragile Families	
	1 month (FANS)	24 months (FITS)	9 months	Birth	12 months
Live in same household with (child)					
Reasons for low/no contact					
How often seen child since stopped living together			X		X
How often talk w/mother about child			X		
How much of time is (child) living w/you					X
Engagement					
Number of hours with child and whether primary caretaker	X	X			
Prenatal support	X		X		
Present at birth, visits soon after	X		X	X	
Held newborn	X		X	X	
Warmth/affection	X	X	X		
Shared activities (e.g., sing songs, take to visit friends, meals together).Includes cog. stimulation items	X	X	X		X
Discipline/parenting style		X			X
Volunteers at child-care program		X			
Violence, abuse, neglect					
Limited setting/monitoring					
School involvement					
Responsibility					
Child-related maintenance (child-care tasks—including baby-sitting)	X	X	X		X
Purchase items for child (including pay for child care)	X	X	X		X

(Continued)

TABLE 19.6
(Continued)

Father Involvement Measures & Constructs	Early Head Start (Father Interview)		ECLS-Father Involvement	Fragile Families	
	1 month (FANS)	24 months (FITS)	9 months	Birth	12 months
Role in deciding about child care	X	X	X		X
Input into child-related decisions	X	X	X		
Provide health insurance coverage, paid for medical insurance, doctorbills, medicine		X	X		X
Given extra money to help out		X	X		
Take child to sitter or child care		X			
How much child support due/ how often paid		X	X		X
Type of child support arrangements (also informal)		X	X	X	X
Whether baby will have father's last name/Whether father's name will be on the birth certificate		X	X	X	
Legal paternity established		X	X	X	
Share common household and child-related expenses		X			
Plans for involvement in the future		X	X		
Discuss child w/doctor, sitter etc.					X
How many children live elsewhere			X		X
Provide support for children living elsewhere			X		X
Efforts to improve life of child					
Fertility, Marital, Partner History					
Number of children ever sired	X	X	X	X	
Age at child's birth (can be calculated)			X		

TABLE 19.6
(Continued)

Father Involvement Measures & Constructs	Early Head Start (Father Interview)		ECLS-Father Involvement	Fragile Families	
	1 month (FANS)	24 months (FITS)	9 months	Birth	12 months
Age when first became father			X		
Marital status at birth of child					X
Ever married/live with child's mother					
Complete fertility history					
Marital/cohabiting history			X		
Number of biological children w/child's mother					X
Health, Mental Health, Stressful Life Events					
Stressful life events	X	X			
Health status	X	X	X	X	X
Depression		X	X	X	X
Cigarette smoking, drug and alcohol use			X	X	X
Family history of: Cigarette smoking, drug & alcohol use, depression, mental disorders, asthma, learning disability			X		
Self-esteem				X	
Locus of control				X	
Limiting conditions			X	X	
Professional treatment for emotional or mental problems			X		
Father–Mother Relationships					
Time w/mom before pregnancy	X			X	
Disagreements concerning child	X	X	X		X
General disagreements	X	X	X	X	X
Rating of relationship w/child's mother	X	X	X	X	
Status of relationship (e.g., romantic/friendship)				X	X

(Continued)

TABLE 19.6
(Continued)

Father Involvement Measures & Constructs	Early Head Start (Father Interview)		ECLS-Father Involvement	Fragile Families	
	1 month (FANS)	24 months (FITS)	9 months	Birth	12 months
Past relationship w/child's mother/why relationship ended				X	X
Plans for relationship in the future (e.g., marriage, cohabitation)				X	X
Mother's view of father's involvement w/child				X	
Quality of current relationship			X		
Feelings about interactions (w/spouse) (may not be bio. mom)					X
Relationships With Family Members					
Dad's relationship with other relatives	X	X			X
Experiences w/own father/father-figure		X		X	X
Present relationship w/own father/father-figure		X	X		X
Experiences w/own mother/mother-figure		X			
Present relationship w/own mother/mother-figure		X	X		X
How problems w/family members are resolved					
Knowledge and Attitudes About Fatherhood					
Feelings about pregnancy	X		X	X	
Perceptions of fatherhood	X	X	X		
Feelings about child	X	X	X	X	
Rating of self as father	X	X	X		
Plans for involvement w/child	X			X	
Knowledge about raising a child	X	X	X		
Stress related to fatherhood		X			

(Continued)

TABLE 19.6
(Continued)

Father Involvement Measures & Constructs	Early Head Start (Father Interview)		ECLS-Father Involvement	Fragile Families	
	1 month (FANS)	24 months (FITS)	9 months	Birth	12 months
Importance of things dads do	X	X	X	X	
Perceived rights and obligations of dads				X	
Social Support Network					
Support of parenting role	X				
Guidance/parenting advice	X				
Material support from relatives and friends				X	X
Emotional support					
Social involvement (excluding church attendance)			X		
Neighborhood & Environment					
Public houisng				X	X
Neighborhood problems (e.g., litter, crime, traffic)				X	X
Safe play areas					
Housing and/or financial problems					X
Child-Related Services and Government Programs					
Attends/invited to parenting training	X	X			
Attends/invited to programs for fathers/men		X			
Attends program's board meeting		X			
Where receive information about caring for child	X				
Program affiliated child care					
Program/agency visits home	X	X			
Welfare and child support policy in father's state				X	
Received help from agency or program					X

(Continued)

TABLE 19.6
(Continued)

Father Involvement Measures & Constructs	Early Head Start (Father Interview)		ECLS-Father Involvement	Fragile Families	
	1 month (FANS)	24 months (FITS)	9 months	Birth	12 months
Received income from program (e.g., welfare, food stamps, unemployment)					X
Criminal Justice System Experience					
Criminal charges					X
Criminal convictions					X
Incarceration/probation					X
Custodial Fatherhood					
Mother/child contact					CO-C5
Child support from mother					X

Note. The X indicates that the item is measured in the study; FANS = Father and Newborn Study; FITS = Father Involvement with Toddlers Study.

conducting in-home interviews (this estimate does not take into consideration the costs of obtaining access to the hospitals, which are substantial and amounted to approximately $300,000 over 2 years in the Fragile Families Study). Sampling from hospitals rather than from birth certificates probably results in higher response rates.

Usually, because both mothers and fathers were to be interviewed and because there was generally more than one birth per hospital per day, multiple interviews could be conducted during each field worker hospital visit. In-home interviews, on the other hand, require a substantial amount of time for locating, scheduling, and traveling. Finally, researchers learned something substantive about the nature of the relationships between unwed mothers and fathers. According to the unwed mothers' reports, over 40% were living with the father. An additional one third were still in a romantic relationship with the father. Over half of the mothers believed that their chances of marrying the father were 50% or greater. Two thirds of the fathers provided some type of financial support during the pregnancy. All told, over 75% of unwed fathers either had a continuing romantic relationship or they (or their kin) provided support to the mother during pregnancy (Teitler, 2001).

In the ECLS-B, two large-scale field tests of the ECLS-B 9-month home visit design have been conducted, one in fall 1999 and a second in fall 2000. During the 1999 field test, different variations of incentive payments were explored to determine if more money increased response rates and if giving the father a check before or after completing a questionnaire made any difference in response rate. Resident fathers received either a $10 or $15 dollar incentive, and some fathers received a check before completing a questionnaire and some afterward. The amount and timing of the incentive were randomly selected by case. The amount of money did not seem to have much effect on the response rates of fathers, and no consistent pattern in response rate was discerned by whether fathers received their check prior to or after completing the questionnaire.

In the 1999 field test, resident fathers were generally cooperative in completing the self-administered questionnaire. Of the total 452 resident fathers identified, 326 (72%) completed a resident father questionnaire. About 50% of the resident fathers either completed the questionnaire during the home visit or returned it to the home office without prompting by the field staff. About 20% were completed after being prompted by telephone. Although lower than the expected 80%, this rate was considered to be primarily the result of a delay in following up with nonresponding resident fathers within 2 weeks of the home visit as originally planned. In the second field test, more resources were put into shortening the gap between the completion of the home visit and following up with fathers who had not completed and returned the resident father questionnaire. In this field test, 85% of the resident fathers completed and returned the questionnaire.

Both the 1999 and 2000 ECLS-B 9-month field tests examined the feasibility of identifying, locating, and contacting nonresident biological fathers of the sampled children and determining whether a questionnaire could be completed. The findings from these field tests suggest that the contact information provided by mothers is often problematic. For example, in 10 of the 40 nonresponse follow-up cases in the 1999 field test, the interviewer recontacted or attempted to recontact the child's mother because the contacting information she had given previously was not current. For six of these cases the mother said she had no way of contacting the father.

Other findings from the 1999 field test pointed to the value of using mothers to hand nonresident fathers a self-administered questionnaire and to encourage father participation and giving the resident father the questionnaire at the beginning of a home visit when possible. Giving a short self-administered questionnaire rather than a long questionnaire tended to increase response rates of nonresident fathers.

Findings from the 2000 field test further suggest that response rates for nonresident fathers will lag behind those of resident fathers. About 67% of the nonresident fathers identified by mothers and for whom she gave her permission for field staff to contact, completed a questionnaire. This was a higher rate than in the 1999 field test and may be due in part to the shortened length of the questionnaire used in the 2000 field test and to the procedure of leaving the nonresident father questionnaire with the mother after the parent interview.

Lessons learned from Early Head Start fall into two main categories: (a) increasing father participation, and (b) facilitating rapport with both the mother and the father. Interviewers reported that the faster they were able to schedule the father interview after the mother interview was completed, the more likely they were able to locate the father and conduct the interview with him. In some cases, interviewers were able to identify the father prior to conducting the mother interview, and both interviews were scheduled for the same time. This strategy only works for mothers and fathers who live together. Another way to increase father participation is to be as flexible as possible in scheduling the interview. Many of the FITS sites chose to conduct the father interview by telephone, and this option facilitated flexible scheduling. One drawback is that for the sites participating in the FACITS, they had to meet the father in person to conduct the father–child videotaped assessment. As the period for completing an interview with a father came to an end, some FACITS sites had to decide whether to make the trade-off of either completing the father interview by phone and not completing the video assessment or not completing either.

Feedback from Early Head Start interviewers also demonstrates how important it is to be sensitive to parents' concerns about being treated similarly. For example, when we separately pretested either the mother interview or the father interview with non-Early Head Start study parents (in cases where we just did one or the other with a given family and not both), mothers and fathers who did not participate in the pretest commented that they wanted to participate and that they felt left out. We received similar comments from fathers in the sites that did not conduct a video assessment. They also wanted the opportunity to play with their children and be videotaped, as the mothers had. The work group also decided that to increase rapport, the incentives offered to mothers and fathers should be the same.

CONCLUSION

Including unwed fathers in a study of families is critical to our understanding of family and child well-being. Nearly one third of all children born in the United States today are born to unmarried parents. The proportions are even higher among poor and minority populations, at 40% among Hispanics and 70% among African Americans (Ventura et al., 1995). In some instances, the parents of these children are living together in a marriagelike relationship. In others, they have a close relationship, but the father lives in a separate household. In still other cases, the father has virtually no contact with either the mother or child. Previous studies indicate that men who father children outside marriage are younger, are less likely to have a high school degree, are less likely to attend college, work fewer hours per week and have much lower hourly wages, and have lower average incomes than that of married fathers (Garfinkel et al., 1998). The difference is even more striking when we look at men in the lower tail of the income distribution. Garfinkel and his colleagues estimated that 40% of unwed fathers have annual incomes less than $7,000. Finally, unwed fathers report more disability, more depression, and more frequent drug and alcohol use than men who father children within marriage, as illustrated in Table 19.7 (taken from Wilson & Brooks-Gunn, 2001). The table summarizes some of the capacities of fathers at the time of their child's birth by the relationship status of the mother and father. Findings such as these are indicative of the types of information that are being generated by these new studies.

Underreporting is also a common problem, as absent male parents are included in survey interviews without any or with inadequate information about their parental status. Issues include response burden, the length of questionnaires, and item difficulty. Another issue is the sensitivity of some items (sexuality, drug use; Turner et al., 1996). Changing family structures also represent a challenge for data collection. Many previous surveys have not measured the varied family forms that now exist, such as cohabiting unions, unmarried couples, single-parent families with nonresident fathers, never-married fathers, families with other relatives playing important parenting roles in children's lives, and families with extended networks beyond the household. Methods for addressing these challenges are often inadequate (Cherlin & Griffith, 1998; Garfinkel et al., 2001).

Mothers are able to report on paternal education, age, and work status quite accurately, as assessed by comparisons of mother and father report in the Fragile Families Study (Teitler, 2001). In the Fragile Families Study, for example, the concordance between maternal report of fathers' education, age, and work status and the fathers' report is very high (Teitler, 2001). However, maternal report of fathers' attitudes, mental health, and drug use is not as accurate. Unwed mothers and fathers are usually, but not always, in agreement as to the nature of their relationship (cohabiting, living apart but still in a romantic relationship, having an on-and-off again romantic relationship, and just being friends (Garfinkel et al., 2001).

Given the recent impetus to include fathers in research programs and in policies, questions are being asked, such as: Who are fathers? How are they involved in their children's lives? What impact does this involvement have on children's development? How does this happen? And how can public policies maximize father's involvement? The result is an emerging body of research on fathers that will advance our understanding of how mothers and fathers influence their children's well-being and how can public policies maximize fathers' involvement. To address these questions, a body of research on fathers is emerging that will advance our understanding of how mothers and fathers influence their children's well-being. Despite methodological advances, there are still barriers to overcome. These include (a) the validity of fathers' self-report, because this relies on respondents' estimates as opposed to full-scale time diaries; (b) the reporting of generic father-

TABLE 19.7

Description of Fathers' Capacities by Couple Relationship Status from Seven
Fragile Family Study Cities

	Married N = 478	Cohabiting N = 678	Stable Romantic N = 347	Unstable Romantic N = 95	Just Friends N = 101	Not Friends N = 35
HEALTH BEHAVIOR						
Health Status						
Poor-Fair	7	8	4	9	13	14
Depression						
Moderate-High	10	20	25	34	20	29
Alcohol Use						
Several times/wk.	17	17	18	23	17	26
Drug Use						
Several times/month	3	11	10	15	12	20
Tobacco Use						
Current Smoker	23	43	43	41	38	49
Domestic Violence						
Yes	2	3	3	5	7	11
DEMOGRAPHICS						
Age						
Less than 20	0	9	18	13	12	20
30 and older	60	30	22	31	33	17
Education						
Less than H.S.	22	37	39	39	31	51
College Degree	26	3	1	3	5	3
Race/Ethnicity						
Non-Hisp. White	32	10	3	3	7	6
Non-Hisp. Black	37	61	81	84	81	77
Hispanic	25	26	13	11	8	14

(From Wilson & Brooks-Gunn, 2001)

ing versus specific fathering, because large-scale surveys do not always identify a target child so fathers evaluate generic fathering rather than child-specific fathering; and (c) the generalization of findings from middle-class European-American groups to other cultural groups. The design of measures that capture what fathers do and that are sensitive to variations across families, cultures, and ethnicities remains a challenge in father involvement research (Cabrera et al., 2000).

Despite these conceptual and methodological barriers, much is being learned that will advance both our substantive understanding and our ability to collect data in the future on fathers. These data will be critical to answer today's pressing policy questions: How do we strengthen families that include mothers and fathers, regardless of family structure? How do low-income fathers engage with their children? What are major barriers (lack of employment, substance abuse, etc.) to positive father involvement? How can we design interventions that improve father/mother/child interactions that ultimately lead to better outcomes for children and parents?

ACKNOWLEDGMENTS

We appreciate the contribution of our collaborators in the three studies highlighted in this chapter. These include the members of the Early Head Start Research and Evaluation Project Fatherhood Study Workgroup (Robert Bradley, Carollee Howes, Shira Rosenblatt, Paul Spicer, JoAnn Robinson, Jeffrey Shears, Jon Korfmacher, Trinidad Sanchez, Shavaun Wall, Nancy Smith, Nancy Taylor, Carla Peterson, JeanAnn Summers, Cynthia Gibbons, Rachel Schiffman, Hiram Fitzgerald, Kathy Thornburg, Kathy Fuger, Mark Fine, Catherine Tamis-LeMonda, Mark Spellman, Jacqueline Shannon, Barbara Greenstein, Brian Wilcox, Ross Thompson, Carol McAllister, James Butler, Monique Bethae, Laurie Mulvey, Susan Pickrel, Lori Roggman, Lisa Boyce, Jerry Cook, Barbara Pan, Mark Langager, Sarah Shaw, Dake Coker, Eduardo Armigo, Joe Stowitschek, Susan Spieker, Anthippy Petras, Gina Barclay McLaughlin, Kimberly Boller, John Love, Welmoet van Kammen, Susan Sprachman, Kathleen Coolahan, Cheri Vogel, Charles Nagatoshi, Jeanne Brooks-Gunn, Allison Filigni, Rebecca Ryan, Lisa Berlin, Helen Raikes, Louisa Tarullo, Frankie Gibson, Rachel Chazan Cohen, Linda Mellgren, Martha Moorehouse, Natasha Cabrera, Michael Lamb, and Ron Mincy). The Fragile Families and Child Wellbeing Study Team has also contributed to this chapter (Sarah McLanahan, Irwin Garfinkel, Marta Tienda, Jeanne Brooks-Gunn, Julien Teitler, and Nancy Reichman). Additionally, the members of the NICHD Research Network on Child and Family Well-Being Workgroup on Fatherhood's counsel is appreciated, especially that of Tamara Halle, Jacinta Bronte-Tinkew, Elizabeth Peters, Jeffrey Evans, and Sandra Hofferth. We are grateful for the work of the DADS Consortium as well as the Interagency Forum on Child and Family Statistics. We would also like to thank several members of the Early Childhood Longitudinal Study—Birth Cohort team, in particular Christine Nord and Kirsten Ellingsen, both of Westat, and Naomi Richman and Liza Reaney from the Education Statistics Services Institute. We are also appreciative of Laura Mielcarek's contribution to manuscript preparation. The writing of this chapter has been funded through the NICHD Research Network on Child and Family Well-Being.

REFERENCES

Amato, P. R., & Gilbreth, J. G. (1999). Nonresidential fathers and children's well-being: A meta-analysis. *Journal of Marriage and the Family, 56,* 555–573.

Berlin, L. J., Brady-Smith, C., & Brooks-Gunn, J. (in press). Links between childbearing age and observed maternal behaviors with 14-month-olds in the Early Head Start Research and Evaluation Project. *Infant Mental Health Journal [Special Issue on Early Head Start].*

Booth, A., & Crouter, A. C. (1998). *Men in families: When do they get involved? What difference does it make?* Mahwah, NJ: Lawrence Erlbaum Associates.

Brooks-Gunn, J., Berlin, L. J., Leventhal, T., & Fuligni, A. (2000). Depending on the kindness of strangers: Current national data initiatives and developmental research. [Special Issue on "New Directions for Child Development in the Twenty-First Century"]. *Child Development, 71,* 257–267.

Burton, L. M., & Snyder, A. R. (1998). The invisible man revisited: Comments on the life course, history, and men's roles in American families. In A. Booth & A. C. Crouter (Eds.), *Men in Families.* Hillsdale, NJ: Lawrence Erlbaum Associates.

Cabrera, N. (1999, August). *How are we measuring father involvement in the Early Head Start Evaluation?* (PHS 00–1025). Proceedings of the National Conference on Health Statistics. Health in the New Millennium: Making Choices, Measuring Impact, Washington, DC.

Cabrera, N. J., Tamis-LeMonda, C. S., Bradley, R. H., Hofferth, S., & Lamb, M. E. (2000). Fatherhood in the twenty-first century. *Child Development, 71,* 127–136.

Cherlin, A. J., & Griffith, J. (1998). Report of the working group on the methodology of studying fathers. In *Nurturing fatherhood: Improving data and research on male fertility, family formation and fatherhood.* Washington, DC: U.S. Government Printing Office.

Eggebeen, D. J., & Knoester, C. (2001). Does fatherhood matter for men? *Journal of Marriage and Family, 63,* 381–393.

Federal Interagency Forum on Child and Family Statistics. (1998). *Nurturing fatherhood: Improving data and research on male fertility, family formation and fatherhood.* Washington, DC: U.S. Government Printing Office.

Fuligni, A. F., & Brooks-Gunn, J. (in press). Family support initiatives. In A. F. Fuligni & J. Brooks-Gunn (Eds.), *Synthesis and profiles of early education and development: Research and intervention initiatives.* Washington, DC: U.S. Department of Education.

Garfinkel, I., McLanahan, S. S., & Hanson, T. L. (1998). A patchwork portrait of nonresident fathers. In I. Garpike, S. McLanahan, D. R. Meyer, & J. A. Seltzer (Eds.), *Fathers under fire.* New York: Russell Sage Foundation.

Garfinkel, I., McLanahan, S., Tienda, M., & Brooks-Gunn, J. (2001). Fragile families and welfare reform. *Children and Youth Services Review, 23,* 277–301.

Greene, A. D., Halle, T. G., LeMenestrel, S., & Moore, K. A. (1998). *Father involvement in young children's lives: Recommendations for a fatherhood module for the ECLS-B.* Paper prepared for the National Center for Education and Statistics by Child Trends, Inc., Washington, DC.

Lamb, M. E. (2000). The history of research on father involvement: An overview. *Marriage and Family Review, 29,* 23–42.

Lamb, M. E., Pleck, J. H., Charnov, E. L., & Levine, J. A. (1985). The role of the father in child development: The effects of increased paternal involvement. In B. B. Lahey & A. E. Kazdin (Eds.), *Advances in clinical child psychology* (Vol. 8, pp. 229–266). New York: Plenum.

Levine, D. B., & Bryant, E. C. (1997). *An examination of alternative approaches to selecting a sample of new births.* Paper prepared for the National Center for Education Statistics, Office of Educational Research & Improvement. U.S. Department of Education.

Marsiglio, W. (1995). *Fatherhood: Contemporary theory, research, and social policy.* Thousand Oaks, CA: Sage.

National Center for Education Statistics. (1999). *Early Childhood Longitudinal Study: Birth Cohort 2000.* http://nces.ed.gov

Nord, C. W., Brimhall, D., & West, J. (1997). *Father's involvement in schools.* Washington, DC: U.S. Department of Education.

Nord, C. W., & West, J. (2001). *Fathers' and mothers' involvement in their children's schools by family type and resident status.* (NCES Publication No. 2001032). Washington, DC: National Center for Education Statistics.

Parke, R. (1995). Father and families. In M. Bornstein (Ed.), *Handbook of parenting: Vol. 3. Status and social conditions of parenting* (pp. 27–64). Mahwah, NJ: Lawrence Erlbaum Associates.

Raikes, H. H., & the EHS Research Consortium Father Studies Workgroup. (2000, April). *Father involvement in Early Head Start: Listening to the voices of fathers, mothers, and program staff.* Invited presentation at the annual meeting of the National Head Start Association, Washington, DC.

Reichman, N., Teitler, J., Garfinkel, I., & McLanahan, S. (2001). The Fragile Families and Child Wellbeing Study: Background, research design, and sampling issues. *Children and Youth Services Review, 23,* 303–326.

Robertson, J. (1995). Are young noncustodial fathers left behind in the labor market? Ph.D. Dissertation, Columbia University, New York.

Sorensen, E. (1997, March). *Nonresident fathers: What we know and what's left to learn?* Paper presented at Conference on Fathering and Male Fertility: Improving Data and Research, Bethesda, MD.

Tamis-LeMonda, C. S., & Cabrera, N. (1999). Perspectives on father involvement: Research and policy. *Social Policy Report, 13*(2), 1–26.

Teitler, J. (2001). Father involvement, child health and maternal health behavior. *Children and Youth Services Review, 23,* 403–425.

Turner, C., Forsyth, B., Reilly, J., & Miller, H. (1996, December). *Automated self-interviewing in surveys.* Paper presented at the International Conference on Computer Assisted Survey Information Collection, San Antonio, TX.

Ventura, S. J., Bachrach, C. A., Hill, L., Kay, K., Holcomb, P., & Koff, E. (1995). *The demography of out-of-wedlock childbearing.* Report to Congress on Out-of-Wedlock Births, Washington, DC.

Western, B., & McLanahan, S. (2000). Fathers behind bars: The impact of incarceration on family formation. In G. L. Fox & M. L. Benson (Eds.), *Families, crime, and criminal justice: Vol. 2. Charting the linkages* (pp. 307–322). New York: JAI Press.

Wilson, M., & Brooks-Gunn, J. (2001). Health status and behaviors of unwed fathers. *Children and Youth Services Review, 23*(4–5), 377–401.

20

Sustaining Fragile Fatherhood

Father Involvement Among Low-Income, Noncustodial African-American Fathers in Philadelphia

Timothy J. Nelson
Northwestern University

Susan Clampet-Lundquist
University of Pennsylvania

Kathryn Edin
Northwestern University

New census data on family living arrangements suggest that fewer fathers may be participating in their children's lives than in any period since the United States began keeping reliable statistics. Many fathers disengage economically and emotionally with their children when they separate or divorce. This is particularly true of low-income fathers, many of whom have never been married to their child's mother or have even lived in the same household. However, recent evidence from the Fragile Families and Child Wellbeing Study shows that the majority of unwed fathers—most of whom are low income—are very involved in their children's lives early on. In fact, half live with the mothers when the child is born, and most provide economic support during pregnancy. Furthermore, when interviewed shortly after their child's birth, most want to remain involved with the child and intend to continue their financial support (Carlson & McLanahan, 2001). Despite these good intentions, father involvement fades dramatically over time, and in the end, most of these children spend the majority of their childhood without the economic and emotional support of fathers.

As welfare time limits have loomed ever closer, the issue of fathers' responsibility has taken on a new importance, and there is tremendous interest in identifying factors that predict whether a father will remain financially and emotionally supportive of his child, as well as the impact that such involvement has on children. An array of public and private initiatives has attempted to find ways to encourage the participation of noncustodial fathers in their children's lives and include components such as mediation between the parents, workforce development, parent training, and modification of child support orders. Although some programs show significant effects on some aspects of father involvement, few of these effects are large, and they are not consistent across studies or even across program sites within studies (e.g., see Johnson, Levine, & Doolittle, 1999).

Why has it proven so difficult to get fathers to become and/or remain involved with their children? One lesson we take from these results is that we may still know too little about the lives of low-income noncustodial fathers and the barriers to involvement they face. We focus our analysis on three themes: (a) what impact fatherhood has on fathers' lifestyles, identities, and aspirations, and on how men construct the fatherhood role; (b) the social forces that work for or against men as they try to fulfill the fathering role to their own, their children's mothers', or their children's, satisfaction; and (c) how fathers manage their desire to fulfill their roles as fathers given the limitations they face.

LITERATURE REVIEW

Though there is a surge of recent interest in the lives of low-income noncustodial fathers, relatively little is known about them. This is partly due to their lack of adequate representation in locally or nationally representative surveys (Cherlin, Griffith, & McCarthy, 1983; Seltzer & Brandreth, 1994). Though low-income fathers, minority fathers, and never-married fathers are most seriously underrepresented in such surveys, there is no group of noncustodial fathers for which there are not large underrepresentation problems (Garfinkel, McLanahan, & Hanson, 1998; Sorensen, 1997).[1] This underrepresentation happens for at least two reasons. First, some fathers apparently respond to surveys but do not admit to interviewers that they are fathers. Second, some fathers are apparently not represented at all, because standard sampling techniques miss them (Garfinkel et al., 1998).

---

[1]Scholars estimate underrepresentation by assuming assortive mating (see Garfinkel, McLanahan, & Hanson, 1998). Because surveys do seem to adequately represent single mothers, assumptions about fathers are made based on the characteristics of mothers. When 50% of women in a particular demographic group admit to being mothers and only 25% of fathers, for example, we might reasonably suspect that only 50% of fathers are represented. Although it could be true that this method overestimates the underrepresentation problem (in this scenario, there would be two groups of fathers; one with a lot of children and one with no children, and the men who were fathers would have greater numbers of children than the women who were mothers), we know of no evidence to suggest this is true. Indeed, the opposite case could just as easily be made.

Much of the literature on fathers has been spurred by a policy interest in child support. As the social safety net for poor single mothers and children has unraveled, state and federal governments have placed increasing importance on reconnecting the fathers of welfare-reliant children economically with their families. In the late 1970s, only 60% of all potentially eligible mothers nationwide had a court-ordered child support award. Of those mothers who had such an award, only half reported that they received the full amount owed. One quarter got only a portion of the amount owned, and the other quarter got nothing (U.S. Census Bureau, 1983, 1995). Of the 40% with no formal child support award, less than 20% told survey researchers they received any support informally (Seltzer, 1995; Teachman, 1991).

The factors behind these dismal statistics are complex, but scholars have argued that for many fathers, inability to pay is not the issue. One study argued that noncustodial fathers as a group could pay nearly twice the amount they paid in 1996 (Sorensen, 1997), whereas another concluded that they could pay roughly three times what they actually contribute (Garfinkel & Oellerich, 1992). Of course, fathers' characteristics do influence their ability to pay. The average non-White father has half the income of a typical White father, and a never-married father has half the income of his divorced counterpart (Garfinkel & Oellerich, 1989; Miller, Garfinkel, & McLanahan, 1997). Garfinkel et al. (1998) estimate that 31% of nonresident fathers are African American, and 53% were not married to the mother when the child was born. Thus, large numbers of noncustodial fathers may have difficulty making substantial contributions toward the care of their noncustodial children.[2]

Although *ability* to pay is an issue for some fathers, their *willingness* to pay varies along several dimensions. One study of divorced fathers in Wisconsin showed that payments are affected by the existence of a court order, both the father's and the mother's income, and the degree of state-imposed punishment for noncompliance (Del Boca & Flinn, 1995). A longitudinal analysis of divorced fathers in an Arizona county shows that noncustodial fathers who feel they have some control over parenting decisions also tend to pay more (Braver et al., 1993).

We also have survey data on levels of father involvement, with the general finding that involvement among all noncustodial fathers is rather low (Furstenberg & Harris, 1992). In general, divorced and separated fathers see their children more often than never-married fathers (King, 1994). However, there is one important exception to this pattern: rates of involvement are extraordinarily high among African-American fathers with very young children (Isaacs & Leon, 1987; Mott,

---

[2]It is also true that the child support system is regressive. Among those fathers who are subject to a court-ordered child support award, low-income fathers are assessed a significantly higher proportion of their income than more affluent fathers. When we look at actual payment rates for those fathers who do pay, we find that low-income fathers pay 28% of their income, as opposed to 10% for more affluent fathers (Sorensen, 1997).

1990; Stier & Tienda, 1993; see also King, 1994). In general, fathers of younger children are more likely to visit than are fathers of older children (Furstenberg & Harris, 1992; Leadbeater, Way, & Raden, 1988; Lerman, 1993), and in fact, father involvement drops off dramatically as children age and as the time since the father last lived with his child increases.

METHOD

We draw data from 40 African-American fathers in the Philadelphia metropolitan area whom we interviewed in-depth on at least two occasions between 1996 and 1998. They were between 16 and 50 years of age, had at least one noncustodial child under the age of 18, and earned less than $8 an hour in the formal economy. All of the respondents lived in one of nine target neighborhoods throughout Philadelphia and its poorest inner suburb (Camden, NJ) which we identified using 1990 census data. For each ethnic group (the larger study encompasses three ethnic groups), we used two criteria to select these neighborhoods: the proportion of the population of a particular race and ethnic group within a cluster of census tracts, and that group's poverty rate averaged across these tracts.

In each target neighborhood, we conducted several months of fieldwork to establish local contacts. By talking with employers, grassroots community leaders, and social service providers, we attempted to establish the range of unskilled and semiskilled noncustodial fathers we might expect to find in these neighborhoods. Using these contacts, we began to garner referrals to fathers. However, these sources were not sufficient, because few low-income noncustodial fathers seemed to have ties with these community leaders and institutions. After contacting these men, we found establishing rapport to be difficult and time consuming because fathers often mistrusted the referring agencies.

By trial and error, we were generally able to sort out the least problematic of our referral sources, but we also utilized street contacts (cold contacts made on street corners that may serve as hangouts, informal sector day labor corners, and so on) and snowball referrals (from fathers who participated to other fathers). To strike a balance between the need for trust and the necessity of recruiting as heterogeneous a sample as possible, we adopted the rule that within each study subcell, our goal was to recruit no more than five fathers from any given social network. The advantage of our neighborhood-specific approach was that our faces became familiar to neighborhood residents, and through word of mouth, fathers became more trusting of us as time went on. The lesson that we learned from these difficulties was that there is no substitute for old-fashioned fieldwork when approaching members of a highly stigmatized group.

After a father agreed to participate in the study, we made an appointment to meet him at his home or, more commonly, at a public place within his neighborhood, as many fathers were living with girlfriends, sisters, and their own mothers, and wanted more privacy than these settings would afford. To protect confidentiality, we asked each father to choose a pseudonym, which we attached to all of the data we gathered for each father (and which we use in this chapter). Interviewers typically engaged each father in two or more conversations. These conversations were semistructured, so that the interviewer eventually covered an extensive list of predetermined topics, but tried to make these conversations as natural as possible by following up on cues given by respondents in the course of the conversation. Therefore, respondents generally determined the order in which the topics were covered. The precise way in which the question was asked also varied from interview to interview. This study of Philadelphia low-income noncustodial fathers is ongoing and will eventually capture data from in-depth interviews with fathers in three cities representing each major ethnic group within that city for a total sample of 480.

FINDINGS

We divide our analysis of interview data into three basic sections. First we look at what fathers say about the impact of children on their lives. Despite their marginal economic circumstances and their sometimes minimal commitment to the child's mother, most of these men initially welcomed the opportunity to become fathers. They also recognized at least some of the requirements of fathering and were determined to embrace these responsibilities. However, despite these good intentions, fathers often fail to live up to these standards for reasons described in the second section. Finally, most fathers persevere in their attempts to partially fulfill the fathering role for at least one of their children by "doing the best" they can.

Lifestyles and Identities: Before and After

One common theme that emerged from our interviews was the often dramatic impact of becoming a father on men's lifestyles. The stories fathers told us sometimes had the flavor of testimonies and were structured into "before" and "after" accounts. Typically, these men had been involved in selling or using drugs, hanging out on the corner, and "messing with" several different women; however, many reported a dramatic change in their behavior when they became fathers. Ahmad,[3] a 19-year-old Camden high school graduate who works in the formal sector and regularly spends time with his daughter (though he provides only intermittent financial help), described the impact the birth of his daughter had on his life as follows:

---

[3]All names have been changed.

She changed my life a lot. I was headed down the wrong path. I grew up on the streets, everything from drugs to this and that. I mean, I've been in jail before. But ever since she's been born, I slowed down a lot. You know. . . . 'Cause it's like, before her, I didn't really care too much about anything. I really just lived every day for that day. But as of now, I'm living every day for today and tomorrow. . . . Until she was born, you couldn't tell me nothing, you know.

These sentiments were echoed by Bucket, a 46-year-old father of one adult daughter and one 12-year-old daughter. Bucket has a GED and does odd jobs (mostly window washing) and sees his youngest daughter twice a month, yet offers no financial support.

I always wanted to be a father. I always wanted a child. I waited until I was 25 years old before I had my first child, but I always wanted to be a father. Before I had her, [I was] in trouble. I was doing wrong things. I was wild, crazy. It always seems as though I was getting in some kind of trouble.

Fathers often embraced these lifestyle changes brought about by their new role enthusiastically and did not merely accept them with reluctance. Robert, a 23-year-old father, sees his 6-month-old son frequently and contributes a portion of his earnings from his full-time formal-sector job intermittently. When we asked him how the pregnancy of his girlfriend and birth of his son had affected him, he told us,

Yeah, it has definitely changed my day-to-day life because I know that for the whole nine months my girl was pregnant and to this date, I have been like totally with her, if not physically at least like on the phone, [asking] "How is everything?" I don't talk to anybody like my friends and how I used to go to parties and things like that. And it is not because I feel like "Oh darn, I can't go out." I want to be there. I want to be with my son, you know. I would rather know what is going on with him then be somewhere, because even when I am out, I am like thinking about him. [I have] reoriented [my life].

According to many of these fathers, their child's birth literally "saved" them from the streets. The salvation theme was fairly strong in virtually all of the interviews with fathers who maintained some level of involvement with their child. Even for those fathers whose involvement had lapsed, many still used this salvation motif to describe how their lives had been transformed by a child's birth.[4] For some fathers the first child was a sufficient impetus to leave the streets, while for others, the transformation did not occur until a second or third child was born (and he was older).

---

[4]Few of our fathers told us they had never been involved in their child's lives. Those that did viewed the "lack of that bond" as a tragic loss and said they regretted that they were just "daddies" and not "real fathers."

In addition to these retrospective accounts of lifestyle changes, the impact of fatherhood is also apparent from the answers fathers gave when we asked them to imagine what their lives would be like if they had never had children. Despite a few stories of thwarted plans for schooling or a missed job opportunity, the overwhelming majority of fathers we interviewed believed strongly (even passionately) that their situations would be much worse without the presence of children in their lives. The most involved fathers spoke most poignantly to this point, but many less-involved fathers (and even some completely uninvolved fathers) said their lives would mean very little if they had not yet fathered a child. Kevin, a 21-year-old father with a GED, does not work regularly but "baby-sits" his toddler each day while the child's mother works. Kevin contributes financially when he picks up odd jobs on weekends.

> I think [my life] would be a lot different to tell you the truth. Yeah, [I would be] getting into trouble. No, I wouldn't be settled. I'd probably, you know, honestly, I'd probably be in jail or something like that, you know. [Having a kid] calms you down.

Bucket, whom we described previously, told us,

> I'd probably still be doing the things I was doing. 'Cause when I did have my first child, it changed me. It stopped me from doing all this stuff I was doing before. So maybe I'd still be doing the things I was doing before if I didn't have her. (Q: What stuff?) Oh, you know, I was on the weed, drinking. If I didn't have [my children], I'd still be doing that. . . . Because [of them] I stopped hanging with different people, I stopped going certain places, you know what I mean. And I got an outlook on life that was different.

Some men claimed that their status as fathers was incompatible with selling drugs, something many had been involved in before they became fathers. Nelson asked Robert, also described earlier, if he would consider selling drugs again to clear up his financial problems. He replied:

> [No], I want to keep it clean, and that is the hardest thing. I could do that and probably make three times over [what I'm making now], and probably get out of all of this [financial mess]. But I don't think that it would make me a better person because it would make me paranoid, and plus I would be bringing an environment around my child that I just do not want. Beeping at 12:00 at night and things of that nature—because I used to do that type of thing when I was younger. I experienced it.

This change in lifestyle was not so immediate for some fathers as it was for Robert. Several told us how they continued to sell or use drugs and "party" after the birth of a child, and a few had even entered the drug trade (usually briefly) specifically to buy a bassinet and/or crib, a changing table, a stroller or "baby coach," blankets, bibs, clothing, and other standard accoutrements of babyhood. Because part of how women demonstrate their adequacy as mothers is predicated on the quality of these items, fathers said that a secondhand crib or hand-me-down stroller wasn't generally up to her standard and that only new items would suffice.

Those fathers who stayed in the drug trade or continued to abuse drugs or alcohol believed strongly that such activity was incompatible with their parenting role. Some said they kept a distance from their children at these points in their lives, while others said it was the mothers who kept them away from their children. This was especially important once the children were old enough to make moral judgments about their fathers' behavior. Peanut, a 35-year-old father who is addicted to both crack and alcohol, dropped out of high school in the 10th grade and relied on hustling odd jobs to get by. Though he supported his daughter both emotionally and economically during the first few years of her life, he seldom sees his daughter now and contributes nothing to her support. He described the conflict between his drug addition and his ability to parent in this way.

> I didn't want [my daughter staying by] me, 'cause I meet with a bunch of dudes and crazy females. So I didn't want her around me. She don't know about my drug addiction, but she know I drink, and that's about it.

Maurice, a 38-year-old father of four, had been severely drug addicted and homeless for several years. Now clean and holding a steady job, he both visits his children and contributes toward their support. He recalled how his drug addiction affected his relationship with his children:

> The lifestyle I was leading at that time . . . my kids played no role in my life at all. I ducked them every chance. I would [do that] because I didn't want them to see me the way that I was. No child support this whole time, no child support whatsoever and it was a lot of years—years away from my kids that I can't make up.

During the "drug years," many fathers told us they cut themselves off from virtually all contact with their own close kin, and for the same reasons they distanced themselves from their children. Those men whose lifestyles didn't change immediately on becoming parents did generally "settle down" after a few years, at which point they attempted to become more involved with their children and other kin. Seven is a 37-year-old father of five children, ranging from ages 1 to 19 years. He lives with the mother of his youngest child but has little contact with his older children, financial or otherwise.

> I try to be a good dad. I try to be a well-rounded father. I don't drink [though] I do smoke cigarettes. I don't smoke marijuana. My drug use—when I was using drugs my kids were infants and so they have no knowledge of me using any drugs. As they got older [and started to pick up on things], my life started to change and the things that I used to do I didn't do any more.

For fathers who did not change their "street" lifestyle early in their child's life, that decision usually had a profound effect on their ability to reinsert themselves into their children's lives when they were older. This is a point we return to later in this chapter.

Fathers' retrospective descriptions of the months following a revelation of their girlfriend's pregnancy also attest to their perceived ability and willingness to become parents. We asked our respondents to think back to that time and to tell us two things: if they had discussed having children prior to the pregnancy, and to describe what went through their minds when they found out about the pregnancy, including whether they had considered abortion or adoption. Only a few of the fathers we spoke to talked of actually "planning" these pregnancies. On the other hand, many freely admitted that they knew such pregnancies were a distinct possibility, given the fact that almost none of them used birth control. For that reason, we characterize many of these pregnancies as unplanned but not accidental (see Nelson, Edin, & Torres, 2001). Peanut spoke for many fathers when he said,

> I knew it could happen, but I wasn't think[ing] about it. I wasn't thinking nothing about it, but I knew it could happen. We were both adults. I was 21 and she was 23. So it wasn't like we were two kids. We knew there was a chance. We didn't use no protection so—(Q: Why not?) I don't know really, I was only messing with her. And she wasn't messing with nobody [else either]. You know what I mean? So you could say that it was not unplanned but not planned. We took a chance. (Q: Did you sit down and talk about it?) No, not really. She had said once that she would like to have kids, but I laughed at her. I wasn't ready for no children. But she did hit me with it. And then when it did happen, I was like "Oh shit!"

Despite the casual way in which Peanut became a father, once he knew that a child was on the way, he claimed he unequivocally and proudly accepted his new role as a father.

> [This was] my first child. I wanted it. I was proud. And it was her first child—she wanted it. Now what happened after that [in our relationship] was a little screwed up. But at the time, we both wanted that child. Once she found out and once she told me, there wasn't no abortion [talk] or nothing [like that] at all.

Bucket forcefully reiterated the fact that he had wanted to become a father at many points during the interview. When asked about his reaction to his girlfriend's pregnancy, he replied, "I was happy. My first child, you know what I mean? I'm 25. I'm on my own. Ready to have a kid. Shoot, I was happy, man. I wanted her, man. I wanted my child. . . . She's a good girl. I wanted her, man."

For many of the men we spoke to, their decision to accept the responsibility of parenthood came out of a desire to rectify the failings of their own fathers. Andre was a 36-year-old Camden resident whose own father abandoned the family right after his mother died, when he was 3 years old. His eldest sister, a senior in high school at the time, raised Andre and his four siblings. Andre described his reaction to his girlfriend's pregnancy as follows:

> After we went together for a while I got her pregnant, and the first thing that hit my mind, was—I was 18—and first thing that hit my mind was, "I do not want to be like my dad. I got to get a job." I graduated the 11th grade and was going to the 12th grade, but this is the summer between the 11th and 12th grade, and I said, "Look, ain't no sense in me going back to school. I need a job."

Although his drug addiction ultimately prevented Andre from holding to this promise, he told one of our interviewers how the absence of his own father had made him resolve not to repeat the pattern with his own children:

> I have resentment towards my father because he wasn't in the household like other people I knew. I knew a father was supposed to be in the household at a real early age, and I promised myself when I was like nine or ten years old that when I had a child . . . I would be there for them all the time. I would be in the household.

Another factor that may serve as an indication of these fathers' attachment to the fathering role was that they almost always desired their sons and daughters to have their last names, a wish that the children's mothers sometimes agreed to and complied with, and sometimes did not. When Nelson asked Martinis if he was excited or worried when he found out he was going to become a father, he replied, "Both. I realized one thing—I'm your dad no matter what, so . . . I wanted her to have my last name." Forty-year-old Martinis has three children (18, 17, and 2) including the 2-year-old daughter he refers to, but only sees them rarely because of a recent spell in prison. Yet, he insisted he had a deeper bond with his youngest child because she carried his last name (unlike the older two).

Such declarations about the irrevocable nature of one's status as a father ("I'm your dad, no matter what") and the responsibilities that it entails are quite common among the men we interviewed. Dayton, a 30-year-old Philadelphia resident, has three children under the age of 7. He has no high school diploma, works sporadically, and sees his children "off and on." Two of the three mothers of his children have formal child support orders, and Dayton is deeply in arrears. He feels it is almost impossible for him to pay child support on a regular basis because he cannot find a steady job and has been in and out of prison. Yet, Dayton states emphatically that, "Once you have [children], then you got to live for them. It ain't just about you no more, it's about them." Lavelle is a 34-year-old Camden resident and father of a 6-year-old daughter who he sees each weekend and supports financially. When Nelson asked him if being a father was more difficult than he had expected, he responded, "Well, you brought a little life into this world that you wanna be responsible for, everybody say 'til [they are] 18, but [I say] for the rest of your life. You are responsible for them for the rest of your life, and you gotta make sure [they are okay]." Robert, a college dropout with a steady job who both visits and supports his 6-month-old son, wanted to send a message to other men in his situation:

> Just say to all the young fathers out there, black, white or whatever, you got to work, you got to support your responsibilities. You are fifty percent responsible, regardless of whatever the situation is and if you are going to be with the girl or without the girl, you still going to have the kid, so you still got to act accordingly and be a man and be a father.

One of the reasons that men place such a high value on having children is that their offspring present virtually the only possibility (in their view) of achieving any sort of upward mobility. Living vicariously through one's children and sacrificing so that they can have more is a powerful theme in countless American narratives. For these fathers, producing a child who might grow up to be successful also had powerful symbolic value, even if they were only minimally involved in the lives of these offspring. Albert, a 23-year-old high school graduate who works as a prep cook, reflects on his 7-year-old daughter (who he frequently sees and consistently supports) and on his hopes for her future:

> So it's just funny, it's somebody so much like you and it's like being in a room with yourself. . . . Maybe—I mean, you could say maybe a better image of me, you know. What I accomplished, I feel she could do twice as better. So it's like basically making a duplicate of yourself but just making it better, you know. Certain flaws you have in yourself aren't [there]. So I can see, whatever I accomplished I know she can accomplish three times over or two times over.

The idea that children represent extensions of one's self and the desire that these children go on to achieve greater things is often connected to the physical resemblance between father and child. In fathers' accounts, this "immortality" theme is often interwoven with the mobility theme. For example, Robert said, "I like having a son because he looks like me, and he is a lot of fun. I look at him and I think of all the things that I want him to be and do. Like more things than I did— different things." Sometimes these fathers' desires seemed to center simply on their children not repeating the mistakes they felt that they had made in life.

In some fathers' accounts, the immortality theme was tied into a fear that, given the violence that permeated their neighborhoods, they might not live much longer. In case of their death, they wanted to leave behind "some evidence that I was on the planet." A few fathers told us that it was this sense of mortality that led them to choose "strong and independent" women to bear their children. Maurice recounted:

> When I was sixteen and seventeen years old, I didn't never think I was going to make it to be 35 years old. I thought I was going to be shot in the streets somewhere.

I thought I would be dead somewhere by now. . . . I always tell they mother, "That is the reason that I chose you to be my kids' mother, because you are strong enough. You are a strong, independent black woman that you can raise these kids by yourself if you had to."

As some of the quotes indicate, fathers often felt an especially close attachment to their male children. This seemed to be not only because of the legacy that a son could carry on, but also because they felt that they could identify with a son more than a daughter, because they felt more adequate and able in their dealings with sons than with daughters, and because they felt that their sons needed them more than their daughters did. Martinis, who was in prison when his son was born, described his feelings about his children and how their sex affected his behavior toward them, even though he was unable to be around for his sons:

I was kind of happy that [my first child was a son]. When [my daughter] was born, I didn't really feel the same. . . . I mean, I appreciated her and everything, she was a beautiful little girl and I cared for her and I loved her too, but it was like, I wanted a son for some reason. . . . It was like my first son and I did a lot of things for him and spent a lot of time with him.

Martinis went on to connect his involvement with his son to his belief that male children need their fathers around more than female children do.

[Fathers need] to be able to give the children guidance, especially the male children. Yeah, they [males] need to have their dads around, especially little guys to know what it is to be a guy. Dads do give them guidance on a lot of different things. Instead of just being a dad, also you can be a friend. I think it is very important to guys to be with they dad, to be there and give them guidance.

Lamont, a 33-year-old Camden father, is a factory worker whose sons (ages 8 and 10) stay with him each weekend. Lamont told Nelson, "A son always look for the man, you know what I'm saying, 'cause that's who he has to try to step after, you know what I'm saying. It's following steps that women can't carry him into." Ahmad related the importance of fathers to his own lack of a father figure when he was growing up:

[I] was rebellious because I didn't have a father . . . to keep me in line or to keep me motivated, or even keep me aspired or inspired. And that is a very important part of a young man's upbringing, because a woman cannot necessarily give a son the things that a father can give a son. Just like a father can't give necessarily some of the things to his daughter that a mother can give a daughter.

To summarize, fathers' accounts suggest that children may play a powerful role in their lives. In general, fathers report that fatherhood motivates them to leave street life and engage in more mainstream pursuits. Fathers' descriptions of children's ongoing roles in their lives suggest that children have tremendous value to fathers irrespective of the level of father involvement. Fathers do, however, voice strong beliefs about the responsibilities fatherhood entails and generally intend to fulfill these responsibilities to the best of their ability.

Forces Contributing to Role Failure

Despite the willingness and strong sense of commitment with which most men approached the fathering role, many of the low-income noncustodial fathers we spoke with admitted that they had failed to live up to this commitment at various points in their lives. In this section we examine some of the forces that work against men as they try, some more and some less successfully, to live up to their own expectations as fathers.

For almost all of the men we interviewed, their involvement with their children is profoundly affected by the status of their relationship with the child's mother. Fathers who are still in a romantic relationship with their child's mother show high levels of financial and emotional support. However, once these fathers separate from their children's mothers, this becomes much more problematic. Issues of access to the child, doubts about their paternity, control and authority over the child's upbringing, and financial stability and support come between mothers and fathers and tend to weaken father involvement. In addition, spells of imprisonment, drug and alcohol addiction, and other aspects of the "street" lifestyle, as well as the difficulties with finding stable employment in a weak labor market, all inhibit men in fulfilling their roles as fathers.

Perhaps the biggest obstacle that men face is dealing with their children's mothers who, they claimed, often actively try to keep them from their children. Several fathers reported attempts on the mother's part to legally terminate visitation rights, keep them away through subterfuge or intimidation, or to deny that the child was even theirs. John, a Camden father of three, said that he wanted to develop a close relationship with his child but was prevented from doing so by his child's mother: "We never really had the chance to really get the closeness that I expected. I tried, but his mother was like a (turncoat). That's what I'm saying. I didn't get the chance the way I wanted to. She started keeping him away." Donald, age 37, had a high school diploma and a steady job (though he was currently in a halfway house following imprisonment) and paid child support for his 14-year-old daughter. He said,

[My daughter's mother and I] went back and forth to court more than once. As a matter of fact, we are getting ready to go back again. Not for the [child support] amount, but for the visitation rights. We are going through a thing with that. She is trying to get me out of my daughter's life, [because] she got married.

Ahmad complained about a similar situation with his son:

Unfortunately, since his mother and I are no longer affiliated, she seems to feel that she doesn't necessarily want him and I to have the relationship that we had initially—I would say about maybe three or four years ago. Now he is presently six years of age now, and I haven't seen him for over a year. And that is because, like I said, she and I are no longer in communication. And I have been trying my hardest to contact her but she is making it difficult for that contact to even take place. It is sort of like a retaliation and a malice-type situation.

Even when the mother did not actively try to keep the father away from his child, fathers often report that her actions could make it difficult to maintain involvement with their children. For example, several fathers said that their child's mother initially named another man as the father, and that this confusion hindered their involvement, even after issues of paternity were finally resolved. Steven discussed the bond between himself and his daughter and how it was affected by the mother's actions:

We have a good relationship, don't get me wrong. I am saying on my behalf, I feel as though it was too late. She (his daughter) knew back then what happened because I told her, and she knew that her mom did certain things to prevent me from being a part of her life. Like telling me that she is not my child, then come back two or three years later and say "Well, your daughter, such and such and such a such." I was being confused by this. I call them "the wonder years" [because] I was wondering [whether or not she was mine].

Similarly, if the mother does not give the man's child his last name or place his name on the birth certificate, it can weaken his attachment. For many men, refusing to give a child the father's last name is a mark of profound disrespect for him. Maurice stated,

I want to be a part of this child's life because it is my child. But I got some feelings because of the fact that my name is not on the birth certificate. . . . All my other children have my last name and this one [from a different relationship] doesn't. This one does not even have my name on the birth certificate.

The fathers we spoke to often expressed frustration at what they perceived as the mother's total control over their children's upbringing. Peanut, for example, bitterly complained, "I had no say-so bringing [my daughter] up or nothing. Like I said, the first year was just giving money—going to the store, buying shit. No say-so." Lavelle said, "It is [difficult negotiating with my daughter's mother.] But she's . . . she gave birth to her so, 'It's my way or the highway.' " In Lavelle's situation, this control extended to conditions surrounding visits with his daughter:

She wants to play it off like a package deal, like, "You can't go here without me, you can't take her here without me, you can't take her there without me." I said "Okay, then I'm going to get visitation so I can take her when I want to take her!"

One of the biggest factors contributing to the breakdown in men's relationships with women, one that continues to affect father involvement as the child grows up, is mistrust and disagreements concerning money. Several fathers spoke with frustration and bitterness about their experiences and their perception that all that women wanted from them was money. For example, Donald, who pays child support, said,

> Yeah, their whole thing is "What can you give me?" and "What can I get from you and how fast can I get it?" More or less money-wise. There is no commitment to a real relationship. Particularly in black women, their whole goal is, "Let me see how much I can get for it and how good I can look" and you know. . . . There is no source of commitment in a relationship. Their thing is, "When things go bad [financially], I am out of here." To me, that was my experience and I am not taking it [anymore].

"Boy Boy," a 20-year-old Philadelphia father who has dealt drugs for a living since he was age 10, expressed similar feelings when he exclaimed, "It is about the 'Benjamins' now; if you don't got no hundred dollar bills, you don't got no woman!" This perception of the mercenary nature of women, including their children's mother(s), contributes toward an attitude of mistrust when it comes to giving financial support to their children. Lee has three children. He neither sees nor supports his older two children, but lives with his youngest child's mother and pays some of the household bills. He reports that he used to give his youngest child's mother cash to buy things that she needed for that child, but that he stopped this practice because she would spend it on herself or her friends:

> Oh God, okay. She went shopping. She might spend some on her friends. Spend some on our daughter, her [other] daughter, [and] spend the rest on herself. Okay, she bought food for the house, alcohol, and drugs. If she is with some friends who are trying to sucker her for some dope, they'll suck [the money] up.

John, a disabled 31-year-old father of one child, offers irregular financial support (from his SSI check and his side jobs) to a 6-year-old daughter. Yet, he seldom sees her due to ongoing acrimony with her mother. He lamented,

> I have been hurt so many times . . . by different women taking advantage of my money. I give them money to buy clothes and get [the children] stuff and take care of they sneakers, shoes, whatever they want. But they take advantage and try to get the whole [SSI] check. And they lie and say they misplaced the money and they don't misplace it, they spend it on theyselves, and then they want to come back and ask me for [more] money and then didn't buy nothing [for the kids].

Such experiences and perceptions impede fathers' willingness to contribute financially to their children. Many feel that they have little control over how their children's mothers are raising their children or spending the money they give toward their children's support.

Most fathers reported that conflicts with their children's mothers came from demands for more money. However, a few reported that mothers' attempts to keep them out of their children's lives stemmed from an attitude of self-sufficiency once the mother had achieved a certain level of economic stability. Rick is a 26-year-old Camden father who works through several day labor agencies and supports his 2-year-old son financially when he is employed. He relates how the upward mobility of his son's mother changed her attitude toward him and his involvement with his son:

> When I met her, she was on welfare, and she was just, ya know, one of those girls who didn't wanna do nothin.' . . . No, she didn't work then, but she got into this program where, you know, you had to work or go to some kind of classes in order to stay on welfare. . . . So she graduated the classes last year, and they got her a job in—what is it?—Housing Authority. Yeah, they pay real good. She a secretary now. . . . That's a good job. She got a house over here on 23rd St. It's a big house. They pay good. Pretty much now, she too good for me and this and that. So she kept puttin' that image out like she was too good for me. . . . She figured, ya know, that ain't nobody else gonna want me because, ya know, I ain't have no steady job and this and that. But she figure she's so well off, you know, she don't really need me.

Self, a 21-year-old high school dropout with a GED, works part time in a nightclub. He has two sons under the age of 2. The children's mother has a child support order, but Self ignores it because he views his children's mother as financially better off than he is. He tells of his feelings of resentment toward his own mother because her own attitude of self-sufficiency had kept his father out of his life:

> I met my [own] father and he told he the story of what happened with my own mother. He . . . came to see me one day and she was just like, "I can handle this. I don't need any help," and just shut the door. And that one decision lasted for 21 years. . . . Had she expressed love . . . that would have changed the whole course of things. But since she decided to not express love and shut the door when he came to see me, I never knew my father.

Several fathers felt that that it was not so much their children's mother as *her* mother who prevented them from maintaining contact with their children. These fathers often attributed the failure of their relationships with their children's mothers to interference by their "mother-in-law," and that the conflictive relationship continued to affect their ties to their children. For example, Peanut bitterly recounted his experience with his girlfriend's mother:

> What broke [our relationship] up was her mother. Her mother didn't like me. . . . After the baby was born, her mom intervened and [my girlfriend] kept trying to tell her [to stop interfering], but her mom wouldn't allow it 'cause she was living with her mother. She still living with her mother. I mean, she's a momma's child.

(Q: What was her mother's reaction when she found out she was pregnant?) As far as I know, her mother said "Okay, but why him? You could have picked somebody else." That was the way that was. She was proud of her daughter. She was almost 23 years old and ain't have no kids yet. . . . [Having the baby] just gave [my daughter's mother's] mother something stronger to put out there to get her away from me. . . . So I wasn't feeling like a real father. . . . [My daughter] has her mother's last name. We ain't married, [but] she could have still gave her my name, but she didn't. [My daughter's] grandmother [was like], "No!"

One respondent told of his relationship with his girlfriend's mother and how it affected his fathering status:

She was a "Miz Alice," a churchgoing lady, one of them ladies that need to be cursed out for real for real. But [my girlfriend was] hiding behind Miz Alice. You know what I mean? Like when we told her—my son's mother was 28 when she had my son. I was like twenty-five. Our first child. We go to tell her [mother] that she's pregnant. She told me to shut my mouth and told her daughter, "What can [he] offer a child?" Yeah, her daughter sat there on the bed and cried in front of her mother, and I said, "I'm a leave [sic] because I don't want to disrespect your mother because she'll never have the opportunity to talk to me like that again."

As we indicated earlier, many of the men who didn't change their "street" lifestyles on becoming fathers found themselves involuntarily sacrificing involvement with their children later in life, most often through imprisonment or severe drug and/or alcohol addiction. Martinis described his feelings about being separated from his young son during imprisonment.

I was ripping [and] running and got incarcerated, and was gone away from [my child's mother] for awhile and I came home and had to like be back in my son's life all over again and that was kind of hard. . . . I missed all that time with [my son] when he was an infant. He was born May of last year and he didn't know who I was and [my girlfriend] was like, "That is your dad." She came twice [to visit me in prison] but she didn't bring him. I was very disappointed that she didn't bring him. It was lovely seeing her, I had a nice visit with her, but I really wanted to see [my son]. But she did bring pictures. . . . I didn't really get a chance to see him personally until I came home in May.

Mark, a 32-year-old father of an 11-year-old, has a high school diploma and is steadily employed. He sees his daughter three weekends out of each month and pays informal child support to her mother. He recounts,

[When my daughter was five, I was incarcerated for drug dealing and sent to a] prison where it is murders and rapists and people not coming home for three hundred years, and it totally sent me ballistic. I thought I was going to go crazy and I didn't think I was going to make it and the only thing that kept me going was my daughter. . . . My daughter came to see me every weekend, every weekend my daughter's mom brought her to see me every weekend, when I was in the state. [Then I got transferred out of state.]

One short period of incarceration convinced Rick, a 26-year-old father of a 2-year-old son, to change his lifestyle. He went on to express disdain for other men who kept up this behavior and risked imprisonment, thus missing out on seeing their own children's development:

I don't see how these guys wanna keep goin' to jail. That's crazy to me. That's what I be tellin' these guys, man. The most I did was three [months] in jail. . . . That's a place I don't wanna be, I know that. 'Cause that was last August, and my son had just—ya know, was [just] start walkin' and talkin'. And when I went there, they barely let me see him. And when I got out, he was walkin' and talkin'. I was like, "Damn!" That crushed me. 'Cause you know, I wanted to see all that, you know. My first son, and—I don't see how these guys'll just take little times of their life out. You missin' a lot, man. When they get out, things have changed.

Spells of imprisonment not only prevented these men from fulfilling their father role while in prison, but often had lasting effects on their relationships with their children, even when they became much older. Because of their absence while imprisoned, many of their children's mothers become attached to other men. These other fathers then "play daddy" to the children of the jailed father, complicating the biological father's relationship to his children when he is released. Dayton, father of three, was still on parole at the time of the interviews. He told Nelson, "I got locked up and that messed me up with [my daughter]. Because now she's like, she told me the other day—when I first came home, rather—she told me she got two dads—her mother's boyfriend and me. And I am like, "You ain't got no two dads!"

A few of the fathers we interviewed had been to jail repeatedly or for one long spell. These men often experienced such a profound disruption of the tie between themselves and their children that a deep distrust developed on the child's part, one that generally persisted despite their efforts to dispel it. These fathers felt they were helpless to overcome the distrust when they finally came home. Martinis spoke poignantly about the effects of repeated imprisonment on his daughter and how he was trying to make up for the years he was away:

We weren't close. Well, in the beginning we were. All the way up until the age of eight or nine, we were close. But after me keep getting myself in trouble [and going back and forth to jail], I guess she kind of gave up on me. I am never around and I guess it hurted her. We just recently had a conversation on the phone and I had to explain to her where I was. Not just where I was literally, but my mindset and why I made the decisions I made and why I was incarcerated and why I did certain things. It wasn't like I wanted to be away from her. I told her that I loved her dearly and we had a little rapport. She had a little daughter, I went to see my granddaughter. I had to go ahead and [visit her] and we talked and she cried and she explained why she feel the way she feel. She feel that she didn't have no dad and it hurted me to hear that but it was the truth. I don't blame her in a way, because I wasn't there, so now I have been trying to incorporate myself in her life again and in her daughter's life. She is coming around now, she is coming to accept me more, but I don't think she is putting her all in it because she maybe feels as though she don't know if I am going to disappear again.

Some fathers talked about severe drug or alcohol habits that took them away from their children. Donald said,

> I haven't [been in my daughter's life consistently]. I been in and out. At one time I was very consistent, but when I started using again, you know what came first. Basically she was in there for the whole picture. I think the rough part, which has been the last ten [years], but the last three [years] has been the rough of the roughest.

Sometimes past drug use played into the previously discussed desire of mothers to keep children from fathers. J. J., a Philadelphia father, explained,

> I can't get a chance. . . . [My child's mother] has had a restraining order for a year and I am going back and forth to court [to get visitation with my daughter]. I already had partial custody of her but she don't want to give her up to me. She don't want to give her. She is looking at my past, my past of getting high.

Role Compromise: "Doing the Best I Can"

One can see that many forces inhibit these men from being the kind of father that they want to be. However, despite these obstacles, the men we interviewed managed to negotiate the expectations of their children, their children's mothers, and themselves. Many of the fathers we interviewed expressed their ideal of fatherhood and what made for a "good father" by emphasizing the concept of "being there" for their children. J. J. said that a good father means, "Being there for your child when she falls, spending a lot of time with your child. At any age, it don't matter how old you is. Just being there for her constantly when she needs your help." Dayton responded along similar lines: "Being there for your children— financially, emotionally, mentally—the whole thing. Being there for them." Robert asked rhetorically, "Sure babies are cute and fun, but are you ready for the work, are you ready for the dedication of the getting up—the 'twenty-four/seven' of it?" Forty-one-year-old Michael, father of two children (ages 24 and 4 months), relies on SSI and odd jobs and rarely sees either of his children. He responded to our question of what makes for a good father by emphasizing this aspect of it (but qualifying it as well):

[A good father is] a man that can take responsibilities—it got mostly to do with responsibility. To be there. How can I put this? [A lot of] men know they're daddies but not fathers. Anybody can hug their children and they're going to hear that "daddy" thing. But see, a father is someone who is always there—not always, but most of the time.

Despite such declarations, however, the fathers we spoke to generally do not see their children on a day-to-day basis, usually for the reasons discussed in the previous section. In spite of these difficulties, many fathers talked of how they would like to "be there" for their children on a more regular basis. For example, when Nelson asked Dayton what the hardest part of being a father was, he replied, "Not being able to spend time with them, like taking them to school and putting them to bed. And that is the hardest part for me—being away from them." Martinis, prohibited from seeing his children during his incarceration, said:

I am not a bad dad, [my children] tell me that they love me and everything, but it is just that I am not always there for them when they really need me around. . . . I try to spend more time with them so that they can get to know me as dad and I feel good about being a dad. It is just that some things that I don't like about myself as far as being there. I am not there all the time whereas though I want to be and it hurts me and it upsets me, and I know that it upsets the mother also—that she wants me to be part of his life. She tells me now, and she says, "Marty, Rahmere doesn't really even know you," 'cause I am not around him a lot. He is only two but seems that he knows me but I don't think that he knows that I am dad because I am not constantly around a lot or with him or doing things.

Given the difficulty of "being there," many fathers told us of their efforts to spend what they call "quality time" with their children. This concept came up with surprising frequency in our interviews and is one that these fathers take quite seriously. For most of the fathers who used the phrase, "quality time" seemed to describe their efforts to take their children out for a special activity, often something educational. Dayton described the things that he did with his children and how such activities validated his status as a father:

I just want to be more than just a dad, I want to take care of them. I will buy them materialistic things and things of that nature, but I think that it is more important to spend that quality time with them and that is what I am trying to get together now. . . . We go to the park here, we go in the house and play games, or I will take them around the playground around the corner and take them to Discovery Land and Chuck E. Cheese, just have fun. I be tiring them out because I just have fun with them all day so that when they come home they just crash right out. It is real fun, but now I want to get into the reading and everything with them and things like that. I was trying to get them into this book but it is hard when they ain't getting it back home [where] they might play Sega all day, or the PlayStation. [So] I need to find out some different ways to get that into them, the books. They be out here wasting time with this PlayStation and television and all this type of stuff [because] the key is . . . knowledge—it is going to be the key for later on in life when they get older, because it is getting deep out here and you can't get that deep with them 'cause they don't understand yet. But I be trying to just be an example for when they come around and reading with them. I am going to get more into that with them because I see that is what I should of had when I was coming up—books and computers and things of that nature.

Andre remarked that, "Even though I'm [not there] everyday . . . there is still something which is called 'quality time.' " Mark used this phrase several times in describing the kinds of things he did with his daughter:

[What] I do is, sometimes I get off work and I probably go down to her school and hang out with her after school, go up to the playground with her, just a little quality time. Actually it was last Friday I got her from school and we went and did a book report. Her book report was due and we set down and did a book report and it was kind of nice. It was just a quality time that we spend.

J. J. said "I would take [my daughter] out places, take her to the park and take her out to dinner, and sometimes I took her to the movies and left the mother at home, and it would just be me and her." Seven talked about the importance of reading to his youngest son:

I like to read to him a lot. Before he was born I read to him in the womb so he likes being read to. He likes me to hold him and all. That is why I read to my son right now, so that when he goes to school he will be adapted to reading. He will know that reading is fundamental. He will know that education is paramount and these are the things that you have to do to succeed in life.

Regarding his older children, Seven stated:

I try to be a good father. I try to emulate my father, because I had a good dad, and I try to treat my kids well and I try to instill in them the right things to do. I try to be a good example with them because we grew up together practically. I have teenage boys and I am still fairly young so we do a lot of things together when they come around. Just a couple of weeks ago me and my son, we put a bike together. We spent a couple of days together [working on that bike].

Andre listed the activities he had done with his youngest son, including ". . . taking him to the store and taking him to the amusement parks and taking him to the zoo and taking him to the Please Touch museum and taking him to the Franklin Institute. These were a lot of places that we went."

Maurice talked about the things that he did with his children after responding to a question about how his life would be different if he had never had children:

I can't even conceive what it is like not having kids. Yeah, it is rewarding. It is very rewarding to see your kids graduate, to see them in a play. This Saturday I get to go see my son in his drill team practice. I mean, actually perform, so I am going to be out there watching my son perform with his drill team. No matter how bad they are, I am still doing to be there. . . . I see my kids three times a week. Normally when I see my son he is over the house. He will come in and go, "What's up, dad?" and I will say, "Hey son, how are you doing? What is going on?" And he will go on about doing his business and we will talk about some things and we will talk about wrestling. Not too long ago we went to a Phillies game together and it was just good. [Another time] I rode down the street and I [saw] my youngest daughter. We got this thing where this summer we were going around trying to find the perfect water ice, and I would pick her up and be like, "We will be back—we are going out to get our water ice." And we would go out and get our water ice and we would talk and everything.

Spending quality time, however, generally requires that a father have some money in his pocket. Even fathers who take their children to the park have to have a few dollars for "water ice," or Italian Ice, that is a favorite summer treat among Philadelphia children. Philadelphia's Children's Museum and Science Museum were favorites among fathers, but an outing for a father and one child could easily cost $20. Fathers without any money in their pocket often felt they couldn't even "go around" their children. Peanut explained,

Part of being a father is that you're going to have to spend money on them. That's what you got to do. You got to be there, you got to have the "paper" to do things for your child. That child's going to need things, the mother's going to need things. You got to be cool.

When Lee was asked about the responsibilities of fatherhood, one of the things he mentioned was that "[You have] to provide for your kids. When you take a walk with them or walk around the neighborhood [and] they say, 'Hey daddy, I want a water ice or a popsicle,' you can't say, 'I can't do that right now.' You have to be able to provide for your kids." Michel works through a temporary employment agency, pays regular child support and sees his children (ages 4, 17 months, and 8 months) each weekend. Michel spoke of how a good father will always make sure that his children "look good," even if he doesn't take care of his own appearance:

I am grown, and it don't take much for me. Now my children is something different. You tend to want your children to look better than you. (Q: Why is that?) Because your children are a product of you—you are done, [so] why you got to be runnin' around looking good? Only time you need to run around looking good is if you got a job that specifies that you have a dress code or whatever the case may be. I don't have that. . . . Children, you tend to want them to be a reflection of you. Someone looks at your child and see your child look good—you could have just crawled up out of the sewer [but] they say, "Well Mike looks bad, but he keep them kids looking good." Simple—that's how I look at it.

Given that most fathers we interviewed felt responsible for giving financial support to their children, it is not surprising that they reported attempting to meet these obligations. However, because these fathers were unemployed or working for low wages, they said that it was hard for them to make substantial or regular financial contributions. Before he went to prison, Martinis reported that his girlfriend

> . . . was really pressuring me about money. I was pressuring myself because I wasn't making enough to be able to give her and the kids all these nice things. I did the best I could but I knew I needed more so I did other things, hustled on the side, to be able to provide her with all these things. Rahmere when he was born, I brought [my girlfriend] all that stuff. I brought her bassinet, blankets, everything. She hardly had to do anything, and she had her own money [as well].

This account echoes many other statements our fathers made: John said, "I'm glad I have [my kids]. I'm doing the best I can." Lee said, "[I have had] moving jobs, I done cut trees, I did roofing jobs. Whatever I can do, I contribute to my family." Self commented, "I offer my [first son] as much love as I possibly can. As far as financially, when I have, I'm definitely willing to share whatever I have." Michel's self-imposed rules regarding the disbursement of his odd-job earnings are as follows;

> [I support my kids] the best way that I know how. I do stuff like . . . little odd jobs—painting, cleaning somebody basement or something—anything. I give them whatever I can and I help everybody. Last month between the two of [my children's mothers] both of them got $100 each.

Lee's practices are similar.

> Somebody gave me $2 for helping them move a couch. And later on, the little money I made I split it. I said, I'll give [my child's mother] a dollar, keep 50 cents for myself, and gave my daughter 50 cents. So I try to break it down all the way around.

The fathers who were able to make regular contributions were proud of their ability to do so. For example, when Nelson asked Mark how long he had worked at his job as a sandwich maker for a local deli, he said:

> It has been almost a year—ten months actually. [I]t is a job, that is all I consider it as. It was basically about my daughter. My daughter is eleven years old and the whole thing was about her. [As long as] I had a steady income coming in I could give her

[things] and I could take care of her to the best of my ability. And no court orders or nothing like that. It is just [to] a point where as though my daughter means a lot to me. It was no one upholding me and saying, "Well you got to pay this child support."

Jimmy, who is 40 and has a 9th-grade education, has two teenage children in foster care. Though he works steadily now, he had been severely drug addicted for a number of years. He now contributes to his children's expenses and says that these contributions represented a turning point in his life and his ability to reactivate his role as a father. When Nelson asked him if he gave his children money, he replied, "Oh, yes I do, yes I do. That's why [my kids] love me today. Not just for the money, but because daddy got himself together."

Fathers who want to make substantial contributions to their children's material well-being but are hampered by low and/or sporadic income often resolve this dilemma by buying a few symbolically important items (see also Edin & Lien, 1997; Rainwater, 1970). They often purchased such things as baby furniture for their pregnant girlfriends, "Pampers" (used generically for all brands of disposable diapers) for infants, and clothes and "sneaks" (sneakers) for their older children. Although the dollar amount that such contributions represent is sometimes small, their cultural significance is more substantial because they indicate the father's willingness to try and support his children to the best of his ability. Such symbolic declarations begin as soon as he learns that he is to become a father and continue as the child grows and develops. When Lee found out that he was to become a father, he received the following bit of advice from two friends: "They said, 'Get a job and provide some Pampers and milk and stuff.' "

For the most part, the fathers we interviewed had managed to sustain this minimum level of contribution. For example, Lacey, a 42-year-old father of three who works as a prep cook, said, "[Now that I am out of jail] I give my children money. *(Q: How much?)* I give them little dollars or fives. Sometimes my son might need sneaks and clothes. I buy that." Lacey now has custody of his youngest child and regularly sees and buys sneakers and clothing for one of his older children. Ahmad said, "For my youngest son, [I am] just doing a lot of the basic things that were required. Buying him outfits, buying him Pampers." Maurice reported, "I was giving [my child's mother] $50 a week, but I buy the kids sneakers [on top of that. If] they need clothes, I buy them clothes. I try to provide the best I can for them for what I make." Kevin proudly stated, "My first priority was always my daughter, you know, so whatever she needed, I got it, you know—Pampers or baby lotion, or something."

Peanut reported how his life and his finances changed when he became a father and how he had to struggle to make these contributions:

I [stopped dealing and went] on welfare. I paid my aunt $35 for my little room. My daughter got the rest. You know what I mean? Well every time I got my check I bought her Pampers, milk, juice, food, little outfits and shit like that. I did what I thought was right. And I would come out with maybe $20 on the end. I was only getting $96 [every two weeks].

Seven said,

> I told you earlier about me taking some painting jobs. It happened during the middle of the school year and the kids were getting ready to go back to school and I was financially stable [enough] to go out and buy them shoes. I bought my daughter two pair and I bought the boys a pair, and so it kind of worked out.

Although most fathers reported that they were doing the best that they could, many are frustrated because they feel that their efforts are either not appreciated or that their children's mothers' expectations are unreasonably high. When one of our interviewers asked Michael if there were disadvantages to being a father, he replied:

> The money. The money's not always there. . . . When the baby was first born, [my girlfriend] was telling me how she wanted a baby coach. I said, "Okay, no problem. We'll get one." She said, "Well, I seen this nice one for $150." I said, "Man, that's a used car! $150! What that baby going to be in there? Two years at the most." And she got highly upset about [me saying] that.

Mark said:

> [D]on't call me a day before you need something. You are putting me on the spot. And [my child's mother] is the type of person that if she wants something she is going to call that day or that week and expect it to be there. And then if you say you can't do it, it is a problem.

For those fathers who are not paying through the formal child support system, their children's mothers often threaten to turn them in if they do not live up to their standards. For example, Mark said,

> She feels as though she can whip me with that whenever she gets mad. She says, "I'll just take you down to court," or "I can take you to court." I have gotten to the point where I say, "Do what you want to do." [S]he threatened me the other day. "Well, I am going to have to take you to court!" and I said, "Okay if that is what you want to do." She is the type of person she can be very cunning.

Those fathers who did pay child support through the formal system had strong feelings about the inflexibility and, in their perspective, unreasonably high payments they had been ordered to make. Seven said,

> They told me to pay $500 and I didn't have the money and so I didn't go to court and they issued a bench warrant. [T]hat's where we are at. I don't pay no support now because [her mother and I were never] together. [But I do] pay support for the [other] four. [Right now] I am supposed to [pay $272 a month] but I am not. I don't have the funds for it.

Self told of his experiences:

> The guy who gave me this paperwork was like "Here's a list. Write down every job that you go look for and bring back this list." It was so crazy. And then, like looking for a job. . . . If you're looking for a job then nine times out of ten, you're on a budget. You need money to get the job. You need money to get clothes for the job interview. You need money to eat lunch once you get the job. . . . So with me, I had this district attorney not listening to anything I'm saying, not explaining anything to me, just speaking into my face "Here, bring this paper back. If you don't bring it back the next time you come back, you're going to jail. You don't have a job next time you come back, you don't pay a certain amount of money, we're locking you up!"

CONCLUSION

Low-income noncustodial African-American fathers are seriously underrepresented in surveys, so we know little about them. Survey data are also limited in that they cannot fully describe how fathers think about fathering nor how they define fatherhood as individuals and as members of cultural and class groups within society. Furthermore, survey data may miss the cultural symbolism inherent in some of the smaller ways in which economically marginalized fathers fulfill their fathering duties (by purchasing Pampers and "sneaks," for example). Surveys may also miss a large portion of child support payments that fathers make informally (directly to the mother and/or child) rather than through the formal system.

This analysis of data drawn from repeated in-depth interviews with 40 low-income noncustodial African-American fathers residing in nine target neighborhoods throughout the Philadelphia metropolitan area seeks to begin to remedy some of these deficiencies. Drawing from an inductive analysis of these data, we describe how fathers come to define (or "construct") the father role and the ways in which they seek to fulfill the duties they associate with that role in the face of severe economic, social, and personal constraints.

These low-income African-American fathers define fatherhood as having both economic and relational aspects. Whereas working-class White men have traditionally viewed breadwinning as the primary responsibility of fathers, these African-American fathers seem to place equal value on the relational aspect of fathering (see also Waller, 1997). In reading through interview transcripts, we were often struck by how often fathers' descriptions of the relational aspects of their fathering reflected the practices of affluent divorced fathers—visiting (or having children come and stay) them on weekends and trying to jam the weekend with special "quality time" events. However, even quality time was expensive, and maintaining contact with children generally required fathers to have something in their pockets.

Fathers spoke poignantly about the meaning their children had for them. Children provided them with a set of attachments to the social mainstream that many said they lacked prior to fatherhood. Many times, the onset of pregnancy and the resulting birth provided fathers who had been "rippin' and runnin' the streets" with a strong motive to leave their fast and dangerous street lives for more conventional ones. For this reason, fathers often claimed that their children had literally "saved" them. The sense of attachment that children afforded fathers can be thought of as a last-ditch life preserver for fathers whose economic and social marginality meant they had metaphorically jumped ship (or been forced to walk the plank). The sense of attachment children provided was sometimes enough to bring fathers back on board, at least marginally. This is presumably why though fathers sometimes admitted that having children had impeded their efforts to further their education, most credited their children with any small successes they had had in life (especially moving from criminal to more mainstream employment).

Furthermore, fathers who felt they had not accomplished all that they had hoped during their own adolescence and adulthood looked to their children to fulfill those dreams. Children carried the physical features and personality traits, if not the actual last name, of their fathers on into the next generation, giving evidence that a father was "on the planet." This was particularly true for male children who, fathers believe, were more likely to carry both the physical likeness and name of their fathers forward. If children were successful, a father could take partial credit, even if his only contribution was biological (and if the children failed, he could blame the mother). Fathers often felt that their children were better versions of themselves, and for many, vicarious success was far better than no success at all.

In short, children did a lot for fathers. However, fathers sometimes did very little for their children in return, particularly as these children aged. Oftentimes, fathers described bleak scenarios in which they were barred from fulfilling the fathering role because of their economic marginality and personal problems (drug addiction, for example). Fathers sometimes said that when they could not contribute, they felt too guilty to have ongoing contact with their children, and those who did not visit or support any of their children usually viewed their own behavior with great shame. These men managed the conflict between their idealized image of fatherhood and their actual performance by continuing to make attempts to support and visit at least one of their children in some fashion. Fathers were constantly on the lookout for better jobs, but were hard pressed to find and keep them, and they often resented the fact that their children's mothers (or even their children) didn't seem to appreciate their efforts.

Past studies of African-American fathers have often focused on their absence and their inability to live up to their familial responsibilities. These qualitative data offer insight into how low-income African-American nonresident fathers construct the fathering role and strive to fulfill the duties they associate with this role in the face of tremendous sociocultural barriers. Both structural and behavioral factors, such as unemployment, drug use, criminal activity, and relational conflicts, hinder or enhance fathers' ability to fulfill these duties at various points during the life course.

ACKNOWLEDGMENTS

This research was funded by grants from the W. T. Grant Foundation, the Russell Sage Foundation, and the Department of Health and Human Services. Antwi Akom, Timothy Nelson, Susan Clampet-Lundquist, David Mitchell, Jennifer Morgan, Magaly Sanchez, Eric K. Shaw, and Kimberly Torres conducted the interviews with fathers. Susan Clampet-Lundquist, Heidi Heimstra, Mirella Landriscina, Rechelle Paranal, and Kelly Pennington coded transcripts of the interviews.

REFERENCES

Braver, S. L., Wolchik, S. A., Sandler, I. N., Sheets, V. L., Fogan, B., & Bay, R. C. (1993). A longitudinal study of non-custodial parents: Parents without children. *Journal of Family Psychology, 7*(1), 9–23.

Carlson, M. J., & McLanahan, S. S. (2001). Father involvement in fragile families. Working Paper 2001–08-FF. Bendheim-Thoman Center for Child Well-Being, Princeton University, Princeton, NJ.

Cherlin, A., Griffith, J., & McCarthy, J. (1983). A note on maritally-disrupted men's reports of child support in the June 1980 Current Population Survey. *Demography, 20*(3), 385–389.

Del Boca, D., & Flinn, C. J. (1995). Rationalizing child-support decisions. *American Economic Review, 85*(5), 1241–1262.

Edin, K., & Lien, L. (1997). *Making ends meet: How single mothers survive welfare and low-wage work*. New York: Russell Sage Foundation.

Furstenburg, F. F., & Harris, K. M. (1992). The disappearing American father? Divorce and the waning significance of biological parenthood. In S. J. South & S. E. Tolnay (Eds.), *The changing American family: Sociological and demographic perspectives* (pp. 197–223) Boulder, CO: Westview Press.

Garfinkel, I., McLanahan, S. S., & Hanson, T. L. (1998). A patchwork portrait of nonresident fathers. In I. Garfinkel, S. S. McLanahan, D. R. Meyer, & J. A. Seltzer (Eds.), *Fathers under fire* (pp. 31–60) New York: Russell Sage Foundation.

Garfinkel, I., & Oellerich, D. T. (1989, May). Noncustodial fathers' ability to pay child support. *Demography, 26*(2), 219–233.

Garfinkel, I., & Oellerich, D. T. (1992). Noncustodial fathers' ability to pay child support. In I. Garfinkel, S. S. McLanahan, & P. K. Robins (Eds.), *Child support assurance: Design issues, expected impacts, and political barriers as seen from Wisconsin* (pp. 55–77). Washington, DC: Urban Institute Press.

Isaacs, M. B., & Leon, G. H. (1987). Race, marital dissolution, and visitation: An examination of adaptive family strategies. *Journal of Divorce, 11*(2), 17–31.

Johnson, E. S., Levine, A., & Doolittle, F. C. (1999). *Father's fair share: Helping poor men manage child support and fatherhood*. New York: Russell Sage Foundation.

King, V. (1994). Variation in the consequences of nonresident father involvement for children's well-being. *Journal of Marriage and the Family, 56*(4), 963–972.

Leadbeater, B. J., Way, N., & Raden, A. (1988). Why not marry your baby's father? Answers from

African American and Hispanic adolescent mothers. In B. J. Leadbeater & N. Way (Eds.), *Urban girls: Resisting stereotypes, creating identities* (pp. 193–207) New York: New York University Press.

Lerman, R. I. (1993). A national profile of young unwed fathers. In R. I. Lerman & T. J. Ooms (Eds), *Young unwed fathers: Changing roles and emergent policies* (pp. 27–61). Philadelphia: Temple University Press.

Miller, C., Garfinkel, I., & McLanahan, S. S. (1997). Child support in the United States: Can fathers afford to pay more? *Review of Income and Wealth, 43*(3), 261–281.

Mott, F. L. (1990). When is a father really gone? Paternal-child contact in father-absent homes. *Demography, 27*(4), 499–518.

Nelson, T. J., Edin, K., & Torres, K. (2001, March). *Unplanned but not accidental: Low-income, non-custodial fathers' participation in childbearing decisions.* Paper presented at the annual meeting of the Population Association of America, Washington, DC.

Rainwater, L. (1970). *Behind ghetto walls.* Hawthorne, NY: Aldine.

Seltzer, J. A. (1995). Demographic change, children's families, and child support policy in the United States. In *Families, human resources, and social development* (pp. 31–54). H.-H. N. Chen, Y.-l. Liu, & M. Hsueh (Eds). Taipei, Taiwan: National Chengchi University.

Seltzer, J., & Brandreth, Y. (1994). What fathers say about involvement with their children after separation. *Journal of Family Issues, 15*(1), 49–77.

Sorensen, E. (1997). A national profile of nonresident fathers and their ability to pay child support. *Journal of Marriage and the Family, 59*, 785–797.

Stier, H., & Tienda, M. (1993). Are men marginal to the family? Insights from Chicago's inner city. In J. C. Hood (Ed.), *Men, work, and families* (pp. 23–44). Newbury Park, CA: Sage.

Teachman, J. D. (1991). Contributions to children by divorced fathers. *Social Problems, 38*(3), 358–71.

U.S. Census Bureau. (1983). Child support and alimony: 1978. *Current Population Reports* (Series P23-112). Washington, DC: U.S. Government Printing Office.

U.S. Census Bureau. (1995). Child support for custodial mothers and fathers: 1991. *Current Population Reports* (Series P60-187). Washington, DC: U.S. Government Printing Office.

Waller, M. R. (1997). *Redefining fatherhood: Paternal involvement, masculinity, and responsibility in the other america.* Unpublished doctoral dissertation, Princeton University.

21

The Responsible Fatherhood Field: Evolution and Goals

Ronald B. Mincy
Columbia University

Hillard W. Pouncy
Princeton University

For much of the last century the American father was regarded primarily as an economic provider. Officially, in census reports and legally in law books, the American father was head of the house. As Michael Katz might have put it, able-bodied fathers could never become subjects of the American social safety net, because the culture believed a father's role was to provide, not to be provided for (Katz, 1989).

This imagery of American fatherhood changed radically in the 1960s. One important factor was the women's movement, which in its drive for economic independence shattered the myth that the father was the only provider and therefore the logical head of the house (Mansbridge, 1986). The well-documented decline in male earnings since the 1970s also undermined the single-earner family (McLanahan & Casper, 1995). It reduced the wage premium long enjoyed by men and decreased the ubiquity of single-earner households. The combined effect of the women's consciousness movement and the labormarket changes of the 1970s slowed rates of family formation while increasing rates of family dissolution (McLanahan & Casper, 1995). Meanwhile, the widespread use of the birth-control pill and other forms of contraception reduced premarital abstinence, led to fewer shotgun marriages, and may have raised rates of cohabitation (Akerlof, Yellen, & Katz, 1995).

Another important factor in changing images of the American father was the expansion of the welfare system. Under some circumstances the welfare system encouraged some mothers who were dissatisfied with their marriages and relationships to end them (U.S. Department of Health and Human Services, 1983; McLanahan & Casper, 1995). In the 1970s welfare's expansion also brought the establishment of a national child support enforcement system. However, the system was implemented so unevenly that Irwin Garfinkel of the School of Social Work at Columbia University concluded, "poor nonresident fathers who were legally obligated to pay child support were required to pay a substantially higher proportion of their income than middle- and, especially, upper-income nonresident fathers" (Garfinkel, 1992, p. 8).

The final blow to the "Father Knows Best" image came when historians confirmed that the stereotypically patriarchal family of the 1950s was a historical anomaly, not a norm (Grishold, 1998). Indeed, for African-American families it had never been the norm. Historically, African-American families based on marriage (as distinct from cohabiting couples or never-married single parents) could best be characterized as dual-earner couples displaying a high degree of economic parity (Mincy & Pouncy, in press). The news that traditional fatherhood was neither traditional nor universal robbed the patriarchal 1950s family of its last justification—the "we do it because it is natural" argument.

By the early 1990s many believed that not only had patriarchy been debunked, but that American family life now excluded fathers more generally. Matters had gone too far. Reversing this trend became an important end-of-century project of a new social entity—responsible fatherhood groups (Gavanas, 1998)—that asked: How should fathers respond the new constellation of social and economic forces? For the most part, these groups reacted by focusing on the goal of increasing the positive involvement of fathers in the lives of their children and families. How this goal was met and why it was chosen are the subject of this chapter.

SCOPE OF THE FIELD

Responsible fatherhood service providers have been a pragmatic, fragmented, and highly focused lot working to meet discrete needs and provide specific services for different kinds of fathers. The types of clients they serve range from noncustodial fathers who seek access and custodial rights to their children (Pearson & Theonnes, 1998) to married and divorced fathers who would like to become more involved with their children (Levine, Murphy, & Wilson, 1993). Some fathers are low-income, noncustodial men who have difficulty meeting their child support obligations (Johnson, Levine, & Doolittle, 1999). Others are never-married fathers attempting to complete a stillborn family formation process (Mincy & Pouncy, 1997).

Fatherhood-related events have increased at such a rapid pace in the last 10 years that some now believe the field has spawned a responsible fatherhood social movement, and at least one intermediary organization dedicated itself to ensuring the possibility (Horn, 1999; Morehouse Research Institute and Institute for American Values, 1999). This view is significant because a social movement might yield greater impact on policy and, perhaps, greater success in promoting responsible fatherhood than could be achieved by the most sweeping social welfare reforms.

There are, however, numerous barriers to the creation of such a movement: philosophical differences, power struggles, and the difficulty of enlarging demonstration programs to function on a national level are among the most challenging issues faced by the nascent fatherhood movement. All leaders of larger fatherhood organizations share the goal of promoting responsible fathers; how to achieve that goal and what to do beyond that point stymie the field.

This chapter identifies the different types of major fatherhood organizations and describes their goals. It discusses the role of patrons: the government, nonprofit foundations, and businesses. It examines the impact that responsible fatherhood programs have had on men, on government policy, and on the public's view of fatherhood. Finally, it assesses where the field stands in terms of creating a social movement and whether this is a reasonable objective for the field to sustain.

A word on terminology: This discussion is mostly about relatively large organizations[1] that we term *intermediaries*. Most of these intermediaries stand between local groups and the national foundations, federal and state authorities, and private groups that fund fatherhood activities. Intermediaries coordinate services and provide technical assistance to networks of local fatherhood programs. They operate as leaders, advocate fatherhood policies, and publicize research results and policy ideas. They create the field's infrastructure (see Fig. 21.1).

Two other reserved terms are *local service provider* and *demonstration project*. *Local service provider* is our term for a community-level, individual responsible fatherhood program. By one estimate, the number of these small, community-based programs has grown from 200 in the mid-1990s to more than 2,000 today (Wade Horn interview, March 27, 2001). Demonstration projects are single-purpose national efforts that assemble several local service providers to test a policy innovation.

A "fatherhood movement" implies a united national effort to encourage responsible behavior among all married and unmarried fathers toward their children through government policy and/or cultural change. Many observers think that such a movement is a shared goal of fatherhood programs generally, but other intermediaries, especially those in low-income and minority communities, question

---

[1]We focus on intermediaries because most local-level fatherhood programs are too early in their development to have had measurable impacts. If measures for assessing the impact of local programs do become available, it will likely be because the intermediaries we discuss have mounted credible demonstrations that they then evaluated with the best available resources. Some of these intermediaries also provide technical assistance that builds the capacity of local providers to provide quality service.

FIG. 21.1.   The Fatherhood Field's Infrastructure Erected in the Mid-1990s
by Foundation and Government Grantmakers

Fatherhood Intermediaries	Pregnancy Prevention	Child-Support Enforcement	Nurturing	Marriage
Established poverty organizations that expanded fatherhood-related work in the 1990s				
Center on Budget and Policy Priorities		■		
Center for Law and Social Policy		■		
National Conference of State Legislators		■		
Urban Institute		■		
Established fatherhood organizations expanded by mid-1990s infrastructure building				
*Families and Work Institute	■		■	
*Institute for Responsible Fatherhood		■	■	■
*National Center for Fathering			■	■
*National Fatherhood Initiative			■	■
New fatherhood organizations created during the infrastructure building period				
**Center for Fathers, Families and Public Policy		■		
**National Center for Fathers and Families		■		
National Latino Fatherhood and Family Institute			■	
**NPCL		■		
**NPNFF		■		

whether a unified social movement is desirable. Because this is an unsettled issue, we distinguish such a movement from the intermediaries, local service providers, and demonstration projects discussed next. We refer to the latter as the field.

ATTRIBUTES OF THE FATHERHOOD FIELD

This chapter reviews development of modern responsible fatherhood programs in their formative period, 1974–2000. It is based on interviews, foundation reports,[2]

---

[2]Sylvester and Reich (2001) is a particularly helpful recent report, which was completed for the Annie E. Casey Foundation.

archival searches, literature reviews, public records, and publications of individual fatherhood groups. Through these sources, we identified over 160 events and activities directly associated with fatherhood programs. We recorded the dates when key actors entered and left the field, as well as the most significant conferences and rallies. We collected the beginning and ending dates of government programs. We also took note of significant research reports and evaluations. In this section, we attempt to answer the major who, what, when, where, and why questions as these relate to fatherhood intermediaries.

A notable feature of the field, one that may affect its potential for becoming a social movement, is that its activities have grown amoebalike from a variety of sources. The 1974 Social Security Act was particularly important in this regard, because it created the Office of Child Support Enforcement (OCSE). Under certain conditions, the Office of Child Support Enforcement regulates the access that noncustodial fathers have to their children. One wing of the fatherhood field exists solely in reaction to OCSE; this segment operates primarily as a traditional interest group, responding to the office as though it were a regulatory agency. Other sources of responsible fatherhood activity include such environmental factors as changes in the family, the workplace, and gender relations.

Local programs offering services to targeted groups of fathers began to appear in the 1980s. Throughout the 1980s we counted 16 important events, including the first two federally sponsored fatherhood demonstration projects. In the 1990s the pace of fatherhood activity increased very rapidly; between 1990 and 1993 the field matched its accomplishments of the previous decade. By the mid-1990s there was as much fatherhood activity in 1 year (1995) as there had been throughout the 1980s. By 2000 the same amount of activity was occurring within a few months (see Fig. 21.2).

The fatherhood field can be divided according to four main themes—pregnancy prevention, child support enforcement, the encouragement of involvement and nurturing, and the promotion of marriage. For one type of practitioner serving male teenagers who are not yet fathers, responsible fatherhood is linked to responsible sexual activity and the prevention of unplanned fatherhood. A second type of practitioner focusing on divorced noncustodial fathers who have failed to pay child support may characterize responsible fatherhood as helping such men meet their child support obligations. In a variation on the child support enforcement theme, a practitioner who works with low-income, never-married men who only recently became fathers may define responsible fatherhood as encouraging such men to engage in a postpregnancy family formation process. A third type of practitioner may view a responsible father as a nurturer who is involved with his children as he strikes a balance between work and family obligations. A fourth type of practitioner may equate fatherhood with marriage and suggest that responsible fatherhood can be practiced only within the bounds of marriage.

In all four thematic areas, the main objective of the fatherhood field is the same: counseling fathers on how to be fathers. How the ideal father is defined, however, determines not only the program's goals but also its approach. Some

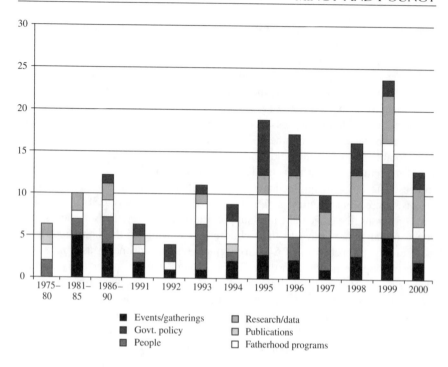

FIG. 21.2.   Growth of the Fatherhood Field, 1979–2000

Source: Sylvester, K., & Reich, K. (2001). *Making fathers count: Reviewing 25 years of father-hood efforts.* Baltimore: Annie E. Casey Foundation.

counsel fathers one-on-one. Others provide a coach, mentor, or professional who guides discussions within a group of fathers. Many set up peer-to-peer counseling sessions in which fathers determine the content, guided by a coach or professional. Some local providers include mothers as well as fathers, either in groups or as couples. Some are based on highly structured curricula; others are fluid and informal. These varied approaches reflect goals that range from assisting married fathers in remaining married to motivating responsible fatherhood behavior by helping men remember what it felt like to be abandoned by their own fathers.

Within the four thematic areas, local providers combine counseling with a wide variety of other services to achieve one or more of the following purposes (Doherty, Kouneski, & Erickson 1996):

- Involve mothers and, especially for unmarried fathers, families of origin whenever possible
- Promote collaborative coparenting inside and outside marriage
- Emphasize critical transitions such as the birth of the child and the divorce of the parents

- Deal with employment, economic issues, and community systems
- Provide opportunities for fathers to learn from other fathers
- Promote the viability of caring, committed, and collaborative marriages

In the subsections that follow, we look at each theme in turn, identifying large intermediaries associated with that theme and examining how the theme determines intermediary goals, approach, and selection of tasks from the preceding list. The first theme focuses on preventing young men from becoming fathers before they are ready to behave responsibly toward their children.

Pregnancy Prevention

The nation's first fatherhood demonstration project, the Teen Fathers Collaboration (TFC), was designed to address this theme. The demonstration's three notable features were as follows: (a) it was the only funded pregnancy prevention project for men, (b) it pioneered the use of a "fathers learn from fathers" component, and (c) it was the first fatherhood program to include employment services. Two research organizations, the Bank Street School of Education and the Manpower Demonstration Research Corporation, operated the project in eight sites between 1983 and 1985 (Hayes, 1987; Hevesi-Sander & Rosen, 1987).

As often happens in demonstrations, the project soon expanded its original goals beyond teenage pregnancy prevention. It began providing services to single teenaged mothers to help them move forward with their lives. As a component of that new goal, some sites also provided services to fathers to keep them involved with their children as they, too, moved on with their lives. The menu of services included parenting classes, job training and job placement, tutoring and educational assistance, individual and group counseling, and family planning classes.

The demonstration provided several lessons for future fatherhood programs:

- "An adolescent father's involvement in his partner's pregnancy increases the young mother's sense of confidence in her nurturing skills, heightens her sense of security after delivery, and raises the father's self-esteem" (Hevesi-Sander & Rosen, 1987).
- "Although inner-city teenage men generally have few economic resources, many contribute financially to support the children they have fathered" (Hevesi-Sander & Rosen, 1987).
- Contrary to stereotypes, relatively few of the inner-city teenaged fathers were sexual predators. Most claimed to be romantically involved with the mother of their children (Levine interview, 2001).
- Although young, never-married parents frequently sought to remain involved with each other, other family members—particularly grandparents—were often hostile to their continued relationship (Levine interview, 2001).

- The mothers were teenagers. Often the father was not a teenager, but in most respects his problems matched those of the young mother. Most were unemployed or underemployed, and many lacked a high school diploma. A significant number of the men were involved with the criminal justice system (author's review of Ford internal memoranda on the demonstration).

The demonstration offered few lessons on preventing unplanned pregnancies. Work continues on pregnancy prevention (Levine & Pitt, 1995), but at present no intermediary has made prevention a major focus of its work.

Child Support Enforcement

Intermediaries, demonstration projects, and local service providers under this theme operate in two different areas. Fathers' rights groups primarily work with divorced or separated fathers on custody and child visitation issues. For other intermediaries, the primary issue is the increasing number of low-income fathers who are as poor as mothers on welfare but are being drawn into an enforcement apparatus that was designed for divorced or separated fathers who are able but unwilling to pay. Put differently, a policy designed for middle- and higher-income fathers, for whom willingness to pay has been the key issue, is increasingly being applied to low-income and impoverished noncustodial fathers for whom ability to pay is the key issue.

The main contribution from both subareas is the idea that policy systems should be transformed in ways that remove barriers to responsible fatherhood. Policy systems in need of reform include the welfare system, the criminal justice system, and the child support enforcement system.

Custody and Visitation. In 1984 the U.S. Congress passed the first important legislation on noncustodial fathers that went beyond simple child support collection. It called on state and local governments to enforce a noncustodial father's access and visitation rights in the same way as they enforced the father's child support obligations. Having agreed to lend a helping hand to custodial parents seeking child support from "deadbeat dads" in 1974, Congress now chose to balance the ledger and encourage action on behalf of fathers who met their child support obligations but faced uncooperative ex-spouses when it came to access and visitation issues. In response, some states created commissions to study such issues, whereas others set up court-sponsored visitation mechanisms (Pearson & Thoennes, 1998).

After years of advocacy by fathers' rights groups, Congress became a full-fledged fatherhood service program patron in 1988 when it funded a series of access and visitation demonstration programs under the 1988 Family Support Act (Pearson & Thoennes, 1998). These demonstrations were to "test methods and techniques to resolve child access and visitation problems" (p. 224). The Office of Child Support Enforcement sponsored Access Demonstration Projects that explored four types of interventions between custodial and noncustodial parents as techniques for resolving access and visitation disputes. This included nondirective mediation between involved parents. In a second type, termed an educational intervention, the project sent one or both "offending" parents to classes where they reviewed laws and procedures governing access and visitation. In a third variant, parents met with a mediator who resolved disputes on a directive basis. The fourth intervention strategy was monitoring the implementation of a visitation order. The first of these intervention strategies—mediation—was to become a staple of fatherhood service programs.

Although fathers' rights groups have the longest tradition of programming within the fatherhood field, most responsible fatherhood intermediaries hold them at arm's length. The latter believe that siding with fathers' rights groups is likely to erode public support for larger responsible fatherhood goals. Fathers' rights groups often present themselves in public as angry men embroiled in contentious, self-defeating battles with their ex-spouses and the court system. In such conflicts the larger message of the fatherhood field that a father's involvement in the lives of his children is important is lost. In addition, other fatherhood organizations wish to avoid becoming enmeshed in the sustained conflicts fathers' rights organizations have had with national women's rights organizations, even though several fatherhood intermediaries have lost support from women's groups on other grounds.

Nonetheless, the father's rights groups associated with Access Demonstration projects contributed the idea to the fatherhood field that systemic public policy changes are necessary to remove social welfare barriers to fathering. In the early 1990s, they argued that there should be a parallel agency to the Office for Child Support Enforcement for the rights of noncustodial parents. Congress and the president established a commission to review the option, but the proposal was never enacted.

Paternity Establishment and Payment.   Child support enforcement is the theme around which more work has been done than any other, primarily because this theme's most important sponsor, government, has had a keen interest in collecting child support from noncustodial fathers and the resources with which to undertake experiments with this end in mind.

In the 1990s partnerships between government agencies and nonprofit foundations sponsored a series of demonstrations exploring methods to address the issue of "dead broke" noncustodial fathers (men too poor to pay even minimum child support awards). True "dead broke" dads are low-income fathers with problems similar to single-parent never-married mothers on welfare. Such fathers are likely to need many of the same services as poor mothers—for example, job training and education. However, the delivery of such services to "dead broke" dads is impeded by a number of problems. Unlike deadbeat fathers, who avoid the child support system because they do not want to pay, "dead broke" fathers are likely to avoid the system because they cannot afford their child support obligations and because they generally avoid mainstream society. In avoiding the system, they create debts for themselves (arrearages), and federal law as well as child support enforcement practice requires penalties and other sanctions for arrearages. When child support authorities discover "dead broke" fathers with an arrearage, such a father is in effect a criminal, and it is difficult for child support to be lenient even when they want to be.

The 1988 Family Support Act introduced a policy tool initially applied to welfare mothers but with potential limited application to "dead broke" fathers. The Family Support Act formalized the doctrine of reciprocal obligation (Mead, 1997). For mothers, this is famously known as welfare-to-work, in which the mother's obligation to work is matched by government provision of benefits and services. The equivalent for fathers would be: If you establish paternity, you will get services. The problem for child support authorities has been distinguishing true "dead broke" fathers from deadbeat fathers pretending to be "dead broke."

Although not authorized by the Family Support Act, the Young Unwed Fathers Project (YUFP) spoke to this need. The demonstration project operated in six sites from 1992 to 1994 and was sponsored by a partnership involving several foundations, the Department of Labor, and the Department of Agriculture. Like the Teen Fathers Collaboration of 1983, this project worked with young, "dead broke," never-married fathers and offered counseling, job placement, and access to job training programs to help young fathers meet their child support obligations (Achatz & McAllum, 1994).

Several important lessons came out of the Young Unwed Fathers Project. First, community-based fatherhood service providers were rarely able to secure effective cooperation either from child support enforcement authorities or from job training providers. When project staff wanted to modify a client's child support orders—delay order start dates, order suspensions, set a new minimum order, or ask that in-kind support be counted toward child support—they usually failed. Child support enforcement authorities often denied such requests, unaware that in many cases they were based on a young father's genuine needs (Johnson & Pouncy, 1998). Meanwhile, the eligibility rules of the Job Training Partnership Act (JTPA), a major training program for the poor, posed severe barriers for these clients. The housing circumstances of many low-income fathers left them ineligible for JTPA services. For example, some lived with a parent who was not poor, and some had no permanent address. Second, to receive complete program services, fathers were required to establish paternity. An 18-year obligation to pay child support followed. Employment and training services, however, were financed through JTPA, the program for which many were ineligible. Thus, many were unable to meet the obligation that the program encouraged them to assume (Achatz & McAllum, 1994).

In its 1988 Family Support Act, Congress also provided funds for a second fatherhood demonstration. The Department of Health and Human Services, in partnership with the Department of Labor and several foundations, awarded a contract to the Manpower Demonstration Research Corporation (MDRC) to operate a demonstration titled Parents' Fair Share (Johnson, Levine, & Doolittle, 1999).

Although Parents' Fair Share (PFS) lasted from 1988 to 1996, it was able to incorporate lessons from the Young Unwed Fathers Project because its pilot phase lasted until 1994. It operated at nine sites and targeted older noncustodial parents who had already been required by a court to meet their child support obligations. In the pilot phase of the program, two thirds of the fathers were 26 years old or older, and 5% of the noncustodial parents were women. The program's components included:

- Peer support group sessions to inform participants about their roles as noncustodial parents, sexual responsibility, commitment to work, and life skills
- Employment and training to secure long-term, stable employment at good wages
- Enhanced child support enforcement featuring reduced child support orders so long as participants remained in the program and swift enforcement should they fail to pay after becoming employed
- Mediation between custodial and noncustodial parents about visitation, household expenditures, and other issues through services modeled on family court programs offered to divorced couples (Doolittle, Knox, Miller, & Rowser, 1998)

To avoid the coordination problems revealed by the Young Unwed Fathers Project, PFS secured its clients through court referrals of men already delinquent in their child support payments. Paternity had already been established, and initially most of the programs were operated directly by child support agencies, not community-based organizations.

PFS sites also had independent funds (JOBS—Jobs Opportunities Basic Skills—funds) to pay for employment and training services. Once in place, Parents' Fair Share enabled child support authorities to resolve the poverty verification problem. A participating judge could give fathers who pled that they were too poor to pay child support a choice: either pay up or go to Parents' Fair Share, where you will receive help finding a job and work with counselors and other fathers and learn to be a responsible father.

One result was a "smoke out" effect—fathers with hidden incomes paid up when forced into such a choice. The average Parents' Fair Share father was more interested in paying than in services that would reattach him to his children (Johnson, Levine, & Doolittle, 1999).

For fathers who opted for training and counseling,

> Parents' Fair Share was moderately successful at increasing earnings among those without a high school diploma and those with little recent work experience. For these men, PFS increased the extent of their employment during the year and helped them get better jobs than they would have otherwise. They were more likely to work in relatively high-wage jobs and in jobs that offered benefits. For the more employable fathers, in contrast, PFS did not affect their earnings on average and caused a slight reduction in employment. The results suggest that fathers who dropped out of the workforce in response to PFS were those who would have worked part-time and earned relatively low wages. For this group, PFS may have increased their expectations about the types of jobs they could obtain, leading them to hold out for better jobs. (Martinez & Miller, 2000)

The intermediaries that administered and evaluated the early demonstration projects in this segment of the field were primarily concerned with research, evaluation, and policy development. Their primary clients were government and foundations. These intermediaries gathered much information about the capacity of responsible fatherhood programs, working with government agencies, to increase child support collections from low-income fathers. However, the use of research intermediaries in this critical role created two problems.

First, the local programs involved in these demonstrations changed with each government- and foundation-sponsored project. When the demonstration ended, most programs lost their funding, and the staff went on to other activities. As a result, few practitioners have worked in the field for more than 5 years, and the expertise that might have been accumulated over time has been lost. In other words, the demonstrations created a great deal of debris in the field, and an infrastructure to support responsible fatherhood never developed. Second, the low-income fathers and families who were the targets of early demonstrations often lived in poor, minority communities, and the staff who operated these programs were often people of color. Well-educated Whites, by contrast, often staffed the research intermediaries. As a result, the flow of information from the community to policymakers and other audiences who lived outside these communities was filtered by class and race differences. Many practitioners who operated programs during these early demonstrations are convinced that they never had the opportunity to develop and implement the kinds of services they felt were needed. They also believe that the story of these communities and their own service efforts has never been accurately told.

Only recently has an intermediary emerged, with government and foundation support, primarily oriented toward building the capacities of practitioners who operate responsible fatherhood programs, especially in low-income communities of color. This intermediary, the National Center for Strategic Nonprofit Planning and Community Leadership (NPCL), is led by Dr. Jeffery Johnson, an educator, trainer, specialist in nonprofit management, and former president of the

Washington, DC–Capital Area United Way. Johnson is also an African American, one of only three people of color who lead intermediaries in the field.

In 1994 the Ford Foundation began work on a demonstration (part of its Strengthening Fragile Families Initiative) targeted at young never-married parents who had not yet entered the child support enforcement system. It, too, responded to the Young Unwed Fathers Project, but it paid attention to the finding that during a pregnancy and for a period of up to 3 years after a birth, some young never-married fathers and mothers were involved in a nontraditional family formation process (Mincy & Pouncy, 1999). In this alternative process, the young couple considered marriage, cohabitation, and long-term family commitments only after a pregnancy and childbirth. Normally, such couples fall apart, but research indicated that family formation and diversion from welfare were also possibilities. Ford termed such couples Fragile Families—capturing an image of their vulnerable state. The Strengthening Fragile Families Initiative hosted a demonstration, the Partners for Fragile Families, that explored methods for strengthening such couples, primarily by working with the father (a young man likely to be a "dead broke" father) to help him solve his problems with the child support enforcement system.

In 1996 the Ford Foundation provided support to develop and coordinate the 10-site Partnership for Fragile Families (PFF) Demonstration. Development included making a case for a federal waiver of section 1115a of the Social Security Act, which was well established as a way of supporting welfare demonstrations but had rarely, if ever, been used to back demonstration projects in child support. Ultimately, the U.S. Department of Health and Human Services, the U.S. Department of Labor, the Charles Stewart Mott Foundation, and several other foundations joined Ford in providing about $20 million for the planning, development, implementation, and assessment of PFF, including $15 million for operations in local sites. This makes PFF the largest demonstration project in the history of the field and NPCL, which the Ford Foundation selected to administer and raise funds for PFF, the leading intermediary working on the child support theme.

Jeffery Johnson of NPCL coauthored the Fatherhood Development Curriculum used for the Young Unwed Fathers Project and initially for Parents' Fair Share. He also helped design the Partnership for Fragile Families based on observations he made while working on those earlier programs. Johnson noted that many "dead broke" fathers were young men with multiple problems, and his insight was that child support enforcement programs had a comparative advantage in reaching them. He theorized that child support was a "big stick" in their lives such that mishandling their child support obligations could send them to prison. Child support could also, however, be the big "carrot," because it might become a means through which such fathers might be reconnected with their children.

In 2000 the Charles Stewart Mott Foundation established the Fathers at Work Demonstration to examine how many resources low-income fathers would need to make them better providers for their children. Because a disproportionate number of young, low-income inner-city males are likely to have a criminal record, be unemployed, and be noncustodial fathers, the eight-site demonstration tries to determine which pathways can lead such fathers from their present locations outside mainstream society back into jobs, relationships with their children, and "legitimate" relationships with public agencies. The demonstration features partnerships of local criminal-justice agencies, child support enforcement authorities, job training providers, and community-based responsible fatherhood groups. NPCL and Private/Public Ventures (P/PV), the research intermediary that administered and evaluated YUFP, jointly administer the demonstration, and P/PV is its sole evaluator. With this partnership of intermediaries, the field is evolving in ways that allow policymakers and foundations to monitor their progress as the local service providers involved in such demonstrations secure assistance in carrying out programming innovations.

In addition to its work on child support enforcement, NPCL provides several other services to the field. First, its expertise in nonprofit management assists emerging national and local fatherhood organizations, especially Ford Foundation grantees, with strategic planning, board development, financial and human-resource management, and tax exemptions. Nonprofit management assistance is critical in this emerging field, where many community-based fatherhood organizations begin life as fatherhood components hosted by organizations that focus on mothers and children. Conflicting missions or competition for funding often require the fatherhood component to seek independence if it is to survive, and independence brings a host of capacity issues that few local service providers are prepared to handle. National organizations that have been underwritten by donors also face capacity issues with which they need help. NPCL has been able to provide this kind of assistance. At different moments, it has provided such assistance to the National Practitioners Network on Fathers and Families (NPNFF); the Center for Fathers, Families, and Public Policy; and the Center for Fathers, Families, and Workforce Development. NPCL also convenes quarterly meetings of these and other organizations to discuss how they can better coordinate their activities.

Second, NPCL is building the field's capacity to deliver quality services. Its Fatherhood Development curriculum, the oldest in the field, trains service providers and the staffs of agencies that presently fund fatherhood programs or seek to fund them. NPCL updates this curriculum to spread promising practices in the field, including new sections on team parenting, how to broach marriage to never-married parents, and how to connect incarcerated fathers with their children. In these efforts, peers learn from peers, and NPCL attempts to take the pulse of the field and disseminate what it learns.

Third, in its role as the nation's institutional voice for low-income parents and their children, NPCL operates public education, communication, and field-building efforts on their behalf. Its public education efforts have been focused on national and state legislators who are considering bills that would support responsible fatherhood services. Its newsletter, *The Collaborator*, reaches community-based responsible-fatherhood practitioners, audiences, and other stakeholders. The organization popularized the term *fragile families* (Pouncy & Steinbock, 2000) and invented terms now widely used in the field such as *dead broke dads* and *marriageability.* In its focus groups, forums, peer-learning colleges, and conferences NPCL builds coalitions between local service providers and stakeholders in the interests of its clients, low-income parents and their children. Its stakeholders include policymakers, advocacy and intermediary organizations working on behalf of women's issues and against domestic violence, professional associations of child support officials and state agency employees, the faith-based community, and Head Start programs.

Its efforts on behalf of low-income parents also extend overseas, most notably to South Africa, where it organized a U.S.–South Africa cross-cultural exchange summit in 1999, and in the United Kingdom, where it has begun to train practitioners based on an adaptation of its Fatherhood Development Curriculum.

Finally, the national contributions of two local service providers should also be noted. The Racine site of Children First, Wisconsin's 1988 child support enforcement demonstration, renamed itself Children UpFront. This Racine program pioneered techniques that would become an important component of Parents' Fair Share's enhanced child support enforcement demonstration. The Racine site was among the first to add "father-friendly" comprehensive services to an enhanced community-based, paternity establishment program. Children UpFront has been included in Parents' Fair Share, the Partners for Fragile Families Demonstration, and the OCSE Responsible Fatherhood Demonstration. Similarly, the Paternal Involvement Project, a local direct-service fatherhood program founded in 1992 in Chicago, heavily influenced the Partners for Fragile Families Demonstration. It inaugurated the idea that programs serving low-income, noncustodial parents should encourage paternal involvement as aggressively as they encourage such fathers to establish paternity and pay child support. In this sense, the Paternal Involvement Project (Paternal Involvement Demonstration Project, 1996) and its successor, Partners for Fragile Families, bridge two responsible fatherhood themes—child support and nurturing. Ultimately, both seek to transform child support enforcement agencies into child well-being agencies that collect child support payments as they promote father involvement. Interestingly, Judge David Grey Ross, Commissioner of the Federal Office of Child Support Enforcement throughout the Clinton administration, endorsed such a transformation.

Nurturing and Involvement

This theme has attracted a number of intermediaries and, unlike efforts in the pregnancy prevention group that try to change individual behavior or child support enforcement intermediaries who seek systemwide changes, intermediaries in this segment focus on changing the culture—each in its own way—and changing a variety of institutions in society (e.g., government, businesses, schools). Because their goals are so far reaching, these intermediaries are also most interested in developing a broad cultural basis for responsible fatherhood.

This theme focuses on increasing fathers' involvement with and nurturing of their children through media campaigns and public messages. Intermediaries in this group specialize in public education campaigns about fatherhood. In this way they seek to transform the customs and practices of mainstream institutions, including the nation's faith-based institutions, schools, government agencies, and most significantly, corporations. One organization—the National Fatherhood Initiative, the intermediary most closely identified with the idea of a social movement—blends strategies for cultural transformation with public policy advocacy. This organization puts great effort into securing public policies and legislation favorable to responsible fatherhood, especially those that encourage fatherhood programs to promote marriage.

The Fatherhood Project was the first responsible fatherhood intermediary focused on nurturing and male-involvement themes.[3] It defined nurturing and male involvement as the male response to rigid gender roles stereotypically ascribed to 1950s-era middle- and upper-income White Americans. In that period, fathers were work centered and mothers were home and child centered, and the twain were never to meet. Movies like *The Man in the Gray Flannel Suit* exposed the dark side of these arrangements for the company man played by Gregory Peck, who is forced to choose between his comfortable nine-to-five job and a high-powered promotion that will destroy his marriage. For women, Betty Friedan's *The Feminine Mystique* exposed similar toxic choices and discontent (Gordon, 2000). The feminist movement of the 1970s is women's well-known political response to rigid gender roles. The less-well-known men's response is a vision of the "new father" hosted by fatherhood programs in this segment of the field (Gordon, 2000).

James Levine, the founding director of the Fatherhood Project, traced the process through which he realized his vision of "new fathers" to the late 1960s. He had been teaching at a preschool in Oakland, California, and noticed that most

---

[3]Strictly speaking, the Fatherhood Project is a project of the Families and Work Institute, an intermediary that addresses the changing nature of work and family life. Its president, Ellen Galinsky, is most noted for her work on the implications of women's increasing participation in the labor force for child well-being and the organization of work. As such, the Fatherhood Project is a father-focused initiative, which is hosted by a nonprofit organization whose primary focus is, arguably, women and children. Like most local fatherhood programs, it has avoided the significant capacity-building and infrastructure costs, by aligning its mission with that of its host. Other intermediaries in the responsible fatherhood field must incur these costs. Because many public and private donors in the larger children youth and family field are committed to gender equity and women's empowerment, the need to cover these costs determines how far intermediaries can go when taking positions on issues that make women's groups uncomfortable. As we shall see, this is an important reason why a unified fatherhood movement has not emerged.

parents of the preschoolers he taught asked him: "What do you really do?" He recalled:

> It was a question that never would have been asked of a woman. My female col-leagues could work with three- and four-year-olds all their lives without anybody expecting they should or might be doing something else. . . . That moment a quarter of a century ago changed my view of the world. It shocked me into realizing that gender stereotypes affect men, as well as women. Intellectually, of course, I knew that such stereotyping was widespread, affecting all sorts of other people. But it was deeply personal. People didn't expect me to teach or care for young children. (Levine, Murphy, & Wilson, 1993)

The Fatherhood Project sees itself as "a solution-oriented research and educa-tional organization" that helps corporations, government agencies, and community-based fatherhood groups adopt male, family- and father-friendly practices, customs, and procedures. It is best known for advocating paternity leave—letting fathers have paid time off from their jobs when they have newborn children or a pregnant spouse. Over the last 10 years the Fatherhood Project developed training programs for more than 50 *Fortune* 500 companies, instructing managers and workers on pro-ductive practices that allow working fathers to improve their balance of work and family life (Levine & Pittinsky, 1998). They also estimate that they have helped over 100 *Fortune* 500 companies integrate attention to fathers into existing family policies. They count Microsoft, IBM, and Merrill Lynch as exemplary corporate clients.

The Fatherhood Project's work with government agencies includes a training program—the Male Involvement Project—for community-based practitioners and the staff of Head Start agencies to "get fathers involved in the lives of their children." The organization also writes guides on how to operate programs for family support agencies, and its State Initiatives on Responsible Fatherhood pro-gram reviews state policies and programs that it hopes "will yield a new under-standing of government's role in fostering responsible fatherhood" (www.father-hoodproject.org).

The National Center for Fathering, founded by Ken Canfield in 1990, also helps corporations and schools incorporate practices encouraging father involve-ment, but it was initially known for its work with faith-based institutions. It holds large seminars of up to 2,000 participants 12 times a year. It uses a 138-item pro-file that characterizes the "new father." In smaller breakout sessions, these pro-files become a tool for discussions between fathers and trainers on how partici-pants can become more involved with their children. Often, sites then operate their own self-sustaining peer-to-peer groups called Dads of Destiny (Canfield, 1996).

In the mid-1990s the center began its Urban Initiative, a six-site demonstration meant to help the organization reach a more diverse population of fathers. The initiative gave the center access to "fragile families" and other types of fathers it normally did not serve. The initiative works with schools, courts, and urban faith-based institutions. It sponsors programs at schools that encourage awareness of fathering and helps teachers understand how to encourage a dialogue about fathers among students whose fathers are absent. They provide mentors for delinquents who have been assigned to them by the courts. They also sponsor father-to-father programs for urban churches.

The initiative also works with corporations and helps companies like Microsoft solve job retention problems. Technology-based start-up firms often offer founding employees stock options that make such employees quite wealthy within a short period. These modern versions of the "Man in the Gray Flannel Suit" give up the firm for the family. The center helps such firms understand which father-friendly policies will keep valued employees from leaving the firm.

The National Fatherhood Initiative (NFI), the third intermediary, takes a more traditional approach to gender roles, although they continue to stress the importance of a father's involvement with his children. The National Fatherhood Initiative argues that the "new father" paradigm destroys the idea of "gendered parental roles" creating an "androgynous father figure." It prefers a vision of the "Good Family Man" who "incorporates some of the attractive nurturing traits of the new father" but retains such older fatherly functions as breadwinner and family protector. It is not clear whether the initiative's version of the "Man in the Gray Flannel Suit" would take the high-powered promotion, but he would want to be the family breadwinner. In the view of NFI, it is also essential that the Good Family Man be married. With this end in view, NFI pursues policy initiatives that promote marriage.

Founded in 1994, the initiative is also committed to cultural transformation. It specializes in public education campaigns promoting its definition of responsible fatherhood. It has, for example, invested heavily in making Fathers' Day a national occasion to rethink the idea of fatherhood. It hosts conferences and an annual fatherhood summit, drawing legislators at local, state, and national levels. It publishes books, articles, and field manuals and operates one direct-service responsible fatherhood program for fathers incarcerated in 85 prisons (Long Distance Dads). Interestingly, despite its success at crafting responsible fatherhood messages for the media, the initiative remains attached to its vision of creating a social movement, because it believes that a social movement is a better medium for its responsible fatherhood message. "Social movements convey ideas and change societies," Wade Horn, its founding executive director, says (Horn interview).

Donald Eberly, who founded NFI, worked with David Blankenhorn, an initiative board member and founder of the Institute for American Values, in the late 1980s on a series of conferences that eventually lead to the initiative's creation. Blankenhorn took the lead in organizing a 1991 fatherhood conference that helped shape his book, *Fatherless America* (1995), and the National Fatherhood Initiative's definition of responsible fatherhood.

NFI claims that national, cultural transformation is its priority, and Horn, for example, characterizes the difference between NFI's cultural agenda and the system transformation agenda of other intermediaries as follows: "There is a difference between creating a social delivery system for fathers and changing the way in which society thinks about fathers. We think the latter is vital" (Horn interview). Nonetheless, the organization has contributed greatly to policymaking aimed at transforming the social welfare system. In the 1999–2000 debate over legislation to fund national responsible fatherhood programs, the initiative anchored the position that such programs should primarily promote marriage. In this sense the organization straddles the nurturing and marriage-promotion segments of the field. In 2000 Donald Eberly and Wade Horn were tapped for appointments within the Bush administration. The National Organization for Women opposed Horn's nomination as Assistant Secretary of the Administration for Children and Families with little effect. As a result, federal efforts in support of the field are likely to have a heavy emphasis on marriage.

Two other efforts that straddle the nurturing/involvement and marriage-promotion lines look even more like a social movement but are not devoted exclusively to promoting responsible fatherhood. The Promise Keepers, a faith-based movement founded in 1994 to encourage fathers' involvement and marriage, staged a large rally in Washington, D.C., attended by hundreds of thousands of men. Its main goal is renewing the faith and religious commitment of its followers. In pursuit of that goal, it asks that members promise to be good husbands and fathers. Although allied to the responsible fatherhood field, its agenda is so extensive that it cannot be regarded simply as a responsible fatherhood program. Similarly, the 1995 Million Man March, a one-time event in Washington, D.C., sponsored by Minister Farrakhan of the Nation of Islam, is not exclusively a responsible fatherhood effort. It encouraged African-American men to be good husbands, but it also wanted them to end racism and contribute to their communities.

The newest intermediary focused on a nurturing theme is also the only responsible fatherhood intermediary focused on Latino culture. The National Latino Fatherhood and Family Institute, founded in 1998 by Jerry Tello, serves communities characterized by high levels of two-parent households, but violent or drunken fathers are a significant problem (Cardenas, 2000). In response the institute defines a responsible father as one who "keeps his word, does not harm his circle of family, friends and community, and holds utmost respect for women" (p. 1).

Marriage for Fathers

This fourth group does not take a completely different stand from the third: both support the idea of cultural transformation, and where the responsibilities of fathers are concerned, they act more as a continuum than as independent structures. What distinguishes this segment of the fatherhood field is its insistence not only that marriage efficiently produces responsible behavior in men but also that responsible fatherhood is possible only in the married state (Gallagher, 1999).

Few intermediaries in this group focus exclusively on responsible fatherhood. Most could be more accurately described as fatherhood outposts of an American marriage movement. Their primary mission is to reduce divorce through various types of premarital counseling. They also work to prolong existing marriages and to reconcile couples that have separated. One such intermediary, Marriage Savers, operates through churches and offers many such counseling programs. Smart Marriages, more formally known as the Coalition for Marriage, Family, and Couples Education, cosponsored with Institute for American Values a Marriage Movement statement of principles (Wetzstein, 2000) and hosts marriage-saving workshops for practitioners. Other groups endorse the enactment of divorce law reform or marriage covenant arrangements by state legislatures.

The National Fatherhood Initiative has been instrumental in proposing that federal funds slated for local responsible fatherhood programs and welfare reform funds be steered into marriage-promotion efforts. It is unclear whether existing fatherhood programs would receive these funds. Rather, marriage practitioners who have little experience working with low-income and minority communities could be the intended recipients of these funds. This is an enormous threat to local programs working on the child support theme.

The one program in this arena that is exclusively a responsible fatherhood program works among low-income men who have children out of wedlock. The Institute for Responsible Fatherhood and Family Revitalization, founded by Charles Ballard in 1982, started in Cleveland, Ohio, now operates out of Washington, D.C. The only marriage-oriented responsible fatherhood intermediary, it operates a six-city demonstration, called Reconnecting Fathers to their Families and to the Workplace, sponsored by the Department of Labor. It explores "how well turning the heart of noncustodial fathers toward their children and family will create jobs for them" (Ballard testimony). The intermediary sets up shops in low-income communities, and the site directors are required to be a married couple that models marriage in neighborhoods with high rates of nonmarriage. They hire "protégés" who recruit noncustodial fathers and provide counseling and similar services. Normally, as they attempt to encourage the father's involvement with his children, the big problem is the mother and unresolved issues between the parents. At this point protégés usually involve the mother and facilitate the man's connection with the mother and his children. Once the program "turns a father's heart toward his children and family," its practitioners argue that marriage, employment, entrepreneurial activities, and "all other things" are possible.

This intermediary sits on a critical fault line in the responsible fatherhood field. It straddles the segment of the field concerned with marriage, usually an area of concern for middle- and upper-income White populations, and the part of the field that addresses low-income never-married minority populations. Critics comment that "dead broke" fathers who do not complete the journey to marriage and employment, as this program intends, risk increasing their debt and legal entanglements (Deparle, 1998). The organization's demonstration should provide useful evidence on the value of its approach.

RECONCILING DIFFERENT
POLICY THEMES

Given their different goals, it would not be surprising if fatherhood intermediaries found it difficult to work together. Intermediaries focused on maintaining marriages have little in common with intermediaries that seek to find jobs for young, unmarried, economically deprived or imprisoned fathers or even with programs that promote the rights of divorced fathers to establish strong, continuing bonds with their children. Some differences are ideological. The Fatherhood Project and its "new father" differ substantially from the National Fatherhood Initiative and its Good Family Man. The "new father" rearranges work/family life to facilitate gender equity at home and in the workplace. The Good Family Man embraces traditional gender roles in his marriage and can only be a Good Family Man if he is married.

For its part, NPCL seeks to avoid taking sides in this disagreement over gender roles for several reasons. The conflict is irrelevant for its clients. The primary concern of the low-income never-married households it serves are males detached from work and family. Second, U.S. welfare policy has traditionally treated poverty as a women's and children's issue and women's groups play influential policymaking roles in the poverty field (Skocpol, 1992). Given this reality, NPCL sees congruence between its mission and the mission of groups working on behalf of low-income women and children. It seeks to avoid conflicts with women's groups who oppose the paternalistic Good Family Man. Finally, the local programs it supports may lose funding if marriage practitioners become the major beneficiaries of funds intended to increase responsible fatherhood and reduce welfare dependency. In these respects, the field's child support segment has its own view of this ideological difference.

The failure to agree even carries over into arguments about definitions and terms of reference. In 1996 James Levine and Edward Pitt of the Fatherhood Project crafted an inclusive statement meant to provide an umbrella description of responsible fatherhood for the entire field (Levine & Pitt, 1995). They suggest that a man who behaves responsibly towards his child does the following:

- He waits to make a baby until he is prepared emotionally and financially to support his child.

- He establishes his legal paternity if and when he does make a baby.
- He actively shares with the child's mother in the continuing emotional and physical care of their child, from pregnancy onward.
- He shares with the child's mother in the continuing financial support of their child, from pregnancy onward.

This definition is relevant to programs serving noncustodial never-married fathers because all four attributes apply to them. It is less relevant to other types of fatherhood. For example, divorced fathers may fulfill the first two conditions but be unlikely to share much with the child's mother. The definition does not mention marriage as a responsible fatherhood act, thus alienating the fourth group of programs from the outset.

Diversity is a centrifugal force operating on the field, pulling organizations away from a common agenda. Because organizations are in competition for scarce resources from Congress, foundations, and business clients, they face pressures to differentiate themselves and to make relative comparisons between themselves and others.

This is especially true for organizations seeking to affect public policy because they are competing for leadership in two critical ways. First, they want local programs to look to them for leadership. This will occur if they can claim credit for congressional and other political decisions to fund these local programs. Second, larger organizations want direct support from Congress for their efforts to lead the field in their chosen direction. This competition maximizes the effects of class, race, and other cleavages.

There are, however, three counterweights that foster the development of a united social movement.

- *Mutual need.* No one program or segment of the field can secure on its own the cultural or systemic transformation it seeks. David Blankenhorn has observed that it is unlikely that a few programs serving only the interests of middle- and upper-income "white guys" would survive Congress. Broad programs that capture the diversity of fathers are more likely to secure bipartisan support. Similarly, Jeffery Johnson, director of NPCL, observes that the fate of his organization is akin to the fate of minorities working in mainstream institutions: "We operate in an environment in which public perceptions of responsible fatherhood are controlled by those for whom the needs of low-income and minority fathers are peripheral. Collaboration, therefore, enables us to advocate for a more inclusive definition of responsible fatherhood" (confirmed in Jeff Johnson interview, January 31, 2002). The risks to all parties in collaboration are also high. They may lose control over their messages and agenda. Their messages may be appropriated. Jeffery Johnson calls his participation in efforts to manage diversity "cooptition—all of us are simultaneously cooperating and competing."

- *Function integration.* Over time, most intermediaries working on one primary theme have grown to understand the importance of the primary themes of other intermediaries. The National Center for Fathering, for example, started by focusing on fathers it could reach in suburban churches, then broadened its work to include fathers accessible through city jails. NPCL began with a concern for "dead broke" fathers and their paternity establishment status, only to confront the salience of marriage after research determined that many of their clients would have liked to marry. After its first few years of focusing exclusively on a broad cultural message, the direct service program launched by NFI focuses on incarcerated fathers.
- *Networks.* Efforts by Vice President Al Gore in 1994 to make the agencies and policies of the executive branch more father friendly led to an organization to network practitioners. The National Practitioners Network for Fathers and Families operates as a conduit among practitioners at the grassroots level, and it, too, bridges divisions and differences.

THE IMPACT OF FATHERHOOD SERVICE PROGRAMS ON MEN

With the exception of the Parents' Fair Share demonstration, there have been no rigorous impact studies of the effects responsible fatherhood programs have on the behavior of men or the well-being of children. Perhaps this indicates the development of the field and its level of funding, but it means that there is little we can say about how these programs affect men or children. Implementation and outcome studies of the three current child support enforcement demonstrations— Fathers at Work, Partners for Fragile Families, and OCSE's Responsible Fatherhood Demonstration—are underway. None has been implemented completely to mount a controlled, experimental evaluation.

We do know that Parents' Fair Share "smoked out" hidden incomes among fathers, increased child support compliance among men who owed it, and increased the earning power of its most needy clients, although men who were better off when they entered the program made fewer gains. The Young Unwed Fatherhood Project also offered lessons that became models for most other major child support enforcement demonstrations.

Representing the fourth theme, Marriage Savers is mounting a study of whether it has affected local divorce rates. Meanwhile, the larger initiatives have produced some interesting possibilities. The Million Man March was credited with increasing African-American electoral turnout in the 1998 congressional elections (Morris, 1997). So far, there has been no formal study of this possibility, but it is consistent with what students find of other teaching or civic events (Verba, Schlozman, & Brady, 1995). It would be worthwhile to study this and other possible effects of responsible fatherhood activity on fathers to see how far the field has come relative to other modern movements. These are particularly interesting possibilities because they suggest that the activities of responsible fatherhood groups could encourage greater civic involvement.

THE IMPACT OF FATHERHOOD PROGRAMS ON GOVERNMENT POLICY AND ON SOCIETY

In addition to changing the behavior of individual men and how they connect with their families and children, parts of the responsible fatherhood field have set themselves the goals of transforming government policy, the workplace, and society. The field has also sought to alter public perception of fathers and their roles, as well as the roles themselves—cultural transformation. These efforts have had varying degrees of success.

Efforts to transform policy systems have attained many of their goals. Congress and most state legislatures have funded demonstrations and programs meant to increase the capacity of low-income fathers to pay child support. Most states have funded "smoke out" programs intended to distinguish "deadbeat" fathers from "dead broke" fathers, by giving the former the choice of paying up or being assigned to a program that offers them simple job search services.

The 1997 Welfare to Work program, which funds the work component of welfare reform, includes funding for noncustodial fathers that may improve employment and training services for "dead broke" noncustodial fathers. The latter is a rare example of a large welfare-related program that shares its funds for low-income mothers with the low-income fathers of their children.

In 2000 the U.S. House of Representatives passed the Fatherhood Counts bill, which would have provided $144 million for fatherhood programs that promote marriage, develop parenting skills, and fund job training. It funded media campaigns and a responsible fatherhood information clearinghouse. It also provided for partnerships based on the PFF model and funded technical assistance by intermediaries. The bill was an outcome of cooptition efforts among most segments of the fatherhood field, including NPCL, the National Fatherhood Initiative, the National Center on Fathering, and the Institute for Responsible Fatherhood. The bill did not pass in the Senate, but in the current legislative session, the Senate will review the legislation in tandem with a similar effort in the House of Representatives.

Intermediaries are also having an impact in the workplace. Several *Fortune* 500 companies have concluded that father-friendly policies will increase productivity. Similarly, in a 1996 Gallup poll, 60% of employed fathers agreed with the statement "if your employer implemented more family-friendly policies, you would be more productive at work." This work by the Fatherhood Project complements the objectives of some women's organizations to make the workplace more accessible to women as the organization achieves its own "new father" goal to make workplaces more supportive of nurturing men.

When it comes to cultural transformation, the effects are more difficult to discern. Fatherhood programs have had a significant impact on the perceptions of the public at large. The National Center for Fathering concludes from its examination of Gallup data that both men and women endorse responsible behavior by fathers, although the Center supplies no trend data indicating how its numbers compare to earlier periods or demonstrating whether there is a link between changes in public opinion and the efforts made by responsible fatherhood groups. A study of Virginia audiences conducted by the National Fatherhood Initiative (NFI) did, however, determine that its media campaigns had had the desired effects (NFI, in press).

One problem in assessing the impact of the field's cultural agendas on society is the organizations' failure to agree on an agenda. Some want the role of fathers to be transformed in accordance with less-rigid gender roles. Others seek a restoration of traditional gender roles. There is no agreement on the place of marriage. Culture is also a more difficult arena because different faiths, races, and classes define culture differently. People maximize their differences and argue over the location of change. Should it be in fathers or in the family? Should it be in how the public perceives the family and fathers? These differences spill over into goals. Should the impact be based on a reduced divorce rate, a rise in contact and involvement, an increased commitment to faith, or a greater commitment to one's community? Each success in this arena, such as the passage of the Louisiana covenant law, represents a failure from the viewpoint of another group. Changes have been made, but whether these are fundamental alterations in the public perception of family formation and fatherhood remains to be seen.

IS THIS A SOCIAL MOVEMENT?

There is a conversation among intermediaries as to whether the field's activities can or should lead to a social movement. For example, would a social movement hosted by the responsible fatherhood field be reactionary, seeking to reestablish the traditional family man in defiance of the changing nature of American families and the claims of feminists and the "new family man"? Or would it be a equality-seeking movement operating in the interests of the powerless—largely, African-American, noncustodial fathers—completing a cycle begun with the 1960s civil rights movement? As with much that has already happened in the responsible fatherhood field, the answer is mixed.

According to the classic definition, social movements are "socially shared demands for change in some aspect of the social order" (Gusfield, 1968). Nineteenth-century political sociologists developed the phrase to describe the behavior of groups that function in the large gap between revolutionary movements, which seek the overthrow of political regimes and political parties, and organized interests which operate within the bounds of ordinary politics (Lorenz Von Stein in 1850, for example, cited in Gusfield, 1968). Some social movements are reactionary, complaining about how society has changed (the Ku Klux Klan). Others demand changes that the public may at best dimly perceive as necessary (millennial movements). Manuals often cite such examples as the aroused villagers in Frankenstein movies, but in formal terms a social movement requires only leaders and associations (the directed elements) and an unaffiliated population (the partisans) in whose interests the movement acts (Blumer, 1969). These attributes usually apply to a movement in its earliest stages. Currently, the phrase is most often associated with efforts by researchers to assess the likely success of insurgent groups that may use violence or the threat of violence to secure their goals (Fording, 2001). The more such groups take on the attributes of a movement, the more successful they are likely to be (Baumgartner & Jones, 1993; Gamson, 1975; Tilly, 1978).

Successful social movements can affect society in many ways, but three are highlighted here. First, social movements may change how partisans think about themselves. The civil rights movement had such an effect on African Americans (Verba & Nie, 1972), and the women's movement had a similar impact on women (Mansbridge, 1986). Second, social movements may change how the public or other third parties regard such groups and appraise their goals (Lipsky, 1968). Finally, social movements may affect public policy and legislation—for good or ill. Most Americans agree that the civil rights and women's movements had necessary and useful impacts on policy (Schuman, Steeh, Bobo, & Krysan, 1997). Few would make the same claims for Prohibition, a policy closely associated with the Women's Christian Temperance Union's public campaign of the 1910s (Gusfield, 1986; Rose, 1996). Normally, powerless groups seeking social change value social movements because by transforming their members' attitudes and public opinion they secure nontraditional resources that allow them to influence policy (Lipsky, 1968).

Judging by these standards—impact on clients, society, and policy—and taking a least-common-denominator view of what the different intermediaries we have discussed agree on, a social movement does appear to be emerging within the fatherhood field. However, we also believe that as intermediaries press for agenda items not commonly shared, they increase the likelihood that their burgeoning movement will self-destruct. We believe that the key intermediaries agree on three items: (a) fathers ought to recognize that they have an important role to play in the family and recognize that they do have important and positive impacts on child well-being, (b) society should endorse these roles for fathers, and (c) public policy ought to help fathers become responsible and help society recognize the value of responsible fatherhood.

We believe that a social movement may be emerging in this field because in each area that one would look for an effect of a social movement, there is evidence of change.

- There is evidence that American fathers have become more committed to responsible fatherhood goals. The National Center on Fathering reports that an advertising agency's private survey found that "the younger generation are more committed to fathering than the older generation." Also, preliminary findings from the national Fragile Families and Child Wellbeing Study surprised policymaking audiences with its finding that the large majority of young low-income fathers said they wanted to be involved in the lives of their children. Previously the perception of young low-income fathers—particularly young never-married low-income African-American fathers—had been that they were uninterested in becoming involved in the lives of their children (Wilson, 1996).

- There is some evidence that public support for responsible fatherhood goals has increased. Between 1992 and 1996 the number of respondents to a Gallup poll who agreed or strongly agreed with the statement "The most significant family or social problem facing America is the physical absence of the father from the home" grew from 70% to 80%. Similarly, in that poll there was broad agreement that fathers make unique contributions in the lives of their children and that fathers need to increase their skills. There is also evidence that media attention to the fatherhood field has increased. Media attention to the term *fragile family,* for example, grew from one article in 1984—long before demonstration projects addressing the problem had begun—to 111 by 1999 (Pouncy & Steinbock, 2000).

- Legislative support for responsible fatherhood policies has increased at federal and state levels. Congress has moved in a large arc from its original interests in finding and enforcing obligations on "deadbeat" dads to its current interest in increasing father involvement, including its growing ability to distinguish between "deadbeat" and "dead broke" dads. We suggest that Congress is midway between its early 1970s stance toward fathers and some imaginary point in the future when it might support a full array of father- and family-friendly policies ranging from welfare policies more supportive of contemporary family formation patterns to government–employer partnerships supportive of working families. With some significant exceptions, most state legislatures can be characterized as lagging behind Congress with their enactments of early 1990s-style enhanced child support enforcement programs. The intermediaries we have discussed were significant at both federal and state levels in securing these policy transformations.

Although we see evidence of an emerging responsible fatherhood social movement, it is not clear how seriously the field itself values the idea of a social movement. The National Fatherhood Initiative and the Institute for American Values, the two organizations leading the call for a Fatherhood Movement, recently moved on and issued similar calls for a Marriage Movement (NFI, 2000). Without a leadership structure that goes beyond the loose "counterweights" described, we believe that the emerging social movement we perceive will falter as the field moves beyond its least-common-denominator agenda that all intermediaries now embrace.

SUMMARY

The field has been most successful in its efforts to change government policy and to remove public policy barriers to responsible fatherhood. It has also enjoyed some success in changing behavior in the corporate workplace and in convincing the public that fathers should be held responsible for their children's support, not only financially but emotionally as well. Separation and conflict have been most evident in its cultural agendas. The importance of marriage as a precondition for or accompaniment to responsible fatherhood continues to divide the field, as does the separation between programs for "deadbeat" versus "dead broke" fathers. Preventing irresponsible fatherhood through family planning programs that target men remains a largely unexplored area. Despite significant differences in perspective, goals, and service populations, the field's initial pattern of social impact resemble those made by an emerging social movement, but as currently structured the field seems unlikely to sustain the cohesion necessary to become a mature movement.

APPENDIX

A time line for selected programs, publications, research or data collection efforts, government policies, and events or gatherings that contributed significantly to the growth and development of the fatherhood field. [Source: Kate Sylvester and Kathy Reich. (2001). *Making fathers count: Reviewing 25 years of fatherhood efforts*. Report for the Annie E. Casey Foundation.]

Year	Programs	Publications	Research/Data Collections	Government Policies	Events/Gatherings
1975		*Who Will Raise the Children? New Options for Fathers (and Mothers)* [James Levine]		President Ford signed the Social Services Amendments of 1974.	
1976			The U.S. Census Bureau collected first national data on divorce, child custody, and child support and issued a report in June 1979.		
1977					
1978					
1979			The U.S. Census Bureau began the regular biannual collection of national data on child support and alimony.		
1980					
1981	James Levine founded The Fatherhood Project® at Bank Street College of Education in New York City.				

(Continued)

Year	Programs	Publications	Research/Data Collections	Government Policies	Events/Gatherings
1982	Charles Ballard founded the Institute for Responsible Fatherhood and Family Revitalization.				
1983			The U.S. Department of Health and Human Services funded data collection on divorce, child support, and fathers' involvement with their children.		
1984		• *Fatherhood USA* [Debra Klinman & Rhiana Kohl] • *Where's Dad?* [Dr. James Dobson]		The White House hosted meeting on creating strong communities, with a special emphasis on fathers.	
1985	• The National Urban League began its Male Responsibility Project. • The Fatherhood Project started the Teen Father Project, later known as the Adolescent Family Life Collaboration. • The Kindering Center opened the National Fathers Network.				

Year					
1986					The U.S. Department of Health and Human Services and the Family Impact Seminar hosted a seminar on young unwed fathers.
1987		*The Truly Disadvantaged: The Inner City, The Underclass, and Public Policy* [William Julius Wilson]		U.S. Representative Patricia Schroeder (D-Colorado) held hearings on fathers and work: "Babies and Briefcases."	
1988	Greg Bishop founded Boot Camp for New Dads.				
1989	James Levine relocated The Fatherhood Project to the Families and Work Institute.	• *Single Mothers and Their Children: A New American Dilemma* [Sara McLanahan & Irwin Garfinkle] • *Second Chances: Men, Women, and Children a Decade After Divorce* [Judith Wallerstein & Sandra Blakeslee]		The U.S. Congress enacted the Family Support Act.	
1990	• Ralph Smith founded The Philadelphia Children's Network. • Dr. Ken Canfield founded the National Center for Fathering. • The Minnesota Early Learning Development (MELD) sponsored				

(Continued)

Year	Programs	Publications	Research/Data Collections	Government Policies	Events/Gatherings
	parenting support groups and developed a new curriculum specifically for young fathers ages 15 to 25.				
1991	• Dr. Robert Austin launched the African-American Men and Boys Initiative (AAMB). • Public/Private Ventures launched the Young Unwed Fathers pilot project at six sites.	*Divided Families: What Happens to Children When Parents Part* [Dr. Frank Furstenberg & Dr. Andrew Cherlin]		Dr. Louis Sullivan, then Secretary of Health and Human Services, began a national male-involvement initiative, including grants to Head Start agencies.	The National Center for Fathering inaugurated its annual fatherhood essay contest.
1992	The Manpower Demonstration Research Corporation began testing the Parents' Fair Share service model. A seven-site demonstration project began two years later.		The National Center for Fathering commissioned the first national poll on the public's attitudes toward fathering.	Democratic Presidential candidate Bill Clinton promised to "end welfare as we know it," in part by encouraging men to take responsibility for their families.	
1993	• Joe Jones began work with low-income new and expectant fathers as part of the Baltimore City Healthy Start Initiative. It	• "Dan Quayle Was Right" [Barbara Dafoe Whitehead, *Atlantic Monthly*] • *America's Fathers and Public Policy* [National		The U.S. Congress required states to allow unwed fathers to voluntarily declare their paternity in hospitals.	The Philadelphia Children's Network and the Center for the Study of Social Policy convened a roundtable on African-American fathers.

	evolved into the Center for Fathers, Families, and Workforce Development. • The Fatherhood Project launched a national early childhood training program concentrating on low-income communities.	Academy of Sciences] • *Getting Men Involved: Strategies for Early Childhood Programs* [The Fatherhood Project] • *FatherLove* [Richard Louv]		• The Philadelphia Children's Network and the National Center on Fathers and Families convened a Practitioners Roundtable before the third Family Re-Union conference. • The third annual Family Re-Union Conference, sponsored by Vice President and Mrs. Gore, focused on "The Role of Men in Children's Lives."
1994	• Don Eberly and Dr. Wade F. Horn founded the National Fatherhood Initiative (NFI). • The National Center on Fathers and Families (NCOFF) was established at the University of Pennsylvania.	• *World Without Work: The Causes and Consequences of Black Male Joblessness* [Ralph Smith & Tom Joe of the Center for the Study of Social Policy] • *Growing Up with a Single Parent: What Hurts, What Helps* [Sara McLanahan & Gary Sandefur] • *The Young Unwed Fathers' Project: Report from the Field* [M. Achatz & C. A. MacAllum] • NFI began publishing *Father Facts*.		

(Continued)

Year	Programs	Publications	Research/Data Collections	Government Policies	Events/Gatherings
1995	• The National Practitioners Network for Fathers and Families was founded with core support from the fatherhood funders' collaborative and housed at The Fatherhood Project. • The Center on Fathers, Families, and Public Policy was founded.	• The annual *KIDS COUNT* report [Annie E. Casey Foundation] • *New Expectations: Community Strategies for Responsible Fatherhood* [James Levine & Edward Pitt] • *Disconnected Dads: Strategies for Promoting Responsible Fatherhood* [Theodora Ooms, Elana Cohen, & John Hutchins] • *Fatherless America: Confronting Our Most Urgent Social Problem* [David Blankenhorn] • NCOFF FatherLit Research Database	The Federal Interagency Forum on Child and Family Statistics identified the lack of research on fatherhood as a major issue and launched a public/private partnership to identify gaps in the research.	• President Clinton issued an Executive Memorandum urging federal agencies to focus on fatherhood issues. • Colorado Governor Roy Romer appointed a task force on responsible fatherhood.	• Numerous Father's Day celebrations and conferences included "The Role of Men in Children's Lives" at the White House. • The Annie E. Casey Foundation, Ford Foundation, Charles Stewart Mott Foundation, and Danforth Foundation created a funders' collaborative. • The National Fatherhood Initiative received a commitment from the Ad Council for a national public-awareness campaign on the importance of fathers. • The Nation of Islam sponsored the Million Man March in Washington, D.C. • NFI and the Washington Family Council sponsored

1996				
• The Ford Foundation launched the Strengthening Fragile Families initiative—a coordinated effort to promote research, policy development, and practice. • The National Center for Strategic Non-Profit Planning and Community Leadership	• *Seven Things States Can Do to Promote Responsible Fatherhood* [Wade F. Horn & Eric Brenner] • *When Work Disappears: The World of the New Urban Poor* [William Julius Wilson] • *The Heart of a Father* [Ken Canfield] • *A Call to Fatherhood* [NFI, the Institute for American Values, and the Center of the American Experiment]	• A Gallup poll sponsored by the National Center on Fathering found that 79% of respondents say the nation's most significant family or social problem is father absence. • The Early Head Start Research and Evaluation Program added a major father studies component to its activities.	• Virginia Governor George Allen, in collaboration with NFI, launched the Virginia Fatherhood Campaign. • President Clinton's Domestic Policy Council, in collaboration with NCOFF, the National Performance Review, and the U.S. Department of Health and Human Services, convened a conference of federal agencies. • President Clinton signed the Personal	nationwide public service announcements about the importance of fathers. • NCOFF and the Institute for Mental Health Initiatives convened a conference for the media: "Fathers and Families in Focus: Exposing Stereotypes and Myths." • NCOFF established the Fathers and Families Roundtable Series. • Radio America and NFI launched a series of radio public service announcements. • NFI hosted an interfaith conference on fatherhood promotion in Washington, D.C. • NFI, the Institute for American Values, and the Center of the American Experiment sponsored a conference in Minneapolis to set a fatherhood agenda. • Coalition of Community

(Continued)

Year	Programs	Publications	Research/Data Collections	Government Policies	Events/Gatherings
	(NPCL) was founded as part of the Ford Foundation's Strengthening Fragile Families Initiative. • Robert Hamrin founded Great Dads.			Responsibility and Work Opportunity Act. • The U.S. House of Representatives formed a bipartisan Congressional Task Force on Fatherhood to examine the issue of fatherlessness and its role in public policy.	Foundations for Youth and the Funders' Collaborative initiated community-wide fatherhood events.
1997	• The HHS Office of Child Support Enforcement funded eight responsible fatherhood demonstration projects. • David Hirsch founded The Illinois Fatherhood Initiative.	• *Map and Track: State Initiatives to Encourage Responsible Fatherhood* [Jane Knitzer & Stephen Page, with Eric Brenner & Vivian Gadsden] • *Fathers, Marriage, and Welfare Reform* [Wade F. Horn & Andrew Bush for Hudson Institute] • PBS aired *Fatherhood USA*, a two-hour documentary produced by The Fatherhood Project. • *Working Fathers: New Strategies for*		• The U.S. Congress enacted the Welfare-to-Work block grant. • NCOFF established the State Policy Series.	The Promise Keepers, a faith-based movement to encourage marriage and father involvement, staged a rally in Washington, D.C.

1998					
• Bienvenidos Family Services and the National Compadres Network founded the National Latino Fatherhood and Family Institute, directed by Jerry Tello. • Texas, The Hogg Foundation and the Center for Public Policy Priorities launched the Texas Fragile Families Initiative. The Sisters of Charity Foundation in South Carolina commited $6 million over six years to community programs to strengthen the role of fathers in families.	• *Balancing Work and Family* [Fatherhood Project] • Preliminary results from Urban Institute and Fragile Families began to support "Fragile Families hypothesis." • *Nurturing Fatherhood: Improving Data and Research on Male Fertility, Family Formation, and Fatherhood* [The Federal Interagency Forum on Child and Family Statistics] • MDRC released interim findings from the Parents' Fair Share demonstration. • *Fathers Under Fire: The Revolution in Child Support Enforcement* [edited by Irwin Garfinkel, Sara McLanahan, Daniel Meyer, & Judith Seltzer for the Russell Sage Foundation]	• Baseline interviews began for the Fragile Families and Child Well-Being study. • NCOFF established the Family Development Study Group. • The Fatherhood Project began a Mott Foundation-supported study of the work-family needs of "working poor" fathers and of public and private initiatives to assist them.	• The NGA formed the Governors' Task Force on Fatherhood Promotion. • U.S. Representative Clay Shaw introduced the first Fathers Count bill, which would have authorized a $2 billion block grant for states to promote responsible fatherhood. The bill died in committee. • The National Governors' Association Human Services Committee devoted its winter meeting to state programs that promote responsible fatherhood. • Wisconsin Governor Tommy Thompson, in collaboration with NFI, launched the Wisconsin Fatherhood Initiative.	• NFI released its analysis of the portrayal of fatherhood on broadcast television and found that fathers are negatively portrayed on most shows. • NFI hosted its second national summit on fatherhood with 500 attendees. • Morehouse College and the Institute for American Values sponsored a three-day conference, "African-American Fathers and Their Families in the 21st Century." • NCOFF began the second tier of the Fathers and Families Roundtable Series.

(Continued)

Year	Programs	Publications	Research/Data Collections	Government Policies	Events/Gatherings
1999	• The Partners for Fragile Families Project announced selection of demonstration sites. • The Father-to-Father initiative's administrative home for technical assistance was housed at the National Center for Fatherhood. • NPNFF became a fully independent organization. • NCSL created the Advisory Committee on Responsible Fatherhood—the only national advisory committee to look at the issue of fatherhood from a state and federal policy context.	• *Developing Innovative Child Support Demonstrations for Non-Custodial Parents* [Wendell Primus] • *Map and Track: State Initiatives to Promote Responsible Fatherhood* (2nd ed.) • *Ten Things Mayors Can Do to Promote Responsible Fatherhood* [NFI] • *The Faith Factor in Fatherhood: Renewing the Sacred Vocation of Fatherhood* [edited by Don Eberly] • *Broke But Not Deadbeat*, a handbook for states on responsible fatherhood programs [Dana Reichert] • *The Fatherhood Movement: A Call to Action* [a collection of essays edited by Wade		• Senators Evan Bayh and Pete Domenici introduced The Responsible Fatherhood Act of 1999. The bill sought to create a $50 million annual block grant to states to promote responsible fatherhood and marriage, increase the child support pass-through, establish a $25 million annual challenge-grant program for fatherhood public awareness campaigns, and establish a national fatherhood clearinghouse. • Senator Joseph Lieberman and 24 senators sponsored a resolution encouraging greater involvement of fathers in their children's lives.	• HHS launched a nationwide public awareness campaign, "They're Your Kids. Be Their Dad." • NFI and the Mayors' Task Force on Fatherhood Promotion hosted the National Summit on Supporting Urban Fathers. • *Fathers Matter!* teleconference was hosted by U.S. Department of Education Secretary Richard Riley and U.S. Department of Health and Human Services Secretary Donna Shalala.

- The Institute for Responsible Fatherhood and Family Revitalization announced that it received a second Welfare-to-Work competitive grant.

F. Horn, David Blankenhorn, & Mitchell B. Pearlstein]
- *Father's Fair Share: Helping Poor Men Manage Child Support and Fatherhood* [Earl Johnson, Ann Levine, & Fred Doolittle]
- *Setting Support When the Non-Custodial Parent Is Low-Income* [Paula Roberts of the Center for Law and Social Policy]
- *Obligating Dads: Helping Low Income Noncustodial Fathers Do More for Their Children* [Elaine Sorenson]

- U.S. Representative Nancy Johnson introduced a limited version of the Fathers Count bill, cosponsored by a bipartisan group of 14 representatives. The Fathers Count bill passed the House of Representatives by a strongly bipartisan 328-93 margin.
- Congress and the President enacted changes to the Welfare-*to*-Work block grant that make it easier for states to offer job training and placement services to low-income, noncustodial fathers.
- North Carolina Governor Jim Hunt and Pennsylvania Governor Tom Ridge launched fatherhood initiatives in their states. Ridge collaborated with NFI in establishing his initiative.

(Continued)

Year	Programs	Publications	Research/Data Collections	Government Policies	Events/Gatherings
2000	• The U.S. Department of Health and Human Services granted waivers to the 10 states with Partners for Fragile Families sites. • The Mott Foundation launched the three-year, six-site Fathers At Work demonstration project, which aims to reduce poverty by supporting interventions.	• *Connecting Low-Income Fathers and Families: A Guide to Practical Policies* [Dana Reichart, with contributions from Daniel Ash, Jenna Davis, & Matt O'Connor] • *Role of Men in Children's Learning* [The U.S. Department of Education] • *Role of Non-Custodial Fathers Tip Guide* [U.S. Department of Health and Human Services] • *Restoring Fathers to Families and Communities: Six Steps for Families and Communities* [Social Policy Action Network]		• President Clinton announced the Fathers Work/Families Win initiative. • The White House announced that child support collections in FY1999 amounted to $15.5 billion, up from $8 billion in 1992. • Representative Nancy Johnson introduced the Child Support Distribution Act of 2000. • The Child Support Distribution Act passed the House of Representatives on a vote of 405-18. Senator Olympia Snowe introduced a similar bill in the House in October, but both bills died at the conclusion of the 106th Congress in December.	• President Clinton devoted his Saturday radio address to Father's Day and directed federal agencies to reach out to state and local governments, community providers, and families to let them know about federal resources available to promote responsible fatherhood.

REFERENCES

Achatz, M., & MacAllum, C.A. (1994). *Young unwed fathers: Report from the field.* Philadelphia: Public/Private Ventures.

Akerlof, George A., Yellen, Janet L., & Katz, Michael L. (1996). An analysis of out-of-wedlock child-bearing in the United States. *Quarterly Journal of Economics, 111*(2), 277–317.

Baumgartner, F. R., & Jones, B. D. (1993). *Agendas and instability in American politics.* Chicago: University of Chicago Press.

Blankenhorn, D. (1995). *Fatherless America: Confronting our most urgent social problem.* New York: Basic Books.

Blumer, H. (1969). Collective behavior. In A. M. Lee & H. Blumer (Eds.), *New outline of the principles of sociology* (pp. 166–222). New York: Barnes and Noble.

Canfield, K. (1996). *The heart of a father: How dads are shaping the destiny of America.* Chicago: Northfield Publishing.

Cardenas, J. (2000, July 25). Building a bridge to reconnect fathers and sons: With an east L.A. institute's help, Latino men learn the realities and rewards of parenthood. *Los Angeles Times*, E1.

Deparle, J. (1998, September 3). Welfare overhaul initiatives focus on fathers. *New York Times*, A1.

Doherty, W. J., Kouneski, E. F., & Erickson, M. F. (1996). *Responsible fathering: An overview and conceptual framework* (Report to the Administration for Children and Families and the Office of the Assistant Secretary for Planning and Evaluation of the U.S. Department of Health and Human Services). Minneapolis: University of Minnesota.

Doolittle, F., Knox, V., Miller, C., & Rowser, S. (1998). *Building opportunities, enforcing obligations: Implementation and interim impacts of Parents' Fair Share.* New York: Manpower Demonstration Research Corporation.

Fording, R. C. (2001, March). The political response to Black insurgency: A critical test of competing theories of the state. *American Political Science Review, 95,*1.

Gallagher, M. (1999). The importance of being married. In W. F. Horn, D. Blankenhorn, & M. B. Pearlstein (Eds.), *The fatherhood movement: A call to action* (pp. 57–69). Lanham, MD: Lexington Books.

Gamson, W. (1975). *The strategy of social protest.* Burr Ridge, IL: Dorsey.

Garfinkel, Irwin. (1992). *Assuring child support: An extension of social security.* New York: Russell Sage Foundation.

Gavanas, A. (1998). Making fathers into role models: The "Fatherhood Responsibility Movement" and African American Masculinities. Manuscript in preparation.

Gordon, M. (2000). The fifties: Fear, sex and discontent. Course Syllabus. University of Wisconsin–Milwaukee.

Grishold, R. L. (1998). The history and politics of fatherlessness. In *Lost Fathers*, C. R. Daniels. New York: St. Martin's Press.

Gusfield, J. R. (1968). Social movements. In D. Sills (Ed.). *The international encyclopedia of the social sciences,* New York: Macmillan.

Gusfield, J. R. (1986). *Symbolic crusade: Status politics and the American temperance movement* (2nd ed.). Urbana: University of Illinois Press.

Hayes, C. D. (Ed.). (1987). *Risking the future: Adolescent sexuality, pregnancy, and childbearing.* Washington, DC: National Academy Press.

Hevesi-Sander, J., & Rosen, J. L. (1987, May/June). Teenage fathers: Working with the neglected partner in adolescent childbearing. *Family Planning Perspectives, 19,* 107–110.

Horn, W. F. (1999). Did you say 'movement'? In W. F. Horn, D. Blankenhorn, & M. B. Pearlstein (Eds.). *The fatherhood movement: A call to action* (pp. 1–15). Lanham, MD: Lexington Books.

Johnson, E. S., Levine, A., & Doolittle, F. C. (1999). *Fathers' fair share: Helping poor men manage child support and fatherhood.* New York: Russell Sage Foundation.

Johnson, J., & Pouncy, H. (1998). Developing creative ways to address the needs of fathers and fragile families. *Harvard Journal of African American Public Policy, IV,* 5–22.

Katz, Michael B. (1989). *The undeserving poor: From the war on poverty to the war on welfare.* New York: Pantheon.

Levine, J., Murphy, D. T., & Wilson, S. (1993). *Getting men involved: Strategies for early childhood programs.* New York: Scholastic.

Levine, J., & Pitt, E. W. (1995). *New expectations: Community strategies for responsible fatherhood.* New York: Families and Work Institute.

Levine, J., & Pittinsky, T. L. (1998). *Working fathers: New strategies for balancing work and family.* New York: Harcourt Brace and Company.

Lipsky, M. (1968). Protest as a political resource. *American Political Science Review, 62,* 1144–1158.

Mansbridge, J. J. (1986). *Why we lost the ERA.* Chicago: University of Chicago Press.

Martinez, J., & Miller, C. (2000). *Working and earning: The impact of Parents' Fair Share on low-income fathers' employment.* New York: Manpower Demonstration Research Corporation.

McLanahan, S., & Casper, L. (1995). Growing diversity and inequality in the American family. In R. Farley (Ed.), *State of the Union: America in the 1990s* (pp. 1–46). New York: Russell Sage Foundation.

Mead, L. (1997). The rise of paternalism. In L. Mead (Ed.), *The new paternalism: Supervisory approaches to fighting poverty* (pp. 1–38). Washington, DC: Brookings Institute.

Miller, D. B. (1997). Adolescent fathers: What we know and what we need to know. *Child and Adolescent Social Work Journal, 14*(1), 55–69.

Mincy, R., & Pouncy, H. (1997). Paternalism, child support enforcement, and fragile families. In L. Mead (Ed.), *The new paternalism: Supervisory approaches to fighting poverty* (pp. 130–180). Washington, DC: Brookings Institute.

Mincy, R., & Pouncy, H. (1999). There must be fifty ways to start a family. In W. F. Horn, D. Blankenhorn, & M. B. Pearlstein (Eds.), *The fatherhood movement: A call to action* (pp. 83–104). Lanham, MD: Lexington Books.

Mincy, R., and Pouncy, H. (in press). The marriage mystery: Marriage, assets, and the expectations of African-American families. In O. Clayton, D. Blankenhorn, and R. Mincy (Eds.), *Are Black fathers necessary?* New York: Russell Sage Foundation.

Morehouse Research Institute and Institute for American Values. (1999). *Turning the corner on father absence in Black America: A statement from the Morehouse conference on African American fathers.* Atlanta: Morehouse Research Institute.

Morris, L. (1997). Million man march and presidential politics. *Government and Politics, 2.*

National Fatherhood Initiative (NFI). (in press). *Father Facts.* Vol. 4. www.fatherhood.org

Paternal Involvement Demonstration Project. (1996). *Statistical summary of direct service sites.* Chicago: Paternal Involvement Demonstration Project.

Pearson, J., & Thoennes, N. (1998). Programs to increase fathers' access to their children. In I. Garfinkel, S. S. McLanahan, D. R. Meyer, & J. A. Seltzer (Eds.), *Fathers under fire: The revolution in child support enforcement* (pp. 220–254). New York: Russell Sage Foundation.

Pouncy, H., & Steinbock, A. (2000). *Field report on media attention to fragile families.* Unpublished Research Report for the Ford Foundation.

Rose, K. D. (1996). *American women and the repeal of prohibition.* New York: New York University Press.

Schuman, H., Steeh, C., Bobo, L., & Krysan, M. (1997). *Racial attitudes in America: Trends and interpretations* (rev. ed.). Cambridge, MA: Harvard University Press.

Skocpol, T. (1992). *Protecting soldiers and mothers: The political origins of social policy in the United States.* Cambridge, MA: Harvard University Press.

Sylvester, K., & Reich, K. (2001). *Making fathers count: Reviewing 25 years of fatherhood efforts.* Baltimore: Annie. E. Casey Foundation.

Tilly, C. (1978). *From mobilization to revolution.* Reading, MA: Addison-Wesley.

U.S. Department of Health and Human Services. (1983). Overview of the final report of the Seattle-Denver Income Maintenance Experiment. Prepared by the Office of Income Security Policy and Office of the Assistant Secretary for Planning and Evaluation. http://aspe.hhs.gov/hsp/SIME-DIME83/index.htm

Verba, S., & Nie, N. H. (1972). *Participation in America: Political democracy and social equality.* New York: Harper and Row.

Verba, S., Schlozman, K. L. & Brady, H. 1995. *Voice and equality: Civic voluntarism in American politics.* Cambridge, MA: Harvard University Press.

Wetzstein, C. (2000, June 30). Coalition pledges to strengthen marriage. *Washington Times,* A11.

Wilson, W. J. (1996). *When work disappears: The world of the new urban poor.* New York: Alfred A. Knopf.

22

Cross-Disciplinary Challenges to the Study of Father Involvement

Catherine S. Tamis-LeMonda
New York University

Natasha Cabrera
*National Institute of Child Health
and Human Development*

Exposure to the perspectives of distinct traditions in the social sciences challenges researchers to confront their own epistemological assumptions and to grapple with the discipline-specific, theoretical, and methodological discourse of others. This approach inevitably leads to a different type of scientific inquiry, one that not only stimulates a different set of research questions, but also presents a more integrative, complex, but perhaps less-tidy, picture of the phenomenon under study. These purposes lay at the core of this collection of writings. Each of the scientific disciplines represented in this *Handbook of Father Involvement* offer unique methodological and theoretical approaches to the study of fathering and to the interpretation of behavioral patterns that characterize ecological systems that include as well as extend beyond family units. Together, the chapters in this handbook offer provocative and challenging insight into the nature and meaning of fatherhood and father involvement by questioning longstanding assumptions about fathers' roles in the lives of families and children in current history.

In the context of disparate orientations, researchers struggle with similar issues that suggest common starting points in the study of father involvement. For the most part, research on fathering is motivated by concern for children's well-being, and social scientists share a core set of questions, including: Who are fathers? What is father involvement and how does it affect children and families? What are the determinants of father involvement? How do cultural contexts shape fathers' roles in families? In this closing chapter, we examine whether and how a cross-disciplinary approach has advanced knowledge about these fundamental questions. What have we learned about father involvement? Where do we go from here?

WHO ARE FATHERS?

The multidisciplinary nature of this handbook sheds light on the complexity of what initially appears to be the most straightforward and fundamental question—Who are fathers? This question is the starting point of almost all chapters (e.g., chaps. 1, 3, 5, 19, and 21), suggesting that it is neither straightforward nor settled. We thus intentionally began this handbook with the section on demography, which from a quantitative perspective illustrates the complexity of defining the "subjects" of this book—fathers. Demographers rely on large-scale data sets to examine population-based process such as fertility, mortality, and immigration that determine population size, growth, composition, and distribution. Generally, national surveys collect data on biological fathers or use mothers as proxies for fathers. However, these large-scale surveys miss absent fathers and nontraditional fathers. Psychologists interested in fatherhood have tended to focus on biological fathers in two-parent families. Hence, what we know about fathers, for theoretical and methodological reasons, comes from a very select sample of men and continues to be limited. However, this trend is changing, and the chapters in this handbook exemplify new directions in fatherhood research across scientific disciplines.

Today, the complexity of defining fathers lies at the foreground of scientific inquiry, and Hernandez and Brandon (chap. 2) and Hofferth, Pleck, and colleagues (chap. 3) succinctly and comprehensively characterize the array of fathers in current U.S. history. Without minimizing the biological basis for fatherhood, cultural prescriptions of who are fathers are often limiting, yet its definition has been boldly expanded to embrace the range of social ecologies that characterizes family life within and across cultures. Fathers vary along lines of biological relatedness, residency status, and paternity establishment, and many of the previously assumed requisites for being a father have become blurred. A father may or may not be biologically related to his child, may or may not be married to his child's mother, may or may not have a relationship with his child's mother, may or may not reside with his child, may or may not have legal ties to his child, may or may not have custody of his child, may or may not support his child (either emotionally or economically), and may or may not establish paternity. Who, then, are fathers? At one extreme, overly narrow definitions of fathering are unduly exclusionary, precluding understanding of the social circumstances that characterize the lives of the adults who care for children today. At the other extreme, exceedingly broad definitions cast doubt on the utility of the term *father* and make predictions of impact difficult to ascertain. How do social scientists strike a balance between breadth and clarity of construct?

In general, researchers assume that through an understanding of family networks, agreements, ideologies, roles, practices, and so forth, it is possible to identify who are fathers to children. Depending on the purpose of the study, if a biological father is not present in a child's life, but an uncle or some other man is, researchers may shift the spotlight to include this father figure in their studies. Terms such as *social father* have been adopted to refer to males in children's lives who assume fathering roles. This approach is eloquently illustrated in the qualitative work of Jarrett and colleagues (chap. 9), in which they demonstrate the range of sociological fathers found in the lives of children and youth from poor African-American families. These include biological fathers, male companions, stepfathers, foster fathers, uncles, grandfathers, older brothers, unrelated family friends and mentors, and fictive kin. Empirical evidence suggests that many of these men, when caring and positively involved, exert a powerful influence on children's life trajectories.

WHAT IS FATHER INVOLVEMENT AND HOW DOES IT INFLUENCE CHILDREN AND FAMILIES?

Inextricably linked to the question of "who" are fathers is the challenge of defining what fathers do in family life today and how those roles affect the lives of children and families. What does it mean to be an "involved father"? How involved should fathers be if they are to positively influence their children's development? What are thresholds of father involvement below which children's well-being is at risk? Does the nature of involvement change when different father types are considered—resident/nonresident, biological/social? Should different criteria be utilized to assess involvement in different types of fathers? The cross-disciplinary nature of this handbook advances an understanding of the multitude of ways in which fathers affect children, the outcomes in children that are affected, under which circumstances fathers matter, and how and why. Indeed, the initial motivation for this handbook rests on the assumption that fathers are a powerful force in children's lives, and the section on child development most notably supports this proposition. Father involvement affects infant–father attachments, children's peer relations and friendships, academic achievement, and social development (see chaps. 4 and 6).

Although the bulk of research on father involvement is atheoretical, researchers in this handbook each adopt unique, discipline-specific frameworks in their study of father involvement. For example, economists view *child support dollars* and *visitation* as important indicators of father involvement. Graham and Beller (chap. 17) examine determinants of these two indicators and link these trends to aspects of children's well-being, most notably educational achievement. Sigle-Rushton and Garfinkel (chap. 16) rely on *marital status* as a proxy for father involvement, based on evidence that married fathers coreside with their children and spend more time with them than do nonresident fathers. They utilize a cost-benefit analysis to explain this ubiquitous pattern. Their analyses reveal that nonresident fathers allocate greater resources to spend time with their children than do resident fathers, by incurring costs associated with visiting arrangements, travel expenses, and sometimes arranging a venue for visits. In contrast, coresidency allows for shared consumption of goods (e.g., housing), thereby lowering the costs of involvement for resident fathers. The net effect of these patterns is that time spent with children is priced at a higher cost to nonresident fathers. This cost-benefit analysis explains why low-income fathers with fewer economic resources might not be as either involved as nonresident fathers who have resources or resident fathers in general.

However, inability to pay child support is not always indicative of father indifference. In their investigation of parental bargaining, England and Folbre (chap. 15) extend the definition of father involvement to include financial support, time, and emotional care. They emphasize the role of emotional attachment (to children) in reducing the bargaining power of primary caregivers, underscoring the synergy among different aspects of father involvement. Their variegated approach to father involvement blends traditional economic indicators with emotional aspects of fathering.

In contrast to a principal focus on economic provisioning, researchers of child development focus on the importance of the *quality of father–child relationships*, how such relationships develop and change over time, and how they affect children's lives. Lamb (chap. 4) discusses the formation and course of infants' attachment to fathers and asserts that similar mechanisms operate to explain father–infant relationships as mother–infant relationships. Likewise, Parke emphasizes the importance of the father–child relationship, but broadens the scope to include complex linkages among father–child, mother–child, and child–peer relationships. Palkovitz (chap. 5) tackles the complexity of the father involvement construct by directly addressing the question: What is meant by more or less father involvement? In his comprehensive overview, he examines components of emotional climate, father–child connection, time investment, discipline, teaching, and financial support, as well as psychological aspects of father involvement, such as energy, responsibility, and commitment. He argues that a fuller understanding of father involvement must consider the meanings of various forms of father involvement for both children and fathers themselves.

The most illuminating example of how conceptualizations of father involvement vary across disciplines is evidenced in the evolutionary section (chaps.

12–14). Evolutionary psychologists have adopted the term *father investment* (rather than *involvement*), reflecting an orientation that links behavior to biology and hence offers a different theoretical understanding of how, why, when, and under what circumstances men "invest" in their offspring. Together, the contributors to this section advanced the notion that children benefit from fathers in a multitude of ways, including but not limited to fathers' enhancement of their offspring's biological fitness and reproductive success. Their foci on unique populations, such as the multiethnic Okavango Delta peoples of Botswana (chaps. 12 and 13) and 19th-century Mormons (chap. 14), challenge orthodoxy (see Section IV opening) and raise consciousness as to how fathering practices fit the long term (i.e., transgenerational) goals of societies. Also central to an evolutionary perspective is the notion of "trade-offs" in fathering: By investing in certain aspects of fathering (e.g., quantity of offspring), fathers may be unable to invest in other ways (e.g., quality of time spent). In addition, Waynforth's categories of direct/indirect care add a new lens to the study of fathers and offer a reproductive interpretation of father absence.

Bock and Johnson (chap. 12) propose a model of embodied capital (e.g., physical strength and growth to actual tissue), which is related to human capital. In this model, fathers are seen as influencing children through investment in activities or experiences that tend to increase their children's embodied capital. Their study includes male labor migrants in the United States who, as characteristic of many poor men from developing countries, send remittances home but spend little time with their children and families (Lucas & Stark, 1985). They predict that children of migrants acquire fewer traditional skills and knowledge than children of nonmigrant laborers due to father absence. However, children of migrants benefit from an increase in resources, which could be used for the acquisition of growth-based embodied capital and experience-based embodied capital in the form of schooling. Although only certain aspects of their model are supported with data, their approach to fathers' effects on children underscores realms of behavior that extend beyond traditional conceptions of fathering and shed light on the role of culture in shaping the meaning of fatherhood.

WHAT ARE THE DETERMINANTS OF FATHER INVOLVEMENT?

A fundamental focus of many chapters in this handbook is on the determinants of fatherhood. What factors, in fathers, children, families, communities, and larger social–cultural contexts influence the process and quality of fathering? What factors support and predict positive father involvement? What factors obstruct involvement? Father involvement is affected by multiple interacting systems operating over the life course, including mental health, expectations, family relations, support networks, education, economic status, children's characteristics, and even public policies (Tamis-LeMonda & Cabrera, 1999).

Chapters in this handbook move beyond enumerating determinants of father involvement toward identifying and modeling mechanisms that underlie associations. Consider the example of father residency, which is considered a key determinant of the quality and quantity of father involvement. Fathers who reside with their children generally spend more time with them and are more emotionally involved (e.g., chaps. 4, 7, and 16). A focus on mechanisms prompts researchers to explore factors that contribute to heightened involvement in resident fathers. Do resident fathers have more resources? Are they more likely to be biologically related to their children? Are their relationships to their children's mothers less conflicted? What are the factors that explain variability in type and amount of father involvement among resident and nonresident fathers? A mother's role as gatekeeper may act as a barrier to the involvement of nonresident fathers (Allen & Doherty, 1996), expeditiously leading to father resentment and withdrawal (Furstenberg, Sherwood, & Sullivan, 1992). There are also instances in which maternal gatekeeping is critical to the safety and well-being of children.

A multidisciplinary approach sheds further light on processes and underlying mechanisms by tackling the question of why certain factors affect fathering through different scientific lenses. Economists, such as Sigle-Rushton and Garfinkel, for example, point to the financial benefits of coresidency for fathers and translate those benefits into more resources for children and less cost to fathers. From a developmental perspective, Lamb suggests that because nonresidential fathers are unable to participate regularly in the daily routines of children's lives (e.g., helping children dress, helping with schoolwork), they become less integral to children's life trajectories over time. The absence of participation in everyday activities might serve as a constant barrier to the development of strong father–child relationships. He also emphasizes the impact of pre- and postmarital conflict on fathers' involvement with and effect on children. Demographers, such as Hofferth and colleagues, build on these observations by emphasizing the role of fathers' legal obligations and connections to children. They point out that cohabiters who are romantically connected to the mother but are neither biologically or legally bound to children do not monitor children's behaviors as much as biological fathers or stepfathers who have adopted their partners' children. They partly ascribe these different patterns of engagement to societal standards or mores about what is and is not appropriate in various legal and biological circumstances. As researchers in this volume point out, the cultural nuances surrounding different types of mother–father unions may also account for variation in father involvement.

Aside from focusing on different sets of fathering determinants, scientists from different disciplines adopt unique methodological approaches. Economists, demographers, and developmentalists, for the most part, look at covariance among predetermined measures (e.g., Do residency, father resources, and time spent with children significantly covary?). In contrast, sociologists and anthropologists seek to understand the perspectives of fathers themselves. For example, Townsend (chap. 10) and Jarrett and colleagues (chap. 9) utilize in-depth interviews to provide insights into fathers' perceptions of the factors that affect their fathering. They explore African-American fathers' views of how neighborhood contexts, relationships to their children's mothers, and negotiations among family members lead to paternal involvement or disengagement; their perceptions of how involvement with their children changes over time; and whether and how they believe their own involvement is affected by existing social policies.

HOW DO CULTURAL CONTEXTS SHAPE FATHER INVOLVEMENT?

An important theme of this handbook is how culture, broadly defined, shapes fathering. The notion of culture encompasses the norms, practices, language, and beliefs that are collectively shared in a society. Sociocultural ideologies and prescriptions about father involvement, together with the economic structure of societies, affect fathers' roles (e.g., breadwinner, caregiver, emotional nurturer) and the investment they make in their children and families, all of which varies substantially across societies (Hewlett, 1992). What fathers do, when, and why, are integrally bound to the cultural contexts of their lives. The study of culture, in particular foreign cultures, has been imperative to the work of anthropologists, sociologists, and evolutionary psychologists (e.g., chaps. 10–14), who have explored the nature and meaning of father involvement in societies strikingly different from mainstream United States. Given the changing demographics of the United States, research on culture, race, and ethnicity is central to other scientific disciplines as well, including that of psychology and economics.

Current immigration and migration patterns have led to enormous cultural and ethnic variation in U.S. families. Today, 20% of fathers with dependent children live in immigrant families, primarily from Hispanic or Asian countries of origin. Fathers' roles are being transformed in parallel with the dramatic rise in racial, ethnic, and cultural diversity in the United States (chap. 2). Because these demographic trends will persist into the future, the cultural content and meaning of fathering and the ways in which we conceptualize and measure father involvement will continue to evolve.

To date, however, most of what we know about father involvement comes from investigations of middle-class men of European decent, a sample more of convenience than of import for families most targeted by social programs and public policy (Cabrera, Tamis-LeMonda, Bradley, Hofferth, & Lamb, 2000; Greene, Hearn, & Emig, 1996; Tamis-LeMonda & Cabrera, 1999). In response to these limitations, contributors to this handbook examine variation in fathering both across societies, as well as within the United States. Consequently, they raise cultural awareness about the roles of fathers and families across groups, challenge mono-cultural assumptions about fathering (e.g., Who is a "good" father? What does it mean to be positively involved?), and highlight interrelations between culture and individual differences. To survive (and hopefully thrive), fathers and families must accommodate the social realities of markedly different political, economic, and demographic regimes.

In the study of U.S. fathers, researchers are confronted with complex interrela-tions among culture, minority status, education, income, and family configuration—codependencies that pervade multicultural societies. Culture is often intertwined with family and socioeconomic structures, making it enormously difficult to disen-tangle cultural factors from family characteristics. For example, Hispanic fathers, and especially Black fathers, are less likely than White fathers to be living with their children. When living with their children Black fathers are much more likely to be caring for stepchildren in a blended family situation. When they do reside with their children, both Black and Hispanic fathers are more likely to be living with a larger number of children (chap. 2). These patterns unfold in a context of limited educa-tional and socioeconomic resources available to Black and Hispanic fathers. Conse-quently, poverty rates among Black and Hispanic fathers with dependent children are two or three times greater than the rates for White fathers (chap. 2). The different economic and structural contexts of family life will undoubtedly affect the nature of father–child relationships, perhaps beyond that of race or ethnicity per se.

Studies conducted on populations outside the United States examine the experi-ences of fathers and families in societies that differ dramatically in terms of histo-ry, politics, economics, and philosophy. Rooparnine's research (chap. 11) demon-strates how men's mating behaviors and investment in children are driven by cultural ideologies about roles and responsibilities and concepts of manhood and fatherhood. As a poignant illustration, he describes the sociocultural practice of progressive mating and childbearing in multiple unions characteristic of Caribbean fathers, patterns that have led some researchers to assert that fatherhood is in "cri-sis" in certain developing areas of the world (Roopnarine & Brown, 1997).

Similarly, Townsend demonstrates how cultural expectations determine the appropriate behavior of men and fathers in families. His anthropological research draws on intensive fieldwork with men in the San Francisco Bay region of north-ern California and those from a village in the southern African country of Botswana (Twasana). In the Tswana cultural model, men provide economic, social, and emotional supports to a variety of children, including their own off-spring, grandchildren, nieces, and nephews, enabling collective, shared invest-ment in children's lives. This contrasts with U.S. fathers' tendency to focus on the well-being of their own offspring. Additionally, in Botswana, father involvement takes on different forms and intensities over children's life course, as fathers pass through a series of culturally prescribed roles and relationships. For example, fathers in Botswana are expected to provide a home for their daughters and their children; children live with their grandparents while their mother is away working. In middle-class U.S. society, in contrast, fathers are expected to support their children early on, but to be less central as their children grow into self-sufficient adults. Townsend points out that these distinct profiles of fathering might reflect situations of economic instability (e.g., Botswana) versus situations where a strong economy affords relative stability and economic well-being.

WHERE DO WE GO FROM HERE?

At minimum, the assemblage of chapters in this handbook admonishes unitary perspectives of fathering by offering multiple scientific lenses through which to understand fatherhood and the pathways through which fathers affect children (e.g., by enhancing reproductive success, supporting academic achievement). Sensitivity to the multidimensionality of father involvement promises to stimulate theoretical models and empirical testing of the synergistic relations among measures of fathering; how dimensions of fathering vary across time, culture, and development; and how they jointly affect the life trajectories of children and families. A significant barrier to engaging in multidisciplinary research derives from the language-specific (jargon) characteristic of disciplines. This challenges scientists to come up with a shared language and urges researchers to speak to a broader audience than is customary within the bounds of specific scientific traditions. Ideally, a cross-disciplinary perspective provides a catalyst for integrating theories on the well-being of children and families and stimulates innovative methodologies, constructs, and theoretical orientations. Cross-disciplinary collaboration impresses researchers to work outside of their academic boxes and to construct models that are flexible, are comprehensive, and shed light on how fathers, mothers, children, and extended kin negotiate and develop relationships in the dynamic contexts of their families, economic circumstances, and communities.

What research directions evolve from this collection of writings? How might collaboration across disciplines advance the broader field of human development and parenting? What challenges remain? In this closing section, we raise several additional considerations that lay at the foreground of future research on fathers—directions that are largely inspired by the contributors to this handbook.

Group Trends Versus Individual Differences: Consequence of Averaging

The standard of scientific evidence in extant research traditionally rests on the ubiquitous "correlation." In fatherhood research, we typically ask whether fathers matter by correlating a particular measure of involvement with a particular developmental outcome in children. Investigations of interactions among variables or subgroups of the study population are rare, most likely because most studies of fathers lack adequate power to test such effects. The conceptual underpinning to the main effect, correlational model is the assumption that father involvement, the way it is measured, benefits children equally: Children who see their fathers have better developmental outcomes. Fathers who engage in more of a certain activity enhance their children's current and future prospects for success. Although empirical evidence lends some support to this notion, fathers' effects on children are typically modest and in certain studies altogether absent. Lamb and Palkovitz (chaps. 4, 5, and 7) aptly caution against a simple appraisal of father involvement as always a "good" thing. Palkovitz (1997; see also chap. 5) notes that because father involvement carries an array of significant qualitative components (e.g., developmental appropriateness, emotional climate) more involvement is not always better. Fathers and children may hit saturation points in which father involvement becomes redundant and a drain on fathers' resources of time and energy, rather than enhancing children's development (see chap. 5). Moreover, these simple correlations do not address variability within and across groups. Not all fathers who reside with their children exert a positive effect on their development. Therefore, the empirical quest for linear associations between fathering and child outcomes may be misleading, potentially masking the richness of individuals' lives and the variety of circumstances under which fathers do and do not benefit their children. Moreover, because correlations cannot be equated with causation, they do not tell us what factor (or set of factors) caused which outcome or set of outcomes.

Lamb's chapter on noncustodial fathers (chap. 7) most aptly illustrates the consequences of group averaging. He notes that modest to small associations exist between children's contact with their noncustodial fathers and various measures of child development. This may be due to the fact that not all father involvement is positive and that some children experience negative or ineffective fathering. As Lamb points out, children do not gain from sheer contact with fathers, but rather thrive in rich, multifaceted father–child relationships. He cites research that suggests that 15 to 25% of the children who experience their parents' divorce are perhaps harmed by regular and extended contact with their noncustodial parents (Greif, 1997; Johnston, 1994). In contrast, when nonresidential fathers are fully integrated into their children's lives, they are more likely to contribute economically to their children's support and to positively affect their children's development.

Consequently, researchers are urged to move beyond questions of main effects and group trends by inquiring into processes that operate at the level of the individual: Under which circumstances do fathers matter? For whom? And why? Practitioners and policymakers, in turn, are challenged to identify when it may be unsuitable to encourage a father's involvement or reinvolvement in his child's life, such as in cases of domestic violence and child abuse, situations in which a mother's role as gatekeeper should be respected (Tamis-LeMonda & Cabrera, 1999).

Multidimensionality and Trade-offs in Fathering

How do different aspects of father involvement codetermine developmental outcomes in children? As yet we have done a better job at exploring single paths of influence than at modeling interrelations among multiple aspects of fathering and children's outcomes. If a particular measure of father involvement is deemed important, does it uniquely contribute to children's well-being or does it exert an influence vis-à-vis other paths? Graham and Beller's account (chap. 17) of the beneficial effects of child support payments on the academic achievement of children illustrates this point. They note that child support dollars predict child outcomes more so than other sources of income, but do not account for all of the variance. Moreover, given the nature of the data, these associations cannot speak to causation. This suggests that a direct, linear account of child support dollars in relation to child development is simplistic. Rather, fathers who pay child support may be more committed or dedicated to their children, may have better relationships with their children's mothers, and may visit their children more often. Or, it may be that fathers who are more committed to their children and have the means to support them are more likely to do so than those who are not.

A multidimensional view of father involvement, in the context of associations among aspects of involvement, dovetail with the notion of trade-offs in parenting (raised in the evolutionary section). Fathers cannot be all things to children, but rather make choices, either implicitly or explicitly, about where to direct their energies and resources. Moreover, these decisions are constrained by a limited set of (perceived) choices that are determined by many factors, including number of children, economic conditions, quality of parental relationship, and personal characteristics. These decisions have costs and benefits that are not always apparent. For instance, the quality of father–child relationships might positively predict the time fathers spend with children, financial provisioning, and even the quality of the mother–child relationship, yet they inversely relate to a father's bargaining power and the number of offspring he bears. Similarly, fathers who are committed to their role as breadwinners may have to compromise other aspects of involvement—such as the actual time they spend with their children. A statement made by a participant in our study of low-income, New York City fathers captures the essence of trade-offs in fathering. In an effort to describe the various ways this father involved himself in his infant's life, we asked him an extensive series of questions about the activities he engaged in with his baby (e.g., diapering, feeding, singing, playing, holding). His responses to question after question about frequency of participation were: "Not at all," "rarely," "not at all," "rarely." After continuing along these lines for some time, he interrupted our experimenter in an exasperated tone and asked, "And when do you get to the part of the questionnaire where you ask me about how hard I break my back working so that I can support my child?" (Picker, Tamis-LeMonda, & Shannon, 2001).

The multiple roles that fathers are expected to play versus the roles that they are actually able to fulfill illustrates the necessity of exploring multiple dimensions of fathering, fathers' views about aspects of fathering, family decision making and motivation, and the mechanisms through which parents exert influence on their children. By elucidating associations among different aspects of fathering and recognizing how and when a father's attention to certain areas of involvement compromises and limits his ability to be involved in other ways, researchers will come closer to understanding the unique and synergistic confluence of factors that affects the course of children's development, as well as the multitude of configurations that characterizes positively involved fathers.

Toward a Dynamic Model of Father Involvement

A notable limitation in current research on fathering is the lack of a life-span theory of how fathers affect children at different stages of development, and why. The complexity of understanding father involvement and its effect on children and families is intensified by the empirical demands of studying a system that is in constant flux: What fathers do, why they engage in certain activities, the ways in which they affect their offspring and families, their perspectives about fathering, and so forth are continually changing as fathers and children grow. Views about what it means to be a father and the roles of fatherhood are constructed over many years; fathering is a process that unfolds over the course of a child's conception, birth, infancy, childhood, and adulthood (Cabrera et al., 2000). Yet relatively little has been documented about the course of becoming a father and the factors that contribute to changes in the quality and quantity of fathers' involvement over time. To date, there is no unified theory explaining the complex set of developmental processes that give meaning to and shape the practice of fatherhood in its many forms and circumstances across the life course (Cabrera et al., 2000; Lamb, 1997; Roggman et al., chap. 1; Tanfer & Mott, 1998).

Scientists from different traditions tend to emphasize fathering at different stages of fathers' and children's lives, partly because of availability of data and partly because of constraints in theory and methodologies. In general, developmental psychologists emphasize fathers' roles in children's early development by focusing on outcomes in infants (e.g., attachment, regulation, cognitive growth), school-age children (e.g., academic performance), and adolescents (e.g., substance use, delinquency). However, little attention is paid to fathering beyond adolescence, or to how father involvement transforms across developmental epochs. How do fathers make the transition between parenting a school-aged child and parenting an adolescent? How do they allocate resources once their children reach adolescence? What role do fathers play when their children reach adulthood?

In contrast, anthropologists tend to focus on fathers' roles across the life span. Anthropological studies on fathering indicate that in certain societies fathers may assume greater importance and responsibilities when their children reach adulthood (chap. 10). Cross-cultural psychologists speak to the evolving mating patterns men adopt over their life course in certain societies, leaving children born by partners in earlier, casual relationships, but later committing and investing greatly in children born from later partners (e.g., chap. 11).

Unique to both these orientations is that of economists, who emphasize choice, decision-making, and the well-being of the family unit, rather than child per se. Hence, economists focus on decision making between parents, allocation of resources within families, and the impact of resources (both human and social capital) on outcomes. Clearly, a research agenda that blends the orientations of these scientific disciplines will provide a more complex picture of fatherhood and a fuller appreciation for the changing nature of fathering across the life course of fathers, children, and families.

New Family Forms and Underrepresented Fathers

Given the array of lifestyles that characterize current U.S. families, fathers' roles are best understood in the context of new and shifting family structures. New family structures challenge long-standing assumptions about different types of fathers and their roles in children's lives. For instance, the notion that biological relatedness explains fathers' investment in children is brought into question by evidence that some biological fathers can be quite indifferent to their children, whereas some stepfathers, or other father figures, can be extremely involved (Tamis-LeMonda & Cabrera, 1999). This points to the variability that exists within groups and urges researchers to search further for factors that underlie these observations. As yet, social scientists are farther along in describing the array of fathers and family types than they are in understanding the pathways through which children are affected in nontraditional families.

An example of a nontraditional family is one that includes a "social father" who is either substituting for a biological father or is an additional male presence in the child's life. The current ecologies of human experience have led to appreciation for the potential role of social fathers in children's development. However, research on the roles of these social fathers is in its infancy. At a very fundamental level, defining a man as a "social father" is a circular process. In order to be a social father, a man should behave fatherly to a child, and what this entails is still unknown. We lack a theoretical framework to guide research on social fathers; hence the question of what is an effective social father versus an ineffective one is open for debate. Can a social father fail his/her child? What is expected of a social father? Why do men choose to invest in someone else's children? Are romantic ties to the mother the only reason that social fathers choose to care for other

men's children? Studies on social fathers must also address the personal, subjective experiences of both children and fathers—of being fathered by someone
other than one's biological father and of being a father to someone else's children.

Aside from the category of social fathers, knowledge on economically disadvantaged and minority fathers is also limited. National studies of men and fathers
have generally excluded those who have unstable housing, do not live with their
families, or are homeless. Little is known about nonresident fathers (see chap. 7),
in part because most national household surveys do not collect information from
fathers who are uncounted, incarcerated, or in the military (chap. 2). This "male
undercount" calls into question the accuracy of the information we have about all
fathers (Tamis-LeMonda & Cabrera, 1999). Moreover, small-scale studies of
underrepresented men have focused largely on negative aspects of behavior, such
as those who do not pay child support, and negative outcomes in children.
Research on potential strengths in less-advantaged families is much needed. Many
of the contributors to this volume rose to the challenge of studying the personal
experiences of hard-to-reach fathers in order to portray their experiences from a
more personalized, less-prescriptive perspective (e.g., chaps. 9, 17, 18, and 20).

The complexities of identifying, describing, and studying different types of
fathers might soon extend to mothers. A decade or so ago it was possible to argue
that unlike the study of motherhood, in which parenthood is clear because it is tied
to women's biological role in the process of birth, fatherhood is an ambiguous
process that is heavily tied to social norms and prescriptions. However, this argument is no longer viable. Given recent reproductive technologies (e.g., in vitro
fertilization and sperm donors bank) and a social and cultural shift that is redefining parenthood (e.g., surrogate parenthood, "rent a womb"), defining who are
mothers is increasingly fraught with the same difficulties as defining fathers. This
blurring of biology and social prescription challenges Margaret Mead's assertion
that "motherhood is a biological necessity, but fatherhood is a social invention."

He said—She said—Child said

A comprehensive understanding of fatherhood necessitates inquiry into multiple
perspectives—at minimum, that of fathers, mothers, and children. Although the
contributors to this handbook impressively met their charge of focusing on the
nature, antecedents, and consequences of father involvement, their accounts
inspire numerous questions about the related views and roles of mothers, as well
as how children perceive their experiences with their fathers and families. Past
research on fathers has used mothers as proxy for fathers, and so the information
we had on fathers was obtained from mothers. Absent from many accounts were
the voices of mothers—how mothers regard and experience their roles as mothers, how they view the roles of their children's fathers, and how they negotiate
family decisions with their partners. Many studies today are remedying this situation not only by collecting data from fathers themselves, but also by gathering

parallel information from mothers (chap. 19). Similarly, although children are often the end goal of fathering studies, we know little about their reflections on the actions of their biological (and sometimes social) fathers and mothers and how those vary across family structures. These limitations characterize the broader parenting and developmental literatures; relatively speaking, few studies examine mothers, fathers, and children together.

Simultaneous emphasis on mothers is critical to research on father involvement, because the roles fathers play in family life and whether or not they reside with mothers often depend on mothers' attitudes and expectations about their roles (and vice versa). Mothers are gatekeepers to nonresidential fathers' access to children and likely gatekeep the roles and responsibilities of both residential and nonresidential fathers. A mother communicates what she expects of her partner by handing over their baby for diapering, or instead by diapering the baby herself. A mother's subtle grimace as a father fails to console a crying infant may lead him to expeditiously "leave the nurturing to mom." In some cases, mothers use children as bait to get what they want (money, sexual interest) from their partners (chap. 20). Reciprocally, it is also unclear how fathers' subtle or overt reactions influence mothers' roles and behaviors and how fathers' thoughts and actions serve to constrain (or expand) mothers' possibilities.

The complexities of engaging in research that focuses on multiple family perspectives are obvious. What should researchers do under circumstances of "he said—she said"? In our own research on low-income mothers and fathers, we were surprised to learn that responses to the most fundamental questions diverged, including whether or not a father resided with his child and whether or not he was the child's biological father. For example, a straightforward question about "coresidency" yields different answers and reveals the transitory nature of family structure. Fathers "reside" with their children one month, or week, or day, are absent the next, only to reunite with their families again in the near (or distant) future. Moreover, mothers and fathers don't always agree on the residential status of fathers (chap. 18). Although fathers may believe they reside in the house, mothers may believe they do not (chap. 20). Indeed, one of the defining features of contemporary family life today is its fluidity (chap. 8), and fathers and mothers might have different perceptions about different aspects of their family life.

What are the empirical and methodological implications of these realities? What does it mean to make statements about father "residency," when residency itself is ephemeral? At a national level, father–mother discrepancies have profound implications for the census, which seeks to ascertain household composition. Although there are estimates of the percentage of the population that is missing from national surveys, analysis and decisions about public policy are often made on available data. Future research should aim to clarify for whom findings apply and, in instances where data are available for different groups, to elucidate areas in which mothers' and fathers' reports converge or diverge, explore reasons for divergences, and offer ways to treat multiple perspectives in analyses. Likewise, we need methodologies that capture the dynamic nature and circumstances of family life and ways to study the effects of change on children's development from the perspectives of both mothers and fathers.

Similarly, various methodological and analytic challenges confront the successful integration of children's perspectives into fatherhood research. A father who works long hours may be personally and emotionally committed to his child, but his child may experience him as "never being there." What do children need? How do children perceive various forms of fathering? Unfortunately, children's voices, especially very young children, are absent from most accounts of father involvement, perhaps due to the difficulty in validly assessing the perspectives of young children. We have yet to understand how children construct meaning about different types of fathers—biological, stepfathers, relatives, and other types of social fathers—and yet to develop reliable ways to ask children the "right" questions. Under which familial, social, economic, and cultural circumstances do children welcome father figures as substitutes and under which circumstances are they rejected? How do children, at different developmental periods, define the various male (and female) members of their social networks? Individual characteristics of children, including gender and temperament, must also be considered in children's personal reactions to family circumstances. One child might incessantly dwell on the rejection of a biological father, despite the presence of a nurturing, involved uncle or stepfather. For another child, an uncle or stepfather might circumvent a sense of rejection. A future challenge to researchers will be to better understand how children make sense of the unique family structures that characterize their lives in the context of changing constructs about fathering.

Universals of Fathering?

The collection of writings in this handbook eloquently portrays the ways that fathers' roles vary across cultural, ethnic, and economic groups. The role that culture plays in development and other outcomes is undisputed. However, there still exists debate about the key elements of a particular culture that are linked to "good" outcomes for children and what these "good" outcomes are. To avoid succumbing into eternal relativism, research is needed that explores whether there exist *universals* in fathering that transcend sociocultural boundaries. What aspects of fathering are critical to child well-being and operate similarly for all families and fathers? Should theoretical models be defined separately for every subgroup within the larger population (including boys vs. girls, specific cultures, different income groups)? Certainly, aspects of fathering that enhance children's well-being may be integrally woven with cultural ways of life and ideologies. However, overly specific models are narrow and often circumvent theory building and modeling of what matters for human development more generally. How might social scientists pursue inclusive, parsimonious models of fathering while retaining their cultural sensitivity?

Although social scientists are profoundly aware of the nuances that characterize fathering in different socialcultural niches, there exists caution about the proposal of generic models of fathering. In general, the impact of father absence and/or poor father–child relationships on childhood development may not differ dramatically across societies (e.g., see Rooparnine's discussion of children in Caribbean families in chap. 11). Although the level and quality of father–child relationships must be considered within sociocultural and economic conditions; patterns of mating, migration, and immigration; and cultural views and ideologies, it is inconceivable that the presence of a warm, nurturing, supportive father will not impress enormous benefit on children, just as it is inconceivable that abusive fathers will not harm the well-being of their children and families. As Ropparnine (chap. 11) notes, one of the absolutely crucial characteristics of family systems is that they provide predictable patterns of relationships and expectations of support and involvement that are generally shared and internalized. The particulars of supportive environments will vary across social, economic, and cultural contexts, yet the ultimate goals of families to raise children who positively contribute to society are shared. Hence, researchers must strike a balance between understanding how fathers and families universally come to construct positive, beneficial environments for children and how the circumstances and settings of individuals' lives shape such constructions.

Integrating Methodologies

One of the most important contributions of this handbook is its presentation of the various methods used across scientific fields. It is apropos that the opening chapter provides a multidisciplinary overview of issues such as sample selection, measurement, design, and analyses in the study of father involvement. Methodological approaches in this handbook range from Townsend's in-depth portrayal of Botswanian fathers, to the use of time diaries and social surveys conducted by demographers (e.g., chap. 3) and sociologists (chap. 8) on thousands of men. As researchers in this handbook have shown, scientific disciplines have different tools and by definition focus on different aspects of the phenomena in question. Consistent with their methodological orientations, certain scholars adopt a priori, theoretical frameworks in their conceptualization of father involvement (e.g., the frequent use of Lamb's tripartite framework of father involvement), whereas others rely on the voices of fathers to infuse meaning into the construct of father involvement (e.g., chaps. 9 and 20).

In part, because multidisciplinary research is a relatively new trend, there is little comparability of constructs, measures, and methodologies within disciplines, let alone across disciplines. Consequently, researchers have yet to benefit fully from the rich array of scientific approaches. The study of social phenomena is at a point in time during which single-discipline scientific inquiry is inadequate to answer emerging questions, especially those that bear on public policy. Multidisciplinary work is at a starting point (see chap. 19). As an example, the ongoing debate on "quantitative" versus "qualitative" approaches is fraught with tension, and successful integration of the two is rare. Clearly, research on fathers stands to benefit from the creative combination of qualitative and quantitative methodologies by capitalizing on the advantages of each while offsetting their disadvantages (chap. 1). Quantitative methodologies, such as those utilized in social survey research, offer the opportunity to examine population-based processes and statistically test formal hypotheses and models of fathering. Qualitative methods probe the deeper meaning of fathers' experiences and can shed light on patterns of fathering in underrepresented populations, about which little is known (e.g., fragile families, low-income fathers, stepfathers, nonresidential fathers, social fathers).

As an example of the synergistic relations between the two methodologies, survey studies have opened researchers' eyes to the male undercount problem. In addressing this phenomenon, qualitative studies have shed light on the experiences of the absentee fathers who are missing from national studies. Through the merging of research methodologies, investigators have come closer to understanding why fathers disengage from their families and how they personally feel about their actions (e.g., chap. 18). Ethnographic studies have dispelled certain myths about absentee fathers and fathers who do not pay child support. We know that such fathers are not ubiquitously "deadbeat" and apathetic, and that the absence of child support payments does not necessarily mean that fathers do not care, or that they are not providing for children in other ways. Similarly, the presence of child support dollars does not guarantee that a father is emotionally committed to his role as a father. Ideally, findings yielded from qualitative studies will feed back into models of fathering and will inform the questions and design of future large-scale studies.

Reaching Out to Fathers and Families

Although national surveys suggest that there is an increasing trend, albeit small, of single fathers seeking sole custody of their children, findings from smaller studies suggest that fewer fathers may be participating in their children's lives today than in any period since the United States began keeping reliable statistics (chap. 20). In contrast to findings from national surveys in which minority and poor fathers are underrepresented, Edin's findings are based on the experiences of smaller samples of poor, minority men. Fathers continue to disengage from their children, both economically and emotionally, sometime after separation or divorce.

Unfortunately, despite a burgeoning knowledge base on fathers and families, researchers, policymakers, and practitioners have made little progress in effecting social change and in designing fatherhood programs that address the explicit and unspoken needs of fathers and families. Part of the problem is lack of information about these fathers. Public policies focus mainly on the economic provisioning of nonresident fathers, assuming that these men are able to pay but choose not to. Although there are some fathers who refuse to pay child support despite economic means, there is a large group of fathers who would like to support their children but are unable to do so due to various circumstances (e.g., unemployment, substance abuse). The rhetoric has moved from *deadbeat* to *dead broke*. Social policies are for the most part punitive and do little to nurture or support other roles that a father may play in his family.

This moderate success with fathers cannot be blamed on a lack of fatherhood programs and initiatives. Paralleling the growing awareness and research surrounding fathers, there has been a geometric progression in the number of programs offering services to targeted groups of fathers over the past 20 years (chap. 21). As an example, the mid-1990s was characterized by as much fatherhood activity in one year (1995) as throughout the entire 1980s. By the year 2000, the same amount of activity occurred within a few months. Evaluation of many such programs indicates much room for improvement; the emerging science on father involvement needs to inform program design and implementation so that they can tailor their services to meet the needs of the fathers and families they serve. Practitioners and researchers alike must listen closely to what fathers themselves deem to be necessary to their roles as fathers.

What recommendations for program development evolve from the current collection of writings? The first, most obvious suggestion speaks to the timing of outreach to at-risk families and fathers. Preliminary findings from the Fragile Families Study suggest that fatherhood programs are likely to make a difference when implemented soon after the transition to fatherhood (chap. 18). Outreach to fathers should ideally begin at the birth of children, as new fathers tend to be highly motivated to advantage themselves of services and fatherhood programs. When interviewed shortly after their child's birth, most fathers from fragile families want to remain involved with their children and intend to financially support their children (chap. 18). Despite such admirable goals, father involvement decreases appreciably over time. This suggests that fatherhood programs might increasingly rely on preventive interventions by providing services to new fathers before children are left without economic and emotional support. The late timing of program services might also explain the disappointing results of programs such as Parents' Fair Share, which drew its clientele from men who had *already* fallen behind in their child support obligations and who were no longer involved in their children's lives (chap. 21). Practitioners who run employment programs for disadvantaged men also indicate that motivation is important in determining whether men can sustain their participation in program long enough to reap their benefits (chap. 18), and practitioners are instrumental in determining the types and effectiveness of services offered to fathers (chap. 1).

In addition to the timing of fatherhood programs, researchers in this handbook suggest that programs treat fathers within the larger context of their families (chaps. 1 and 18). Programs should be ready to address the multiple needs of mothers and fathers by being equipped to expand parents' educational and employment opportunities, support and develop their parenting skills, and assist them in overcoming substance abuse or mental health problems (chap. 18). Finally, evaluation research on the effectiveness of fatherhood programs, on what is being done with fathers, what does and does not work, and why is urgent. There have been virtually no rigorous impact studies of the effects of responsible fatherhood programs on the behavior of men or the well-being of children, and even current demonstration projects (e.g., Fathers at Work; Fragile Families) do not include controlled, experimental evaluations (chap. 21). Consequently, researchers, practitioners and policymakers remain unable to pinpoint whether, how, and why different types of fatherhood programs affect men, families, and children.

Interfacing with Policy

The integration of research and policy on fathers is in its infancy. Researchers should be encouraged to attend to constructs and variables that not only have theoretical relevance for policy and practice but can also be readily translated and incorporated into policy and program initiatives. Social trends are useful markers that help us gain a broad picture of the ecological contexts in which families live. Both researchers and policymakers need to be cognizant of the dynamic interplay between research and policy and of how knowledge about father involvement and well-targeted policy initiatives together feed the process of support to all family members, most notably children (Tamis-LeMonda & Cabrera, 1999; see also chaps. 18 and 19).

Research and social policies are synergistic: Social trends and policies are catalysts for the recent surge in research initiatives pertaining to fathers, and research initiatives on father involvement promise to provide a rich foundation on which to base future policy directions (Tamis-LeMonda & Cabrera, 1999). It is thus apt that the closing section of this handbook emphasizes the policy and program implications of research on father involvement, demonstrates how research and policy might be integrated, and highlights the ways in which program initiatives might benefit from research findings (chaps. 18, 19, and 21). How can knowledge about father involvement, the predictors of involvement, and the influences of involvement on children be translated into policies that support fathers, families, and children? How do current social policies shape the research questions that are (or should be) asked? What role have sociocultural and historical trends played in determining the nature of research and policies on father involvement? How might research guide programs for fathers, and how in turn might the effects of such programs be evaluated?

Although research on fathers has lagged significantly behind that of mothers, the last two decades have witnessed an unprecedented surge of studies on fathers. Despite several shortcomings to earlier studies on fathers, including a predominant focus on middle-income groups, ongoing data collection efforts such as

EHS, ECLS-B, and Fragile Families will soon be available to researchers and policymakers. These national-level data will address many of the shortcomings of past research and should extend our knowledge about the antecedents and consequences of father involvement for children from underrepresented, low-income families. Collectively, the knowledge we gain will give us a better understanding of what it means to be a father under economic, social, and personal strain, and this information will be critical to developing and implementing policies for low-income fathers (chap. 19).

Researchers in this handbook were keenly aware of the links between policy and research. They raised questions that promise to be increasingly central to future policy decisions, such as those concerning child custody, visitation, child-support dollars, and the structure and scheduling of welfare benefits to families. Some authors made implicit policy recommendations; others tackled current policy issues heads on; still others researched the consequences of current policies; and certain investigators examined the translation of policy to program initiatives.

The closing section of this handbook raises the critical question of whether current policies benefit fathers and families, or whether they sometimes lead some fathers to drift away from and out of the lives of their children (e.g., chap. 18). When and under which circumstances do we as a society limit and restrict fathers' access to children? Does society marginalize fathers who do not reside with their children? How do we encourage involved fathers to remain active in their children's lives? Which trends are beneficial and supportive to families? Have we listened enough to fathers? Can the adverse effects of certain policies be ameliorated so as to support the healthy development of children, fathers, and families? We anticipate that the future sharing of theories, expertise, and methodologies among scientific disciplines will bring us closer to adequately addressing these policy-relevant questions and hope that the collection of writings in this multidisciplinary handbook represents a first step in such a collaborative process.

REFERENCES

Allen, W. D., & Doherty, W. J. (1996). The responsibilities of fatherhood as perceived by African-American teenage fathers. *Families in Society, 77,* 142–155.

Cabrera, N., Tamis-LeMonda, C. S., Bradley, R. H., Hofferth, S., & Lamb, M. E. (2000). Fatherhood in the 21st century. *Child Development, 71*(1), 127–136.

Furstenberg, F. F., Jr., Sherwood, K. E., & Sullivan, M. L. (1992). *Caring and paying: What fathers and mothers say about child support.* New York: Manpower Demonstration Research Corporation.

Greene, A. D., Hearn, G. & Emig, C. (1996, June 11–12). *Developmental, ethnographic, and demographic perspectives on fatherhood: Summary of report of the conference.* Paper prepared for the NICHD Family and Child Well-Being Research Network by Child Trends, Bethesda, MD.

Greif, G. L. (1997). *Out of touch: When parents and children lose contact after divorce.* New York: Oxford University Press.

Hewlett, B. S. (1992). Husband–wife reciprocity and the father–infant relationship among Aka pygmies. In B. S. Hewlett (Ed.), *Father–child relations: Cultural and biosocial contexts* (pp. 153–176). New York: Aldine de Gruyter.

Johnston, J. R. (1994). High-conflict divorce. *The Future of Children, 4,* 165–182.

Lamb, M. E. (1997). *The role of the father in child development* (3rd ed.). New York: Wiley.

Lucas, R. E., & Stark, O. (1985). Motivations to remit: Evidence from Botswana. *Journal of Political Economy, 93,* 901–918.

Palkovitz, R. (1997). Reconstructing "involvement": Expanding conceptualizations of men's caring in contemporary families. In A. J. Hawkins & D. C. Dollahite (Eds.), *Generative fathering: Beyond deficit perspectives* (pp. 200–216). Thousand Oaks, CA: Sage.

Picker, R., Tamis-LeMonda, C. S., & Shannon, J. D. (2000, August). *"Being Somebody": A Qualitative Exploration of the Impact of Fatherhood.* Paper presented to the American Psychological Association Conference, Washington, D.C.

Roopnarine, J. L., & Brown, J. (Eds.). (1997). *Carribbean families: Diversity among ethnic groups.* Norwood, NJ: Ablex.

Tamis-Le-Monda, C. & Cabrera, N. (1999). Perspectives on father involvement: Research and policy. *Social Policy Report. Society for Research in Child Development, 13*(2), 1–26.

Tanfer, K., & Mott, F. (1998). The meaning of fatherhood for men. In *Nurturing fatherhood: Improving data and research on male fertility, family formation and fatherhood* (pp. 243–293). Washington, DC: Federal Interagency Forum on Child and Family Statistics.

Author Index

All page numbers in italic type refer to multiple-author works. All page numbers in roman type refer to single-author works.

A

Abbey, B. B., *148*

Achatz, M., *213, 216, 220, 222, 223, 226, 227, 229, 230, 232, 234, 237, 242, 401, 564*

Adams, M., *161*

Ahmeduzzaman, M., *283, 286, 288*

Ainsworth, M., 287

Ainsworth, M. D. S., *94, 104*

Akabayashi, H., *312*

Akamatsu, S., *350*

Akerlof, G. A., *555*

Alderman, H., *397*

Alexander, G., *287*

Allen, A., 295

Allen, W., *211, 226, 227, 228, 230, 232, 237*

Allen, W. D., *604*

Allison, K., *215, 238*

Allison, P., *471*

Allison, P. D., *172, 191, 198, 202, 440, 443, 447*

Amato, P., *2, 17, 18, 211, 350*

Amato, P. A., *190, 191, 194, 197, 204*

Amato, P. R., 7, 8, *127, 171, 171, 172, 173, 174, 175, 180, 190, 194, 194, 195, 198, 254, 472, 472, 490*

Ames, G. J., *94, 97*

An, C., *417*

Anderson, B., *102*

Anderson, E., *212, 216, 217, 218, 219, 221, 223, 227, 235, 236, 238, 239, 241*

Anderson, K., *69, 78, 79*

Anderson, K. G., *69, 310*

Anderson, P., *280, 282, 283, 284, 285, 286, 288, 291, 294, 296*

Andersson, M., 360, 361

Appel, A. E., *175*

Arendell, T., 257

Argys, L. M., *175, 198, 332, 389, 402, 446, 447, 448*

Arnold, E., 288, 289, 292

Aschenbrenner, J., 219, 220, 221, 224, 226, 232, 234, 240

Asher, S. R., *141*

Auerbach, C. F., *283*

Aughinbaugh, A., 447

Auletta, K., 211

Austin, B., *98*

Axelrod, R., *279*

B

Baca Zinn, M., 211, 257

Bachrach, C. A., *462, 463, 464, 518*

Bachu, A., 464

Back, K. W., *290*

Bader, A. P., 94, *94*

Bales, R., 7

Bales, R. F., *152*

Ball, R. E., 288

Ballard, M., *157*

U

Udry, J., 344
Uhlenberg, P., *200*
Underwood, M. K., *148*
U.S. Census Bureau, 36, 57, 58, 62, 127, 175, 261, 432, 445, 527
U.S. Department of Health and Human Services, 483, 556
Unyk, A. M., *95*
Uzgiris, I., *103*

V

Valentine, B. L., 212, 221
Valentine, R. L., 213
van der Klaaw, W., *424*
Van Egeren, L. A., *12*
Van IJzendoorn, M. H., *104, 105,* 105
Vega-Lahr, N., *102*
Veherencamp, S. L., *360*
Veneziano, R. A., *254*
Ventura, S. J., *462, 463, 464, 518*
Verba, S., *577, 580*
Verdonck, A., *345*
Verschueren, K., *105*
Veum, J. R., 198
Vietze, P. M., *101, 103*
Vincent, A., *360, 361*
Vincent, J. P., *174*
Vitaro, F., *141*
Voland, E., *364*
Volkmer, H. J., *98*
Volling, B., *104*
Volling, B. L., *96, 104*
von Bertalanffy, L., 6
von Eye, A., *5, 25,* 25

W

Wachs, T., *103*
Wadsworth, E. M., *155*
Waldfogel, J., 393, *423, 425, 449*
Wales, T. J., *397*
Walker, H., *101*
Wall, S., *94, 104*
Waller, M., 226, 232, *242, 449*

Waller, M. R., *479, 480,* 550
Walsh, C. J., *94, 96*
Walzer, S., 257
Wang, S., *154, 160, 161*
Wang, S. J., *154, 156*
Ward, C. D., *95*
Wark, L., *198*
Warren-Leubecker, A., *95*
Warshak, R. A., 178
Wasik, B., *280*
Waters, E., *94, 104*
Way, N., *528*
Waynforth, D., *341, 342, 343, 344,* 349, *350, 352*
Webb, W., *12, 284, 290*
Weiderman, M., 350
Weingarten, K., *121, 253*
Weinraub, M., *97, 98*
Weis, L., *216, 217, 223, 238*
Weisner, T., 257
Weisner, T. S., 332
Weiss, Y., *402, 411, 433, 434, 437, 474*
Wells, R., *398*
Welsh, M., *160, 161*
West, J., *11, 490*
West, M. M., *98*
Westerman, M. A., *160*
Western, B., 480, *504*
Weston, D. M., *105*
Wetzstein, C., 574
Wheaton, L., *57, 58, 59*
Whitbeck, L., *471, 472*
White, D., *98*
White, L. K., 425
White, R. T., 213, 215, 217, 239
Whitehead, B. D., 170
Whiting, B. B., 255, *255, 280, 292*
Whiting, J., *255,* 338
Whiting, J. W. M., *280, 292*
Wikoff, R. L., *95*
Wild, M., *157*
Wild, M. N., *157*
Willard, D. E., *306, 362, 377*
Wille, D., 94
Willemsen, E., *99*
Williams, C. W., 212, 214, 215, 219, 221, 226, 232, 233
Williams, G. A., *141*
Williams, G. C., 360
Williams, J., 258, 262

Subject Index